Introduction to Probability for Computing

Computer science students can find probability challenging and remote from their computing interests. Maximize student engagement and understanding with this uniquely rigorous yet accessible undergraduate text, which is written specifically for computing students. It combines probability basics with a wide range of computing-relevant topics, including statistical inference, computer system simulation, randomized algorithms, and Markov modeling of queueing systems. The book has been class-tested, and will be an invaluable learning tool whether your course covers probability with statistics, with simulation, with randomized algorithms, or with stochastic processes.

- Motivates students with numerous real-world computer science applications, such as hash table design, capacity provisioning in data centers, web page ranking, disk modeling, virus propagation, deducing signals in noisy environments, error-correcting codes, caching, and primality testing.
- Written as a sequence of questions and answers to engage students and encourage them actively to think about and better understand definitions, equations, and fundamental concepts.
- Includes full-color illustrations and almost 400 exercises.

Mor Harchol-Balter is the Bruce J. Nelson Professor of Computer Science at Carnegie Mellon University. She is a Fellow of both ACM and IEEE. She has received numerous teaching awards, including the Herbert A. Simon Award for teaching excellence at CMU. She is also the author of the popular textbook *Performance Analysis and Design of Computer Systems* (Cambridge, 2013).

"Based on 20 years of teaching Computer Science and Operations Research at Carnegie Mellon University, Professor Harchol-Balter provides a unique presentation of probability and statistics that is both highly engaging and also strongly motivated by real-world computing applications that students will encounter in industry. This book is approachable and fun for undergraduate students, while also covering advanced concepts relevant to graduate students."

Eytan Modiano, Massachusetts Institute of Technology

"This book provides a fantastic introduction to probability for computer scientists and computing professionals, addressing concepts and techniques crucial to the design and analysis of randomized algorithms, to performing well-designed simulations, to statistical inference and machine learning, and more. Also contains many great exercises and examples. Highly recommend!"

Avrim Blum, Toyota Technological Institute at Chicago

"Mor Harchol-Balter's new book does a beautiful job of introducing students to probability! The book is full of great computer science-relevant examples, wonderful intuition, simple and clear explanations, and mathematical rigor. I love the question-answer style she uses, and could see using this book for students ranging from undergraduate students with zero prior exposure to probability all the way to graduate students (or researchers of any kind) who need to brush up and significantly deepen (and/or broaden) their knowledge of probability."

Anna Karlin, University of Washington

"Probability is at the heart of modeling, design, and analysis of computer systems and networks. This book by a pioneer in the area is a beautiful introduction to the topic for undergraduate students. The material in the book introduces theoretical topics rigorously, but also motivates each topic with practical applications. This textbook is an excellent resource for budding computer scientists who are interested in probability."

R. Srikant, University of Illinois at Urbana-Champaign

"I know probability theory, and have taught it to undergrads and grads at MIT, UC Berkeley, and Carnegie Mellon University. Yet this book has taught me some wonderfully interesting important material that I did not know. Mor is a great thinker, lecturer, and writer. I would love to have learned from this book as a student — and to have taught from it as an instructor!"

Manuel Blum, University of California, Berkeley, and Carnegie Mellon University

Introduction to Probability for Computing

MOR HARCHOL-BALTER

Carnegie Mellon University, Pennsylvania

CAMBRIDGE
UNIVERSITY PRESS

Shaftesbury Road, Cambridge CB2 8EA, United Kingdom

One Liberty Plaza, 20th Floor, New York, NY 10006, USA

477 Williamstown Road, Port Melbourne, VIC 3207, Australia

314–321, 3rd Floor, Plot 3, Splendor Forum, Jasola District Centre,
New Delhi – 110025, India

103 Penang Road, #05–06/07, Visioncrest Commercial, Singapore 238467

Cambridge University Press is part of Cambridge University Press & Assessment,
a department of the University of Cambridge.

We share the University's mission to contribute to society through the pursuit of
education, learning and research at the highest international levels of excellence.

www.cambridge.org
Information on this title: www.cambridge.org/highereducation/isbn/9781009309073

DOI: 10.1017/9781009309097

© Mor Harchol-Balter 2024

First published 2024

Printed in the United Kingdom by TJ Books Limited, Padstow, Cornwall, 2024

A catalogue record for this publication is available from the British Library.

Library of Congress Cataloging-in-Publication Data
Names: Harchol-Balter, Mor, 1966- author.
Title: Introduction to probability for computing / Mor Harchol-Balter,
    Carnegie Mellon University, Pennsylvania.
Description: Cambridge, United Kingdom ; New York, NY, USA : Cambridge
    University Press, 2023. | Includes bibliographical references and index.
Identifiers: LCCN 2023002753 | ISBN 9781009309073 (hardback)
Subjects: LCSH: Computer science–Mathematics. | Probabilities.
Classification: LCC QA76.9.M35 H36 2023 | DDC 004.01/51–dc23/eng/20230210
LC record available at https://lccn.loc.gov/2023002753

ISBN 978-1-009-30907-3 Hardback

Additional resources for this publication at www.cambridge.org/harchol-balter

*To the students at CMU's
School of Computer Science
whose curiosity and drive
inspire me every day
to keep writing.*

Contents

Preface

Probability theory has become indispensable in computer science. It is at the core of machine learning and statistics, where one often needs to make decisions under stochastic uncertainty. It is also integral to computer science theory, where most algorithms today are randomized algorithms, involve random coin flips. It is a central part of performance modeling in computer networks and systems, where probability is used to predict delays, schedule jobs and resources, and provision capacity.

Why This Book?

This book gives an introduction to probability as it is used in computer science theory and practice, drawing on applications and current research developments as motivation and context. This is not a typical counting and combinatorics book, but rather it is a book centered on distributions and how to work with them.

Every topic is driven by what computer science students need to know. For example, the book covers distributions that come up in computer science, such as heavy-tailed distributions. There is a large emphasis on variability and higher moments, which are very important in empirical computing distributions. Computer systems modeling and simulation are also discussed, as well as statistical inference for estimating parameters of distributions. Much attention is devoted to tail bounds, such as Chernoff bounds. Chernoff bounds are used for confidence intervals and also play a big role in the analysis of randomized algorithms, which themselves comprise a large part of the book. Finally, the book covers Markov chains, as well as a bit of queueing theory, both with an emphasis on their use in computer systems analysis.

Intended Audience

The material is presented at the advanced undergraduate level. The book is based on an undergraduate class, Probability and Computing (PnC), which I have been teaching at Carnegie Mellon University (CMU) for almost 20 years. While PnC is primarily taken by undergraduates, several Masters and PhD students choose to take the class. Thus we imagine that instructors can use the book for different levels of classes, perhaps spanning multiple semesters.

Question/Answer Writing Style

The book uses a style of writing aimed at engaging the reader to be active, rather than passive. Instead of large blocks of text, we have short "Questions" and "Answers." In working through the book, you should cover up the answers, and write down your own answer to each question, before looking at the given answer. The goal is "thinking" rather than "reading," where each chapter is intended to feel like a conversation.

Exercises

The exercises in this book are an integral part of learning the material. They also introduce many of the computer science and statistics applications. Very few of the exercises are rote. Every problem has important insights, and the insights often build on each other. Exercises are (very roughly) organized from easier to harder. Several of the exercises in the book were contributed by students in the class!

To aid in teaching, solutions to a large subset of the exercises are available *for instructors only* at www.cambridge.org/harchol-balter. Instructors who need solutions to the remaining exercises can request these from the author. The solutions are for the personal use of the instructor only. They should not be distributed or posted online, so that future generations can continue to enjoy the exercises.

Organization of the Material

The book consists of eight parts. Parts I, II, and III provide an introduction to basic probability. Part IV provides an introduction to computer systems modeling and simulation. Part V provides an introduction to statistical inference. Parts VI and VII comprise a course in randomized algorithms, starting with tail bound inequalities and then applying these to analyze a long list of randomized algorithms. Part VIII provides an introduction to stochastic processes as they're used in computing.

Before we describe the parts in more detail, it is worth looking at the *dependency structure* for the book, given in Figure P1. Aside from Parts I, II, and III, most of the parts can be taught in any order.

In particular, it is possible to imagine at least *four different courses* being taught from this book, depending on the parts that an instructor might choose to teach. Figure P2 depicts different courses that one might teach. All the courses start with Parts I, II, and III, but then continue with Simulation, or Statistics, or Randomized Algorithms, or Stochastic Processes, depending on the particular course.

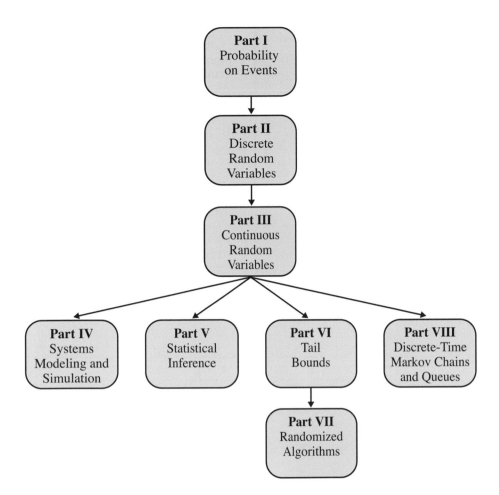

Figure P1 *The dependency structure between the parts of this book. Most parts are independent of other parts and can be taught in any order.*

Description of Each Part

Part I: Foundations and Probability on Events: Part I starts by reviewing the prerequisites for the book. These include series, calculus, elementary combinatorics, and asymptotic notation. Exercises and examples are provided to help in reviewing the prerequisites. The main focus of Part I is on defining probability on events, including conditioning on events, independence of events, the Law of Total Probability, and Bayes' Law. Some examples of applications covered in Part I are: faulty computer networks, Bayesian reasoning for healthcare testing, modeling vaccine efficacy, the birthday paradox, Monty Hall problems, and modeling packet corruption in the Internet.

Part II: Discrete Random Variables: Part II introduces the most common discrete random variables (Bernoulli, Binomial, Geometric, and Poisson), and then

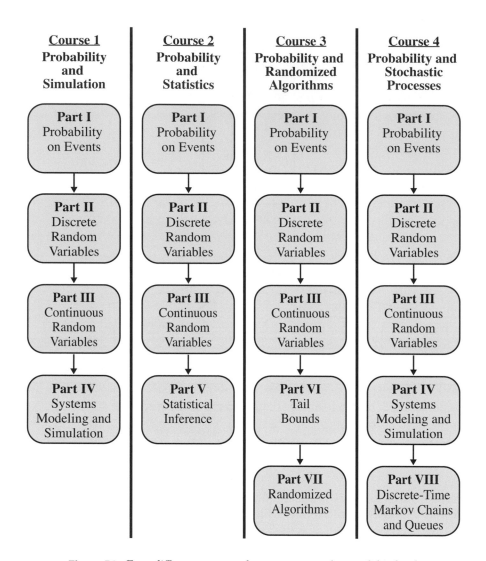

Figure P2 *Four different courses that one can teach out of this book.*

continues with the standard material on random variables, such as linearity of expectation, conditioning, conditional probability mass functions, joint distributions, and marginal distributions. Some more advanced material is also included, such as: variance and higher moments of random variables; moment-generating functions (specifically z-transforms) and their use in solving recurrence relations; Jensen's inequality; sums of a random number of random variables; tail orderings, and simple tail inequalities. Both Simpson's paradox and the inspection paradox are covered. Some examples of applications covered in Part II are: noisy reading from a flash storage, the binary symmetric channel, approximating a Binomial distribution by a Poisson, the classical marriage algorithm, modeling the time until a disk fails, the coupon collector problem, properties of random graphs, time until k consecutive failures, computer virus propagation, epidemic growth modeling, hypothesis testing in data analysis, stopping times, total variation distance, and polygon triangulation.

Part III: Continuous Random Variables: Part III repeats the material in Part II, but this time with continuous random variables. We introduce the Uniform, Exponential, and Normal distributions, as well as the Central Limit Theorem. In addition, we introduce the Pareto heavy-tailed distribution, which is most relevant for empirical computing workloads, and discuss its relevance to today's data center workloads. We cover failure rate functions and the heavy-tail property and their relevance to computing workloads. We again cover moment-generating functions, but this time via Laplace transforms, which are more commonly used with continuous random variables. Some applications covered in Part II are: classifying jobs in a supercomputing center, learning the bias of a coin, dart throwing, distributions whose parameters are random variables, relating laptop quality to lifetime, modeling disk delays, modeling web file sizes, modeling compute usage, modeling IP flow durations, and Internet node degrees.

Part IV: Computer Systems Modeling and Simulation: Part IV covers the basics of what is needed to run simulations of computer systems. We start by defining and analyzing the Poisson process, which is the most commonly used model for the arrival process of jobs into computer systems. We then study how to generate random variables for simulation, using the inverse transform method and the accept–reject method. Finally, we discuss how one would program a simple event-driven or trace-driven simulator. Some applications that we cover include: Malware detection of infected hosts, population modeling, reliability theory, generating a Normal random variable, generating Pareto and Bounded Pareto random variables, generating a Poisson random variable, simulation of heavy-tailed distributions, simulation of high-variance distributions, simulation of jointly distributed random variables, simulation of queues, and simulation of networks of queues.

Part V: Statistical Inference: Part V switches gears to statistics, particularly statistical inference, where one is trying to estimate some parameters of an experiment. We start with the most traditional estimators, the sample mean and sample variance. We also cover desirable properties of estimators, including zero bias, low mean squared error, and consistency. We next cover maximum likelihood estimation and linear regression. We complete this part with a discussion of maximum a posterior (MAP) estimators and minimum mean square error (MMSE) estimators. Some applications that we cover include: estimating voting probabilities, deducing the original signal in a noisy environment, estimating true job sizes from user estimates, estimation in interaction graphs, and estimation in networks with error correcting codes.

Part VI: Tail Bounds and Applications: Part VI starts with a discussion of tail bounds and concentration inequalities (Markov, Chebyshev, Chernoff), for which we provide full derivations. We provide several immediate applications for these tail bounds, including a variety of classic balls-and-bins applications. The balls and bins framework has immediate application to dispatching tasks to servers in a server farm, as well as immediate application to hashing algorithms, which we also study extensively. We cover applications of tail bounds to defining confidence intervals in statistical estimation, and well as bias estimation, polling schemes, crowd sourcing, and other common settings from computing and statistics.

Part VII: Randomized Algorithms: Part VII introduces a wide range of randomized algorithms. The randomized algorithms include Las Vegas algorithms, such as randomized algorithms for sorting and median finding, as well as Monte Carlo randomized algorithms such as MinCut, MaxCut, matrix multiplication checking, polynomial multiplication, and primality testing. The exercises in this part are particularly relevant because they introduce many additional randomized algorithms such as randomized dominating set, approximate median finding, independent set, AND/OR tree evaluation, knockout tournaments, addition of n-bit numbers, randomized string exchange, path-finding in graphs, and more. We use the tail bounds that we derived earlier in Part VI to analyze the runtimes and accuracy of our randomized algorithms.

Part VIII: Markov Chains with a Side of Queueing Theory: Part VIII provides an introduction to stochastic processes as they come up in computer science. Here we delve deeply into discrete-time Markov chains (both finite and infinite). We discuss not only how to solve for limiting distributions, but also when they exist and why. Ergodicity, positive-recurrence and null-recurrence, passage times, and renewal theory are all covered. We also cover time averages versus ensemble averages and the impact of these different types of averages on running simulations. Queueing theory is integral to Part VIII. We define the performance metrics that computer scientists care about: throughput, response time, and load. We cover Little's Law, stability, busy periods, and capacity provisioning. A huge number of applications are covered in Part VIII, including, for example, the classic PageRank algorithm for ranking web pages, modeling of epidemic spread, modeling of caches, modeling processors with failures, Brownian motion, estimating the spread of malware, reliability theory applications, population modeling, server farm and data center modeling, admission control, and capacity provisioning.

Acknowledgments

Most textbooks begin with a class, and this book is no exception. I created the Probability and Computing (called "PnC" for short) class 20 years ago, with the aim of teaching computer science undergraduates the probability that they need to know to be great computer scientists. Since then I have had a few opportunities to co-teach PnC with different colleagues, and each such opportunity has led to my own learning. I would like to thank my fantastic co-instructors: John Lafferty, Klaus Sutner, Rashmi Vinayak, Ryan O'Donnell, Victor Adamchik, and Weina Wang. I'm particularly grateful to Weina, who collaborated with me on three of the chapters of the book and who is a kindred spirit in Socratic teaching. The book has also benefited greatly from many spirited TAs and students in the class, who proposed fun exercises for the book, many referencing CMU or Pittsburgh.

I would also like to thank my illustrator, Elin Zhou, who painstakingly created every image and figure in the book, while simultaneously managing her undergraduate classes at CMU. I chose Elin as my illustrator because her artwork embodies the spirit of fun and inclusiveness that permeates the PnC class. One of the themes of PnC is chocolate, which is tossed out throughout the class to students who answer questions. This chocolate would not be possible if it weren't for our class sponsor, Citadel, who even paid to have chocolate mailed directly to student homes throughout the pandemic, while classes were online.

I have been fortunate to have several excellent editors at Cambridge University Press: Julie Lancashire, Ilaria Tassistro, and Rachel Norridge. Thanks to their recommendations, the statistics chapters were added, redundant material was removed, and the style and layout of the book improved immensely. My copy editor, Gary Smith, was also fantastic to work with and meticulous!

On a personal note, I want to thank my family. In particular, I'm grateful to my son, Danny Balter, for always telling me that I'm good at explaining things. I'm also grateful to my mom, Irit Harchol, who is one of my best friends, and who takes the time to talk with me every day as I walk to and from work. Thanks to my inlaws, Ann and Richard Young, who are my cheering squad. Finally, I have infinite love and gratitude for my husband, Ary Young, for always making me their top priority and for never leaving my side, even if it means sleeping on my sofa as I sit here typing away.

Part I

Fundamentals and Probability on Events

In this first part of the book we focus on some basic tools that we will need throughout the book.

We start, in Chapter 1, with a review of some mathematical basics: series, limits, integrals, counting, and asymptotic notation. Rather than attempting an exhaustive coverage, we instead focus on a select "toolbox" of techniques and tricks that will come up over and over again in the exercises throughout the book. Thus, while none of this chapter deals with probability, it is worth taking the time to master its contents.

In Chapter 2, we cover the fundamentals of probability. Here we define probability based on an experiment and events. We discuss the axioms of probability, conditioning, independence, the Law of Total Probability, and Bayes' Law.

1 Before We Start ... Some Mathematical Basics

This book assumes some mathematical skills. The reader should be comfortable with high school algebra, including logarithms. Basic calculus (integration, differentiation, limits, and series evaluation) is also assumed, including nested (3D) integrals and sums. We also assume that the reader is comfortable with sets and with simple combinatorics and counting (as covered in a discrete math class). Finally, we assume versatility with "big-O" and "little-o" notation. To help the reader, in this chapter we review a few basic concepts that come up repeatedly throughout the book. Taking the time to understand these *now* will make it much easier to work through the book.

1.1 Review of Simple Series

There are several series that come up repeatedly in the book, starting in Chapter 3.

Question: Try evaluating the following in closed form. (Don't peek at the answers until you've tried these yourself.) We provide the full derivations below.

(a) $S = 1 + x + x^2 + x^3 + \cdots + x^n$.
(b) $S = 1 + x + x^2 + x^3 + \cdots$, where $|x| < 1$.
(c) $S = 1 + 2x + 3x^2 + 4x^3 + \cdots + nx^{n-1}$.
(d) $S = 1 + 2x + 3x^2 + 4x^3 + \cdots$, where $|x| < 1$.

Example 1.1 *Evaluate:* $S = 1 + x + x^2 + x^3 + \cdots + x^n$.

Solution: The trick here is to multiply both sides by the quantity $(1 - x)$:

$$(1 - x)S = S - xS$$
$$= 1 + x + x^2 + x^3 + \cdots + x^n$$
$$\quad -x - x^2 - x^3 - \cdots - x^{n+1}$$
$$= 1 - x^{n+1}.$$

Hence,

$$S = \frac{1 - x^{n+1}}{1 - x}. \tag{1.1}$$

Note that (1.1) assumes that $x \neq 1$. If $x = 1$, then the answer is clearly $S = n + 1$.

Example 1.2 *Evaluate:* $S = 1 + x + x^2 + x^3 + \cdots$ *where* $|x| < 1$.

Solution: This is the same as series (a) except that we need to take the limit as $n \to \infty$:

$$S = \lim_{n \to \infty} 1 + x + x^2 + \cdots + x^n = \lim_{n \to \infty} \frac{1 - x^{n+1}}{1 - x} = \frac{1}{1 - x}. \tag{1.2}$$

Question: Why did we need $|x| < 1$? What would happen if $|x| \geq 1$?

Answer: If $|x| \geq 1$, then the infinite sum diverges.

Example 1.3 *Evaluate:* $S = 1 + 2x + 3x^2 + 4x^3 + \cdots + nx^{n-1}$.

Approach 1: One approach is to again use the $(1 - x)$ trick:

$$
\begin{aligned}
(1 - x)S &= 1 + 2x + 3x^2 + 4x^3 + \cdots + nx^{n-1} \\
&\quad - x - 2x^2 - 3x^3 - 4x^4 - \cdots - nx^n \\
&= 1 + x + x^2 + x^3 + \cdots + x^{n-1} - nx^n \\
&= \frac{1 - x^n}{1 - x} - nx^n \\
&= \frac{1 - (n + 1)x^n + nx^{n+1}}{1 - x}.
\end{aligned}
$$

Hence,

$$S = \frac{1 - (n + 1)x^n + nx^{n+1}}{(1 - x)^2}. \tag{1.3}$$

Approach 2: An easier approach is to view the sum as the derivative of a known sum:

$$
\begin{aligned}
S &= \frac{d}{dx}\left(1 + x + x^2 + x^3 + \cdots + x^n\right) \\
&= \frac{d}{dx}\left(\frac{1 - x^{n+1}}{1 - x}\right) \\
&= \frac{(1 - x) \cdot (-(n + 1)x^n) + (1 - x^{n+1})}{(1 - x)^2} \\
&= \frac{1 - (n + 1)x^n + nx^{n+1}}{(1 - x)^2}.
\end{aligned}
$$

The above assumes that $x \neq 1$. If $x = 1$, then the answer is $S = 1 + 2 + \cdots + n = \frac{n(n+1)}{2}$.

Example 1.4 *Evaluate: $S = 1 + 2x + 3x^2 + 4x^3 + \cdots$ where $|x| < 1$.*

Solution: We again view S as a derivative of a sum:

$$
\begin{aligned}
S &= \frac{d}{dx}\left(1 + x + x^2 + x^3 + \cdots\right) \\
&= \frac{d}{dx}\left(\frac{1}{1-x}\right) \\
&= \frac{1}{(1-x)^2}.
\end{aligned}
\tag{1.4}
$$

1.2 Review of Double Integrals and Sums

Integrals, nested integrals, and nested sums come up throughout the book, starting in Chapter 7. When evaluating these, it is important to pay attention to the area over which you're integrating and also to remember tricks like integration by parts.

Question: Try deriving the following three expressions (again, no peeking at the answers).

(a) $\int_0^\infty y e^{-y} dy$.

(b) $\int_0^\infty \int_0^y e^{-y} dx dy$. Do this both with and without changing the order of integration.

(c) $\int_1^e \int_0^{\ln x} 1 \, dy dx$. Do this both with and without changing the order of integration.

Below we provide the derivations.

Example 1.5 *Derive: $\int_0^\infty y e^{-y} dy$.*

Solution: We start by reviewing integration by parts:

$$
\int_a^b u \, dv = (uv)\Big|_a^b - \int_a^b v \, du.
\tag{1.5}
$$

Applying (1.5), let $u = y$, and $du = dy$. Let $dv = e^{-y}dy$, and $v = -e^{-y}$. Then,

$$\int_0^\infty ye^{-y} = -ye^{-y}\Big|_{y=0}^{y=\infty} - \int_{y=0}^\infty (-e^{-y})dy$$

$$= 0 - (-0) - e^{-y}\Big|_{y=0}^\infty$$

$$= 0 + 0 - (0 - 1)$$

$$= 1.$$

Example 1.6 *Derive:* $\int_0^\infty \int_0^y e^{-y}dxdy.$

Solution: Without changing the order of integration, we have:

$$\int_{y=0}^{y=\infty} \int_{x=0}^{x=y} e^{-y}dxdy = \int_{y=0}^{y=\infty} xe^{-y}\Big|_{x=0}^{x=y}dy$$

$$= \int_{y=0}^{y=\infty} ye^{-y}dy$$

$$= 1.$$

To change the order of integration, we first need to understand the space over which we're integrating. The original region of integration is drawn in Figure 1.1(a), where y ranges from 0 to ∞, and, for each particular value of y, we let x range from 0 to y.

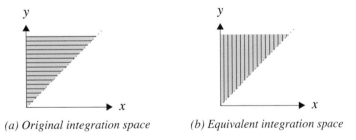

(a) Original integration space　　*(b) Equivalent integration space*

Figure 1.1 *Region of integration drawn two ways.*

We can visualize this instead as shown in Figure 1.1(b), where x now ranges from 0 to ∞, and, for each particular value of x, we let y range from x to ∞:

$$\int_{x=0}^{x=\infty} \int_{y=x}^{y=\infty} e^{-y}dydx = \int_{x=0}^{x=\infty} -e^{-y}\Big|_{y=x}^{y=\infty}dx$$

$$= \int_{x=0}^{x=\infty} (0 + e^{-x})dx$$

$$= -e^{-x}\Big|_{x=0}^{x=\infty}$$

$$= 1.$$

Example 1.7 *Derive:* $\int_1^e \int_0^{\ln x} 1 \, dy \, dx.$

Solution: Without changing the order of integration, we have:

$$\int_{x=1}^{x=e} \int_{y=0}^{y=\ln x} 1 \, dy \, dx = \int_{x=1}^{x=e} \ln x \, dx$$

$$\text{(applying integration by parts)}$$

$$= (\ln x \cdot x)\Big|_{x=1}^{x=e} - \int_{x=1}^{x=e} x \cdot \frac{1}{x} \, dx$$

$$= e - 0 - (e - 1)$$

$$= 1.$$

To change the order of integration, we first need to understand the space over which we're integrating. This is drawn in Figure 1.2(a).

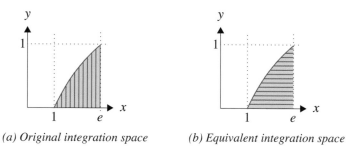

(a) *Original integration space*   (b) *Equivalent integration space*

Figure 1.2 *Region of integration drawn two ways.*

We can visualize this instead as shown in Figure 1.2(b), which leads to the nested integrals:

$$\int_{y=0}^{y=1} \int_{x=e^y}^{x=e} 1 \, dx \, dy = \int_{y=0}^{y=1} x \Big|_{x=e^y}^{x=e} \, dy$$

$$= \int_{y=0}^{y=1} (e - e^y) \, dy$$

$$= (ey - e^y)\Big|_{y=0}^{y=1}$$

$$= (e - e) - (0 - e^0)$$

$$= 1.$$

1.3 Fundamental Theorem of Calculus

The Fundamental Theorem of Calculus (FTC) will come up in the book starting in Chapter 7. We state it here and provide some intuition for why it holds.

Theorem 1.8 (FTC and extension) *Let $f(t)$ be a continuous function defined on the interval $[a, b]$. Then, for any x, where $a < x < b$,*

$$\frac{d}{dx} \int_a^x f(t)dt = f(x). \tag{1.6}$$

Furthermore, for any differentiable function $g(x)$,

$$\frac{d}{dx} \int_a^{g(x)} f(t)dt = f(g(x)) \cdot g'(x). \tag{1.7}$$

We start with intuition for (1.6):

The integral $\int_a^x f(t)dt$ represents the area under the curve $f(t)$ between $t = a$ and $t = x$. We are interested in the rate at which this area changes for a small change in x.

It helps to think of the integral as a "box" parameterized by x.

$$\text{Box}(x) = \boxed{\int_a^x f(t)dt}.$$

$$
\begin{aligned}
\frac{d}{dx} \int_a^x f(t)dt = \frac{d}{dx}\text{Box}(x) &= \lim_{\Delta \to 0} \frac{\text{Box}(x+\Delta) - \text{Box}(x)}{\Delta} \\
&= \lim_{\Delta \to 0} \frac{\int_a^{x+\Delta} f(t)dt - \int_a^x f(t)dt}{\Delta} \\
&= \lim_{\Delta \to 0} \frac{\int_x^{x+\Delta} f(t)dt}{\Delta} \\
&\approx \lim_{\Delta \to 0} \frac{f(x) \cdot \Delta}{\Delta} \qquad f(x) \approx f(x+\Delta) \text{ for tiny } \Delta \\
&= f(x).
\end{aligned}
$$

The same argument applies to (1.7):

$$\text{Box}(x) = \boxed{\int_a^{g(x)} f(t)dt}.$$

$$\frac{d}{dx} \int_a^{g(x)} f(t)dt = \frac{d}{dx} \text{Box}(x) = \lim_{\Delta \to 0} \frac{\text{Box}(x + \Delta) - \text{Box}(x)}{\Delta}$$

$$= \lim_{\Delta \to 0} \frac{\int_a^{g(x+\Delta)} f(t)dt - \int_a^{g(x)} f(t)dt}{\Delta}$$

$$= \lim_{\Delta \to 0} \frac{\int_{g(x)}^{g(x+\Delta)} f(t)dt}{\Delta}$$

$$\approx \lim_{\Delta \to 0} \frac{f(g(x)) \cdot (g(x + \Delta) - g(x))}{\Delta}$$

$$= f(g(x)) \cdot \lim_{\Delta \to 0} \frac{g(x + \Delta) - g(x)}{\Delta}$$

$$= f(g(x)) \cdot g'(x).$$

1.4 Review of Taylor Series and Other Limits

There are certain limits and limiting series which come up repeatedly in this book, so we discuss these here.

Question: What is the famous limit in (1.8) called, and how should we interpret it?

$$\lim_{n \to \infty} \left(1 + \frac{1}{n}\right)^n. \tag{1.8}$$

Answer: Expression (1.8) is the definition of Euler's number, e, which is an irrational, transcendental number having value approximately 2.7183.

It helps to think about (1.8) in terms of money. Suppose you have m dollars. You are promised a 100% interest rate yearly. If the interest is compounded annually, you will have $2m$ dollars after one year. If the interest is compounded every 6 months, you will have $\left(1 + \frac{1}{2}\right)^2 m = \frac{9}{4}m$ dollars after one year. If the interest is compounded every 4 months, you will have $\left(1 + \frac{1}{3}\right)^3 m = \frac{64}{27}m$ dollars after one year. Notice how this keeps going up. If the interest is compounded continuously, you will have

$$\lim_{n \to \infty} \left(1 + \frac{1}{n}\right)^n \cdot m = e \cdot m$$

dollars after one year. Big difference!

Question: What, then, is this limit (assume x is a constant):

$$\lim_{n \to \infty} \left(1 + \frac{x}{n}\right)^n \ ?$$

Answer:

$$\lim_{n \to \infty} \left(1 + \frac{x}{n}\right)^n = e^x. \qquad (1.9)$$

To see this, let $a = \frac{n}{x}$. As $n \to \infty$, we also have $a \to \infty$:

$$\lim_{n \to \infty} \left(1 + \frac{x}{n}\right)^n = \lim_{a \to \infty} \left(1 + \frac{1}{a}\right)^{ax} = \lim_{a \to \infty} \left(\left(1 + \frac{1}{a}\right)^a\right)^x = e^x. \qquad (1.10)$$

Question: Let $0 < x < 1$. Let's do some comparisons:

(a) What is bigger, $1 + x$ or e^x?
(b) What is bigger, $1 - x$ or e^{-x}?

Hint: It helps to think about the Taylor series expansion of e^x around $x = 0$.

Answer: For $0 < x < 1$, it turns out that $e^x > 1 + x$ and $e^{-x} > 1 - x$. To see this, we start with a brief reminder of the Taylor series expansion around 0, also known as a Maclaurin series. Consider any function $f(x)$ which is infinitely differentiable at $x = 0$. Let us define

$$p(x) = f(0) + \frac{f'(0)}{1!}x + \frac{f''(0)}{2!}x^2 + \frac{f'''(0)}{3!}x^3 + \cdots .$$

Observe that the multiplier $\frac{x^n}{n!}$ gets very small for large n. It is easy to see that $p(x)$ is a polynomial that approximates $f(x)$ very well around $x = 0$. In particular, you can see via differentiation that the following are true:

$$\begin{aligned}
p(0) &= f(0) \\
p'(0) &= f'(0) \\
p''(0) &= f''(0) \\
p'''(0) &= f'''(0)
\end{aligned}$$

etc.

In fact, Taylor's theorem [71, p.678] says roughly that if x is within the radius of convergence of $p(\cdot)$, then $p(x)$ approaches $f(x)$ as we write out more and more terms of $p(x)$. Expressing $p(x)$ with an infinite number of terms allows us to say that $f(x) = p(x)$.

Returning to our question, we can see that the function $f(x) = e^x$ is infinitely differentiable around 0, and thus, for any x, we can express:

$$e^x = f(x) = 1 + \frac{x}{1!} + \frac{x^2}{2!} + \frac{x^3}{3!} + \cdots . \qquad (1.11)$$

Thus clearly for any $x > 0$, we have that

$$e^x > 1 + x, \qquad (1.12)$$

where $1 + x$ is a very good approximation for e^x when x is very small.

Likewise, we can express $f(x) = e^{-x}$ as

$$e^{-x} = 1 - \frac{x}{1!} + \frac{x^2}{2!} - \frac{x^3}{3!} + \frac{x^4}{4!} - \cdots . \qquad (1.13)$$

Now, when $0 < x < 1$, we see that

$$e^{-x} > 1 - x, \qquad (1.14)$$

because $\frac{x^2}{2!} > \frac{x^3}{3!} > \frac{x^4}{4!} > \cdots$. Again, $1 - x$ is a very good approximation for e^{-x} when x is very small.

We end with a discussion of the harmonic series.

Definition 1.9 *The **nth harmonic number** is denoted by H_n, where*

$$H_n = 1 + \frac{1}{2} + \frac{1}{3} + \frac{1}{4} + \cdots + \frac{1}{n}. \qquad (1.15)$$

Example 1.10 (Approximating H_n)

Question: How can we find upper and lower bounds on H_n?

Answer: Figure 1.3 shows the function $f(x) = \frac{1}{x}$ in red. We know how to exactly compute the area under the red curve. Now observe that the area under the red curve is upper-bounded by the sum of the areas in the blue rectangles, which form a harmonic sum. Likewise, the area under the red curve is lower-bounded by the sum of the rectangles with the yellow border, which form a related harmonic sum. Specifically, summing the area in the blue rectangles, we have that:

$$H_n = 1 + \frac{1}{2} + \frac{1}{3} + \cdots + \frac{1}{n} > \int_1^{n+1} \frac{1}{x} \, dx = \ln(n+1).$$

Likewise, summing the area in the yellow rectangles, we have that:

$$\ln n = \int_1^n \frac{1}{x} \, dx > \frac{1}{2} + \frac{1}{3} + \cdots + \frac{1}{n}.$$

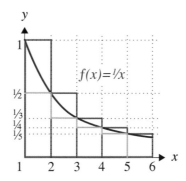

Figure 1.3 *The area under the red curve $f(x) = \frac{1}{x}$ is upper-bounded by $1 + \frac{1}{2} + \frac{1}{3} + \frac{1}{4} + \frac{1}{5}$ (in blue), and it is lower-bounded by $\frac{1}{2} + \frac{1}{3} + \frac{1}{4} + \frac{1}{5}$ (in yellow).*

Adding 1 to both sides,

$$1 + \ln(n) > 1 + \frac{1}{2} + \frac{1}{3} + \cdots + \frac{1}{n} = H_n.$$

Hence:

$$\ln(n + 1) < H_n < 1 + \ln(n). \tag{1.16}$$

From (1.16),

$$H_n \approx \ln(n), \quad \text{for high } n. \tag{1.17}$$

Furthermore,

$$\lim_{n \to \infty} H_n = 1 + \frac{1}{2} + \frac{1}{3} + \cdots = \infty. \tag{1.18}$$

1.5 A Little Combinatorics

Counting is the basis of discrete probability and will be assumed right from the beginning. It's important to differentiate between combinations and permutations.

Example 1.11 (Combinations versus permutations)

Suppose Baskin-Robins has n flavors of ice cream. You are building a cone with $k < n$ scoops. How many different cones can you make if each flavor can only be used once? There are two cases:

(a) The ordering of the flavors matters.
(b) The ordering of the flavors does not matter.

Question: Which of (a) and (b) is counting permutations? Which is counting combinations?

Answer:

(a) Each ordering is called a **permutation**. There are n choices for the bottom flavor, then $n - 1$ for the next flavor, then $n - 2$ for the next one, and so on, with $n - (k - 1)$ for the kth and final flavor. Hence there are

$$n \cdot (n - 1) \cdot (n - 2) \cdots (n - (k - 1)) = \frac{n!}{(n - k)!}$$

possible permutations.
(b) Each choice of k flavors is called a **combination**. We can think of the number of combinations as equal to the number of permutations divided by $k!$, since the ordering of flavors doesn't matter:

$$ABC = ACB = CAB = CBA = BAC = BCA.$$

Thus the number of combinations is:

$$\frac{n!}{(n - k)! \cdot k!}.$$

We write

$$\binom{n}{k} = \frac{n!}{(n - k)! \cdot k!}$$

and call this "n choose k" to denote all the ways of choosing k flavors out of n.

Note that the number of combinations is smaller than the number of permutations by a factor of $k!$.

There are certain sums of combinations which come up a lot in this book. Try these yourself without peeking at the answers:

Question: Evaluate $S_1 = \binom{n}{0} + \binom{n}{1} + \binom{n}{2} + \cdots + \binom{n}{n}$.

Answer: Imagine you have n elements. Then S_1 represents the total number of possible subsets of the n elements (all subsets of size 0 plus all subsets of size 1 plus all subsets of size 2, etc.). But the total number of subsets of n elements is 2^n, because there are two choices for each of the n elements: each element can either be "in the subset" or "out of the subset." Hence $S_1 = 2^n$.

Question: Evaluate $S_2 = \binom{n}{0}y^n + \binom{n}{1}xy^{n-1} + \binom{n}{2}x^2y^{n-2} + \cdots + \binom{n}{n}x^n$.

Answer: Consider the *binomial expansion* of $(x+y)^n$. In this expansion, the term $x^k y^{n-k}$ appears exactly $\binom{n}{k}$ times, because you're picking k of the n parentheses from which to draw an x. Thus, $S_2 = (x+y)^n$.

Question: Evaluate $S_3 = \binom{n}{0} + \binom{n}{1}x + \binom{n}{2}x^2 + \cdots + \binom{n}{n}x^n$.

Answer: S_3 is the same as S_2, where we substitute $y = 1$. Hence $S_3 = (x+1)^n$.

It is often useful to be able to approximate $\binom{n}{k}$. Theorem 1.12 provides easy-to-use upper and lower bounds.

Theorem 1.12 (Simple bounds on $\binom{n}{k}$)

$$\left(\frac{n}{k}\right)^k < \binom{n}{k} < \left(\frac{ne}{k}\right)^k. \tag{1.19}$$

Proof:

First we prove the upper bound:

$$
\begin{aligned}
\binom{n}{k} &= \frac{n(n-1)(n-2)\cdots(n-k+1)}{k!} \\
&= \frac{\frac{n}{n} \cdot \frac{n-1}{n} \cdot \frac{n-2}{n} \cdots \frac{n-k+1}{n} \cdot n^k}{k!} \\
&= \frac{1 \cdot \left(1 - \frac{1}{n}\right) \cdot \left(1 - \frac{2}{n}\right) \cdots \left(1 - \frac{k-1}{n}\right) \cdot n^k}{k!} \\
&< \frac{n^k}{k!}.
\end{aligned}
\tag{1.20}
$$

Now the Taylor series expansion of e^k for positive integer k tells us that $e^k > \frac{k^k}{k!}$.

Thus:

$$\binom{n}{k} < \frac{n^k}{k!} = \frac{n^k}{k^k} \cdot \frac{k^k}{k!} < \frac{n^k}{k^k} \cdot e^k = \left(\frac{ne}{k}\right)^k.$$

Next we prove the lower bound:

Starting from (1.20),

$$
\binom{n}{k} = \frac{1 \cdot \left(1 - \frac{1}{n}\right) \cdot \left(1 - \frac{2}{n}\right) \cdots \left(1 - \frac{k-1}{n}\right) \cdot n^k}{k \cdot (k-1) \cdot (k-2) \cdots (k - (k-1))}
$$

$$
= \frac{1 \cdot \left(1 - \frac{1}{n}\right) \cdot \left(1 - \frac{2}{n}\right) \cdots \left(1 - \frac{k-1}{n}\right) \cdot n^k}{\frac{k}{k} \cdot \frac{k-1}{k} \cdot \frac{k-2}{k} \cdots \frac{k-(k-1)}{k} \cdot k^k}
$$

$$
= \frac{1 \cdot \left(1 - \frac{1}{n}\right) \cdot \left(1 - \frac{2}{n}\right) \cdots \left(1 - \frac{k-1}{n}\right)}{1 \cdot \left(1 - \frac{1}{k}\right) \cdot \left(1 - \frac{2}{k}\right) \cdots \left(1 - \frac{k-1}{k}\right)} \cdot \left(\frac{n}{k}\right)^k
$$

$$
> \left(\frac{n}{k}\right)^k .
$$

The last line follows since $k < n$. Thus $1 - \frac{i}{n} > 1 - \frac{i}{k}$ for $0 < i < k$. ∎

Another useful combinatorial identity is called **Vandermonde's identity**.

Theorem 1.13 (Vandermonde's identity)

$$
\binom{m+n}{r} = \sum_{k=0}^{r} \binom{m}{k} \cdot \binom{n}{r-k}.
$$

Question: What is the logic behind Vandermonde's identity?

Answer: Suppose you are trying to pick r leaders from a set of m women and n men. There are $\binom{m+n}{r}$ ways of picking the r leaders, which is the left-hand side of Vandermonde's identity. However, we can also view the picking of the r leaders as first picking k leaders from the set of m women, where $0 \le k \le r$, and then picking $r - k$ leaders from the set of n men. We now need to sum over all possible values of k. But this latter view represents the right-hand side of Vandermonde's identity.

Question: What does Vandermonde's identity say about $\binom{2n}{n}$?

Answer: By Vandermonde's identity,

$$
\binom{2n}{n} = \sum_{k=0}^{n} \binom{n}{k}^2 .
\tag{1.21}
$$

We end with a final useful result when working with factorials, known as the **Stirling bounds**, whose proof can be found in [76].

> **Theorem 1.14 (Stirling)** *For all positive integers n,*
> $$\sqrt{2\pi n}\left(\frac{n}{e}\right)^n \leq n! \leq e\sqrt{n}\left(\frac{n}{e}\right)^n. \tag{1.22}$$

The power of Stirling's result lies in the fact that the upper and lower bounds given in (1.22) differ by a multiplicative constant of less than 1.1.

1.6 Review of Asymptotic Notation

Asymptotic notation primarily comes up starting in Chapter 18. Asymptotic notation is a convenient way to summarize the rate at which a function $f(n)$ grows with n, without getting into the specifics. For example, we'd like to be able to say that $f(n) = 3n$ grows linearly with n, while $f(n) = \sqrt{5}n^2$ grows quadratically with n. The asymptotic notation below will help us do this.

In words:

- $O(g(n))$ is the set of functions that grow no faster than $g(n)$.
- $o(g(n))$ is the set of functions that grow strictly slower than $g(n)$.
- $\Theta(g(n))$ is the set of functions that grow at the same rate as $g(n)$.
- $\Omega(g(n))$ is the set of functions that grow no slower than $g(n)$.
- $\omega(g(n))$ is the set of functions that grow strictly faster than $g(n)$.

Throughout our discussion we will assume that $f(n)$ and $g(n)$ are functions that map *positive* integers n to *positive* real numbers. If $f(n)$ is negative (e.g., $f(n) = -3n$) we classify it based on its absolute value.

We typically write $f(n) = O(g(n))$ to denote that $f(n)$ is in the set of functions $O(g(n))$. We follow this same convention for the other sets.

1.6.1 Big-O and Little-o

> **Definition 1.15** *We say that $f(n) = O(g(n))$, pronounced as $f(n)$ is "**big-O**" of $g(n)$, if there exists a constant $c \geq 0$, s.t.,*
> $$\lim_{n \to \infty} \frac{f(n)}{g(n)} = c.$$

Example 1.16 (Big-O)

- $n = O(3n)$
- $3n = O(n)$
- $-3n^2 \neq O(n)$
- $n \lg n + 18n = O(n^2)$
- $\frac{3 \lg \lg n}{\lg n} = O(1)$

Definition 1.17 *We say that $f(n) = o(g(n))$, pronounced as $f(n)$ is "**little-o**" of $g(n)$, if*

$$\lim_{n \to \infty} \frac{f(n)}{g(n)} = 0.$$

Corollary 1.18 $f(n) = o(1)$ *if and only if* $f(n) \to 0$ *as* $n \to \infty$.

Example 1.19 (Little-o)

- $3n \neq o(n)$
- $n \lg n + 18n = o(n^2)$
- $n^2 = o(n^3)$
- $\lg n = o(n^{0.01})$
- $\frac{3 \lg \lg n}{\lg n} = o(1)$

Question: If $f(n) = o(g(n))$, does that imply that $f(n) = O(g(n))$? How about the converse?

Answer: $f(n) = o(g(n))$ implies that $f(n) = O(g(n))$. The converse is not true.

When comparing complicated functions, it is often helpful to first think about simpler functions. Consider the following example.

Example 1.20 (More complicated functions)

Let $f(n) = n$. Let $g(n) = \frac{\log \log n}{\log \log \log n}$.

Question: Is it the case that $f(n) = o(g(n))$? Or is $g(n) = o(f(n))$?

Hint: Rather than take limits, consider an easier question: how do n and $\log \log n$ compare?

Answer: It is easy to see that

$$\log \log n = o(n).$$

Thus it is also true that if we make the left-hand side smaller, the relationship still holds. By dividing the left-hand side by $\log \log \log n$, we are dividing it by something that is ≥ 1, and hence we are only making it smaller. Thus we also have

$$\frac{\log \log n}{\log \log \log n} = o(n).$$

1.6.2 Big-Omega and Little-omega

Definition 1.21 *We say that $f(n) = \Omega(g(n))$, pronounced as $f(n)$ is "big-Omega" of $g(n)$, if*

$$\lim_{n \to \infty} \frac{f(n)}{g(n)} > 0.$$

Example 1.22 (Big-Omega)

- $3n = \Omega(n)$
- $n \lg n + 18n = \Omega(n \lg n)$
- $n^2 = \Omega(n \lg n)$
- $\frac{3 \lg \lg n}{\lg n} \neq \Omega(1)$

Definition 1.23 *We say that $f(n) = \omega(g(n))$, pronounced as $f(n)$ is "little-omega" of $g(n)$, if*

$$\lim_{n \to \infty} \frac{f(n)}{g(n)} = \infty.$$

Example 1.24 (Little-omega)

- $3n \neq \omega(n)$
- $n \lg n + 18n = \omega(n)$
- $n^2 = \omega(n \lg n)$
- $\frac{3 \lg \lg n}{\lg n} \neq \omega(1)$

Question: If $f(n) = \omega(g(n))$, does that imply that $f(n) = \Omega(g(n))$? How about the converse?

Answer: $f(n) = \omega(g(n))$ implies that $f(n) = \Omega(g(n))$, but the converse is not true.

1.6.3 Big-Theta

> **Definition 1.25** *We say that* $f(n) = \Theta(g(n))$, *pronounced as* $f(n)$ *is "big-Theta" of* $g(n)$, *if both*
>
> $$f(n) = O(g(n)) \text{ and } f(n) = \Omega(g(n)).$$

Example 1.26 (Big-Theta)

- $3n = \Theta(n)$
- $n \lg n + 18n \neq \Theta(n)$

Question: Can we have $f(n) = o(g(n))$ and $f(n) = \omega(g(n))$?

Answer: No. This would require $\lim_{n \to \infty} \frac{f(n)}{g(n)}$ to be both 0 and ∞.

We end with a harder example:

Example 1.27 *Prove that* $3^{\log_2(n^2)} = o(n^4)$.

Solution:

$$\lim_{n \to \infty} \frac{3^{\log_2(n^2)}}{n^4} = \lim_{n \to \infty} \frac{3^{2\log_2 n}}{2^{\log_2(n^4)}} = \lim_{n \to \infty} \frac{9^{\log_2 n}}{2^{4\log_2 n}} = \lim_{n \to \infty} \frac{9^{\log_2 n}}{16^{\log_2 n}} = \lim_{n \to \infty} \left(\frac{9}{16}\right)^{\log_2 n} = 0.$$

1.7 Exercises

1.1 **Choosing ice-cream flavors**
   There are n distinct flavors of ice-cream. Jin and Jong each pick two distinct flavors. Count the number of possibilities where Jin and Jong share exactly one flavor. In this problem the order of the flavors does not matter. An example of a possibility that "counts" is:

   Jin gets {Chocolate, Vanilla}   *and*   Jong gets {Chocolate, Strawberry}.

1.2 **Evaluating a single integral**

Evaluate the following integral:

$$\int_0^\infty 5xe^{-5x}\,dx.$$

1.3 **Evaluating a double integral**

Evaluate this double integral:

$$\int_0^{10} \int_0^y x\,dx\,dy.$$

Do this in two different ways. For each way, draw the region of integration:

(a) Without changing the order of integration.

(b) By changing the order of integration.

1.4 **Evaluating a double integral**

Evaluate this double integral:

$$\int_1^{10} \int_1^{x^2} dy\,dx.$$

Do this in two different ways. For each way, draw the region of integration:

(a) Without changing the order of integration.

(b) By changing the order of integration.

1.5 **Practice with Taylor series**

Let $f(x) = \ln(1 + x)$. Follow the procedure in the chapter to express the Taylor series expansion of $f(\epsilon)$, where $0 < \epsilon \le 1$.

1.6 **Counting balls and bins**

You are throwing n identical balls into n distinct (numbered) bins, where each ball is thrown into one bin.

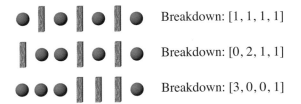

Breakdown: $[1, 1, 1, 1]$

Breakdown: $[0, 2, 1, 1]$

Breakdown: $[3, 0, 0, 1]$

Figure 1.4 *Some examples of Exercise 1.6 where n = 4.*

(a) How many ways are there to distribute the n balls among the n bins? [Hint: Figure 1.4 illustrates that each way of distributing balls can be viewed as an arrangement of $n - 1$ "sticks" and n balls.]

(b) How many ways are there to distribute the n balls among the n bins such that bin 1 has $\geq k$ balls?

1.7 Permutations

Consider all permutations of the numbers $\{1, 2, 3, \ldots, n\}$.

(a) How many permutations are there?

(b) What fraction of all permutations have a 1 in the first position?

(c) What fraction of all permutations have a 1 in the first position and a 2 in the second position?

(d) What fraction of all permutations have a 1 somewhere before a 2?

1.8 Practice with asymptotic notation

(a) Let $a(n) = n$. Let $b(n) = n \log n$. Which of the following are true?

   (i) $a(n) = O(b(n))$

   (ii) $a(n) = o(b(n))$

   (iii) $a(n) = \Theta(b(n))$

   (iv) $a(n) = \omega(b(n))$

   (v) $a(n) = \Omega(b(n))$

(b) Repeat the problem where now $a(n) = \frac{3 \log 3}{\ln \ln n}$ and $b(n) = 1$.

(c) Repeat the problem where now $a(n) = 2^n$ and $b(n) = n^{\ln n}$.

1.9 Harder practice with asymptotic notation

Use the definitions for asymptotic notation to prove the following statements:

(a) Show that $5^{\log_2(n^3)} = \omega(n^6)$.

(b) Show that $(\ln n)^{\frac{3 \ln n}{\ln \ln n}} = \Omega(n^3)$.

(c) Given that $k = \dfrac{9 \ln n}{\ln \ln n}$, show that for large n we have $k \ln k \geq 8 \ln n$.

2 Probability on Events

In this chapter we introduce probability on events. We follow an axiomatic approach that uses elementary set theory.

2.1 Sample Space and Events

Probability is typically defined in terms of some **experiment**. The **sample space**, Ω, of the experiment is the set of all possible outcomes of the experiment.

> **Definition 2.1** *An **event**, E, is any subset of the sample space, Ω.*

For example, in an experiment where a die is rolled twice, each outcome (a.k.a. sample point) is denoted by the pair (i, j), where i is the first roll and j is the second roll. There are 36 sample points. The event

$$E = \{ (1, 3) \text{ or } (2, 2) \text{ or } (3, 1) \}$$

denotes that the sum of the die rolls is 4.

In general, the sample space may be *discrete*, meaning that the number of outcomes is finite, or at least countably infinite, or *continuous*, meaning that the number of outcomes is uncountable.

One can talk of unions and intersections of events, because they are also sets. For example, we can talk of $E \cup F$, $E \cap F$, and $\overline{E}$. Here, E and F are events and $\overline{E}$, the complement of E, denotes the set of points in Ω but not in E, also written $\Omega \setminus E$.

Question: For the die-rolling experiment, consider events E_1 and E_2 defined on Ω in Figure 2.1. Do you think that E_1 and E_2 are independent?

Answer: No, they are not independent. We get to this later when we define independence. We say instead that E_1 and E_2 are mutually exclusive.

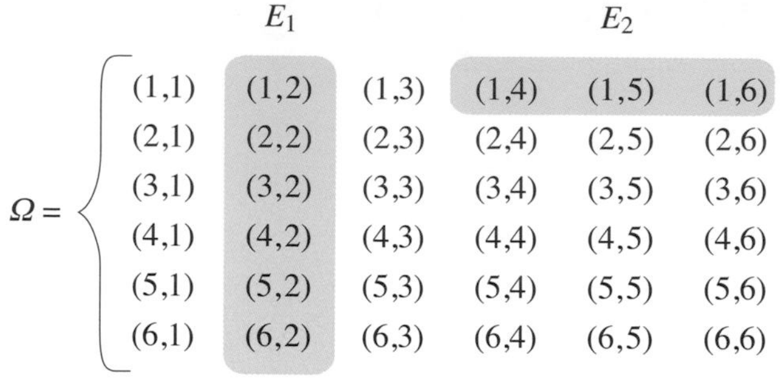

$$
\Omega = \left\{
\begin{array}{cccccc}
(1,1) & (1,2) & (1,3) & (1,4) & (1,5) & (1,6) \\
(2,1) & (2,2) & (2,3) & (2,4) & (2,5) & (2,6) \\
(3,1) & (3,2) & (3,3) & (3,4) & (3,5) & (3,6) \\
(4,1) & (4,2) & (4,3) & (4,4) & (4,5) & (4,6) \\
(5,1) & (5,2) & (5,3) & (5,4) & (5,5) & (5,6) \\
(6,1) & (6,2) & (6,3) & (6,4) & (6,5) & (6,6)
\end{array}
\right.
$$

$$E_1 \qquad\qquad E_2$$

Figure 2.1 *Illustration of two mutually exclusive events in sample space Ω.*

Definition 2.2 *If $E_1 \cap E_2 = \emptyset$, then E_1 and E_2 are* **mutually exclusive**.

Definition 2.3 *If E_1, E_2, ..., E_n are events such that $E_i \cap E_j = \emptyset$, $\forall i \neq j$, and such that $\bigcup_{i=1}^{n} E_i = F$, then we say that events E_1, E_2, ..., E_n* **partition** *set F.*

2.2 Probability Defined on Events

Given a sample space Ω, we can talk about the probability of event E, written $\mathbf{P}\{E\}$. The probability of event E is the probability that the outcome of the experiment lies in the set E.

Probability on events is defined via the Probability Axioms:

Axiom 2.4 (The Three Probability Axioms)
Non-negativity: $\mathbf{P}\{E\} \geq 0$, *for any event E.*
Additivity: *If $E_1, E_2, E_3, \ldots$ is a countable sequence of events, with $E_i \cap E_j = \emptyset$,*
$\quad\quad\forall i \neq j$, *then*

$$\mathbf{P}\{E_1 \cup E_2 \cup E_3 \cup \cdots\} = \mathbf{P}\{E_1\} + \mathbf{P}\{E_2\} + \mathbf{P}\{E_3\} + \cdots .$$

Normalization: $\mathbf{P}\{\Omega\} = 1$.

From the three Probability Axioms, it is easy to reason that if we roll a die, where each side is equally likely, then, by symmetry, $\mathbf{P}\{\text{roll is 3}\} = \frac{1}{6}$. Likewise, $\mathbf{P}\{\text{roll is} \leq 3\} = \mathbf{P}\{\text{roll is 1 or 2 or 3}\} = \frac{3}{6}$.

Question: Is something missing from these Axioms? What if $E \cap F \neq \emptyset$?

Answer: The case where events E and F overlap can be derived from the Additivity Axiom, as shown in Lemma 2.5.

Lemma 2.5

$$\mathbf{P}\{E \cup F\} = \mathbf{P}\{E\} + \mathbf{P}\{F\} - \mathbf{P}\{E \cap F\}.$$

Lemma 2.5 is illustrated in Figure 2.2, where events E and F are depicted as sets. The subtraction of $\mathbf{P}\{E \cap F\}$ term is necessary so that those sample points in the intersection are not counted twice.

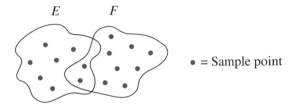

Figure 2.2 *Venn diagram.*

Proof: We can express the set $E \cup F$ as a union of two mutually exclusive sets:

$$E \cup F = E \cup (F \setminus (E \cap F)),$$

where $F \setminus (E \cap F)$ denotes the points that are in F but are *not* in $E \cap F$. Then, by the Additivity Axiom, we have:

$$\mathbf{P}\{E \cup F\} = \mathbf{P}\{E\} + \mathbf{P}\{F \setminus (E \cap F)\}. \tag{2.1}$$

Also by the Additivity Axiom we have:

$$\mathbf{P}\{F\} = \mathbf{P}\{F \setminus (E \cap F)\} + \mathbf{P}\{E \cap F\}. \tag{2.2}$$

We can rewrite (2.2) as:

$$\mathbf{P}\{F \setminus (E \cap F)\} = \mathbf{P}\{F\} - \mathbf{P}\{E \cap F\}. \tag{2.3}$$

Substituting (2.3) into (2.1), we get:

$$\mathbf{P}\{E \cup F\} = \mathbf{P}\{E\} + \mathbf{P}\{F\} - \mathbf{P}\{E \cap F\}. \qquad \blacksquare$$

Lemma 2.6 (Union bound) $\mathbf{P}\{E \cup F\} \leq \mathbf{P}\{E\} + \mathbf{P}\{F\}.$

Proof: This follows immediately from Lemma 2.5. $\qquad \blacksquare$

Question: When is Lemma 2.6 an equality?

Answer: When E and F are mutually exclusive.

Question: Suppose your experiment involves throwing a dart, which is *equally likely* to land anywhere in the interval $[0, 1]$. What is the probability that the dart lands at exactly 0.3?

Answer: The probability of landing at exactly 0.3 is defined to be 0. To see why, suppose that the probability were some $\epsilon > 0$. Then the probability of landing at 0.5 would also be ϵ, as would the probability of landing at any rational point. But these different outcomes are mutually exclusive events, so their probabilities add. Thus, the probability of landing in $[0, 1]$ would be greater than 1, which contradicts $\mathbf{P}\{\Omega\} = 1$. While the probability of landing at exactly 0.3 is 0, the probability of landing in the interval $[0, 0.3]$ is defined to be 0.3.

2.3 Conditional Probabilities on Events

Definition 2.7 *The* **conditional probability** *of event E given event F is written as* $\mathbf{P}\{E \mid F\}$ *and is given by the following, where we assume* $\mathbf{P}\{F\} > 0$:

$$\mathbf{P}\{E \mid F\} = \frac{\mathbf{P}\{E \cap F\}}{\mathbf{P}\{F\}}. \tag{2.4}$$

$\mathbf{P}\{E \mid F\}$ should be thought of as the probability that event E occurs, given that we have narrowed our sample space to points in F.

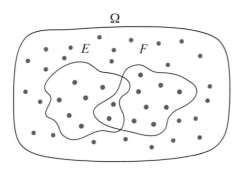

Figure 2.3 *Sample space with 42 sample points, all equally likely.*

To visualize $\mathbf{P}\{E \mid F\}$, consider Figure 2.3, where $\mathbf{P}\{E\} = \frac{8}{42}$ and $\mathbf{P}\{F\} = \frac{10}{42}$. If we imagine that we narrow our space to the 10 points in F, then the probability that the outcome of the experiment is in set E, given that the outcome is in set

F, should be 2 out of 10. Indeed,

$$\mathbf{P}\{E \mid F\} = \frac{2}{10} = \frac{\frac{2}{42}}{\frac{10}{42}} = \frac{\mathbf{P}\{E \cap F\}}{\mathbf{P}\{F\}}.$$

Example 2.8 (Sandwich choices)

Table 2.1 shows my sandwich choices each day. We define the "first half of the week" to be Monday through Wednesday (inclusive), and the "second half of the week" to be Thursday through Sunday (inclusive).

Mon	Tue	Wed	Thu	Fri	Sat	Sun
Jelly	Cheese	Turkey	Cheese	Turkey	Cheese	None

Table 2.1 *My sandwich choices.*

Question: What is $\mathbf{P}\{\text{Cheese} \mid \text{Second half of week}\}$?

Answer: We want the fraction of days in the second half of the week when I eat a cheese sandwich. The answer is clearly 2 out of 4. Alternatively, via (2.4):

$$\mathbf{P}\{\text{Cheese} \mid \text{Second half of week}\} = \frac{\mathbf{P}\{\text{Cheese \& Second half}\}}{\mathbf{P}\{\text{Second half}\}} = \frac{\frac{2}{7}}{\frac{4}{7}} = \frac{2}{4}.$$

Example 2.9 (Two offspring)

The offspring of a horse is called a foal. A horse couple has at most one foal at a time. Each foal is equally likely to be a "colt" or a "filly." We are told that a horse couple has two foals, and at least one of these is a colt. Given this information, what's the probability that both foals are colts?

Question: What is $\mathbf{P}\{\text{both are colts} \mid \text{at least one is a colt}\}$?

Answer:

$$\mathbf{P}\{\text{both are colts} \mid \text{at least one is a colt}\}$$
$$= \frac{\mathbf{P}\{\text{both are colts } and \text{ at least one is a colt}\}}{\mathbf{P}\{\text{at least one is a colt}\}}$$
$$= \frac{\mathbf{P}\{\text{both are colts}\}}{\mathbf{P}\{\text{at least one is a colt}\}}$$
$$= \frac{\frac{1}{4}}{\frac{3}{4}} = \frac{1}{3}.$$

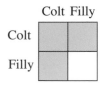

Figure 2.4 *In Example 2.9, we've conditioned on being in the shaded region.*

Question: How might the question read if you wanted the answer to be $\frac{1}{2}$?

Answer: The question would ask what is $\mathbf{P}$ {both are colts | first born is a colt}.

Question: Consider again the example of the couple with two colts, but where we're given the additional information that 10% of horse couples only produce colts, 10% of horse couples only produce fillies, and 80% are equally likely to produce either gender. Does this change your answer to $\mathbf{P}$ {both are colts | at least one is a colt}?

Answer: Yes! See Exercise 2.11(b).

We now look at generalizing the notion of conditioning. By Definition 2.7, if E_1 and E_2 are events, where $\mathbf{P}\{E_1 \cap E_2\} > 0$, then

$$\mathbf{P}\{E_1 \cap E_2\} = \mathbf{P}\{E_1\} \cdot \mathbf{P}\{E_2 \mid E_1\} = \mathbf{P}\{E_2\} \cdot \mathbf{P}\{E_1 \mid E_2\}.$$

That is, the probability that the outcome is both in E_1 and in E_2 can be computed by multiplying two quantities: (1) first restrict the outcome to being in E_1 (probability $\mathbf{P}\{E_1\}$); (2) then further restrict the outcome to being in E_2, given that we've already restricted it to being in E_1 (probability $\mathbf{P}\{E_2 \mid E_1\}$). The next theorem presents a useful "chain rule" for conditioning. This chain rule will be proved in Exercise 2.9.

Theorem 2.10 (Chain rule for conditioning) *Let* $E_1, E_2, \ldots, E_n$ *be events, where* $\mathbf{P}\left\{\bigcap_{i=1}^{n} E_i\right\} > 0.$ *Then*

$$\mathbf{P}\left\{\bigcap_{i=1}^{n} E_i\right\} = \mathbf{P}\{E_1\} \cdot \mathbf{P}\{E_2 \mid E_1\} \cdot \mathbf{P}\{E_3 \mid E_1 \cap E_2\} \cdots \mathbf{P}\left\{E_n \mid \bigcap_{i=1}^{n-1} E_i\right\}.$$

2.4 Independent Events

> **Definition 2.11** *Events E and F are* **independent,** *written* $E \perp F$, *if*
>
> $$\mathbf{P}\{E \cap F\} = \mathbf{P}\{E\} \cdot \mathbf{P}\{F\}.$$

The above definition might seem less-than-intuitive to you. You might prefer to think of independence using the following definition:

> **Definition 2.12 (Alternative)** *Assuming that* $\mathbf{P}\{F\} \neq 0$, *we say that events E and F are* **independent** *if*
>
> $$\mathbf{P}\{E \mid F\} = \mathbf{P}\{E\}.$$

Definition 2.12 says that $\mathbf{P}\{E\}$ is not affected by whether F is true or not.

> **Lemma 2.13** *Definitions 2.11 and 2.12 are equivalent.*

Proof:
Definition 2.11 $\Rightarrow$ *Definition 2.12*: Assuming that $\mathbf{P}\{F\} > 0$, we have:

$$\mathbf{P}\{E \mid F\} = \frac{\mathbf{P}\{E \cap F\}}{\mathbf{P}\{F\}} \overset{\text{by 2.11}}{=} \frac{\mathbf{P}\{E\} \cdot \mathbf{P}\{F\}}{\mathbf{P}\{F\}} = \mathbf{P}\{E\}.$$

Definition 2.12 $\Rightarrow$ *Definition 2.11*:

$$\mathbf{P}\{E \cap F\} = \mathbf{P}\{F\} \cdot \mathbf{P}\{E \mid F\} \overset{\text{by 2.12}}{=} \mathbf{P}\{F\} \cdot \mathbf{P}\{E\}. \qquad \blacksquare$$

Generally people prefer Definition 2.11 because it doesn't require that $\mathbf{P}\{F\} > 0$ and because it shows clearly that a null event is independent of every event.

Question: Can two mutually exclusive (non-null) events ever be independent?

Answer: No. If E and F are mutually exclusive, then $\mathbf{P}\{E \mid F\} = 0 \neq \mathbf{P}\{E\}$.

Question: Suppose one is rolling a die twice. Which of these pairs of events are independent?

(a) E_1 = "First roll is 6" and E_2 = "Second roll is 6"
(b) E_1 = "Sum of the rolls is 7" and E_2 = "Second roll is 4"

Answer: They are both independent!

Question: Suppose we had defined: E_1 = "Sum of the rolls is 8" and E_2 = "Second roll is 4." Are they independent now?

Answer: No.

Example 2.14 (The unreliable network)

Suppose you are routing a packet from the source node to the destination node, as shown in Figure 2.5. On the plus side, there are 8 possible paths on which the packet can be routed. On the minus side, each of the 16 edges in the network independently only works with probability p. What is the probability that you are able to route the packet from the source to the destination?

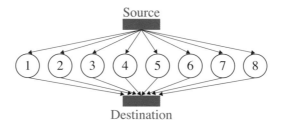

Figure 2.5 *Unreliable network. Each edge only works with probability p.*

We want to figure out the probability that at least one path is working. We will first demonstrate an intuitive, but wrong, solution.

Solution 1 (WRONG!):

There are eight possible two-hop paths to get from source to destination.

Let E_1 denote the event that the first two-hop path works, E_2 denote the event that the second two-hop path works, and E_i denote the event that the ith two-hop path works:

$$\mathbf{P}\{E_i\} = p^2, \ \forall i.$$

Now the probability that at least one path works is the union of these eight events, namely:

$$\mathbf{P}\{\text{At least one path works}\} = \mathbf{P}\{E_1 \cup E_2 \cup \cdots \cup E_8\}$$
$$= \mathbf{P}\{E_1\} + \mathbf{P}\{E_2\} + \cdots + \mathbf{P}\{E_8\}$$
$$= 8p^2.$$

Question: What is wrong with Solution 1?

Answer: We cannot say that the probability of the union of the events equals the sum of their probabilities, unless the events are mutually exclusive. However, we know that the E_i's are independent, and hence they *cannot* be mutually exclusive.

Question: How does the answer given in Solution 1 compare to the correct answer? Higher? Lower?

Answer: The answer given in Solution 1 is an upper bound on the correct answer, via the Union Bound in Lemma 2.6.

There's a lesson to be learned from Solution 1. When dealing with the probability of a *union* of independent events, it helps to turn the problem into an *intersection of independent events*. We will illustrate this idea in Solution 2.

Solution 2 (CORRECT!):

$$
\begin{aligned}
\mathbf{P}\{\text{At least one path works}\} &= \mathbf{P}\{E_1 \cup E_2 \cup \cdots \cup E_8\} \\
&= 1 - \mathbf{P}\{\text{All paths are broken}\} \\
&= 1 - \mathbf{P}\{\overline{E_1} \cap \overline{E_2} \cap \cdots \cap \overline{E_8}\} \\
&= 1 - \mathbf{P}\{\overline{E_1}\} \cdot \mathbf{P}\{\overline{E_2}\} \cdots \mathbf{P}\{\overline{E_8}\}.
\end{aligned}
$$

$$
\mathbf{P}\{\overline{E_1}\} = \mathbf{P}\{\text{path 1 is broken}\} = 1 - \mathbf{P}\{\text{path 1 works}\} = 1 - p^2.
$$

Thus,

$$
\mathbf{P}\{\text{At least one path works}\} = 1 - \left(1 - p^2\right)^8.
$$

Question: Suppose we have three events: A, B, and C. Given that

$$
\mathbf{P}\{A \cap B \cap C\} = \mathbf{P}\{A\} \cdot \mathbf{P}\{B\} \cdot \mathbf{P}\{C\}, \tag{2.5}
$$

can we conclude that A, B, and C are independent?

Answer: No. The problem is that (2.5) does not ensure that any *pair* of events are independent, as required by Definition 2.15.

Definition 2.15 *Events $A_1, A_2, \ldots, A_n$ are **independent** if, for every subset S of $\{1, 2, \ldots, n\}$,*

$$
\mathbf{P}\left\{\bigcap_{i \in S} A_i\right\} = \prod_{i \in S} \mathbf{P}\{A_i\}.
$$

A weaker version of independence is called *pairwise independence* and is defined in Definition 2.16.

Definition 2.16 *Events $A_1, A_2, \ldots, A_n$ are* **pairwise independent** *if every pair of events is independent, i.e.,*

$$\forall i \neq j, \qquad \mathbf{P}\{A_i \cap A_j\} = \mathbf{P}\{A_i\} \cdot \mathbf{P}\{A_j\}.$$

Although pairwise independence is weaker than full independence, it still admits some nice properties, as we'll see in Exercise 5.38.

A different notion of independence that comes up frequently in problems (see for example, Exercise 2.14) is that of conditional independence.

Definition 2.17 *Two events E and F are said to be* **conditionally independent** *given event G, where $\mathbf{P}\{G\} > 0$, if*

$$\mathbf{P}\{E \cap F \mid G\} = \mathbf{P}\{E \mid G\} \cdot \mathbf{P}\{F \mid G\}.$$

Independence does not imply conditional independence and vice-versa, see Exercise 2.19.

2.5 Law of Total Probability

Observe that the set E can be expressed as

$$E = (E \cap F) \cup \left(E \cap \overline{F}\right).$$

That is, E is the union of the set $E \cap F$ and the set $E \cap \overline{F}$, because any point in E is also either in F or not in F.

Now observe that $E \cap F$ and $E \cap \overline{F}$ are mutually exclusive. Thus,

$$\mathbf{P}\{E\} = \mathbf{P}\{E \cap F\} + \mathbf{P}\left\{E \cap \overline{F}\right\}$$

$$= \mathbf{P}\{E \mid F\}\mathbf{P}\{F\} + \mathbf{P}\left\{E \mid \overline{F}\right\}\mathbf{P}\left\{\overline{F}\right\},$$

where $\mathbf{P}\left\{\overline{F}\right\} = 1 - \mathbf{P}\{F\}$.

Theorem 2.18 is a generalization of this idea:

> **Theorem 2.18 (Law of Total Probability)** *Let $F_1, F_2, \ldots, F_n$ partition the state space Ω. Then,*
>
> $$P\{E\} = \sum_{i=1}^{n} P\{E \cap F_i\}$$
>
> $$= \sum_{i=1}^{n} P\{E \mid F_i\} \cdot P\{F_i\}.$$
>
> *Remark: This also holds if $F_1, F_2, \ldots, F_n$ partition E.*
> *This also extends to the case where there are countably infinite partitions.*

Proof:

$$E = \bigcup_{i=1}^{n} (E \cap F_i).$$

Now, because the events $E \cap F_i$, $i = 1, \ldots, n$ are mutually exclusive, we have that

$$P\{E\} = \sum_{i=1}^{n} P\{E \cap F_i\} = \sum_{i=1}^{n} P\{E|F_i\} \cdot P\{F_i\}. \qquad \blacksquare$$

Question: Suppose we are interested in the probability of a transaction failure. We know that if there is a caching failure, that will lead to transaction failures with probability $5/6$. We also know that if there is a network failure then that will lead to a transaction failure with probability $1/4$. Suppose that a caching failure occurs with probability $1/100$ and a network failure occurs with probability $1/100$. What is the probability of a transaction failure?

Answer: It is tempting to write (WRONGLY):

$$P\{\text{transaction fails}\} = P\{\text{transaction fails} \mid \text{caching failure}\} \cdot \frac{1}{100}$$

$$+ P\{\text{transaction fails} \mid \text{network failure}\} \cdot \frac{1}{100}$$

$$= \frac{5}{6} \cdot \frac{1}{100} + \frac{1}{4} \cdot \frac{1}{100}.$$

Question: What is wrong with that solution?

Answer: The two events that we conditioned on – a network failure and a caching failure – do not partition the space. The sum of the probabilities of these events is clearly < 1. Furthermore, there may be a non-zero probability that *both* a network failure and a caching failure occur.

One needs to be very careful that the events that we condition on are (1) mutually exclusive and (2) sum to the whole space under consideration.

We can generalize the Law of Total Probability to apply to a conditional probability, as in Theorem 2.19.

> **Theorem 2.19 (Law of Total Probability for conditional probability)** *Let $F_1, F_2, \ldots, F_n$ partition the sample space Ω. Then:*
>
> $$\mathbf{P}\{A \mid B\} = \sum_{i=1}^{n} \mathbf{P}\{A \mid B \cap F_i\} \cdot \mathbf{P}\{F_i \mid B\}.$$

Proof:

$$\mathbf{P}\{A \mid B\} = \frac{\mathbf{P}\{A \cap B\}}{\mathbf{P}\{B\}}$$

$$= \frac{\sum_i \mathbf{P}\{A \cap B \cap F_i\}}{\mathbf{P}\{B\}}$$

$$= \frac{\sum_i \mathbf{P}\{B\} \cdot \mathbf{P}\{F_i \mid B\} \cdot \mathbf{P}\{A \mid B \cap F_i\}}{\mathbf{P}\{B\}} \qquad \text{(chain rule)}$$

$$= \sum_i \mathbf{P}\{F_i \mid B\} \cdot \mathbf{P}\{A \mid B \cap F_i\}. \qquad \blacksquare$$

2.6 Bayes' Law

Sometimes, one needs to know $\mathbf{P}\{F \mid E\}$, but all one knows is the reverse direction: $\mathbf{P}\{E \mid F\}$. Is it possible to get $\mathbf{P}\{F \mid E\}$ from $\mathbf{P}\{E \mid F\}$? It turns out that it is possible, assuming that we also know $\mathbf{P}\{E\}$ and $\mathbf{P}\{F\}$.

> **Theorem 2.20 (Bayes' Law)** *Assuming $\mathbf{P}\{E\} > 0$,*
>
> $$\mathbf{P}\{F \mid E\} = \frac{\mathbf{P}\{E \mid F\} \cdot \mathbf{P}\{F\}}{\mathbf{P}\{E\}}.$$

Proof:

$$\mathbf{P}\{F \mid E\} = \frac{\mathbf{P}\{E \cap F\}}{\mathbf{P}\{E\}} = \frac{\mathbf{P}\{E \mid F\} \cdot \mathbf{P}\{F\}}{\mathbf{P}\{E\}}. \qquad \blacksquare$$

The Law of Total Probability can be combined with Bayes' Law as follows: Let

$F_1, F_2, \ldots, F_n$ partition Ω. Then we can write: $\mathbf{P}\{E\} = \sum_{j=1}^{n} \mathbf{P}\{E \mid F_j\} \cdot \mathbf{P}\{F_j\}$. This yields:

> **Theorem 2.21 (Extended Bayes' Law)** *Let* $F_1, F_2, \ldots, F_n$ *partition* Ω. *Assuming* $\mathbf{P}\{E\} > 0$,
>
> $$\mathbf{P}\{F \mid E\} = \frac{\mathbf{P}\{E \mid F\} \cdot \mathbf{P}\{F\}}{\mathbf{P}\{E\}} = \frac{\mathbf{P}\{E \mid F\} \cdot \mathbf{P}\{F\}}{\sum_{j=1}^{n} \mathbf{P}\{E \mid F_j\} \mathbf{P}\{F_j\}}.$$

Example 2.22 (Cancer screening)

Suppose that there is a rare child cancer that occurs in one out of one million kids. There's a test for this cancer, which is 99.9% effective (see Figure 2.6).

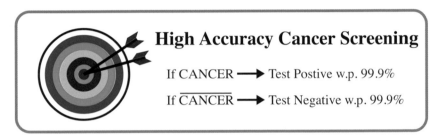

Figure 2.6 *High accuracy cancer screening.*

Question: Suppose that my child's test result is positive. How worried should I be?

Answer:

$\mathbf{P}\{\text{Cancer} \mid \text{Test pos.}\}$

$$= \frac{\mathbf{P}\{\text{Test pos.} \mid \text{Cancer}\} \cdot \mathbf{P}\{\text{Cancer}\}}{\mathbf{P}\{\text{Test pos.} \mid \text{Cancer}\} \cdot \mathbf{P}\{\text{Cancer}\} + \mathbf{P}\{\text{Test pos.} \mid \text{No Cancer}\} \cdot \mathbf{P}\{\text{No Cancer}\}}$$

$$= \frac{0.999 \cdot 10^{-6}}{0.999 \cdot 10^{-6} + 10^{-3} \cdot \left(1 - 10^{-6}\right)}$$

$$\approx \frac{10^{-6}}{10^{-6} + 10^{-3}}$$

$$= \frac{1}{1001}.$$

Thus, the probability that the child has the cancer is less than 1 in 1000.

Question: What was the key factor in obtaining the result?

Answer: There are two things going on here. First, the cancer is very rare: 10^{-6} likelihood. Second, there is a very low probability of error in the test: 10^{-3} chance of error. The *key* determining factor in the chance that the child has cancer is the *ratio* of these two. Consider the ratio of the rareness of the cancer, 10^{-6}, to the low error probability of the test, 10^{-3}. This ratio yields 10^{-3}, which is (roughly) the probability that the child has the cancer. If the cancer were even rarer, say 10^{-7} likelihood, then the probability that the child has cancer would be approximately the ratio $\frac{10^{-7}}{10^{-3}} = 10^{-4}$.

2.7 Exercises

2.1 **Bombs and alarms**
   A bomb detector alarm lights up with probability 0.99 if a bomb is present. If no bomb is present, the bomb alarm still (incorrectly) lights up with probability 0.05. Suppose that a bomb is present with probability 0.1. What is the probability that there is no bomb and the alarm lights up?

2.2 **More on independent events**
   Suppose that we roll a die twice. Consider the following three events:

$$E_1 = \text{Second roll is 4}$$
$$E_2 = \text{Difference between the two rolls is 4}$$
$$E_3 = \text{Difference between the two rolls is 3}$$

   (a) Are E_1 and E_2 independent?
   (b) Are E_1 and E_3 independent?

2.3 **How much do vaccines help?**
   The US Surgeon General recently declared that 99.5% of COVID deaths are among the unvaccinated [40]. Given that I'm vaccinated, what are my chances of dying from COVID? You may use any of the facts below:
   • The fraction of people who are currently vaccinated in the United States is 50%.
   • The fraction of people who die from COVID in the United States is 0.2%.

2.4 **Bayesian reasoning for weather prediction**
   In the hope of having a dry outdoor wedding, John and Mary decide to get married in the desert, where the average number of rainy days per year is 10. Unfortunately, the weather forecaster is predicting rain for tomorrow, the day of John and Mary's wedding. Suppose that the weather forecaster is not perfectly accurate: If it rains the next day, 90% of the time the forecaster predicts rain. If it is dry the next day, 10% of the time the forecaster still

(incorrectly) predicts rain. Given this information, what is the probability that it will rain during John and Mary's wedding?

2.5 **Assessing risk**

Airlines know that on average 5% of the people making flight reservations do not show up. They model this by assuming that each person independently does not show up with probability of 5%. Consequently, their policy is to sell 52 tickets for a flight that can only hold 50 passengers. What is the probability that there will be a seat available for every passenger who shows up?

2.6 **When one event implies another**

Suppose that we are told that event A implies event B. Which of the following *must* be true:

(a) $\mathbf{P}\{A\} \le \mathbf{P}\{B\}$
(b) $\mathbf{P}\{A\} > \mathbf{P}\{B\}$
(c) Neither

2.7 **Wearing masks and COVID**

This problem analyzes mask wearing and COVID via Figure 2.7.

(a) Does consistently wearing masks reduce your chance of catching COVID? Let C (respectively, M) denote the event that a randomly chosen person catches COVID (respectively, consistently wears a mask). Compare $\mathbf{P}\{C \mid M\}$ with $\mathbf{P}\{C \mid \overline{M}\}$.

(b) Your friend comes down with COVID. Based on your answer to part (a), do you think it's more likely that they didn't consistently wear a mask, or that they did? Do the computation to see if you're right.

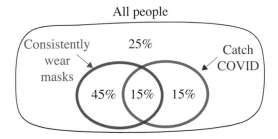

Figure 2.7 *Venn diagram showing fraction of people who wear masks consistently and fraction of people who catch COVID, for Exercise 2.7.*

2.8 **Positive correlation**

We say that events A and B are *positively correlated* if

$$\mathbf{P}\{A \mid B\} > \mathbf{P}\{A\}. \tag{2.6}$$

Prove or disprove that (2.6) implies

$$\mathbf{P}\{B \mid A\} > \mathbf{P}\{B\}. \tag{2.7}$$

Assume that $\mathbf{P}\{A\} > 0$ and $\mathbf{P}\{B\} > 0$.

2.9 Chain rule for conditioning

Let $E_1, E_2, \ldots, E_n$ be n events, where $\mathbf{P}\left\{\bigcap_{i=1}^{n} E_i\right\} > 0$. Prove via induction that

$$\mathbf{P}\left\{\bigcap_{i=1}^{n} E_i\right\} = \mathbf{P}\{E_1\} \cdot \mathbf{P}\{E_2 \mid E_1\} \cdot \mathbf{P}\{E_3 \mid E_1 \cap E_2\} \cdots \mathbf{P}\left\{E_n \mid \bigcap_{i=1}^{n-1} E_i\right\}.$$

2.10 Birthday paradox

The famous birthday paradox considers the situation of a room of $m = 30$ people, where we ask what is the probability that no two have the same birthday. Let A be the event that no two people have the same birthday. It would seem that $\mathbf{P}\{A\}$ is high, given that there are $n = 365$ possible birthdays, but it turns out that $\mathbf{P}\{A\} < e^{-1}$; hence with high likelihood at least two people have the same birthday.

Assume that all n birthdays are equally likely. Prove the above claim via the following conditioning approach: Imagine that the people in the room are ordered, from 1 to m. Let A_i be the event that person i has a different birthday from each of the first $i - 1$ people. Now observe that $A = \bigcap_{i=1}^{m} A_i$, and use the chain rule from Exercise 2.9. [Hint: Leave everything in terms of n and m until the final evaluation. You will need to use (1.14), which says that $1 - \frac{i}{n} \le e^{-\frac{i}{n}}$ for high n.]

2.11 It's a colt!

The offspring of a horse is called a foal. A horse couple has at most one foal at a time. Each foal is equally likely to be a "colt" or a "filly." We are told that a horse couple has two foals, and at least one of these is a colt. Given this information, what's the probability that both foals are colts?

(a) Compute the answer to the above question, assuming only that each foal is equally likely to be a colt or a filly.

(b) Now re-compute the answer given the latest discovery: Scientists have discovered that 10% of horse couples only produce colts, 10% of couples only produce fillies, and 80% are equally likely to produce either gender.

(c) Is your answer for (b) different from that for (a)? Why?

2.12 It's a Sunday colt!

As in Exercise 2.11, we are told that a horse couple has two foals. Additionally, we are told that at least one of these foals is a colt that was born on a Sunday. Given this information, what's the probability that both foals are colts? Assume that a foal is equally like to be born on any day of the week, and is equally likely to be a colt or a filly, and births are independent.

2.13 **Happy or sad**
Independently, on any given day, with probability 50% Mor is happy, and with probability 50% she is sad. While it's hard to know how Mor is feeling, her clothes offer a clue. On her happy days, Mor is 90% likely to wear red and 10% likely to wear black. On her sad days, Mor is 90% likely to wear black and 10% likely to wear red. For the last two days, Mor has worn black. What is the likelihood that Mor has been sad both of the last two days?

2.14 **Bayesian reasoning for healthcare testing**
A pharmaceutical company has developed a potential vaccine against the H1N1 flu virus. Before any testing of the vaccine, the developers assume that with probability 0.5 their vaccine will be effective and with probability 0.5 it will be ineffective. The developers do an initial laboratory test on the vaccine. This initial lab test is only partially indicative of the effectiveness of the vaccine, with an accuracy of 0.6. Specifically, if the vaccine is effective, then this laboratory test will return "success" with probability 0.6, whereas if the vaccine is ineffective, then this laboratory test will return "failure" with probability 0.6.
(a) What is the probability that the laboratory test returns "success"?
(b) What is the probability that the vaccine is effective, given that the laboratory test returned "success"?
(c) The developers decide to add a second experiment (this one on human beings) that is more indicative than the original lab test and has an accuracy of 0.8. Specifically, if the vaccine is effective, then the human being test will return "success" with probability 0.8. If the vaccine is ineffective, then the human being test will return "failure" with probability 0.8. What is the probability that the vaccine is effective, given that both the lab test and the human being test came up "success"? How useful was it to add this additional test? Assume that the two tests (human test and lab test) are conditionally independent on the vaccine being effective or ineffective.

2.15 **Independence of three events**
Natassa suggests the following definition for the independence of three events: Events A, B, and C are independent if

$$\mathbf{P}\{A \cap B \cap C\} = \mathbf{P}\{A\} \cdot \mathbf{P}\{B\} \cdot \mathbf{P}\{C\}.$$

Is Natassa correct? Specifically, does the above definition also ensure that any *pair* of events are independent? Either provide a proof or a counter-example. Assume that your events each have non-zero probability.

2.16 Does independence imply independence of the complement?
Haotian reasons that if event E is independent of event G, then E should also be independent of $\overline{G}$. He argues that if E is not affected by whether G is true, then it should also not be affected by whether G is not true. Either provide a formal proof via the definition of independence, or find a counter-example where you define E, G, and $\overline{G}$.

2.17 Corrupted packets
CMU has two campuses: one in Pittsburgh and one in Qatar. Suppose all packets of a flow originate in either Pittsburgh or in Qatar. Packets originating in Pittsburgh are (independently) corrupted with probability p. Packets originating in Qatar are (independently) corrupted with probability q. We are watching a flow of packets (all from the same origin). At first, we don't know the origin, so we assume that each origin is equally likely. So far, we've seen two packets in the flow, both of which were corrupted. Given this information:
(a) What is the probability that the flow originated in Pittsburgh?
(b) What is the probability that the next packet will be corrupted?

2.18 Pairwise independence and the mystery novel principle
The mystery novel principle considers three events, A, B, and C, where:
- A tells us nothing about C;
- B tells us nothing about C;
- But A and B together tell us everything about C!

Another way of phrasing this is that A, B, and C are "pairwise independent," meaning that any pair of these is independent. However, the three events together are not independent. Provide a simple example of three events with this property. [Hint: You shouldn't need more than two tosses of a coin.]

2.19 Independence does not imply conditional independence
Produce an example of two events, A and B, that are independent, but are no longer independent once we condition on some event C. [Hint: Your example can be very simple. Consider, for instance, the simple experiment of flipping a coin two times, and define events based on that experiment.]

2.20 Does conditional independence imply conditional independence on the complement?
Jelena reasons that if events E and F are conditionally independent of event G, then they should also be conditionally independent of event $\overline{G}$. Either provide a formal proof, or find a counter-example.

2.21 **Another definition of conditional independence?**

Recall that events E and F are conditionally independent on event G if

$$\mathbf{P}\{E \cap F \mid G\} = \mathbf{P}\{E \mid G\} \cdot \mathbf{P}\{F \mid G\}.$$

Taegyun proposes an alternative definition: events E and F are conditionally independent on event G if

$$\mathbf{P}\{E \mid F \cap G\} = \mathbf{P}\{E \mid G\}.$$

Taegyun argues that "knowing F gives no additional information about E, given that we already know G." Is Taegyun's definition equivalent to the original definition (i.e., each definition implies the other) or not? If so, prove it. If not, find a counter-example. Assume that $\mathbf{P}\{F \cap G\} > 0$.

2.22 **The famous Monty Hall problem**

A game show host brings the contestant into a room with three closed doors. Behind one of the doors is a car. Behind the other two doors is a goat. The contestant is asked to pick a door and state which door she has chosen (we'll assume she picks the door at random, because she has no insider knowledge).

Now the game show host, knowing what's behind each door, picks a door that was not chosen by the contestant and reveals that there is a goat behind that door (the game show host will always choose to open a door with a goat). The contestant is then asked, "Would you like to switch from your chosen door?"

One would think that it shouldn't matter whether the contestant switches to the other unopened door, since the car is equally likely to be behind the originally chosen door and the remaining unopened door. This intuition is wrong. Derive the probability that the contestant gets the car, both in the case that the contestant switches doors and the case that the contestant sticks with her original door.

2.23 **Weighty coins**

Imagine that there are two coins of weight w_1 and eight coins of weight w_2, where $w_1 \neq w_2$. All the coins look identical. We pick two pairs of coins, without replacement, from the pile of 10 coins. What is the probability that all the chosen coins have weight w_2, given that the weights of the two pairs are equal?

2.24 **Winning streak**

Assume that the Pittsburgh Steelers win a game with probability p irrespective of the opponent, and that the outcome of each game is independent of the others.

(a) Suppose you are told that the Steelers won four out of the eight games they played in a season. What is the probability that Steelers had a winning streak (i.e., continuous wins) of at least three matches in that season?

(b) Suppose $p = 0.5$. Suppose the Steelers play six games in a particular season. What is the probability that the Steelers will have a winning streak of at least three matches? (Is the hype that a winning streak receives by the media worth it?)

2.25 **Monty Hall with five doors**

A game show host brings the contestant into a room with five closed doors. Behind one of the doors is a car. Behind the other four doors is a goat. The contestant is asked to pick a door and state which door she has chosen (we'll assume she picks the door at random, because she has no insider knowledge).

Now the game show host, knowing what's behind each door, picks a door that was not chosen by the contestant and reveals that there is a goat behind that door (the game show host will always choose to open a door with a goat). The contestant is then asked, "Would you like to switch from your chosen door?"

Derive the probability that the contestant gets the car, both in the case that the contestant switches doors and the case that the contestant sticks with her original door.

2.26 **Another fun door problem**

Imagine there are two doors. Both doors have money behind them, but one contains twice as much money as the other. Suppose you choose one door randomly, and before you look behind the door you are given the chance to switch doors. Should you switch?

(a) Explain what is wrong with the following argument that favors switching:

Suppose M is the money behind the door I chose. Then with probability $\frac{1}{2}$, I chose the door with less money and the other door contains $2M$. Also with probability $\frac{1}{2}$, I chose the door with more money and the other door contains $\frac{M}{2}$. Therefore the expected value of money in the other door is

$$\frac{1}{2} \cdot 2M + \frac{1}{2} \cdot \frac{M}{2} = \frac{5}{4}M > M.$$

So we should switch.

(b) Prove that there is no point to switching.

2.27 **Prediction with an unknown source**

You have two dice. Die A is a fair die (each of the six numbers are equally likely) and die B is a biased die (the number six comes up with probability $\frac{2}{3}$ and the remaining $\frac{1}{3}$ probability is split evenly across all the other numbers).

Kaige picks a die at random and rolls that die three times. Given that the first two rolls are both sixes, what is the probability that the third roll will also be a six?

2.28 **Modeling packet corruption**

Packet switched networks are the backbone of the Internet. Here, data is transferred from a source to a destination by encapsulating and transferring data as a series of packets. There are a number of reasons due to which packets get lost in the network and never reach the destination. Consider two models for packet losses in the network.

Model 1: Each packet is lost with probability p independently.

Model 2: A packet is lost with probability p_1 if its previous packet was transmitted successfully, and is lost with probability p_2 if its previous packet was lost.

Suppose a source sends exactly three packets over the network to a destination. For this setup, under Model 2, assume that the probability of the first packet getting lost is p_1. Further assume $p = p_1 = 0.01$ and $p_2 = 0.5$.

(a) What is the probability that the second packet is lost under Model 1 and Model 2?

(b) Suppose you are told that the third packet is lost. Given this additional information, what is the probability that the second packet is lost under Model 1 and Model 2?

(c) Suppose we represent the loss pattern for the three packets using 0s and 1s, where 0 represents the packet being lost and 1 represents the packet being transferred successfully. For example, loss pattern 110 corresponds to the scenario when the first two packets are transferred successfully and the third packet is lost. What is the probability of loss patterns {010, 100, 001} under Model 1 and Model 2?

(d) What do you observe from your answer to the above question? Specifically, what kind of loss patterns have higher probability in Model 2 as compared to Model 1?

Aside: Extensive measurements over the Internet have shown that packet losses in real-world networks are correlated. Models similar to Model 2 are used to model such correlated packet-loss scenarios. For example, one such model is called the Gilbert–Elliot model [23, 32].

Part II

Discrete Random Variables

In Part I, we saw that experiments are classified as either having a discrete sample space, with a countable number of possible outcomes, or a continuous sample space, with an uncountable number of possible outcomes. In this part, our focus will be on the discrete world. In Part III we will focus on the continuous world.

We start, in Chapter 3, by introducing the notion of a discrete random variable. We then show that everything that we've learned about probability on events applies to random variables as well. In this chapter, we cover the most common discrete distributions: the Bernoulli, Binomial, Geometric, and Poisson.

Chapter 4 is devoted to understanding expectation of discrete random variables. This includes linearity of expectation and conditional expectation. We end with a discussion of Simpson's paradox.

In Chapter 5, we move on to variance and higher moments of discrete random variables. We also introduce the notion of a sum of random variables, where the number being summed is itself a random variable. We next turn to the tail of a random variable, namely the probability that the random variable exceeds some value, introducing some very simple tail bounds, as well as the concept of stochastic dominance. We end with a discussion of the inspection paradox, which is one of the more subtle consequences of high variability.

Finally, in Chapter 6, we finish off our unit on discrete random variables by introducing the z-transform, a moment-generating function which is tailored for discrete random variables. The z-transform allows us to quickly compute all higher moments of random variables. It also has many other applications, including solving recurrence relations.

3 Common Discrete Random Variables

While the previous chapter covered probability on events, in this chapter we will switch to talking about random variables and their corresponding distributions. We will cover the most common discrete distributions, define the notion of a joint distribution, and finish with some practical examples of how to reason about the probability that one device will fail before another.

3.1 Random Variables

Consider an experiment, such as rolling two dice. Suppose that we are interested in the sum of the two rolls. That sum could range anywhere from 2 to 12, with each of these events having a different probability. A *random variable*, X, associated with this experiment is a way to represent the value of the experiment (in this case the sum of the rolls). Specifically, when we write X, it is understood that X has many instances, ranging from 2 to 12 and that different instances occur with different probabilities. For example, $\mathbf{P}\{X = 3\} = \frac{2}{36}$.

Formally, we say,

> **Definition 3.1** *A* **random variable** *(r.v.) is a real-valued function of the outcome of an experiment involving randomness.*

For the above experiment, r.v. X could be the sum of the rolls, while r.v. Y could be the sum of the squares of the two rolls, and r.v. Z could be the value of the first roll only. Any real-valued function of the outcome is legitimate.

As another experiment, we can imagine throwing two darts at the interval $[0, 1]$, where each dart is equally likely to land anywhere in the interval. Random variable D could then represent the distance between the two darts, while r.v. L represents the position of the leftmost dart.

> **Definition 3.2** *A* **discrete random variable** *can take on at most a countably infinite number of possible values, whereas a* **continuous random variable** *can take on an uncountable set of possible values.*

Question: Which of these random variables is discrete and which is continuous?

(a) The sum of the rolls of two dice
(b) The number of arrivals at a website by time t
(c) The time until the next arrival at a website
(d) The CPU requirement of an HTTP request

Answer: The sum of rolls can take on only a finite number of values – those between 2 and 12 – so it clearly is a discrete r.v. The number of arrivals at a website can take on the values: $0, 1, 2, 3, \ldots$ namely a countable set; hence this is discrete as well. Time, in general, is modeled as a continuous quantity, even though there is a non-zero granularity in our ability to measure time via a computer. Thus quantities (c) and (d) are continuous random variables.

We use capital letters to denote random variables. For example, X could be a r.v. denoting the sum of two dice, where

$$\mathbf{P}\{X = 7\} = \mathbf{P}\{(1, 6) \text{ or } (2, 5) \text{ or } (3, 4), \ldots, \text{ or } (6, 1)\} = \frac{1}{6}.$$

Key insight: Because the "outcome of the experiment" is just an event, all the theorems that we learned about events apply to random variables as well. For example, $X = 7$ above is an event. In particular, the Law of Total Probability (Theorem 2.18) holds. For example, if N denotes the number of arrivals at a website by time t, then $N > 10$ is an event. We can then use conditioning on events to get

$$\mathbf{P}\{N > 10\} = \mathbf{P}\{N > 10 \mid \text{ weekday }\} \cdot \frac{5}{7} + \mathbf{P}\{N > 10 \mid \text{ weekend }\} \cdot \frac{2}{7}.$$

All of this will become more concrete when we study examples of random variables.

3.2 Common Discrete Random Variables

Discrete random variables take on a countable number of values, each with some probability. A discrete r.v. is associated with a discrete probability distribution that represents the likelihood of each of these values occurring. We will sometimes go so far as to define a r.v. by the distribution associated with it, omitting the whole discussion of an "experiment."

Definition 3.3 *Let X be a discrete r.v. Then the* **probability mass function (p.m.f.)**, *$p_X(\cdot)$ of X, is defined as:*

$$p_X(a) = \mathbf{P}\{X = a\} \qquad where \qquad \sum_x p_X(x) = 1.$$

The **cumulative distribution function** *of X is defined as:*

$$F_X(a) = \mathbf{P}\{X \le a\} = \sum_{x \le a} p_X(x).$$

The **tail** *of X is defined as:*

$$\overline{F}_X(a) = \mathbf{P}\{X > a\} = \sum_{x > a} p_X(x) = 1 - F_X(a).$$

Common discrete distributions include the Bernoulli, the Binomial, the Geometric, and the Poisson, all of which are discussed next.

3.2.1 The Bernoulli(p) Random Variable

Consider an experiment involving a single coin flip, where the coin has probability p of coming up heads and $1 - p$ of coming up tails.

Let r.v. X represent the outcome of the experiment, that is, the value of the coin. We say that the value is 1 if the coin comes up heads and 0 otherwise. Then,

$$X = \begin{cases} 1 & \text{w/ prob } p \\ 0 & \text{otherwise} \end{cases}.$$

We say that X is a r.v. *drawn from* the Bernoulli(p) distribution, and we write:

$$X \sim \text{Bernoulli}(p).$$

The p.m.f. of r.v. X is defined as follows:

$$p_X(1) = p$$
$$p_X(0) = 1 - p.$$

The p.m.f. is depicted in Figure 3.1.

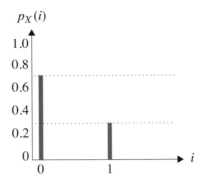

Figure 3.1 *Probability mass function of the Bernoulli($p = 0.3$) distribution.*

3.2.2 The Binomial(n,p) Random Variable

Now consider an experiment where we again have a coin with probability p of coming up heads (success). This time we flip the coin n times (these are independent flips).

Let r.v. X represent the number of heads (successes). Observe that X can take on any of these (discrete) values: $0, 1, 2, \ldots, n$.

The p.m.f. of r.v. X is defined as follows:

$$p_X(i) = \mathbf{P}\{X = i\}$$
$$= \binom{n}{i} p^i (1 - p)^{n-i}, \text{ where } i = 0, 1, 2, \ldots, n.$$

A r.v. X with the above p.m.f. is said to be drawn from the Binomial(n, p) distribution, written: $X \sim$ Binomial(n, p). The p.m.f. is shown in Figure 3.2.

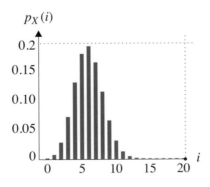

Figure 3.2 *Probability mass function of the Binomial($n = 20, p = 0.3$) distribution.*

Observe that the sum of the p.m.f. is 1, as desired:

$$\sum_{i=0}^{n} p_X(i) = \sum_{i=0}^{n} \binom{n}{i} p^i (1-p)^{n-i} = (p + (1-p))^n = 1. \quad \checkmark$$

Here we've used the binomial expansion from Section 1.5.

3.2.3 The Geometric(p) Random Variable

Again consider an experiment where we have a coin with probability p of coming up heads (success). We now flip the coin until we get a success; these are independent trials, each distributed Bernoulli(p).

Let r.v. X represent the number of flips until we get a success.

The p.m.f. of X is defined as follows:

$$p_X(i) = \mathbf{P}\{X = i\}$$
$$= (1-p)^{i-1} p, \text{ where } i = 1, 2, 3, \ldots.$$

A r.v. X with the above p.m.f. is said to be drawn from the Geometric(p) distribution, written: $X \sim$ Geometric(p). The p.m.f. is shown in Figure 3.3.

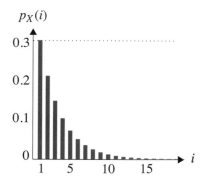

Figure 3.3 *Probability mass function of the Geometric($p = 0.3$) distribution.*

Question: What is $\overline{F}_X(i)$?

Answer:

$$\overline{F}_X(i) = \mathbf{P}\{X > i\} = \mathbf{P}\{\text{First } i \text{ flips were tails}\} = (1-p)^i.$$

Observe that the sum of the p.m.f. is 1, as desired:

$$\sum_{i=1}^{\infty} p_X(i) = \sum_{i=1}^{\infty} (1-p)^{i-1} \cdot p = \sum_{i=0}^{\infty} (1-p)^i \cdot p = p \cdot \frac{1}{1-(1-p)} = 1. \quad \checkmark$$

Here we've used the Geometric series sum from Section 1.1.

Question: Let's review. Suppose you have a room of n disks. Each disk independently dies with probability p each year. How are the following quantities distributed?

(a) The number of disks that die in the first year
(b) The number of years until a particular disk dies
(c) The state of a particular disk after one year

Answer: The distributions are: (a) Binomial(n, p); (b) Geometric(p); (c) Bernoulli(p).

3.2.4 The Poisson(λ) Random Variable

We define the Poisson(λ) distribution via its p.m.f. Although the p.m.f. does not appear to have any meaning at present, we will show many applications of this distribution to computer systems in Chapter 12. In particular, the Poisson distribution occurs naturally when looking at a mixture of a very large number of independent sources, each with a very small individual probability. It can therefore be a reasonable approximation for the distribution of the number of arrivals to a website (or a router) per second, when the average rate of arrivals to the website is λ arrivals per second.

If $X \sim$ Poisson(λ), then

$$p_X(i) = \frac{e^{-\lambda} \lambda^i}{i!}, \quad \text{where } i = 0, 1, 2, \ldots.$$

The p.m.f. for the Poisson(λ) distribution is shown in Figure 3.4.

The sum of the p.m.f. is again 1, as desired:

$$\sum_{i=0}^{\infty} p_X(i) = \sum_{i=0}^{\infty} \frac{e^{-\lambda} \lambda^i}{i!} = e^{-\lambda} \sum_{i=0}^{\infty} \frac{\lambda^i}{i!} = e^{-\lambda} \cdot e^{\lambda} = 1. \quad \checkmark$$

Here we've used the Taylor series expansion from (1.11) of Section 1.4.

Question: Does the shape of the Poisson distribution remind you of other distributions?

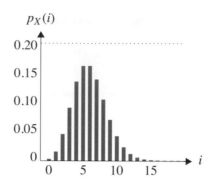

Figure 3.4 *Probability mass function of the Poisson($\lambda = 6$) distribution.*

Answer: The Poisson distribution does not look all that different from the Binomial distribution. It too has a bell-like shape. However, it has an infinite range. In Exercise 3.8 we will see that if n is large and p is small, then Binomial(n, p) is actually very close to Poisson(np). The Poisson distribution is also similar to the Normal distribution (Chapter 9), except that it is lower-bounded by 0.

3.3 Multiple Random Variables and Joint Probabilities

We are often interested in probability statements concerning two or more random variables simultaneously. For example, imagine that we have n disks, each of which fails with probability p every day. We might want to know the probability that all n disks fail on the same day, or the probability that disk 1 fails before disk 2. In asking such questions, we often are assuming that the failure of disks is **independent** (in which case we often say that the disks "independently fail" with probability p on each day). By independent, we mean that the fact that one disk fails doesn't influence the failure of the other disks. However, it could be that the failures are **positively correlated**. By this we mean that the fact that one disk fails makes it more likely that other disks fail as well (for example, maybe the fact that a disk failed means there are mice in the building, which in turn can influence other disks).

In the above scenario, the state of each disk (working or failed) is a r.v. There are several ways to reason about multiple random variables. We introduce two techniques in this section. The first technique involves using the joint p.m.f. and is illustrated in Example 3.6. The second involves conditioning one r.v. on another and is illustrated in Example 3.8.

> **Definition 3.4** *The* **joint probability mass function** *between discrete random variables X and Y is defined by*
>
> $$p_{X,Y}(x, y) = \mathbf{P}\{X = x \ \& \ Y = y\}.$$
>
> *This is equivalently written as* $\mathbf{P}\{X = x, Y = y\}$ *or as* $\mathbf{P}\{X = x \cap Y = y\}$.
> *By definition:*
>
> $$\sum_x \sum_y p_{X,Y}(x, y) = 1.$$

Question: What is the relationship between $p_X(x)$ and $p_{X,Y}(x, y)$?

Answer: Via the Law of Total Probability, we have:

$$p_X(x) = \sum_y p_{X,Y}(x, y) \quad \text{and} \quad p_Y(y) = \sum_x p_{X,Y}(x, y).$$

When written this way, $p_X(x)$ is often referred to as the **marginal probability mass function** of X. The term "marginal" comes from the fact that $p_X(x)$ here would appear in the margins of a joint p.m.f. table, after summing an entire column over all y values.

Similarly to the way we defined two events E and F as being independent, we can likewise define two random variables as being independent. This is because $X = x$ and $Y = y$ are events.

> **Definition 3.5** *We say that discrete random variables X and Y are* **independent**, *written $X \perp Y$, if*
>
> $$\mathbf{P}\{X = x \ \& \ Y = y\} = \mathbf{P}\{X = x\} \cdot \mathbf{P}\{Y = y\}, \quad \forall x, y$$
>
> *or, equivalently,*
>
> $$p_{X,Y}(x, y) = p_X(x) \cdot p_Y(y).$$

Question: If X and Y are independent, what does this say about $\mathbf{P}\{X = x \mid Y = y\}$?

Answer: Again, since $X = x$ and $Y = y$ are events, we can apply the simple conditioning formula that we learned in Chapter 2. As expected,

$$\mathbf{P}\{X = x \mid Y = y\} = \frac{\mathbf{P}\{X = x \ \& \ Y = y\}}{\mathbf{P}\{Y = y\}} = \frac{\mathbf{P}\{X = x\} \cdot \mathbf{P}\{Y = y\}}{\mathbf{P}\{Y = y\}} = \mathbf{P}\{X = x\}.$$

Example 3.6 (Who fails first?)

Here's a question that commonly comes up in industry, but isn't immediately obvious. You have a disk with probability p_1 of failing each day. You have a CPU which independently has probability p_2 of failing each day.

Question: What is the probability that your disk fails *before* your CPU?

Before you look at the answer, try to think for yourself what the answer might be. Is it $|p_1 - p_2|$, or $\frac{p_1}{p_2}$, or $p_1(1 - p_2)$?

Answer: We model the problem by considering two Geometric random variables and deriving the probability that one is smaller than the other. Let $X_1 \sim$ Geometric(p_1) and $X_2 \sim$ Geometric(p_2), where $X_1 \perp X_2$. We want $\mathbf{P}\{X_1 < X_2\}$.

$$\mathbf{P}\{X_1 < X_2\} = \sum_{k=1}^{\infty} \sum_{k_2=k+1}^{\infty} p_{X_1,X_2}(k, k_2)$$

$$= \sum_{k=1}^{\infty} \sum_{k_2=k+1}^{\infty} p_{X_1}(k) \cdot p_{X_2}(k_2) \quad \text{(by independence)}$$

$$= \sum_{k=1}^{\infty} \sum_{k_2=k+1}^{\infty} (1 - p_1)^{k-1} p_1 \cdot (1 - p_2)^{k_2-1} p_2$$

$$= \sum_{k=1}^{\infty} (1 - p_1)^{k-1} p_1 \sum_{k_2=k+1}^{\infty} (1 - p_2)^{k_2-1} p_2$$

$$= \sum_{k=1}^{\infty} (1 - p_1)^{k-1} p_1 (1 - p_2)^{k} \sum_{k_2=1}^{\infty} (1 - p_2)^{k_2-1} p_2$$

$$= \sum_{k=1}^{\infty} (1 - p_1)^{k-1} p_1 (1 - p_2)^{k} \cdot 1$$

$$= p_1(1 - p_2) \sum_{k=1}^{\infty} [(1 - p_2)(1 - p_1)]^{k-1}$$

$$= \frac{p_1(1 - p_2)}{1 - (1 - p_2)(1 - p_1)}. \tag{3.1}$$

Question: Explain why your final expression (3.1) makes sense.

Answer: Think about X_1 and X_2 in terms of coin flips. Notice that all the flips are irrelevant until the final flip, since before the final flip both the X_1 coin and the X_2 coin only yield tails. $\mathbf{P}\{X_1 < X_2\}$ is the probability that on that final flip, where by definition at least one coin comes up heads, it is the case that the X_1

coin is heads and the X_2 coin is tails. So we're looking for the probability that the X_1 coin produces a heads and the X_2 coin produces a tails, conditioned on the fact that they're not both tails, which is derived as:

$$\mathbf{P}\{\text{Coin } 1 = H \text{ \& Coin } 2 = T \mid \text{not both } T\} = \frac{\mathbf{P}\{\text{Coin } 1 = H \text{ \& Coin } 2 = T\}}{\mathbf{P}\{\text{not both } T\}}$$

$$= \frac{p_1(1 - p_2)}{1 - (1 - p_2)(1 - p_1)}. \quad \checkmark$$

Another way to approach Example 3.6 is to use conditioning. In computing the probability of an event, we saw in Chapter 2 that it is useful to condition on other events. We can use this same idea in computing probabilities involving random variables, because $X = k$ and $Y = y$ are just events. Thus, Theorem 3.7 follows immediately from the Law of Total Probability (Theorem 2.18).

Theorem 3.7 (Law of Total Probability for Discrete R.V.) *We can express the probability of an event E by conditioning on a discrete r.v. Y as follows:*

$$\mathbf{P}\{E\} = \sum_y \mathbf{P}\{E \cap Y = y\} = \sum_y \mathbf{P}\{E \mid Y = y\} \cdot \mathbf{P}\{Y = y\}.$$

Likewise, for discrete random variables X and Y, we can express the probability of the event X = k by conditioning on the value of Y as follows:

$$\mathbf{P}\{X = k\} = \sum_y \mathbf{P}\{X = k \cap Y = y\} = \sum_y \mathbf{P}\{X = k \mid Y = y\} \cdot \mathbf{P}\{Y = y\}.$$

As always, being able to condition is a *huge* tool! It allows us to break a problem into a number of simpler problems. The trick, as usual, is knowing what to condition on.

Example 3.8 (Who fails first, revisited)

Suppose again that your disk has probability p_1 of failing each day, and your CPU independently has probability p_2 of failing each day.

Question: What is the probability that your disk fails *before* your CPU? This time use conditioning to determine this probability.

Answer: Again, let $X_1 \sim \text{Geometric}(p_1)$ and $X_2 \sim \text{Geometric}(p_2)$, where $X_1 \perp X_2$.

$$\mathbf{P}\{X_1 < X_2\} = \sum_{k=1}^{\infty} \mathbf{P}\{X_1 < X_2 \mid X_1 = k\} \cdot \mathbf{P}\{X_1 = k\}$$

$$= \sum_{k=1}^{\infty} \mathbf{P}\{k < X_2 \mid X_1 = k\} \cdot \mathbf{P}\{X_1 = k\}$$

$$= \sum_{k=1}^{\infty} \mathbf{P}\{X_2 > k\} \cdot \mathbf{P}\{X_1 = k\} \quad \text{(by independence)}$$

$$= \sum_{k=1}^{\infty} (1 - p_2)^k \cdot (1 - p_1)^{k-1} \cdot p_1$$

$$= p_1(1 - p_2) \sum_{k=1}^{\infty} [(1 - p_2)(1 - p_1)]^{k-1}$$

$$= \frac{p_1(1 - p_2)}{1 - (1 - p_2)(1 - p_1)}.$$

Unsurprisingly, conditioning leads to a simpler solution.

3.4 Exercises

3.1 ORs and ANDs
Two fair coins are flipped. Let X represent the logical OR of the two flips. Let Y represent the logical AND of the two flips.
(a) What is the distribution of X?
(b) What is the distribution of Y?
(c) What is the distribution of $X + Y$?

3.2 If at first you don't succeed
Every day, independently at random, I win a prize with probability $\frac{1}{100}$. What is the probability that it takes more than 100 days to win a prize?

3.3 Independence
We're given a joint p.m.f. for two discrete random variables X and Y.

	$Y = 1$	$Y = 2$	$Y = 3$
$X = 0$	1/8	1/4	1/8
$X = 1$	1/8	0	3/8

(a) What is $p_{X,Y}(0, 1)$? What is $p_X(0)$? What is $p_Y(1)$?
(b) Are X and Y independent?

3.4 From 10 disks to 1
Today you have 10 working disks. Suppose that each disk independently dies with probability p each day. What is the probability that tomorrow you have just 1 working disk?

3.5 Independence of random variables
Sachit has been studying the definition of independence of discrete random variables (Definition 3.3). He's wondering if the following statement is a corollary of the definition:

If $X \perp Y$, then $\mathbf{P}\{X > i \ \& \ Y > j\} = \mathbf{P}\{X > i\} \cdot \mathbf{P}\{Y > j\}$.

Prove or disprove this statement.

3.6 More independence practice
We're given a joint p.m.f. for two random variables X and Y.

	$Y = 1$	$Y = 2$	$Y = 3$
$X = 1$	3/8	3/16	1/4
$X = 2$	1/8	1/16	0

(a) Are X and Y independent?
(b) What is $\mathbf{P}\{X = 1 \mid Y > 1\}$?
(c) Find an event A where X and Y are conditionally independent given A.

3.7 Sum of two independent Binomials
Let $X \sim \text{Binomial}(n, p)$ and $Y \sim \text{Binomial}(n, p)$, where $X \perp Y$. What is the distribution of $Z = X + Y$? [Hint: Don't try to do this via math. Think about the experiment.]

3.8 Poisson approximation to Binomial
You will prove that the Binomial(n, p) distribution is well approximated by the Poisson(np) distribution when n is large and p is small. Let $X \sim$ Binomial(n, p) and consider $p_X(i)$, for an arbitrary fixed value of $i \geq 0$. In your expression for $p_X(i)$, set $p = \lambda/n$ so that $p_X(i)$ is expressed in terms of only λ and n. Expand out all the "choose" terms. Now take the limit as $n \to \infty$, while remembering that i is a fixed constant. Show that $p_X(i)$ approaches the p.m.f. of a Poisson(λ) r.v.

3.9 COVID testing
[Proposed by Vanshika Chowdhary] On day 0, you take a long-distance flight and you are infected with COVID with probability $\frac{1}{2}$. Being a responsible citizen, you decide to quarantine for 14 days. You also visit a wizard, who gives you some special beans to help cure you, just in case you are sick. You take the beans every day, starting on day 1 of your quarantine. Each day, the beans have a $\frac{1}{8}$ chance of immediately curing you. Suppose

you are tested at the end of day 14 (after 14 days of taking beans) and the test comes back negative. What is the probability that you were actually infected with COVID on day 0? Assume that the test is fully accurate.

3.10 Marginal probability

An urn contains n balls, which are numbered $1, 2, \ldots, n$. Suppose that we draw $k < n$ balls *without replacement* from the urn. Each ball is selected at random. Specifically, in the first draw, each ball has probability $\frac{1}{n}$ of being selected. In the second draw, each of the remaining $n - 1$ balls has probability $\frac{1}{n-1}$ of being selected, and so on. Let X_i denote the number on the ith ball drawn. Your goal is to prove that

$$\mathbf{P}\{X_i = \ell\} = \frac{1}{n}.$$

To do that, follow these steps:
(a) Are the X_i's independent?
(b) Write an expression for $\mathbf{P}\{X_1 = a_1, X_2 = a_2, \ldots, X_k = a_k\}$, where $1 \leq a_i \leq n$.
(c) Express the marginal probability, $\mathbf{P}\{X_i = \ell\}$, as a sum

$$\mathbf{P}\{X_i = \ell\} = \sum \mathbf{P}\{X_1 = a_1, \ldots, X_{i-1} = a_{i-1}, X_i = \ell, \ldots, X_k = a_k\}.$$

What is the sum over?
(d) Evaluate the summation from (c). Start by evaluating the term inside the sum. Then determine the number of terms being summed.

3.11 Binary symmetric channel (BSC)

A binary symmetric channel is a communications model used in coding theory. There is a transmitter who wishes to send a bit, B. There is noise, N, which may corrupt the bit, and there is a final output Y, where

$$Y = B \oplus N.$$

Here, $\oplus$ is a binary sum. Assume that $B \sim \text{Bernoulli}(p)$ and that $N \sim \text{Bernoulli}(0.5)$ and that $N \perp B$. Can we say that $B \perp Y$? Why or why not?

3.12 Noisy reading from flash storage

Flash memories are a type of storage media which provide orders of magnitude faster access to data as compared to hard disks. However, one of the downsides of flash memories is that they are prone to error when reading. You have two flash memory devices, F1 and F2. The noisy readings from F1 and F2 are modeled as follows:
• F1: For any stored bit, the value read is flipped with probability p_1.
• F2: For any stored bit, the value read is flipped with probability p_2.
Suppose you write a bit into both F1 and F2 (i.e., the same bit is written into both devices), and that F1 and F2 act independently on that bit. A day

later, you read the bit that you wrote from F1 and from F2. Represent the value read from F1 by the r.v. Y_1 and the value read from F2 by Y_2. Assume that the stored bit is represented by X, where X is equally likely to be 0 or 1, barring any other information.

(a) Assume that $p_1 = 0.1$ and $p_2 = 0.2$, that is, the probability of flipping is low. Are Y_1 and Y_2 dependent? Explain using the definition of independence of random variables.

(b) Repeat when $p_1 = 0.5$ and $p_2 = 0.2$. Now are Y_1 and Y_2 dependent?

(c) Repeat when $p_1 = 0.7$ and $p_2 = 0.8$. Now are Y_1 and Y_2 dependent?

(d) For what values of p_1 and p_2 do you conjecture that Y_1 and Y_2 are dependent? Why do you think this is?

3.13 **Correlated basketball**
A basketball player attempts a shot and makes it. She attempts another shot and misses it. Her subsequent shots have success probability based on the proportion of her previous successful shots. What's the probability she makes 50 out of 100 shots? [Hint: Try looking for a pattern.]

3.14 **How to find a mate**
Imagine that there are n people in the world. You want to find the best spouse. You date one person at a time. After dating a person, you must decide if you want to marry them. If you decide to marry, then you're done. If you decide not to marry, then that person will never again agree to marry you (they're on the "burn list"), and you move on to the next person.

Suppose that after dating a person you can accurately rank them in comparison with all the other people you've dated so far. You do not, however, know their rank relative to people you haven't dated. So, for example, you might early on date the person who is the best of the n, but you don't know that – you only know that this person is better than the people you've dated so far.

For the purpose of this problem, assume that each candidate has a unique score, uniformly distributed between 0 and 1. Your goal is to find the candidate with the highest score.

> **Algorithm 3.9 (Marriage algorithm)**
> 1. Date $r \ll n$ people. Rank those r to determine the "best of r."
> 2. Now keep dating people until you find a person who is better than that "best of r" person.
> 3. As soon as you find such a person, marry them. If you never find such a person, you'll stay unwed.

What value of r maximizes $\mathbf{P}$ {end up marrying the best of n}? When using that r, what is the probability that you end up marrying the best person? In your analysis, feel free to assume that n is large and thus $H_n \approx \ln(n)$, by (1.17).

4 Expectation

In Chapter 3, we studied several common discrete distributions. In this chapter we will learn how to obtain their mean, or expectation. We will also cover some useful tools that help us to simplify deriving expectations, such as the linearity of expectation result and deriving expectations by conditioning.

4.1 Expectation of a Discrete Random Variable

The probability mass function (p.m.f.) of a random variable (r.v.) specifies the possible values of the r.v., each with a probability ("weight"). The *expectation* of the random variable, also known as its *mean* or *average*, is a way of summarizing all these different values into a single number. This single number is the sum of all the values, each weighted by its probability of occurring. Expectation is typically used to give us a single value when trading off different options.

Example 4.1 (Choosing between startups)

Suppose you have to choose between startups to join. Startup A will give you a win of ten million dollars with probability 10%, but will cost you one million dollars with probability 90%. Startup B will give you a win of one million dollars with probability 50%, but will cost you half a million with probability 50%.

Question: Which do you choose?

Answer: One way of comparing the two options is to think of A and B as random variables and compare their expectations:

$$\text{Expected value of A } = 10^7 \cdot (0.1) + (-10^6) \cdot (0.9) = 10^5.$$
$$\text{Expected value of B } = 10^6 \cdot (0.5) + (-0.5 \cdot 10^6) \cdot (0.5) = 2.5 \cdot 10^5.$$

By this metric, one might choose startup B. On the other hand, one could also say that expectation is not the right view, since no startup is worth joining if there isn't a potential upside of at least 10 million dollars.

> **Definition 4.2** *The **expectation of a discrete random variable** X, written* $\mathbf{E}[X]$, *is the sum of the possible values of X, each weighted by its probability:*
>
> $$\mathbf{E}[X] = \sum_x x \mathbf{P}\{X = x\}.$$
>
> *We can also think of $\mathbf{E}[X]$ as representing the mean of the distribution from which X is drawn.*

The following example illustrates why expectation is thought of as an average.

Example 4.3 (Average cost of lunch)

Table 4.1 shows the daily cost of my lunch. What is the average cost of my lunch?

Mon	Tues	Wed	Thurs	Fri	Sat	Sun
$7	$7	$12	$12	$12	$0	$9

Table 4.1 *Cost of lunch example.*

We can think of *Cost* as a r.v. that takes on each of the values in Table 4.1 with probability $\frac{1}{7}$. Then,

$$\text{Average Cost} = \frac{7 + 7 + 12 + 12 + 12 + 0 + 9}{7}$$

$$|||$$

$$\mathbf{E}[\text{Cost}] = 7 \cdot \left(\frac{2}{7}\right) + 12 \cdot \left(\frac{3}{7}\right) + 9 \cdot \left(\frac{1}{7}\right) + 0 \cdot \left(\frac{1}{7}\right).$$

In the expectation view, each possible value (7, 12, 9, and 0) is weighted by its probability.

Question: If $X \sim \text{Bernoulli}(p)$, what is $\mathbf{E}[X]$?

Answer: $\mathbf{E}[X] = 0 \cdot (1 - p) + 1 \cdot (p) = p$.

Example 4.4 (Expected time until disk fails)

Question: Suppose a disk has probability $\frac{1}{3}$ of failing each year. On average, how many years will it be until the disk fails?

Answer: This is simply $\mathbf{E}[X]$, where $X \sim$ Geometric(p), with $p = \frac{1}{3}$. Assuming $X \sim$ Geometric(p), we have:

$$\mathbf{E}[X] = \sum_{n=1}^{\infty} n(1-p)^{n-1}p$$

$$= p \cdot \sum_{n=1}^{\infty} n \cdot q^{n-1} \quad \text{where } q = (1-p)$$

$$= p \cdot \left(1 + 2q + 3q^2 + 4q^3 + \ldots\right)$$

$$= p \cdot \frac{1}{(1-q)^2} \quad \text{using (1.4)}$$

$$= p \cdot \frac{1}{p^2}$$

$$= \frac{1}{p}.$$

So when $p = \frac{1}{3}$, the expected number of years until the disk fails is 3. (This type of analysis will be repeated throughout the book, so commit it to memory.)

Question: If $X \sim$ Poisson(λ), what is $\mathbf{E}[X]$?

Answer:

$$\mathbf{E}[X] = \sum_{i=0}^{\infty} i \frac{e^{-\lambda}\lambda^i}{i!}$$

$$= \sum_{i=1}^{\infty} i \frac{e^{-\lambda}\lambda^i}{i!}$$

$$= \lambda e^{-\lambda} \sum_{i=1}^{\infty} \frac{\lambda^{i-1}}{(i-1)!}$$

$$= \lambda e^{-\lambda} \sum_{k=0}^{\infty} \frac{\lambda^k}{k!}$$

$$= \lambda e^{-\lambda} e^{\lambda} \quad \text{using (1.11)}$$

$$= \lambda.$$

It is interesting to note that the λ parameter for the Poisson distribution is also its mean. The same holds for the p parameter of the Bernoulli distribution. By contrast, the p parameter of the Geometric distribution is the reciprocal of its mean.

One can also consider the expectation of a function of a random variable.

> **Definition 4.5** *The* **expectation of a function** $g(\cdot)$ *of a discrete random variable X is defined as follows:*
> $$\mathbf{E}[g(X)] = \sum_x g(x) \cdot p_X(x).$$

Example 4.6 (Volume of sphere)

Consider a sphere, where the radius is a random variable, R, where

$$R = \begin{cases} 1 & \text{w/ prob. } \frac{1}{3} \\ 2 & \text{w/ prob. } \frac{1}{3} \\ 3 & \text{w/ prob. } \frac{1}{3} \end{cases}.$$

Question: What is the expected volume of the sphere?

Answer:

$$\mathbf{E}[\text{Volume}] = \mathbf{E}\left[\frac{4}{3}\pi R^3\right]$$
$$= \frac{4}{3}\pi \cdot 1^3 \cdot \frac{1}{3} + \frac{4}{3}\pi \cdot 2^3 \cdot \frac{1}{3} + \frac{4}{3}\pi \cdot 3^3 \cdot \frac{1}{3}$$
$$= 16\pi.$$

Observe that

$$\mathbf{E}\left[R^3\right] \neq (\mathbf{E}[R])^3.$$

Question: Suppose X is defined as follows:

$$X = \begin{cases} 0 & \text{w/ prob. } 0.2 \\ 1 & \text{w/ prob. } 0.5 \\ 2 & \text{w/ prob. } 0.3 \end{cases}.$$

What is $\mathbf{E}[X]$ and what is $\mathbf{E}\left[2X^2 + 3\right]$?

Answer:

$$\mathbf{E}[X] = 0 \cdot (0.2) + 1 \cdot (0.5) + 2 \cdot (0.3).$$
$$\mathbf{E}\left[2X^2 + 3\right] = \left(2 \cdot 0^2 + 3\right)(0.2) + \left(2 \cdot 1^2 + 3\right)(0.5) + \left(2 \cdot 2^2 + 3\right)(0.3).$$

You may have noticed that $\mathbf{E}\left[2X^2 + 3\right] = 2\mathbf{E}\left[X^2\right] + 3$. This is no coincidence and is due to Linearity of Expectation, to be discussed in Section 4.2.

We can also consider the expectation of a function of multiple random variables.

Definition 4.7 *Let X and Y be random variables. The* **expectation of the product** *XY is defined by summing over all possible outcomes (x, y) as follows:*

$$\mathbf{E}[XY] = \sum_x \sum_y xy \cdot p_{X,Y}(x, y),$$

where $p_{X,Y}(x, y) = \mathbf{P}\{X = x \,\&\, Y = y\}$.

Theorem 4.8 (Expectation of a product) *If $X \perp Y$, then*

$$\mathbf{E}[XY] = \mathbf{E}[X] \cdot \mathbf{E}[Y].$$

Proof:

$$\mathbf{E}[XY] = \sum_x \sum_y xy \cdot \mathbf{P}\{X = x, Y = y\}$$

$$= \sum_x \sum_y xy \cdot \mathbf{P}\{X = x\}\mathbf{P}\{Y = y\} \quad \text{(by definition of } \perp\text{)}$$

$$= \sum_x x\mathbf{P}\{X = x\} \cdot \sum_y y\mathbf{P}\{Y = y\}$$

$$= \mathbf{E}[X]\mathbf{E}[Y]. \qquad\qquad\blacksquare$$

The same proof shows that if $X \perp Y$, then

$$\mathbf{E}[g(X)f(Y)] = \mathbf{E}[g(X)] \cdot \mathbf{E}[f(Y)], \tag{4.1}$$

for arbitrary functions g and f. A consequence of (4.1) is that if $X \perp Y$, then:

$$\mathbf{E}\left[\frac{X}{Y}\right] = \mathbf{E}[X] \cdot \mathbf{E}\left[\frac{1}{Y}\right].$$

Question: If $\mathbf{E}[XY] = \mathbf{E}[X]\mathbf{E}[Y]$, does that imply that $X \perp Y$?

Answer: No, see Exercise 4.7.

We end this section with Theorem 4.9, which offers an alternative way of computing expectations that can be very useful in practice. *Remember this!*

Theorem 4.9 (Alternative definition of expectation) *Let r.v. X be non-negative, discrete, and integer-valued. Then*

$$\mathbf{E}[X] = \sum_{x=0}^{\infty} \mathbf{P}\{X > x\}. \tag{4.2}$$

Proof: See Exercise 4.16. $\qquad\qquad\blacksquare$

4.2 Linearity of Expectation

The following is one of the most powerful theorems of probability:

> **Theorem 4.10 (Linearity of Expectation)** *For random variables X and Y,*
>
> $$\mathbf{E}[X+Y] = \mathbf{E}[X] + \mathbf{E}[Y].$$

Question: Does Theorem 4.10 require $X \perp Y$?

Answer: Surprisingly not!

Proof: Theorem 4.10 holds for both discrete and continuous random variables. We show below a proof for the case of discrete random variables and will re-prove this in Chapter 8 for the case of continuous random variables.

$$\mathbf{E}[X+Y] = \sum_y \sum_x (x+y)p_{X,Y}(x,y)$$

$$= \sum_y \sum_x x p_{X,Y}(x,y) + \sum_y \sum_x y p_{X,Y}(x,y)$$

$$= \sum_x \sum_y x p_{X,Y}(x,y) + \sum_y \sum_x y p_{X,Y}(x,y)$$

$$= \sum_x x \sum_y p_{X,Y}(x,y) + \sum_y y \sum_x p_{X,Y}(x,y)$$

$$= \sum_x x p_X(x) + \sum_y y p_Y(y)$$

$$= \mathbf{E}[X] + \mathbf{E}[Y]. \qquad \blacksquare$$

Observe that the same proof can also be used to show that

$$\mathbf{E}[f(X) + g(Y)] = \mathbf{E}[f(X)] + \mathbf{E}[g(Y)].$$

Linearity of Expectation can simplify many proofs. We show some examples.

Example 4.11 (Mean of Binomial)

Let $X \sim \text{Binomial}(n, p)$. What is $\mathbf{E}[X]$?

Recall $\mathbf{E}[X] = \sum_{i=0}^{n} i\binom{n}{i}p^i(1-p)^{n-i}$. This expression may appear daunting.

Question: Can we instead think of Binomial(n, p) as a sum of random variables?

Answer:

$$X = \text{number of heads (successes) in } n \text{ trials} = X_1 + X_2 + \cdots + X_n,$$

where

$$X_i = \begin{cases} 1 & \text{if trial } i \text{ is successful} \\ 0 & \text{otherwise} \end{cases}$$

$$\mathbf{E}[X_i] = p.$$

Then,

$$\mathbf{E}[X] = \mathbf{E}[X_1] + \mathbf{E}[X_2] + \cdots + \mathbf{E}[X_n] = n\mathbf{E}[X_i] = np.$$

Question: What is the intuition behind this result?

Answer: There are n coin flips, each with probability p of coming up heads, which should result in an average of np heads.

The X_i's above are called **indicator random variables** because they take on values 0 or 1. In the previous example, the X_i's were **independent and identically distributed** (**i.i.d.**). However, even if the trials were *not* independent, we would still have

$$\mathbf{E}[X] = \mathbf{E}[X_1] + \cdots + \mathbf{E}[X_n].$$

The following example makes this clear.

Example 4.12 (Drinking from your own cup)

At a party, n people put their drink on a table. Later that night, no one can remember which cup is theirs, so they simply each grab any cup at random (Figure 4.1). Let X denote the number of people who get back their own drink. Think of this as a random permutation of cups across people.

Question: What is $\mathbf{E}[X]$? How do you imagine that $\mathbf{E}[X]$ might depend on n?

Hint: Start by trying to express X as a sum of indicator random variables?

Answer: $X = I_1 + I_2 + \cdots + I_n$, where

$$I_i = \begin{cases} 1 & \text{if the } i\text{th person gets their own drink} \\ 0 & \text{otherwise} \end{cases}.$$

Although the I_i's have the same distribution (by symmetry), they are *not* independent of each other! Nevertheless, we can still use Linearity of Expectation to

Figure 4.1 *Each person picks up a random cup.*

say

$$\begin{aligned}
\mathbf{E}\left[X\right] &= \mathbf{E}\left[I_1\right] + \mathbf{E}\left[I_2\right] + \cdots + \mathbf{E}\left[I_n\right] \\
&= n\mathbf{E}\left[I_i\right] \\
&= n\left(\frac{1}{n} \cdot 1 + \frac{n-1}{n} \cdot 0\right) \\
&= 1.
\end{aligned}$$

Interestingly, the expected number of people who get back their own drink is independent of n!

Example 4.13 (Coupon collector)

Imagine there are n distinct coupons that we are trying to collect (Figure 4.2). Every time that we draw a coupon, we get one of the n coupons at *random*, with each coupon being equally likely. (You can think of this as draws with replacement, or you can imagine that there are an infinite number of each of the n coupon types.) Thus it is quite likely that the same coupon will be drawn more than one time. The coupon collector question asks:

How many draws does it take in expectation until I get all n distinct coupons?

Let D denote the number of draws needed to collect all coupons.

Question: What is $\mathbf{E}\left[D\right]$?

Answer: It is not at all obvious how to get $\mathbf{E}\left[D\right]$. The trick is to try to express

Figure 4.2 *The goal of the coupon collector problem is to collect all n coupons.*

D as a sum of random variables:

$$D = D_1 + D_2 + \cdots + D_n. \tag{4.3}$$

Question: What should D_i represent?

Answer: One might think that D_i should be the number of draws needed to get coupon number i. But this doesn't work, because while I'm trying to get coupon i, I might be drawing other coupons.

Question: Is there a better definition for D_i that doesn't result in over-counting?

Answer: Let D_i denote the number of draws needed to get the ith *distinct* coupon, after getting $i - 1$ distinct coupons. That is, D_1 is the number of draws needed to get any coupon (namely $D_1 = 1$). D_2 is the number of *additional* draws needed to get a coupon which is distinct from the first coupon. D_3 is the number of *additional* draws needed to get a coupon which is distinct from the first two distinct coupons.

Question: How is D_i distributed?

Answer:

$$D_1 \sim \text{Geometric}(1) = 1$$
$$D_2 \sim \text{Geometric}\left(\frac{n-1}{n}\right)$$
$$D_3 \sim \text{Geometric}\left(\frac{n-2}{n}\right)$$
$$\vdots$$
$$D_n \sim \text{Geometric}\left(\frac{1}{n}\right).$$

We are now finally ready to apply Linearity of Expectation to (4.3).

$$\mathbf{E}[D] = \mathbf{E}[D_1 + D_2 + \cdots + D_n]$$
$$= \mathbf{E}[D_1] + \mathbf{E}[D_2] + \cdots + \mathbf{E}[D_n]$$
$$= 1 + \frac{n}{n-1} + \frac{n}{n-2} + \cdots + \frac{n}{1}.$$

But we can express this in terms of the harmonic series (see Section 1.4) as follows:

$$\mathbf{E}[D] = n \cdot \left(\frac{1}{n} + \frac{1}{n-1} + \frac{1}{n-2} + \cdots + 1\right) = n \cdot H_n, \qquad (4.4)$$

where

$$H_n = 1 + \frac{1}{2} + \frac{1}{3} + \ldots + \frac{1}{n}.$$

Question: What is $\mathbf{E}[D]$ approximately equal to for large n?

Answer: From (1.17), it follows that $\mathbf{E}[D] \approx n \ln n$.

4.3 Conditional Expectation

One is often interested in the expected value of a random variable conditioned on some event. For example, if X is a random variable denoting the price of a hotel room and A is the event that the month is March, one might be interested in $\mathbf{E}[X \mid A]$, which is the expected price of the room given that the month is March.

Recall that $p_X(\cdot)$ is the p.m.f. for r.v. X, where

$$p_X(x) = \mathbf{P}\{X = x\}.$$

To understand conditional expectation, rather than working with the p.m.f., we need to work with the *conditional p.m.f.*

> **Definition 4.14** *Let X be a discrete r.v. with p.m.f. $p_X(\cdot)$ defined over a countable sample space. Let A be an event s.t. $\mathbf{P}\{A\} > 0$. Then $p_{X|A}(\cdot)$ is the* **conditional p.m.f.** *of X given event A. We define*
>
> $$p_{X|A}(x) = \mathbf{P}\{X = x \mid A\} = \frac{\mathbf{P}\{(X = x) \cap A\}}{\mathbf{P}\{A\}}.$$

A conditional probability thus involves narrowing down the probability space. To see this, let's consider some examples.

Example 4.15 (Conditioning on an event)

Let X denote the size of a job. Suppose that

$$X = \begin{cases} 1 & \text{w/ prob. } 0.1 \\ 2 & \text{w/ prob. } 0.2 \\ 3 & \text{w/ prob. } 0.3 \\ 4 & \text{w/ prob. } 0.2 \\ 5 & \text{w/ prob. } 0.2 \end{cases}.$$

Let A be the event that the job is "small," meaning that its size is ≤ 3. Our goal is to understand the conditional p.m.f. of X given event A, which is colored in blue.

Question: What is $p_X(1)$?

Answer: $p_X(1) = 0.1$.

Question: What is $p_{X|A}(1)$?

Answer: Intuitively, if we condition on the job being small (blue), we can see that, of the blue jobs, one-sixth of them have size 1. Algebraically:

$$\begin{aligned} p_{X|A}(1) = \mathbf{P}\{X = 1 \mid A\} &= \frac{\mathbf{P}\{X = 1 \,\&\, A\}}{\mathbf{P}\{A\}} \\ &= \frac{\mathbf{P}\{X = 1\}}{\mathbf{P}\{A\}} \\ &= \frac{\frac{1}{10}}{\frac{6}{10}} \\ &= \frac{1}{6}. \end{aligned}$$

We have normalized $\mathbf{P}\{X = 1\}$ by the probability of being in A.

Question: What is $p_{X|A}(x)$, if $x \notin A$?

Answer: 0.

Lemma 4.16 *A conditional p.m.f. is a p.m.f., that is,*

$$\sum_x p_{X|A}(x) = \sum_{x \in A} p_{X|A}(x) = 1.$$

Proof: See Exercise 4.12. ■

We can also consider the case where the event, A, is an instance of a r.v. For example, A might be the event $Y = y$.

Example 4.17 (Conditioning on the value of a random variable)

Two discrete random variables X and Y taking the values $\{0, 1, 2\}$ have a joint p.m.f. given by Table 4.2.

$Y = 2$	0	$\frac{1}{6}$	$\frac{1}{8}$
$Y = 1$	$\frac{1}{8}$	$\frac{1}{6}$	$\frac{1}{8}$
$Y = 0$	$\frac{1}{6}$	$\frac{1}{8}$	0
	$X = 0$	$X = 1$	$X = 2$

Table 4.2 *Joint p.m.f.,* $p_{X,Y}(x, y)$.

Question: What is $p_{X|Y=2}(1)$?

Answer:

$$p_{X|Y=2}(1) = \mathbf{P}\{X = 1 \mid Y = 2\} = \frac{\mathbf{P}\{X = 1 \ \& \ Y = 2\}}{\mathbf{P}\{Y = 2\}} = \frac{\frac{1}{6}}{\frac{1}{6} + \frac{1}{8}} = \frac{4}{7}.$$

Question: What is $p_{X|Y=2}(2)$?

Answer: By the fact that $p_{X|Y=2}(x)$ is a p.m.f., and observing that $p_{X|Y=2}(0) = 0$, it must be the case that

$$p_{X|Y=2}(2) = 1 - p_{X|Y=2}(1) = \frac{3}{7}.$$

Definition 4.18 *For a discrete r.v. X, the* **conditional expectation** *of X given event A is as follows:*

$$\mathbf{E}[X \mid A] = \sum_x x p_{X|A}(x) = \sum_x x \cdot \frac{\mathbf{P}\{(X = x) \cap A\}}{\mathbf{P}\{A\}}.$$

Simply put, the conditional expectation is the same as the expectation, but rather than using the p.m.f., we use the conditional p.m.f., which likely has a different range.

Example 4.19 (Conditional expectation)

Again let X denote the size of a job. Suppose that

$$X = \begin{cases} 1 & \text{w/ prob. } 0.1 \\ 2 & \text{w/ prob. } 0.2 \\ 3 & \text{w/ prob. } 0.3 \\ 4 & \text{w/ prob. } 0.2 \\ 5 & \text{w/ prob. } 0.2 \end{cases}.$$

Let A be the event that the job is "small," meaning that its size is ≤ 3.

Question: What is $\mathbf{E}[X]$?

Answer:

$$\mathbf{E}[X] = 1 \cdot \frac{1}{10} + 2 \cdot \frac{2}{10} + 3 \cdot \frac{3}{10} + 4 \cdot \frac{2}{10} + 5 \cdot \frac{2}{10} = \frac{32}{10}.$$

Question: What is $\mathbf{E}[X|A]$?

Answer: Note that this should be a smaller value than $\mathbf{E}[X]$.

$$\begin{aligned} \mathbf{E}[X|A] &= 1 \cdot p_{X|A}(1) + 2 \cdot p_{X|A}(2) + 3 \cdot p_{X|A}(3) \\ &= 1 \cdot \frac{1}{6} + 2 \cdot \frac{2}{6} + 3 \cdot \frac{3}{6} \\ &= \frac{14}{6}. \end{aligned}$$

Example 4.20 (More conditional expectation practice)

Two discrete random variables X and Y taking the values $\{0, 1, 2\}$ have a joint p.m.f. given by Table 4.3.

	$X = 0$	$X = 1$	$X = 2$
$Y = 2$	0	$\frac{1}{6}$	$\frac{1}{8}$
$Y = 1$	$\frac{1}{8}$	$\frac{1}{6}$	$\frac{1}{8}$
$Y = 0$	$\frac{1}{6}$	$\frac{1}{8}$	0

Table 4.3 *Joint p.m.f., $p_{X,Y}(x, y)$.*

Question: Compute the conditional expectation $\mathbf{E}[X \mid Y = 2]$.

Answer:

$$\mathbf{E}\left[X \mid Y = 2\right] = 0 \cdot p_{X|Y=2}(0) + 1 \cdot p_{X|Y=2}(1) + 2 \cdot p_{X|Y=2}(2)$$
$$= 1 \cdot \frac{4}{7} + 2 \cdot \frac{3}{7} = \frac{10}{7}.$$

Example 4.21 (Indicators: an alternative to conditioning)

Let S be a discrete r.v., without loss of generality, say:

$$S = \begin{cases} 1 & \text{w/prob } p_S(1) \\ 2 & \text{w/prob } p_S(2) \\ 3 & \text{w/prob } p_S(3) \\ 4 & \text{w/prob } p_S(4) \\ \vdots \end{cases}.$$

Let $I_{S \leq x}$ be an indicator r.v. which is 1 when $S \leq x$ and 0 otherwise. Likewise, let $I_{S > x}$ be an indicator r.v. which is 1 when $S > x$ and 0 otherwise.

Question: Argue that

$$S \stackrel{d}{=} S \cdot I_{S \leq x} + S \cdot I_{S > x}. \tag{4.5}$$

The $\stackrel{d}{=}$ is indicating that the left-hand side and right-hand side of (4.5) are **equal in distribution**, that is, they take on the same values with the same probabilities.

Answer: $S \cdot I_{S \leq x}$ is a r.v. that returns the same values of S if those values are $\leq x$, and otherwise returns 0. Think of this as the r.v. S with a bunch of 0's where the terms for $S > x$ would be. For example, if $x = 2$, then:

$$S \cdot I_{S \leq 2} = \begin{cases} 1 & \text{w/prob } p_S(1) \\ 2 & \text{w/prob } p_S(2) \\ 0 & \text{w/prob } p_S(3) \\ 0 & \text{w/prob } p_S(4) \\ \vdots \end{cases} \qquad S \cdot I_{S > 2} = \begin{cases} 0 & \text{w/prob } p_S(1) \\ 0 & \text{w/prob } p_S(2) \\ 3 & \text{w/prob } p_S(3) \\ 4 & \text{w/prob } p_S(4) \\ \vdots \end{cases}.$$

Adding together $S \cdot I_{S \leq x}$ and $S \cdot I_{S > x}$, we get exactly the distribution of S.

Question: How does $S \cdot I_{S \leq 2}$ compare to the r.v. $[S \mid S \leq 2]$?

Answer:

$$S \cdot I_{S \leq 2} = \begin{cases} 1 & \text{w/prob } p_S(1) \\ 2 & \text{w/prob } p_S(2) \\ 0 & \text{w/prob } 1 - \mathbf{P}\{S \leq 2\} \end{cases}.$$

By contrast,

$$[S \mid S \le 2] = \begin{cases} 1 & \text{w/prob } p_S(1)/\mathbf{P}\{S \le 2\} \\ 2 & \text{w/prob } p_S(2)/\mathbf{P}\{S \le 2\} \end{cases}.$$

Question: How is $\mathbf{E}\left[S \cdot I_{S \le 2}\right]$ related to $\mathbf{E}\left[S \mid S \le 2\right]$?

Answer:

$$\mathbf{E}\left[S \cdot I_{S \le 2}\right] = 1 \cdot p_S(1) + 2 \cdot p_S(2).$$

More generally,

$$\mathbf{E}\left[S \cdot I_{S \le x}\right] = \sum_{i=1}^{x} i p_S(i). \tag{4.6}$$

By contrast,

$$\mathbf{E}\left[S \mid S \le x\right] = \sum_{i=1}^{x} i \frac{p_S(i)}{\mathbf{P}\{S \le x\}} = \frac{1}{\mathbf{P}\{S \le x\}} \cdot \sum_{i=1}^{x} i p_S(i). \tag{4.7}$$

Comparing (4.6) and (4.7), we have:

$$\mathbf{E}\left[S \cdot I_{S \le x}\right] = \mathbf{E}\left[S \mid S \le x\right] \cdot \mathbf{P}\{S \le x\}. \tag{4.8}$$

Question: Express $\mathbf{E}\left[S\right]$ in two ways: (1) using indicator random variables and (2) via conditioning on $S \le x$.

Answer: For (1), we use (4.5) and take expectations of both sides as follows:

$$\mathbf{E}\left[S\right] = \mathbf{E}\left[S \cdot I_{S \le x}\right] + \mathbf{E}\left[S \cdot I_{S > x}\right]. \tag{4.9}$$

For (2) we use the result from (4.8) to replace each term in (4.9), obtaining:

$$\mathbf{E}\left[S\right] = \mathbf{E}\left[S \mid S \le x\right] \cdot \mathbf{P}\{S \le x\} + \mathbf{E}\left[S \mid S > x\right] \cdot \mathbf{P}\{S > x\}. \tag{4.10}$$

4.4 Computing Expectations via Conditioning

Recall the Law of Total Probability, which says that the probability of an event can be computed as a sum of conditional probabilities. In the same way, an expectation can be computed as a sum of conditional expectations – we saw an example of this in (4.10). Conditioning is often the easiest way to compute an expectation.

Theorem 4.22 *Let events $F_1, F_2, F_3, \ldots$ partition the state space Ω. Then,*

$$\mathbf{E}[X] = \sum_{i=1}^{\infty} \mathbf{E}[X \mid F_i] \cdot \mathbf{P}\{F_i\}.$$

Given a discrete r.v. Y, if we think of $Y = y$ as an event, then we have:

$$\mathbf{E}[X] = \sum_{y} \mathbf{E}[X \mid Y = y] \mathbf{P}\{Y = y\}.$$

Proof: We show the proof for the second expression in the theorem. The proof for the first expression follows the same lines.

$$\mathbf{E}[X] = \sum_{x} x \mathbf{P}\{X = x\}$$

$$= \sum_{x} x \sum_{y} \mathbf{P}\{X = x \mid Y = y\} \mathbf{P}\{Y = y\}$$

$$= \sum_{x} \sum_{y} x \mathbf{P}\{X = x \mid Y = y\} \mathbf{P}\{Y = y\}$$

$$= \sum_{y} \sum_{x} x \mathbf{P}\{X = x \mid Y = y\} \mathbf{P}\{Y = y\}$$

$$= \sum_{y} \mathbf{P}\{Y = y\} \sum_{x} x \mathbf{P}\{X = x \mid Y = y\}$$

$$= \sum_{y} \mathbf{P}\{Y = y\} \mathbf{E}[X \mid Y = y] \quad \text{(by Definition 4.18).} \quad \blacksquare$$

Example 4.23 (Expectation of Geometric, revisited)

Recall that in Example 4.4 we computed the mean of a Geometric with parameter p. How can we redo this more simply via conditioning? Specifically, we seek $\mathbf{E}[N]$, where N is the number of flips required to get the first head.

Question: What do we condition on?

Answer: We condition on the value of the first flip, Y, as follows:

$$\mathbf{E}[N] = \mathbf{E}[N \mid Y = 1] \mathbf{P}\{Y = 1\} + \mathbf{E}[N \mid Y = 0] \mathbf{P}\{Y = 0\}$$
$$= 1 \cdot p + (1 + \mathbf{E}[N]) \cdot (1 - p)$$
$$p\mathbf{E}[N] = p + (1 - p)$$
$$\mathbf{E}[N] = \frac{1}{p}.$$

The difficult step here is reasoning that $\mathbf{E}[N \mid Y = 0] = 1 + \mathbf{E}[N]$. That is, knowing that we already got a tail on the first flip adds 1 to the expected time to get a head, because the *remaining* time needed to get a head "restarts" after that tail. This is the same idea as a person who has been trying to win the lottery for the last 100 days. Their remaining time to win the lottery is the same as if they started today. The fact that they already tried for 100 days just adds 100 to their total time spent trying to win the lottery. The property that your past doesn't affect your future is called **memorylessness** and will come up again.

Note how conditioning greatly simplifies the original derivation given in Example 4.4.

The proof of Theorem 4.22 generalizes to Theorem 4.24:

Theorem 4.24

$$\mathbf{E}[g(X)] = \sum_y \mathbf{E}[g(X) \mid Y = y] \mathbf{P}\{Y = y\}.$$

Theorem 4.24 will be particularly useful in Chapter 5's discussion of higher moments.

4.5 Simpson's Paradox

We end this chapter with Simpson's paradox [70]. The paradox is counter-intuitive because people *mistakenly* think it is related to conditioning, when it is not.

The best way to understand Simpson's paradox is via an example. A common example from the healthcare area involves the evaluation of two potential treatments for kidney stones: call these Treatment A and Treatment B. Suppose that patients are classified as having "small" kidney stones or "large" ones. It turns out that Treatment A is more effective than B on small stones, and also that Treatment A is more effective than B on large stones. However, paradoxically, if we ignore patient classifications, we find that Treatment B is the more effective treatment. The fact that the "winner" changes when we remove the classification is called Simpson's paradox.

Question: Spend some time asking yourself: How can this be?

Answer: Table 4.4 shows a numerical instance of the paradox. Looking at the top left box, (small, A), we see that Treatment A is 90% effective on small stones – it is effective on 90 out of the 100 small-stone patients who receive

	Treatment A	Treatment B
Small stones	90% effective (**winner!**) (successful on 90 out of 100)	80% effective (successful on 800 out of 1000)
Large stones	60% effective (**winner!**) (successful on 600 out of 1000)	50% effective (successful on 50 out of 100)
Aggregate mix	63% effective (successful on 690 out of 1100)	77% effective (**winner!**) (successful on 850 out of 1100)

Table 4.4 *Simpson's paradox: Treatment A is more effective than Treatment B both on small stones and on large stones. But Treatment B is more effective than Treatment A when we ignore stone size.*

it. By contrast, Treatment B is only 80% effective on small stones, as shown in box (small, B) – it is effective on 800 out of the 1000 small-stone patients who receive it. Thus Treatment A is more effective than Treatment B on small-stone patients. The large stone row of the table shows that Treatment A is 60% effective on large-stone patients, while Treatment B is only 50% effective on large-stone patients. Based on the above data, it seems that Treatment A is best.

In the last line of the table, labeled "aggregate mix," we mix up all the small-stone and large-stone patients, so that they are no longer classified by their stone size. We now look at the 1100 patients that received Treatment A and ask how many of them had success. We find that only 690 of the 1100 patients had success, meaning that Treatment A is 63% effective. By contrast, of the 1100 patients that received Treatment B, we find that 77% of them had success. Based on this, it seems that Treatment B is best.

Question: Which treatment is actually best, A or B?

Answer: Treatment A is best. Treatment A is best when used for patients with small stones, and it is also best when used for patients with large stones. In practice, doctors know that Treatment A is best, and they thus reserve it for patients with large stones, which are the more difficult cases. This is why we see bigger studies (1000 patients) where Treatment A is applied to patients with large stones. Treatment B is more typically reserved for the easier patients, which is why we see bigger studies (1000 patients) where Treatment B is applied to patients with small stones.

Question: But if Treatment A is best, why does it turn out to look bad in the "mix," where we ignore the patient classification?

Answer: Mathematically, the paradox is caused by a combination of two things:

1. The biggest contributors to the "mix" are quadrants [large, A] and [small, B], since these both involve tests with 1000 patients.
2. But [small, B] has a higher effectiveness percentage than [large, A] because, although Treatment A is the better treatment, this fact is dwarfed by the fact that small stones are so much easier to handle than large ones.

Together, these leave us believing that Treatment B is better when we look at the aggregate mix.

4.6 Exercises

4.1 **Socks**
Socks come in two colors: red and blue. There are an infinite number of socks of each color. Each time we pick a sock, we get a random sock. What is the expected number of picks until we have a pair (two of the same color)?

4.2 **Random graphs**
Consider a "random graph" on n vertices, where each pair of vertices is connected by an edge with probability p.
(a) What is the expected number of edges in the random graph?
(b) What is the distribution of the degree of vertex i?

4.3 **Multi-round gamble**
[Proposed by Rashmi Vinayak] At a casino, you're attracted to an "amazing" offer. Every round you bet, you either triple your bet with probability half or lose your bet with probability half.
(a) What is the obvious betting strategy, that is, how much of your money should you bet in each round to maximize your winnings?
(b) For this strategy, what is the probability that you end up with no money? (Are you surprised by the answers to the above two questions?)

4.4 **Probability bounds**
You are told that the average file size in a database is 6K bytes.
(a) Explain why it follows (from the definition of expectation) that fewer than half of the files can have size > 12K.
(b) You are now given the additional information that the minimum file size is 3K. Derive a tighter upper bound on the percentage of files of size > 12K.

4.5 **Shared birthdays**
There are n people in a room. A person is "happy" if he/she shares a birthday with another person in the room. What is the expected number of happy people?

4.6 **Identities**
Let A and B be independent random variables. Assume that $B \neq 0$ and that $\mathbf{E}[B] \neq 0$. Prove or disprove the following statement:

$$\mathbf{E}\left[\frac{A}{B}\right] = \frac{\mathbf{E}[A]}{\mathbf{E}[B]}.$$

4.7 **Expectation of product**
Prove or disprove the following claim: If

$$\mathbf{E}[XY] = \mathbf{E}[X] \cdot \mathbf{E}[Y],$$

then X and Y are independent random variables.

4.8 **Coin pattern**
Your coin produces heads with probability p. You flip your coin $n \geq 3$ times. What is the expected number of times that the pattern HTH appears? Example: If the n flips are $\langle H, T, H, T, H, T, H \rangle$ then the pattern HTH appears three times.

4.9 **Random word generation: I love to love**
Every minute, a random word generator spits out one word uniformly at random from the set { I, love, to }. Suppose we let the generator run for n minutes. What is the expected number of times that the phrase "I love to love" appears?

4.10 **Permutations**
Let π be a permutation on $[n] = \{1, \ldots, n\}$, where $n \geq 3$. Here $\pi(i)$ denotes the number in the ith position of permutation π. We say that π has a local maximum at $i \in [n]$ if all these are true:
- $\pi(i) > \pi(i+1)$, if $i = 1$
- $\pi(i-1) < \pi(i)$ and $\pi(i) > \pi(i+1)$, if $1 < i < n$
- $\pi(i-1) < \pi(i)$, if $i = n$

What is the expected number of local maxima of a random permutation π on $[n]$? [Hint: Use Linearity of Expectation and indicator random variables.]

4.11 **Triangles in random graphs**
Consider a "random graph," G, on n vertices, where each pair of vertices is connected by an edge with probability $p = \frac{d}{n}$. Let Y denote the number of triangles in G. Derive $\mathbf{E}[Y]$. What does $\mathbf{E}[Y]$ look like for high n?

4.12 **A conditional p.m.f. is a p.m.f**
Prove that the conditional p.m.f. $p_{X|A}(\cdot)$ is a p.m.f. by showing that

$$\sum_x p_{X|A}(x) = 1.$$

4.13 **Tail of Geometric and memorylessness**
Let $X \sim \text{Geometric}(p)$.
(a) Derive $\mathbf{E}[X \mid X > 5]$ by summing over the conditional p.m.f. Be careful to get the indices correct.
(b) Your final answer should be extremely simple in light of the memorylessness property of the Geometric distribution. Explain your final answer.

4.14 **Practice with conditional expectation**
For the joint p.m.f. in Table 4.2, compute $\mathbf{E}[X \mid Y \neq 1]$.

4.15 **More conditional expectation practice**
We're given a joint p.m.f. for two random variables X and Y.

	$Y = 1$	$Y = 2$	$Y = 3$
$X = 0$	$1/4$	$3/16$	$1/16$
$X = 1$	$1/8$	0	$3/8$

What is $\mathbf{E}\left[\frac{X}{Y} \mid X^2 + Y^2 \leq 4\right]$?

4.16 **Alternative definition of expectation: summing the tail**
Let X be a non-negative, discrete, integer-valued r.v. Prove that

$$\mathbf{E}[X] = \sum_{x=0}^{\infty} \mathbf{P}\{X > x\}.$$

4.17 **Simpson's paradox for PhD admissions**
A total of 110 Berkeley undergrads and 110 CMU undergrads apply for PhD programs in CS at Berkeley and CMU. Assume that all the students started their grad applications at the very last minute, and as a result were only able to apply to their first choice between Berkeley PhD or CMU PhD (not both). Below are the acceptance rates for each group at each university:

	Berkeley Undergrad	CMU Undergrad
Berkeley PhD	32% (32 out of 100 applicants)	40% (4 out of 10 applicants)
CMU PhD	10% (1 out of 10 applicants)	18% (18 out of 100 applicants)
Either PhD	30% (33 out of 110 applicants)	20% (22 out of 110 applicants)

(a) Which group of students, CMU students or Berkeley students, had a higher acceptance rate into the Berkeley PhD program?
(b) Which group of students, CMU students or Berkeley students, had a higher acceptance rate into the CMU PhD program?
(c) Which group of students, CMU students or Berkeley students, were more likely to be admitted into a PhD program?
(d) What was Berkeley's overall acceptance rate and what was CMU's overall acceptance rate (assume that no students outside Berkeley or CMU applied)?
(e) What proportion of the students admitted to either the CMU or Berkeley PhD programs were admitted to the Berkeley PhD program?
(f) How is it possible that CMU students had a higher acceptance rate at each of the PhD programs than Berkeley students, and yet a lower chance of getting into a PhD program overall?

4.18 k heads in a row
Stacy's fault-tolerant system only crashes if there are k *consecutive* failures. Assume that every minute a failure occurs independently with probability p. What is the expected number of minutes until Stacy's system crashes? This is equivalent to $\mathbf{E}[T_k]$, where T_k denotes the number of flips needed to get k heads in a row when flipping a coin with probability p of heads. [Hint: Write a recurrence relation for the r.v. T_k in terms of T_{k-1}.]

4.19 Virus propagation
We start with a network of three computers. Unbeknownst to us, two of the computers are infected with a hidden virus and the other is not. A sequence of new uninfected computers now join the network, one at a time. Each new computer joins the existing network by attaching itself to a random computer in the network (all computers in the network are equally likely attachment points). If the new computer attaches itself to an infected computer, then it immediately becomes infected with the virus; otherwise the new computer does not get the virus. At the point where the network consists of k total computers, what is the expected fraction of these that is infected? Assume $k > 3$.

4.20 Coupon collector, time to repeat
In the coupon collection problem, there are n distinct coupons that we are trying to collect. Every time we draw a coupon, we get one of the n at random, with each coupon being equally likely (the coupon we get is replaced after each drawing). Thus it is likely that we quickly see a repeat. Define N to be the r.v., where

N = Number of coupons collected until we first get a repeat.

What is $\mathbf{E}[N]$? [Note: You can leave your answer in the form of a sum.]

4.21 **Minimum of n dice**

Your goal is to derive a simple expression for the expected minimum value of n independent rolls of a die. Below are some steps to help:

(a) You roll a die twice. What's the expected value of the minimum of the rolls? Compute this by simple counting and/or conditioning.

(b) Now redo the problem in (a), but use the result of Exercise 4.16 to compute your answer.

(c) Now repeat (b), but for the case of n rolls. What does your expression for the expected minimum value become as $n \to \infty$?

4.22 **The counter-intuitive nature of conditional independence**

A fair coin is flipped N times, and H heads are obtained (both N and H are random variables in the experiment). Suppose we are told that $H = 5$. What is $\mathbf{E}\,[N \mid H = 5]$?

(a) If you had to guess, what would you guess is $\mathbf{E}\,[N \mid H = 5]$?

(b) Write out $\mathbf{E}\,[N \mid H = 5]$ based on Definition 4.18. Go as far as you can in evaluating the expression. What is missing?

(c) Suppose we're now given a "prior" distribution on N, namely that

$$N = \begin{cases} 10 & \text{w/prob } 0.5 \\ 20 & \text{w/prob } 0.5 \end{cases}.$$

Use this information to finish evaluating $\mathbf{E}\,[N \mid H = 5]$. You will need a computer for the final evaluation. Is this the answer you originally expected?

4.23 **Revisiting die rolls**

Recall Exercise 2.27, where you have two dice. Die A is a fair die (each of the six numbers is equally likely) and die B is a biased die (the number six comes up with probability $\frac{2}{3}$ and the remaining $\frac{1}{3}$ probability is split evenly across all the other numbers). Kaige picks a die at random and rolls that die three times. Given that the first two rolls are both sixes, what is the expected value of the third roll?

4.24 **Expectation of a product**

[Proposed by Priyatham Bollimpalli] In his spare time, Priyatham likes to sit around multiplying random numbers. After studying probability, he has become interested in the expected value of the product.

(a) Priyatham multiplies two single-digit, non-equal, positive numbers. If each number is equally likely to be picked from $\{1, 2, 3, \ldots, 9\}$ (without replacement), what is the expected value of the product? [Note: This formula may come in handy: $\sum_{i=1}^{n} i^2 = \frac{n(n+1)(2n+1)}{6}$]

(b) What is the expectation of a product of two two-digit numbers, where all four digits are non-zero, unique, and picked uniformly at random?

For example 45 and 76 are two valid numbers, whereas 45 and 59 are not since 5 is repeated. [Hint: Solution is short.]
(c) Suppose we didn't need to assume the digits were unique. Explain in one line what the answer to part (a) would be now.

4.25 Socks for multi-footed animals
Socks come in two colors: red and blue. There are an infinite number of socks of each color. Every time we pick a sock, we get a random sock.
(a) A human has two feet. What is the expected number of picks until we have a pair (sock for each foot) of a single color?
(b) The three-toed sloth needs a sock for each toe. What is the expected number of picks until we have three socks of the same color?
(c) Prof. Veloso's new soccer-playing robot has n feet (more feet helps it win). What is the expected number of picks until the robot has a sock for each foot, where all socks must be of the same color? [Note: Don't worry about trying to come up with a closed-form expression.]

4.26 The three rivers of Pittsburgh
[Proposed by Lea Herzberg] In Pittsburgh, three rivers meet as shown in Figure 4.3. Assume that, for every boat traveling up the Ohio River, with probability $\frac{2}{3}$ the boat continues up the Allegheny and, independently, with probability $\frac{1}{3}$, the boat continues up the Monongahela.

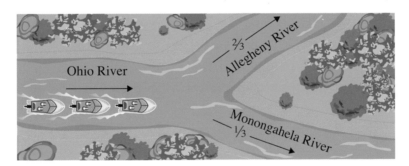

Figure 4.3 *The three rivers of Pittsburgh, where the arrows represent the direction of the boats.*

Let X denote the number of boats approaching the fork from the Ohio in the last hour. Let A (respectively, M) denote the number of boats entering the Allegheny (respectively, Monongahela) in the last hour.
Suppose $X \sim \text{Poisson}(\lambda = 100)$. Your goal is to derive $\mathbf{E}[X \mid M = 100]$.
(a) Do you have any intuition about what $\mathbf{E}[X \mid M = 100]$ should be?
(b) Using Definition 4.18 for conditional expectation, write an expression for $\mathbf{E}[X \mid M = 100]$ using all the information given in the problem. Express your answer in terms of an expression involving λ's and x's and some sums. Do not worry about simplifying your expression.

(c) Your expression in (b) is very unwieldy and hard to evaluate. Instead, we will follow a different approach to get to the answer. In following this approach, assume $p = \frac{1}{3}$ and $\lambda = 100$, but express your answers generally in terms of p and λ until the last part.

(i) Let $Z = [M \mid X = x]$. How is Z distributed?

(ii) Using step (i), what is the joint probability $p_{X,M}(x, m)$?

(iii) Use step (ii) to prove that $M \sim \text{Poisson}(\lambda p)$.

(iv) Combine steps (ii) and (iii) to derive $p_{X \mid M=m}(x)$, and then use that to get the distribution of the r.v. $[X - m \mid M = m]$.

(v) Use the result in (iv) to get $\mathbf{E}[X \mid M = m]$.

(vi) Returning to the original problem, given that in the last hour 100 boats entered the Monongahela, what is the expected number of boats leaving the Ohio in the last hour? Note that you will likely find your intuition from part (a) was incorrect.

5   Variance, Higher Moments, and Random Sums

In Chapter 4 we devoted a lot of time to computing the expectation of random variables. As we explained, the expectation is useful because it provides us with a single summary value when trading off different options. For example, in Example 4.1, we used the "expected earnings" in choosing between two startups.

However one might want more information than just the expected earnings. For example, two companies, say Microsoft and Startup X could both have expected earnings of 100K, but at Microsoft your earnings are unlikely to deviate much from 100K, whereas at Startup X your earnings could range from 0 to 1M. Although both companies offer the same expected earnings, Startup X feels "riskier." The purpose of this chapter is to formalize what we mean by "risk" or "variability." Before we start, it will be useful to go over the definition of moments.

5.1 Higher Moments

Definition 5.1 *For a random variable, X, we say that the **kth moment** of X is $\mathbf{E}\left[X^k\right]$. Observe that $\mathbf{E}\left[X\right]$ is the first moment of X.*

Example 5.2 (Second moment of Geometric)

Let $X \sim \text{Geometric}(p)$. What is $\mathbf{E}\left[X^2\right]$?

Formally,

$$\mathbf{E}\left[X^2\right] = \sum_{i=1}^{\infty} i^2 p_X(i) = \sum_{i=1}^{\infty} i^2 (1-p)^{i-1} p.$$

It is not obvious how to compute this sum.

Question: Can we use Theorem 4.8 to express $\mathbf{E}\left[X^2\right] = \mathbf{E}\left[X\right] \cdot \mathbf{E}\left[X\right]$?

Answer: No, because X is certainly not independent of X.

Fortunately, there is something we can do: Since $\mathbf{E}\left[X^2\right]$ is an expectation, we can compute it via conditioning. We will condition on the value of the first flip.

$$\begin{aligned}
\mathbf{E}\left[X^2\right] &= \mathbf{E}\left[X^2 \mid \text{1st flip is head}\right] \cdot p + \mathbf{E}\left[X^2 \mid \text{1st flip is tail}\right] \cdot (1-p) \\
&= 1^2 \cdot p + \mathbf{E}\left[(1+X)^2\right] \cdot (1-p) \\
&= p + \mathbf{E}\left[1 + 2X + X^2\right] \cdot (1-p) \\
&= p + \left(1 + 2\mathbf{E}\left[X\right] + \mathbf{E}\left[X^2\right]\right)(1-p) \\
&= p + (1-p) + 2(1-p) \cdot \frac{1}{p} + \mathbf{E}\left[X^2\right](1-p)
\end{aligned}$$

$$p\mathbf{E}\left[X^2\right] = 1 + 2 \cdot \frac{1-p}{p}$$

$$\mathbf{E}\left[X^2\right] = \frac{2-p}{p^2}.$$

Question: In the above, observe that we write:

$$\mathbf{E}\left[X^2 \mid \text{1st flip is tail}\right] = \mathbf{E}\left[(1+X)^2\right].$$

Why didn't we write $\mathbf{E}\left[X^2 \mid \text{1st flip is tail}\right] = 1 + \mathbf{E}\left[X^2\right]$?

Answer: Consider the random variable (r.v.) Y, where

$$Y = [X \mid \text{1st flip is tail}] = [X \mid X > 1].$$

That is, we define Y to be the r.v. X conditioned on the fact that we know that $X > 1$. Given that the first flip is a tail, everything starts from scratch, that is, we've wasted one flip, and we get a new draw of X. It thus makes sense that

$$Y \stackrel{d}{=} 1 + X, \tag{5.1}$$

that is, Y is equal in distribution to $1 + X$. In Exercise 5.18, we formally prove (5.1) by showing that $\mathbf{P}\left\{Y = i\right\} = \mathbf{P}\left\{1 + X = i\right\}$ for all i.

From (5.1), it follows that:

$$\mathbf{E}\left[X \mid \text{1st flip is tail}\right] = \mathbf{E}\left[Y\right] = \mathbf{E}\left[(1+X)\right] = 1 + \mathbf{E}\left[X\right]$$
$$\mathbf{E}\left[X^2 \mid \text{1st flip is tail}\right] = \mathbf{E}\left[Y^2\right] = \mathbf{E}\left[(1+X)^2\right].$$

Question: Could we use the same approach to compute the third moment of X?

Answer: Sure:

$$\mathbf{E}\left[X^3\right] = 1^3 \cdot p + \mathbf{E}\left[(1+X)^3\right] \cdot (1-p).$$

Now expand out the cube and then again apply Linearity of Expectation.

5.2 Variance

We are often interested in how much an experiment is likely to deviate from its mean.

> **Definition 5.3** *The **variance** of r.v. X, written as **Var**(X), is the expected squared difference of X from its mean.*
>
> $$\mathbf{Var}(X) = \mathbf{E}\left[(X - \mathbf{E}[X])^2\right].$$

A depiction of variance is given in Figure 5.1.

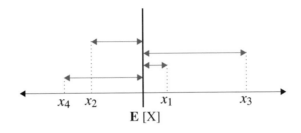

Figure 5.1 *Variance of X. For each value of X, we square its distance to* $\mathbf{E}[X]$, *and take the appropriate weighted average of these.*

Example 5.4 (Variance of Bernoulli)

Let $X \sim$ Bernoulli(p). Our goal is to determine **Var**(X). Here X represents a single flip of a coin, where the coin has probability p of heads. That is:

$$X = \begin{cases} 1 & \text{w/prob } p \\ 0 & \text{w/prob } 1 - p \end{cases}.$$

Question: What is $\mathbf{E}[X]$? What is $\mathbf{Var}(X)$?

Answer:

$$\mathbf{E}[X] = p \cdot 1 + (1 - p) \cdot 0 = p$$

$$\begin{aligned}
\mathbf{Var}(X) &= \mathbf{E}\left[(X - p)^2\right] \\
&= \mathbf{E}\left[X^2 - 2Xp + p^2\right] \\
&= \mathbf{E}\left[X^2\right] - 2p\mathbf{E}[X] + p^2 \\
&= \left(p \cdot 1^2 + (1 - p) \cdot 0^2\right) - 2p \cdot p + p^2 \\
&= p(1 - p).
\end{aligned} \tag{5.2}$$

Formula (5.2) is worth memorizing.

Question: Can we compute $\mathbf{Var}(X)$ via conditioning?

Answer: There is a right and a wrong way to do this.

The WRONG way is to say:

$$\mathbf{Var}(X) = p \cdot \mathbf{Var}(X \mid X = 1) + (1 - p) \cdot \mathbf{Var}(X \mid X = 0)$$
$$= p \cdot 0 + (1 - p) \cdot 0 = 0.$$

This is incorrect, because no theorem says that we can condition on variance. We only have Theorem 4.24, which allows us to condition on expectation.

That said, if we can leave variance in the form of an expectation, then we can use conditioning. Here's the CORRECT way to condition:

$$\mathbf{Var}(X) = \mathbf{E}\left[(X - p)^2\right]$$
$$= \mathbf{E}\left[(X - p)^2 \mid X = 1\right] \cdot p + \mathbf{E}\left[(X - p)^2 \mid X = 0\right] \cdot (1 - p)$$
$$= (1 - p)^2 \cdot p + p^2 \cdot (1 - p)$$
$$= p(1 - p).$$

Question: For any r.v. X, how does $\mathbf{Var}(-X)$ compare to $\mathbf{Var}(X)$?

Answer: Looking at Figure 5.1, we see that every value of X is now negated, including the mean of X. Thus the distance of each value to the mean doesn't change. Hence the sum of the squares of the distances doesn't change either. So $\mathbf{Var}(X) = \mathbf{Var}(-X)$.

5.3 Alternative Definitions of Variance

Question: How else might you want to define variance?

Answer: There are many answers possible. One thing that is bothersome about the existing definition is the squaring, since the units of $\mathbf{Var}(X)$ are then different from the units of X. One might instead choose to define $\mathbf{Var}(X)$ as

$$\mathbf{E}\left[X - \mathbf{E}\left[X\right]\right],$$

without the square term.

Question: What's wrong with this?

Answer: By Linearity of Expectation: $\mathbf{E}\left[X - \mathbf{E}\left[X\right]\right] = \mathbf{E}\left[X\right] - \mathbf{E}\left[X\right] = 0$. Hence this definition doesn't work.

Another possibility is to define **Var**(X) as

$$\mathbf{E}\left[\left|X - \mathbf{E}[X]\right|\right],$$

using the absolute value instead of the square.

This alternative definition is totally legitimate. The only problem is that it is missing the convenient linearity property that we'll see shortly in Theorem 5.8.

One more idea is to consider the square root of variance, which has the same units as X. This is actually so common that it has a name.

Definition 5.5 *We define the* **standard deviation of** X *as*

$$\sigma_X = \mathbf{std}(X) = \sqrt{\mathbf{Var}(X)}.$$

We often write

$$\mathbf{Var}(X) = \sigma_X^2.$$

There's something disturbing about the definition of variance: The same measurement taken in different scales will end up with different values of variance. For example, suppose that X and Y are measuring the same quantity, but X is measured in centimeters and Y is measured in millimeters. As a result, we find that:

$$X = \begin{cases} 3 & \text{w/prob } \frac{1}{3} \\ 2 & \text{w/prob } \frac{1}{3} \\ 1 & \text{w/prob } \frac{1}{3} \end{cases} \qquad Y = \begin{cases} 30 & \text{w/prob } \frac{1}{3} \\ 20 & \text{w/prob } \frac{1}{3} \\ 10 & \text{w/prob } \frac{1}{3} \end{cases}.$$

We would like to believe that X and Y have the same variance, in that they're measuring the same quantity, just in different units.

Question: How do **Var**(X) and **Var**(Y) compare?

Answer: Var$(X) = \frac{2}{3}$, while **Var**$(Y) = \frac{200}{3}$. Since units are not typically shown, we are left with very different values.

The problem is not fixed by switching to the standard deviation.

Question: How do **std**(X) and **std**(Y) compare?

Answer: std$(X) = \sqrt{\frac{2}{3}}$, while **std**$(Y) = \sqrt{\frac{200}{3}}$.

Again, this feels less than satisfactory. For these reasons, researchers use a normalized version of variance, which is *scale-invariant* (insensitive to scaling), called the squared coefficient of variation.

Definition 5.6 *The* **squared coefficient of variation** *of r.v. X is defined as*

$$C_X^2 = \frac{\text{Var}(X)}{\text{E}[X]^2}.$$

Question: How do C_X^2 and C_Y^2 compare?

Answer: Both are $\frac{1}{6}$.

Note that C_X^2 is not defined if $\text{E}[X] = 0$. In practice, the C_X^2 metric is used when modeling empirical quantities like job sizes, flow durations, memory consumption, etc., whose values are typically positive with positive means.

5.4 Properties of Variance

Lemma 5.7 provides another way of computing variance.

Lemma 5.7 (Equivalent definition of variance) *The variance of r.v. X can equivalently be expressed as follows:*

$$\text{Var}(X) = \text{E}[X^2] - (\text{E}[X])^2.$$

Proof:

$$\text{Var}(X) = \text{E}\left[(X - \text{E}[X])^2\right] = \text{E}\left[X^2 - 2X\text{E}[X] + \text{E}[X]^2\right]$$
$$= \text{E}\left[X^2\right] - 2\text{E}[X]\text{E}[X] + \text{E}[X]^2$$
$$= \text{E}\left[X^2\right] - \text{E}[X]^2. \qquad \blacksquare$$

Even with this easier formulation, variance is often hard to compute. Fortunately, the Linearity of Variance Theorem helps us break down the variance of a random variable into easier subproblems.

Theorem 5.8 (Linearity of Variance) *Let X and Y be random variables where $X \perp Y$. Then,*

$$\text{Var}(X + Y) = \text{Var}(X) + \text{Var}(Y).$$

This generalizes to show that if $X_1, X_2, \ldots, X_n$ are independent, then

$$\text{Var}(X_1 + X_2 + \cdots + X_n) = \text{Var}(X_1) + \text{Var}(X_2) + \cdots + \text{Var}(X_n).$$

Proof: We prove the first statement of the theorem:

$$\mathbf{Var}(X+Y) = \mathbf{E}\left[(X+Y)^2\right] - (\mathbf{E}\left[(X+Y)\right])^2$$
$$= \mathbf{E}\left[X^2\right] + \mathbf{E}\left[Y^2\right] + 2\mathbf{E}\left[XY\right] - (\mathbf{E}\left[X\right])^2 - (\mathbf{E}\left[Y\right])^2 - 2\mathbf{E}\left[X\right]\mathbf{E}\left[Y\right]$$
$$= \mathbf{Var}(X) + \mathbf{Var}(Y) + \underbrace{2\mathbf{E}\left[XY\right] - 2\mathbf{E}\left[X\right]\mathbf{E}\left[Y\right]}_{\text{equals 0 if } X \perp Y}. \qquad \blacksquare$$

Theorem 5.8 is hugely powerful, assuming that X and Y are independent. One of the key reasons for the chosen definition of variance (as opposed to using absolute values, for example) is that the chosen definition lends itself to this linearity property.

It turns out that Theorem 5.8 can be extended to the case where the X_i's are not independent but rather only *pairwise independent*, which means that each *pair* of variables X_i and X_j are independent. This generalization is proven in Exercise 5.38.

We now present some examples of the benefits of Linearity of Variance.

Example 5.9 (Second moment of Binomial)

Let $X \sim \text{Binomial}(n, p)$. Our goal is to derive $\mathbf{E}\left[X^2\right]$.

If we work directly from the definition of the second moment, we have:

$$\mathbf{E}\left[X^2\right] = \sum_{i=0}^{n} i^2 \binom{n}{i} p^i (1-p)^{n-i}.$$

This is not an easy sum to work with. On the other hand, we can write X as a sum of indicator random variables, as we've done in the past:

$$X = \text{number of successes in } n \text{ trials} = X_1 + X_2 + \cdots + X_n,$$

where

$$X_i \sim \text{Bernoulli}(p) \qquad \text{and} \qquad \mathbf{E}\left[X_i\right] = p.$$

Then

$$\mathbf{Var}(X) = \mathbf{Var}(X_1) + \mathbf{Var}(X_2) + \cdots + \mathbf{Var}(X_n)$$
$$= n\mathbf{Var}(X_i)$$
$$= np(1-p).$$

Now, invoking Lemma 5.7, we have:

$$\mathbf{E}\left[X^2\right] = \mathbf{Var}(X) + \mathbf{E}\left[X\right]^2 = np(1 - p) + (np)^2.$$

Question: Recall the drinks example from Section 4.2, where n people put their drinks on a table, and each picks up a random cup. Let X denote the number of people who get back their own cup. Can we use indicator random variables to derive $\mathbf{Var}(X)$?

Answer: We could define X_i to be an indicator r.v. on whether person i gets back their own drink or not. Unfortunately, these X_i's are *not* independent, so we can't apply the Linearity of Variance Theorem as we did in computing the variance of the Binomial. In Exercise 5.36 you will see that you can nonetheless deduce $\mathbf{Var}(X)$ by writing out $\mathbf{E}\left[X^2\right] = \mathbf{E}\left[(X_1 + X_2 + \cdots + X_n)^2\right]$ and reasoning about the $\mathbf{E}\left[X_i X_j\right]$ terms.

Example 5.10 (Sums versus copies)

Consider two independent and identically distributed (i.i.d.) random variables, X_1 and X_2, which are both distributed like X. Let

$$Y = X_1 + X_2 \qquad \text{and} \qquad Z = 2X.$$

Question: Do Y and Z have the same distribution?

Answer: No. Suppose, for example, that your experiment is flipping a fair coin, where heads is 1 and tails is 0. In the case of Y, you flip the coin two independent times and look at the sum. The possible values for Y are 0, 1, or 2. In the case of Z, you flip the coin one time, and return double your result. The only possible values for Z are 0 or 2.

Question: How do $\mathbf{E}\left[Y\right]$ and $\mathbf{E}\left[Z\right]$ compare?

Answer: They are the same. $\mathbf{E}\left[Y\right] = \mathbf{E}\left[Z\right] = 2\mathbf{E}\left[X\right]$. In the case of the coin experiment, $\mathbf{E}\left[Y\right] = \mathbf{E}\left[Z\right] = 2 \cdot \frac{1}{2} = 1$.

Question: How do $\mathbf{Var}(Y)$ and $\mathbf{Var}(Z)$ compare?

Answer: $\mathbf{Var}(Y) = 2\mathbf{Var}(X)$, but $\mathbf{Var}(Z) = 4\mathbf{Var}(X)$.

Question: Does it make sense that $\mathbf{Var}(Y)$ is smaller than $\mathbf{Var}(Z)$?

Answer: In the case of Y, you are adding two independent results, which tends to yield a result that is often closer to the average. By contrast, in the case of Z you are taking one result and doubling it. This yields more extreme values. The variance is higher when we see extreme values.

5.5 Summary Table for Discrete Distributions

It is worth memorizing the mean and variance of the common distributions, because they come up over and over again. Table 5.1 shows these quantities.

Distribution	p.m.f.	Mean	Variance
Bernoulli(p)	$p_X(0) = 1 - p \; ; \; p_X(1) = p$	p	$p(1-p)$
Binomial(n,p)	$p_X(x) = \binom{n}{x}p^x(1-p)^{n-x}, \quad x = 0,1,\ldots,n$	np	$np(1-p)$
Geometric(p)	$p_X(x) = (1-p)^{x-1}p, \quad x = 1,2,3,\ldots$	$\frac{1}{p}$	$\frac{1-p}{p^2}$
Poisson(λ)	$p_X(x) = e^{-\lambda} \cdot \frac{\lambda^x}{x!}, \quad x = 0,1,2,\ldots$	λ	λ

Table 5.1 *Common discrete distributions.*

5.6 Covariance

Suppose we now have two random variables, X and Y.

Definition 5.11 *The **covariance** of any two random variables X and Y, denoted by **Cov**(X,Y), is defined by*

$$\mathbf{Cov}(X,Y) = \mathbf{E}\left[(X - \mathbf{E}\left[X\right])(Y - \mathbf{E}\left[Y\right])\right].$$

Lemma 5.12 provides an alternative definition of covariance.

Lemma 5.12 $\mathbf{Cov}(X,Y) = \mathbf{E}\left[XY\right] - \mathbf{E}\left[X\right]\mathbf{E}\left[Y\right].$

Proof:

$$\begin{aligned}
\mathbf{Cov}(X,Y) &= \mathbf{E}\left[(X - \mathbf{E}\left[X\right])(Y - \mathbf{E}\left[Y\right])\right] \\
&= \mathbf{E}\left[XY\right] - \mathbf{E}\left[\mathbf{E}\left[X\right] \cdot Y\right] - \mathbf{E}\left[X \cdot \mathbf{E}\left[Y\right]\right] + \mathbf{E}\left[\mathbf{E}\left[X\right] \cdot \mathbf{E}\left[Y\right]\right] \\
&= \mathbf{E}\left[XY\right] - \mathbf{E}\left[X\right]\mathbf{E}\left[Y\right] - \mathbf{E}\left[X\right]\mathbf{E}\left[Y\right] + \mathbf{E}\left[X\right]\mathbf{E}\left[Y\right] \\
&= \mathbf{E}\left[XY\right] - \mathbf{E}\left[X\right]\mathbf{E}\left[Y\right]
\end{aligned}$$

$\blacksquare$

Intuitively, the covariance between X and Y indicates something about the joint distribution between X and Y. If the larger-than-average values of X tend to happen with the larger-than-average values of Y, then $(X - \mathbf{E}[X])(Y - \mathbf{E}[Y])$ is positive on average, so the $\mathbf{Cov}(X,Y)$ is positive, and we say that the random variables X and Y are **positively correlated**. If the larger-than-average values of X mainly tend to happen together with the smaller-than-average values of Y, then $(X - \mathbf{E}[X])(Y - \mathbf{E}[Y])$ is negative on average, so the $\mathbf{Cov}(X,Y)$ is negative, and we say that the random variables X and Y are **negatively correlated**.

Thus the *sign* of $\mathbf{Cov}(X,Y)$ tells us the direction of the relationship between X and Y. Note that the magnitude of $\mathbf{Cov}(X,Y)$ is meaningless because it is too influenced by the magnitudes of X and Y.

Question: What is a nice name for $\mathbf{Cov}(X,X)$?

Answer: $\mathbf{Var}(X)$.

We will explore properties of covariance in Exercises 5.13–5.17.

5.7 Central Moments

The variance of a r.v. X is the second moment of the difference of X from its mean. In the same way, we can define higher moments of the difference of X from its mean.

> **Definition 5.13** *The* **kth moment** *of a r.v. X is*
> $$\mathbf{E}\left[X^k\right] = \sum_i i^k \cdot p_X(i).$$
> *The* **kth central moment** *of a r.v. X is*
> $$\mathbf{E}\left[(X - \mathbf{E}[X])^k\right] = \sum_i (i - \mathbf{E}[X])^k \cdot p_X(i).$$

Question: What do we call the second central moment?

Answer: Variance.

We've discussed the intuition behind the second central moment in terms of capturing the variability of the distribution. The third central moment is related to the "skew" of the distribution, namely whether it leans right or leans left.

Question: Consider the three distributions shown in Figure 5.2. Which have positive skew? Negative skew? Zero skew?

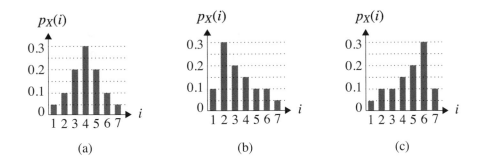

Figure 5.2 *Which of these distributions has positive/negative/zero skew?*

Answer: It is easy to see that the distribution in (a) has **zero skew**. Here, X is symmetric about its mean so $\mathbf{E}\left[(X - \mathbf{E}[X])^3\right] = 0$. The distribution in (b) has **positive skew** because it is "skewed" above its mean, so there will be more positive terms than negative ones in computing $\mathbf{E}\left[(X - \mathbf{E}[X])^3\right]$. Likewise the distribution in (c) has **negative skew** because it is "skewed" below its mean.

Question: Does having a zero third central moment guarantee that the distribution is symmetric?

Answer: No. This is why "skew" is not a perfect term. There are also plenty of distributions that don't look skewed one way or the other.

Question: Is there intuition behind the fourth central moment?

Answer: The fourth central moment is very similar to the second central moment, except that "outliers" count a lot more, because their difference from the mean is accentuated when raised to the fourth power.

5.8 Sum of a Random Number of Random Variables

In many applications one needs to add up a number of i.i.d. random variables, where the number of these variables is itself a r.v. Let $X_1, X_2, X_3, \ldots$ be i.i.d. random variables, where $X_i \sim X$. Let S denote the sum:

$$S = \sum_{i=1}^{N} X_i, \quad \text{where } N \perp \{X_1, X_2, \ldots\},$$

where N is not a constant, but rather a non-negative, integer-valued r.v.

Figure 5.3 shows an example where a game show contestant gets a prize each day. Here, X_i represents the prize on day i. After receiving the prize, the wheel is spun. If the wheel lands on STOP then the game ends; otherwise the contestant is invited to come back tomorrow. The number of times that the wheel is spun is a r.v., N. In this story $N \sim$ Geometric $\left(\frac{1}{6}\right)$. The total earnings of the contestant is $S = \sum_{i=1}^{N} X_i$. We are interested in understanding $\mathbf{E}[S]$ and $\mathbf{Var}(S)$.

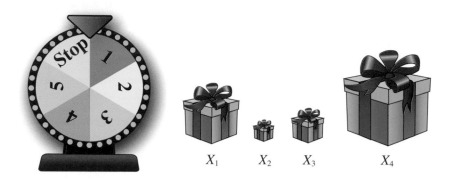

Figure 5.3 *Keep getting prizes until the wheel says STOP.*

Question: In computing $\mathbf{E}[S]$, why can't we directly apply Linearity of Expectation?

Answer: Linearity of Expectation only applies when N is a constant. But this suggests that we can condition on the value of N, and then apply Linearity of Expectation.

$$
\begin{aligned}
\mathbf{E}[S] = \mathbf{E}\left[\sum_{i=1}^{N} X_i\right] &= \sum_{n} \mathbf{E}\left[\sum_{i=1}^{N} X_i \ \Big| \ N = n\right] \cdot \mathbf{P}\{N = n\} \\
&= \sum_{n} \mathbf{E}\left[\sum_{i=1}^{n} X_i\right] \cdot \mathbf{P}\{N = n\} \\
&= \sum_{n} n\mathbf{E}[X] \cdot \mathbf{P}\{N = n\} \\
&= \mathbf{E}[X] \cdot \mathbf{E}[N].
\end{aligned}
\tag{5.3}
$$

Question: Let's try the same approach to get $\mathbf{Var}(S)$. What is $\mathbf{Var}(S \mid N = n)$?

Answer:

$$\mathbf{Var}(S \mid N = n) = n \cdot \mathbf{Var}(X), \qquad \text{by Linearity of Variance.}$$

Unfortunately, we there's no "Total Law of Variance" the way there's a "Total

Law of Expectation." So we cannot write:

$$(\text{WRONG}) \quad \mathbf{Var}(S) = \sum_n \mathbf{Var}(S \mid N = n) \cdot \mathbf{P}\{N = n\}$$

$$= \sum_n n \cdot \mathbf{Var}(X) \cdot \mathbf{P}\{N = n\}$$

$$= \mathbf{E}[N] \cdot \mathbf{Var}(X).$$

We can't use conditioning to get $\mathbf{Var}(S)$, but we can use it to get $\mathbf{E}[S^2]$:

$$\mathbf{E}[S^2] = \sum_n \mathbf{E}[S^2 \mid N = n] \cdot \mathbf{P}\{N = n\}$$

$$= \sum_n \mathbf{E}\left[\left(\sum_{i=1}^{n} X_i\right)^2\right] \cdot \mathbf{P}\{N = n\}$$

$$= \sum_n \mathbf{E}\left[(X_1 + X_2 + \cdots + X_n)^2\right] \cdot \mathbf{P}\{N = n\}$$

$$= \sum_n \left(n \cdot \mathbf{E}[X_1^2] + (n^2 - n) \cdot \mathbf{E}[X_1 X_2]\right) \cdot \mathbf{P}\{N = n\}$$

$$= \sum_n n\mathbf{E}[X^2]\,\mathbf{P}\{N = n\} + \sum_n (n^2 - n)\mathbf{E}[X]^2\,\mathbf{P}\{N = n\}$$

$$= \mathbf{E}[N]\,\mathbf{E}[X^2] + \mathbf{E}[N^2]\,\mathbf{E}[X]^2 - \mathbf{E}[N]\,\mathbf{E}[X]^2$$

$$= \mathbf{E}[N]\,\mathbf{Var}(X) + \mathbf{E}[N^2]\,\mathbf{E}[X]^2.$$

Now,

$$\mathbf{Var}(S) = \mathbf{E}[S^2] - \mathbf{E}[S]^2$$

$$= \mathbf{E}[N]\,\mathbf{Var}(X) + \mathbf{E}[N^2]\,\mathbf{E}[X]^2 - (\mathbf{E}[N]\,\mathbf{E}[X])^2$$

$$= \mathbf{E}[N]\,\mathbf{Var}(X) + \mathbf{Var}(N)\mathbf{E}[X]^2.$$

We have proven Theorem 5.14.

Theorem 5.14 *Let $X_1, X_2, X_3, \ldots$ be i.i.d. random variables, where $X_i \sim X$.*
Let

$$S = \sum_{i=1}^{N} X_i, \quad where\ N \perp \{X_1, X_2, \ldots\}.$$

Then,

$$\mathbf{E}[S] = \mathbf{E}[N]\,\mathbf{E}[X], \tag{5.4}$$

$$\mathbf{E}[S^2] = \mathbf{E}[N]\,\mathbf{Var}(X) + \mathbf{E}[N^2]\,(\mathbf{E}[X])^2, \tag{5.5}$$

$$\mathbf{Var}(S) = \mathbf{E}[N]\,\mathbf{Var}(X) + \mathbf{Var}(N)\,(\mathbf{E}[X])^2. \tag{5.6}$$

While we were able to derive $\mathbf{E}\left[S^2\right]$, with some effort, you may be wondering how we would manage if we needed $\mathbf{E}\left[S^3\right]$, or some higher moment. It turns out that there's a much easier way to handle this type of analysis, by leveraging z-transforms, which we cover in Chapter 6.

Example 5.15 (Epidemic growth modeling)

A common way of modeling epidemic growth is via a tree.

Imagine that at time $t = 0$ we start with a single node (leaf). At each time step, every leaf independently either forks off two children with probability $\frac{1}{2}$, or stays inert (does nothing) with probability $\frac{1}{2}$.

We will be interested in

$$X_t = \text{Total number of leaves in the tree after } t \text{ steps.}$$

Specifically, what is $\mathbf{E}\left[X_t\right]$ and $\mathbf{Var}(X_t)$?

Figure 5.4 provides one example of how our tree might grow.

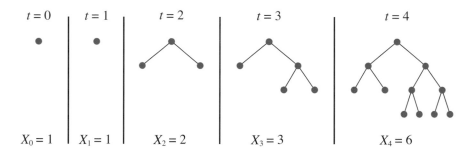

Figure 5.4 *Example of tree growth.*

Question: How can we model X_t?

It is tempting to try to write $X_t = C \cdot X_{t-1}$ for some C.

Question: Certainly the number of leaves at time t are related to the number of leaves at time $t - 1$, so how can we relate X_t to X_{t-1}?

Hint: Think of X_t as a sum of a random number of random variables.

Answer: The key insight is that each of the X_{t-1} leaves contributes either 1 or 2 to X_t. Specifically, if the leaf is inert in the current round, then it contributes 1 to the next round. If the leaf forks children in the current round, then it contributes

2 to the next round. Thus we can write:

$$X_t = \sum_{i=1}^{X_{t-1}} Y_i,$$

where

$$Y_i \sim Y = \begin{cases} 1 & \text{w/prob } 0.5 \\ 2 & \text{w/prob } 0.5 \end{cases}$$

and where $X_0 = 1$.

Question: Do the conditions of Theorem 5.14 apply?

Answer: Yes, the Y_i's are all i.i.d. and are independent of X_{t-1}.

Observe that

$$\mathbf{E}[Y] = \frac{3}{2} \quad \text{and} \quad \mathbf{Var}(Y) = \frac{1}{4}.$$

Question: Applying Theorem 5.14, what are $\mathbf{E}[X_t]$ and $\mathbf{Var}(X_t)$?

Answer:

$$\mathbf{E}[X_t] = \mathbf{E}[X_{t-1}] \cdot \mathbf{E}[Y] = \mathbf{E}[X_{t-1}] \cdot \frac{3}{2}.$$

Therefore,

$$\mathbf{E}[X_t] = \mathbf{E}[X_0] \cdot \left(\frac{3}{2}\right)^t = \left(\frac{3}{2}\right)^t.$$

$$\mathbf{Var}(X_t) = \mathbf{E}[X_{t-1}] \cdot \mathbf{Var}(Y) + \mathbf{Var}(X_{t-1}) \cdot \mathbf{E}[Y]^2$$
$$= \left(\frac{3}{2}\right)^{t-1} \cdot \frac{1}{4} + \mathbf{Var}(X_{t-1}) \cdot \frac{9}{4}.$$

This recursion simplifies to:

$$\mathbf{Var}(X_t) = \left(\frac{9}{4}\right)^t \cdot \frac{1}{3}\left(1 - \left(\frac{2}{3}\right)^t\right).$$

5.9 Tails

The mean, the variance, and higher moments are all ways of summarizing a distribution. For a discrete r.v., X, when we refer to the **distribution associated** with **X**, we are typically talking about either the p.m.f. of X, namely, $p_X(i) = \mathbf{P}\{X = i\}$ or the cumulative distribution function (c.d.f.) of X, namely, $F_X(i) = \mathbf{P}\{X \le i\}$.

It is also common to talk about the **tail** of X, which is defined as

$$\overline{F}_X(i) = \mathbf{P}\{X > i\} = 1 - F_X(i).$$

The tail comes up in quality-of-service guarantees for computer systems and in capacity provisioning. Consider, for example, a router buffer that is designed to hold no more than 10,000 packets. We might be interested in the probability that the number of packets exceeds 10,000 and thus no longer fits within the buffer.

5.9.1 Simple Tail Bounds

A **tail bound** provides an upper bound on the tail of a distribution. We will spend considerable time on motivating and developing tail bounds in Chapter 18, but for now we only state the two simplest tail bounds. The first, Markov's inequality, relies only on the mean of the distribution, but requires the assumption that the distribution only takes on non-negative values.

> **Theorem 5.16 (Markov's inequality)** *Let X be a non-negative r.v., with finite mean $\mu = \mathbf{E}[X]$. Then, $\forall a > 0$,*
>
> $$\mathbf{P}\{X \ge a\} \le \frac{\mu}{a}.$$

Proof:

$$\mu = \sum_{x=0}^{\infty} x p_X(x)$$

$$\ge \sum_{x=a}^{\infty} x p_X(x)$$

$$\ge \sum_{x=a}^{\infty} a p_X(x)$$

$$= a \sum_{x=a}^{\infty} p_X(x)$$

$$= a\mathbf{P}\{X \ge a\}. \qquad \blacksquare$$

The second tail bound, Chebyshev's inequality, is based on the variance of the distribution. Chebyshev's inequality is derived by applying Markov's inequality to the deviation of a r.v. from its mean.

Theorem 5.17 (Chebyshev's inequality) *Let X be a r.v. with finite mean* $\mu = \mathbf{E}[X]$ *and finite variance* $\mathbf{Var}(X)$. *Then,* $\forall a > 0$,

$$\mathbf{P}\{|X - \mu| \geq a\} \leq \frac{\mathbf{Var}(X)}{a^2}.$$

Proof:

$$\mathbf{P}\{|X - \mu| \geq a\} = \mathbf{P}\{(X - \mu)^2 \geq a^2\}$$

$$\leq \frac{\mathbf{E}\left[(X - \mu)^2\right]}{a^2} \quad \text{(by Markov's inequality)}$$

$$= \frac{\mathbf{Var}(X)}{a^2}. \qquad\qquad \blacksquare$$

5.9.2 Stochastic Dominance

Question: Suppose that r.v. X and r.v. Y are defined on the same sample space, but $X \neq Y$ in distribution. Is it possible that

$$\mathbf{P}\{X > i\} \geq \mathbf{P}\{Y > i\} \quad \forall \text{ values of } i?$$

Answer: Yes! In fact this has a name.

Definition 5.18 *Given two random variables X and Y, if*

$$\mathbf{P}\{X > i\} \geq \mathbf{P}\{Y > i\}, \quad \forall i$$

we say that X **stochastically dominates** *Y. We write this as* $X \geq_{st} Y$.

Example 5.19 (Stochastic dominance)

Figure 5.5 illustrates stochastic dominance of X over Y. Let

$$X = \begin{cases} 1 & \text{w/prob } 0.3 \\ 2 & \text{w/prob } 0.2 \\ 3 & \text{w/prob } 0.4 \\ 4 & \text{w/prob } 0.1 \end{cases} \quad \text{and} \quad Y = \begin{cases} 1 & \text{w/prob } 0.4 \\ 2 & \text{w/prob } 0.4 \\ 3 & \text{w/prob } 0.2 \\ 4 & \text{w/prob } 0 \end{cases}.$$

When looking at the p.m.f. of X and the p.m.f. of Y, it is not at all obvious that

X dominates Y. However, when looking at the tails of the distributions, we see that the tail of X (purple function) is always above or equal to that of Y (red function).

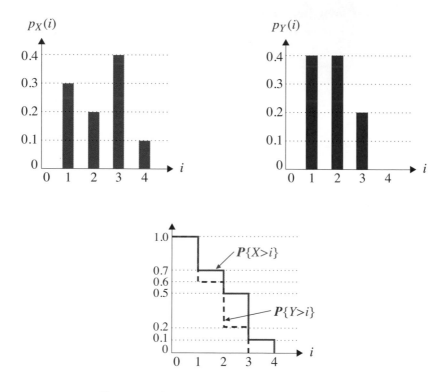

Figure 5.5 $X \geq_{st} Y$, where X is shown in purple and Y is shown in red.

Question: When looking at the tail part of Figure 5.5, what does the area under the red (dashed) $\mathbf{P}\{Y > i\}$ function represent?

Answer: The area under the red function is $\mathbf{E}[Y]$ and the area under the purple (solid) $\mathbf{P}\{X > i\}$ function is $\mathbf{E}[X]$. To understand this, recall Exercise 4.16.

Example 5.20 (More shoes are better!)

As another example of stochastic dominance, let's look at shoes. My husband likes to tell me that I own way too many shoes (Figure 5.6), but I argue that women stochastically dominate men when it comes to the number of pairs of shoes they own.[1] Let X be a random variable representing the number of pairs of shoes owned by women, where X is reasonably approximated by a Poisson distribution with mean 27. Similarly let $Y \sim \text{Poisson}(12)$ denote the number of

---

[1] According to a study of shoe brands in the United States, the average man owns 12 pairs of shoes, while the average woman owns 27 pairs [81].

Figure 5.6 *The shoes in my closet.*

pairs of shoes owned by men. While a given man might have more shoes than a given woman, the number of shoes owned by an arbitrary woman stochastically dominates the number owned by an arbitrary man.

Figure 5.7 shows an illustration of two Poisson distributions: $Y \sim$ Poisson(20) (red/dashed) and $X \sim$ Poisson(50) (purple/solid). In Figure 5.7(a), we see that $p_X(i)$ is above $p_Y(i)$ for large values of i (although it is below for small values of i). In Figure 5.7(b), we see that $\mathbf{P}\{X > i\}$ is always at least equal to $\mathbf{P}\{Y > i\}$. Thus, we say that Poisson(50) (purple/solid) stochastically dominates Poisson(20) (red/dashed).

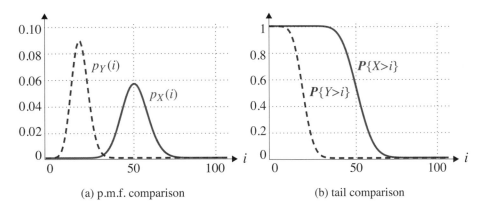

(a) p.m.f. comparison   (b) tail comparison

Figure 5.7 *The purple (solid) curve represents $X \sim$ Poisson(50) while the red (dashed) curve represents $Y \sim$ Poisson(20). The purple curve stochastically dominates the red one.*

Question: If X stochastically dominates Y, and both are non-negative, then it feels like the mean of X should be at least that of Y. Is this true? What about higher moments of X versus Y?

Answer: The answer is yes! See Exercise 5.37.

5.10 Jensen's Inequality

By the definition of variance, and the fact that it must be positive, we know that

$$\mathbf{E}\left[X^2\right] \geq \mathbf{E}\left[X\right]^2.$$

Question: Does it also hold that $\mathbf{E}\left[X^3\right] \geq \mathbf{E}\left[X\right]^3$? Is $\mathbf{E}\left[X^4\right] \geq \mathbf{E}\left[X\right]^4$?

Answer: Yes! Specifically, if X is a positive random variable, then

$$\mathbf{E}\left[X^a\right] \geq \mathbf{E}\left[X\right]^a, \qquad \forall a \in \mathbb{R}, \text{ where } a > 1. \tag{5.7}$$

The proof of (5.7) is given in Exercise 5.32 and follows immediately from Jensen's inequality (Theorem 5.23). Before we can describe Jensen's inequality, we need to review convex functions.

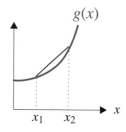

Figure 5.8 *Illustration of convex function $g(x)$.*

Informally a convex function is an upturned curve. More precisely, if we pick any two points on the curve and draw a line segment between these, then the line segment will lie above the curve (see Figure 5.8).

> **Definition 5.21** *A real-valued function $g(\cdot)$ defined on an interval $S \subseteq \mathbb{R}$ is said to be **convex** on S if, for any $x_1, x_2 \in S$ and any $\alpha \in [0, 1]$, we have*
>
> $$g\left(\alpha x_1 + (1 - \alpha)x_2\right) \leq \alpha g(x_1) + (1 - \alpha)g(x_2).$$

To visualize Definition 5.21, observe that

- $\alpha x_1 + (1 - \alpha)x_2$ is a weighted average of x_1 and x_2; and
- $\alpha g(x_1) + (1 - \alpha)g(x_2)$ is a weighted average of $g(x_1)$ and $g(x_2)$.

Thus Definition 5.21 is saying that if z is any weighted average of x_1 and x_2, then the point $g(z)$ on the curve will always lie below the corresponding point on the line, namely the weighted average of $g(x_1)$ and $g(x_2)$.

Suppose now that X is a r.v. where

$$X = \begin{cases} x_1 & \text{w/prob } p_X(x_1) \\ x_2 & \text{w/prob } p_X(x_2) \end{cases}.$$

Then, for any convex function $g(\cdot)$, Definition 5.21 says that

$$g\left(p_X(x_1)x_1 + p_X(x_2)x_2\right) \le p_X(x_1)g(x_1) + p_X(x_2)g(x_2). \tag{5.8}$$

Question: What does (5.8) say about $g(\mathbf{E}[X])$?

Answer:

$$g(\mathbf{E}[X]) \le \mathbf{E}[g(X)].$$

It is easy to generalize Definition 5.21 using induction to obtain Definition 5.22:

Definition 5.22 *A real-valued function $g(\cdot)$ defined on an interval $S \subseteq \mathbb{R}$ is said to be **convex** on S if, for any points $x_1, x_2, \ldots, x_n \in S$ and any $\alpha_1, \alpha_2, \ldots, \alpha_n \in [0, 1]$, where $\alpha_1 + \alpha_2 + \cdots + \alpha_n = 1$, we have*

$$g(\alpha_1 x_1 + \alpha_2 x_2 + \cdots + \alpha_n x_n) \le \alpha_1 g(x_1) + \alpha_2 g(x_2) + \cdots + \alpha_n g(x_n).$$

Let X be a r.v. where

$$X = \begin{cases} x_1 & \text{w/prob } p_X(x_1) \\ x_2 & \text{w/prob } p_X(x_2) \\ \vdots \\ x_n & \text{w/prob } p_X(x_n) \end{cases}.$$

Question: What does Definition 5.22 say about $\mathbf{E}[g(X)]$?

Answer: Again

$$g\left(p_X(x_1)x_1 + \cdots + p_X(x_n)x_n\right) \le p_X(x_1)g(x_1) + \cdots + p_X(x_n)g(x_n),$$

so again $g(\mathbf{E}[X]) \le \mathbf{E}[g(X)]$.

This is summarized by Jensen's inequality:

Theorem 5.23 (Jensen's inequality) *Let X be a r.v. that takes on values in an interval S, and let $g : S \to \mathbb{R}$ be convex on S. Then,*

$$g(\mathbf{E}[X]) \le \mathbf{E}[g(X)]. \tag{5.9}$$

We have proven Theorem 5.23 in the case of a discrete r.v. X with finite support.

The theorem also generalizes to the case where X has infinite support and further to the case where X is a continuous r.v. We omit the proof.

Important: A useful method for determining that a function is convex is to check its second derivative. Specifically, $g(\cdot)$ is convex on S if and only if $g''(x) \geq 0$ for all $x \in S$. For example, $g(x) = x^2$ is convex over $\mathbb{R}$, because $g''(x) = 2 \geq 0$.

5.11 Inspection Paradox

We end this chapter by describing one of the more subtle consequences of variability, called the inspection paradox. The inspection paradox says that the mean seen by a random observer can be very different from the true mean. This is best illustrated via examples.

Example 5.24 (Waiting for the bus)

The 61C bus arrives at my bus stop every 10 minutes on average. Specifically, if S denotes the time between buses, then $\mathbf{E}[S] = 10$. I arrive at the bus stop at random times. I would expect that my average wait time for a bus is five minutes. However, I've been monitoring it, and my average wait time is actually eight minutes.

Question: How can this be?

Hint: The answer has to do with the variability of S, specifically its squared coefficient of variation, C_S^2.

Question: If $C_S^2 = 0$, what should the average waiting time of a random arrival be?

Answer: Five minutes, since the person is equally likely to arrive anywhere in $[0, 10]$.

Question: So what goes wrong when C_S^2 is high?

Hint: Looking at Figure 5.9, we see that there are short intervals and long intervals between buses. The average length of an interval is 10 minutes. But which interval is a random arriving person more likely to "land" in?

Answer: A random arriving person is more likely to land in a large interval, thus experiencing an extra-long waiting time. This difference between the true average and the average experienced by a randomly arriving person is what we call the inspection paradox. For a concrete example involving buses, see Exercise 5.20.

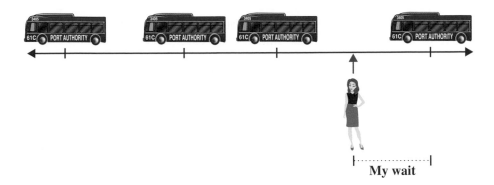

Figure 5.9 *Inspection paradox. The mean time between buses is 10 minutes, so why is my average wait so high?*

Example 5.25 (Class size)

As another example, suppose we ask every student at CMU about the sizes of their classes and we take the average of all these numbers. You will probably hear that the average is somewhere around 100 students in a class. But when you talk to the dean, the dean will tell you that the average class size is 30.

Question: Can the dean and the students both be right?

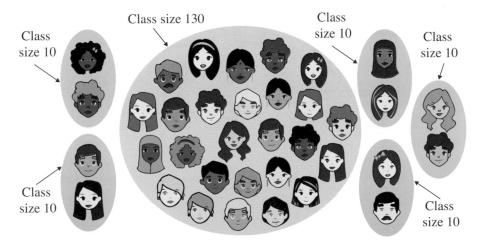

Figure 5.10 *Inspection paradox. The average class size is 30, so why is my average class size so large?*

Answer: Yes! This again is a classic example of the inspection paradox. Figure 5.10 provides an illustration. Say we have five classes of size 10 students and one class of size 130 students. The average across classes is indeed 30. However, most students are in the 130 person class, so they experience a high average.

Question: Suppose that each student takes just one class and there are $50 + 130 = 180$ students in the school. What is the average *observed* class size?

Answer: $\frac{50}{180}$ fraction of students observe a class size of 10, while $\frac{130}{180}$ fraction of students observe a class size of 130. Thus,

$$\text{Average observed class size} \ = \ \frac{50}{180} \cdot 10 + \frac{130}{180} \cdot 130 \approx 97.$$

Example 5.26 (My friends have more Facebook friends than I do!)

As a final example, we consider a study done by Allen Downey which samples 4,000 Facebook users [20]. For each person, p, the study computes the number of friends of p, and the number of friends of each of p's friends. The study found that an average user has 44 friends. However, your average friend has 104 friends. Furthermore, the probability that your friend is more popular than you is 76%.

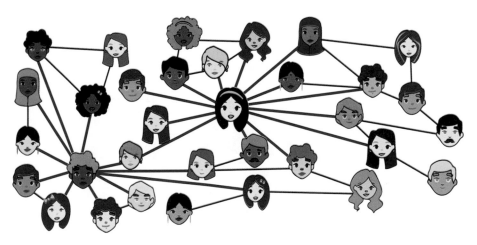

Figure 5.11 *Inspection paradox. Popular people (shown with red links) are more likely to be your friends.*

Question: How can this be?

Answer: This is again an inspection paradox, which stems from the fact that there is variability in the number of friends that people have. As shown in Figure 5.11, most people have a few friends, but a few people have a lot of friends. Let's call a person who has lots of friends a "popular" person. Popular people are simply counted more and thus are more visible to an observer. Consider two potential friends: one popular and one unpopular. The popular person is more likely to be included among your friends than the unpopular one, because the popular person has *lots* of friends. Now, whenever a popular person is included as one of your friends, this ends up raising the average number of friends that your friends have. The friends phenomenon was originally studied by Scott Feld [26].

5.12 Exercises

5.1 **Simplifying variance**
Simplify each of the following expressions into its simplest form using either definition of variance. Also provide an interpretation of your result by explaining what changes in Figure 5.1.
(a) $\mathbf{Var}(X + 5)$
(b) $\mathbf{Var}(X - 5)$
(c) $\mathbf{Var}(5X)$
(d) $\mathbf{Var}(-X + 3)$

5.2 **Difference of independent random variables**
Let X and Y be discrete random variables where $X \perp Y$. Express $\mathbf{Var}(X - Y)$ in terms of $\mathbf{Var}(X)$ and $\mathbf{Var}(Y)$. Prove it!

5.3 **Sums versus copies**
Let X, Y, and Z be i.i.d. random variables, all distributed as Bernoulli(p). Evaluate the following:
(a) $\mathbf{E}[X + Y + Z]$
(b) $\mathbf{E}[3X]$
(c) $\mathbf{E}[X + Y + Z]^2$
(d) $\mathbf{E}\left[(X + Y + Z)^2\right]$
(e) $\mathbf{E}\left[(3X)^2\right]$

5.4 **The coveted 212 area code**
There are eight million people in NYC. Suppose that each independently is given a phone number with a 212 area code with probability 2%. What is the standard deviation on the number of people who get the coveted 212 area code?

5.5 **Variance of Poisson**
Let $X \sim \text{Poisson}(\lambda)$. Derive $\mathbf{Var}(X)$.

5.6 **Die throws**
Let X_1 and X_2 be the results of two independent die throws. Which is larger $\mathbf{E}[X_1 X_2]$ or $\mathbf{E}[X_1^2]$? Or are they the same? Compute each.

5.7 Understanding variance and risk
Let $X_1, X_2, \ldots, X_c$ be i.i.d. instances of r.v. X.

(a) Which is lower: $\mathbf{Var}(X_1 + X_2 + \cdots + X_c)$ or $\mathbf{Var}(cX)$? Compute each.

(b) A mutual fund allows you to buy a small piece of many different companies, as opposed to buying a large piece of a single company. It is said that investing in a mutual fund is less risky than investing in a single company. Explain this statement via your analysis in part (a).

5.8 Grade of A
The average grade on the first probability exam is 70%. The "A" grade cutoff is 90%. What is an upper bound on the fraction of students who get an "A"?

(a) Assume that we have no other knowledge, and use Markov's inequality.

(b) Assume that we know the standard deviation of grades is 5%, and apply Chebyshev's inequality.

5.9 Chebyshev's inequality
Show that Chebyshev's inequality guarantees that the probability of deviating from the mean by more than k standard deviations is less than $\frac{1}{k^2}$. Specifically, if X is any random variable with mean μ and finite variance σ^2, then for any real number $k > 0$,

$$\mathbf{P}\{|X - \mu| \geq k\sigma_X\} \leq \frac{1}{k^2}.$$

5.10 Stochastic dominance of Geometrics
Let $X \sim \text{Geometric}(0.2)$, $Y \sim \text{Geometric}(0.4)$, where $X \perp Y$. What is $\mathbf{P}\{X > Y\}$? Is $X \geq_{st} Y$?

5.11 Applications of Jensen's inequality
Let X be a positive random variable.

(a) How do $\mathbf{E}\left[X^{-1}\right]$ and $\mathbf{E}\left[X\right]^{-1}$ compare?

(b) How do $\mathbf{E}\left[e^X\right]$ and $e^{\mathbf{E}[X]}$ compare?

5.12 Zero covariance
(a) Prove that if X and Y are independent random variables, then $\mathbf{Cov}(X, Y) = 0$.

(b) Show that the converse is not true. That is, $\mathbf{Cov}(X, Y) = 0$ does *not* imply that $X \perp Y$. [Hint: Find a counter-example.]

5.13 Using covariance to express variance of a sum
Let X and Y be random variables. Prove that

$$\mathbf{Var}(X + Y) = \mathbf{Var}(X) + \mathbf{Var}(Y) + 2\mathbf{Cov}(X, Y). \qquad (5.10)$$

Equation (5.10) can be generalized to:

$$\mathbf{Var}\left(\sum_{i=1}^{n} X_i\right) = \sum_{i=1}^{n} \mathbf{Var}(X_i) + 2 \sum_{1 \le i < j \le n} \mathbf{Cov}(X_i, X_j) \qquad (5.11)$$

for random variables $X_1, X_2, \ldots, X_n$. You do not have to prove (5.11).

5.14 Covariance and events

Let X and Y be indicator random variables, where

$$X = \begin{cases} 1 & \text{if event } A \text{ occurs} \\ 0 & \text{otherwise} \end{cases} \qquad Y = \begin{cases} 1 & \text{if event } B \text{ occurs} \\ 0 & \text{otherwise} \end{cases}.$$

Prove that $\mathbf{Cov}(X, Y) > 0$ if and only if events A and B are positively correlated (see Exercise 2.8 for the definition of positively correlated events).

5.15 Cauchy–Schwarz inequality

In this problem, you will prove the Cauchy–Schwarz inequality for random variables which says that for any two random variables X and Y,

$$\left| \mathbf{E}\left[XY \right] \right| \le \sqrt{\mathbf{E}\left[X^2 \right] \mathbf{E}\left[Y^2 \right]}. \qquad (5.12)$$

Follow these steps:
(a) Let $Z = (X - cY)^2$, where c is a constant. Explain why $\mathbf{E}\left[Z \right] \ge 0$.
(b) Now substitute in $c = \frac{\mathbf{E}[XY]}{\mathbf{E}[Y^2]}$ and simplify until you get (5.12).

5.16 Correlation coefficient

Recall that $\mathbf{Cov}(X, Y)$ can be arbitrarily high or low depending on the magnitude of X and Y. In practice, it is common to use a normalized version on covariance called the correlation coefficient, $\rho(X, Y)$, where

$$\rho(X, Y) \equiv \frac{\mathbf{Cov}(X, Y)}{\sigma_X \sigma_Y},$$

where σ_X and σ_Y represent the standard deviations of X and Y respectively. Prove that the magnitude of $\mathbf{Cov}(X, Y)$ is bounded, specifically

$$-1 \le \rho(X, Y) \le 1.$$

[Hint 1: It helps to use the Cauchy–Schwarz inequality from Exercise 5.15.]
[Hint 2: Start by working with $V = \frac{1}{\sigma_X}(X - \mathbf{E}\left[X \right])$ and $W = \frac{1}{\sigma_Y}(Y - \mathbf{E}\left[Y \right])$.]

5.17 Sampling without replacement: variance and covariance

Suppose that we have an urn that contains b balls numbered $1, 2, \ldots b$. We draw $n \le b$ balls at random from the urn, one at a time, without replacement. Let X_i denote the number on the ith ball drawn.
(a) What is $\mathbf{P}\{X_i = k\}$?

(b) Show that

$$\mathbf{Var}(X_i) = \frac{(b-1)(b+1)}{12}. \tag{5.13}$$

[Hint: Use the identity that $\sum_{i=1}^{b} i^2 = \frac{1}{6}b(b+1)(2b+1)$.]
(c) Follow the steps below to show that:

$$\mathbf{Cov}(X_i, X_j) = -\frac{b+1}{12}. \tag{5.14}$$

(i) What is $\mathbf{P}\{X_i = k_1, X_j = k_2\}$?
(ii) Explain why $\mathbf{Var}\left(\sum_{i=1}^{b} X_i\right) = 0$.
(iii) Apply $\mathbf{Var}\left(\sum_{i=1}^{b} X_i\right) = \sum_{i=1}^{b} \mathbf{Var}(X_i) + 2\sum_{1 \le i < j \le b} \mathbf{Cov}(X_i, X_j)$
from (5.11) to get $\mathbf{Cov}(X_i, X_j)$.
(iv) Explain why it makes sense that $\mathbf{Cov}(X_i, X_j)$ is negative.

5.18 Memorylessness of Geometric
Let $X \sim \text{Geometric}(p)$. Let $Y = [X \mid X > 1]$. You will prove that

$$Y \stackrel{d}{=} 1 + X.$$

(a) Argue that Y and $1 + X$ have the same sample space of possible values.
(b) Write a simple expression for $\mathbf{P}\{Y = i\}$, where $i \ge 2$.
(c) Write a simple expression for $\mathbf{P}\{1 + X = i\}$, where $i \ge 2$.
Your answers for parts (b) and (c) should be the same.

5.19 Variance of the Geometric
Let $X \sim \text{Geometric}(p)$. Derive $\mathbf{Var}(X) = \frac{1-p}{p^2}$. [Hint: Use conditioning.]

5.20 Buses and the inspection paradox
Suppose that half of all buses arrive 5 minutes after the previous bus, and half arrive 15 minutes after the previous bus. Let r.v. S denote the time between buses.
(a) What is $\mathbf{E}[S]$?
(b) If you arrive at a random time, what is the expected length of the inter-bus interval that you find yourself in?
(c) Let's consider a more extreme example where half of all buses arrive $\epsilon > 0$ minutes after the previous bus, while half arrive $20 - \epsilon$ minutes after the previous bus. How do your answers to (a) and (b) change? Derive the answers in the limit as $\epsilon \to 0$.

5.21 Happy gambling
At the Happy Casino, at every turn you earn a dollar with probability 0.6 and lose a dollar with probability 0.4. Let W denote your total money won after n games (this could be positive or negative).

(a) What is $\mathbf{E}[W]$?

(b) What is $\mathbf{Var}(W)$?

5.22 Good chips versus lemons

A chip supplier produces 95% good chips and 5% lemons (bad chips). The good chips fail with probability 0.0001 each day. The lemons fail with probability 0.01 each day. You buy a random chip. Let T be the time until your chip fails. Compute $\mathbf{E}[T]$ and $\mathbf{Var}(T)$.

5.23 Napster

As a present for my brother, I decided to create a collection of all 50 songs from his favorite band. Unfortunately, whenever I typed in the band name, I was sent a *random* song from the band. Let D denote the number of downloads required to get all 50 songs.

(a) What is $\mathbf{E}[D]$? Give a closed-form approximation.

(b) What is $\mathbf{Var}(D)$? (No need for closed-form here.)

5.24 Ensuring Internet connectivity

Janice manages the wireless Internet connection in a building. Let N denote the number of occupants in the building each day, where $\mathbf{E}[N] = 100$ and $\sigma_N = 10$. Each occupant needs Internet connectivity. Suppose that one wireless access point can serve $m = 10$ occupants. Janice wants to use as few access points as possible, while ensuring all occupants of the building get Internet connectivity.

(a) Suppose that on a given day Janice wants to ensure that, with probability at least 80%, all occupants get Internet connectivity. According to Markov's inequality, how many access points, n, does she need?

(b) Repeat part (a), this time using the Chebyshev bound.

5.25 Hypothesis testing in data analysis

In hypothesis testing, a decision between two alternatives, one of which is called the "null hypothesis" (H_0) and the other the "alternative hypothesis" (H_1), is to be made. You are given a coin with probability p of heads, and you want to test if it is fair or biased in favor of heads. Here,

H_0: Coin is fair (that is, $p = 0.5$).

H_1: Coin is biased toward heads (that is, $p > 0.5$).

You perform an experiment of tossing the coin $n = 10$ times and observe $k = 8$ heads. Based on this outcome, you have to decide whether to "reject H_0" (that is, choose H_1). A popular approach used in making such decisions is based on the "p-value." The p-value of an outcome is the probability that the observed outcome, *or something more extreme* than the observed outcome, occurs under the assumption that H_0 is true. Here, "more extreme" means more in favor of H_1.

(a) What is the p-value for the outcome of your experiment?

(b) To be more confident in choosing between hypotheses H_0 and H_1, should the associated p-value be higher or lower?

(c) To be confident of your decision, you set the p-value at 0.01. How many heads do you need to observe in the experiment in order to choose H_1.

5.26 Mouse in a maze

[Problem adapted from Sheldon Ross.] A mouse is trapped in a maze. Initially it has to choose one of two directions. If it goes to the right, then it will wander around in the maze for three minutes and will then return to its initial position. If it goes to the left, then with probability $\frac{1}{3}$ it will depart the maze after two minutes of traveling, and with probability $\frac{2}{3}$ it will return to its initial position after five minutes. The mouse is at all times equally likely to go to the left or the right. Let T denote the number of minutes that it will be trapped in the maze.

(a) What is $\mathbf{E}[T]$?

(b) What is $\mathbf{Var}(T)$?

5.27 Central moments

Recall that when X and Y are independent random variables, we have:

$$\mathbf{Var}(X + Y) = \mathbf{Var}(X) + \mathbf{Var}(Y).$$

Let $\mathbf{Skew}(X)$ denote the third central moment of X, that is,

$$\mathbf{Skew}(X) = \mathbf{E}\left[(X - \mathbf{E}[X])^3\right].$$

Either prove or disprove (via a counter-example) that, for independent X and Y:

$$\mathbf{Skew}(X + Y) = \mathbf{Skew}(X) + \mathbf{Skew}(Y).$$

[Hint: It may help to define $X' = X - \mathbf{E}[X]$ and $Y' = Y - \mathbf{E}[Y]$ and then restate the problem in terms of X' and Y'.]

5.28 All I do is sleep and work

A typical CMU student's life consists of alternating between home and school every hour, according to Figure 5.12. If the student is home, with probability p she will switch to school at the next hour (otherwise she will stay home). If the student is at school, with probability q she will switch to home at the next hour (otherwise she will stay at school). Assuming the student just got to school, let T be the time (in hours) until the student goes home. What is $\mathbf{Var}(T)$?

5.29 Dominance

[Proposed by Weina Wang] Suppose that X and Y represent the result of coin flips, where

$$X \sim \text{Bernoulli}(0.5) \qquad \text{and} \qquad Y \sim \text{Bernoulli}(0.6).$$

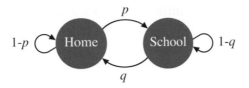

Figure 5.12 *Figure for Exercise 5.28.*

Clearly sometimes the value of X exceeds that of Y, although slightly more often the value of Y exceeds that of X. Define a joint probability distribution, $p_{X,Y}(x, y)$ where the marginal distributions are $p_X(x) \sim$ Bernoulli(0.5) and $p_Y(y) \sim$ Bernoulli(0.6), but $\mathbf{P}\{X \leq Y\} = 1$.

5.30 **All I do is sleep, work, and drink coffee**

Imagine a poor student caught in an endless cycle between sleeping, working, and drinking coffee at the coffee house. The student's life is described by Figure 5.13, where the student is always in one of three states, and every hour the student transitions (possibly back to the same state) with the probability shown. For example, after drinking a cup of coffee, the student will, at the next hour, with probability $\frac{1}{3}$ go back to work, or with probability $\frac{2}{3}$ stay to drink another cup of coffee. Assuming that the student is at work, let T denote the number of hours until she goes home to sleep.

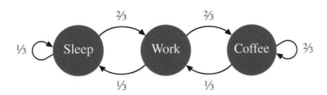

Figure 5.13 *Figure for Exercise 5.30.*

(a) What is $\mathbf{E}[T]$?
(b) What is $\mathbf{Var}(T)$?

5.31 **Average of random number of random variables**

Let $X_1, X_2, X_3, \ldots$ be i.i.d. random variables with distribution X. Let N be a positive, integer-valued r.v., where $N \perp X$. Let

$$A = \frac{1}{N} \sum_{i=1}^{N} X_i.$$

(a) Derive $\mathbf{E}[A]$.
(b) Derive $\mathbf{Var}(A)$.

5.32 **Higher moment inequalities**
Use Jensen's inequality to prove that for any positive r.v. X,

$$\mathbf{E}\left[X^a\right] \geq \mathbf{E}\left[X\right]^a, \qquad \forall a \in \mathbb{R}, \text{ where } a > 1.$$

5.33 **Summing up to a stopping time**
[Proposed by Tianxin Xu] Imagine I roll a fair three-sided die.
  • If the die comes up 1, I give you one dollar, and I role again.
  • If the die comes up 2, I give you two dollars, and I role again.
  • If the die comes up 3, I give you three dollars, but we stop playing.
Let S denote the total amount of money that I give you during the game.
Observe

$$S = \sum_{i=1}^{N} X_i,$$

where X_i is the result of the ith role, and N is the number of rolls until we
see a 3 (inclusive). Your goal is to compute $\mathbf{E}\left[S\right]$ and $\mathbf{Var}(S)$.
(a) Explain why we can't apply Theorem 5.14.
(b) Compute $\mathbf{E}\left[S\right]$. [Hint: Condition on the first roll.] Is your answer the
    same as in Theorem 5.14?
(c) Now compute $\mathbf{Var}(S)$. Is your answer the same as in Theorem 5.14?
The r.v. N in this problem is called a "stopping time" because its value only
depends on the X_i's that were seen so far, and not on the future. When N
is a stopping time, and the X_i's are i.i.d. with $X_i \sim X$, an identity called
Wald's equation says that $\mathbf{E}\left[\sum_{i=1}^{N} X_i\right] = \mathbf{E}\left[N\right] \cdot \mathbf{E}\left[X\right]$ [74].

5.34 **Skewering the Binomial**
Let $\mathbf{Skew}(X) = \mathbf{E}\left[(X - \mathbf{E}\left[X\right])^3\right]$. If $Y \sim \text{Binomial}(n, p)$, what is
$\mathbf{Skew}(Y)$?

5.35 **Race to win**
Obama and Romney are counting votes as they come in. Suppose that each
incoming vote is for Obama with probability $p = 0.6$ and is for Romney
with probability $1 - p = 0.4$. At the moment when Obama has 100 votes,
we'd like to understand how many votes Romney has. Let R denote the
number of Romney votes at the moment when Obama gets his 100th vote.[2]
(a) What is $p_R(i)$? (We want the probability of the event that there are
    i Romney votes *and* 100 Obama votes *and* that the last vote is for
    Obama.)
(b) What is $\mathbf{E}\left[R\right]$? [Hint: If you try to derive $\mathbf{E}\left[R\right]$ from $p_R(i)$, you will
    find it hard. Look for the much easier way. Hint: Linearity.]
(c) What is $\mathbf{Var}(R)$? [Hint: This should be easy after (b).]

---

[2] This is an instance of a Negative Binomial distribution.

5.36 **Cups at a party**

There are n people at a party. Each person puts their cup down on the table. Then they each pick up a random cup.
(a) What is the expected number of people who get back their own cup?
(b) Derive the variance of the number of people who get back their own cup.

5.37 **Stochastic dominance**

Let X and Y be non-negative, discrete, integer-valued random variables. We are given that $X \geq_{st} Y$.
(a) Prove that $\mathbf{E}[X] \geq \mathbf{E}[Y]$.
(b) Prove that $\mathbf{E}[X^2] \geq \mathbf{E}[Y^2]$.
[Hint: Compare $\sum_i i \cdot \mathbf{P}\{X > i\}$ with $\sum_i i \cdot \mathbf{P}\{Y > i\}$.]

5.38 **Pairwise independence**

Consider n random variables: $X_1, X_2, \ldots, X_n$. We say that these are *pairwise independent* if any two of these are independent, that is,

$$\forall i \neq j, \qquad \mathbf{P}\{X_i = i \ \& \ X_j = j\} = \mathbf{P}\{X_i = i\} \cdot \mathbf{P}\{X_j = j\}.$$

We will show that if $X_1, X_2, \ldots, X_n$ are pairwise independent, then:

$$\mathbf{Var}(X_1 + X_2 + \cdots + X_n) = \mathbf{Var}(X_1) + \mathbf{Var}(X_2) + \cdots + \mathbf{Var}(X_n).$$

(a) Prove the desired linearity theorem in the case where $\mathbf{E}[X_i] = 0, \forall i$.
(b) For the rest of the problem, assume that $\mathbf{E}[X_i] \neq 0$. Define $Y_i = X_i - \mathbf{E}[X_i]$. What is $\mathbf{E}[Y_i]$?
(c) What does your result from part (a) say about the linearity of $\mathbf{Var}(Y_1 + Y_2 + \cdots + Y_n)$? After writing down the linearity statement for the Y_i's, substitute back $Y_i = X_i - \mathbf{E}[X_i]$. You will see that you can claim a linearity result for the X_i's as well.

5.39 **Total variation distance**

We often want to express the "distance" between two distributions. There are many ways to define such a distance. One way is the total variation distance (TVD). Given two discrete distributions, X and Y, we write:

$$\mathbf{TVD}(X, Y) = \frac{1}{2} \sum_i \left| \mathbf{P}\{X = i\} - \mathbf{P}\{Y = i\} \right|.$$

Prove two properties of $\mathbf{TVD}(X, Y)$:
(a) Prove that $\mathbf{TVD}(X, Y) \leq 1$.
(b) Prove that $\mathbf{TVD}(X, Y) \leq \mathbf{P}\{X \neq Y\}$.

6   z-Transforms

This chapter is a very brief introduction to the wonderful world of transforms. Transforms come in many varieties. There are z-transforms, moment-generating functions, characteristic functions, Fourier transforms, Laplace transforms, and more. All are very similar in their function. In this chapter, we will study *z-transforms*, a variant particularly well suited to common *discrete* random variables. In Chapter 11, we will study Laplace transforms, a variant ideally suited to common continuous random variables.

Transforms are an extremely powerful analysis technique. In this chapter we will cover two of the most common uses of transforms:

1. Computing higher moments of random variables (see Sections 6.1 – 6.6).
2. Solving recurrence relations, particularly recurrences that will come up later when we study Markov chains. This will be discussed in Section 6.7 and then again when we get to infinite-state Markov chains in Chapter 26.

6.1 Motivating Examples

Suppose that you want to know the third moment of a Binomial(n, p) distribution. Let $X \sim \text{Binomial}(n, p)$. Then,

$$\mathbf{E}\left[X^3\right] = \sum_{i=0}^{n} \binom{n}{i} p^i (1 - p)^{n-i} i^3.$$

This is a daunting expression.

As another example, you might want to know the fifth moment of a Poisson(λ) distribution. Let $Y \sim \text{Poisson}(\lambda)$. Then,

$$\mathbf{E}\left[X^5\right] = \sum_{i=0}^{\infty} \frac{e^{-\lambda} \lambda^i}{i!} \cdot i^5.$$

Again, it's not easy to see how to derive this. One of the most important uses of transforms is that they allow us to obtain *all* moments of a random variable, as we now explain.

6.2 The Transform as an Onion

One can think of the transform of a random variable as an onion, shown in Figure 6.1. This onion contains inside it all the moments of the random variable. Getting the moments out of the onion is not an easy task, however, and may involve some tears as the onion is peeled, where the "peeling process" involves differentiating the transform. The first moment is stored in the outermost layer of the onion and thus does not require too much peeling to reach. The second moment is stored a little deeper, the third moment even deeper (more tears), etc. Although getting the moments is painful, it is entirely straightforward how to do it – just keep peeling the layers.

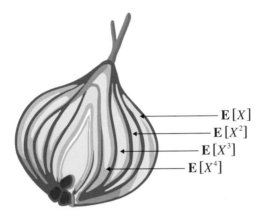

Figure 6.1 *The z-transform onion.*

Definition 6.1 *The* **z-transform***, $G_p(z)$, of a discrete function, $p(i)$, $i = 0, 1, 2, \ldots$ is defined as*

$$G_p(z) = \sum_{i=0}^{\infty} p(i)z^i.$$

Observe that the z-transform is a polynomial in z. Here, z should be thought of as a placeholder that keeps $p(i)$ separated from $p(i+1)$, by multiplying $p(i)$ by z^i and multiplying $p(i+1)$ by z^{i+1}.

When we speak of the z-transform of a discrete random variable (r.v.) X, we are referring to the z-transform of the probability mass function (p.m.f.), $p_X(\cdot)$, associated with X.

> **Definition 6.2** *Let X be a non-negative discrete r.v. with p.m.f. $p_X(i)$, where $i = 0, 1, 2, \ldots$. Then the **z-transform of r.v.** X is written as $\widehat{X}(z)$, where*
>
> $$\widehat{X}(z) = G_{P_X}(z) = \mathbf{E}\left[z^X\right] = \sum_{i=0}^{\infty} p_X(i)z^i.$$
>
> *Throughout, we assume that z is a constant and we will assume that $|z| \le 1$.*

Note that the z-transform can be defined for any random variable. However, convergence is *guaranteed* when the r.v. is *non-negative* and $|z| \le 1$, as we'll see in Theorem 6.6. That does not mean that convergence doesn't happen in other settings as well.

Question: What is $\widehat{X}(1)$?

> **Theorem 6.3** *For all discrete random variables, X,*
>
> $$\widehat{X}(1) = 1.$$

Proof:

$$\widehat{X}(1) = \mathbf{E}\left[z^X\right]\Big|_{z=1} = \sum_{i=-\infty}^{\infty} p_X(i) \cdot 1^i = 1. \qquad \blacksquare$$

6.3 Creating the Transform: Onion Building

The z-transform is defined so as to be really easy to compute for all the commonly used discrete random variables. Below are some examples.

Example 6.4 *Derive the z-transform of $X \sim Binomial(n, p)$:*

$$\widehat{X}(z) = \mathbf{E}\left[z^X\right] = \sum_{i=0}^{n} \binom{n}{i} p^i (1-p)^{n-i} z^i$$

$$= \sum_{i=0}^{n} \binom{n}{i} (zp)^i (1-p)^{n-i}$$

$$= (zp + (1-p))^n.$$

Example 6.5 *Derive the z-transform of* $X \sim Geometric(p)$:

$$\widehat{X}(z) = \mathbf{E}\left[z^X\right] = \sum_{i=1}^{\infty} p(1-p)^{i-1} z^i$$

$$= zp \sum_{i=1}^{\infty} (z(1-p))^{i-1}$$

$$= zp \sum_{i=0}^{\infty} (z(1-p))^i$$

$$= \frac{zp}{1-z(1-p)}.$$

Question: Can you see where we used the fact that $|z| \leq 1$ above?

Answer: We needed $|z(1-p)| < 1$ to get $\sum_{i=1}^{\infty}(z(1-p))^{i-1}$ to converge.

In both the above cases, notice how much easier it is to create the transform than to compute higher moments.

One might wonder if the series defined by $\widehat{X}(z)$ might in some cases diverge. This is not the case.

Theorem 6.6 (Convergence of z-transform) $\widehat{X}(z)$ *is bounded for any non-negative discrete r.v. X, assuming* $|z| \leq 1$.

Proof: We are given that

$$-1 \leq z \leq 1.$$

Because $i \geq 0$, this implies that

$$-1 \leq z^i \leq 1.$$

Multiplying all terms by $p_X(i)$, we have

$$-p_X(i) \leq z^i p_X(i) \leq p_X(i).$$

Now summing over all i, we have

$$-\sum_i p_X(i) \leq \sum_i z^i p_X(i) \leq \sum_i p_X(i),$$

which evaluates to

$$-1 \leq \widehat{X}(z) \leq 1.$$

So $\widehat{X}(z)$ is bounded between -1 and 1. ∎

6.4 Getting Moments: Onion Peeling

Once we have created the onion corresponding to a r.v., we can "peel its layers" to extract the moments of the random variable.

Theorem 6.7 (Onion Peeling Theorem) *Let X be a discrete, integer-valued, non-negative r.v. with p.m.f. $p_X(i)$, $i = 0, 1, 2, \ldots$. Then we can get the moments of X by differentiating $\widehat{X}(z)$ as follows:*

$$\widehat{X}'(z)\Big|_{z=1} = \mathbf{E}[X]$$

$$\widehat{X}''(z)\Big|_{z=1} = \mathbf{E}[X(X-1)]$$

$$\widehat{X}'''(z)\Big|_{z=1} = \mathbf{E}[X(X-1)(X-2)]$$

$$\widehat{X}''''(z)\Big|_{z=1} = \mathbf{E}[X(X-1)(X-2)(X-3)]$$

$$\vdots$$

Note: If the above moments are not defined at $z = 1$, one can instead consider the limit as $z \to 1$, where evaluating the limit may require using L'Hospital's rule.

Proof: Below we provide a sketch of the proof argument. This can be obtained formally via induction and can also be expressed more compactly. However, we choose to write it out this way so that you can visualize exactly how the moments "pop" out of the transform when it's differentiated:

$$\widehat{X}(z) = p_X(0)z^0 + p_X(1)z^1 + p_X(2)z^2 + p_X(3)z^3 + p_X(4)z^4 + p_X(5)z^5 + \cdots$$

$$\widehat{X}'(z) = p_X(1) + 2p_X(2)z^1 + 3p_X(3)z^2 + 4p_X(4)z^3 + 5p_X(5)z^4 + \cdots$$

$$\widehat{X}'(z)\Big|_{z=1} = 1p_X(1) + 2p_X(2) + 3p_X(3) + 4p_X(4) + 5p_X(5) + \cdots$$

$$= \mathbf{E}[X] \checkmark$$

$$\widehat{X}''(z) - 2p_X(2) + 3 \cdot 2p_X(3)z + 4 \cdot 3p_X(4)z^2 + 5 \cdot 4p_X(5)z^3 + \cdots$$

$$\widehat{X}''(z)\Big|_{z=1} = 2 \cdot 1p_X(2) + 3 \cdot 2p_X(3) + 4 \cdot 3p_X(4) + 5 \cdot 4p_X(5) + \cdots$$

$$= \mathbf{E}[X(X-1)] \checkmark$$

$$\widehat{X}'''(z) = 3 \cdot 2p_X(3) + 4 \cdot 3 \cdot 2p_X(4)z + 5 \cdot 4 \cdot 3p_X(5)z^2 + \cdots$$

$$\widehat{X}'''(z)\Big|_{z=1} = 3 \cdot 2 \cdot 1p_X(3) + 4 \cdot 3 \cdot 2p_X(4) + 5 \cdot 4 \cdot 3p_X(5) + \cdots$$

$$= \mathbf{E}[X(X-1)(X-2)] \checkmark$$

And so on ...   ■

Question: What is the insight behind the above proof? How does the transform hold all these moments?

Answer: The insight is that the "z" term separates the layers, allowing us to get each successive moment when differentiating. One can think of the z's as the pasta in the lasagna that keeps everything from running together.

Let's consider an example of applying the Onion Peeling Theorem.

Example 6.8 (Variance of Geometric) *Let $X \sim$ Geometric(p). Compute* **Var**(X).

$$\widehat{X}(z) = \frac{zp}{1 - z(1 - p)}$$

$$\mathbf{E}[X] = \frac{d}{dz}\left(\frac{zp}{1 - z(1 - p)}\right)\Bigg|_{z=1} = \frac{p}{(1 - z(1 - p))^2}\Bigg|_{z=1} = \frac{1}{p}$$

$$\mathbf{E}\left[X^2\right] = \widehat{X}''(z)\Big|_{z=1} + \mathbf{E}[X] = \frac{2p(1 - p)}{(1 - z(1 - p))^3}\Bigg|_{z=1} + \frac{1}{p} = \frac{2 - p}{p^2}$$

$$\mathbf{Var}(X) = \mathbf{E}\left[X^2\right] - (\mathbf{E}[X])^2 = \frac{1 - p}{p^2}.$$

Question: As we've seen, the z-transform of X is an onion that contains all moments of X. But does it also contain the distribution of X? Specifically, can you get the p.m.f., $p_X(i)$, from the onion, $\widehat{X}(z)$?

Answer: The answer is yes! In Exercise 6.14 you will derive an algorithm for extracting $p_X(i)$ from $\widehat{X}(z)$ for any non-negative discrete r.v. X. This tells us that there is an injective mapping from the set of discrete non-negative random variables to the set of z-transforms. Put another way, the z-transform uniquely determines the distribution.

6.5 Linearity of Transforms

Since transforms are just expectations, it makes sense that one might have a law similar to Linearity of Expectation. However, since transforms encompass *all* moments, it also makes sense that such a law might require independence of the random variables being added. Theorem 6.9 encapsulates these points.

Theorem 6.9 (Linearity) *Let X and Y be independent discrete random variables. Let $W = X + Y$. Then the z-transform of W is $\widehat{W}(z) = \widehat{X}(z) \cdot \widehat{Y}(z)$.*

Proof:

$$\widehat{W}(z) = \mathbf{E}\left[z^W\right]$$
$$= \mathbf{E}\left[z^{X+Y}\right]$$
$$= \mathbf{E}\left[z^X \cdot z^Y\right]$$
$$= \mathbf{E}\left[z^X\right] \cdot \mathbf{E}\left[z^Y\right]$$
$$= \widehat{X}(z) \cdot \widehat{Y}(z). \qquad \blacksquare$$

Question: Where did we use the fact that $X \perp Y$?

Answer: In splitting up the expectation into a product of expectations.

Example 6.10 (From Bernoulli to Binomial)

Let $X \sim$ Bernoulli(p). Let $Y \sim$ Binomial(n, p).

Question: (a) What is $\widehat{X}(z)$? (b) How can we use $\widehat{X}(z)$ to get $\widehat{Y}(z)$?

Answer:

(a) $\widehat{X}(z) = (1 - p) \cdot z^0 + p \cdot z^1 = 1 - p + pz$.
(b) $Y = \sum_{i=1}^{n} X_i$. Given that $X_i \sim X$, for all i, and the X_i's are independent,

$$\widehat{Y}(z) = \left(\widehat{X}(z)\right)^n = (1 - p + pz)^n.$$

Example 6.11 (Sum of Binomials)

Let $X \sim$ Binomial(n, p) and $Y \sim$ Binomial(m, p), where $X \perp Y$.

Question: What is the distribution of $Z = X + Y$?

Answer:

$$\widehat{Z}(z) = \widehat{X}(z) \cdot \widehat{Y}(z)$$
$$= (zp + (1 - p))^n \cdot (zp + (1 - p))^m$$
$$= (zp + (1 - p))^{m+n}.$$

Observe that $(zp + (1 - p))^{m+n}$ is the z-transform of a Binomial r.v. with parameters $m + n$ and p. Thus, the distribution of Z must be Binomial($m + n, p$), which should make sense.

6.6 Conditioning

> **Theorem 6.12** *Let X, A, and B be discrete random variables where*
>
> $$X = \begin{cases} A & w/prob\ p \\ B & w/prob\ 1 - p \end{cases}.$$
>
> *Then,*
>
> $$\widehat{X}(z) = p \cdot \widehat{A}(z) + (1 - p) \cdot \widehat{B}(z).$$

Theorem 6.12 should be interpreted as first tossing a p-coin (coin with probability p of heads). If that coin comes up heads, then set $X = A$. Otherwise set $X = B$.

Proof:

$$\begin{aligned}
\widehat{X}(z) &= \mathbf{E}\left[z^X\right] \\
&= \mathbf{E}\left[z^X \,\middle|\, X = A\right] \cdot p + \mathbf{E}\left[z^X \,\middle|\, X = B\right] \cdot (1 - p) \\
&= \mathbf{E}\left[z^A\right] \cdot p + \mathbf{E}\left[z^B\right] \cdot (1 - p) \\
&= p\widehat{A}(z) + (1 - p)\widehat{B}(z).
\end{aligned}$$
■

Question: In the examples in the previous section, we considered the sum of a constant number (n) of random variables. How can we use conditioning to derive the z-transform of the sum of a r.v. number (N) of random variables?

Answer: Exercise 6.10 walks you through the proof of Theorem 6.13, which generalizes Theorem 5.14 to all higher moments.

> **Theorem 6.13 (Summing a random number of i.i.d. random variables)**
> *Let $X_1, X_2, X_3, \ldots$ be i.i.d. discrete random variables, where $X_i \sim X$. Let N be a positive, integer-valued, discrete r.v., where $N \perp X_i$ for all i. Let*
>
> $$S = \sum_{i=1}^{N} X_i.$$
>
> *Then,*
>
> $$\widehat{S}(z) = \widehat{N}\left(\widehat{X}(z)\right),$$
>
> *that is, we substitute in $\widehat{X}(z)$ as the z-parameter in $\widehat{N}(z)$.*

6.7 Using z-Transforms to Solve Recurrence Relations

Recurrence relations are prevalent throughout computer science, biology, signal processing, and economics, just to name a few fields. One of the most common types of recurrence relations is a linear homogeneous recurrence, of the form:

$$f_{i+n} = a_1 f_{i+n-1} + a_2 f_{i+n-2} + \cdots + a_n f_i.$$

A popular example of such a recurrence relation is the following:

$$f_{i+2} = f_{i+1} + f_i, \tag{6.1}$$

where $f_0 = 0$ and $f_1 = 1$.

Question: Do you recognize the relation?

Figure 6.2 *Fibonacci sequence.*

Answer: Equation (6.1) is the Fibonacci sequence. It was used to model the growth in the population of rabbits, where f_i denotes the number of rabbits in month i.

Solving a recurrence relation means finding a closed-form expression for f_n. While (6.1) seems very simple to solve by just "unraveling the recurrence," it turns out to be impossible to do this. It also is hard to imagine how one might "guess" the form of the solution. Fortunately, z-transforms provide an excellent technique for solving these recurrence relations. In this section, we see how to derive a closed-form expression for f_n using z-transforms. This method may seem overly complex. However it's the easiest technique known for handling recurrences. We start by defining the z-transform of a sequence.

Definition 6.14 *Given a sequence of values:* $\{f_0, f_1, f_2, \ldots\}$. *Define*

$$F(z) = \sum_{i=0}^{\infty} f_i z^i.$$

*$F(z)$ is the **z-transform of the sequence**. Note that z just functions as a placeholder, for the purpose of separating out the f_i's. Note that the f_i's here are **not** probabilities, and there is no r.v. associated with this z-transform.*

We illustrate the method on a recurrence relation of this form:

$$f_{i+2} = b f_{i+1} + a f_i, \tag{6.2}$$

where we assume f_0 and f_1 are given and a and b are constants. However, the method can be applied more generally. Our goal is to derive a closed-form expression for f_n.

Step 1: Derive $F(z)$ as a ratio of polynomials.

The goal in Step 1 is to derive $F(z)$. It will be useful to represent $F(z)$ as a ratio of two polynomials in z. From (6.2), we have:

$$f_{i+2} = b f_{i+1} + a f_i$$
$$f_{i+2} z^{i+2} = b f_{i+1} z^{i+2} + a f_i z^{i+2}$$
$$\sum_{i=0}^{\infty} f_{i+2} z^{i+2} = b \sum_{i=0}^{\infty} f_{i+1} z^{i+2} + a \sum_{i=0}^{\infty} f_i z^{i+2}$$
$$F(z) - f_1 z - f_0 = b z \sum_{i=0}^{\infty} f_{i+1} z^{i+1} + a z^2 \sum_{i=0}^{\infty} f_i z^i$$
$$F(z) - f_1 z - f_0 = b z (F(z) - f_0) + a z^2 F(z)$$
$$\left(1 - b z - a z^2\right) F(z) = f_1 z + f_0 - b z f_0$$
$$F(z) = \frac{f_0 + z (f_1 - b f_0)}{1 - b z - a z^2}. \tag{6.3}$$

Step 2: Rewrite $F(z)$ via partial fractions.

The goal in Step 2 is to apply partial fractions to $F(z)$. Specifically, we want to write

$$F(z) = \frac{N(z)}{D(z)} = \frac{A}{h(z)} + \frac{B}{g(z)},$$

where $D(z) = h(z) \cdot g(z)$ and h, g are (hopefully) linear in z.

Lemma 6.15 *If $D(z) = a z^2 + b z + 1$, then*

$$D(z) = \left(1 - \frac{z}{r_0}\right)\left(1 - \frac{z}{r_1}\right),$$

where r_0 and r_1 are the (real) roots of $D(z)$.

Proof: To see that the two ways of writing $D(z)$ are equivalent, we note that the two quadratic expressions have the same two roots (r_0 and r_1) and furthermore have the same constant term, 1. ∎

In our case, see (6.3), $D(z) = -az^2 - bz + 1$, so

$$(r_0, r_1) = \left(\frac{-b - \sqrt{b^2 + 4a}}{2a}, \frac{-b + \sqrt{b^2 + 4a}}{2a} \right) \tag{6.4}$$

$$D(z) = h(z) \cdot g(z)$$
$$h(z) = 1 - \frac{z}{r_0}$$
$$g(z) = 1 - \frac{z}{r_1}.$$

We now use $N(z) = f_0 + z(f_1 - f_0 b)$ from (6.3) to solve for A and B:

$$F(z) = \frac{A}{1 - \frac{z}{r_0}} + \frac{B}{1 - \frac{z}{r_1}} \tag{6.5}$$

$$= \frac{A\left(1 - \frac{z}{r_1}\right) + B\left(1 - \frac{z}{r_0}\right)}{\left(1 - \frac{z}{r_0}\right)\left(1 - \frac{z}{r_1}\right)}$$

$$= \frac{(A + B) + z\left(-\frac{A}{r_1} - \frac{B}{r_0}\right)}{\left(1 - \frac{z}{r_0}\right)\left(1 - \frac{z}{r_1}\right)} = \frac{N(z)}{D(z)} = \frac{f_0 + z(f_1 - f_0 b)}{D(z)}. \tag{6.6}$$

Matching the z-coefficients in the numerators of (6.6), we have

$$A + B = f_0$$
$$-\frac{A}{r_1} - \frac{B}{r_0} = f_1 - f_0 b,$$

which solves to

$$B = \frac{r_0 f_0 + (f_1 - f_0 b) r_0 r_1}{r_0 - r_1} \tag{6.7}$$
$$A = f_0 - B. \tag{6.8}$$

Step 3: Rewrite $F(z)$ via series expansion.

Returning to (6.5), we assume that z is chosen such that $0 < z < r_0$ and $0 < z < r_1$. This allows us to write:

$$\frac{A}{1 - \frac{z}{r_0}} = A \sum_{i=0}^{\infty} \left(\frac{z}{r_0} \right)^i \quad \text{and} \quad \frac{B}{1 - \frac{z}{r_1}} = B \sum_{i=0}^{\infty} \left(\frac{z}{r_1} \right)^i.$$

Thus, the geometric series expansion of $F(z)$ can be rewritten as follows:

$$F(z) = \sum_{i=0}^{\infty} f_i z^i = A \sum_{i=0}^{\infty} \left(\frac{z}{r_0} \right)^i + B \sum_{i=0}^{\infty} \left(\frac{z}{r_1} \right)^i. \qquad (6.9)$$

Step 4: Match terms to obtain f_n.

Finally, we match the z-coefficients in (6.9) to obtain the f_n's:

$$f_n = \frac{A}{r_0^n} + \frac{B}{r_1^n}, \qquad (6.10)$$

where A and B are obtained from (6.8) and (6.7) and r_0 and r_1 are obtained from (6.4).

To get a final form, recall that we are given that $f_0 = 0$ and $f_1 = 1$. Furthermore, $a = 1$ and $b = 1$. Then, from (6.4), we have that

$$r_0 = -\phi$$
$$r_1 = \phi^{-1}$$

where

$$\phi = \frac{1 + \sqrt{5}}{2}.$$

Finally, from (6.8) and (6.7), we get:

$$A = -\frac{1}{\sqrt{5}} \quad \text{and} \quad B = \frac{1}{\sqrt{5}}.$$

Substituting these into (6.10), we get

$$f_n = \frac{1}{\sqrt{5}} \left(\phi^n - (-\phi)^{-n} \right).$$

6.8 Exercises

6.1 Moments of Poisson
Use z-transforms to derive $\mathbf{E}\left[X(X-1)(X-2)\cdots(X-k+1)\right]$, for $k = 1, 2, 3, \ldots$, where $X \sim \text{Poisson}(\lambda)$.

6.2 Sum of Poissons
Let $X_1 \sim \text{Poisson}(\lambda_1)$. Let $X_2 \sim \text{Poisson}(\lambda_2)$. Suppose $X_1 \perp X_2$. Let $Y = X_1 + X_2$. How is Y distributed? Prove it using z-transforms. Note that the parameter for the Poisson denotes its mean.

6.3 Moments of Binomial
Use z-transforms to derive $\mathbf{E}\left[X(X-1)(X-2)\cdots(X-k+1)\right]$, for $k = 1, 2, 3, \ldots$, where $X \sim \text{Binomial}(n, p)$.

6.4 Sums of Binomials
Suppose that $X \sim \text{Binomial}(n, p)$ and $Y \sim \text{Binomial}(n, q)$ and $X \perp Y$. Let $Z = X + Y$. Can we say that $Z \sim \text{Binomial}(n, p + q)$? If so, prove it via z-transforms. If not, explain why not.

6.5 z-Transform of linear combination
Suppose X and Y are independent random variables. What is the z-transform of $aX + bY$, where a and b are arbitrary integers. Express your answer as a function of $\widehat{X}(\cdot)$ and $\widehat{Y}(\cdot)$.

6.6 Scaling up random variables via transforms
Let X_1, X_2, and X_3 be i.i.d. random variables, all with distribution X. Let $S = X_1 + X_2 + X_3$ and let $Y = 3X$. Suppose we are told that the z-transform of X is some function $g_X(z)$. What can you say about the z-transform of S? What can you say about the z-transform of Y? Express both of these in terms of $g_X(\cdot)$.

6.7 Matching random variables and their z-transforms
Assume that X, Y, Z, and T are independent random variables, where:
- $X, Y, Z \sim \text{Binomial}(3, 0.5)$
- $T \sim \text{Bernoulli}(0.5)$
Match each expression on the left to its z-transform on the right.

1._____ $3T$	a.	$2^{-9} \cdot (z+1)^9$
2._____ $X + 3$	b.	$2^{-3} \cdot (z+1)^3 \cdot z^3$
3._____ $X + Y + Z$	c.	$2^{-4} \cdot (z+1)^3 + 0.5$
4._____ $X \cdot T$	d.	$0.5 \cdot (z^3 + 1)$

6.8 Difference transform
Let $W = X - Y$, where $X \perp Y$. Which of the following represents $\widehat{W}(z)$:

(a) $\widehat{X}(z) \cdot \widehat{Y}(z)$

(b) $\frac{\widehat{X}(z)}{\widehat{Y}(z)}$

(c) $\widehat{X}(z) \cdot \widehat{Y}\left(\frac{1}{z}\right)$

(d) $\widehat{X}(z) - \widehat{Y}(z)$

(e) None of the above.

Justify your answer.

6.9 **Trip time**

A professor walks all the way down Carnegie St. (Figure 6.3). When she reaches the end, with probability 0.5, she turns down Mellon St. and walks all the way to the end. Otherwise, with probability 0.5 she turns down University St. and walks all the way to the end. We are interested in the professor's total trip time, T.

- Let C be a r.v. denoting the time to walk down Carnegie St.
- Let M be a r.v. denoting the time to walk down Mellon St.
- Let U be a r.v. denoting the time to walk down University St.

Assume that you are given $\mathbf{E}[C]$, $\mathbf{E}[C^2]$, $\mathbf{Var}(C)$, $\widehat{C}(z)$. You are also given these expressions for M and U. Assume that C, M, and U are independent.

(a) Express $\mathbf{E}[T]$ in terms of the given quantities (and constants).

(b) Express $\mathbf{Var}(T)$ in terms of the given quantities (and constants).

(c) Express $\widehat{T}(z)$ in terms of the given quantities (and constants).

You do *not* have to simplify your answers.

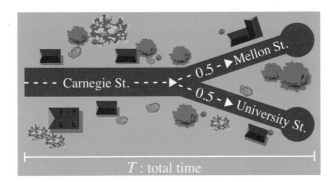

Figure 6.3 *Figure for Exercise 6.9.*

6.10 **Sum of a random number of random variables**

Suppose that $X_1, X_2, \ldots$ are i.i.d. discrete random variables, all distributed as X. Suppose that N is a positive integer-valued discrete r.v., where $N \perp X_i$ for all i. Let

$$S = \sum_{i=1}^{N} X_i.$$

(a) Prove that $\widehat{S}(z) = \widehat{N}\left(\widehat{X}(z)\right)$. [Hint: Condition on N.]

(b) Suppose that each day that the sun shines, I earn 10 dollars with probability $p = \frac{1}{3}$ and 1 dollar with probability $p = \frac{2}{3}$. The sun shines every day with probability $q = \frac{4}{5}$. Today is sunny. Let S denote the total money I earn starting today until it turns cloudy.

  (i) Write an expression for $\widehat{S}(z)$ using part (a).

  (ii) Differentiate your z-transform to get $\mathbf{E}\,[S]$ and $\mathbf{Var}(S)$.

6.11 Geometric number of Geometrics

Suppose that $X_1, X_2, \ldots$ are i.i.d. discrete random variables, all with distribution Geometric(q). Suppose that $N \sim$ Geometric(p), where $N \perp X_i$ for all i. Let

$$S = \sum_{i=1}^{N} X_i.$$

Derive the z-transform $\widehat{Y}(z)$. What does the transform say about the distribution of Y? Provide some intuition for the result.

6.12 Mouse in maze with transforms

A mouse is trapped in a maze. Initially it has to choose one of two directions. If it goes to the right, then it will wander around in the maze for three minutes and will then return to its initial position. If it goes to the left, then with probability $\frac{1}{3}$ it will depart the maze after two minutes of traveling, and with probability $\frac{2}{3}$ it will return to its initial position after five minutes of traveling. Assume that the mouse is at all times equally likely to go to the left or the right. Let T denote the number of minutes that it will be trapped in the maze. In Exercise 5.26 we computed $\mathbf{E}\,[T]$ and $\mathbf{Var}(T)$. This time compute $\widehat{T}(z)$, and then differentiate it to get $\mathbf{E}\,[T]$.

6.13 The wandering frog

[Proposed by Tianxin Xu] There are three lily pads, A, B, and C. A frog sits on lily pad A. At each time step, the frog has an equal probability of jumping from the lily pad that it is currently on to either of the other pads.

(a) What is the expected number of hops before the frog returns to pad A?

(b) What is the z-transform of the number of hops before the frog returns to A?

(c) What is the probability that the frog is on lily pad A after n hops? Check your answer by thinking about the case where $n \to \infty$.

6.14 Getting distribution from the transform

The transform of a r.v. captures all moments of the r.v., but does it also capture the distribution? The answer is yes! You are given the z-transform,

$\widehat{X}(z)$, of a non-negative, discrete, integer-valued r.v., X. Provide an algorithm for extracting the p.m.f. of X from $\widehat{X}(z)$.

6.15 Using z-transforms to solve recurrences

This problem will walk you through the process of solving a recurrence relation:

$$a_{n+1} = 2a_n + 3, \qquad a_0 = 1.$$

(a) Define $A(z) = \sum_{n=0}^{\infty} a_n z^n$ to be the z-transform of the sequence of a_n's. Multiply every term of the recurrence relation by z^{n+1} and sum over all n to obtain an expression for $A(z)$ in terms of $A(z)$'s. You should get:

$$A(z) = \frac{1+2z}{(1-2z)(1-z)}. \tag{6.11}$$

(b) Apply partial fractions to determine the constants v and w that allow you to break up (6.11) into simpler terms:

$$A(z) = \frac{1+2z}{(1-2z)(1-z)} = \frac{v}{1-2z} + \frac{w}{1-z}.$$

(c) Recall from Section 1.1 how we can express $\frac{1}{1-z}$ and $\frac{1}{1-2z}$ as power series in z. Use these, and the correct values of v and w, to express $A(z)$ as a power series in z.

(d) Determine a_n by looking at the coefficient of z^n in your power series.

6.16 Polygon triangulation

In this problem, we are interested in the number of triangulations of an n-sided polygon. Figure 6.4 shows all possible triangulations for $n = 3, 4, 5$. Let

$$a_n = \text{number of triangulations of an } n + 1\text{-sided polygon},$$

where $n \geq 2$. Our goal is to derive a clean expression for a_n. We will use z-transforms, where

$$A(z) = \sum_{n=0}^{\infty} a_n z^n.$$

Follow these steps:

(a) Argue that (6.12) holds for $n \geq 2$:

$$a_n = \sum_{k=0}^{n} a_k a_{n-k}, \qquad n \geq 2, \tag{6.12}$$

where we will set $a_0 = 0$, $a_1 = 1$, and $a_2 = 1$. This is a counting argument. Looking at Figure 6.5, first start by assuming that the pink triangle $(1, k + 1, n + 1)$ is included in your triangulation. Count the number of ways to triangulate, given that constraint. Now consider all possibilities for the $k + 1$ endpoint of the included pink triangle.

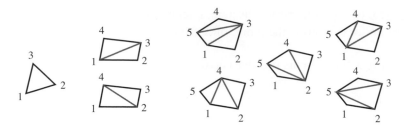

Figure 6.4 *Figure for Exercise 6.16, showing all possible triangulations of n-sided polygons.*

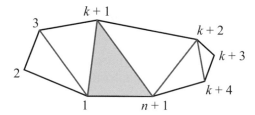

Figure 6.5 *For Exercise 6.16: counting triangulations in an n + 1-sided polygon.*

(b) Using (6.12), argue that

$$A(z) = z + (A(z))^2 . \tag{6.13}$$

The first few steps of the derivation are given below:

$$A(z) = z + \sum_{n=2}^{\infty} a_n z^n$$

$$= z + \sum_{n=2}^{\infty} \left(\sum_{k=0}^{n} a_k a_{n-k} \right) z^n$$

$$= z + \sum_{n=0}^{\infty} \left(\sum_{k=0}^{n} a_k a_{n-k} \right) z^n$$

Explain why each of the above steps is true and then finish the derivation to get (6.13).

(c) Solve (6.13) to get $A(z)$. You will need to use $A(0) = 0$.

(d) All that remains is to express $A(z)$ as a power series of z. To do this, we are providing you with the Taylor series expansion of $\sqrt{1 - 4z}$ in (6.14):

$$\sqrt{1 - 4z} = 1 - 2 \sum_{n=1}^{\infty} \frac{1}{n} \binom{2n - 2}{n - 1} z^n . \tag{6.14}$$

(e) Obtain a_n.

Part III

Continuous Random Variables

In this part of the book, we repeat the material in Part II, but this time we focus on continuous random variables, which can take on an uncountable number of values. Continuous random variables are very relevant to computer systems – how else can we model response time, for example? Working in continuous time also allows us to leverage everything we know about calculus.

Because continuous-time analysis is often harder for students (no one seems to remember how to integrate!), we split up our discussion of continuous random variables into two parts. In Chapter 7, we consider the case of random variables drawn from a single distribution. Here we introduce the two most common continuous distributions: the Uniform and the Exponential. In Chapter 8, we move on to multiple distributions and introduce jointly distributed continuous random variables. All the topics, such as conditioning, Bayes' Law, independence, that were covered in Part II are reintroduced in these two chapters, from the continuous perspective.

Chapter 9 is devoted to one very important continuous distribution, the Normal, a.k.a., Gaussian distribution, which occurs throughout nature. We also introduce the Central Limit Theorem, which we will use multiple times in the book as a tail approximation.

In Chapter 10 we discuss another very important continuous distribution, the Pareto distribution. This distribution also occurs throughout nature and is particularly relevant to computer science. We discuss properties of the Pareto distribution, in particular the heavy-tailed property and decreasing failure rate, and their implications for the design of computer systems.

Finally, Chapter 11 is the counterpart to Chapter 6. While z-transforms are the moment-generating function of choice for discrete random variables, the Laplace transform is the moment-generating function of choice for continuous random variables. We illustrate how the Laplace transform can be used to generate all moments of continuous random variables, and we also show how one can combine Laplace transforms and z-transforms.

7 Continuous Random Variables: Single Distribution

Until now we have only studied discrete random variables. These are defined by a probability mass function (p.m.f.). This chapter introduces continuous random variables, which are defined by a probability density function.

7.1 Probability Density Functions

> **Definition 7.1** *A* **continuous random variable (r.v.)** *has a continuous range of values that it can take on. This might be an interval or a set of intervals. Thus a continuous r.v. can take on an uncountable set of possible values.*

Continuous random variables are extremely common. They might be used to represent the time of an event, the speed of a device, the location of a satellite, or the distance between people's eyeballs. All these quantities can be discretized, of course, but it's more accurate to think of them as continuous random variables, and the math also gets much easier as well, since one can invoke calculus.

The probability that a continuous r.v., X, is equal to any particular value is defined to be zero. We define probability for a continuous r.v. in terms of a density function.

> **Definition 7.2** *The* **probability density function (p.d.f.)** *of a continuous r.v. X is a non-negative function $f_X(\cdot)$, where*
>
> $$\mathbf{P}\{a \leq X \leq b\} = \int_a^b f_X(x)dx \qquad \text{and where} \qquad \int_{-\infty}^{\infty} f_X(x)dx = 1.$$

Definition 7.2 is illustrated in Figure 7.1. To interpret the p.d.f., $f_X(x)$, think about a very skinny rectangle of height $f_X(x)$ and width dx with area $f_X(x)dx$. This area represents a tiny probability:

$$f_X(x)dx \approx \mathbf{P}\{x \leq X \leq x + dx\}.$$

Now the integral from a to b of $f_X(x)dx$ is the sum of all these tiny probabilities.

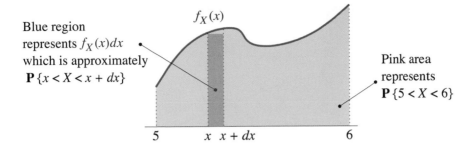

Blue region represents $f_X(x)dx$ which is approximately $\mathbf{P}\{x < X < x + dx\}$

Pink area represents $\mathbf{P}\{5 < X < 6\}$

$f_X(x)$

5 $x \; x + dx$ 6

Figure 7.1 *The area under the curve represents the probability that X is between 5 and 6, namely $\int_5^6 f_X(x)\,dx$.*

Question: How does $\mathbf{P}\{a \leq X \leq b\}$ compare with $\mathbf{P}\{a < X < b\}$?

Answer: These are the same. For continuous distributions we don't have to be careful about differentiating between $<$ and $\leq$, because there is no mass at any particular value.

Question: Does $f_X(x)$ have to be below 1 for all x?

Answer: No, $f_X(x)$ is not a probability.

Density functions are used everywhere, and are not necessarily related to probability. We start with a typical example from a calculus class.

Example 7.3 (Density as a rate)

Imagine that we're filling a bathtub, as in Figure 7.2, where the rate of water out of the faucet starts out slow but increases over time. Specifically, let

$$f(t) = t^2, \qquad t \geq 0$$

denote the rate (in gallons/s) at which water comes out of the faucet.

Question: If we start filling at time 0, what is the total amount of water in the bathtub by time 4 seconds?

Answer: In this example, $f(t) = t^2$ is a density function, where $f(t)$ is the instantaneous rate at time t. If we want to talk about a *total amount of water*, we need to integrate the rate (density) over some period of time:

$$\int_0^4 t^2\,dt = \frac{64}{3} = 21\frac{1}{3} \text{ gallons.}$$

Question: Is $f(t) = t^2$, where $t > 0$, a p.d.f.?

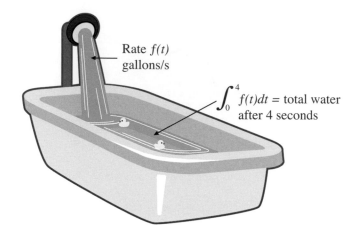

Figure 7.2 *Here, $f(t) = t^2$ represents the gallons/s coming out at time t.*

Answer: No. For $f(t)$ to be a p.d.f., it must be the case that $\int_{-\infty}^{\infty} f(t)dt = 1$, which is not true. Also, in our example $f(t)$ has no relation to probability.

Now for an example involving a p.d.f.

Example 7.4 (Weight of two-year-olds)

Let's say that the weight of two-year-olds can range anywhere from 15 pounds to 35 pounds. Let $f_W(x)$ denote the p.d.f. of weight for two-year-olds, where

$$f_W(x) = \begin{cases} \frac{3}{40} - \frac{3}{4000}(x - 25)^2 & \text{if } 15 \leq x \leq 35 \\ 0 & \text{otherwise} \end{cases}.$$

Question: What is the fraction of two-year-olds who weigh > 30 pounds?

Answer: As illustrated in Figure 7.3,

$$\mathbf{P}\{\text{Two-year-old weighs } > 30 \text{ pounds}\} = \int_{30}^{\infty} f_W(x)dx = \int_{30}^{35} f_W(x)dx \approx 16\%.$$

Definition 7.5 *The **cumulative distribution function (c.d.f.)** $F(\cdot)$ of a continuous r.v. X is defined by*

$$F_X(a) = \mathbf{P}\{-\infty < X \leq a\} = \int_{-\infty}^{a} f_X(x)dx.$$

*We can express the **tail** of X by*

$$\overline{F_X}(a) = 1 - F_X(a) = \mathbf{P}\{X > a\}.$$

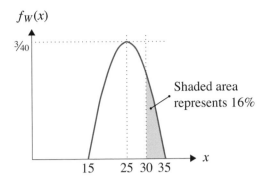

Figure 7.3 *Probability density function for the weight of two-year-olds.*

Question: We know how to get $F_X(x)$ from $f_X(x)$. How do we get $f_X(x)$ from $F_X(x)$?

Answer: By the Fundamental Theorem of Calculus (explained in Section 1.3),

$$f_X(x) = \frac{d}{dx} \int_{-\infty}^{x} f_X(t)\,dt = \frac{d}{dx} F_X(x).$$

7.2 Common Continuous Distributions

There are many common continuous distributions. Below we briefly define just a couple: the Uniform and Exponential distributions.

Uniform(a, b), often written $U(a, b)$, models the fact that any interval of length δ between a and b is equally likely. Specifically, if $X \sim U(a, b)$, then

$$f_X(x) = \begin{cases} \dfrac{1}{b-a} & \text{if } a \leq x \leq b \\[2mm] 0 & \text{otherwise} \end{cases}.$$

Question: For $X \sim U(a, b)$, what is $F_X(x)$?

Answer:

$$F_X(x) = \int_{a}^{x} \frac{1}{b-a}\,dt = \frac{x-a}{b-a}, \qquad a \leq x \leq b.$$

Figure 7.4 depicts $f_X(x)$ and $F_X(x)$ graphically.

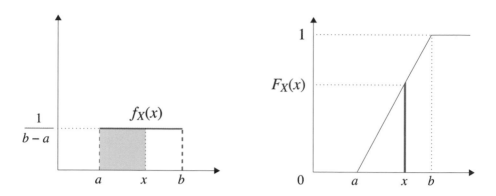

Figure 7.4 *The p.d.f., $f_X(x)$, and c.d.f., $F_X(x)$, functions for $X \sim Uniform(a, b)$. The shaded (pink) region under the p.d.f. has an area equal to the height of the blue segment in the c.d.f.*

Exp(λ) denotes the Exponential distribution, whose p.d.f. drops off exponentially. We say that a r.v. X is distributed Exponentially with *rate $\lambda > 0$*, written $X \sim \text{Exp}(\lambda)$, if

$$f_X(x) = \begin{cases} \lambda e^{-\lambda x} & \text{if } x \geq 0 \\ 0 & \text{if } x < 0 \end{cases}.$$

The graph of the p.d.f. is shown in Figure 7.5.

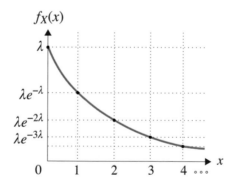

Figure 7.5 *Exponential probability density function, where $\lambda = 0.5$.*

The c.d.f., $F_X(x) = \mathbf{P}\{X \leq x\}$, is given by

$$F_X(x) = \int_{-\infty}^{x} f_X(t)dt = \begin{cases} 1 - e^{-\lambda x} & \text{if } x \geq 0 \\ 0 & \text{if } x < 0 \end{cases}.$$

$$\overline{F}_X(x) = 1 - F_X(x) = e^{-\lambda x}, \quad \text{if } x \geq 0.$$

Both $f_X(x)$ and $\overline{F}_X(x)$ drop off by a *constant* factor, $e^{-\lambda}$, with each unit increase of x.

The Exponential distribution has a property called **memorylessness**.

> **Definition 7.6** *We say that r.v. X has the* **memoryless property** *if*
>
> $$\mathbf{P}\{X > t + s \mid X > s\} = \mathbf{P}\{X > t\} \qquad \forall s, t \geq 0.$$

To understand memorylessness, think of X as representing the time until I win the lottery. Suppose we know that I haven't yet won the lottery by time s. Then the probability that I will need $> t$ more time to win the lottery is independent of s (that is, it's independent of how long I've been trying so far).

Equivalently, we say X is memoryless if

$$[X \mid X > s] \stackrel{d}{=} s + X, \qquad \forall s \geq 0.$$

That is, the r.v. $[X \mid X > s]$ and the r.v. $s + X$ have the same distribution.

Question: Prove that if $X \sim \text{Exp}(\lambda)$, then X has the memoryless property.

Answer:

$$\mathbf{P}\{X > t + s \mid X > s\} = \frac{\mathbf{P}\{X > t + s\}}{\mathbf{P}\{X > s\}} = \frac{e^{\lambda(t+s)}}{e^{-\lambda s}} = e^{-\lambda t} = \mathbf{P}\{X > t\}.$$

Question: What other distribution has the memoryless property?

Answer: The Geometric distribution.

Question: Does the Uniform distribution also have the memoryless property?

Answer: No. If $X \sim \text{Uniform}(a, b)$ and we are given that $X > b - \epsilon$, then we know that X will end very soon.

The memoryless property is a little counter-intuitive, because it says that history doesn't affect the future.

Example 7.7 (The naked mole-rat)

Most living beings have the property that their mortality rate increases as they age. The naked mole-rat is an exception in that its remaining lifetime is independent of its age [65].

Figure 7.6 *The naked mole-rat's mortality rate does not increase with age.*

Question: Let X denote the lifetime of the naked mole-rat in years, where $X \sim \text{Exp}(1)$. If a naked mole-rat is four years old, what is its probability of surviving at least one more year?

Answer:

$$\mathbf{P}\{X > 4 + 1 \mid X > 4\} = \frac{\mathbf{P}\{X > 5\}}{\mathbf{P}\{X > 4\}} = \frac{e^{-5}}{e^{-4}} = e^{-1}.$$

Question: If a naked mole-rat is 24 years old, what is its probability of surviving at least one more year?

Answer: Same thing! $\mathbf{P}\{X > 24 + 1 \mid X > 24\} = e^{-1}$.

Example 7.8 (Post office)

Suppose that a post office has two clerks. When customer A walks in, customer B is being served by one clerk, and customer C is being served by the other clerk. All service times are Exponentially distributed with rate λ.

Question: What is $\mathbf{P}\{A$ is the last to leave$\}$?

Answer: $\frac{1}{2}$. Note that one of B or C will leave first. Without loss of generality, let us say B leaves first. Then C and A will have the same distribution on their remaining service time. It does not matter that C has been served for a while.

We will return to the memoryless property of the Exponential distribution in Chapter 12. There are additional important continuous distributions, including the **Normal** and **Pareto** distributions, which we defer to Chapters 9 and 10, respectively.

7.3 Expectation, Variance, and Higher Moments

The moments of a continuous distribution are derived from its p.d.f., just as we used the p.m.f. in the case of discrete distributions. Likewise, we can also define arbitrary functions of a continuous random variable.

Definition 7.9 *For a continuous r.v. X, with p.d.f.* $f_X(\cdot)$, *we have:*

$$E[X] = \int_{-\infty}^{\infty} x \cdot f_X(x)dx$$

$$E[X^i] = \int_{-\infty}^{\infty} x^i \cdot f_X(x)dx.$$

For any function $g(\cdot)$, *we have:*

$$E[g(X)] = \int_{-\infty}^{\infty} g(x) \cdot f_X(x)dx.$$

In particular,

$$\text{Var}(X) = E\left[(X - E[X])^2\right] = \int_{-\infty}^{\infty} (x - E[X])^2 \cdot f_X(x)dx$$

Example 7.10 (The Uniform distribution)

Question: Derive the mean and variance of $X \sim \text{Uniform}(a, b)$.

Answer: Recall that

$$f_X(x) = \begin{cases} \dfrac{1}{b-a} & \text{if } a \le x \le b \\ \\ 0 & \text{otherwise} \end{cases}.$$

Thus,

$$E[X] = \int_{-\infty}^{\infty} f_X(t)t\,dt = \int_a^b \frac{1}{b-a}t\,dt = \frac{1}{b-a} \cdot \frac{b^2-a^2}{2} = \frac{a+b}{2}.$$

This answer should make sense! Likewise,

$$E[X^2] = \int_{-\infty}^{\infty} f_X(t)t^2\,dt = \int_a^b \frac{1}{b-a}t^2\,dt = \frac{1}{b-a} \cdot \frac{b^3-a^3}{3} = \frac{b^2+ab+a^2}{3}.$$

After some algebra, this yields:

$$\text{Var}(X) = E[X^2] - E[X]^2 = \frac{(b-a)^2}{12}.$$

Example 7.11 (The Exponential distribution)

Question: Derive the mean and variance of $X \sim \text{Exp}(\lambda)$.

Answer: Recall that

$$f_X(x) = \begin{cases} \lambda e^{-\lambda x} & \text{if } x \geq 0 \\ 0 & \text{if } x < 0 \end{cases}.$$

Thus,

$$\mathbf{E}[X] = \int_{-\infty}^{\infty} f_X(t) t \, dt = \int_0^{\infty} \lambda e^{-\lambda t} t \, dt = \frac{1}{\lambda} \qquad \text{(integration by parts)}.$$

Likewise,

$$\mathbf{E}[X^2] = \int_{-\infty}^{\infty} f_X(t) t^2 \, dt = \int_0^{\infty} \lambda e^{-\lambda t} t^2 \, dt = \frac{2}{\lambda^2} \qquad \text{(double integration by parts)}.$$

Thus,

$$\mathbf{Var}(X) = \mathbf{E}[X^2] - \mathbf{E}[X]^2 = \frac{1}{\lambda^2}.$$

Observe that whereas the λ parameter for the Poisson distribution is also its mean, for the Exponential distribution, the λ parameter is the reciprocal of the mean. We thus refer to λ as the **rate** of the Exponential. For example, if the time until the next arrival is Exponentially distributed with rate three arrivals per second, then the expected time until the next arrival is $\frac{1}{3}$ seconds.

Example 7.12 (Time to get from NYC to Boston)

New York City   180 miles   Boston

Figure 7.7 *What is the expected time to get from NYC to Boston?*

Suppose that the distance from NYC to Boston is 180 miles. You decide to buy a motorized bicycle for the trip. Suppose that motorized bikes have speeds that are Uniformly distributed between 30 and 60 m.p.h., and you buy a random motorized bike. Let T be the time to get from NYC to Boston. What is $\mathbf{E}[T]$?

Consider two ideas for figuring this out:

Idea 1: Average speed is 45 m.p.h. Thus, $\mathbf{E}[T] = \frac{180}{45} = 4$ hours.

Idea 2: $\mathbf{E}[T]$ is the average of $\frac{180}{30}$ and $\frac{180}{60}$. Thus $\mathbf{E}[T]$ is the average of 6 and 3, which is 4.5 hours.

Question: Which of ideas 1 and 2 is correct?

Answer: Neither is correct! We are interested in

$$T = \frac{180}{S},$$

where $S \sim \text{Uniform}(30, 60)$ represents the speed of the bike. Then,

$$
\begin{aligned}
\mathbf{E}[T] = \mathbf{E}\left[\frac{180}{S}\right] &= \int_{30}^{60} \frac{180}{s} \cdot f_S(s)\,ds \\
&= \int_{30}^{60} \frac{180}{s} \cdot \frac{1}{60 - 30}\,ds \\
&= 6 \int_{30}^{60} \frac{1}{s}\,ds \\
&= 6 \cdot (\ln(60) - \ln(30)) \\
&\approx 4.15 \text{ hours.}
\end{aligned}
$$

7.4 Computing Probabilities by Conditioning on a R.V.

Recall the Law of Total Probability for discrete random variables (Theorem 3.7) which said the following: For any event A and any *discrete* r.v. X,

$$\mathbf{P}\{A\} = \sum_x \mathbf{P}\{A \cap X = x\} = \sum_x \mathbf{P}\{A \mid X = x\} \cdot p_X(x) \qquad (7.1)$$

The same result holds when conditioning on a continuous r.v., expect that: (1) We are working with densities, rather than probabilities, (2) we need to integrate the densities, rather than summing probabilities, and (3) when we condition on a continuous r.v., we're conditioning on a zero-probability event, which can feel a little odd but is still well defined.

> **Theorem 7.13 (Law of Total Probability: Continuous)** *Given any event A and continuous r.v. X, we can compute $\mathbf{P}\{A\}$ by conditioning on the value of X, as follows:*
>
> $$\mathbf{P}\{A\} = \int_{-\infty}^{\infty} f_X(x \cap A)\,dx = \int_{-\infty}^{\infty} \mathbf{P}\{A \mid X = x\} f_X(x)\,dx.$$
>
> *Here, $f_X(x \cap A)$ is notation that we're adopting to denote the density of the intersection of the event A with $X = x$.*

Theorem 7.13 is analogous to (7.1), except that now the state space that we're conditioning on has been partitioned into an *uncountable* number of events of zero mass.

As an example, suppose A is the event $X > 50$. Then,

$$f_X(x \cap A) = \begin{cases} f_X(x) & \text{if } x > 50 \\ 0 & \text{if } x \le 50 \end{cases}.$$

That is, $\forall x \le 50$, the quantity $f_X(x \cap A)$ is simply 0, because the intersection of $X = x$ and $X > 50$ is zero. Similarly, $\forall x > 50$, the quantity $f_X(x \cap A)$ is just $f_X(x)$ because the event $X > 50$ doesn't add any new information.

Using Theorem 7.13,

$$\mathbf{P}\{X > 50\} = \mathbf{P}\{A\} = \int_{-\infty}^{\infty} f_X(x \cap A)dx = \int_{50}^{\infty} f_X(x)dx.$$

Likewise, we get this same answer by writing:

$$\mathbf{P}\{X > 50\} = \int_{-\infty}^{\infty} \mathbf{P}\{X > 50 \mid X = x\} \cdot f_X(x)dx = \int_{50}^{\infty} 1 \cdot f_X(x)dx.$$

Question: It may seem confusing to think about $\mathbf{P}\{A \mid X = x\}$. How can this possibly be well defined? If we write:

$$\mathbf{P}\{A \mid X = x\} = \frac{\mathbf{P}\{A \cap X = x\}}{\mathbf{P}\{X = x\}},$$

don't we have zero in the denominator?

Answer: Yes, we do have zero in the denominator, but we also have zero in the numerator, so this is not necessarily a problem. Both the numerator and denominator are actually densities. The correct notation is:

$$\mathbf{P}\{A \mid X = x\} = \frac{f_X(x \cap A)}{f_X(x)}.$$

Conditioning on a zero-probability event is best explained via an example.

Example 7.14 (Coin whose probability of heads is a r.v.)

Suppose we have a coin with probability P of heads, where P is drawn from a Uniform$(0, 1)$ distribution.

Question: What is the probability that the next 10 flips are all heads?

Answer:

$$\mathbf{P}\{10 \text{ Heads}\} = \int_0^1 \mathbf{P}\{10 \text{ Heads} \mid P = p\} \cdot f_P(p)dp$$

$$= \int_0^1 \mathbf{P}\{10 \text{ Heads} \mid P = p\} \cdot 1dp$$

$$= \int_0^1 p^{10}dp$$

$$= \frac{1}{11}.$$

As we can see here, the conditional probability $\mathbf{P}\{10 \text{ Heads} \mid P = p\}$ makes perfect sense.

Definition 7.15 defines the conditional p.d.f., $f_{X|A}(x)$.

Definition 7.15 (Conditional p.d.f. and Bayes' Law) *For a continuous r.v. X and an event A, we define the* **conditional p.d.f.** *of r.v. X given event A as:*

$$f_{X|A}(x) = \frac{f_X(x \cap A)}{\mathbf{P}\{A\}} = \frac{\mathbf{P}\{A \mid X = x\} \cdot f_X(x)}{\mathbf{P}\{A\}}.$$

Once again, $f_X(x \cap A)$ denotes the density of the intersection of the event A with X = x.

Observe that $f_{X|A}(x)$ has a value of 0 when x is outside of A. The conditional p.d.f. is still a proper p.d.f. in the sense that:

$$\int_x f_{X|A}(x) = 1.$$

Example 7.16 (Pictorial view of conditional density)

A conditional density function can be viewed as a density function whose domain has been restricted in some way, and then scaled up to compensate. To see this, imagine we have a density function $f_X(x)$, where

$$f_X(x) > 0 \quad \text{for} \quad 0 < x < 100.$$

Now let A be the event that $X > 50$. Figure 7.8 shows $f_X(x)$ in blue/dashed and $f_{X|A}(x)$ in red/solid. The $f_X(x)$ curve is positive over the interval $[0, 100]$. The $f_{X|A}(x)$ curve is positive over the interval $[50, 100]$. The $f_{X|A}(x)$ curve is a scaled-up version of $f_X(x)$, where the scaling factor is $\frac{1}{\mathbf{P}\{X>50\}}$. This allows the

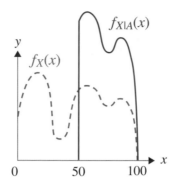

Figure 7.8 *In blue/dashed we see the p.d.f. $f_X(x)$. In red/solid we see the conditional p.d.f. $f_{X|X>50}(x)$.*

area under each curve to be 1, so both are proper probability density functions. Specifically,

$$f_{X|A}(x) = f_{X|X>50}(x) = \frac{f_X(x \cap X > 50)}{\mathbf{P}\{X > 50\}} = \begin{cases} \frac{f_X(x)}{\mathbf{P}\{X>50\}} & \text{if } x > 50 \\ 0 & \text{if } x \le 50 \end{cases}.$$

Here we've used the fact that

$$f_X(x \cap X > 50) = \begin{cases} f_X(x) & \text{if } x > 50 \\ 0 & \text{if } x \le 50 \end{cases}.$$

We furthermore see that the conditional p.d.f. integrates to 1:

$$\int_{x=0}^{100} f_{X|A}(x)\,dx = \int_{x=50}^{100} \frac{f_X(x)}{\mathbf{P}\{X > 50\}}\,dx = \frac{\mathbf{P}\{X > 50\}}{\mathbf{P}\{X > 50\}} = 1.$$

7.5 Conditional Expectation and the Conditional Density

One is often interested in the expected value of a random variable, conditioned on some event, A. In the continuous world this could, for example, be the expected height of people if we're restricted to people of height greater than 6 feet.

It is useful to start by recalling the definition of conditional expectation for the **discrete** space, given in Definitions 4.18 and 4.14: For a *discrete* r.v. X, and an event A, where $\mathbf{P}\{A\} > 0$, the conditional expectation of X given event A is:

$$\mathbf{E}[X \mid A] = \sum_x x \cdot p_{X|A}(x), \tag{7.2}$$

where

$$p_{X|A}(x) = \mathbf{P}\{X = x \mid A\} = \frac{\mathbf{P}\{(X = x) \cap A\}}{\mathbf{P}\{A\}}. \tag{7.3}$$

Definition 7.17 provides the corresponding definitions for a *continuous* r.v. X and an event A. Note the use of a **conditional p.d.f.** for the continuous case, where we used a conditional p.m.f. for the discrete case.

Definition 7.17 *For the case of a continuous r.v. X, corresponding to (7.2), we similarly define the* **conditional expectation** *of r.v. X given event A, where $\mathbf{P}\{A\} > 0$, as:*

$$\mathbf{E}[X \mid A] = \int_x x \cdot f_{X|A}(x)dx,$$

where $f_{X|A}(x)$ is the conditional p.d.f. defined in Definition 7.15.

Example 7.18 (Pittsburgh Supercomputing Center)

The Pittsburgh Supercomputing Center (PSC) runs large parallel jobs for scientists from all over the country. Jobs are grouped into different bins based on their *size*, where "size" denotes the required number of CPU-hours. Suppose that job sizes are Exponentially distributed with *mean* 1000 CPU-hours. Further suppose that all jobs of size less than 500 CPU-hours are sent to bin 1, and all remaining jobs are sent to bin 2.

Question: Consider the following questions:

(a) What is $\mathbf{P}\{$Job is sent to bin 1$\}$?
(b) What is $\mathbf{P}\{$Job size $< 200 \mid$ job is sent to bin 1$\}$?
(c) What is $f_{X|A}(x)$, where X is the job size and A is the event that the job is sent to bin 1?
(d) What is $\mathbf{E}[$Job size $\mid$ job is in bin 1$]$?

Answer: Start by recalling that for $X \sim \text{Exp}\left(\frac{1}{1000}\right)$ we have

$$f_X(x) = \begin{cases} \frac{1}{1000}e^{-\frac{x}{1000}} & \text{if } x > 0 \\ 0 & \text{otherwise} \end{cases}$$

$$F_X(x) = \mathbf{P}\{X \le x\} = 1 - e^{-\frac{1}{1000}x}.$$

(a)

$$\mathbf{P}\{\text{Job is sent to bin 1}\} = F_X(500) = 1 - e^{-\frac{500}{1000}} = 1 - e^{-\frac{1}{2}} \approx 0.39.$$

(b)

$$\mathbf{P}\{\text{Job size} < 200 \mid \text{job is sent to bin 1}\} = \frac{\mathbf{P}\{X < 200 \cap \text{bin 1}\}}{\mathbf{P}\{\text{bin 1}\}}$$

$$= \frac{F_X(200)}{F_X(500)} \approx 0.46.$$

(c)

$$f_{X|A}(x) = \frac{f_X(x \cap A)}{\mathbf{P}\{A\}} = \frac{f_X(x \cap A)}{F_X(500)} = \begin{cases} \frac{f_X(x)}{F_X(500)} = \frac{\frac{1}{1000}e^{-\frac{x}{1000}}}{1 - e^{-\frac{1}{2}}} & \text{if } x < 500 \\ 0 & \text{otherwise} \end{cases}.$$

We have used the fact that $f_X(x \cap A) = f_X(x)$ if and only if $x < 500$.

(d)

$$\mathbf{E}\,[\text{Job size} \mid \text{job in bin 1}] = \int_{-\infty}^{\infty} x f_{X|A}(x) dx = \int_{0}^{500} x \frac{\frac{1}{1000}e^{-\frac{x}{1000}}}{1 - e^{-\frac{1}{2}}} dx \approx 229.$$

Question: Why is the expected size of jobs in bin 1 less than 250?

Answer: Consider the shape of the Exponential p.d.f. Now truncate it at 500, and scale everything by a constant needed to make it integrate to 1. There is still more weight on the smaller values, so the expected value is less than the midpoint.

Question: How would the answer to question (d) change if the job sizes were distributed Uniform$(0, 2000)$, still with mean 1000?

Answer: Logically, given that the job is in bin 1 and the distribution is Uniform, we should find that the expected job size is 250 CPU-hours. Here is an algebraic argument:

$$f_{X|A}(x) = \frac{f_X(x \cap A)}{\mathbf{P}\{A\}} = \frac{f_X(x \cap A)}{F_X(500)} = \begin{cases} \frac{f_X(x)}{F_X(500)} = \frac{\frac{1}{2000}}{\frac{500}{2000}} = \frac{1}{500} & \text{if } x < 500 \\ 0 & \text{otherwise} \end{cases}.$$

$$\mathbf{E}\,[\text{Job size} \mid \text{job in bin 1}] - \int_{-\infty}^{\infty} x f_{X|A}(x) dx = \int_{0}^{500} x \frac{1}{500} dx = 250.$$

This next example talks about a coin. However, it represents the type of math used all the time when learning the bias of humans, such as a human's likelihood for clicking on a particular type of ad, or their likelihood for buying a particular brand of shoes, etc.

Example 7.19 (Learning the bias of a coin, or a human)

Suppose that we have a biased coin, with probability P of heads. P is a r.v. in that we don't know what it is. Since we know nothing, our initial assumption is that $P \sim \text{Uniform}(0, 1)$. We are interested in the expected value of P, given that the coin has resulted in 10 heads out of the first 10 flips.

At first, one might think that the best estimator of P is the fraction of heads obtained. For example, if the coin has resulted in 7 heads and 3 tails out of 10 flips, then one might be tempted to say that $\mathbf{E}[P] = 0.7$. Likewise, if the coin has resulted in 10 heads out of 10 flips, one might be tempted to say that $\mathbf{E}[P] = 1$. However, this reasoning seems shakier if you've only seen 1 flip so far, and in fact the reasoning is incorrect.

We define A as the event that 10 heads have occurred in 10 flips. By Definition 7.17,

$$\mathbf{E}[P \mid A] = \int_0^1 f_{P|A}(p) \cdot p \, dp,$$

where, by Definition 7.15,

$$f_{P|A}(p) = \frac{\mathbf{P}\{A \mid P = p\} \cdot f_P(p)}{\mathbf{P}\{A\}} = \frac{p^{10} \cdot 1}{\mathbf{P}\{A\}},$$

and where

$$\mathbf{P}\{A\} = \int_0^1 \mathbf{P}\{A \mid P = p\} \cdot f_P(p) \, dp = \int_0^1 p^{10} \cdot 1 \, dp = \frac{1}{11}.$$

Putting these together, we have:

$$
\begin{aligned}
\mathbf{E}[P \mid A] &= \int_0^1 f_{P|A}(p) \cdot p \, dp \\
&= \int_0^1 \frac{p^{10} \cdot 1}{\mathbf{P}\{A\}} \cdot p \, dp \\
&= \int_0^1 11 p^{10} \cdot p \, dp \\
&= \frac{11}{12}.
\end{aligned}
$$

Thus, the expected bias of the coin is not 1 but is close to 1, as one would intuit. Observe that the answer depends on our initial assumption that $P \sim \text{Uniform}(0, 1)$. That initial assumption is referred to as **"the prior"** and will be the focus of Chapter 17.

7.6 Exercises

7.1 Valid p.d.f.s

Which of the following are plausible probability density functions?

$$f_X(x) = \begin{cases} 0.5x^{-.5} & \text{if } 0 < x < 1 \\ 0 & \text{otherwise} \end{cases}$$

$$f_X(x) = \begin{cases} 2x^{-2} & \text{if } 0 < x < 1 \\ 0 & \text{otherwise} \end{cases}$$

$$f_X(x) = \begin{cases} x^{-2} & \text{if } 1 < x < \infty \\ 0 & \text{otherwise} \end{cases} .$$

7.2 Translation

Let $X \sim \text{Exp}(\mu)$. Let $Y = 3X$. What is $f_Y(t)$?

7.3 Weight of two-year-olds

For Example 7.4, where W denotes the weight of two-year-olds:
(a) Derive $\mathbf{E}[W]$.
(b) Derive $\mathbf{Var}(W)$.

7.4 Exponential distribution warm-up

Suppose that the time a customer spends in a bank is Exponentially distributed with mean 10 minutes.
(a) What is $\mathbf{P}\{\text{Customer spends} > 5 \text{ min in bank}\}$?
(b) What is $\mathbf{P}\{\text{Customer spends} > 15 \text{ min total} \mid \text{he is there after 10 min}\}$?

7.5 Memorylessness

Let $X \sim \text{Exp}(\lambda)$. What is $\mathbf{E}[X \mid X > 10]$? Solve this in two ways:
(a) By integrating the conditional p.d.f.
(b) By a two-line argument via the memoryless property of Exponential distribution.

7.6 Memorylessness continued

Given $X \sim \text{Exp}(1)$, what is $\mathbf{E}[X^2 \mid X > 10]$?

7.7 Practice with conditional expectations

Let X be a continuous r.v. with the following p.d.f.:

$$f_X(t) = \begin{cases} \frac{3}{2t^2} & \text{if } 1 < t < 3 \\ 0 & \text{otherwise} \end{cases} .$$

Derive $\mathbf{E}[X \mid 1 < X < 2]$.

7.8 **When will I hear back?**
More than 20 days ago, I interviewed at U-co for a software engineer position, but I still haven't heard back. Turns out that this is a common phenomenon. There are two types of recruiters at U-co:
- Type A: Get back to you in time Exponentially distributed with mean 20 days.
- Type B: Never get back to you.

There are an equal number of Type A and Type B recruiters at U-co. What is $\mathbf{P}\{$My recruiter is type B $|$ I've been waiting more than 20 days$\}$?

7.9 **Alternative definition of expectation: summing the tail**
Let X be a non-negative, continuous r.v.
(a) Prove

$$\mathbf{E}[X] = \int_{x=0}^{\infty} \mathbf{P}\{X > x\}\, dx.$$

(b) What is a nicer name for this quantity?

$$\int_{x=0}^{\infty} x\mathbf{P}\{X > x\}\, dx.$$

7.10 **Transformations**
Transforming probability density functions must be handled carefully, through the cumulative distribution functions as illustrated below:
(a) Let $f_X(\cdot)$ denote the p.d.f. of r.v. X and $f_Y(\cdot)$ denote the p.d.f. of r.v. Y. Suppose that

$$Y = aX + b,$$

where $a > 0$ and $b > 0$ are constants. Express $f_Y(\cdot)$ in terms of $f_X(\cdot)$.
(b) Let $X \sim \text{Uniform}(-1, 1)$. Let $Y = e^X$. Derive the p.d.f. of Y from that of X.

7.11 **When the first alarm goes off**
Before I go to bed, I set three alarms.
- Alarm A goes off after X_A time, where $X_A \sim \text{Exp}(\lambda_A)$.
- Alarm B goes off after X_B time, where $X_B \sim \text{Exp}(\lambda_B)$.
- Alarm C goes off after X_C time, where $X_C \sim \text{Exp}(\lambda_C)$.

Assume that $X_A \perp X_B \perp X_C$. Let T denote the time until the first alarm goes off. What is $\mathbf{E}[T]$? What is $\mathbf{Var}(T)$? [Hint: It helps to start by analyzing the tail distribution of T.]

7.12 **Reliability: when the last server dies**
Nivedita has bought two very old servers to host her new online game. At the time of purchase, she was told that each of the servers will fail at some Uniformly distributed random time during the next year, where the servers

fail independently of each other. Half a year later, her game is still up, which means that at least one server did not yet fail. What is the expected time until the last server fails?

(a) Start by solving the following easier problem: Let $X_1 \sim \text{Uniform}(0, 1)$ and $X_2 \sim \text{Uniform}(0, 1)$, where $X_1 \perp X_2$. Let $X = \max(X_1, X_2)$. Derive $\mathbf{E}[X]$.

(b) The original problem is asking, what is: $\mathbf{E}\left[X \mid X > \frac{1}{2}\right]$. Derive this quantity.

8 Continuous Random Variables: Joint Distributions

In the previous chapter, we studied individual continuous random variables. We now move on to discussing multiple random variables, which may or may not be independent of each other. Just as in Chapter 3 we used a joint probability mass function (p.m.f.), we now introduce the continuous counterpart, the joint probability density function (joint p.d.f.). We will use the joint p.d.f. to answer questions about the expected value of one random variable, given some information about the other random variable.

8.1 Joint Densities

When dealing with multiple continuous random variables, we can define a joint p.d.f. which is similar to the joint p.m.f. in Definition 3.4.

> **Definition 8.1** *The* **joint probability density function** *between continuous random variables X and Y is a non-negative function $f_{X,Y}(x, y)$, where*
>
> $$\int_c^d \int_a^b f_{X,Y}(x, y)\, dx\, dy = \mathbf{P}\{a \leq X \leq b \ \& \ c \leq Y \leq d\}$$
>
> *and where*
>
> $$\int_{-\infty}^{\infty} \int_{-\infty}^{\infty} f_{X,Y}(x, y)\, dx\, dy = 1.$$

Definition 8.1 is illustrated in Figure 8.1.

Example 8.2 (Height and weight of two-year-olds)

Let's say that two-year-olds range in weight from 15 pounds to 35 pounds and range in height from 25 inches to 40 inches. Let W be a r.v. denoting the weight of a two-year-old, and H be a r.v. denoting the height. Let $f_{W,H}(w, h)$ denote the joint density function of weight and height.

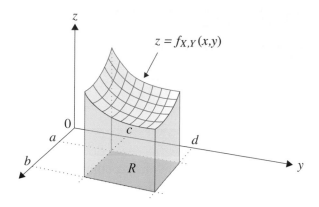

Figure 8.1 *Volume under the curve shows* $\mathbf{P}\{a \le X \le b \ \& \ c \le Y \le d\}$.

Question: What is the fraction of two-year-olds whose weight exceeds 30 pounds, but whose height is less than 30 inches?

Answer:

$$\int_{h=-\infty}^{h=30} \int_{w=30}^{w=\infty} f_{W,H}(w,h)\,dw\,dh = \int_{h=25}^{h=30} \int_{w=30}^{w=35} f_{W,H}(w,h)\,dw\,dh.$$

These are equivalent because the joint density function is only non-zero in the range where $15 \le w \le 35$ and $25 \le h \le 40$.

We can also integrate the joint p.d.f. over just one variable to get a marginal p.d.f.

Definition 8.3 *The* **marginal densities**, $f_X(x)$ *and* $f_Y(y)$, *are defined as:*

$$f_X(x) = \int_{-\infty}^{\infty} f_{X,Y}(x,y)\,dy$$

$$f_Y(y) = \int_{-\infty}^{\infty} f_{X,Y}(x,y)\,dx.$$

Note that $f_X(x)$ and $f_Y(y)$ are densities and not probabilities.

Question: If $f_{W,H}(w,h)$ is the joint p.d.f of weight and height in two-year-olds, what is the fraction of two-year-olds whose height is exactly 30 inches?

Answer: The event of having height exactly 30 inches is a zero-probability event, so the answer is zero. We could write

$$\int_{w=-\infty}^{w=\infty} f_{W,H}(w,30)\,dw = f_H(30), \qquad \text{by Definition 8.3,}$$

but, again, this is a density and hence has zero probability.

Finally, as in Definition 3.3, we can define independence for continuous random variables.

> **Definition 8.4** *We say that continuous random variables X and Y are* **independent***, written $X \perp Y$, if*
> $$f_{X,Y}(x, y) = f_X(x) \cdot f_Y(y) \qquad \forall x, y.$$

Example 8.5 (Joint p.d.f.)

Let
$$f_{X,Y}(x, y) = \begin{cases} x + y & \text{if } 0 \le x, y \le 1 \\ 0 & \text{otherwise} \end{cases}.$$

Note that $f_{X,Y}(x, y)$ is a proper density in that $\int_0^1 \int_0^1 f_{X,Y}(x, y) dx dy = 1$.

Question: (a) What is $\mathbf{E}[X]$? (b) Is $X \perp Y$?

Answer:

(a) To derive $\mathbf{E}[X]$, we first derive $f_X(x)$. We do this using Definition 8.3.

$$f_X(x) = \int_{y=-\infty}^{y=\infty} f_{X,Y}(x, y) dy = \int_{y=0}^{y=1} (x + y) dy = x + \frac{1}{2}$$

$$\mathbf{E}[X] = \int_{x=-\infty}^{x=\infty} f_X(x) \cdot x dx = \int_{x=0}^{1} \left(x + \frac{1}{2} \right) \cdot x dx = \frac{7}{12}.$$

(b) We will show that X and Y are not independent, using Definition 8.4:

$$f_X(x) = \int_{y=-\infty}^{y=\infty} f_{X,Y}(x, y) dy = x + \frac{1}{2} \qquad \text{for } 0 \le x \le 1$$

$$f_Y(y) = \int_{x=-\infty}^{x=\infty} f_{X,Y}(x, y) dx = y + \frac{1}{2} \qquad \text{for } 0 \le y \le 1.$$

Hence, clearly,
$$f_{X,Y}(x, y) \ne f_X(x) \cdot f_Y(y).$$

Example 8.6 (Joint p.d.f. for independent random variables)

Question: What is an example of a joint p.d.f. where X and Y are independent?

Answer: Let
$$f_{X,Y}(x, y) = \begin{cases} 4xy & \text{if } 0 \le x, y \le 1 \\ 0 & \text{otherwise} \end{cases}.$$

Again, this is a proper p.d.f., since it integrates to 1. Furthermore:

$$f_X(x) = \int_{y=0}^{1} 4xy\,dy = 2x \qquad \text{for } 0 \le x \le 1$$

$$f_Y(y) = \int_{x=0}^{1} 4xy\,dx = 2y \qquad \text{for } 0 \le y \le 1.$$

Hence,

$$f_{X,Y}(x, y) = f_X(x) \cdot f_Y(y)$$

as desired.

Example 8.7 (Which Exponential happens first?)

Suppose that the time until server 1 crashes is denoted by $X \sim \text{Exp}(\lambda)$ and the time until server 2 crashes is denoted by $Y \sim \text{Exp}(\mu)$. We want to know the probability that server 1 crashes before server 2 crashes. Assume that $X \perp Y$.

The goal is thus $\mathbf{P}\{X < Y\}$. We will show how to do this by integrating the joint density function between X and Y:

$$\mathbf{P}\{X < Y\} = \int_{x=0}^{\infty} \int_{y=x}^{\infty} f_{X,Y}(x, y)\,dy\,dx$$

$$= \int_{x=0}^{\infty} \int_{y=x}^{\infty} f_X(x) \cdot f_Y(y)\,dy\,dx$$

$$= \int_{x=0}^{\infty} \lambda e^{-\lambda x} \cdot \int_{y=x}^{\infty} \mu e^{-\mu y}\,dy\,dx$$

$$= \int_{x=0}^{\infty} \lambda e^{-\lambda x} \cdot e^{-\mu x}\,dx$$

$$= \lambda \int_{x=0}^{\infty} e^{-(\lambda+\mu)x}\,dx$$

$$= \frac{\lambda}{\lambda + \mu}.$$

Question: Where did we use the fact that $X \perp Y$?

Answer: We used independence in splitting the joint p.d.f. in the second line.

8.2 Probability Involving Multiple Random Variables

We can use the joint p.d.f. to derive expectations involving multiple random variables, via Definition 8.8.

Definition 8.8 *Let X and Y be continuous random variables with joint p.d.f.* $f_{X,Y}(x,y)$. *Then, for any function* $g(X,Y)$, *we have*

$$\mathbf{E}[g(X,Y)] = \int_{-\infty}^{\infty} \int_{-\infty}^{\infty} g(x,y) \cdot f_{X,Y}(x,y) dx dy.$$

We can also use the joint p.d.f. to define the conditional p.d.f. involving two continuous random variables, thus extending Definition 7.15.

Definition 8.9 (Conditional p.d.f. and Bayes' Law: two random variables)
Given two continuous random variables, X and Y, we define the **conditional**
p.d.f. *of r.v. X given event $Y = y$ as:*

$$f_{X|Y=y}(x) = \frac{f_{X,Y}(x,y)}{f_Y(y)} = \frac{f_{Y|X=x}(y) \cdot f_X(x)}{f_Y(y)} = \frac{f_{Y|X=x}(y) \cdot f_X(x)}{\int_x f_{X,Y}(x,y) dx}.$$

The first equality in Definition 8.9 is just the definition of a conditional p.d.f., where now we're conditioning on a zero-probability event, $Y = y$. The second equality is a reapplication of the first equality, but this time with X and Y interchanged. The result is a Bayes' Law, akin to that in Definition 7.15.

Observe that the conditional p.d.f. is still a proper p.d.f. in the sense that:

$$\int_x f_{X|Y=y}(x) = 1.$$

Recall the Law of Total Probability for continuous random variables from Theorem 7.13, which we have repeated below in Theorem 8.10 for easy reference.

Theorem 8.10 (Law of Total Probability: Continuous) *Given any event A*
and any continuous r.v., Y, we can compute $\mathbf{P}\{A\}$ by conditioning on the value
of Y as follows:

$$\mathbf{P}\{A\} = \int_{-\infty}^{\infty} f_Y(y \cap A) dy = \int_{-\infty}^{\infty} \mathbf{P}\{A \mid Y = y\} f_Y(y) dy.$$

Here, $f_Y(y \cap A)$ denotes the density of the intersection of the event A with
$Y = y$.

Analogously to Theorem 8.10, we can express a density of one r.v. by conditioning on another r.v., as shown in Theorem 8.11.

> **Theorem 8.11 (Law of Total Probability: Multiple Random Variables)**
> *Let X and Y be continuous random variables. Then:*
>
> $$f_X(x) = \int_y f_{X,Y}(x,y)dy = \int_y f_{X|Y=y}(x)f_Y(y)dy.$$

As a starting example, let's revisit Example 8.7 and show how it can be solved more simply by conditioning.

Example 8.12 (Which Exponential happens first – revisited)

Suppose that the time until server 1 crashes is denoted by $X \sim \text{Exp}(\lambda)$ and the time until server 2 crashes is denoted by $Y \sim \text{Exp}(\mu)$. We want to know the probability that server 1 crashes before server 2 crashes. Assume that $X \perp Y$.

The goal is thus $\mathbf{P}\{X < Y\}$. This time, we derive the quantity by conditioning on the value of X, as follows:

$$
\begin{aligned}
\mathbf{P}\{X < Y\} &= \int_0^\infty \mathbf{P}\{X < Y \mid X = x\} \cdot f_X(x)dx \\
&= \int_0^\infty \mathbf{P}\{Y > x \mid X = x\} \cdot \lambda e^{-\lambda x}dx \\
&= \int_0^\infty \mathbf{P}\{Y > x\} \cdot \lambda e^{-\lambda x}dx \\
&= \int_0^\infty e^{-\mu x} \cdot \lambda e^{-\lambda x}dx \\
&= \lambda \int_0^\infty e^{-(\lambda+\mu)x}dx = \frac{\lambda}{\lambda+\mu}.
\end{aligned}
$$

Question: Where did we use the fact that $X \perp Y$?

Answer: We used independence to claim that $\mathbf{P}\{Y > x \mid X = x\} = \mathbf{P}\{Y > x\}$; here we assumed that the fact that $X = x$ has no effect on the value of Y.

Now let's consider a more involved example.

Example 8.13 (Relationship between hand-in time and grade)

[Parts of this problem are borrowed from [51]] As a professor, I'm curious about whether there's a relationship between the time when a student turns in their homework and the grade that the student receives on the homework.Let T denote the amount of time prior to the deadline that the homework is submitted. I have noticed that no one ever submits the homework earlier than two days before the homework is due, so $0 \leq T \leq 2$. Let G denote the grade that the homework receives, viewed as a percentage, meaning $0 \leq G \leq 1$. Both G and T are continuous random variables. Suppose their joint p.d.f. is given by

$$f_{G,T}(g,t) = \frac{9}{10}tg^2 + \frac{1}{5}, \qquad \text{where } 0 \leq g \leq 1 \text{ and } 0 \leq t \leq 2.$$

Question:

(a) What is the probability that a randomly selected student gets a grade above 50% on the homework?
(b) What is the probability that a student gets a grade above 50%, given that the student submitted less than a day before the deadline?

Answer: It's easiest to start this problem by determining the marginal density function $f_G(g)$. We will determine $f_T(t)$ as well, for future use:

$$f_G(g) = \int_{t=0}^{t=2} f_{G,T}(g,t)dt = \int_{t=0}^{t=2} \left(\frac{9}{10}tg^2 + \frac{1}{5} \right) dt = \frac{9}{5} \cdot g^2 + \frac{2}{5} \quad (8.1)$$

$$f_T(t) = \int_{g=0}^{g=1} f_{G,T}(g,t)dg = \int_{g=0}^{g=1} \left(\frac{9}{10}tg^2 + \frac{1}{5} \right) dg = \frac{3}{10} \cdot t + \frac{1}{5}. \quad (8.2)$$

To understand the probability that a randomly selected student gets a grade above 50% on the homework, we want $\mathbf{P}\left\{G > \frac{1}{2}\right\}$. We can directly use $f_G(g)$ to get this as follows:

$$\mathbf{P}\left\{G > \frac{1}{2}\right\} = \int_{g=\frac{1}{2}}^{g=1} f_G(g)dg = \int_{g=\frac{1}{2}}^{g=1} \left(\frac{9}{5} \cdot g^2 + \frac{2}{5} \right) dg = \frac{29}{40} = 0.725.$$

To understand the probability that a student gets a grade above 50%, given that the student submitted less than a day before the deadline, we want $\mathbf{P}\left\{G > \frac{1}{2} \mid T < 1\right\}$:

$$\mathbf{P}\left\{G > \frac{1}{2} \mid T < 1\right\} = \frac{\mathbf{P}\{G > 0.5 \ \& \ T < 1\}}{\mathbf{P}\{T < 1\}}$$

$$= \frac{\int_{g=0.5}^{g=1} \int_{t=0}^{t=1} f_{G,T}(g,t)dtdg}{\int_{t=0}^{t=1} f_T(t)dt}$$

$$= \frac{\int_{g=0.5}^{g=1} \int_{t=0}^{t=1} \left(\frac{9}{10}tg^2 + \frac{1}{5} \right) dtdg}{\int_{t=0}^{t=1} \left(\frac{3}{10} \cdot t + \frac{1}{5} \right) dt}$$

$$= \frac{0.23125}{0.35} = 0.66.$$

8.3 Pop Quiz

Density functions can be tricky. Below we quickly summarize what we've learned in the form of a pop quiz. Throughout, assume that X and Y are continuous random variables with joint density function

$$f_{X,Y}(x, y), \qquad \text{where } -\infty < x, y < \infty.$$

Question: What are the marginal densities $f_X(x)$ and $f_Y(y)$?

Answer:

$$f_X(x) = \int_{y=-\infty}^{y=\infty} f_{X,Y}(x, y)dy \qquad f_Y(y) = \int_{x=-\infty}^{x=\infty} f_{X,Y}(x, y)dx.$$

Question: What is the conditional density $f_{X|Y=y}(x)$? How about $f_{Y|X=x}(y)$?

Answer:

$$f_{X|Y=y}(x) = \frac{f_{X,Y}(x, y)}{f_Y(y)} \tag{8.3}$$

$$f_{Y|X=x}(y) = \frac{f_{X,Y}(x, y)}{f_X(x)} \tag{8.4}$$

Question: How can we write $f_{X|Y=y}(x)$ in terms of $f_{Y|X=x}(y)$?

Answer: If we substitute $f_{X,Y}(x, y)$ from (8.4) into (8.3), we get:

$$f_{X|Y=y}(x) = \frac{f_{X,Y}(x, y)}{f_Y(y)} = \frac{f_{Y|X=x}(y) \cdot f_X(x)}{f_Y(y)}.$$

Question: How do we write $\mathbf{P}\{X < a \mid Y = y\}$?

Answer: This is just a question of summing up the conditional density $f_{X|Y=y}(x)$ over all values of x where $x < a$:

$$\mathbf{P}\{X < a \mid Y = y\} = \int_{x=-\infty}^{x=a} f_{X|Y=y}(x)dx.$$

Question: How do we write $f_{Y|Y<a}(y)$ in terms of $f_Y(y)$?

Answer: Intuitively, we're just conditioning on the event that $Y < a$, which narrows the range of values, so the conditional density gets scaled up by a constant factor. Here are all the steps. Let A denote the event that $Y < a$. Then:

$$f_{Y|Y<a}(y) = f_{Y|A}(y)$$
$$= \frac{f_Y(y \cap A)}{\mathbf{P}\{A\}}$$
$$= \frac{f_Y(y \cap Y < a)}{\mathbf{P}\{Y < a\}}$$
$$= \begin{cases} \frac{f_Y(y)}{\mathbf{P}\{Y<a\}} & \text{if } y < a \\ 0 & \text{otherwise} \end{cases}.$$

Question: How do we write $f_{Y|X<a}(y)$ in terms of $f_{X,Y}(x, y)$?

Answer: In the case of $f_{Y|X<a}(y)$, we define A to be the event that $X < a$. Now we are conditioning on an event A that doesn't involve Y. Because of this, we can't simply scale up the density function, and we must instead return to the joint density. Then the steps are as follows:

$$f_{Y|X<a}(y) = f_{Y|A}(y)$$
$$= \frac{f_Y(y \cap A)}{\mathbf{P}\{A\}}$$
$$= \frac{f_Y(y \cap X < a)}{\mathbf{P}\{X < a\}}$$
$$= \frac{\int_{x=-\infty}^{x=a} f_{X,Y}(x, y)dx}{\mathbf{P}\{X < a\}}.$$

8.4 Conditional Expectation for Multiple Random Variables

We now move on to expectation. We will extend the definitions from Section 7.5 on conditional expectation to multiple random variables. As before, the key to defining conditional expectation is to use a conditional p.d.f.

Definition 8.14 *Given continuous random variables X and Y, we define:*

$$\mathbf{E}[X \mid Y = y] = \int_x x \cdot f_{X|Y=y}(x)dx.$$

A typical situation where Definition 8.14 might come up is in computing the expected weight of two-year-olds if their height is 30 inches. Another way in which Definition 8.14 is useful is that it allows us to simplify computations of expectation by conditioning, as in Theorem 8.15.

> **Theorem 8.15** *We can derive* $\mathbf{E}[X]$ *by conditioning on the value of a continuous r.v. Y as follows:*
>
> $$\mathbf{E}[X] = \int_y \mathbf{E}[X \mid Y = y] \cdot f_Y(y)dy.$$

Theorem 8.15 is the direct continuous counterpart to Theorem 4.22. The proof of Theorem 8.15 follows the same lines as that of Theorem 4.22, except that we use Definition 8.14 in place of Definition 4.18.

Let's now return to Example 8.13, this time from the perspective of expectation.

Example 8.16 (Relationship between hand-in time and grade, continued)

Let T denote the number of days prior to the deadline that the homework is submitted. No one ever submits the homework earlier than two days before the homework is due, so $0 \le T \le 2$. Let G denote the grade that the homework receives, viewed as a percentage, meaning $0 \le G \le 1$. Both G and T are continuous random variables. Their joint p.d.f. is given by

$$f_{G,T}(g,t) = \frac{9}{10}tg^2 + \frac{1}{5}.$$

Question: A random student submits at $T = 0$, that is, exactly when the homework is due. What is the student's expected grade?

Answer:

$$\mathbf{E}[G \mid T = 0] = \int_{g=0}^{1} g \cdot f_{G|T=0}(g)dg \qquad \text{by Definition 8.14}$$

$$= \int_{g=0}^{1} g \frac{f_{G,T}(g,0)}{f_T(0)}dg \qquad \text{by Definition 8.9}$$

$$= \int_{g=0}^{1} g \frac{\frac{1}{5}}{\frac{1}{5}}dg$$

$$= \frac{1}{2}. \tag{8.5}$$

Question: Who has a higher expected grade: a student who submits exactly when the homework is due, or a student who submits more than 1 day early?

Answer: To answer this, we must compare $\mathbf{E}[G \mid T = 0]$ from (8.5) with $\mathbf{E}[G \mid 1 < T < 2]$.

We derive $\mathbf{E}\left[G \mid 1 < T < 2\right]$ in the same way as we derived $\mathbf{E}\left[G \mid T = 0\right]$:

$$
\begin{aligned}
\mathbf{E}\left[G \mid 1 < T < 2\right] &= \int_{g=0}^{1} g\, f_{G \mid 1 < T < 2}(g)\, dg \qquad \text{by Definition 7.17} \\
&= \int_{g=0}^{1} g\, \frac{f_G\left(g \cap (1 < T < 2)\right)}{\mathbf{P}\{1 < T < 2\}}\, dg \qquad \text{by Definition 7.15} \\
&= \int_{g=0}^{1} g\, \frac{\int_{t=1}^{t=2} f_{G,T}(g,t)\, dt}{\int_{t=1}^{t=2} f_T(t)\, dt}\, dg \\
&= \int_{g=0}^{1} g\, \frac{\int_{t=1}^{t=2}\left(\frac{9}{10} t g^2 + \frac{1}{5}\right) dt}{\int_{t=1}^{t=2}\left(\frac{3}{10} t + \frac{1}{5}\right) dt}\, dg \qquad f_T(t) \text{ is from (8.2)} \\
&= \int_{g=0}^{1} g\, \frac{\frac{1}{20}\left(27 g^2 + 4\right)}{0.65}\, dg \\
&= 0.673.
\end{aligned}
$$

So the expected grade is higher for those who turn in their homework more than a day early, as compared with those who turn in their homework exactly on time. This makes sense!

8.5 Linearity and Other Properties

In this chapter and the prior one on continuous random variables, we have not bothered to repeat all the prior results that we saw for discrete random variables, such as Linearity of Expectation (Theorem 4.10), Linearity of Variance (Theorem 5.8), and Expectation of a Product (Theorem 4.8). However, all of these results extend to continuous random variables as well. The proofs are straightforward and are deferred to the exercises.

8.6 Exercises

8.1 **Linearity of expectation for continuous random variables**
Let X and Y be continuous random variables. Prove that
$$
\mathbf{E}\left[X + Y\right] = \mathbf{E}\left[X\right] + \mathbf{E}\left[Y\right].
$$

8.2 Product of continuous random variables

Let X and Y be continuous random variables, where $X \perp Y$. Prove that

$$\mathbf{E}[XY] = \mathbf{E}[X] \cdot \mathbf{E}[Y].$$

8.3 Two Uniforms

Let $X \sim \text{Uniform}(0,1)$ and $Y \sim \text{Uniform}(0,2)$ be independent random variables. What is $\mathbf{P}\{X \leq Y\}$?
(a) Solve this via the joint p.d.f. of X and Y.
(b) Solve this by conditioning on X.

8.4 Quality of service

A company pays a fine if the time to process a request exceeds 7 seconds. Processing a request consists of two tasks: (a) retrieving the file, which takes some time X that is Exponentially distributed with mean 5; and (b) processing the file, which takes some time Y that is independent of X and is distributed $\text{Uniform}(1,3)$. Given that the mean time to process a request is clearly 7 seconds, the company views the fine as unfair, because it will have to pay the fine on half its requests. Is this right? What is the actual fraction of time that the fine will have to be paid?

8.5 Meeting up

Eric and Timmy have agreed to meet between 2 and 3 pm to work on homework. They are rather busy and are not quite sure when they can arrive, so assume that each of their arrival times is independent and uniformly distributed over the hour. Each agrees to wait 15 minutes for the other, after which he will leave. What is the probability that Eric and Timmy will be able to meet?

8.6 Practice with joint random variables

Let X and Y be continuous random variables with the following joint p.d.f.

$$f_{X,Y}(x, y) = \begin{cases} e^{-x} & \text{if } 0 \leq y \leq x \\ 0 & \text{otherwise} \end{cases}.$$

(a) Start by drawing the region R where the joint p.d.f. is non-zero. This will help you determine the limits of integration for the remaining parts.
(b) What is $f_X(x)$? State the region over which this p.d.f. is non-zero.
(c) What is $f_Y(y)$? State the region over which this p.d.f. is non-zero.
(d) What is $f_{Y|X=x}(y)$, where $x > 0$? State the region over which this p.d.f. is non-zero.
(e) What is $\mathbf{E}[Y \mid X = x]$, where $x > 0$?

8.7 **Distance between darts**

We are given a line segment, $[0, 1]$. Kristy and Timmy each independently throw a dart uniformly at random within the line segment. What is the expected distance between Kristy's and Timmy's darts?

8.8 **Comparison of two darts**

We are given a line segment, $[0, 1]$. Two darts are each independently thrown uniformly at random within the line segment. What is the probability that the value of one dart is at least three times the value of the other?

8.9 **Sum of independent random variables**

The *convolution* of two functions $f(\cdot)$ and $g(\cdot)$ is defined as

$$f \circ g(z) = \int_{-\infty}^{\infty} f(z - x)g(x)dx.$$

Let X and Y be two independent continuous random variables. Define a new r.v. $Z = X + Y$. In this problem, you will show that the p.d.f. of Z is the convolution of the probability density functions of X and Y. Follow these steps:

(a) Show that $F_Z(z) = \int_{-\infty}^{z} \int_{-\infty}^{\infty} f_X(x) \cdot f_Y(t - x)dxdt$.

(b) Differentiate $F_Z(z)$ to obtain $f_Z(z)$.

[Hint: You will need to invoke the Fundamental Theorem of Calculus from Section 1.3.]

8.10 **Bear problem**

[Proposed by Weina Wang] You stand at a position $X \sim \text{Exp}(1)$ on the line. Your friend stands at position $Y \sim \text{Exp}(2)$. Assume that X and Y are independent. A bear comes from the left. The bear will eat the first person it comes to; however, if the distance between you and your friend is < 1, then the bear will eat both of you. What is the probability that you get eaten?

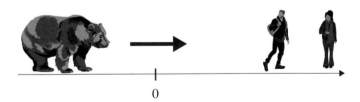

0

Figure 8.2 *Figure for Exercise 8.10.*

8.11 **Bayes of our lives**

The number of seasons in a television series is $N \sim \text{Geometric}(P)$. After each season, there is a fixed probability, P, that the series is canceled. However, the parameter P depends on the popularity of the series, so we don't know what it is in general. For a new series, we assume that $P \sim \text{Uniform}(0, 1)$. A television series has been running for 37 seasons (and renewed for more). Derive the expected value of P, given this information, that is, derive $\mathbf{E}\left[P \mid N > 37\right]$.

8.12 Density of choice
Suppose that X and Y are continuous random variables and let

$$Z = \begin{cases} X & \text{w/prob } p \\ Y & \text{w/prob } 1 - p \end{cases}.$$

(a) Derive the p.d.f. of Z in terms of the probability density functions of X and Y.
(b) The Double Exponential distribution is defined via the random variable W, where $W = ST$ and $T \sim \text{Exp}(\lambda)$ and S is a discrete r.v. with equal probability of being 1 or -1. Use part (a) to derive the p.d.f. of W.

8.13 When the parameters of a distribution are random variables
There are many situations where the parameters of a distribution are themselves random variables. For example, let $X \sim \text{Exp}(\lambda)$ and $Y \sim \text{Uniform}(0, X)$. (a) What is $\mathbf{E}\left[Y\right]$? (b) What is $\mathbf{Var}(Y)$?

8.14 Smallest interval
A dart is thrown uniformly at random at the unit interval $[0, 1]$. The dart splits the interval into two segments, one to its right and one to its left. What is the expected length of the smaller segment?

8.15 Smallest interval with two darts
Two independent darts are thrown uniformly at random at the unit interval $[0, 1]$. The two darts naturally split the interval into three segments. Let S be the length of the smallest segment. What is $\mathbf{E}\left[S\right]$? [Hint: There are several ways to solve this problem. A good way to start is to derive the tail of S, and then integrate the tail to get $\mathbf{E}\left[S\right]$, as in Exercise 7.9. To get the tail, it may help to draw a 2D picture of where each of the darts is allowed to fall.]

8.16 Different views on conditional expectation
[Proposed by Misha Ivkov] Let $X \sim \text{Uniform}(0, 1)$ and $Y \sim \text{Uniform}(0, 1)$. Our goal is to understand

$$\mathbf{E}\left[X \mid X + Y = 1.5\right].$$

(a) Dong makes the realization that $X + Y = 1.5$ implies that $X = 1.5 - Y$. He then reasons that

$$\mathbf{E}\left[X \mid X + Y = 1.5\right] = \mathbf{E}\left[1.5 - Y\right].$$

What's the result via Dong's approach? Is Dong right? Why or why not?

(b) Lisa suggests that one should first compute the conditional density function, $f_{X|X+Y=1.5}(x)$, using Definition 8.14 and then use that to get $\mathbf{E}[X \mid X + Y = 1.5]$. Follow Lisa's approach to derive $\mathbf{E}[X \mid X + Y = 1.5]$.

(c) Misha believes that pictures are the only way to prove things. Draw a 2D plot that allows you to understand $\mathbf{E}[X \mid X + Y = 1.5]$.

8.17 Hiring for tech

At a popular tech company, candidates are rated on two axes: technical skills (T) and communication skills (C). The values of T and C can in theory be any real number from 0 (worst) to 1 (best). In practice, however, it never happens that a candidate gets a rating of less than 0.5 in both categories (that's just too harsh), so candidate scores actually fall within region R in Figure 8.3(a). Assume that candidate scores are uniformly distributed over region R, as shown in Figure 8.3(b).

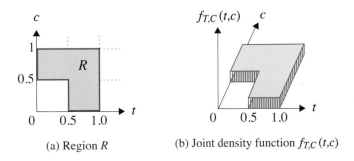

(a) Region R (b) Joint density function $f_{T,C}(t,c)$

Figure 8.3 *For Exercise 8.17.*

(a) What is the joint density function $f_{T,C}(t, c)$?

(b) What is the marginal p.d.f. of T, that is, $f_T(t)$?

(c) What is $\mathbf{E}[C \mid T < 0.75]$? (Write out the full conditional density and then integrate it appropriately.)

8.18 On the probability of a triangle

Suppose we have an interval of length 1. We throw two darts at the interval independently and uniformly at random. The two darts divide our interval into three segments. We want to know the probability that the three segments form a triangle.

(a) Describe the criterion we need in order to achieve our goal.

(b) If the first dart lands at $x \in [0, \frac{1}{2}]$, what's the probability that the resulting segments give us a triangle?

(c) What is the probability that the three segments form a triangle?

8.19 Relating laptop quality to lifetime

[Proposed by Weina Wang] You have a laptop whose quality is represented by $Q \sim \text{Uniform}(1, 2)$, with a larger number representing higher quality. Laptops with higher quality have higher expected lifetimes. Let X be the lifetime of the laptop in years (assume this ranges from 0 to ∞). We are told that, given that $Q = q$, the lifetime of the laptop is $X \sim \text{Exp}\left(\frac{1}{q}\right)$ for $1 \leq q \leq 2$.

(a) Assume $1 \leq q \leq 2$. What is $f_{X|Q=q}(x)$? What is $\mathbf{E}[X \mid Q = q]$?
(b) What is the joint p.d.f. $f_{X,Q}(x, q)$?
(c) Suppose your laptop is still working after one year. What is the expected quality of your laptop given that fact?

[Note: In your final expression, you will get some integrals that you can't compute. Here are approximations to use: $\int_1^2 te^{-\frac{1}{t}} dt \approx 0.78$ and $\int_1^2 e^{-\frac{1}{t}} dt \approx 0.5$.]

8.20 Gambling at the casino

[Proposed by Weina Wang] Your friend Alice is visiting Las Vegas and takes X dollars to a casino, where $X \sim \text{Uniform}(10, 20)$. At the end of the day, she brings back Y dollars. Given that she takes $X = x$ dollars, the density of Y is

$$f_{Y|X=x}(y) = \begin{cases} -\frac{y}{2x^2} + \frac{1}{x} & \text{if } 0 \leq y \leq 2x \\ 0 & \text{otherwise} \end{cases}.$$

(a) What is Alice's expected return from gambling, that is, $\mathbf{E}[Y - X]$? The following steps will help:
  (i) Derive $\mathbf{E}[X]$. This is uncomplicated.
  (ii) Derive $\mathbf{E}[Y \mid X = x]$.
  (iii) Use (ii) to derive $\mathbf{E}[Y]$.
  (iv) Derive $\mathbf{E}[Y] - \mathbf{E}[X]$.
(b) Suppose you know that Alice wins at gambling. What is the expectation of the amount of money she takes to the casino? [Hint: The problem is asking for $\mathbf{E}[X \mid Y > X]$. To get this, you will need $f_{X|Y>X}(x)$.]

8.21 Modeling expected disk delay

The delay to read a single byte from a hard disk consists of two components: (1) *seek time* – this is the time needed to move the disk head to the desired track; and (2) *rotation time* – this is the time needed to rotate the disk head on the track to reach the desired byte (Figure 8.4). Suppose that bytes are uniformly distributed across the disk. Let T be a r.v. denoting the time to reach a single (randomly located) byte. Your goal is to compute $\mathbf{E}[T]$. Assume that the disk has radius r (a constant). Assume that the tracks are infinitely thin. Assume the disk head starts from wherever the last byte was read. Assume that the time to traverse the full radius r is 15 ms. At all

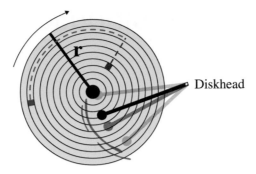

Figure 8.4 *For Exercise 8.21. A disk with radius r. Each circle represents a track. The red square (on the inner track) shows the byte most recently read. The blue square (on the outer track) shows the next byte requested. To read the blue byte, the disk head first seeks to the outer track of the blue byte and then waits for the disk to rotate to the correct byte.*

times, the disk rotates at 6,000 RPM (rotations per minute) in one direction only. Provide your final answer in ms. [Hint: Outer tracks hold more bytes than inner ones.]

8.22 **Hula hoop cutting**

You are holding a hula hoop of unit radius with your hand at its top (12 o'clock; Figure 8.5). In a moment, two points on the hoop will be selected uniformly at random, and the hoop will be cut at those points, splitting it into two arcs.

Figure 8.5 *For Exercise 8.22. The cuts create two arcs: a pink one that you're holding, and a purple one that falls.*

(a) Compute the expected value of the angular difference between the two arcs.

(b) When the cuts are made, one arc falls to the ground while the other one stays in your hand. What is the probability that you are holding the larger arc?

9 Normal Distribution

An important and ubiquitous continuous distribution is the Normal distribution (also called the Gaussian). Normal distributions occur frequently in statistics, economics, natural sciences, and social sciences. For example, IQs approximately follow a Normal distribution. Men's heights and weights are approximately Normally distributed, as are women's heights and weights. Part of what makes the Normal distribution so relevant is the Central Limit Theorem (CLT; Section 9.4), which says that the average of a large number of independent and identically distributed (i.i.d.) quantities converges to a Normal. This explains, for example, why the Binomial random variable (r.v.) has a Normal shape when the number of coin flips is high. It also explains why noise (which is the mixture of many independent factors) is typically Normally distributed.

9.1 Definition

Definition 9.1 *A continuous r.v. X follows a* **Normal** *or* **Gaussian** *distribution, written* $X \sim Normal(\mu, \sigma^2)$, *if X has probability density function (p.d.f.)* $f_X(x)$ *of the form*

$$f_X(x) = \frac{1}{\sqrt{2\pi}\sigma} e^{-\frac{1}{2}\left(\frac{x-\mu}{\sigma}\right)^2}, \qquad -\infty < x < \infty,$$

where $\sigma > 0$. *The parameter* μ *is called the* **mean**, *and the parameter* σ *is called the* **standard deviation**.

Definition 9.2 *X follows a* **standard Normal** *distribution if* $X \sim Normal(0, 1)$, *that is,*

$$f_X(x) = \frac{1}{\sqrt{2\pi}} e^{-\frac{1}{2}x^2}, \qquad -\infty < x < \infty.$$

The $Normal(\mu, \sigma^2)$ p.d.f. has a "bell" shape and is symmetric around μ, as shown in Figure 9.1. The fact that $f_X(x)$ in Definition 9.1 is actually a density function can be seen by proving that it integrates to 1. This integration involves a change into polar coordinates (trust me, you do not want to see the gory details [71]).

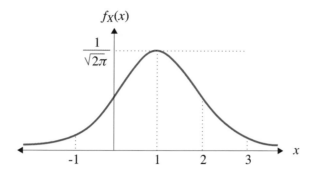

Figure 9.1 *Normal*(1, 1) *p.d.f.*

Theorem 9.3 shows that the parameters of the Normal distribution in fact represent its mean and variance.

Theorem 9.3 *Let $X \sim Normal(\mu, \sigma^2)$, then* $\mathbf{E}[X] = \mu$ *and* $\mathbf{Var}(X) = \sigma^2$.

Proof: Because $f_X(x)$ is symmetric around μ, it is obvious that $\mathbf{E}[X] = \mu$.

$$\mathbf{Var}(X) = \int_{-\infty}^{\infty} (x - \mu)^2 f_X(x) dx$$

$$= \frac{1}{\sqrt{2\pi}\sigma} \int_{-\infty}^{\infty} (x - \mu)^2 e^{-\frac{1}{2}((x-\mu)/\sigma)^2} dx$$

$$= \frac{\sigma^2}{\sqrt{2\pi}} \int_{-\infty}^{\infty} y^2 e^{-y^2/2} dy \qquad (\text{let } y = (x - \mu)/\sigma \text{ and } dx = \sigma dy)$$

$$= \frac{\sigma^2}{\sqrt{2\pi}} \int_{-\infty}^{\infty} y \cdot \left(y e^{-y^2/2} \right) dy$$

$$= \frac{\sigma^2}{\sqrt{2\pi}} \left(-y e^{-y^2/2} \right) \Big|_{-\infty}^{\infty} + \frac{\sigma^2}{\sqrt{2\pi}} \int_{-\infty}^{\infty} e^{-y^2/2} dy \qquad (\text{integration by parts})$$

$$= \frac{\sigma^2}{\sqrt{2\pi}} \int_{-\infty}^{\infty} e^{-y^2/2} dy$$

$$= \sigma^2.$$

The last line was obtained by using the fact that

$$\frac{1}{\sqrt{2\pi}} \int_{-\infty}^{\infty} e^{-y^2/2} dy = 1,$$

because the integrand is the density function of the standard Normal. ∎

One of the things that makes the Normal distribution challenging is that its cumulative distribution function (c.d.f.) is not known in closed form. For the standard Normal, it is common to use the function $\Phi(\cdot)$ to represent the c.d.f., but the value of $\Phi(x)$ must be computed numerically. We will return to this point in Section 9.3.

Definition 9.4 *If $X \sim Normal(0, 1)$, then the c.d.f. of X is denoted by*

$$\Phi(x) = F_X(x) = \mathbf{P}\{X \le x\} = \frac{1}{\sqrt{2\pi}} \int_{-\infty}^{x} e^{-t^2/2} dt.$$

9.2 Linear Transformation Property

The Normal distribution has a very particular property known as the "Linear Transformation Property," which says that if X is a Normal r.v., and you take a linear function of X, then that new r.v. will also be distributed as a Normal. Note that this property is *not* true for other distributions that we have seen, such as the Exponential.

Theorem 9.5 (Linear Transformation Property) *Let $X \sim Normal(\mu, \sigma^2)$. Let*

$$Y = aX + b,$$

where $a > 0$ and $b \in \mathbb{R}$. Then, $Y \sim Normal(a\mu + b, a^2\sigma^2)$.

Proof: Clearly $\mathbf{E}[Y] = a\mathbf{E}[X] + b = a\mu + b$ and $\mathbf{Var}(Y) = a^2\mathbf{Var}(X) = a^2\sigma^2$. All that remains is to show that $f_Y(y)$ is Normally distributed.

Question: What do we want $f_Y(y)$ to look like?

Answer: We want to show that

$$f_Y(y) = \frac{1}{\sqrt{2\pi}(a\sigma)} e^{-\frac{1}{2}\left(\frac{y-(a\mu+b)}{a\sigma}\right)^2}.$$

Question: Can we relate the p.d.f. of Y to the p.d.f. of X as follows:

$$f_Y(y) = \mathbf{P}\{Y = y\} = \mathbf{P}\{aX + b = y\} = \mathbf{P}\left\{X = \frac{y-b}{a}\right\} = f_X\left(\frac{y-b}{a}\right)?$$

Answer: The above is WRONG, because we can't say that $f_Y(y) = \mathbf{P}\{Y = y\}$. To make this argument correctly, we need to go through the c.d.f., which represents a valid probability.

We relate the c.d.f. of Y to the c.d.f. of X as follows:

$$F_Y(y) = \mathbf{P}\{Y \le y\} = \mathbf{P}\{aX + b \le y\} = \mathbf{P}\left\{X \le \frac{y-b}{a}\right\} = F_X\left(\frac{y-b}{a}\right).$$

We now differentiate both sides with respect to y:

$$\frac{d}{dy}F_Y(y) = \frac{d}{dy}\int_{-\infty}^{y} f_Y(t)\,dt \overset{\text{FTC}}{=} f_Y(y)$$

$$\frac{d}{dy}F_X\left(\frac{y-b}{a}\right) = \frac{d}{dy}\int_{-\infty}^{\frac{y-b}{a}} f_X(t)\,dt \overset{\text{FTC}}{=} f_X\left(\frac{y-b}{a}\right)\cdot\frac{d}{dy}\left(\frac{y-b}{a}\right) = \frac{1}{a}f_X\left(\frac{y-b}{a}\right),$$

where FTC denotes the Fundamental Theorem of Calculus (Section 1.3).

Thus we have shown that

$$f_Y(y) = \frac{1}{a}f_X\left(\frac{y-b}{a}\right).$$

Evaluating this, we have

$$f_Y(y) = \frac{1}{a}f_X\left(\frac{y-b}{a}\right)$$

$$= \frac{1}{a\sqrt{2\pi}\sigma}e^{-(\frac{y-b}{a}-\mu)^2/2\sigma^2}$$

$$= \frac{1}{\sqrt{2\pi}(a\sigma)}e^{-(y-b-a\mu)^2/2a^2\sigma^2}$$

$$= \frac{1}{\sqrt{2\pi}(a\sigma)}e^{-(y-(b+a\mu))^2/2a^2\sigma^2}.$$

So $f_Y(y)$ is a Normal p.d.f. with mean $a\mu + b$ and variance $a^2\sigma^2$. ∎

9.3 The Cumulative Distribution Function

As stated earlier, unfortunately we do not know how to compute the c.d.f. of a Normal distribution. We must therefore use a table of numerically integrated results for $\Phi(y)$, such as that given in [82].[1]

---

[1] In practice no one ever goes to the table anymore, because there are approximations online that allow you to compute the $\Phi(\cdot)$ values to within seven decimal places; see, for example, [75].

Here is a snippet of the numerical table for $\Phi(y)$:

y	0.5	1.0	1.5	2.0	2.5	3.0
$\Phi(y)$	0.6915	0.8413	0.9332	0.9772	0.9938	0.9987

Question: Looking at the table you see, for example, that $\Phi(1) = 0.8413$. What does this tell us about the probability that the standard Normal is within one standard deviation of its mean?

Answer: Let $Y \sim \text{Normal}(0, 1)$. Since $\Phi(1) \doteq 0.84$, we know that $\mathbf{P}\{Y < 1\} = 0.84$. We want to know $\mathbf{P}\{-1 < Y < 1\}$.

$$
\begin{aligned}
\mathbf{P}\{-1 < Y < 1\} &= \mathbf{P}\{Y < 1\} - \mathbf{P}\{Y < -1\} \\
&= \mathbf{P}\{Y < 1\} - \mathbf{P}\{Y > 1\} \quad \text{(by symmetry)} \\
&= \mathbf{P}\{Y < 1\} - (1 - \mathbf{P}\{Y < 1\}) \\
&= 2\mathbf{P}\{Y < 1\} - 1 \\
&= 2\Phi(1) - 1 \\
&\doteq 2 \cdot 0.84 - 1 \\
&= 0.68.
\end{aligned}
$$

So with probability approximately 68%, we are within one standard deviation of the mean.

Question: If $Y \sim \text{Normal}(0, 1)$, what's the probability that Y is within k standard deviations of its mean?

Answer:

$$
\mathbf{P}\{-k < Y < k\} = 2\Phi(k) - 1. \tag{9.1}
$$

Equation (9.1) tells us the following useful facts:

- With probability $\approx 68\%$, the Normal is within 1 standard deviation of its mean.
- With probability $\approx 95\%$, the Normal is within 2 standard deviations of its mean.
- With probability $\approx 99.7\%$, the Normal is within 3 standard deviations of its mean.

Question: The "useful facts" were expressed for a standard Normal. What if we do not have a standard Normal?

Answer: We can convert a non-standard Normal into a standard Normal using the Linear Transformation Property. That is:

$$X \sim \text{Normal}(\mu, \sigma^2) \iff Y = \frac{X - \mu}{\sigma} \sim \text{Normal}(0, 1).$$

Thus, if $Y \sim \text{Normal}(0, 1)$, and $X \sim \text{Normal}(\mu, \sigma^2)$, then the probability that X deviates from its mean by less than k standard deviations is:

$$\mathbf{P}\{-k\sigma < X - \mu < k\sigma\} = \mathbf{P}\left\{-k < \frac{X - \mu}{\sigma} < k\right\} = \mathbf{P}\{-k < Y < k\}.$$

This point is summarized in Theorem 9.6.

Theorem 9.6 *If $X \sim \text{Normal}(\mu, \sigma^2)$, then the probability that X deviates from its mean by less than k standard deviations is the same as the probability that the standard Normal deviates from its mean by less than k.*

Theorem 9.6 illustrates why it is often easier to think in terms of standard deviations than absolute values.

Question: Proponents of IQ testing will tell you that human intelligence (IQ) has been shown to be Normally distributed with mean 100 and standard deviation 15. What fraction of people have an IQ greater than 130 ("the gifted cutoff")?

Answer: We are looking for the fraction of people whose IQ is more than two standard deviations *above* the mean. This is the same as the probability that the standard Normal exceeds its mean by more than two standard deviations, which is $1 - \Phi(2) = 0.023$. Thus only about 2.3% of people have an IQ above 130.

Other properties of the Normal distribution will be proven later in the book. A particularly useful property is that the sum of two independent Normal distributions is Normally distributed.

Theorem 9.7 (Sum of two independent Normals) *Let $X \sim \text{Normal}(\mu_x, \sigma_x^2)$. Let $Y \sim \text{Normal}(\mu_y, \sigma_y^2)$. Assume $X \perp Y$. Let $W = X + Y$. Then*

$$W \sim \text{Normal}(\mu_x + \mu_y, \sigma_x^2 + \sigma_y^2).$$

Proof: This will be proven in Exercise 11.10 via Laplace transforms. ∎

9.4 Central Limit Theorem

Consider sampling the heights of 1000 individuals within the country and taking that average. The CLT, which we define soon, says that this average will tend to be Normally distributed. This would be true even if the distribution of individual heights were not Normal. Likewise, the CLT would apply if we took the average of a large number of Uniform random variables. It is this property that makes the Normal distribution so important! We now state this more formally.

Let $X_1, X_2, X_3, \ldots, X_n$ be independent and identically distributed random variables with some mean μ and variance σ^2. Note: We are *not* assuming that these are Normally distributed random variables. In fact we are not even assuming that they are necessarily continuous random variables – they may be discrete.

Let

$$S_n = X_1 + X_2 + \cdots + X_n. \tag{9.2}$$

Question: What are the mean and standard deviation of S_n?

Answer: E $[S_n] = n\mu$ and **Var**$(S_n) = n\sigma^2$. Thus **std**$(S_n) = \sigma\sqrt{n}$.

Let

$$Z_n = \frac{S_n - n\mu}{\sigma\sqrt{n}}.$$

Question: What are the mean and standard deviation of Z_n?

Answer: Z_n has mean 0 and standard deviation 1.

Theorem 9.8 (Central Limit Theorem (CLT)) *Let $X_1, X_2, \ldots, X_n$ be a sequence of i.i.d. random variables with common mean μ and finite variance σ^2, and define*

$$S_n = \sum_{i=1}^{n} X_i \quad and \quad Z_n = \frac{S_n - n\mu}{\sigma\sqrt{n}}.$$

Then the distribution of Z_n converges to the standard normal, Normal$(0, 1)$, as $n \to \infty$. That is,

$$\lim_{n\to\infty} \mathbf{P}\{Z_n \le z\} = \Phi(z) = \frac{1}{\sqrt{2\pi}} \int_{-\infty}^{z} e^{-x^2/2} dx$$

for every z.

Proof: Our proof uses Laplace transforms, so we defer it to Exercise 11.12. ∎

It should seem counter-intuitive to you that Z_n converges to a Normal in distribution, especially when the X_i's might be very skewed and not-at-all Normal themselves.

Question: Does the sum S_n also converge to a Normal?

Answer: This is a little trickier, but, for practical purposes, yes. Since S_n is a linear transformation of Z_n, then by the Linear Transformation Property, S_n gets closer and closer to a Normal distribution too. However, S_n is not well defined as $n \to \infty$, because S_n is getting closer and closer to Normal($n\mu, n\sigma^2$), which has infinite mean and variance as $n \to \infty$. There's another problem with looking at S_n. Suppose all the X_i's are integer-valued. Then S_n will also be integer-valued and hence not exactly Normal (although it will behave close to Normal for high n – see Exercise 9.6). For all these reasons, CLT involves Z_n rather than S_n.

Question: Does the average $A_n = \frac{1}{n} S_n$ converge to a Normal?

Answer: Yes! Applying the Linear Transformation Property to Z_n, we see that A_n gets closer and closer to a Normal with mean μ and variance $\frac{\sigma^2}{n}$.

The CLT is extremely general and explains many natural phenomena that result in Normal distributions. The fact that CLT applies to any sum of i.i.d. random variables allows us to prove that the Binomial(n, p) distribution, which is a sum of i.i.d. Bernoulli(p) random variables, can be approximated by a Normal distribution when n is sufficiently high. In Exercise 9.7 you will use a similar argument to explain why the Poisson(λ) distribution is well represented by a Normal distribution when λ is high.

In the next example, we illustrate how the CLT is used in practice.

Example 9.9 (Signal with noise)

Imagine that we are trying to transmit a signal. During the transmission, there are 100 sources independently making low noise. Each source produces an amount of noise that is Uniformly distributed between $a = -1$ and $b = 1$. If the total amount of noise is greater than 10 or less than -10, then it corrupts the signal. However, if the absolute value of the total amount of noise is under 10, then it is not a problem.

Question: What is the approximate probability that the absolute value of the total amount of noise from the 100 signals is less than 10?

Answer: Let X_i be the noise from source i. Observe that

$$\mu_{X_i} = 0$$

$$\sigma_{X_i}^2 = \frac{(b-a)^2}{12} = \frac{1}{3}$$

$$\sigma_{X_i} = \frac{1}{\sqrt{3}}.$$

Let $S_{100} = X_1 + X_2 + \cdots + X_{100}$.

$$\mathbf{P}\{-10 < S_{100} < 10\} = \mathbf{P}\left\{\frac{-10}{\sqrt{100/3}} < \frac{S_{100} - 0}{\sqrt{100/3}} < \frac{10}{\sqrt{100/3}}\right\}$$

$$\approx \mathbf{P}\left\{-\sqrt{3} < \text{Normal}(0,1) < \sqrt{3}\right\}$$

$$= 2\Phi\left(\sqrt{3}\right) - 1$$

$$\approx 0.91.$$

Hence the approximate probability of the signal getting corrupted is $< 10\%$. In practice, this CLT approximation is excellent, as we'll see in Chapter 18.

9.5 Exercises

9.1 **Practice with the $\Phi(\cdot)$ table**
Let $X \sim \text{Normal}(0, 1)$. Let $Y \sim \text{Normal}(10, 25)$. Using the table for $\Phi(\cdot)$ values given in the chapter, answer the following questions:
(a) What is $\mathbf{P}\{X > 0\}$?
(b) What is $\mathbf{P}\{-1 < X < 1.5\}$?
(c) What is $\mathbf{P}\{-2.5 < Y < 22.5\}$?

9.2 **Total work processed by server**
A server handles 300 jobs per day. Job sizes are i.i.d. and are Uniformly distributed between 1 second and 3 seconds. Let S denote the sum of the sizes of jobs handled by the server in a day. Approximately, what is $\mathbf{P}\{590 < S < 610\}$?

9.3 **Bytes at a server**
A server receives 100 messages a day. Message sizes (in bytes) are i.i.d. from distribution $\text{Exp}(\mu)$. Let S denote the total number of bytes received by the server. Approximately, what is $\mathbf{P}\left\{\frac{90}{\mu} < S < \frac{110}{\mu}\right\}$?

9.4 Estimating failure probability

Suppose that 10% of cars have engine light problems at some point in their lifetime. If a dealer sells 200 cars, what is the (approximate) probability that fewer than 5% of the cars she sells will eventually have engine light problems? Use the appropriate Normal distribution table. Express your answer as a decimal.

9.5 Linear Transformation of Exponential

Recall that the Normal distribution has a pretty Linear Transformation property. Does the Exponential distribution have this as well? Let $X \sim \text{Exp}(\mu)$. Let $Y = aX + b$, where a and b are positive constants. Is Y Exponentially distributed? Prove your answer.

9.6 Accuracy of the Central Limit Theorem

Bill Gater invites 1,000 friends to a dinner. Each is asked to make a contribution. The contributions are i.i.d. Poisson-distributed random variables with mean $1,000 each. Bill hopes to raise $1,000,000. Your job is to compute the probability that Bill raises $< \$999,000$.
(a) Compute this using the Normal approximation from this chapter.
(b) Now write an *exact* expression for this probability, and then use your calculator or small program to evaluate the expression.

9.7 Why a Poisson looks like a Normal

You may have noticed that the Poisson(λ) distribution looks very similar in shape to a Normal with mean λ and variance λ. This is particularly true for high λ. Use the CLT approximation to explain why this is, in the case where λ is a high integer. [Hint: The exercises on the Poisson distribution from Chapter 6 are useful here.]

9.8 Heuristic proof of Stirling's approximation

[Contributed by Ishani Santurkar] Stirling's approximation, Theorem 1.14, says that $n!$ grows in accordance with (9.3) for large n:

$$n! \sim \sqrt{2\pi n} \left(\frac{n}{e}\right)^n. \tag{9.3}$$

In this problem you will come up with a heuristic proof for this fact.
(a) Let $X \sim \text{Poisson}(n)$. What is $p_X(n)$?
(b) Now assume that n is large, and use the Normal approximation from Exercise 9.7 to write an alternative approximate expression for $p_X(n)$. Note that for a continuous r.v. Y we can't talk about $\mathbf{P}\{Y = i\}$, but we can write: $\mathbf{P}\{i < Y < i+1\} \approx f_Y(i) \cdot 1$.
(c) Equate (a) and (b) to get (9.3).

9.9 Fractional moments

Given the ugliness of the Normal distribution, I am happy to say that it never comes up in my research . . . until a few days ago! Here is the story: I had a r.v. $X \sim \text{Exp}(1)$ and I needed to compute $\mathbf{E}\left[X^{\frac{1}{2}}\right]$. Figure out why I needed a Normal distribution to do this and what answer I finally got. [Hint: Start by applying integration by parts. Then make the right change of variables. If you do it right, the standard Normal should pop out. Remember that the Exponential ranges from 0 to ∞, whereas the Normal ranges from $-\infty$ to ∞.]

9.10 Sampling from an unknown distribution

We want to understand some statistics (e.g., mean and variance) of the webpage load time distribution, X. To do that, we randomly choose n websites and measure their load times, $X_1, X_2, \ldots, X_n$. We assume that the X_i's are i.i.d. samples of X, where $X_i \sim X$. Our goal is to use these samples to estimate X's mean, $\mu = \mathbf{E}[X]$, and X's variance, $\sigma^2 = \mathbf{Var}(X)$. Our *sample mean* $\overline{X}$ is defined as

$$\overline{X} \equiv \frac{1}{n} \sum_{i=1}^{n} X_i.$$

Our *sample variance* is defined as

$$S^2 \equiv \frac{1}{(n-1)} \sum_{i=1}^{n} (X_i - \overline{X})^2.$$

(a) If the expectation of the sample mean is the same as the actual mean, that is if $\mathbf{E}\left[\overline{X}\right] = \mu$, then $\overline{X}$ is called an *unbiased estimator of the mean* of the sampling distribution. Prove that $\overline{X}$ is an unbiased estimator of the mean.

(b) If the expectation of the sample variance is the same as the actual variance, that is, if $\mathbf{E}\left[S^2\right] = \sigma^2$, then S^2 is called an *unbiased estimator of the variance* of the sampling distribution. Prove that S^2 is an unbiased estimator of the variance.

It will help to follow these steps:

(i) Start by expressing $(n-1)S^2 = \sum_{i=1}^{n} \left((X_i - \mu) + (\mu - \overline{X})\right)^2$.

(ii) From (i), show that: $(n-1)S^2 = \sum_{i=1}^{n} (X_i - \mu)^2 - n(\mu - \overline{X})^2$.

(iii) Take expectations of both sides of (ii).

10 Heavy Tails: The Distributions of Computing

We have studied several common continuous distributions: the Uniform, the Exponential, and the Normal. However, if we turn to computer science quantities, such as file sizes, job CPU requirements, IP flow times, and so on, we find that none of these are well represented by the continuous distributions that we've studied so far. To understand the type of distributions that come up in computer science, it's useful to start with a story. This chapter is a story of my own experience in studying UNIX jobs in the mid-1990s, as a PhD student at U.C. Berkeley. Results of this research are detailed in [37, 38]. The story serves as both an introduction to empirical measurements of computer workloads and as a case study of how a deeper understanding of computer workloads can inform computer system design. We end with results from 2020 measurements of workloads at Google from [72].

10.1 Tales of Tails

Back in the early 1990s, I was a PhD student happily studying computer science theory. Like many others in the theory area, I had avoided taking my graduate operating systems requirement for as long as possible. When I finally got up the guts to walk into the graduate operating systems class, I looked up at the blackboard (Figure 10.1) and thought, "Hmm ... maybe this isn't going to be so bad."

Figure 10.1 *The blackboard in my operating systems class.*

Sadly the professor wasn't referring to complexity theory. Instead, he was referring to migration for the purpose of CPU load balancing in a Network of Workstations – at U.C. Berkeley this project was coined the "N.O.W. project" [4]. The idea in *CPU load balancing* is that CPU-bound jobs (processes) might benefit from being *migrated* from a heavily loaded workstation to a more lightly loaded workstation (Figure 10.2).

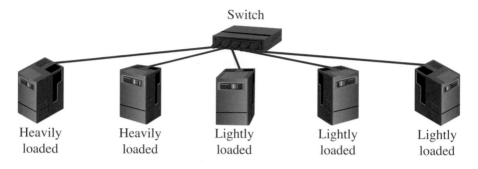

Switch

| Heavily loaded | Heavily loaded | Lightly loaded | Lightly loaded | Lightly loaded |

Figure 10.2 *"Network of Workstations." CPU load balancing migrates jobs from heavily loaded workstations to lightly loaded ones.*

CPU load balancing is still important in today's networks of servers. It is not free, however: Migration can be expensive if the job has a lot of "state" that has to be migrated with it (e.g., lots of open files associated with the job), as is common for jobs that have been running for a while. A job that has accrued a lot of state might not be worth migrating.

There are two types of migration used in load balancing techniques:

NP – non-preemptive migration This is migration of newborn jobs only – also called *initial placement* or *remote execution*, where you don't migrate a job once it has started running.

P – preemptive migration This is migration of jobs that are already active (running) – also referred to as *active process migration*.

In the mid-1990s it was generally accepted that migrating active processes was a bad idea, because of their high migration cost. Except for one or two experimental operating systems, like MOSIX [6], people only migrated newborn jobs.

First, some important terminology used in CPU load balancing:

> **Definition 10.1** *A job's* **size** *(a.k.a.* **lifetime***) refers to the job's total CPU requirement (measured in seconds or CPU cycles). A job's* **age** *refers to its total CPU usage thus far (also measured in seconds or CPU cycles). A job's* **remaining size** *(a.k.a.* **remaining lifetime***) refers to its remaining CPU requirement.*

What we really want to know is a job's remaining lifetime. If the job has a high remaining CPU requirement, then it may pay to migrate the job, even if it has accumulated a lot of state, because the job will get to spend its long remaining lifetime on a lightly loaded machine. Sadly, we do not know a job's remaining lifetime, just its current CPU age.

What we're interested in is the **tail** of the job size, that is, $\mathbf{P}\{\text{Size} > x\}$. More specifically, we want to understand the conditional remaining lifetime given an age a:

$$\mathbf{P}\{\text{Size} > x + a \mid \text{Size} > a\}.$$

Question: Suppose we have two jobs, one with age 2 seconds and the other with age 100 seconds, as in Figure 10.3. Which job is likely to have greater remaining lifetime?

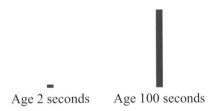

Age 2 seconds   Age 100 seconds

Figure 10.3 *Which job has greater remaining lifetime?*

Answer: We'll find out soon ...

10.2 Increasing versus Decreasing Failure Rate

The obvious question is, then, "How are UNIX job CPU lifetimes distributed?"

The common wisdom at the time, backed up by many research papers, suggested that UNIX job CPU lifetimes were *Exponentially distributed.*

Question: If UNIX job lifetimes are Exponentially distributed, what does that tell us about the question in Figure 10.3?

Answer: Recall from Section 7.1 that if Size is Exponentially distributed, then, by the memoryless property,

$$\mathbf{P}\{\text{Size} > x + a \mid \text{Size} > a\} = \mathbf{P}\{\text{Size} > x\}.$$

Thus the conditional remaining lifetime is independent of the current age. This says that newborn jobs and older (active) jobs have the *same* expected remaining lifetime. Hence, since newborn jobs are much cheaper to migrate, it makes sense to favor migrating the newborn jobs and ignore the older jobs (NP beats P!).

One can imagine, however, that $\mathbf{P}\{\text{Size} > x + a \mid \text{Size} > a\}$ might *not* be independent of a but rather might either decrease with a or might increase with a.

If $\mathbf{P}\{\text{Size} > x + a \mid \text{Size} > a\}$ decreases with a, we call that **increasing failure rate** or **increasing hazard rate**. This is not a typo! The term "failure rate" refers to the probability that the job *terminates*. So we're saying that the older a job is, the sooner it will terminate, that is, the lower its probability of running an additional x seconds. Likewise, if $\mathbf{P}\{\text{Size} > x + a \mid \text{Size} > a\}$ increases with a, we say that the Size has **decreasing failure rate** or **decreasing hazard rate**.

Colloquially, increasing failure rate says, "the older you are, the sooner you'll die," while decreasing failure rate says "the older you are, the longer you'll live."

Question: What are some real-world examples of random variables with increasing failure rate?

Answer: Here are a few:

- the lifetime of a car;
- the lifetime of a washing machine;
- the lifetime of a person.

Actually, almost anything you think of will have increasing failure rate. Aging leads to failing (ending) sooner.

Question: What are some real-world examples of random variables with decreasing failure rate?

Answer: This is a lot harder to think about because we're looking for an example where older is better in the sense of lasting longer. Here are some examples:

- The lifetime of a friendship. Generally, the longer you've been friends with someone, the longer you're likely to continue to be friends.
- The time you've lived in your home. If you've lived in your home for many years, you're more likely to continue to stay there.

To make the concept of failure rate more precise, we define the failure rate function.

> **Definition 10.2** *Given a continuous random variable (r.v.) X with probability density function (p.d.f.) $f_X(t)$ and tail $\overline{F}_X(t) = \mathbf{P}\{X > t\}$, the* **failure rate function***, $r_X(t)$, for X is:*
>
> $$r_X(t) \equiv \frac{f_X(t)}{\overline{F}_X(t)}.$$

Question: $r_X(t)$ looks like a conditional density function. What is that density?

Answer: If we write $\overline{F}_X(t) = \mathbf{P}\{X > t\} = \mathbf{P}\{X \geq t\}$, then we can see that:

$$r_X(t) = \frac{f_X(t)}{\overline{F}_X(t)} = f_{X|X \geq t}(t).$$

This is the density that $X = t$ given that $X \geq t$.

To further interpret $r_X(t)$, consider the probability that a t-year-old item will fail during the next dt seconds:

$$\mathbf{P}\{X \in (t, t + dt) \mid X > t\} = \frac{\mathbf{P}\{X \in (t, t + dt)\}}{\mathbf{P}\{X > t\}}$$

$$\approx \frac{f_X(t) \cdot dt}{\overline{F}_X(t)}$$

$$= r_X(t) \cdot dt.$$

Thus, $r_X(t)$ represents the *instantaneous failure rate* of a t-year-old item, whose lifetime distribution is X.

> **Definition 10.3** *If $r_X(t)$ is strictly decreasing in t, we say that X has* **decreasing failure rate***; if $r_X(t)$ is strictly increasing in t, we say that X has* **increasing failure rate***.*

In general, $r_X(t)$ is not necessarily going to always decrease with t or increase with t; it's common that $r_X(t)$ is decreasing for some t and increasing for others.

Question: Suppose $r_X(t)$ is constant. What do you know about X?

Answer: In Exercise 10.2, we prove that X *must* be Exponentially distributed.

Before we leave our discussion of the Exponential distribution, let's recall the notion of the squared coefficient of variation of a r.v. X. By Definition 5.6, this is

$$C_X^2 = \frac{\mathbf{Var}(X)}{\mathbf{E}[X]^2}$$

and represents the normalized variance. It is the metric of choice for systems measurements because it is scale invariant.

Question: What is C_X^2, when $X \sim \mathrm{Exp}(\lambda)$?

Answer: 1.

10.3 UNIX Process Lifetime Measurements

If UNIX process lifetimes (sizes) are Exponentially distributed, then there is no benefit to active process migration: all jobs have the remaining lifetime distribution, regardless of their age.

Refusing to believe that there were no benefits to active process migration, I decided to measure the distribution of job lifetimes. I collected the CPU lifetimes of millions of UNIX jobs on a wide range of different machines, including instructional, research, and administrative machines, over the course of many months, including only jobs whose size exceeded 1 second. Figure 10.4 shows the tail of my measured distribution.

At first glance Figure 10.4 looks like an Exponential distribution,

$$\overline{F}_{\mathrm{Size}}(x) = e^{-\lambda x}.$$

But on closer examination you can see that it's not Exponential.

Question: How can you tell that job sizes are *not* Exponentially distributed?

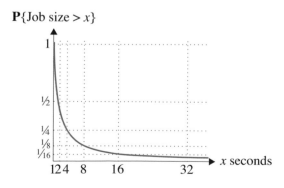

Figure 10.4 *Plot of measured distribution,* $\overline{F}_X(x) = \mathbf{P}\{Job\ size > x\}$, *where $x \geq 1$.*

Answer: For an Exponential distribution, the fraction of jobs remaining should drop by a constant factor with each unit increase in x (constant failure rate). In Figure 10.4, we see that the fraction of jobs remaining decreases by a slower and slower rate as we increase x (decreasing failure rate). In fact, looking at the graph, we see that if we start with jobs of CPU age 1 second, half of them make it to 2 seconds. Of those that make it to 2 seconds, half of those make it to 4 seconds. Of those that make it to 4 seconds, half of those make it to 8 seconds, and so on.

To see the distribution more easily it helps to view it on a log-log plot, as shown in Figure 10.5. The bumpy line shows the data, and the straight line is the best curve-fit. From Figure 10.5 it is apparent that the tail of the distribution of job lifetimes decays like $\frac{1}{x}$. That is, the distribution is well approximated by

$$\mathbf{P}\{\text{Size} > x\} = \frac{1}{x}, \qquad x \geq 1.$$

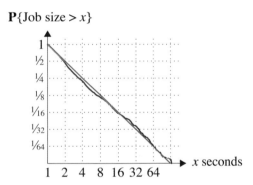

Figure 10.5 *Log-log plot of measured distribution,* $\overline{F}_X(x) = \mathbf{P}\{\textit{Job size} > x\}$, $x \geq 1$.

10.4 Properties of the Pareto Distribution

It turns out that the distribution that I had measured has a name in economic theory. It is called the Pareto distribution, or "power-law distribution," and is named after Vilfredo Pareto, who was an economist in the early 1900s.

Definition 10.4 *We say that X follows a* **Pareto distribution** *with parameter α, written X $\sim$ Pareto(α), if*

$$\overline{F}_X(x) = \mathbf{P}\{X > x\} = x^{-\alpha}, \qquad \textit{for } x \geq 1,$$

where $0 < \alpha < 2$.

Question: So job sizes are distributed as Pareto($\alpha = 1$). What does this say about **E** [Size]? Also, does the job size distribution exhibit increasing failure rate, or decreasing failure rate, or neither?

Answer:

It's easy to see that **E** [Size] $= \infty$ and that the failure rate is decreasing. We derive this below for general $0 < \alpha < 2$.

Let $X \sim$ Pareto(α). Then:

$$\overline{F}_X(x) = \mathbf{P}\{X > x\} = x^{-\alpha}, \qquad x \geq 1$$

$$\Rightarrow F_X(x) = \mathbf{P}\{X < x\} = 1 - x^{-\alpha}, \qquad x \geq 1$$

$$\Rightarrow f_X(x) = \frac{dF_X(x)}{dx} = \alpha x^{-\alpha-1}, \qquad x \geq 1$$

$$\Rightarrow r_X(x) = \frac{f_X(x)}{\overline{F}_X(x)} = \frac{\alpha x^{-\alpha-1}}{x^{-\alpha}} = \frac{\alpha}{x}, \qquad x \geq 1.$$

Because $r_X(x) = \frac{\alpha}{x}$ decreases with x, the Pareto distribution has decreasing failure rate (DFR). Thus the older a job is (the more CPU it has used up so far), the greater its probability of using another second of CPU.

The Pareto($\alpha = 1$) distribution has an interesting *doubling property*.

Question: Given that Job size $\sim$ Pareto($\alpha = 1$), what is the probability that a job of age $t > 1$ survives to age $\geq 2t$?

Answer:

$$\mathbf{P}\{\text{Size} > 2t \mid \text{Size} \geq t\} = \frac{\frac{1}{2t}}{\frac{1}{t}} = \frac{1}{2}.$$

Question: For $X \sim$ Pareto(α), with $0 < \alpha \leq 1$, what are the moments of X?

Answer: The calculations are straightforward, by integration over the density function. It is easy to see that all moments are infinite.

Question: For $X \sim$ Pareto(α), with $1 < \alpha < 2$, what are the moments of X?

Answer: The mean of X is now finite. Higher moments are still infinite.

But something doesn't seem right here. How can our distribution of job sizes have infinite mean? Although the data fits a Pareto($\alpha = 1$) distribution very well, the moments of job size are still finite. To see this we need to introduce the Bounded-Pareto distribution.

10.5 The Bounded-Pareto Distribution

When fitting a curve to *measured (empirical) data*, the data has a *minimum* job lifetime, k, and a *maximum* job lifetime, p. In particular, the measured data has *finite* moments, not infinite ones. To model the empirical data, we therefore want a distribution with a Pareto shape, but that has been truncated between k and p. We refer to such a distribution as a *Bounded-Pareto* distribution.

> **Definition 10.5** *The* **Bounded-Pareto**(k, p, α) *distribution has density function*
> $$f(x) = \alpha x^{-\alpha-1} \cdot \frac{k^\alpha}{1 - \left(\frac{k}{p}\right)^\alpha},$$
> *for $k \le x \le p$ and $0 < \alpha < 2$.*

The factor $\frac{k^\alpha}{1-(k/p)^\alpha}$ in Definition 10.5 is a normalization factor needed to make the integral of the density function between k and p come out to 1. For the Bounded-Pareto distribution, obviously all of the moments are finite.

For the UNIX job sizes that I measured, the squared coefficient of variation, C^2, was finite, ranging between $C^2 = 25$ and $C^2 = 49$, which was considered extremely high in the 1990s.

10.6 Heavy Tails

The following are three properties of the Pareto distribution:

1. **Decreasing failure rate (DFR)** – The more CPU you have used so far, the more you will continue to use.
2. **Infinite variance**
3. **"Heavy-tail property"** – A minuscule fraction of the very largest jobs comprise 50% of the total system load. (Note that this is much more biased than the often quoted 80–20 rule.)

The "heavy-tail property" comes up in many other settings. For example, in economics, when studying people's wealth, it turns out that the richest 1% of all people have more money between them than all the remaining 99% of us combined. The heavy-tailed property is often referred to as "a few big elephants (big jobs) and many, many mice (little jobs)," as illustrated in Figure 10.6. For comparison, in an Exponential distribution, the largest 1% of the jobs comprise only about 5% of the total demand.

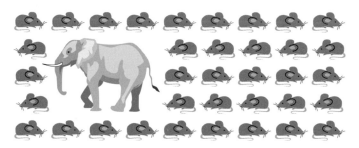

Figure 10.6 *Heavy-tailed property: "Elephants and mice."*

The parameter α can be interpreted as a measure of the variability of the distribution and the heavy-tailedness: $\alpha \to 0$ yields the most variable and most heavy-tailed distribution, whereas $\alpha \to 2$ yields the least variable, and least heavy-tailed distribution. These properties are explored in more depth in the exercises.

These properties largely hold for the Bounded-Pareto distribution as well as the Pareto, although clearly the Bounded-Pareto has finite moments. Also the Bounded-Pareto cannot have strict DFR because there is an upper bound on job size.

10.7 The Benefits of Active Process Migration

Let's return to the original question of CPU load balancing.

Question: What does the DFR property of the Pareto distribution tell us about whether it pays to migrate older jobs?

Answer: DFR says that the older jobs have higher expected remaining lifetimes. This leads us to think that it may pay to migrate *older* jobs. Although an old job may have a high migration cost because it has accumulated a lot of state (memory), if the job is really old then it has a high probability of using a lot more CPU in the future. This means that the cost of migration can be amortized over a very long lifetime, as the job gets to spend its long remaining lifetime running on a lightly loaded machine.

Question: What does the heavy-tail property of the Pareto distribution tell us?

Answer: By the heavy-tail property, it is only necessary to migrate the 1% biggest jobs, because they contain most of the work [38].

10.8 From the 1990s to the 2020s

At this point you might be wondering whether these Pareto distributions still apply to jobs today. To answer this, we look at the jobs scheduled by the Borg scheduler [73], which serves jobs in Google data centers.

Question: How do you imagine that jobs look different today than they did in the 1990s?

Answer: There are many differences, but an important one is that back in the 1990s a job ran on a single CPU. The job's *size* was the time it needed on a single CPU. By contrast, the Google jobs today are all parallel jobs. We can think of a job as holding onto a certain number of processors (CPUs) for an amount of time. The **size of a job** is then measured in CPU-hours (number of CPUs occupied times the number of hours).

Jobs today also often utilize a lot of memory (think about machine learning jobs). We can also view the **size of a job** as measured in memory-unit-hours (number of memory units times hours held).

Question: If you had to guess, would you guess that the distribution of compute usage today is more variable or less variable than in the 1990s? Would you guess that the distribution is more heavy-tailed or less heavy-tailed than in the 1990s?

Answer: The answer to both is "more," but the degree to which the answer is "more" is quite shocking.

Figure 10.7(a) shows the distribution of compute usage, and Figure 10.7(b) shows the distribution of memory usage [72]. Because Google doesn't like to reveal exact numbers, it uses normalized units in expressing compute and memory usage. Thus, per-job compute usage is expressed in units of NCU-hours (normalized CPU times hours) and per-job memory usage is expressed in units of NMU-hours (normalized memory units times hours). Note that a 100 NCU-hour job might have consumed 100 machines for 1 hour, or 5 machines for 20 hours, or various other combinations.

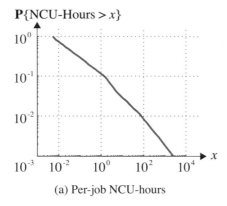

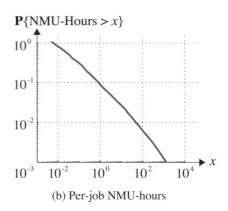

Figure 10.7 *Tail of resource usage based on a trace of millions of jobs run at Google in May 2019 [72, 77]. NCU-hours denotes normalized CPU-hours used. NMU-hours denotes normalized memory-unit-hours used.*

The distribution for compute usage at Google's data centers fits a Pareto($\alpha = 0.69$) distribution, which is much more heavy-tailed than what we saw in the 1990s measurements. We find that, while the mean NCU-hours used per job is about 1.2, the variance is 33,300, which means that the squared coefficient of variation is

$$C^2 = \frac{\text{variance}}{\text{mean}^2} = 23,000,$$

which is huge! The heavy-tailed property is also much more extreme than what we saw in the 1990s: The largest (most compute-intensive) 1% of jobs comprise about 99% of the compute load.

Memory usage follows much the same patterns as compute usage, obeying a Pareto($\alpha = 0.72$) distribution with astronomical variability: $C^2 \approx 43,000$. Again we see an extremely strong heavy-tailed property, with the top 1% of jobs comprising 99% of the total memory usage. Memory and compute usage are also correlated.

10.9 Pareto Distributions Are Everywhere

It is not just computing jobs that fit a heavy-tailed Pareto distribution. Pareto job size distributions are everywhere in computer science and in nature! Here are some more practical and interesting stories:

Web file size: Around 1996–1998, Mark Crovella, Azer Bestavros, and Paul Barford at Boston University were measuring the sizes of files on websites. They found that these file sizes obeyed a Pareto distribution with $\alpha \approx 1.1$. They also found similar results for the sizes of files requested from websites. Their SURGE web workload generator is based on these findings [7, 18, 19].

Internet node degrees: Around the same time, the three Faloutsos brothers were observing a similar distribution when looking at the Internet topology. They observed, for example, that most nodes have low out-degree, but a very few nodes have very high out-degree, and the distribution of the degrees follows a Pareto distribution. Their beautiful 1999 paper won the Sigcomm Test of Time award [25].

IP flow durations: In 1999, Jennifer Rexford, Anees Shaikh, and Kang Shin at AT&T were working on routing IP flows to create better load balancing. Their goal was to reroute only 1% of the IP flows. Would that be enough? Fortunately, their measurements showed that the number of packets in IP flows follows a heavy-tailed Pareto distribution. Consequently, the 1% largest IP flows (those with the most packets) contain about 50% of the bytes in all flows. By rerouting only 1% of the flows, they were able to redistribute half the load. Their paper appeared in Sigcomm 99 [69] and generated a large group of follow-up papers dealing with sampling methods for how to detect which flows are large, based on using the DFR property and the knowledge of how many packets the flow has sent so far.

Implications for designing scheduling policies: Around this same time, my students and I, in collaboration with Mark Crovella at Boston University, started a project called SYNC (Scheduling Your Network Connections). The goal was to improve the performance of web servers by changing the order in which they scheduled their jobs to favor requests for small files over requests for large files. Clearly favoring requests for small files over large ones would decrease mean response time. However, people had not tried this in the past because they were afraid that the requests for large files would "starve" or at least be treated unfairly compared to requests for small files. Using the heavy-tailed property of web file sizes, we were able to prove analytically and in implementation that this fear is unfounded for the distribution of web files. The crux of the argument is that, although short requests do go ahead of long requests, all those short requests together make up very little load (more than half the load is in the top 1% of long requests) and hence do not interfere noticeably with the long requests [5, 17, 39]. In 2004, Ernst Biersack, Idris Rai, and Guillaume Urvoy-Keller extended the SYNC results to TCP flow scheduling by exploiting the DFR property of the Pareto distribution to discern which flows have short remaining duration [58, 59].

Wireless session times, phone call durations, wealth, natural disasters: There are many, many more examples of the Pareto distribution in measured distributions involving jobs created by humans. Wireless session times have been shown to follow a Pareto distribution [8]. Phone call durations have been shown to follow a distribution similar to a Pareto. Human wealth follows a Pareto distribution. Natural phenomena too follow Pareto distributions. For example, John Doyle at Caltech has shown that the damage caused by forest fires follows a Pareto distribution, with most forest fires causing little damage, but the largest few forest fires causing the majority of the damage. The same property holds for earthquakes and other natural disasters.

Given the prevalence of the Pareto distribution, there has been a great deal of research interest in **why** the Pareto distribution comes up everywhere. Ideally, we would like to prove something similar in nature to the Central Limit Theorem (CLT), which explains the ubiquity of the Normal distribution, but this time for the Pareto distribution. If you recall, CLT assumed that we are taking the average of many i.i.d. random variables, each with *finite* variance. Suppose that we're taking the average of i.i.d. random variables, where these have infinite variance. Does that lead to a different distribution than a Normal? Does it lead to a Pareto? If you are interested in this question, and, more generally in the question of why the Pareto distribution comes up, I recommend a book, *The Fundamentals of Heavy Tails* [55].

10.10 Summary Table for Continuous Distributions

At this point, we have seen several continuous distributions. Just as we summarized the mean and variance of our discrete distributions in Table 5.1, it is worth taking the time to do the same for the continuous distributions. Table 10.1 summarizes the common continuous distributions.

10.11 Exercises

10.1 **How variable is a Uniform distribution really?**
The Uniform distribution feels highly variable, particularly when its endpoints are far apart. Consider $X \sim \text{Uniform}(0, b)$, and assume that b is large. What is C_X^2 as a function of b? Do you still think the Uniform is highly variable?

10.2 **Failure rate**
Let X be a continuous random variable with p.d.f. $f_X(t), t \geq 0$ and c.d.f.

Distribution	p.d.f. $f_X(x)$	Mean	Variance
Exp(λ)	$f_X(x) = \lambda e^{-\lambda x}, x \geq 0$	$\frac{1}{\lambda}$	$\frac{1}{\lambda^2}$
Uniform(a, b)	$f_X(x) = \frac{1}{b-a}$, if $a \leq x \leq b$	$\frac{b+a}{2}$	$\frac{(b-a)^2}{12}$
Pareto(α), $0 < \alpha < 2$	$f_X(x) = \alpha x^{-\alpha-1}$, if $x > 1$	$\begin{cases} \infty & \text{if } \alpha \leq 1 \\ \frac{\alpha}{\alpha-1} & \text{if } \alpha > 1 \end{cases}$	∞
Normal(μ, σ^2)	$f_X(x) = \frac{1}{\sqrt{2\pi}\sigma}e^{-\frac{1}{2}\left(\frac{x-\mu}{\sigma}\right)^2}$, $-\infty < x < \infty$	μ	σ^2

Table 10.1 *Common continuous distributions.*

$F_X(t) = \mathbf{P}\{X < t\}$. We define the failure rate of X to be $r_X(t)$, where

$$r_X(t) \equiv \frac{f_X(t)}{\overline{F}_X(t)}.$$

Thus, $r_X(t)dt$ represents the probability that a t-year-old item will fail in the next dt seconds.

(a) Prove that for the Exponential distribution the failure rate is a constant.

(b) Prove that the Exponential distribution is the only non-negative distribution with constant failure rate.

10.3 **Modeling distributions with low variability: the Erlang-k**

The Erlang-k distribution is often used to model distributions, X, where $0 < C_X^2 < 1$. An Erlang-k distribution is a sum of k Exponentially distributed "stages." Formally, we say that $X \sim$ Erlang-$k(\mu)$ if

$$X = X_1 + X_2 + \cdots + X_k,$$

where the X_i's are i.i.d., with $X_i \sim \text{Exp}(k\mu)$.

(a) What is $\mathbf{E}[X]$?

(b) What is $\mathbf{Var}(X)$?

(c) What is C_X^2?

(d) What happens to X as $k \to \infty$?

10.4 **Hyperexponential distribution and DFR**

We say that X follows a two-phase **Hyperexponential** distribution (written H_2) if:

$$X \sim \begin{cases} \text{Exp}(\mu_1) & \text{w/prob } p \\ \text{Exp}(\mu_2) & \text{w/prob } 1-p \end{cases},$$

where $\mu_1 \neq \mu_2$.

(a) Prove that the Hyperexponential distribution has DFR. [Hint: Take the derivative of the failure rate.]

(b) Explain intuitively why the Hyperexponential has DFR.

10.5 Squared coefficient of variation for the Hyperexponential
Consider three different distributions:

(i.) $X \sim \text{Exp}(\mu = 1)$

(ii.) $X \sim \text{Exp}(\mu = .01)$

(iii.)

$$X \sim \begin{cases} \text{Exp}(1) & \text{w/prob. } 0.99 \\ \text{Exp}(\mu = 0.01) & \text{w/prob. } 0.01 \end{cases}.$$

For each distribution:

(a) What is $\mathbf{E}[X]$?

(b) What is $\mathbf{Var}(X)$?

(c) What is C_X^2?

10.6 Why the Hyperexponential is good for modeling high variability
The Hyperexponential is good at modeling high-variability distributions. To gain some intuition for why this is true, let us analyze the simple case of a *Degenerate Hyperexponential* distribution, where one of the phases is identically zero:

$$X \sim \begin{cases} \text{Exp}(p\mu) & \text{w/prob } p \\ 0 & \text{w/prob } 1 - p \end{cases}.$$

(a) What is $\mathbf{E}[X]$?

(b) What is C_X^2?

(c) What values of C_X^2 are possible?

10.7 Bounded-Pareto with negative parameter
A Pareto(α) distribution is defined with $0 < \alpha < 2$. But what happens if you set $\alpha = -1$? Let $X \sim \text{BoundedPareto}(k, p, \alpha)$, where $\alpha = -1$. What is the density function $f_X(x)$? What does this tell you about the distribution of X?

10.8 The heavy-tail property
We explore three distributions for job size, all with mean $3,000$:

(a) Exponential distribution with rate $\frac{1}{3,000}$.

(b) BoundedPareto($k = 0.0009, p = 10^{10}, \alpha = 0.5$).

(c) BoundedPareto($k = 332.067, p = 10^{10}, \alpha = 1.1$).

In each case, compute the fraction of load, q, made up by just the top (largest) 1% of all jobs. For a non-negative job size distribution, X, with density $f_X(\cdot)$,

$$q = \frac{\int_{[t \text{ in top } 1\%]} t f_X(t) dt}{\int_0^\infty t f_X(t) dt}.$$

Also report the size cutoff, x, defining the top 1% of jobs. It may help to use a symbolic math package to do this calculation.

11 Laplace Transforms

In Chapter 6, we covered a type of generating function known as the z-transform, which is particularly well suited to discrete, integer-valued, random variables. In this chapter, we will introduce a new type of generating function, called the Laplace transform, which is particularly well suited to common continuous random variables.

11.1 Motivating Example

We start with a motivating example.

Question: Let $X \sim \text{Exp}(\lambda)$. How can we derive $\mathbf{E}\left[X^3\right]$?

Answer: By definition,

$$\mathbf{E}\left[X^3\right] = \int_0^\infty t^3 \lambda e^{-\lambda t}\, dt.$$

While this is doable, it requires applying integration by parts many times – enough to guarantee that our answer will be wrong. In this chapter, we will see how Laplace transforms can be used to quickly yield the kth moment of $X \sim \text{Exp}(\lambda)$, for any k.

11.2 The Transform as an Onion

As in the case of the z-transform, we can think of the Laplace transform of a random variable (r.v.) as an onion, where the onion is an expression that contains all the moments of the r.v. The Laplace onion (Figure 11.1) looks different than the z-transform onion (Figure 6.1), but the basic point is the same: higher moments are stored deeper inside the onion and thus more peeling (tears) are required to get to them.

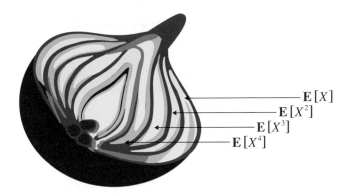

Figure 11.1 *The Laplace transform onion.*

Definition 11.1 *The* **Laplace transform**, $L_f(s)$, *of a continuous function,* $f(t), t \geq 0$, *is defined as*

$$L_f(s) = \int_0^\infty e^{-st} f(t)dt.$$

Observe that the Laplace transform is a function of s. Here s should be thought of as a placeholder that keeps the layers of the onion separate, similar to the function of z in the z-transform.

When we speak of the Laplace transform of a continuous r.v. X, we are referring to the Laplace transform of the probability density function (p.d.f.), $f_X(t)$, associated with X.

Definition 11.2 *Let X be a non-negative continuous r.v. with p.d.f.* $f_X(t)$. *Then the* **Laplace transform** *of X is denoted by* $\widetilde{X}(s)$, *where*

$$\widetilde{X}(s) = L_{f_X}(s) = \int_0^\infty e^{-st} f_X(t)dt = \mathbf{E}\left[e^{-sX}\right].$$

Throughout, we will imagine that s is a constant where $s \geq 0$.

Question: What is $\widetilde{X}(0)$?

Theorem 11.3 *For all continuous random variables, X,*
$$\widetilde{X}(0) = 1.$$

Proof:

$$\widetilde{X}(0) = \mathbf{E}\left[e^{-0 \cdot X}\right] = 1. \qquad \blacksquare$$

11.3 Creating the Transform: Onion Building

The Laplace transform is defined so as to be really easy to compute for all the commonly used continuous random variables. Below are some examples.

Example 11.4 *Derive the Laplace transform of* $X \sim Exp(\lambda)$:

$$\widetilde{X}(s) = \int_0^\infty e^{-st} \lambda e^{-\lambda t} \, dt = \lambda \int_0^\infty e^{-(\lambda+s)t} \, dt = \frac{\lambda}{\lambda + s}.$$

Example 11.5 *Derive the Laplace transform of* $X = a$, *where a is some constant:*

$$\widetilde{X}(s) = e^{-sa}.$$

Example 11.6 *Derive the Laplace transform of* $X \sim Uniform(a, b)$, $a, b \geq 0$:

$$\widetilde{X}(s) = \int_0^\infty e^{-st} f_X(t) dt$$

$$= \int_a^b e^{-st} \frac{1}{b-a} dt$$

$$= \left(\frac{-e^{-sb}}{s} + \frac{e^{-sa}}{s} \right) \frac{1}{b-a}$$

$$= \frac{e^{-sa} - e^{-sb}}{s(b-a)}.$$

Question: How do we know that the Laplace transform converges?

> **Theorem 11.7 (Convergence of Laplace transform)** $\widetilde{X}(s)$ *is bounded for any non-negative continuous r.v. X, assuming* $s \geq 0$.

Proof: Observe that
$$e^{-t} \leq 1,$$
for all non-negative values of t. Since $s \geq 0$, it follows that
$$e^{-st} = \left(e^{-t} \right)^s \leq 1.$$
Thus:
$$\widetilde{X}(s) = \int_0^\infty e^{-st} f_X(t) dt \leq \int_0^\infty 1 \cdot f_X(t) dt = 1. \qquad \blacksquare$$

Question: Why don't we use the z-transform for continuous random variables?

Answer: We could, in theory. It just looks uglier. Consider, for example, the z-transform of $X \sim Exp(\lambda)$:

$$\widehat{X}(z) = \mathbf{E}\left[z^X\right] = \int_{t=0}^{\infty} z^t \cdot \lambda e^{-\lambda t}\, dt.$$

This doesn't look fun to integrate! However, it can be done, if we first express z^t as $e^{t \ln z}$. Try it!

11.4 Getting Moments: Onion Peeling

Once we have created the onion corresponding to r.v., X, we can "peel its layers" to extract the moments of X.

Theorem 11.8 (Onion peeling) *Let X be a non-negative, continuous r.v. with p.d.f. $f_X(t)$, $t \geq 0$. Then:*

$$\left.\widetilde{X}'(s)\right|_{s=0} = -\mathbf{E}[X]$$

$$\left.\widetilde{X}''(s)\right|_{s=0} = \mathbf{E}\left[X^2\right]$$

$$\left.\widetilde{X}'''(s)\right|_{s=0} = -\mathbf{E}\left[X^3\right]$$

$$\left.\widetilde{X}''''(s)\right|_{s=0} = \mathbf{E}\left[X^4\right]$$

$$\vdots$$

Note: If the above moments are not defined at $s = 0$, one can instead consider the limit as $s \to 0$.

Example 11.9 (Higher moments of Exponential) *Derive the kth moment of $X \sim Exp(\lambda)$:*

$$\widetilde{X}(s) = \frac{\lambda}{\lambda + s} = \lambda(\lambda + s)^{-1}$$

$$\widetilde{X}'(s) = -\lambda(\lambda + s)^{-2} \qquad \Longrightarrow \qquad \mathbf{E}[X] = \frac{1}{\lambda}$$

$$\widetilde{X}''(s) = 2\lambda(\lambda + s)^{-3} \qquad \Longrightarrow \qquad \mathbf{E}\left[X^2\right] = \frac{2}{\lambda^2}$$

$$\widetilde{X}'''(s) = -3!\lambda(\lambda + s)^{-4} \qquad \Longrightarrow \qquad \mathbf{E}\left[X^3\right] = \frac{3!}{\lambda^3}$$

We can show via induction that:

$$\mathbf{E}\left[X^k\right] = \frac{k!}{\lambda^k}.$$

Proof: [Theorem 11.8] Below we provide a sketch of the proof argument. A more compact version of this proof is given in Exercise 11.3. However, for now we choose to write it out this way so that you can visualize exactly how the moments "pop" out of the transform when it's differentiated.

We start with the Taylor series expansion of e^{-st}:

$$e^{-st} = 1 - (st) + \frac{(st)^2}{2!} - \frac{(st)^3}{3!} + \frac{(st)^4}{4!} - \cdots$$

$$e^{-st}f(t) = f(t) - (st)f(t) + \frac{(st)^2}{2!}f(t) - \frac{(st)^3}{3!}f(t) + \frac{(st)^4}{4!}f(t) - \cdots$$

$$\int_0^\infty e^{-st}f(t)dt = \int_0^\infty f(t)dt - \int_0^\infty (st)f(t)dt + \int_0^\infty \frac{(st)^2}{2!}f(t)dt - \cdots$$

$$\widetilde{X}(s) = 1 - s\mathbf{E}\left[X\right] + \frac{s^2}{2!}\mathbf{E}\left[X^2\right] - \frac{s^3}{3!}\mathbf{E}\left[X^3\right] + \frac{s^4}{4!}\mathbf{E}\left[X^4\right] - \frac{s^5}{5!}\mathbf{E}\left[X^5\right] + \cdots$$

$$\widetilde{X}'(s) = -\mathbf{E}\left[X\right] + s\mathbf{E}\left[X^2\right] - \frac{1}{2!}s^2\mathbf{E}\left[X^3\right] + \frac{1}{3!}s^3\mathbf{E}\left[X^4\right] - \frac{1}{4!}s^4\mathbf{E}\left[X^5\right] + \cdots$$

$$\widetilde{X}'(0) = -\mathbf{E}\left[X\right] \checkmark$$

$$\widetilde{X}''(s) = \mathbf{E}\left[X^2\right] - s\mathbf{E}\left[X^3\right] + \frac{1}{2!}s^2\mathbf{E}\left[X^4\right] - \frac{1}{3!}s^3\mathbf{E}\left[X^5\right] + \cdots$$

$$\widetilde{X}''(0) = \mathbf{E}\left[X^2\right] \checkmark$$

$$\widetilde{X}'''(s) = -\mathbf{E}\left[X^3\right] + s\mathbf{E}\left[X^4\right] - \frac{1}{2!}s^2\mathbf{E}\left[X^5\right] + \cdots$$

$$\widetilde{X}'''(0) = -\mathbf{E}\left[X^3\right] \checkmark$$

And so on ...   ■

Question: At this point, you might be wondering why we don't define the Laplace transform of X to be $\mathbf{E}\left[e^{sX}\right]$, rather than $\mathbf{E}\left[e^{-sX}\right]$. What would be the pros and cons of using $\mathbf{E}\left[e^{sX}\right]$?

Answer: On the plus side, using $\mathbf{E}\left[e^{sX}\right]$ would obviate the need for the alternating negative signs. On the minus side, we would not have the convergence guarantee from Theorem 11.7.

As in the case of z-transforms, we will assume that the Laplace transform (when it converges) uniquely determines the distribution.

11.5 Linearity of Transforms

Just as we had a linearity theory for z-transforms, we have a similar result for Laplace transforms. Again, the random variables need to be independent!

> **Theorem 11.10 (Linearity)** *Let X and Y be continuous, non-negative, independent random variables. Let Z = X + Y. Then,*
> $$\widetilde{Z}(s) = \widetilde{X}(s) \cdot \widetilde{Y}(s).$$

Proof:

$$\begin{aligned}
\widetilde{Z}(s) = \mathbf{E}\left[e^{-sZ}\right] &= \mathbf{E}\left[e^{-s(X+Y)}\right] \\
&= \mathbf{E}\left[e^{-sX} \cdot e^{-sY}\right] \\
&= \mathbf{E}\left[e^{-sX}\right] \cdot \mathbf{E}\left[e^{-sY}\right] \qquad \text{(because } X \perp Y) \\
&= \widetilde{X}(s) \cdot \widetilde{Y}(s).
\end{aligned}$$
∎

11.6 Conditioning

Conditioning also holds for Laplace transforms, just as it held for z-transforms:

> **Theorem 11.11** *Let X, A, and B be continuous random variables where*
> $$X = \begin{cases} A & w/prob\ p \\ B & w/prob\ 1-p \end{cases}.$$
> *Then,*
> $$\widetilde{X}(s) = p \cdot \widetilde{A}(s) + (1-p) \cdot \widetilde{B}(s).$$

Proof:

$$\widetilde{X}(s) = \mathbf{E}\left[e^{-sX}\right]$$
$$= \mathbf{E}\left[e^{-sX}\,\middle|\, X = A\right] \cdot p + \mathbf{E}\left[e^{-sX}\,\middle|\, X = B\right] \cdot (1-p)$$
$$= p\mathbf{E}\left[e^{-sA}\right] + (1-p)\mathbf{E}\left[e^{-sB}\right]$$
$$= p\widetilde{A}(s) + (1-p)\widetilde{B}(s). \qquad\blacksquare$$

Theorem 11.12 is a generalization of Theorem 11.11, where we condition not just on two options, but a continuum of options. Theorem 11.12 is useful when you have a r.v. that depends on the value of another r.v.

Theorem 11.12 *Let* Y *be a non-negative continuous r.v., and let* X_Y *be a continuous r.v. that depends on* Y. *Then, if* $f_Y(y)$ *denotes the p.d.f. of* Y, *we have that*

$$\widetilde{X_Y}(s) = \int_{y=0}^{\infty} \widetilde{X_y}(s) f_Y(y) dy.$$

Proof: Observe that it is the fact that a transform is just an expectation that allows us to do the conditioning below:

$$\widetilde{X_Y}(s) = \mathbf{E}\left[e^{-sX_Y}\right] = \int_{y=0}^{\infty} \mathbf{E}\left[e^{-sX_Y}\,\middle|\, Y = y\right] \cdot f_Y(y) dy$$

$$= \int_{y=0}^{\infty} \mathbf{E}\left[e^{-sX_y}\right] \cdot f_Y(y) dy$$

$$= \int_{y=0}^{\infty} \widetilde{X_y}(s) \cdot f_Y(y) dy. \qquad\blacksquare$$

An example of where Theorem 11.12 is used is given in Exercise 11.13. We will see many more examples when we get to later chapters on stochastic processes.

11.7 Combining Laplace and z-Transforms

Consider again the sum of a random number of random variables, similarly to what we did in Chapter 6, but this time where the random variables being summed are continuous.

Theorem 11.13 (Summing a random number of i.i.d. random variables)
Let $X_1, X_2, X_3, \ldots$ be i.i.d. continuous random variables, where $X_i \sim X$. Let N be a positive discrete r.v., where $N \perp X_i$ for all i. Let

$$S = \sum_{i=1}^{N} X_i.$$

Then,

$$\widetilde{S}(s) = \widehat{N}\left(\widetilde{X}(s)\right),$$

that is, the z parameter of $\widehat{N}(z)$ has been replaced by $\widetilde{X}(s)$.

Example 11.14 (Transform of a Poisson number of i.i.d. Exponentials)
Derive the Laplace transform of a Poisson(λ) number of i.i.d. Exp(μ) random variables.

Recall that for $N \sim$ Poisson(λ) we have that $\widehat{N}(z) = e^{-\lambda(1-z)}$. Recall likewise that for $X \sim$ Exp(μ) we have that

$$\widetilde{X}(s) = \frac{\mu}{s + \mu}.$$

From this it follows that

$$\widetilde{S}(s) = \widehat{N}(\widetilde{X}(s)) = e^{-\lambda(1-z)}\Big|_{z=\frac{\mu}{s+\mu}} = e^{-\lambda\left(1-\frac{\mu}{s+\mu}\right)} = e^{-\frac{\lambda s}{s+\mu}}.$$

Proof: (Theorem 11.13) Let $\widetilde{S}(s \mid N = n)$ denote the Laplace transform of S given $N = n$. By Theorem 11.10, $\widetilde{S}(s \mid N = n) = \left(\widetilde{X}(s)\right)^n$. By conditioning,

$$\widetilde{S}(s) = \sum_{n=0}^{\infty} \mathbf{P}\{N = n\}\, \widetilde{S}(s \mid N = n) = \sum_{n=0}^{\infty} \mathbf{P}\{N = n\}\left(\widetilde{X}(s)\right)^n$$

$$= \widehat{N}\left(\widetilde{X}(s)\right). \qquad \blacksquare$$

11.8 One Final Result on Transforms

Normally we look at the Laplace transform of the p.d.f., but we could also ask about the Laplace transform of an arbitrary function. Theorem 11.15 considers the Laplace transform of the cumulative distribution function (c.d.f.) and relates that to the Laplace transform of the p.d.f.

> **Theorem 11.15** *Let $B(x)$ be the c.d.f. corresponding to p.d.f. $b(t)$, where $t \geq 0$. That is,*
>
> $$B(x) = \int_0^x b(t)dt.$$
>
> *Let*
>
> $$\widetilde{b}(s) = L_{b(t)}(s) = \int_0^\infty e^{-st} b(t)dt.$$
>
> *Let*
>
> $$\widetilde{B}(s) = L_{B(x)}(s) = \int_0^\infty e^{-sx} B(x)dx = \int_0^\infty e^{-sx} \int_0^x b(t)dt\,dx.$$
>
> *Then,*
>
> $$\widetilde{B}(s) = \frac{\widetilde{b}(s)}{s}.$$

Proof: The proof is just a few lines. See Exercise 11.4.   ∎

11.9 Exercises

11.1 **Conditioning practice**

Let $X_1 \sim \text{Exp}(\mu_1)$. Let $X_2 \sim \text{Exp}(\mu_2)$. Assume $X_1 \perp X_2$. Let

$$X = \begin{cases} X_1 & \text{w/prob } \frac{1}{2} \\ X_1 + X_2 & \text{w/prob } \frac{1}{3} \\ 1 & \text{w/prob } \frac{1}{6} \end{cases}.$$

What is $\widetilde{X}(s)$?

11.2 **Effect of doubling**

Let $X \sim \text{Exp}(\lambda)$. Let $Y = 2X$. What is $\widetilde{Y}(s)$?

11.3 **Compact proof of onion peeling**

In this problem we provide a more compact proof of Theorem 11.8. Let X be a non-negative, continuous r.v. with p.d.f. $f_X(t), t \geq 0$. Prove that:

$$\left. \frac{d^k}{ds^k} \widetilde{X}(s) \right|_{s=0} = (-1)^k \mathbf{E}\left[X^k \right].$$

[Hint: Bring the derivative into the integral of $\widetilde{X}(s)$ and simplify.]

11.4 **Relating the transform of the c.d.f. to the transform of the p.d.f.**

Prove Theorem 11.15.

11.5 **Inverting the transform**
You are given that the Laplace transform of r.v. X is:

$$\widetilde{X}(s) = \frac{3e^{-3s}}{3 + 4s + s^2}.$$

How is X distributed? You can express X in terms of other random variables.

11.6 **Two species of onions**
We have defined two types of onions: the z-transform and the Laplace transform. Show that these are actually the same. Let X be a r.v.
(a) Show that $\widetilde{X}(s)$ becomes $\widehat{X}(z)$ when s is a particular function of z.
(b) Show that $\widehat{X}(z)$ becomes $\widetilde{X}(s)$ when z is a particular function of s.

11.7 **Sum of Geometric number of Exponentials**
Let $N \sim$ Geometric(p). Let $X_i \sim$ Exp(μ), where the X_i's are independent. Let $S_N = \sum_{i=1}^{N} X_i$. Use transforms to prove that S_N is Exponentially distributed and derive the rate of S_N.

11.8 **Downloading files**
You need to download two files: file 1 and file 2. File 1 is available via source A or source B. File 2 is available only via source C. The time to download file 1 from source A is Exponentially distributed with rate 1. The time to download file 1 from source B is Exponentially distributed with rate 2. The time to download file 2 from source C is Exponentially distributed with rate 3. All of these download times are independent. You decide to download from *all three* sources simultaneously, in the hope that you get both file 1 and file 2 as soon as possible. Let T denote the time until you get *both* files. What is $\widetilde{T}(s)$?

11.9 **Two-sided Laplace transform: Normal distribution**
In the case where a distribution can take on negative values, we define the Laplace transform as follows: Let X be a r.v. with p.d.f. $f(t)$, $-\infty < t < \infty$:

$$\widetilde{X}(s) = L_f(s) = \int_{-\infty}^{\infty} e^{-st} f(t)dt.$$

Let $X \sim$ Normal$(0, 1)$ be the standard Normal. Prove that

$$\widetilde{X}(s) = e^{\frac{s^2}{2}}. \tag{11.1}$$

Note: More generally, if $X \sim$ Normal(μ, σ^2), then

$$\widetilde{X}(s) = e^{-s\mu + \frac{1}{2}s^2\sigma^2}. \tag{11.2}$$

You only need to prove (11.1).

11.10 Sum of two Normals

Let $X \sim \text{Normal}(\mu_x, \sigma_x^2)$. Let $Y \sim \text{Normal}(\mu_y, \sigma_y^2)$. Assume $X \perp Y$. Derive the distribution of $X + Y$. First try doing this without Laplace transforms. After you give up, use Laplace transforms, specifically (11.2).

11.11 Those tricky interview questions

Let $X, Y \sim \text{Normal}(0, 1)$ be i.i.d. random variables. Derive $\mathbf{P}\{X < 3Y\}$.

11.12 Heuristic proof of Central Limit Theorem (CLT) via transforms

You will derive a heuristic proof of the CLT. Let $X_1, X_2, \ldots$ be a sequence of i.i.d. non-negative random variables, each with distribution X and mean μ and variance σ^2. CLT says that the distribution of

$$\frac{X_1 + X_2 + \cdots + X_n - n\mu}{\sigma\sqrt{n}} \tag{11.3}$$

tends to the standard Normal as $n \to \infty$. Specifically,

$$\mathbf{P}\left\{\frac{X_1 + X_2 + \cdots + X_n - n\mu}{\sigma\sqrt{n}} \le a\right\} \to \frac{1}{\sqrt{2\pi}}\int_{-\infty}^{a} e^{-x^2/2} dx, \text{ as } n \to \infty.$$

We'll show that the Laplace transform of (11.3) (roughly) converges to that of the standard Normal (11.1), hence the underlying distributions are the same. Let

$$S = \frac{X_1 + X_2 + \cdots + X_n}{\sqrt{n}}.$$

(a) Start with the case where $\mu = 0$ and $\sigma^2 = 1$.
 (i) Show that

$$\widetilde{S}(s) \approx \left(1 - \frac{s\mathbf{E}[X]}{\sqrt{n}} + \frac{s^2\mathbf{E}[X^2]}{2n}\right)^n.$$

 (ii) Using what you know about μ and σ^2, show that

$$\widetilde{S}(s) \to \widetilde{N_{(0,1)}}(s), \text{ as } n \to \infty.$$

(b) Now go back to the case where $\mu \ne 0$ and $\sigma^2 \ne 1$.
 (i) Define $Y_i = \frac{X_i - \mu}{\sigma}$. What are the mean and variance of Y_i?
 (ii) Based on (a), what can you say about $\mathbf{P}\left\{\frac{Y_1 + \cdots + Y_n}{\sqrt{n}} \le a\right\}$?
 (iii) What does (ii) tell us about $\mathbf{P}\left\{\frac{X_1 + X_2 + \cdots + X_n - n\mu}{\sigma\sqrt{n}} \le a\right\}$?

11.13 Random variable with random parameters

The time until a light bulb burns out is Exponentially distributed with mean somewhere between $\frac{1}{2}$ year and 1 year. We model the lifetime using r.v. X_Y where $X_Y \sim \text{Exp}(Y)$ and $Y \sim \text{Uniform}(1, 2)$. Derive $\widetilde{X_Y}(s)$.

Part IV

Computer Systems Modeling and Simulation

The goal of this part of the book is to learn how to run simulations of computer systems. Simulations are an important part of evaluating computer system performance. For example, we might have a new load-balancing algorithm, and we're trying to understand whether it reduces the mean job response time or improves utilization. Or we might have a queueing network, where we want to understand the fraction of packet drops when we double the arrival rate of packets. Being able to simulate the computer system is an easy way to get answers to such questions.

Before we can dive into the art of simulation, we first have to understand a few things about modeling. In Chapter 12 we study the Poisson process, which is the most common model used for the arrival process into a computer system. The Poisson process is not only easy to simulate, it also has many other beneficial properties when it comes to simulation and modeling.

In Chapter 13 we study the art of generating random variables for simulation. This is an extremely important part of simulation, since we often have to generate the interarrival times of jobs and the service requirements of jobs. Each of these is typically modeled by some random variable that is a good estimate of the empirical (true) workload. In our simulation, we need to generate instances of these random variables.

Finally, in Chapter 14 we are ready to understand how to program an event-driven simulation. We discuss several examples of event-driven simulation, focusing on the state that needs to be tracked and also on how to measure the quantities that we need from our simulation.

When simulating a computer system, we're often simulating a queueing network. We cover the basics of queueing networks in Chapter 14. However, we defer a more detailed discussion of queueing networks to Chapter 27, after we've covered Markov chains, which allow us to understand more about the analysis of queueing networks.

12 The Poisson Process

This chapter deals with one of the most important aspects of systems modeling, namely the *arrival process*. When we say "arrival process" we are referring to the sequence of arrivals into the system. The most widely used arrival process model is the Poisson process. This chapter defines the Poisson process and highlights its properties. Before we dive into the Poisson process, it will be helpful to review the Exponential distribution, which is closely related to the Poisson process.

12.1 Review of the Exponential Distribution

Recall we say that a random variable (r.v.) X is distributed Exponentially with *rate* λ, written $X \sim \text{Exp}(\lambda)$, if its probability density function (p.d.f.) is

$$f_X(x) = \begin{cases} \lambda e^{-\lambda x} & x \geq 0 \\ 0 & x < 0 \end{cases}.$$

The cumulative distribution function (c.d.f.), $F_X(x) = \mathbf{P}\{X \leq x\}$, is given by

$$F_X(x) = \int_{-\infty}^{x} f_X(y) dy = \begin{cases} 1 - e^{-\lambda x} & x \geq 0 \\ 0 & x < 0 \end{cases}$$

$$\overline{F}_X(x) = 1 - F_X(x) = e^{-\lambda x}, \ x \geq 0.$$

Observe that both $f_X(x)$ and $\overline{F}_X(x)$ drop off by a *constant* factor, $e^{-\lambda}$, with each unit increase of x.

Recall also that for $X \sim \text{Exp}(\lambda)$, we have:

$$\mathbf{E}[X] = \frac{1}{\lambda} \qquad \text{Var}(X) = \frac{1}{\lambda^2} \qquad C_X^2 = \frac{\text{Var}(X)}{\mathbf{E}[X]^2} = 1.$$

In particular, the **rate** of the Exponential distribution, λ, is the reciprocal of its mean. Also recall that an Exponentially distributed r.v. X exhibits the **memory-less** property, which says that:

$$\mathbf{P}\{X > s + t \mid X > s\} = \mathbf{P}\{X > t\}, \quad \forall s, t \geq 0.$$

Finally, recall that the Exponential distribution has **constant failure rate** equal to λ (Exercise 10.2).

Question: Suppose that the lifetime of a job is Exponentially distributed with rate λ. Suppose that the job has already run for t seconds (its age is t). Consider a very small δ. What does the constant failure rate say about the probability that the job will complete in the next δ seconds?

Answer: The probability that a job of age t will complete in the next δ seconds is $\lambda\delta$, independent of t. See Chapter 10 for a review of the notion of failure rate.

12.2 Relating the Exponential Distribution to the Geometric

It can be proven that the Exponential distribution is the *only* continuous-time memoryless distribution.

Question: What is the only discrete-time memoryless distribution?

Answer: The Geometric distribution.

When reasoning about Exponential random variables, we find it very helpful to instead think about Geometric random variables, for which we have more intuition. We can think of the Exponential distribution as the "continuous counterpart" of the Geometric distribution by making the following analogy:

- The Geometric distribution can be viewed as the *number* of flips needed to get a "success." The distribution of the remaining *number* of flips is independent of how many times we have flipped so far.
- The Exponential distribution is the *time* until "success." The distribution of the remaining *time* is independent of how long we have waited so far.

To unify the Geometric and Exponential distributions, we introduce the notion of a "δ-step proof." Throughout the chapter, we will use this way of thinking to come up with quick intuitions and arguments. The idea is to imagine each unit of time as divided into n pieces, each of duration $\delta = \frac{1}{n}$, and suppose that a trial (coin flip) occurs every δ time period, rather than at unit times.

We now define a r.v. Y, where Y is Geometrically distributed with probability $p = \lambda\delta$ of getting a head, for some small $\delta \to 0$. However, rather than flipping every unit time step, we flip every δ-step. That is,

$$Y \sim \text{Geometric}(p = \lambda\delta \mid \text{Flip every } \delta\text{-step}).$$

Observe that Y denotes the *number* of flips until success. Now define Y^* to be the *time* until success under Y:

$$Y^* = \text{Time associated with } Y.$$

Observe that as $\delta \to 0$ (or $n \to \infty$), Y^* becomes a positive, real-valued r.v., because success can occur at any time.

Question: What is $\mathbf{E}[Y^*]$? How is Y^* distributed?

Answer:

$$\mathbf{E}[Y^*] = (\text{avg. \# trials until success}) \cdot (\text{time per trial})$$
$$= \frac{1}{\delta\lambda} \cdot \delta = \frac{1}{\lambda}.$$

To understand the distribution of Y^*, we express $\mathbf{P}\{Y^* > t\}$ as the probability that all the trials up to at least time t have been failures (i.e., we have had at least t/δ failures).

$$\mathbf{P}\{Y^* > t\} = \mathbf{P}\left\{\text{at least } \frac{t}{\delta} \text{ failures}\right\} = (1 - \delta\lambda)^{\frac{t}{\delta}}$$

$$= \left(1 - \frac{1}{\frac{1}{\delta\lambda}}\right)^{\frac{t}{\delta}}$$

$$= \left(1 - \frac{1}{\frac{1}{\delta\lambda}}\right)^{\frac{1}{\lambda\delta} \cdot \lambda \cdot t}$$

$$= \left[\left(1 - \frac{1}{\frac{1}{\delta\lambda}}\right)^{\frac{1}{\lambda\delta}}\right]^{\lambda t}$$

$$\longrightarrow [e^{-1}]^{\lambda t}, \text{ as } \delta \to 0, \text{ by (1.9)}$$
$$= e^{-\lambda t}.$$

But $\mathbf{P}\{Y^* > t\} = e^{-\lambda t}$ implies that $Y^* \sim \text{Exp}(\lambda)$.

We have thus proven the following theorem, which is depicted in Figure 12.1.

Theorem 12.1 *Let $X \sim \text{Exp}(\lambda)$. Then X represents the time to a successful event, given that an event occurs every δ-step and is successful with probability $\lambda\delta$, where $\delta \to 0$.*

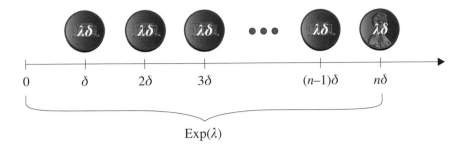

Figure 12.1 *Geometric depiction of the Exp(λ) distribution. Time is divided into steps of duration δ, and a coin (with probability $\lambda\delta$ of "heads") is flipped only at each δ-step.*

12.3 More Properties of the Exponential

Before we continue, here is a useful definition.

Definition 12.2

$$f = o(\delta) \quad \text{if} \quad \lim_{\delta \to 0} \frac{f}{\delta} = 0.$$

For example, $f = \delta^2$ is $o(\delta)$ because $\frac{\delta^2}{\delta} \to 0$ as $\delta \to 0$. Likewise $f = \sqrt{\delta}$ is *not* $o(\delta)$. Basically, a function is $o(\delta)$ if it goes to zero faster than δ, as $\delta \to 0$.

This definition may seem a little odd, because in general asymptotic notation (as in Section 1.6) "big-O" and "little-o" are defined in terms of some $n \to \infty$, not as $\delta \to 0$. When we use $\delta \to 0$, everything is flipped.

We now illustrate how to combine the $o(\delta)$ notation with the discretized view of an Exponential to prove a few properties of the Exponential distribution.

Theorem 12.3 *Given $X_1 \sim Exp(\lambda_1)$, $X_2 \sim Exp(\lambda_2)$, $X_1 \perp X_2$,*

$$\mathbf{P}\{X_1 < X_2\} = \frac{\lambda_1}{\lambda_1 + \lambda_2}.$$

Proof: (Traditional algebraic proof)

$$\mathbf{P}\{X_1 < X_2\} = \int_0^\infty \mathbf{P}\{X_1 < X_2 \mid X_2 = x\} \cdot f_2(x)dx$$

$$= \int_0^\infty \mathbf{P}\{X_1 < x \mid X_2 = x\} \cdot \lambda_2 e^{-\lambda_2 x}dx$$

$$= \int_0^\infty \mathbf{P}\{X_1 < x\} \cdot \lambda_2 e^{-\lambda_2 x}dx, \qquad \text{since } X_1 \perp X_2$$

Continuing,

$$P\{X_1 < X_2\} = \int_0^\infty (1 - e^{-\lambda_1 x})(\lambda_2 e^{-\lambda_2 x}) dx$$

$$= \int_0^\infty \lambda_2 e^{-\lambda_2 x} dx - \lambda_2 \int_0^\infty e^{-(\lambda_1 + \lambda_2)x} dx$$

$$= 1 - \frac{\lambda_2}{\lambda_1 + \lambda_2}$$

$$= \frac{\lambda_1}{\lambda_1 + \lambda_2}. \qquad \blacksquare$$

Now for a more intuitive proof, by analogy with the Geometric distribution:

Proof: (Intuitive Geometric proof) Success of type 1 occurs with probability $\lambda_1 \delta$ on each δ-step. Independently, success of type 2 occurs with probability $\lambda_2 \delta$ on each δ-step. $P\{X_1 < X_2\}$ is really asking, given that a success of type 1 or type 2 has occurred, what is the probability that it is a success of type 1?

$$P\{\text{type 1} \mid \text{type 1 or type 2}\} = \frac{P\{\text{type 1}\}}{P\{\text{type 1 or type 2}\}}$$

$$= \frac{\lambda_1 \delta}{\lambda_1 \delta + \lambda_2 \delta - (\lambda_1 \delta)(\lambda_2 \delta)}$$

$$= \frac{\lambda_1 \delta}{\lambda_1 \delta + \lambda_2 \delta - o(\delta)}$$

$$= \frac{\lambda_1}{\lambda_1 + \lambda_2 - \frac{o(\delta)}{\delta}}$$

$$\rightarrow \frac{\lambda_1}{\lambda_1 + \lambda_2} \text{ as } \delta \rightarrow 0. \qquad \blacksquare$$

Example 12.4 (Which fails first?)

There are two potential failure points for our server: the power supply and the disk. The lifetime of the power supply is Exponentially distributed with mean 500, and the lifetime of the disk is independently Exponentially distributed with mean 1,000.

Question: What is the probability that the system failure, when it occurs, is caused by the power supply?

Answer: $\frac{\frac{1}{500}}{\frac{1}{500} + \frac{1}{1000}}$.

Theorem 12.5 *Given $X_1 \sim Exp(\lambda_1)$, $X_2 \sim Exp(\lambda_2)$, $X_1 \perp X_2$. Let*

$$X = \min(X_1, X_2).$$

Then

$$X \sim Exp(\lambda_1 + \lambda_2).$$

Proof: (Traditional algebraic proof)

$$
\begin{aligned}
\mathbf{P}\{X > t\} &= \mathbf{P}\{\min(X_1, X_2) > t\} \\
&= \mathbf{P}\{X_1 > t \text{ and } X_2 > t\} \\
&= \mathbf{P}\{X_1 > t\} \cdot \mathbf{P}\{X_2 > t\} \\
&= e^{-\lambda_1 t} \cdot e^{-\lambda_2 t} \\
&= e^{-(\lambda_1 + \lambda_2)t}.
\end{aligned}
$$

■

Here is an alternative argument by analogy with the Geometric distribution:

Proof: (Intuitive Geometric proof)

- A trial occurs every δ-step.
- The trial is "successful of type 1" with probability $\lambda_1 \delta$.
- The trial is "successful of type 2" independently with probability $\lambda_2 \delta$.
- We are looking for the time until there is a success of either type.
  A trial is "successful" (either type) with probability

$$\lambda_1 \delta + \lambda_2 \delta - (\lambda_1 \delta) \cdot (\lambda_2 \delta) = \delta \underbrace{\left(\lambda_1 + \lambda_2 - \frac{o(\delta)}{\delta}\right)}_{\text{rate}}.$$

- Thus the time until we get a "success" is Exponentially distributed with rate

$$\lambda_1 + \lambda_2 - \frac{o(\delta)}{\delta},$$

and as $\delta \to 0$ this gives the desired result.

■

Question: In the server from Example 12.4, what is the time until there is a failure of either the power supply or the disk?

Answer: Exponential with rate $\left(\frac{1}{500} + \frac{1}{1000}\right)$.

12.4 The Celebrated Poisson Process

The Poisson process is the most widely used model for arrivals into a system. Part of the reason for this is that it is analytically tractable. However, the Poisson process is also a good model for any process of arrivals which is the aggregation of many independently behaving users. For example, the Poisson process is a good representation of the arrivals of requests into a web server, or the arrivals of jobs into a supercomputing center, or the arrivals of emails into a mail server. The "Limiting Theorem," see [45, pp. 221–228] explains how an aggregate of independent arrival processes leads to a Poisson process. The point is this: If you look at the request stream from an individual user, it will *not* look like a Poisson process. However, if you aggregate the requests from a very large number of users, that *aggregate stream* starts to look like a Poisson process.

Before we define a Poisson process, it helps to recall the Poisson distribution.

Question: If $X \sim \text{Poisson}(\lambda)$, what is $p_X(i)$, $\mathbf{E}[X]$, and $\mathbf{Var}(X)$?

Answer:

$$p_X(i) = \frac{e^{-\lambda}\lambda^i}{i!}, \quad i = 0, 1, 2, \ldots$$

$$\mathbf{E}[X] = \mathbf{Var}(X) = \lambda.$$

A Poisson process is a particular type of arrival sequence. We will need a little terminology. Figure 12.2 shows a sequence of arrivals. Each arrival is associated with a time. The arrival times are called "events."

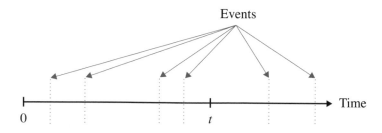

Figure 12.2 *Sequence of events.*

Definition 12.6 *For any sequence of events, we define $N(t)$, $t \geq 0$ to be the* **number of events that occurred by time t** *(including time t).*

Definition 12.7 *An event sequence has* **independent increments** *if the numbers of events that occur in disjoint time intervals are independent. Specifically, for all* $t_0 < t_1 < t_2 < \ldots < t_n$, *the n quantities below are independent:*

$$N(t_1) - N(t_0) \perp N(t_2) - N(t_1) \perp \ldots \perp N(t_n) - N(t_{n-1}).$$

Example 12.8 (Examples of sequences of events)

Consider three sequences of events:

(a) births of children
(b) people entering a store
(c) goals scored by a particular soccer player.

Question: Do these event processes have independent increments?

Answer:

(a) No. The number of births depends on the population size, which increases with prior births.
(b) Yes.
(c) Maybe. Depends on whether we believe in slumps!

Definition 12.9 *The event sequence has* **stationary increments** *if the number of events during a time period depends only on the length of the time period and not on its starting point. That is,* $N(t + s) - N(s)$ *has the same distribution for all s.*

Definition 12.10 (First definition of the Poisson process) *A Poisson process with rate* λ *is a sequence of events such that*

1. $N(0) = 0$.
2. *The process has independent increments.*
3. *The number of events in any interval of length t is Poisson distributed with mean* λt. *That is,* $\forall s, t \geq 0$,

$$\mathbf{P}\{N(t + s) - N(s) = n\} = \frac{e^{-\lambda t}(\lambda t)^n}{n!} \quad n = 0, 1, \ldots$$

Question: Why is λ called the "rate" of the process?

Answer: Observe that $\mathbf{E}[N(t)] = \lambda t$, so the rate of events is $\frac{\mathbf{E}[N(t)]}{t} = \lambda$.

Question: Why only "independent increments"?

Answer: The third item in the definition already implies stationary increments, because the number of events within an interval of length t depends only on t.

Observe that the assumption of stationary and independent increments is equivalent to asserting that, at any point in time, the process *probabilistically restarts itself*. That is, the process from any point on is independent of all that occurred previously (by independent increments) and also has the same distribution as the original process (by stationary increments). Simply put, the process has no memory. This leads us to the second definition of the Poisson process.

> **Definition 12.11 (Second definition of the Poisson process)** *A Poisson process with rate λ is a sequence of events such that the inter-event times are i.i.d. Exponential random variables with rate λ and $N(0) = 0$.*

Question: Which definition of a Poisson process would you use when trying to simulate a Poisson process, the first or the second?

Answer: The Second Definition seems much easier to work with. The times between arrivals are just instances of $\text{Exp}(\lambda)$. We will learn how to generate instances of $\text{Exp}(\lambda)$ in Chapter 13.

First Definition $\Rightarrow$ Second Definition

Let $T_1, T_2, T_3, \ldots$ be the *inter-event* times of a sequence of events. We need to show that $T_i \sim \text{Exp}(\lambda)$, $\forall i$. By the first definition,

$$\mathbf{P}\{T_1 > t\} = \mathbf{P}\{N(t) = 0\} = \frac{e^{-\lambda t}(\lambda t)^0}{0!} = e^{-\lambda t}.$$

Next,

$$\mathbf{P}\left\{T_{n+1} > t \;\Big|\; \sum_{i=1}^{n} T_i = s\right\} = \mathbf{P}\left\{0 \text{ events in } (s, s+t) \;\Big|\; \sum_{i=1}^{n} T_i = s\right\}$$

$$= \mathbf{P}\{0 \text{ events in } (s, s+t)\}, \quad \text{by indpt. increments}$$

$$= e^{-\lambda t}, \quad \text{by stationary increments.}$$

Second Definition $\Rightarrow$ First Definition

Feller [27, p. 11] has a rigorous algebraic proof that the Second Definition implies the First Definition. The idea is to show that the sum of n i.i.d. $\text{Exp}(\lambda)$

random variables has a Gamma, $\Gamma(n, \lambda)$ distribution. Feller then uses the $\Gamma(n, \lambda)$ distribution to show that $N(t)$ follows a Poisson distribution.

Rather than going through this tedious algebraic proof, we instead provide an argument by analogy with the Geometric distribution: $N(t)$ refers to the number of arrivals by time t. Our goal is to prove that $N(t) \sim$ Poisson(λt). Think of an arrival/event as being a "success." The fact that the interarrival times are distributed as Exp(λ) corresponds to flipping a coin every δ-step, where a flip is a success (arrival) with probability $\lambda \delta$:

$$N(t) = \text{Number of successes (arrivals) by time } t$$
$$\sim \text{Binomial}(\# \text{ flips, probability of success of each flip})$$
$$\sim \text{Binomial}\left(\frac{t}{\delta}, \lambda\delta\right).$$

Observe that as $\delta \to 0$, $\frac{t}{\delta}$ becomes very large and $\lambda\delta$ becomes very small.

Question: Now what do you know about Binomial(n, p) for large n and tiny p?

Answer: Recall from Exercise 3.8 that

$$\text{Binomial}(n, p) \to \text{Poisson}(np), \quad \text{as } n \to \infty \text{ and } p \to 0.$$

So, as $\delta \to 0$,

$$N(t) \sim \text{Poisson}\left(\frac{t}{\delta} \cdot \lambda\delta\right) = \text{Poisson}(\lambda t).$$

12.5 Number of Poisson Arrivals during a Random Time

Imagine that jobs arrive to a system according to a Poisson process with rate λ. We wish to understand how many arrivals occur during time S, where S is a r.v. Here, S might represent the time that a job is being processed. Assume that S is independent of the Poisson process. Let A_S denote the number of Poisson arrivals during S. It is useful to first talk about A_t, the number of arrivals during a constant time t. Notice that A_t is what we normally refer to as $N(t)$.

Definition 12.12 *Assume that arrivals occur according to a Poisson process with rate λ. We define*

$$A_t = N(t) = \text{Number of arrivals during time } t$$

and

$$A_S = \text{Number of arrivals during time r.v. } S.$$

Question: What is $\mathbf{E}[A_t]$?

Answer: $\mathbf{E}[A_t] = \mathbf{E}[N(t)] = \lambda t$.

Question: What is $\mathbf{Var}(A_t)$?

Answer: Recall that $A_t = N(t) \sim \text{Poisson}(\lambda t)$. Thus $\mathbf{Var}(A_t) = \lambda t$.

Question: If we want to know the moments of A_S, what should we do?

Answer: Condition on the value of S. For example, to get the first moment of A_S we write:

$$
\begin{aligned}
\mathbf{E}[A_S] &= \int_{t=0}^{\infty} \mathbf{E}[A_S \mid S = t] \cdot f_S(t)dt \\
&= \int_{t=0}^{\infty} \mathbf{E}[A_t] \cdot f_S(t)dt \\
&= \int_{t=0}^{\infty} \lambda t \cdot f_S(t)dt \\
&= \lambda \mathbf{E}[S].
\end{aligned}
\tag{12.1}
$$

12.6 Merging Independent Poisson Processes

In networks, it is common that two Poisson processes are *merged*, meaning that they're interleaved into a single process as shown in Figure 12.3.

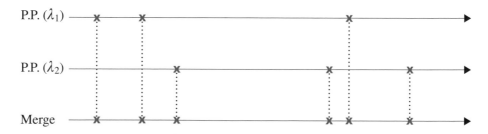

Figure 12.3 *A Poisson process with rate λ_1 is merged with a Poisson process with rate λ_2.*

> **Theorem 12.13 (Poisson merging)** *Given two independent Poisson processes, where process 1 has rate λ_1 and process 2 has rate λ_2, the merge of process 1 and process 2 is a single Poisson process with rate $\lambda_1 + \lambda_2$.*

Proof: Process 1 has $\text{Exp}(\lambda_1)$ interarrival times. Process 2 has $\text{Exp}(\lambda_2)$ interarrival times. The time until the first event from either process 1 or process 2 is the minimum of $\text{Exp}(\lambda_1)$ and $\text{Exp}(\lambda_2)$, which is distributed $\text{Exp}(\lambda_1 + \lambda_2)$ (Theorem 12.5). Likewise, the time until the second event is also distributed $\text{Exp}(\lambda_1 + \lambda_2)$, etc. Thus, using the Second Definition, we have a Poisson process with rate $\lambda_1 + \lambda_2$. ■

Proof: (Alternative) Let $N_i(t)$ denote the number of events in process i by time t:

$$N_1(t) \sim \text{Poisson}(\lambda_1 t)$$
$$N_2(t) \sim \text{Poisson}(\lambda_2 t).$$

Yet the sum of two independent Poisson random variables is still Poisson with the sum of the means, so

$$\underbrace{N_1(t) + N_2(t)}_{\text{merged process}} \sim \text{Poisson}(\lambda_1 t + \lambda_2 t).$$

■

12.7 Poisson Splitting

It is also common that a stream of arrivals is split into two streams, where each arrival is sent to the A stream with probability p and to the B stream with probability $1 - p$. Figure 12.4 illustrates the splitting of a Poisson stream.

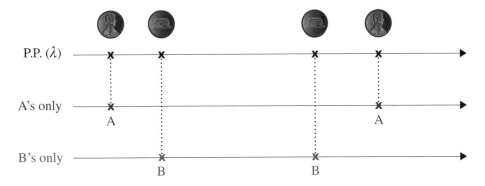

Figure 12.4 *Splitting a Poisson process with rate λ into an A stream and a B stream, based on coin flips.*

Theorem 12.14 (Poisson splitting) *Given a Poisson process with rate λ, suppose that each event is classified "type A" with probability p and "type B" with probability $1 - p$. Then type A events form a Poisson process with rate $p\lambda$, type B events form a Poisson process with rate $(1 - p)\lambda$, and these two processes are independent. Specifically, if $N_A(t)$ denotes the number of type A events by time t, and $N_B(t)$ denotes the number of type B events by time t, then*

$$\mathbf{P}\{N_A(t) = n, N_B(t) = m\} = \mathbf{P}\{N_A(t) = n\} \cdot \mathbf{P}\{N_B(t) = m\}$$
$$= e^{-\lambda t p}\frac{(\lambda t p)^n}{n!} \cdot e^{-\lambda t(1-p)}\frac{(\lambda t(1 - p))^m}{m!}.$$

This is one of those theorems that initially seems very counter-intuitive. It is really not clear why the times between the type A events end up being *Exponentially* distributed with rate λp as opposed to something else. Consider the sequence of events comprising the original Poisson process, where a coin with bias p is flipped at each event. When the coin flip comes up "head," the event is classified as "type A." If we look at just the type A events, we might imagine that some pairs of consecutive type A events are separated by $\text{Exp}(\lambda)$ (where we had two heads in a row) while other pairs of consecutive type A events are separated by multiple $\text{Exp}(\lambda)$ periods (where we didn't have a head for a while). It is not at all clear why the times between type A events are actually $\text{Exp}(\lambda p)$.

Before proving Theorem 12.14, we provide intuition for what's going on, by again making use of δ-step arguments. The original process has $\text{Exp}(\lambda)$ interarrival times, which is equivalent to tossing a coin every $\delta \to 0$ steps, where the coin comes up "success" with probability $\lambda\delta$. We refer to this $\lambda\delta$ coin as the *first* coin. Now we can imagine a *second* coin being flipped, where the second coin has probability p of success. Only if *both* the first and second coins are successes at the same time do we have a type A success. But this is equivalent to flipping just a *single* coin, with probability $\lambda\delta p$ of success. The time between successes for the single coin is then distributed $\text{Exp}(\lambda p)$. This proof is illustrated in Figure 12.5 and can be repeated for type B events.

Proof: [Theorem 12.14] This proof is taken from [64, p. 258]. What makes this proof precise is that (1) it uses no approximations and (2) it explicitly proves independence. Let

$$N(t) = \text{Number of events by time } t \text{ in the original process}$$
$$N_A(t) = \text{Number of type A events by time } t$$
$$N_B(t) = \text{Number of type B events by time } t.$$

We start by computing the joint probability that there are n events of type A and

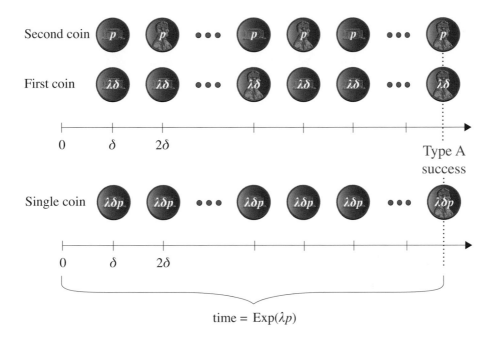

Figure 12.5 *A "type A success" only occurs if both the $\lambda\delta$-coin and the p-coin are heads.*

m events of type B by time t.

$$\mathbf{P}\{N_A(t) = n, N_B(t) = m\}$$

$$= \sum_{k=0}^{\infty} \mathbf{P}\{N_A(t) = n, N_B(t) = m \mid N(t) = k\} \cdot \mathbf{P}\{N(t) = k\}$$

$$= \mathbf{P}\{N_A(t) = n, N_B(t) = m \mid N(t) = n + m\} \cdot \mathbf{P}\{N(t) = n + m\}$$

(because this is the only non-zero term in the above sum)

$$= \mathbf{P}\{N_A(t) = n, N_B(t) = m \mid N(t) = n + m\} \cdot e^{-\lambda t} \frac{(\lambda t)^{n+m}}{(n + m)!}$$

$$= \binom{n + m}{n} p^n (1 - p)^m e^{-\lambda t} \frac{(\lambda t)^{n+m}}{(n + m)!},$$

where the last line comes from the Binomial.

Simplifying, we have:

$$\mathbf{P}\{N_A(t) = n, N_B(t) = m\} = \frac{(m + n)!}{n! m!} p^n (1 - p)^m e^{-\lambda t} \frac{(\lambda t)^{n+m}}{(n + m)!}$$

$$= e^{-\lambda t p} \frac{(\lambda t p)^n}{n!} \cdot e^{-\lambda t (1-p)} \frac{(\lambda t (1 - p))^m}{m!}. \quad (12.2)$$

To illustrate that the type A process and type B process are independent, we now compute the marginal probability $\mathbf{P}\{N_A(t) = n\}$ by summing the joint probability, (12.2), over all values of m:

$$P\{N_A(t) = n\} = \sum_{m=0}^{\infty} P\{N_A(t) = n, N_B(t) = m\}$$

$$= e^{-\lambda t p} \frac{(\lambda t p)^n}{n!} \sum_{m=0}^{\infty} e^{-\lambda t (1-p)} \frac{(\lambda t (1 - p))^m}{m!}$$

$$= e^{-\lambda t p} \frac{(\lambda t p)^n}{n!}.$$

In a similar fashion we compute the marginal probability $P\{N_B(t) = m\}$, obtaining:

$$P\{N_B(t) = m\} = e^{-\lambda t (1-p)} \frac{(\lambda t (1 - p))^m}{m!}.$$

Hence, by (12.2) we have that

$$P\{N_A(t) = n, N_B(t) = m\} = P\{N_A(t) = m\} \cdot P\{N_B(t) = m\}, \quad (12.3)$$

showing that the processes are independent. Now because the other conditions in the First Definition such as independent increments are also obviously satisfied, we have that $\{N_A(t), t \geq 0\}$ forms a Poisson process with rate λp and that $\{N_B(t), t \geq 0\}$ forms an independent Poisson process with rate $\lambda(1 - p)$. ∎

12.8 Uniformity

Theorem 12.15 *Given that one event of a Poisson process has occurred by time t, that event is equally likely to have occurred anywhere in $[0, t]$.*

Proof: Let T_1 denote the time of that one event:

$$P\{T_1 < s \mid N(t) = 1\} = \frac{P\{T_1 < s \text{ and } N(t) = 1\}}{P\{N(t) = 1\}}$$

$$= \frac{P\{1 \text{ event in } [0, s] \text{ and } 0 \text{ events in } [s, t]\}}{\frac{e^{-\lambda t}(\lambda t)^1}{1!}}$$

$$= \frac{P\{1 \text{ event in } [0, s]\} \cdot P\{0 \text{ events in } [s, t]\}}{e^{-\lambda t} \cdot \lambda t}$$

$$= \frac{e^{-\lambda s} \cdot \lambda s \cdot e^{-\lambda(t-s)} \cdot (\lambda(t - s))^0}{e^{-\lambda t} \cdot \lambda t}$$

$$= \frac{s}{t}.$$

∎

Generalization: If k events of a Poisson process occur by time t, then the k events are distributed independently and uniformly in $[0, t]$ [62, pp. 36–38].

12.9 Exercises

12.1 **Doubling Exponentials**
Suppose that job sizes are distributed $\text{Exp}(\mu)$. If job sizes all double, what can we say about the distribution of job sizes now? Prove it.

12.2 **Conditional Exponential**
Let $X \sim \text{Exp}(\lambda)$. What is $\mathbf{E}\left[X^2 \mid X < 1\right]$? [Hint: No integrals, just think!]

12.3 **Stationary and independent increments**
For a Poisson process with arrival rate λ, let $N(t)$ denote the number of arrivals by time t. Simplify the following, pointing out explicitly where you used stationary increments and where you used independent increments:

$$\mathbf{P}\{N(t) = 10 \mid N(3) = 2\} \qquad (\text{assume } t > 3).$$

12.4 **Poisson process definition**
Suppose requests arrive to a website according to a Poisson process with rate $\lambda = 1$ request per ms. What is the probability that there are 5 arrivals in the first 5 ms and 10 arrivals in the first 10 ms?

12.5 **Packets of different colors**
(a) A stream of packets arrives according to a Poisson process with rate $\lambda = 50$ packets/s. Suppose each packet is of type "green" with probability 5% and of type "yellow" with probability 95%. Given that 100 green packets arrived during the previous second, (i) what is the expected number of yellow packets that arrived during the previous second? And (ii) what is the probability that 200 yellow packets arrived during the previous second?
(b) Red packets arrive according to a Poisson process with rate $\lambda_1 = 30$ packets/s. Black packets arrive according to a Poisson process with rate $\lambda_2 = 10$ packets/s. Assume the streams are merged into one stream. Suppose we are told that 60 packets arrived during one second. What is the probability that exactly 40 of those were red?

12.6 **Uniformity**
Packets arrive according to a Poisson process with rate λ. You are told that by time 30 seconds, 100 packets have arrived. What is the probability that 20 packets arrived during the first 10 seconds?

12.7 **Poisson process products**
Suppose customers arrive to a store according to a Poisson process with rate λ customers per second. Let $N(t)$ denote the number of arrivals by time t. What is $\mathbf{E}\left[N(s)N(t)\right]$, where $s < t$?

12.8 **Number of Poisson arrivals during S**
Let A_S denote the number of arrivals of a Poisson process with rate λ during S, where S is a continuous non-negative r.v., and the Poisson process is independent of S. You will derive $\mathbf{Var}(A_S)$ in two different ways:
(a) Do it without transforms.
(b) Derive the z-transform of A_S and differentiate it appropriately.

12.9 **Malware and honeypots**
A new malware is out in the Internet! We want to estimate its spread by time t. Internet hosts get infected by this malware according to a Poisson process with parameter λ, where λ is *not known*. Thrasyvoulos installs a honeypot security system to detect whether hosts are infected. Unfortunately there is a *lag time* between when a computer is infected and the honeypot detects the damage. Assume that this lag time is distributed $\text{Exp}(\mu)$. Suppose that the honeypot system has detected $N_1(t)$ infected hosts by time t. Thrasyvoulos worries that, because of the lag, the number of infected hosts is actually much higher than $N_1(t)$. We ask: How many *additional* hosts, $N_2(t)$, are expected to also be infected at time t.
(a) Suppose that an infection happens at time s, where $0 < s < t$. What is the probability that the infection is detected by time t?
(b) Consider an arbitrary infection that happens before time t. What is the (unconditional) probability, p, that the infection is detected by the honeypot by time t?
(c) How can we use our knowledge of $N_1(t)$ to estimate λ as a function of $N_1(t)$?
(d) Use your estimate of λ to determine the expected value of $N_2(t)$ as a function of $N_1(t)$.

12.10 **Sum of Geometric number of Exponentials**
Let $N \sim \text{Geometric}(p)$. Let $X_i \sim \text{Exp}(\mu)$. Let $S_N = \sum_{i=1}^{N} X_i$.
(a) What is the distribution of S_N? Prove this using a δ-step argument.
(b) Based on what you learned in (a), what is $\mathbf{P}\left\{S_N > t\right\}$?
(c) For a Poisson process with rate λ, where packets are colored "red" with probability q, what is the variance of the time between red packets?

12.11 **Reliability theory: max of two Exponentials**
Redundancy is often built into systems so that if a disk fails there is no catastrophe. The idea is to have the data on two disks, so that a catastrophe

only occurs if *both* disks fail. The time until a catastrophe occurs can be viewed as the "max" of two random variables.

(a) Let $X_1 \sim \text{Exp}(\lambda)$. Let $X_2 \sim \text{Exp}(\lambda)$. Suppose $X_1 \perp X_2$. What is $\mathbf{E}\left[\max(X_1, X_2)\right]$?

(b) Let $X_1 \sim \text{Exp}(\lambda_1)$. Let $X_2 \sim \text{Exp}(\lambda_2)$. Suppose $X_1 \perp X_2$. What is $\mathbf{E}\left[\max(X_1, X_2)\right]$?

12.12 Exponential downloads

You need to download two files: file 1 and file 2. File 1 is available via source A or source B. File 2 is available only via source C. The time to download file 1 from source A is $\text{Exp}(1)$. The time to download file 1 from source B is $\text{Exp}(2)$. The time to download file 2 from source C is $\text{Exp}(3)$. You decide to download from *all three* sources simultaneously, in the hope that you get both file 1 and file 2 as soon as possible. Let T denote the time until you get *both* files.

(a) What is $\mathbf{E}[T]$?

(b) What is $\mathbf{P}\{T < t\}$?

12.13 Reliability theory: max of many Exponentials

Let $X_1, X_2, \ldots, X_n$ be i.i.d. with distribution $\text{Exp}(\lambda)$. Let

$$Z = \max(X_1, X_2, \ldots, X_n).$$

(a) What is $\mathbf{E}[Z]$?

(b) Roughly, what does $\mathbf{E}[Z]$ look like as a function of n and λ when n is reasonably high?

(c) Derive the distribution of Z.

12.14 Conditional distribution

Let $X \sim \text{Exp}(\lambda_X)$ and $Y \sim \text{Exp}(\lambda_Y)$, where $X \perp Y$. Let $Z = \min(X, Y)$. Prove that

$$(X \mid X < Y) \sim Z.$$

That is, show that $\mathbf{P}\{X > t \mid X < Y\} = \mathbf{P}\{Z > t\}$.

Before you start, take a minute to think about what this problem is saying: Suppose for simplicity that X and Y are both drawn from $\text{Exp}(\lambda)$. Say I put X in one hand and Y in the other, without looking. If you ask to see a random hand, the value you get is distributed $\text{Exp}(\lambda)$. However, if you ask me to look inside my hands and hand over the smaller of the two values, then the value that I give you will no longer be distributed $\text{Exp}(\lambda)$.

12.15 Two two-stage jobs

We have two jobs, X and Y, where each has two stages, as shown in Figure 12.6. Both stages of a job must be completed in order. That is, to complete job X, we need to first run X_1 and then run X_2. Similarly, to complete job Y we must run Y_1 followed by Y_2. Assume that X_1, X_2, Y_1, and Y_2 are i.i.d. with distribution $\text{Exp}(\mu)$. Suppose that job X and job Y start running at the same time.

Figure 12.6 *Figure for Exercise 12.15.*

(a) What is the expected time until the first of these jobs completes?
(b) What is the expected time until the last of these jobs completes?

12.16 **Population modeling**
Naveen is interested in modeling population growth over time. He figures it is reasonable to model the birth process as a Poisson process with some average rate λ. He also assumes that a person's lifespan follows some distribution, T, with c.d.f. $F_T(t)$ and tail $\overline{F}_T(t) = 1 - F_T(t)$, where he assumes that lifespans of individuals are independent. Let $N(t)$ denote the population (number of people who are alive) at time t.
(a) Prove that $\mathbf{E}\left[N(t)\right] = \lambda \int_{k=0}^{t} \overline{F}_T(t - k)dk$.
(b) Naveen reads that approximately $\lambda = 4$ million people are both in the United States per year. He can't find a good distribution for lifespan, T, but he notes that the average life expectancy is $\mathbf{E}\left[T\right] = 75$ years. He decides to approximate lifespan by the Uniform$(50, 100)$ distribution. Given these numbers, what can Naveen say about $\mathbf{E}\left[N(t)\right]$? Provide formulas for the three cases: $t < 50$; $50 < t < 100$; and $t > 100$.
(c) What does Naveen's model say about $\mathbf{E}\left[N(t)\right]$ as $t \to \infty$, meaning we're in steady state.

13 Generating Random Variables for Simulation

At this point, we have discussed many discrete and continuous distributions. This chapter shows how we can generate instances of these distributions and others. This is helpful when performing simulations of computer systems, as in Chapter 14. For example, we might have a computer system where the inter-arrival times of jobs are well modeled by an Exponential distribution and the job sizes (service requirements) are well modeled by a Pareto distribution. To simulate the system, we need to be able to generate instances of Exponential and Pareto random variables. This chapter presents the two basic methods used for generating instances of random variables. Both of these methods assume that we already have a generator of Uniform(0, 1) random variables,[1] as is provided by most operating systems.[2]

13.1 Inverse Transform Method

To generate instances of a random variable (r.v.), X, this method assumes that:

1. We know the cumulative distribution function (c.d.f.) of X, that is, we know
   $F_X(x) = \mathbf{P}\{X \le x\}$.
2. We can easily invert $F_X(x)$, that is, we can get x from $F_X(x)$.

The high-level plan is that we will generate a random instance of Uniform(0, 1) (this is already available from our operating system), and then find a way to translate that to an instance of X.

---

[1] Actually, most operating systems provide a random integer between 1 and $N = 2^{32} - 1$. This is easy to convert into a Uniform(0, 1) by just dividing by N.

[2] One cannot always trust the random number generator provided by one's operating system. It is worth reading the literature on what guarantees different random number generators provide and on how to "seed" the random number generator [10].

13.1.1 The Continuous Case

We assume without loss of generality that X ranges from 0 to ∞. The method works just as well when X has some finite upper bound.

Idea: Let u be our random instance from $U(0, 1)$. We want to map u to x, where x is an instance of the r.v. X. The key point is that the x that we output needs to be consistent with the distribution of X.

Let's suppose there is some mapping which takes each u and assigns it a unique x. Such a mapping is illustrated by $g^{-1}(\cdot)$ in Figure 13.1. Here, the y-axis shows u, between 0 and 1, being mapped to an x on the x-axis between 0 and ∞.

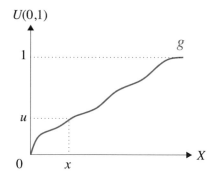

Figure 13.1 *Illustration of mapping $g(\cdot)$.*

Question: Can you figure out what the mapping, $g^{-1}(\cdot)$, should be?

Hint: Think about what property we want for our output. What should be the probability of outputting a value between 0 and x?

Answer: A value in $(0, x)$ should be output with probability $F_X(x)$.

Question: What is the actual probability that $g^{-1}(\cdot)$ outputs a value in $(0, x)$?

Answer: Because $g^{-1}(\cdot)$ only maps values in $(0, u)$ to values in $(0, x)$, the probability of outputting a value in $(0, x)$ is the probability that the uniform instance is in $(0, u)$.

Question: And what is the probability that the uniform instance is in $(0, u)$?

Answer: u.

So we want that

$$u = \mathbf{P}\left\{0 < U < u\right\} = \mathbf{P}\left\{0 < X < x\right\} = F_X(x).$$

That is, we want

$$u = F_X(x) \quad \text{or equivalently} \quad x = F_X^{-1}(u). \tag{13.1}$$

Question: So what was the $g(\cdot)$ function in Figure 13.1?

Answer: $g(\cdot) = F_X(\cdot)$, the c.d.f. of X.

Algorithm 13.1 (Inverse Transform method to generate continuous r.v. X)

1. *Generate $u \in U(0, 1)$.*
2. *Return $x = F_X^{-1}(u)$. That is, return x such that $F_X(x) = u$.*

Example 13.2 *Generate $X \sim Exp(\lambda)$:*

For the $Exp(\lambda)$ distribution,

$$F(x) = 1 - e^{-\lambda x}.$$

So, by (13.1) we want,

$$x = F^{-1}(u)$$
$$F(x) = u$$
$$1 - e^{-\lambda x} = u$$
$$-\lambda x = \ln(1 - u)$$
$$x = -\frac{1}{\lambda} \ln(1 - u). \tag{13.2}$$

Given $u \in U(0, 1)$, setting $x = -\frac{1}{\lambda} \ln(1-u)$ produces an instance of $X \sim Exp(\lambda)$.

13.1.2 The Discrete Case

The discrete case follows the same basic idea as the continuous case (see Figure 13.2). This time, we want to generate a discrete r.v., X, with the following probability mass function (p.m.f.):

$$X = \begin{cases} x_0 & \text{w/prob } p_0 \\ x_1 & \text{w/prob } p_1 \\ \cdots \\ x_k & \text{w/prob } p_k \end{cases}.$$

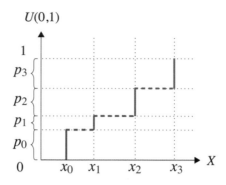

Figure 13.2 *Generating a discrete r.v. with four values.*

Algorithm 13.3 (Inverse Transform method to generate discrete r.v. X)

1. *Arrange $x_0, \ldots, x_k$, the possible values of X, s.t. $x_0 < x_1 < \ldots < x_k$.*
2. *Generate $u \in U(0, 1)$.*
3. *If $0 < u \leq p_0$, then output x_0.*
   If $p_0 < u \leq p_0 + p_1$, then output x_1.
   If $p_0 + p_1 < u \leq p_0 + p_1 + p_2$, then output x_2.
   If $\sum_{i=0}^{\ell-1} p_i < u \leq \sum_{i=0}^{\ell} p_i$, then output x_ℓ, where $0 \leq \ell \leq k$.

Notice that again our $g(\cdot)$ function, shown in blue in Figure 13.2, is $F_X(\cdot)$, the c.d.f.

This sounds easy enough, but it is not always practical. If X can take on many values, then we have to compute many partial sums: $\sum_{i=0}^{\ell} p_i$ for all $0 \leq \ell \leq k$. For this method to be practical, we therefore need closed-form expressions for $\sum_{i=0}^{\ell} p_i$ for all ℓ. Equivalently, we need a closed form for $F_X(x) = \mathbf{P}\{X \leq x\}$ for any x. Then we could do the same thing as in the continuous case, as in (13.1): generate $u \in U(0, 1)$, and set $x = F_X^{-1}(u)$, where a ceiling may be necessary since x is discrete. Thus, as in the continuous case, we need *both* have a closed-form expression for the c.d.f. and also know how to invert this function.

13.2 Accept–Reject Method

The Inverse Transform method required both knowing the c.d.f., $F_X(x)$, of the r.v. X that we're trying to generate, and also being able to invert $F_X(x)$. However, there are many cases where we aren't able to satisfy both of these requirements.

The Accept–Reject method has easier requirements:

1. We need the p.d.f., $f_X(t)$ (or p.m.f.) of the r.v. X that we're trying to generate.
2. We need to know how to generate some other r.v. Y, where Y and X take on the same set of values, that is,

$$f_X(t) > 0 \iff f_Y(t) > 0.$$

The Accept–Reject method is very simple. We generate an instance of Y. Then with some probability we return that value as our instance of X, and otherwise we reject that value and try again.

13.2.1 Discrete Case

Here's the algorithm for a discrete r.v. X, with p.m.f. $p_X(i) = \mathbf{P}\{X = i\}$.

Algorithm 13.4 (Accept-Reject algorithm to generate discrete r.v. X)
1. *Find a discrete r.v. Y, which we already know how to generate, where*

$$p_Y(i) > 0 \iff p_X(i) > 0.$$

2. *Let $c > 1$ be the smallest constant such that*

$$\frac{p_X(i)}{p_Y(i)} \le c, \quad \forall i \text{ s.t. } p_X(i) > 0.$$

3. *Generate an instance of Y. Call this instance i.*
4. *With probability Accept-Ratio$(i) = \frac{p_X(i)}{c\,p_Y(i)}$, accept i and return $X = i$. Else, reject i and return to step 3.*

Question: In Step 4 of the Accept–Reject algorithm, how do we implement accepting i with probability Accept-Ratio(i)?

Answer: We generate a Uniform$(0, 1)$ r.v. and accept if the generated Uniform is smaller than Accept-Ratio(i).

Question: What's the intuition behind Accept-Ratio(i) in Step 4?

Answer: We can think of

$$\text{Accept-Ratio}(i) = \frac{p_X(i)}{c\,p_Y(i)}$$

as representing the *relative likelihood* of i being an instance of X versus Y. If this likelihood is high, then we are more likely to trust i as a reasonable instance of X. If the likelihood is low, then even if i is a common instance for Y, it is not a common instance for X and hence we are more likely to reject i as an instance of X.

Question: What role does c play in the accept ratio?

Answer: c is just a normalizing constant which is needed to ensure that the accept ratio is a probability (< 1).

Formally, we have the following argument:

Fraction of time i is generated and accepted

$= \mathbf{P}\{i \text{ is generated}\} \cdot \mathbf{P}\{i \text{ is accepted given } i \text{ is generated}\}$

$= p_Y(i) \cdot \dfrac{p_X(i)}{c p_Y(i)}$

$= \dfrac{p_X(i)}{c}.$ \hfill (13.3)

Fraction of time any value is accepted

$= \displaystyle\sum_i \text{Fraction of time } i \text{ is generated and is accepted}$

$= \displaystyle\sum_i \dfrac{p_X(i)}{c}$

$= \dfrac{1}{c}.$ \hfill (13.4)

Combining (13.3) and (13.4), we have:

$$\mathbf{P}\{X \text{ is set to } i\} = \frac{\text{Frac. time } i \text{ is generated and accepted}}{\text{Frac. time any value is accepted}} = \frac{\frac{p_X(i)}{c}}{\frac{1}{c}} = p_X(i),$$

as desired.

Question: On average, how many values of Y are generated before one is accepted?

Answer: c. Because the fraction of time any value is accepted is $\frac{1}{c}$.

13.2.2 Continuous Case

The Accept–Reject method works the same way for continuous random variables, except that we now use the p.d.f. instead of the p.m.f.

> **Algorithm 13.5 (Accept-Reject algorithm to generate continuous r.v. X)**
>
> 1. *Find a continuous r.v. Y, which we already know how to generate, where*
>
> $$f_Y(t) > 0 \iff f_X(t) > 0.$$
>
> 2. *Let $c > 1$ be the smallest constant such that*
>
> $$\frac{f_X(t)}{f_Y(t)} \le c, \quad \forall t \text{ s.t. } f_X(t) > 0.$$
>
> 3. *Generate an instance of Y. Call this instance t.*
> 4. *With probability Accept-Ratio$(t) = \frac{f_X(t)}{c \cdot f_Y(t)}$, accept t and return $X = t$.*
>   *Else, reject t and return to step 3.*

Similarly to the Accept–Reject algorithm for the discrete case, we can show that:

Density of returning t on an iteration = Density of generating $t \cdot \mathbf{P}\{\text{accept } t\}$

$$= f_Y(t) \cdot \frac{f_X(t)}{c \cdot f_Y(t)}$$

$$= f_X(t) \cdot \frac{1}{c}.$$

Hence,

$$\mathbf{P}\{\text{Return some value on a given iteration}\} = \int_t f_X(t) \cdot \frac{1}{c} dt = \frac{1}{c},$$

so the expected number of iterations needed to get an instance of X is c.

Example 13.6 *Generate r.v. X with p.d.f. $f_X(t) = 20t(1-t)^3, \quad 0 < t < 1$.*

If you plot $f_X(t)$, it looks like Figure 13.3. Observe that X has positive p.d.f. only in the interval $(0, 1)$. Thus we want to choose a Y that is easy to generate and also has positive p.d.f. only in $(0, 1)$.

Question: Any ideas for what $f_Y(t)$ should be?

Answer: Consider simply $f_Y(t) = 1$, where $0 < t < 1$.

Question: Suppose we now apply the Accept–Reject method. What will c be?

Answer: Based on the plot, c should not be too bad – just over 2. To determine c precisely, we want to determine

$$\max_t \left\{ \frac{f_X(t)}{f_Y(t)} \right\} = \max_t \left\{ 20t(1-t)^3 \right\}.$$

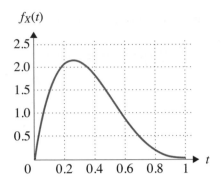

Figure 13.3 *Plot of $f_X(t)$.*

Taking the derivative with respect to t, and setting it equal to zero, we have

$$\frac{d}{dt}(20t(1-t)^3) = 0 \iff t = \frac{1}{4}.$$

So the maximum value is obtained when $t = \frac{1}{4}$:

$$c = \frac{f_X\left(\frac{1}{4}\right)}{f_Y\left(\frac{1}{4}\right)} = 20\left(\frac{1}{4}\right)\left(\frac{3}{4}\right)^3 = \frac{135}{64}. \tag{13.5}$$

Observe how easy it was to make a good guess for $f_Y(t)$ just by looking at the plot of $f_X(t)$.

Question: Could we have used the Inverse Transform method to generate X?

Answer: No. While it is easy to get $F_X(x)$, unfortunately $F_X(x)$ is not easy to invert. Thus we won't be able to solve $u = F_X(x)$ for x.

Example 13.7 (Generating a Normal r.v.)

We now turn to generating the Normal distribution. By the Linear Transformation Property (Theorem 9.5), it suffices to generate a standard Normal. Here it's clearly impossible to use the Inverse Transform method since we don't know the c.d.f.

Goal: Generate $N \sim \text{Normal}(0, 1)$.

Idea: It suffices to generate $X = |N|$ and then multiply N by -1 with probability 0.5.

So how do we generate such an X? A plot of X is shown in Figure 13.4.

$$f_X(t) = \frac{2}{\sqrt{2\pi}}e^{-\frac{t^2}{2}}, \quad 0 < t < \infty.$$

Question: What is a good choice for a r.v. Y that we know how to generate, such that $f_Y(t)$ fits $f_X(t)$ reasonably well?

Answer: Let $Y \sim \text{Exp}(1)$.

$$f_Y(t) = e^{-t}, \quad 0 < t < \infty.$$

Observe that $f_X(t)$ is not too much higher than $f_Y(t)$, according to Figure 13.4.

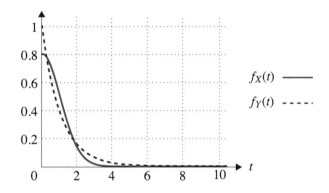

Figure 13.4 *Solid line shows $f_X(t)$. Dashed line shows proposed $f_Y(t)$.*

Question: How many iterations are needed on average?

Answer: We need to determine c.

$$\frac{f_X(t)}{f_Y(t)} = \frac{2}{\sqrt{2\pi}}e^{-\frac{t^2}{2}+t} = \sqrt{\frac{2}{\pi}}e^{t-\frac{t^2}{2}}.$$

So, the maximum value occurs when $t - \frac{t^2}{2}$ is maximized.

$$0 = \frac{d}{dt}\left(t - \frac{t^2}{2}\right) = 1 - t \quad \Longrightarrow \quad t = 1.$$

So,

$$c = \frac{f_X(1)}{f_Y(1)} = \sqrt{\frac{2e}{\pi}} \approx 1.3.$$

Thus we only need 1.3 iterations on average!

13.2.3 A Harder Problem

Consider $X \sim \text{Poisson}(\lambda)$, with $p_X(i) = \frac{e^{-\lambda}\lambda^i}{i!}$.

Question: Can we use the Inverse Transform method to generate an instance of a Poisson r.v.?

Answer: There is no closed form for $F(x) = \mathbf{P}\{X \leq x\}$ so the Inverse Transform method will not work.

Question: Can we use the Accept–Reject method?

Answer: It looks like we should be able to apply the Accept–Reject method, but it is hard to find the right Y distribution to match up to (see [48, p. 503]).

We will show a different way to generate $X \sim \text{Poisson}(\lambda)$ in Exercise 13.5 by relating X to a Poisson process with rate λ.

13.3 Readings

A lot more is known about generating random variables than we have described in this chapter. Some particularly well-written texts are [63] and [48].

13.4 Exercises

13.1 **Generating random variables for simulation** – (from [63])
Give an algorithm for generating X with p.d.f. $f_X(x) = 30(x^2 - 2x^3 + x^4)$ where $0 < x < 1$.

13.2 **Inverse Transform method**
Provide a simple algorithm for generating values from a continuous distribution with p.d.f. $f(t) = \frac{5}{4}t^{-2}$, where $1 < t < 5$.

13.3 **Generating a Geometric distribution**
Give a simple and efficient algorithm for generating values from a Geometric(p) distribution. Now use your algorithm to generate 50 instances of Geometric(0.2). Determine the sample mean (the average of the 50 generated instances). Compare the sample mean with the desired answer.

13.4 **Simulation of heavy-tailed distributions**

Write a short program to generate 100 instances of

$$X \sim \text{BoundedPareto}(k = 332.067, p = 10^{10}, \alpha = 1.1),$$

as defined in Definition 10.5. Take their average. Record your answer. Now generate 1000 instances of this distribution, and again take their average and record your answer. Keep going. This time, generate 10,000 instances of this distribution and take their average and record it. Next, generate 100,000 instances. Keep going until you run out of patience. You should find that your sample averages are well below the true average (compute this!). Explain why this is. What trend do you see in your sample averages?

13.5 **Generating a Poisson r.v.**

Describe an efficient algorithm for generating instances of a Poisson r.v. with mean 1. It will be helpful to start by recalling what you learned in Chapter 12 about the Poisson process and where the Poisson distribution comes up in the context of a Poisson process.

13.6 **Simulating jointly distributed random variables**

Let X and Y be non-negative, continuous random variables whose joint density is given by:

$$f_{X,Y}(x, y) = \lambda e^{-\lambda x} x e^{-xy}, \quad x \geq 0, \ y \geq 0.$$

Provide a simple algorithm, using the Inverse Transform method, that generates a point (x, y) drawn from the above joint p.d.f. Explain your reasoning.

14 Event-Driven Simulation

Having covered how to generate random variables in the previous chapter, we are now in good shape to move on to the topic of creating an event-driven simulation. The goal of simulation is to predict the performance of a computer system under various workloads. A big part of simulation is modeling the computer system as a queueing network. Queueing networks will be revisited in much more detail in Chapter 27, where we *analytically* address questions of performance and stability (analysis is easier to do after covering Markov chains and hence is deferred until later).

For now, we only explain as much as we need to about queueing networks to enable simulation. We will start by discussing how to simulate a single queue.

14.1 Some Queueing Definitions

Figure 14.1 depicts a queue. The circle represents the **server** (you can think of this as a CPU). The red rectangles represent **jobs**. You can see that one of the jobs is currently being served (it is in the circle) and three other jobs are queueing, waiting to be served, while three more jobs have yet to arrive to the system. The red rectangles have different heights. The height of the rectangle is meant to represent the **size** of a job, where size indicates the job's service requirement (number of seconds needed to process the job). You can see that some jobs are large, while others are small. Once the job finishes **serving** (being processed) at the server, it leaves the system, and the next job starts serving. We assume that new jobs arrive over time. The time between arrivals is called the **interarrival time**. Unless otherwise stated, we assume that jobs are served in first-come-first-served (FCFS) order.

Question: If the arrival process to a queue is a Poisson process, what can we say about the interarrival times?

Answer: The interarrival times are independent and identically-distributed (i.i.d.) $\sim \text{Exp}(\lambda)$ where $\frac{1}{\lambda}$ represents the mean interarrival time and λ can be viewed as the **rate of arrivals** in jobs/s.

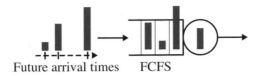

Future arrival times   FCFS

Figure 14.1 *Single queue with arrivals.*

We will generally assume a **stochastic setting** where all quantities are i.i.d. random variables. We will denote a job's size by the random variable (r.v.) S. For example, if $S \sim \text{Uniform}(0, 10)$, then jobs each require independent service times ranging between 0 and 10 seconds. The interval times between jobs is denoted by the r.v. I, where again we assume that these are independent. For example, if $I \sim \text{Exp}(\lambda)$, where $\lambda = 0.1$, then the average time between arrivals is 10 seconds. When running a simulation based on distributions for interarrival times and job sizes, we are assuming that these distributions are reasonable approximations of the **observed workloads** in the actual computer system being simulated.

However, it is also possible to assume that job sizes and interarrival times are taken from a **trace**. In that case, the simulation is often referred to as a **trace-driven simulation**. The trace typically includes information collected about the system over a long period of time, say a few months or a year.

Question: What are some advantages of using a trace to drive the simulation as opposed to generating inputs from distributions?

Answer: The trace captures correlations between successive interarrival times and/or successive job sizes. For example, it might be the case that a small job is more likely to be followed by another small job, or that arrivals tend to occur in bursts. This is harder to capture with independent random variables, although one can certainly try to create more complex probabilistic models of the workload [33].

We define the **response time of job**, typically denoted by r.v. T, to be the time from when the job first arrives until it completes service. We can also talk about the **waiting time** (a.k.a. **delay**) of a job, denoted by r.v. T_Q, which is the time from when the job first arrives until it first receives service. We define the **number of jobs in system**, denoted by r.v. N, to be the total number of jobs in the system. We define the **server utilization**, denoted by ρ, as the long-run fraction of time that the server is busy.

The goal of a simulation is typically to understand some aspect of the system performance. As an example, suppose that we are interested in the **mean response time**, $\mathbf{E}\left[T\right]$. We can think of this as follows. Let T_1 denote the response time of the first job, T_2 the response time of the second job, etc. Then,

$$\mathbf{E}\,[T] = \frac{1}{n}\sum_{i=1}^{n}T_i,$$

where it is assumed that n is sufficiently large that the mean response time is not changing very much. Thus, to get the mean response time, we can imagine having each of the first n jobs record its response time, where we then average over all of these.

14.2 How to Run a Simulation

Imagine that we want to simulate the queue shown in Figure 14.1, where the interarrival times are i.i.d. instances of r.v. I and the job sizes (service requirements) are i.i.d. instances of some r.v. S. Assume that we know how to generate instances of I and S using the techniques described in Chapter 13.

Question: Do we run this system in real time?

Answer: No, that would take forever.

The whole point is to be able to process millions of arrivals in just a few hours. To do this, we use an **event-driven simulation**. The idea is to maintain the **system state** at all times and also maintain a **global clock**. Then we ask,

   "What is the next event that will cause a change in the system state?"

We then increase the time on the global clock by the time until this next event, and we update the system state to reflect the next event. We also update the times until the next events. We then repeat this process, stepping through events in near-zero time.

For example, let's consider an event-driven simulation of the queue in Figure 14.1.

Question: What is the system state?

Answer: The state is the current number of jobs in the system.

Question: What are events that change the state?

Hint: There are only two such events.

Answer: A new arrival or a job completion.

The interarrival times will need to be generated according to r.v. I. The job sizes (service requirements) will need to be generated according to r.v. S.

Question: Do we generate all the arrival times and all the job sizes for the whole simulation in advance and store these in a large array?

Answer: No, it's much simpler to generate these as we need them.

Let's run through how this works. We are going to maintain four variables:

1. Clock: represents the time;
2. State: represents the current number of jobs in the system;
3. Time-to-next-completion;
4. Time-to-next-arrival.

The simulation starts here: State is 0 jobs. Clock = 0. There's no job serving, so Time-to-next-completion = ∞. To determine the time to the next arrival, we generate an instance of I, let's say $I = 5.3$, and set Time-to-next-arrival = 5.3.

We ask which event will happen first. Since $\min(\infty, 5.3) = 5.3$, we know the next event is an arrival.

We now update everything as follows: State is 1 job. Note that this job starts serving immediately. Clock = 5.3. To determine the time to the next completion, we generate an instance of S representing the service time of the job in service, say $S = 10$, and set Time-to-next completion = 10. To determine the next arrival we generate an instance of I, say $I = 2$, and set Time-to-next-arrival = 2.

We again ask which event will happen first. Since $\min(10, 2) = 2$, we know the next event is an arrival.

We now update everything as follows: State is 2 jobs. Clock = $5.3 + 2 = 7.3$. Time-to-next-completion = $10 - 2 = 8$, because the job that was serving has completed 2 seconds out of its 10 second requirement. To determine the next arrival we generate an instance of I, say $I = 9.5$, and set Time-to-next-arrival = 9.5.

We again ask which event will happen first. Since $\min(8, 9.5) = 8$, we know the next event is a completion.

We now update everything as follows: State is 1 job. Clock = $7.3 + 8 = 15.3$. To determine the time to the next completion, we generate an instance of S, say $S = 1$, and set Time-to-next-completion = 1. Time-to-next-arrival = $9.5 - 8 = 1.5$ because 8 seconds have already passed since the last arrival, decreasing the previous time from 9.5 down to 1.5.

We continue in this manner, with updates to the state happening only at job arrival times or completions. Note that we only generate new instances of I or S as needed.

Question: When exactly do we generate a new instance of I?

Answer: There are two times: The main time we generate a new instance of I is immediately after a new job arrives. However, we also generate a new instance of I at the very start of the simulation when there are 0 jobs.

Question: When exactly do we generate a new instance of S?

Answer: The main time we generate a new instance of S is immediately after a job completes service. However, there is an exception to this rule, which occurs when the system moves from State 1 (one job) to State 0 (zero jobs). At that time, the Time-to-next-completion is set to ∞. Additionally, we generate a new instance of S at the time when the system moves from State 0 to State 1.

Question: What changes if a trace is used to provide interarrival times and/or job sizes – that is, we run a trace-driven simulation?

Answer: Nothing, really. The same approach is used, except that rather than generating a new instance of I or S when we need it, we just read the next value from the trace.

14.3 How to Get Performance Metrics from Your Simulation

So now you have your simulation running. How do you figure out the **mean response time**? We propose two methods, the first of which we already discussed briefly.

Method 1: Every job records the clock time when it arrives and then records the clock time when it completes. Taking the difference of these gives us the job's response time. We now just need to average the response time over all the jobs.

Question: Should we write each job's response time into a file and then take the average at the end of our simulation?

Answer: No, the writing wastes time in our simulation. You should be able to maintain a running average. Let $\overline{T}_n$ denote the average over the first n jobs:

$$\overline{T}_n = \frac{1}{n} \sum_{i=1}^{n} T_i.$$

Then $\overline{T}_{n+1}$ can easily be determined from $\overline{T}_n$ as follows:

$$\overline{T}_{n+1} = \frac{1}{n+1} \cdot \left(\overline{T}_n \cdot n + T_{n+1}\right).$$

Method 2: We perform several runs of the simulation. A single **run** involves running the simulation, without bothering to have jobs record their response time, until we get to the 10,000th job (we've picked this number arbitrarily). We then record the response time of that 10,000th job. We now start the simulation from scratch, repeating this process for, say, 1000 runs. Each run provides us with just a single number. We now take the average of all 1000 numbers to obtain the mean response time.

Question: What are some benefits to Method 1?

Answer: Method 1 is simpler because we don't have to keep restarting the simulation from scratch.

Question: What are some benefits to Method 2?

Answer: Method 2 provides independent measurements of response time. Notice that Method 1 does not provide independent measurements, because if a job has high response time then it is likely that the subsequent job also has high response time (the queue is currently long). Having independent measurements has the advantage that we can create a **confidence interval** around our measured mean response time. We defer discussion of how to obtain confidence intervals to Chapter 19.

If one runs a simulation for long enough, it really doesn't matter whether one uses Method 1 or Method 2, assuming that your system is well behaved.[1] This brings us to another question.

Question: How long is "long enough" to run a simulation?

Answer: We want to run the simulation until the metric of interest, in this case mean response time, appears to have stabilized (it's not going up or down substantially). There are many factors that increase the time it takes for a simulation to converge. These include load, number of servers, and any type of variability, either in the arrival process or the job service times. It is not uncommon to need to run a simulation with a billion arrivals before results stabilize.

Now suppose the goal is not the mean response time, but rather the **mean number**

---

[1] Technically, by well behaved we mean that the system is "ergodic." It suffices that the system empties infinitely often. For a more detailed discussion of ergodicity, see Chapter 25 and Section 27.7.

of jobs in the system, $\mathbf{E}[N]$. Specifically, we define the mean number as a time-average, as follows: Let $M(s)$ denote the number of jobs in the system at time s. Then,

$$\mathbf{E}[N] = \lim_{t \to \infty} \frac{\int_{s=0}^{s=t} M(s)ds}{t}. \qquad (14.1)$$

Think of this as summing the number of jobs in the system over every moment of time s from $s = 0$ to $s = t$ and then dividing by t to create an average. Obviously we're not really going to take t to infinity in our simulation, but rather just some high enough number that the mean number of jobs stabilizes.

Question: But how do we get $\mathbf{E}[N]$ from our simulation? We're not going to look at the number at every single time s. Which times do we use? Can we simply measure the number of jobs in the system as seen by each arrival and average all of those?

Answer: This is an interesting question. It turns out that if the arrival process is a Poisson process, then we can simply record the number of jobs as seen by each arrival. This is due to a property called PASTA (Poisson arrivals see time averages), explained in [35, section 13.3]. Basically this works because of the memoryless property of a Poisson process, which says that the next arrival can come at any time, which can't in any way be predicted. Thus the arrival times of a Poisson process are good "random" points for sampling the current number of jobs.

Unfortunately, if the arrival process is not a Poisson process, then having each arrival track the number of jobs that it sees can lead to very wrong results.

Question: Can you provide an example for what goes wrong when we average over what arrivals see?

Answer: Suppose that $I \sim \text{Uniform}(1, 2)$. Suppose that $S = 1$. Then every arrival finds an empty system and thus we would conclude that the mean number of jobs is 0, when in reality the mean number of jobs is: $\frac{2}{3} \cdot 1 + \frac{1}{3} \cdot 0 = \frac{2}{3}$.

Question: So how do we measure the mean number of jobs in the system if the arrival process is *not* a Poisson process?

Answer: The easiest solution is to simulate a Poisson process (independent of the arrival process) and sample the number of jobs at the times of that simulated Poisson process. This adds more events since we now have arrivals, completions, and Poisson events.

14.4 More Complex Examples

We now turn to some more complex examples of queueing networks.

Example 14.1 (Router with finite buffer)

Figure 14.2 shows a router with finite (bounded) buffer space. There is room for $n = 6$ packets, one in service (being transmitted) and the others waiting to be transmitted. Note that all the packets are purposely depicted as having the same size, as is typical for packets. When a packet arrives and doesn't find space, it is dropped.

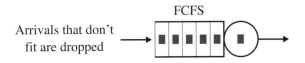

Figure 14.2 *Queue with finite buffer space.*

In terms of running the simulation, nothing changes. The system state is still the number of packets in the system. As before we generate packet sizes and interarrival times as needed. One of the common reasons to simulate a router with finite buffer space is to understand how the buffer space affects the fraction of packets that are dropped. We will investigate this in Exercise 14.4.

Question: Suppose we are trying to understand mean response time in the case of the router with finite buffer space. What do we do with the dropped packets?

Answer: Only the response times of packets that enter the system are counted.

Example 14.2 (Packet-routing network)

Figure 14.3 shows a network of three queues, where all queues are unbounded (infinite buffer space). A packet may enter either from queue 1 or from queue 2. If the packet enters at queue 2, it will serve at queue 2 and leave without joining any other queues. A packet entering at queue 1 will serve at queue 1 and then move to either queue 2 or queue 3, each with probability 0.5. We might be interested here in the response time of a packet entering at queue 1, where response time is the time from when the packet arrives at queue 1 until it leaves the network (either at server 2 or at server 3).

Question: What is the state space for Figure 14.3?

Answer: The system state is the number of packets at each of the three queues.

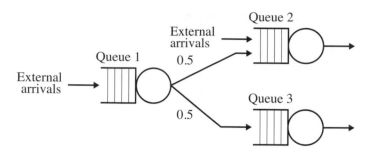

Figure 14.3 *Network of queues.*

Question: How many possible events do we need to watch for now?

Answer: We need to track five possible events. For queue 1, we need to track Time-to-next-arrival and Time-to-next-completion. For queue 3, we only need to track Time-to-next-completion. The arrival times at queue 3 are determined by flipping a fair coin after each completion at queue 1. Likewise, for queue 2, the internal arrival times at queue 2 are determined by flipping a fair coin after each completion at queue 1. However, queue 2 also has *external* arrivals. These external arrivals need to be tracked. Thus, for queue 2 we need to track the Time-to-next-external-arrival and Time-to-next-completion.

Example 14.3 (Call center)

Figure 14.4 shows an example of a call center, as might be operated by a company like Verizon. There is an arrival stream of incoming calls. There are k servers (operators) ready to accept calls. When a call comes in, it goes to any operator who is free (we imagine that all operators are homogeneous). If no operators are free, the call has to queue. Whenever an operator frees up, it takes the call at the head of the queue (i.e., calls are served in FCFS order). We assume that the service times of calls are i.i.d., represented by r.v. S. Here we might be interested in the average or variance of the queueing time experienced by calls.

Question: Do calls leave in the order that they arrived?

Answer: No. Calls enter service in the order that they arrived, but some calls might be shorter than others, and hence may leave sooner, even though they entered later.

Question: What is the state space for Figure 14.4?

Answer: The system state is the total number of jobs in the system (we do not need to differentiate between those in service and those queued), plus the remaining service time for each of the jobs in service.

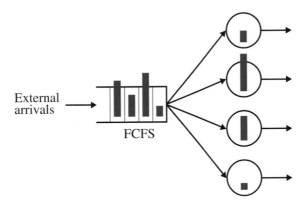

Figure 14.4 *Call center with k = 4 servers.*

Question: What are the events that we need to track?

Answer: We need to track $k + 1$ events. These are the Time-to-next-completion at each of the k servers and the Time-to-next-arrival for the system.

We will explore additional examples in the exercises.

14.5 Exercises

14.1 **Mean response time in an M/M/1 queue**
In this problem you will simulate a queue, as shown in Figure 14.1, and measure its mean job response time, $\mathbf{E}[T]$. Job sizes are i.i.d. instances of $S \sim \text{Exp}(\mu)$, where $\mu = 1$. The arrival process is a Poisson process with rate λ. The queue is called an M/M/1 to indicate that both interarrival times and job sizes are memoryless (M). For each value of $\lambda = 0.5, 0.6, 0.7, 0.8, 0.9$, record both $\mathbf{E}[T]$ and $\mathbf{E}[N]$. Draw curves showing what happens to $\mathbf{E}[T]$ and $\mathbf{E}[N]$ as you increase λ. To check that your simulation is correct, it helps to verify that Little's Law ($\mathbf{E}[N] = \lambda \cdot \mathbf{E}[T]$) holds. Little's Law will be covered in Chapter 27.

14.2 **Server utilization of an M/M/1 queue**
Repeat Exercise 14.1, but this time measure the server utilization, ρ, which is the long-run fraction of time that the server is busy. To get ρ, you will sample the server at the times of job arrivals to determine the average fraction of arrivals that see a busy server.

14.3 **Doubling the arrival rate and the service rate**
Repeat Exercises 14.1 and 14.2, but this time double each of the original

arrival rates and simultaneously double the service rate. Specifically, in these "new" runs, our arrival rates will be: $\lambda = 1.0, 1.2, 1.4, 1.6, 1.8$, and our job sizes will be i.i.d. instances of $S \sim \text{Exp}(\mu)$, where $\mu = 2$.

(a) How does ρ_{new} compare with ρ_{orig}?

(b) How does $\mathbf{E}[N_{\text{new}}]$ compare with $\mathbf{E}[N_{\text{orig}}]$?

(c) How does $\mathbf{E}[T_{\text{new}}]$ compare with $\mathbf{E}[T_{\text{orig}}]$?

Try to provide intuition for your findings. [Hint: Think about how doubling the arrival rate and service rate affects time scales.]

14.4 Effect on loss probability of various improvements
As in Exercise 14.1, we have a queue whose arrivals are a Poisson process with rate λ, and whose job sizes are i.i.d. instances of r.v. $S \sim \text{Exp}(\mu)$. Let $\mu = 1$ and $\lambda = 0.9$. Now suppose that the queue is bounded so that at most $n = 5$ jobs can be in the system (one serving and the other four queueing).

(a) Simulate the system to determine the loss probability, namely the fraction of arriving jobs that are dropped because they don't fit.

(b) That loss probability is deemed too high, and you are told that you must lower it. You are considering two possible improvements:

(i) Double the capacity of your system by setting $n = 10$.

(ii) Double the speed of your server (double μ) to $\mu = 2$.

Which is more effective at reducing loss probability? Simulate and find out.

(c) Conjecture on why you got the answer that you got for part (b). Do you think that your answer to part (b) is always true? If you can't decide, run some more simulations with different values of λ.

14.5 Effect of variability of job size on response time
In this problem, we will study the effect of variability of job sizes on response time by using a DegenerateHyperexponential(μ, p) distribution, which will allow us to increase the variability in job size, S, by playing with μ and p parameters. The **Degenerate Hyperexponential** with parameters μ and p is defined as follows:

$$S \sim \begin{cases} \text{Exp}(p\mu) & \text{w/prob } p \\ 0 & \text{w/prob } 1 - p \end{cases}.$$

(a) What is $\mathbf{E}[S]$? Is this affected by p?

(b) What is the squared coefficient of variation of S, namely C_S^2?

(c) What is the range of possible values for C_S^2, over $0 < p < 1$?

(d) Create a simulation to determine mean queueing time, $\mathbf{E}[T_Q]$, in a single queue. The arrival process to the queue is a Poisson process with rate $\lambda = 0.8$. The job sizes are denoted by $S \sim$ DegenerateHyperexponential($\mu = 1, p$). You will run multiple simulations, each with the appropriate value of p to create the cases of $C_S^2 = 1, 3, 5, 7, 9$. Draw a graph with $\mathbf{E}[T_Q]$ on the y-axis and C_S^2 on the x-axis. Note that a job of size 0 may still experience a queueing time, even though its service time is 0.

(e) What happens when C_S^2 increases? Why do you think this is? Think about it from the perspective of the time that the average job waits.

14.6 Favoring short jobs over long ones

Consider a queue with a Poisson arrival process and mean interarrival time of 110. Job sizes are drawn i.i.d. from

$$S \sim \begin{cases} 1 & \text{w/prob } 0.5 \\ 200 & \text{w/prob } 0.5 \end{cases}.$$

(a) Simulate the queue where the jobs are served in FCFS order. What is the mean response time, $\mathbf{E}[T]$?

(b) Now consider a different scheduling policy, called Non-Preemptive Shortest Job First (NP-SJF). Like FCFS, NP-SJF is *non-preemptive*, meaning that once we start running a job, we always finish it. However, in NP-SJF the jobs of size 1 always have priority over the jobs of size 200. Specifically, NP-SJF maintains two FCFS queues, one with jobs of size 1 and the other with jobs of size 200, where, whenever the server is free, it picks to run the job at the head of the queue of jobs of size 1. Only if there is no job of size 1 does the server run a job of size 200. Note that among jobs of a given size, the service order is still FCFS. Simulate NP-SJF and report $\mathbf{E}[T]$. Try to use as little state as you can get away with.

(c) You should find that $\mathbf{E}[T]$ is much lower under NP-SJF scheduling than under FCFS scheduling. Why do you think this is?

14.7 SRPT queue versus FCFS queue

The Shortest Remaining Processing Time (SRPT) scheduling policy minimizes mean response time, $\mathbf{E}[T]$ [66, 67]. Under SRPT, at all times the server is working on that job with the shortest *remaining* processing time. The SRPT policy is *preemptive*, meaning that jobs can be stopped and restarted with no overhead. Under SRPT, a new arrival will preempt the current job serving if and only if the new arrival has size which is smaller than the remaining time on the job in service.

(a) Suppose we have an SRPT queue and job j is currently running. Can job j be preempted by any of the other jobs currently in the queue?

(b) In an SRPT queue, can there be multiple jobs which have each received partial service so far?

(c) Simulate an SRPT queue, with Poisson arrival process with rate $\lambda = 0.45$. Assume that the job sizes are $S \sim \text{BoundedPareto}(k = 0.004, p = 1000, \alpha = 0.5)$ (see Definition 10.5). What is $\mathbf{E}[T]^{\text{SRPT}}$?

(d) Perform the same simulation but for a FCFS queue. What is $\mathbf{E}[T]^{\text{FCFS}}$?

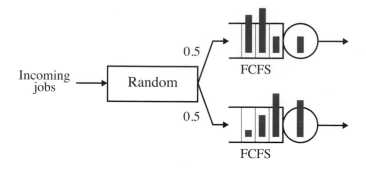

(a) Random Task Assignment

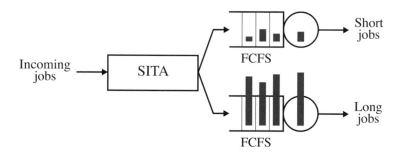

(b) Size-Interval Task Assignment

Figure 14.5 *Random dispatching versus SITA dispatching.*

14.8 Size-Interval Task Assignment versus Random

Figure 14.5 illustrates a server farm with two identical FCFS queues. In Figure 14.5(a), every incoming arrival is dispatched (assigned) with probability 0.5 to the first queue and probability 0.5 to the second queue. This is called Random task assignment (Random). In Figure 14.5(b), if the incoming arrival is "small" then it is dispatched to the top queue, and if it is "large" it is dispatched to the bottom queue. This is called Size-Interval Task Assignment (SITA) [36, 34]. Suppose that arrivals occur according to a Poisson process with rate $\lambda = 0.5$. Assume that job sizes are i.i.d. and follow a BoundedPareto($k = 0.004, p = 1000, \alpha = 0.5$) distribution (see Definition 10.5) with mean $\mathbf{E}[S] = 2$.

(a) Simulate Random assignment and report the mean queueing time $\mathbf{E}[T_Q]$.

(b) Simulate SITA. Use a size cutoff of 58.3, where jobs smaller than this cutoff are deemed "small." Report $\mathbf{E}[T_Q]$.

(c) Which was better? Why do you think this is?

Part V

Statistical Inference

The focus until now in the book has been on *probability*. We can think of probability as defined by a probabilistic model, or distribution, which governs an "experiment," through which one *generates* samples, or events, from this distribution. One might ask questions about the probability of a certain event occurring, under the known probabilistic model.

We now turn our attention to *statistics*. In statistics, we go the other direction. We are given some data, and our goal is to *infer* the underlying probabilistic model that generated this data.

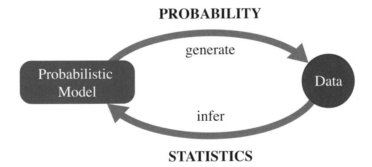

The figure above illustrates the difference in direction. While statistics and probability may sound different, they are actually closely linked. In particular, when a statistician is trying to "infer" (estimate) the underlying probabilistic model that generated some data, they might start by computing the probability that certain candidate models produced that data.

Because the data that we see is limited, either in quantity (there may only be a few samples) or in accuracy (the data may be somewhat noisy or corrupted), there is often some subjectivity involved in determining the best estimator for the underlying probabilistic model. In this sense, statistics is sometimes viewed as more of an art, where statisticians might argue with each other over which estimator is more "correct." We will see several examples of this in our study of statistical inference.

We start in Chapter 15 by discussing the most commonly used estimators, namely those for mean and variance. In Chapter 16 we move on to parameter estimation following the classical inference approach of maximum likelihood estimation. In Chapter 17 we continue looking at parameter estimation, but this time via the Bayesian inference approach, where we discuss maximum a posteriori estimators and minimum mean square error estimators. Along the way, we also touch on a few related topics like linear regression (see Section 16.7).

Although this is the main statistics part of the book, statistical topics come up throughout the book. In particular, the important topic of confidence intervals on estimators is deferred to Chapter 19, since it is better treated after a more in-depth discussion of tail probabilities.

15 Estimators for Mean and Variance

The general setting in statistics is that we observe some data and then try to infer some property of the underlying distribution behind this data. The underlying distribution behind the data is unknown and represented by random variable (r.v.) X. This chapter will briefly introduce the general concept of estimators, focusing on estimators for the mean and variance.

15.1 Point Estimation

Point estimation is an estimation method which outputs a single value. As an example of a point estimation, suppose we are trying to estimate the number of books that the average person reads each year. We sample n people at random from the pool of all people and ask them how many books they read annually. Let $X_1, X_2, \ldots, X_n$ represent the responses of the n people. We can assume that the pool of people is sufficiently large that it's reasonable to think of the X_i's as being independent and identically distributed (i.i.d.), where $X_i \sim X$ for all i. We would like to estimate $\theta = \mathbf{E}[X]$. A reasonable point estimator for θ is simply the average of the X_i's sampled.

> **Definition 15.1** *We write*
>
> $$\hat{\theta}(X_1, X_2, \ldots, X_n)$$
>
> *to indicate an* **estimator** *of the unknown value θ. Here $X_1, \ldots, X_n$ represent the sampled data and our estimator is a function of this data. Importantly, $\hat{\theta}(X_1, X_2, \ldots, X_n)$ is a* **random variable***, since it is a function of random variables. We sometimes write $\hat{\theta}$ for short when the sample data is understood. We write*
>
> $$\hat{\theta}(X_1 = k_1, X_2 = k_2, \ldots, X_n = k_n)$$
>
> *to indicate the* **constant** *which represents our estimation of θ based on a specific instantiation of the data where $X_1 = k_1, X_2 = k_2, \ldots, X_n = k_n$.*

15.2 Sample Mean

While $\hat{\theta}$ is the notation most commonly used for an estimator of θ, there are certain estimators, like the "sample mean," that come up so frequently that they have their own name.

Definition 15.2 (Mean estimator) *Let $X_1, X_2, \ldots, X_n$ be i.i.d. samples of r.v. X with unknown mean. The **sample mean** is a point estimator of $\theta = \mathbf{E}[X]$. It is denoted by $\overline{X}$ or by M_n, and defined by:*

$$\hat{\theta}(X_1, X_2, \ldots, X_n) = M_n = \overline{X} \equiv \frac{X_1 + X_2 + \cdots + X_n}{n}. \tag{15.1}$$

The notation M_n is attractive because it specifies the number of samples, while the notation $\overline{X}$ is attractive because it specifies the underlying distribution whose mean we are estimating.

15.3 Desirable Properties of a Point Estimator

For any unknown parameter θ that we wish to estimate, there are often many possible estimators.

As a running example, throughout this section, let $X_1, X_2, \ldots, X_n$ be i.i.d. random samples from a distribution represented by r.v. X, with finite mean $\mathbf{E}[X]$ and finite variance σ^2.

In estimating $\theta = \mathbf{E}[X]$, consider two possible estimators:

$$\hat{\theta}_A = \overline{X} = \frac{X_1 + X_2 + \cdots + X_n}{n}$$

$$\hat{\theta}_B = X_2.$$

What makes one estimator better than another? In this section we define some desirable properties of a point estimator.

Definition 15.3 *Let $\hat{\theta}(X_1, X_2, \ldots X_n)$ be a point estimator for θ. Then we define the **bias** of $\hat{\theta}$ by*

$$\mathbf{B}(\hat{\theta}) = \mathbf{E}[\hat{\theta}] - \theta.$$

*If $\mathbf{B}(\hat{\theta}) = 0$, we say that $\hat{\theta}$ is an **unbiased estimator** of θ.*

Clearly we would like our estimator to have zero bias.

Question: How do $\hat{\theta}_A$ and $\hat{\theta}_B$ compare with respect to bias?

Answer: They are both unbiased estimators.

Question: Nevertheless, why do you favor $\hat{\theta}_A$ over $\hat{\theta}_B$?

Answer: $\hat{\theta}_A$ feels less variable. This brings us to the second desirable property of an estimator, which is low mean squared error.

Definition 15.4 *The* **mean squared error** *(MSE) of an estimator* $\hat{\theta}(X_1, X_2, \ldots, X_n)$ *is defined as:*

$$\mathbf{MSE}(\hat{\theta}) = \mathbf{E}\left[(\hat{\theta} - \theta)^2\right].$$

Lemma 15.5 *If $\hat{\theta}(X_1, X_2, \ldots, X_n)$ is an unbiased estimator, then*

$$\mathbf{MSE}(\hat{\theta}) = \mathbf{Var}(\hat{\theta}).$$

Proof:

$$\mathbf{MSE}(\hat{\theta}) = \mathbf{E}\left[(\hat{\theta} - \theta)^2\right] = \mathbf{E}\left[(\hat{\theta} - \mathbf{E}\left[\hat{\theta}\right])^2\right] = \mathbf{Var}(\hat{\theta}). \qquad \blacksquare$$

Question: How do $\hat{\theta}_A$ and $\hat{\theta}_B$ compare with respect to their MSE?

Answer: Using Lemma 15.5,

$$\mathbf{MSE}(\hat{\theta}_A) = \mathbf{Var}(\hat{\theta}_A) = \frac{1}{n^2} \cdot n\mathbf{Var}(X) = \frac{\mathbf{Var}(X)}{n}.$$

By contrast,

$$\mathbf{MSE}(\hat{\theta}_B) = \mathbf{Var}(\hat{\theta}_B) = \mathbf{Var}(X_2) = \mathbf{Var}(X).$$

Thus $\hat{\theta}_A$ has much lower MSE.

Finally, it is desirable that our estimator has the property that it becomes more accurate (closer to θ) as the sample size increases. We refer to this property as **consistency**.

Definition 15.6 *Let $\hat{\theta}_1(X_1), \hat{\theta}_2(X_1, X_2), \hat{\theta}_3(X_1, X_2, X_3), \ldots$ be a sequence of point estimators of θ, where $\hat{\theta}_n(X_1, X_2, \ldots, X_n)$ is a function of n i.i.d. samples. We say that r.v. $\hat{\theta}_n$ is a* **consistent estimator** *of θ if, $\forall \epsilon > 0$,*

$$\lim_{n \to \infty} \mathbf{P}\left\{|\hat{\theta}_n - \theta| \geq \epsilon\right\} = 0.$$

Lemma 15.7 Let $\hat{\theta}_1(X_1), \hat{\theta}_2(X_1, X_2), \hat{\theta}_3(X_1, X_2, X_3), \ldots$ be a sequence of point estimators of θ, where $\hat{\theta}_n(X_1, X_2, \ldots, X_n)$ is a function of n i.i.d. samples. Assume that all the estimators have finite mean and variance. If

$$\lim_{n \to \infty} \mathbf{MSE}(\hat{\theta}_n) = 0,$$

then $\hat{\theta}_n$ is a consistent estimator.

Proof: For any constant $\epsilon > 0$,

$$\mathbf{P}\left\{\left|\hat{\theta}_n - \theta\right| \geq \epsilon\right\} = \mathbf{P}\left\{\left|\hat{\theta}_n - \theta\right|^2 \geq \epsilon^2\right\}$$

$$\leq \frac{\mathbf{E}\left[\left|\hat{\theta}_n - \theta\right|^2\right]}{\epsilon^2} \qquad \text{by Markov's inequality (Theorem 5.16)}$$

$$= \frac{\mathbf{E}\left[\left(\hat{\theta}_n - \theta\right)^2\right]}{\epsilon^2}$$

$$= \frac{\mathbf{MSE}(\hat{\theta}_n)}{\epsilon^2}.$$

Taking limits of both sides as $n \to \infty$, we have:

$$\lim_{n \to \infty} \mathbf{P}\left\{\left|\hat{\theta}_n - \theta\right| \geq \epsilon\right\} = \lim_{n \to \infty} \frac{\mathbf{MSE}(\hat{\theta}_n)}{\epsilon^2} = 0. \qquad \blacksquare$$

Question: In the proof of Lemma 15.7, why didn't we apply Chebyshev's inequality (Theorem 5.17)?

Answer: We don't know that $\theta = \mathbf{E}\left[\hat{\theta}_n\right]$, so we can't say that $\mathbf{MSE}(\hat{\theta}_n) = \mathbf{Var}(\hat{\theta}_n)$.

Question: Is $\hat{\theta}_A = \overline{X} = M_n$ a consistent estimator of $\mathbf{E}[X]$?

Answer: Yes. By Lemma 15.7, it suffices to show that

$$\lim_{n \to \infty} \mathbf{MSE}(M_n) = 0.$$

Given that we know that M_n is an unbiased estimator of $\mathbf{E}[X]$, Lemma 15.5 tells us that it suffices to show that

$$\lim_{n \to \infty} \mathbf{Var}(M_n) = 0.$$

But this latter fact is obviously true because $\mathbf{Var}(X)$ is finite and thus

$$\mathbf{Var}(M_n) = \frac{\mathbf{Var}(X)}{n} \to 0 \qquad \text{as } n \to \infty.$$

Hence, M_n is a consistent estimator.

15.4 An Estimator for Variance

Again let $X_1, X_2, \ldots, X_n$ denote n i.i.d. samples of an unknown distribution denoted by r.v. X, where $X_i \sim X$, and where $\mathbf{E}[X] = \mu$ and $\mathbf{Var}(X) = \sigma_X^2$ are finite. We have seen that $\overline{X} = \frac{X_1 + X_2 + \cdots + X_n}{n}$ is a good estimator for $\mathbf{E}[X]$, satisfying all three desirable properties. We now turn to the question of a good estimator for $\mathbf{Var}(X)$.

There are two distinct cases to consider:

1. The case where we already know the mean and want to estimate $\theta = \mathbf{Var}(X)$.
2. The case where we do not know the mean and want to estimate $\theta = \mathbf{Var}(X)$.

It turns out that the best estimator is different for these two cases.

15.4.1 Estimating the Variance when the Mean is Known

Starting with the first case, suppose that μ is known. We can then define an estimator which computes the squared distance of each sample from μ and takes the average of these squared distances:

$$\hat{\theta}(X_1, X_2, \ldots, X_n) = \overline{S^2} \equiv \frac{1}{n} \sum_{i=1}^{n} (X_i - \mu)^2 . \tag{15.2}$$

Question: Is $\overline{S^2}$ as defined in (15.2) an unbiased estimator for $\theta = \mathbf{Var}(X)$?

Answer: Yes!

$$\mathbf{E}\left[\overline{S^2}\right] = \frac{1}{n} \sum_{i=1}^{n} \mathbf{E}\left[(X_i - \mu)^2\right] = \frac{1}{n} \sum_{i=1}^{n} \mathbf{Var}(X_i) = \mathbf{Var}(X).$$

15.4.2 Estimating the Variance when the Mean is Unknown

Now consider the second case, where μ is not known. This case is way more common but also trickier.

Question: Given that we don't know $\mu = \mathbf{E}[X]$, how can we replace μ in our definition of the estimator?

Answer: We can replace μ by $\overline{X} = \frac{X_1 + X_2 + \cdots + X_n}{n}$, which we already saw was a good estimator for $\mathbf{E}[X]$.

This leads us to an updated definition of our estimator, which now computes the squared distance of each sample from $\overline{X}$ and takes the average of these squared distances:

$$\hat{\theta}(X_1, X_2, \ldots, X_n) = \overline{S^2} \equiv \frac{1}{n} \sum_{i=1}^{n} \left(X_i - \overline{X} \right)^2 \tag{15.3}$$

Question: Is $\overline{S^2}$ as defined in (15.3) an unbiased estimator for $\theta = \mathbf{Var}(X)$?

Answer: Unfortunately, and surprisingly, the answer is no. In Exercise 15.4, you will prove that

$$\mathbf{E}\left[\overline{S^2}\right] = \frac{n-1}{n} \cdot \mathbf{Var}(X). \tag{15.4}$$

Question: Given (15.4), what is an unbiased estimator for $\theta = \mathbf{Var}(X)$ in the case where we don't know $\mathbf{E}[X]$?

Answer: We need to multiply $\overline{S^2}$ by $\frac{n}{n-1}$. The sample variance, defined next, does this.

Definition 15.8 (Variance Estimator) *Let $X_1, X_2, \ldots, X_n$ be i.i.d. samples of r.v. X with unknown mean and variance. The* **sample variance** *is a point estimator of $\theta = \mathbf{Var}(X)$. It is denoted by S^2 and defined by:*

$$\hat{\theta}(X_1, X_2, \ldots, X_n) = S^2 \equiv \frac{1}{n-1} \sum_{i=1}^{n} \left(X_i - \overline{X} \right)^2 \tag{15.5}$$

Lemma 15.9 *The sample variance, S^2, from Definition 15.8 is an unbiased estimator of* $\mathbf{Var}(X)$.

Proof:

$$\mathbf{E}\left[S^2\right] \stackrel{(15.3)}{=} \frac{n}{n-1} \mathbf{E}\left[\overline{S^2}\right] \stackrel{(15.4)}{=} \frac{n}{n-1} \cdot \frac{n-1}{n} \cdot \mathbf{Var}(X) = \mathbf{Var}(X) \qquad \blacksquare$$

Question: The difference between the estimators $\overline{S^2}$ in (15.3) and S^2 in (15.5) is very slight. Does it really matter which we use?

Answer: Assuming that the number of samples, n, is large, in practice it shouldn't matter which of these two estimators we use.

15.5 Estimators Based on the Sample Mean

Simple estimators, like the sample mean, can sometimes be useful in estimating other, more complex quantities. We provide one example here and another in Exercise 15.6.

Example 15.10 (Estimating the number of tanks)

In World War II, the Allies were trying to estimate the number of German tanks. Each tank was assigned a serial number when it was created. When the Allies captured a tank, they would record its serial number.

Question: If the Allies captured the tanks with serial numbers shown in Figure 15.1, what is a good estimate for the total number of German tanks?

Figure 15.1 *Captured tanks with serial numbers shown.*

We are trying to estimate a *maximum*, call it θ, based on seeing n samples, $X_1, X_2, \ldots, X_n$, each of which are randomly picked *without replacement* from the integers $1, 2, \ldots, \theta$. Our goal is to determine $\hat{\theta}(X_1, X_2, \ldots, X_n)$.

Question: Are the n samples independent?

Answer: No. Once serial number k is seen, it will never be seen again.

There are many ways to estimate the max, θ. We will use the sample mean to estimate θ, by expressing the expectation of the sample mean as a function of θ.

$$\overline{X} = \frac{1}{n}(X_1 + X_2 + \cdots + X_n)$$

$$\mathbf{E}\left[\overline{X}\right] = \frac{1}{n}(\mathbf{E}[X_1] + \mathbf{E}[X_2] + \cdots + \mathbf{E}[X_n]).$$

Although the X_i's are not independent, they all have the same marginal distribution:

$$\mathbf{P}\{X_i = k\} = \frac{1}{\theta}, \quad \text{where } 1 \le k \le \theta.$$

Hence,

$$\mathbf{E}[X_i] = \frac{1}{\theta} \cdot 1 + \frac{1}{\theta} \cdot 2 + \cdots + \frac{1}{\theta} \cdot \theta = \frac{\theta + 1}{2}.$$

But this implies

$$\mathbf{E}\left[\overline{X}\right] = \frac{\theta + 1}{2}.$$ (15.6)

Equivalently, we can write

$$\theta = 2\mathbf{E}\left[\overline{X}\right] - 1.$$

Hence, a reasonable estimator for θ could be

$$\hat{\theta}(X_1, X_2, \ldots, X_n) \equiv 2\overline{X} - 1.$$ (15.7)

Question: Is $\hat{\theta}$ from (15.7) an unbiased estimator?

Answer: Yes, by (15.6), we see that $\mathbf{E}\left[\hat{\theta}\right] = 2\mathbf{E}\left[\overline{X}\right] - 1 = \theta$.

Question: Is $\hat{\theta}$ from (15.7) a good estimator of θ?

Answer: Not necessarily. If the number of samples, n, is small, we could end up in the perverse situation where there is one very high sample, while most of the samples are far below the mean. In this case, our sample mean, $\overline{X}$, would be particularly low, so $\hat{\theta} = 2\overline{X} - 1$ might actually be smaller than the largest sample.

Now suppose we want to determine $\mathbf{MSE}(\hat{\theta})$. Since $\hat{\theta}$ is an unbiased estimator, by Lemma 15.5, $\mathbf{MSE}(\hat{\theta}) = \mathbf{Var}(\hat{\theta})$. Thus,

$$\mathbf{MSE}(\hat{\theta}) = \mathbf{Var}(\hat{\theta}) = \mathbf{Var}\left(2\overline{X} - 1\right)$$

$$= \frac{4}{n^2}\mathbf{Var}(X_1 + X_2 + \cdots + X_n)$$

$$= \frac{4}{n^2} \cdot \left(\sum_{i=1}^{n}\mathbf{Var}(X_i) + 2\sum_{1 \leq i < j \leq n}\mathbf{Cov}(X_i, X_j)\right) \quad \text{(by (5.11))}$$

$$= \frac{4}{n} \cdot \left(\mathbf{Var}(X_1) + (n-1)\mathbf{Cov}(X_1, X_2)\right),$$

where the last line follows from the fact that all the X_i's have the same distribution, and all the pairs (X_i, X_j) have the same distribution.

From (5.13) and (5.14), we know that:

$$\mathbf{Var}(X_1) = \frac{(\theta - 1)(\theta + 1)}{12} \qquad \text{and} \qquad \mathbf{Cov}(X_1, X_2) = -\frac{\theta + 1}{12}.$$

Hence,

$$\mathbf{MSE}(\hat{\theta}) = \frac{4}{n} \cdot \left(\frac{(\theta - 1)(\theta + 1)}{12} - (n - 1) \cdot \frac{\theta + 1}{12}\right) = \frac{1}{3n}(\theta + 1)(\theta - n).$$

So we see that the MSE of our estimate increases with the square of the highest value, θ, and decreases linearly with the number of samples, n.

15.6 Exercises

15.1 Practice computing sample mean and sample variance
The following 10 job sizes are measured: $5, 2, 6, 9, 1.5, 2.3, 7, 15, 8, 8.3$.
What is the sample mean, $\overline{X}$? What is the sample variance, S^2?

15.2 Accuracy of sample mean and sample variance
Generate 30 instances of each of the following distributions – recall (13.2):
   (i) $X \sim \text{Exp}(1)$
   (ii) $X \sim \text{Exp}(.01)$
   (iii)

$$X \sim \begin{cases} \text{Exp}(1) & \text{w/prob } 0.99 \\ \text{Exp}(.01) & \text{w/prob } 0.01 \end{cases}.$$

For each distribution, answer the following questions:
   (a) What is the sample mean? Compare this with the true mean, $\mathbf{E}[X]$.
   (b) What is the sample variance? Compare this with $\mathbf{Var}(X)$.
   (c) For which distribution was the sample mean most (least) accurate? How about the sample variance? Provide some thoughts on why.
Now repeat the problem, generating 100 instances of each distribution.

15.3 Variance–bias decomposition
Given an estimator $\hat{\theta}(X_1, \ldots, X_n)$, prove that
$$\mathbf{MSE}(\hat{\theta}) = \mathbf{Var}(\hat{\theta}) + (\mathbf{B}(\hat{\theta}))^2, \tag{15.8}$$
where $\mathbf{B}(\hat{\theta}) \equiv \mathbf{E}[\hat{\theta}] - \theta$ is the bias of $\hat{\theta}$.

15.4 Estimating variance is tricky
Let $X_1, X_2, \ldots, X_n$ be i.i.d. samples of r.v. X with unknown finite mean and variance. Let $\overline{X}$ denote the sample mean. Define
$$\overline{S^2} \equiv \frac{1}{n} \sum_{i=1}^{n} \left(X_i - \overline{X}\right)^2.$$

Prove that $\overline{S^2}$ is *not* an unbiased estimator of $\mathbf{Var}(X)$. Follow these steps:
   (a) Prove that $\mathbf{E}\left[\overline{S^2}\right] = \frac{1}{n} \sum_{i=1}^{n} \mathbf{Var}\left(X_i - \overline{X}\right)$.
   (b) Show that $\mathbf{Var}\left(X_i - \overline{X}\right) = \frac{n-1}{n} \mathbf{Var}(X)$.
   (c) Combine (a) and (b) to show that $\mathbf{E}\left[\overline{S^2}\right] = \frac{n-1}{n} \mathbf{Var}(X)$.

15.5 Sample standard deviation

Let $X_1, X_2, \ldots, X_n$ be i.i.d. samples of r.v. X with unknown finite mean and variance. Define the **sample standard deviation**, S, as

$$S = \sqrt{S^2},$$

where S^2 is the sample variance, given by (15.5). Is S an unbiased estimator of **std**(X)? Prove your answer. [Hint 1: S is not a constant, so **Var**$(S) > 0$.] [Hint 2: Use the fact that $\mathbf{E}\left[S^2\right] = \mathbf{Var}(X)$.]

15.6 Arrivals at a web server: two estimators

The arrival process of requests to a web server is well-modeled by a Poisson process with some average rate λ requests/minute. We're interested in

$p_0 = $ Fraction of minutes during which there are 0 requests.

If we know λ, then we know from Chapter 12 that $p_0 = e^{-\lambda}$. But how can we estimate p_0 if we don't know λ? Let's suppose that we have sampled n minutes and let $X_1, X_2, \ldots, X_n$ denote the number of arrivals during each of the n minutes.

(a) One idea is to first define an estimator for λ, namely

$$\hat{\lambda}(X_1, \ldots, X_n) = \overline{X} = \frac{1}{n}(X_1 + X_2 + \cdots + X_n),$$

and then define our estimator for p_0 to be

$$\hat{p}_0(X_1, \ldots, X_n) = e^{-\hat{\lambda}} = e^{-\overline{X}}.$$

Prove that $\hat{p}_0$ is a biased estimator of p_0. Follow these steps:
  (i) What does Jensen's inequality (Theorem 5.23) tell us about $\mathbf{E}\left[\hat{p}_0\right]$ as compared to p_0?
  (ii) Prove that $\mathbf{E}\left[\hat{p}_0\right] = e^{-n\lambda(1-e^{-1/n})}$. [Hint: Recall $X_i \sim $ Poisson(λ). What does this say about the distribution of $X_1 + X_2 + \cdots + X_n$?]
  (iii) Show that $\mathbf{E}\left[\hat{p}_0\right]$ converges to p_0 from above as $n \to \infty$.
(b) An alternative idea is to look at the average fraction of minutes with 0 arrivals and use that as our estimator. That is,

$$\hat{p}_0^{\text{alt}}(X_1, \ldots, X_n) = \frac{\text{number of } X_i \text{ equal to } 0}{n}.$$

Prove that $\hat{p}_0^{\text{alt}}$ is an unbiased estimator of p_0.

15.7 Acknowledgment

This chapter was written in collaboration with Weina Wang, who was a major contributor to the chapter contents and the exercises.

16 Classical Statistical Inference

In Chapter 15, we focused on estimating the mean and variance of a distribution given observed samples. In this chapter and the next, we look at the more general question of statistical inference, where this time we are estimating the parameter(s) of a distribution or some other quantity. We will continue to use the notation for estimators given in Definition 15.1.

16.1 Towards More General Estimators

We start the chapter with another example of point estimation.

Example 16.1 (Estimating the number of pink jelly beans)

Consider the jar of jelly beans shown in Figure 16.1. Suppose that we know that the jar has 1000 jelly beans. Our goal is to estimate the number of pink jelly beans. Let

$$\theta = \text{Number of pink jelly beans in the jar.}$$

To estimate θ, we randomly sample $n = 20$ jelly beans with replacement.

Figure 16.1 *This jar has 1000 jelly beans. How many of them are pink?*

Let X be the number of pink jelly beans that we observe in our sample of $n = 20$.

Observe that X is a random variable (r.v.) since the experiment is random. X can take on values from 0 to n. We use r.v. $\hat{\theta}(X)$ to denote our estimator of θ.

Question: What is a reasonable guess for what $\hat{\theta}(X)$ might look like?

Hint: It is easier to think about a specific instantiation of X. For example, suppose we observe $X = x$ pink jelly beans.

Answer: If we observe x jelly beans in our sample, then a reasonable estimate for the *fraction* of pink jelly beans is $\frac{x}{n}$. Hence we estimate the *number* of pink jelly beans is

$$\hat{\theta}(X = x) = \left(\frac{x}{n}\right) \cdot 1000, \qquad 0 \le x \le n. \tag{16.1}$$

Now, since (16.1) holds for every value of x, it follows that we can define

$$\hat{\theta}(X) = \left(\frac{X}{n}\right) \cdot 1000. \tag{16.2}$$

Question: Is $\hat{\theta}(X)$, as defined in (16.2), an unbiased estimator of θ?

Hint: It helps to start by considering the distribution of X.

Answer: Let us define

$$p = \frac{\theta}{1000}$$

to be the true fraction of pink jelly beans. Then,

$$X \sim \text{Binomial}(n, p),$$

and hence

$$\mathbf{E}[X] = np = n \cdot \frac{\theta}{1000}.$$

From this it follows that

$$\mathbf{E}\left[\hat{\theta}(X)\right] = \mathbf{E}\left[\frac{X}{n} \cdot 1000\right] = \mathbf{E}[X] \cdot \frac{1000}{n}$$

$$= n \cdot \frac{\theta}{1000} \cdot \frac{1000}{n}$$

$$= \theta. \qquad \checkmark$$

Thus, $\hat{\theta}(X)$ is an unbiased estimator of θ.

Question: Is $\hat{\theta}(x)$ a consistent estimator of θ?

Answer: Yes! To see this, we will show that $\mathbf{MSE}(\hat{\theta}) \to 0$, as $n \to \infty$. Note that n can be arbitrarily high because we're sampling with replacement.

We start by observing that $\mathbf{MSE}(\hat{\theta}) = \mathbf{Var}(\hat{\theta})$, by Lemma 15.5. Hence,

$$
\begin{aligned}
\mathbf{MSE}(\hat{\theta}) = \mathbf{Var}(\hat{\theta}) &= \left(\frac{1000}{n}\right)^2 \cdot np(1-p) \\
&= \left(\frac{1000}{n}\right)^2 \cdot n \cdot \frac{\theta}{1000}\left(1 - \frac{\theta}{1000}\right) \\
&= \frac{\theta(1000 - \theta)}{n}.
\end{aligned}
$$

Clearly, $\mathbf{MSE}(\hat{\theta}) \to 0$ as $n \to \infty$, so $\hat{\theta}$ is a consistent estimator, by Lemma 15.7.

16.2 Maximum Likelihood Estimation

In the previous section, we came up with what seemed like a reasonable estimator. However, there was no specific *method* for coming up with this estimator, nor the estimators in the prior chapter. In this section we describe a specific *methodology* for deriving an estimator. The methodology is called **maximum likelihood estimation (MLE)**. It is the *classical inference methodology* adopted by statisticians who consider themselves to be *frequentists*. In the next chapter we will investigate a different methodology for coming up with estimators which is preferred by the *Bayesian* statisticians.

In explaining the MLE method, to simplify notation we will assume that the sample data is just a single r.v., X, but in general it can be $X_1, X_2, \ldots, X_n$. For now we will assume that we have a single unknown, θ, that we are trying to estimate; we will later consider multiple unknowns. The goal is to derive $\hat{\theta}(X)$, which is a maximum likelihood estimator of θ based on the sample data X; we refer to this as an **ML estimator**. To create an ML estimator, we first consider an *arbitrary specific value* of the sample data, $X = x$, and ask,

"What is the value of θ which maximizes the likelihood of seeing $X = x$?"

The expression that we derive will be a function of x. Since x is chosen *arbitrarily*, this allow us to define $\hat{\theta}$ as a function of the r.v. X.

> **Algorithm 16.2 (Creating an ML estimator)** *Our goal is to estimate an un-known value, θ, given sample data represented by r.v. X.*
>
> *1. Define*
> $$\hat{\theta}_{ML}(X = x) = \underset{\theta}{argmax}\, \mathbf{P}\{X = x \mid \theta\}.$$
>
> $\mathbf{P}\{X = x \mid \theta\}$ *is called the* **likelihood function** *and represents the proba-bility that $X = x$, given a particular θ. The value of θ which maximizes the likelihood function is denoted by $\hat{\theta}_{ML}(X = x)$.*
>
> *2. Convert $\hat{\theta}_{ML}(X = x)$, which is a function of x, for any arbitrary x, into r.v. $\hat{\theta}_{ML}(X)$, which is a function of a r.v., by replacing x with X.*

The MLE method is best illustrated via an example. Returning to Example 16.1, suppose that in our sample of $n = 20$ jelly beans we observe $X = 3$ jelly beans.

Question: What is $\mathbf{P}\{X = 3 \mid \theta\}$?

Answer: If we're given that there are θ pink jelly beans, then the fraction of pink jelly beans is $p = \frac{\theta}{1000}$. Hence, given $n = 20$, we have

$$\mathbf{P}\{X = 3 \mid \theta\} = \binom{20}{3}\left(\frac{\theta}{1000}\right)^{3}\cdot\left(1 - \frac{\theta}{1000}\right)^{17}.$$

Figure 16.2 shows the probability that $X = 3$ under all possible values of θ from 0 to 1000, assuming $n = 20$.

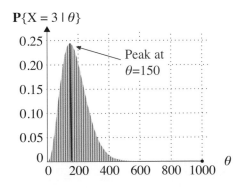

Figure 16.2 $\mathbf{P}\{X = 3 \mid \theta\}$ *as a function of θ, assuming $n = 20$.*

Question: Based on Figure 16.2, what value of θ maximizes $\mathbf{P}\{X = 3 \mid \theta\}$?

Answer: $\theta = 150$. So

$$\hat{\theta}_{ML}(X = 3) = \underset{\theta}{argmax}\,\mathbf{P}\{X = 3 \mid \theta\} = 150.$$

Question: What is the likelihood function, $\mathbf{P}\{X = x \mid \theta\}$?

Answer:

$$\mathbf{P}\{X = x \mid \theta\} = \binom{n}{x}\left(\frac{\theta}{1000}\right)^x \cdot \left(1 - \frac{\theta}{1000}\right)^{n-x}.$$

Question: What is $\hat{\theta}_{\text{ML}}(X = x) = \underset{\theta}{\text{argmax}}\, \mathbf{P}\{X = x \mid \theta\}$?

Answer: To answer this, we'll need to solve for the value of θ which maximizes the likelihood function:

$$0 = \frac{d}{d\theta}\mathbf{P}\{X = x \mid \theta\}$$

$$= \frac{d}{d\theta}\binom{n}{x}\left(\frac{\theta}{1000}\right)^x \cdot \left(1 - \frac{\theta}{1000}\right)^{n-x}$$

$$= \binom{n}{x} \cdot \left(\frac{\theta}{1000}\right)^x \cdot (n - x) \cdot \left(1 - \frac{\theta}{1000}\right)^{n-x-1} \cdot \frac{-1}{1000}$$

$$+ \binom{n}{x} \cdot x\left(\frac{\theta}{1000}\right)^{x-1} \cdot \frac{1}{1000}\left(1 - \frac{\theta}{1000}\right)^{n-x}.$$

If we divide both sides by $\binom{n}{x} \cdot \left(\frac{\theta}{1000}\right)^{x-1} \cdot \left(1 - \frac{\theta}{1000}\right)^{n-1-x}$, we are left with:

$$0 = -\frac{n-x}{1000} \cdot \frac{\theta}{1000} + \frac{x}{1000} \cdot \left(1 - \frac{\theta}{1000}\right)$$

$$0 = -(n - x)\theta + x(1000 - \theta)$$

$$\theta = \frac{1000x}{n}.$$

It is easily shown that the second derivative of the likelihood function is negative, and thus

$$\theta = \frac{1000x}{n}$$

is in fact the value of θ that maximizes the likelihood function. Hence,

$$\hat{\theta}_{\text{ML}}(X = x) = \frac{1000x}{n}. \tag{16.3}$$

Question: Given that

$$\hat{\theta}_{\text{ML}}(X = x) = \frac{1000x}{n}, \quad \text{for all } 0 \leq x \leq n,$$

what does this say about $\hat{\theta}_{\text{ML}}(X)$?

Answer:

$$\hat{\theta}_{\text{ML}}(X) = \frac{1000X}{n}.$$

Notice that this is the same estimator that we arrived at in (16.2); however, this time we followed a specific method (MLE) for coming up with the estimator.

16.3 More Examples of ML Estimators

Example 16.3 (Submissions to the Pittsburgh Supercomputing Center)

The number of jobs submitted daily to the Pittsburgh Supercomputing Center (PSC) follows a Poisson distribution with unknown parameter λ. Suppose that the numbers of job submissions on different days are independent. We observe the number of job submissions each day for a month, and denote these by $X_1, X_2, \ldots, X_{30}$. Our goal is to derive $\hat{\lambda}_{\text{ML}}(X_1, X_2, \ldots, X_{30})$, the ML estimator for λ.

Question: Before we do the computation, ask yourself: What do you expect the answer to be?

Hint: Recall that the parameter λ represents the mean of the Poisson distribution.

Answer: We are being asked to estimate the unknown parameter λ, which is the mean number of arrivals. It would make sense if this was simply the sample mean. That is:

$$\hat{\lambda}_{\text{ML}}(X_1, X_2, \ldots, X_{30}) = \frac{X_1 + X_2 + \cdots + X_{30}}{30}.$$

We now proceed to follow the MLE method, which will lead us to find that our intuition is in fact correct.

We write

$$\hat{\lambda}_{\text{ML}}(X_1 = x_1, X_2 = x_2, \ldots, X_{30} = x_{30})$$
$$= \underset{\lambda}{\text{argmax}} \; \mathbf{P}\{X_1 = x_1, X_2 = x_2, \ldots, X_{30} = x_{30} \mid \lambda\}$$
$$= \underset{\lambda}{\text{argmax}} \; \frac{\lambda^{x_1} e^{-\lambda}}{x_1!} \cdot \frac{\lambda^{x_2} e^{-\lambda}}{x_2!} \cdots \frac{\lambda^{x_{30}} e^{-\lambda}}{x_{30}!}$$
$$= \underset{\lambda}{\text{argmax}} \; \frac{\lambda^{x_1+x_2+\cdots+x_{30}} e^{-30\lambda}}{x_1! x_2! \cdots x_{30}!}.$$

To find the maximizing λ, we set the derivative of the likelihood function to 0:

$$0 = \frac{d}{d\lambda}\left(\frac{\lambda^{x_1+\cdots+x_{30}}e^{-30\lambda}}{x_1!x_2!\cdots x_{30}!}\right)$$

$$= \frac{(x_1+\cdots+x_{30})\,\lambda^{x_1+\cdots+x_{30}-1}\cdot e^{-30\lambda} + \lambda^{x_1+\cdots+x_{30}}\cdot e^{-30\lambda}\cdot(-30)}{x_1!\cdots x_{30}!}$$

Dividing both sides by the appropriate constants leaves us with

$$0 = (x_1+\cdots+x_{30}) + \lambda\cdot(-30). \qquad (16.4)$$

Solving (16.4), and verifying that the second derivative is negative, yields

$$\lambda = \frac{x_1+\cdots+x_{30}}{30}$$

as the value of λ which maximizes the likelihood function.

Hence,

$$\hat{\lambda}_{\mathrm{ML}}(X_1 = x_1, X_2 = x_2, \ldots, X_{30} = x_{30}) = \frac{x_1+\cdots+x_{30}}{30}, \quad \forall x_1,\ldots,x_{30} \geq 0.$$

So

$$\hat{\lambda}_{\mathrm{ML}}(X_1, X_2, \ldots, X_{30}) = \frac{X_1 + X_2 + \ldots X_{30}}{30},$$

as predicted.

16.4 Log Likelihood

Sometimes, rather than finding the value of θ that maximizes some probability, it is more convenient to maximize the log of that probability. Lemma 16.4 makes this clear.

Lemma 16.4 (Maximizing the log likelihood) *Given an unknown value, θ, that we are trying to estimate, suppose that we have sample data represented by r.v. X. Then,*

$$\hat{\theta}_{ML}(X = x) \equiv \underset{\theta}{argmax}\, \mathbf{P}\{X = x \mid \theta\} = \underset{\theta}{argmax}\, \log \mathbf{P}\{X = x \mid \theta\}.$$

Here, $\log \mathbf{P}\{X = x \mid \theta\}$ is referred to as the **log likelihood function**.

Proof: Maximizing the log likelihood is equivalent to maximizing the likelihood since log is a strictly increasing function. ∎

Example 16.5 (Submissions to the PSC, revisited!)

Let's revisit Example 16.3, where the goal is to estimate λ. This time, however, we derive the estimator that maximizes the log likelihood:

$$\hat{\lambda}_{\text{ML}}(X_1 = x_1, X_2 = x_2, \ldots, X_{30} = x_{30})$$

$$= \underset{\lambda}{\text{argmax}} \ \ln\left(\mathbf{P}\{X_1 = x_1, X_2 = x_2, \ldots, X_{30} = x_{30} \mid \lambda\}\right)$$

$$= \underset{\lambda}{\text{argmax}} \ \ln\left(\mathbf{P}\{X_1 = x_1 \mid \lambda\} \cdot \mathbf{P}\{X_2 = x_2 \mid \lambda\} \cdots \mathbf{P}\{X_{30} = x_{30} \mid \lambda\}\right).$$

Hence,

$$\hat{\lambda}_{\text{ML}}(X_1 = x_1, X_2 = x_2, \ldots, X_{30} = x_{30})$$

$$= \underset{\lambda}{\text{argmax}} \ \sum_{i=1}^{30} \ln \mathbf{P}\{X_1 = x_1 \mid \lambda\}$$

$$= \underset{\lambda}{\text{argmax}} \ \sum_{i=1}^{30} \ln\left(\frac{e^{-\lambda}\lambda^{x_i}}{x_i!}\right)$$

$$= \underset{\lambda}{\text{argmax}} \ \left(-30\lambda + \sum_{i=1}^{30} x_i \ln(\lambda) - \sum_{i=1}^{30} \ln(x_i!)\right)$$

$$= \underset{\lambda}{\text{argmax}} \ \left(-30\lambda + \sum_{i=1}^{30} x_i \ln(\lambda)\right).$$

To find the maximizing λ, we set the derivative of the log likelihood function to 0:

$$0 = \frac{d}{d\lambda}\left(-30\lambda + \sum_{i=1}^{30} x_i \ln(\lambda)\right) = -30 + \left(\sum_{i=1}^{30} x_i\right) \cdot \frac{1}{\lambda}.$$

Hence,

$$\lambda = \frac{x_1 + x_2 + \cdots + x_{30}}{30}.$$

Thus again,

$$\hat{\lambda}_{\text{ML}}(X_1 = x_1, X_2 = x_2, \ldots, X_{30} = x_{30}) = \frac{x_1 + x_2 + \cdots + x_{30}}{30}.$$

16.5 MLE with Data Modeled by Continuous Random Variables

When data is modeled by continuous random variables, we replace the probability mass function (p.m.f.) with the probability density function (p.d.f.) in expressing the likelihood. Definitions 16.6 and 16.7 provide a summary.

Definition 16.6 (MLE summary: single variable) *Given an unknown value, θ, that we wish to estimate:*
If the sample data is represented by **discrete** *r.v. X, then we define*

$$\hat{\theta}_{ML}(X = x) \equiv \underset{\theta}{argmax}\, \mathbf{P}\{X = x \mid \theta\}.$$

If the sample data is represented by **continuous** *r.v. X, we instead define*

$$\hat{\theta}_{ML}(X = x) \equiv \underset{\theta}{argmax}\, f_{X \mid \theta}(x).$$

Definition 16.7 (MLE summary: multiple variables) *Given an unknown value, θ, that we wish to estimate:*
If the sample data is represented by **discrete** *random variables $X_1, X_2, \ldots, X_n$, we define*

$$\hat{\theta}_{ML}(X_1 = x_1, X_2 = x_2, \ldots, X_n = x_n) \equiv \underset{\theta}{argmax}\, \mathbf{P}\{X_1 = x_1, \ldots, X_n = x_n \mid \theta\}.$$

If the sample data is represented by **continuous** *random variables $X_1, X_2, \ldots, X_n$, we define*

$$\hat{\theta}_{ML}(X_1 = x_1, X_2 = x_2, \ldots, X_n = x_n) \equiv \underset{\theta}{argmax}\, f_{X_1, X_2, \ldots, X_n \mid \theta}(x_1, x_2, \ldots, x_n).$$

Example 16.8 (Time students spend on their probability homework)

Students often ask, "How long can I expect to spend on homework if I take the PnC probability class?" It turns out that the distribution of the time that students spend on homework is approximately distributed as Uniform$(0, b)$, where students can be viewed as independent in the time that they spend doing the homework. To get a feel for what b is, we survey three students. Let X_1, X_2, X_3 denote the times reported by the three students.

What is the ML estimator $\hat{b}_{ML}(X_1, X_2, X_3)$ for b?

$$\hat{b}_{\mathrm{ML}}(X_1 = x_1, X_2 = x_2, X_3 = x_3) = \underset{b}{\mathrm{argmax}}\ f_{X_1,X_2,X_3|b}(x_1,x_2,x_3).$$

$$f_{X_1,X_2,X_3|b}(x_1,x_2,x_3) = \begin{cases} \frac{1}{b^3} & \text{if } 0 < x_1,x_2,x_3 \le b \\ 0 & \text{otherwise} \end{cases}$$

$$= \begin{cases} \frac{1}{b^3} & \text{if } b \ge \max\{x_1,x_2,x_3\} \\ 0 & \text{otherwise} \end{cases}.$$

Clearly $f_{X_1,X_2,X_3|b}(x_1,x_2,x_3)$ achieves its maximum when $b = \max\{x_1,x_2,x_3\}$. Therefore,

$$\hat{b}_{\mathrm{ML}}(X_1 = x_1, X_2 = x_2, X_3 = x_3) = \max\{x_1,x_2,x_3\}$$

and

$$\hat{b}_{\mathrm{ML}}(X_1, X_2, X_3) = \max\{X_1, X_2, X_3\}.$$

Question: Does $\hat{b}_{\mathrm{ML}}$ feel like a good estimator of b? Is it what you would have expected?

Answer: Clearly, our estimate for b must be at least equal to the maximum of the samples. But it's not clear that our estimate shouldn't be *higher* than the maximum observed. In fact, if we've only made a few observations, one would expect b to be higher than the highest observation so far.

Question: Is $\hat{b}_{\mathrm{ML}}$ an unbiased estimator?

Answer: This will be explored in Exercise 16.5, where you will show that $\hat{b}_{\mathrm{ML}}$ is not an unbiased estimator, but can be made into one pretty easily.

We now turn to one more example involving continuous random variables.

Example 16.9 (Estimating the standard deviation of temperature)

The high temperature in Pittsburgh in June is (approximately) Normally distributed with a mean of $\mu = 79$ F. Suppose we would like to estimate the standard deviation, σ, of temperature. To do this, we observe the temperature on n randomly sampled independent June days, denoted by $X_1, X_2, \ldots, X_n$. Derive $\hat{\theta}_{\mathrm{ML}}(X_1, X_2, \ldots, X_n)$, the ML estimator of σ.

We will use the log likelihood formulation:

$$\hat{\sigma}_{\mathrm{ML}}(X_1 = x_1, X_2 = x_2, \ldots, X_n = x_n) = \underset{\sigma}{\mathrm{argmax}}\ \ln\left(f_{X_1,X_2,\ldots,X_n|\sigma}(x_1,x_2,\ldots,x_n)\right),$$

where

$$\ln \left(f_{X_1,\ldots,X_n \mid \sigma}(x_1,\ldots,x_n) \right)$$

$$= \ln \left(\prod_{i=1}^{n} f_{X_i \mid \sigma}(x_i) \right)$$

$$= \sum_{i=1}^{n} \ln \left(f_{X_i \mid \sigma}(x_i) \right)$$

$$= \sum_{i=1}^{n} \ln \left(\frac{1}{\sqrt{2\pi}\sigma} e^{-\frac{(x_i-\mu)^2}{2\sigma^2}} \right)$$

$$= \sum_{i=1}^{n} \left(-\frac{(x_i-\mu)^2}{2\sigma^2} - \ln \sigma - \ln \sqrt{2\pi} \right)$$

$$= -\frac{1}{2\sigma^2} \sum_{i=1}^{n} (x_i - \mu)^2 - n \ln \sigma - n \ln \sqrt{2\pi}. \qquad (16.5)$$

To find the maximizing σ, we set the derivative of (16.5) to 0:

$$0 = \frac{d}{d\sigma} \left(-\frac{1}{2\sigma^2} \sum_{i=1}^{n} (x_i - \mu)^2 - n \ln \sigma - n \ln \sqrt{2\pi} \right)$$

$$= \frac{1}{\sigma^3} \sum_{i=1}^{n} (x_i - \mu)^2 - \frac{n}{\sigma}$$

$$= \frac{1}{\sigma^2} \sum_{i=1}^{n} (x_i - \mu)^2 - n \qquad \text{(multiplying both sides by } \sigma\text{)}.$$

This yields

$$\sigma = \sqrt{\frac{\sum_{i=1}^{n} (x_i - \mu)^2}{n}}.$$

Hence,

$$\hat{\sigma}_{\mathrm{ML}}(X_1 = x_1, X_2 = x_2, \ldots, X_n = x_n) = \sqrt{\frac{\sum_{i=1}^{n} (x_i - \mu)^2}{n}},$$

and thus it follows that

$$\hat{\sigma}_{\mathrm{ML}}(X_1, X_2, \ldots, X_n) = \sqrt{\frac{\sum_{i=1}^{n} (X_i - \mu)^2}{n}}. \qquad (16.6)$$

Question: How does $\hat{\sigma}_{\text{ML}}(X_1, X_2, \ldots, X_n)$ in (16.6) compare with $\sqrt{S^2}$ from (15.2)?

Answer: These are the same.

16.6 When Estimating More than One Parameter

Sometimes we want to estimate more than one parameter of a distribution. This is done by defining an MLE that jointly optimizes over multiple parameters.

To see how this works, let's return to Example 16.9. Suppose this time we need to estimate both the mean, μ, and the standard deviation, σ, of the Normal distribution of temperature. Again we have n randomly sampled temperatures: $X_1, X_2, \ldots, X_n$. This time, we wish to derive a pair of ML estimators: $\hat{\mu}_{\text{ML}}(X_1, X_2, \ldots, X_n)$ and $\hat{\sigma}_{\text{ML}}(X_1, X_2, \ldots, X_n)$, where

$$\left(\begin{array}{l} \hat{\mu}\,(X_1 = x_1, \ldots, X_n = x_n) \\ \hat{\sigma}\,(X_1 = x_1, \ldots, X_n = x_n) \end{array} \right) = \underset{\mu, \sigma}{\text{argmax}}\ \ln\left(f_{X_1, \ldots, X_n | \mu, \sigma}(x_1, \ldots, x_n) \right).$$

Our likelihood function, $g(\mu, \sigma)$, now depends on two parameters:

$$g(\mu, \sigma) = f_{X_1, X_2, \ldots, X_n | \mu, \sigma}(x_1, x_2, \ldots, x_n).$$

To find the pair (μ, σ) that maximizes $g(\mu, \sigma)$, we set both of the partial derivatives below to 0:

$$\frac{\partial \ln g(\mu, \sigma)}{\partial \mu} = 0 \qquad \text{and} \qquad \frac{\partial \ln g(\mu, \sigma)}{\partial \sigma} = 0.$$

From (16.5), we know that

$$\ln\left(g(\mu, \sigma)\right) = -\frac{1}{2\sigma^2} \sum_{i=1}^{n} (x_i - \mu)^2 - n \ln \sigma - n \ln \sqrt{2\pi}.$$

Taking partial derivatives, we have that:

$$\frac{\partial \ln g(\mu, \sigma)}{\partial \mu} = \frac{1}{\sigma^2} \sum_{i=1}^{n} (x_i - \mu), \tag{16.7}$$

$$\frac{\partial \ln g(\mu, \sigma)}{\partial \sigma} = \frac{1}{\sigma^3} \sum_{i=1}^{n} (x_i - \mu)^2 - \frac{n}{\sigma}. \tag{16.8}$$

Setting $\frac{\partial \ln g(\mu, \sigma)}{\partial \mu} = 0$ in (16.7) and $\frac{\partial \ln g(\mu, \sigma)}{\partial \sigma} = 0$ in (16.8) yields

$$\mu = \frac{x_1 + x_2 + \cdots + x_n}{n} \qquad \text{and} \qquad \sigma = \sqrt{\frac{1}{n} \sum_{i=1}^{n} (x_i - \mu)^2}.$$

Substituting the expression $\mu = \frac{x_1 + x_2 + \cdots + x_n}{n}$ into the expression for σ, we get

$$\sigma = \sqrt{\frac{1}{n} \sum_{i=1}^{n} \left(x_i - \frac{x_1 + x_2 + \cdots + x_n}{n} \right)^2}.$$

Hence we have that

$$\hat{\mu}(X_1 = x_1, \ldots, X_n = x_n) = \frac{x_1 + x_2 + \cdots + x_n}{n}$$

and

$$\hat{\sigma}(X_1 = x_1, \ldots, X_n = x_n) = \sqrt{\frac{1}{n} \sum_{i=1}^{n} \left(x_i - \frac{x_1 + x_2 + \cdots + x_n}{n} \right)^2}.$$

Since these hold for all values of $x_1, \ldots, x_n$, we have that:

$$\hat{\mu}(X_1, \ldots, X_n) = \frac{X_1 + X_2 + \cdots + X_n}{n}$$

and

$$\hat{\sigma}(X_1, \ldots, X_n) = \sqrt{\frac{1}{n} \sum_{i=1}^{n} \left(X_i - \frac{X_1 + X_2 + \cdots + X_n}{n} \right)^2}.$$

16.7 Linear Regression

We now turn to a different kind of estimation optimization problem, which is very common in data analysis. We are given n data points generated through some experiment. We can think of the ith data point as a pair of random variables, (X_i, Y_i) with value $(X_i = x_i, Y_i = y_i)$. We want to find the line that best fits the specific values: $(x_1, y_1), (x_2, y_2), \ldots, (x_n, y_n)$, as shown in Figure 16.3. This is called **linear regression**.

As a concrete example, a company might be trying to understand how advertising is related to revenue. The company has data showing different periods where advertising was lower or higher, and the corresponding revenue during those periods. The company would like to use this data to create a linear approximation of the relationship between advertising (x value) and revenue (y value).

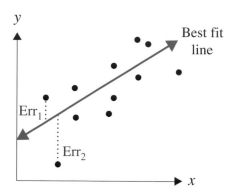

Figure 16.3 *An example of linear regression.*

Recall that a line in the x–y plane is determined by two parameters a and b, where

$$y = ax + b.$$

Our goal is to determine the values of a and b which define a line that best fits our data, where "best" is defined in Definition 16.10.

Definition 16.10 (Linear regression) *Let* $\{(X_1, Y_1), (X_2, Y_2), \ldots, (X_n, Y_n)\}$ *be a set of data sample points. Suppose that* $\hat{a}$ *and* $\hat{b}$ *are estimators for the* a *and* b *parameters of a line fitting the sample points. For the purpose of estimation,* Y_i *is viewed as the* **dependent r.v.** *and* X_i *as the* **independent r.v.** *The* **estimated dependent r.v.** *is* $\hat{Y}_i$, *where*

$$\hat{Y}_i \equiv \hat{a} X_i + \hat{b}.$$

The **point-wise error** *is defined as the difference between the value of the estimated dependent r.v. and the true value for the ith point:*

$$\text{Err}_i = Y_i - \hat{Y}_i.$$

The **sample average squared error (SASE)** *is then:*

$$\text{SASE}(\hat{Y}_1, \ldots, \hat{Y}_n) = \frac{1}{n} \sum_{i=1}^{n} (\text{Err}_i)^2 = \frac{1}{n} \sum_{i=1}^{n} (Y_i - \hat{Y}_i)^2. \qquad (16.9)$$

The goal of **linear regression** *is to find estimates* $\hat{a}$ *and* $\hat{b}$ *that minimize* $\text{SASE}(\hat{Y}_1, \ldots, \hat{Y}_n)$.

Our plan is to derive estimators

$$\hat{a}\left((X_1,Y_1),\ldots(X_n,Y_n)\right) \qquad \text{and} \qquad \hat{b}\left((X_1,Y_1),\ldots(X_n,Y_n)\right),$$

which are functions of the data and which minimize $\textbf{SASE}(\hat{Y}_1,\ldots,\hat{Y}_n)$ in (16.9).[1]

Question: What goes wrong if we try to set up $\hat{a}$ and $\hat{b}$ as ML estimators?

Answer: Observe that the likelihood function doesn't make sense here. There is no probability:

$$\textbf{P}\left\{(X_1 = x_1, Y_1 = y_1),\ldots,(X_n = x_n, Y_n = y_n) \mid a, b\right\}$$

because once the X_i's are specified and a and b are specified, then the Y_i's are immediately specified.

The point is that we are not trying to maximize a likelihood function, but rather we're finding the $\hat{a}$ and $\hat{b}$ estimators that minimize the **SASE**. Other than that change in objective, however, the optimization setup is very similar to what we do under MLE, which is why we've included the topic in this chapter.

Question: How do we set up the optimization problem, replacing the likelihood function by the **SASE**?

Answer: For a given set of specific points, $(x_1, y_1),\ldots,(x_n, y_n)$, and a given choice of a and b, we define

$$g(a,b) = \textbf{SASE} = \frac{1}{n}\sum_{i=1}^{n}\left(y_i - (ax_i + b)\right)^2.$$

Then,

$$\left(\begin{array}{l} \hat{a}\left((X_1 = x_1, Y_1 = y_1),\ldots,(X_n = x_n, Y_n = y_n)\right) \\ \hat{b}\left((X_1 = x_1, Y_1 = y_1),\ldots,(X_n = x_n, Y_n = y_n)\right) \end{array}\right) = \operatorname*{argmin}_{a,b} g(a,b)$$

$$= \operatorname*{argmin}_{a,b}\left(\frac{1}{n}\sum_{i=1}^{n}\left(y_i - (ax_i + b)\right)^2\right)$$

$$= \operatorname*{argmin}_{a,b}\left(\sum_{i=1}^{n}\left(y_i - (ax_i + b)\right)^2\right). \qquad (16.10)$$

---

[1] The **SASE** is reminiscent of the **MSE** that we define in Chapters 15 and 17, and in fact many books write **MSE** here. The main difference is that **SASE** is a *sample average* of squares, while **MSE** is an expectation of squares.

Question: How do we find the minimizing (a, b)?

Answer: To find the pair (a, b) that minimizes $g(a, b)$, we set both of the partial derivatives below to 0:

$$\frac{\partial g(a, b)}{\partial a} = 0 \quad \text{and} \quad \frac{\partial g(a, b)}{\partial b} = 0.$$

We start with finding the minimizing b. By (16.10),

$$0 = -\sum_{i=1}^{n} \frac{\partial}{\partial b} (y_i - (ax_i + b))^2$$

$$= 2 \sum_{i=1}^{n} (y_i - (ax_i + b))$$

$$= \sum_{i=1}^{n} (y_i - (ax_i + b)) \qquad \text{(divide both sides by 2)}$$

$$= \sum_{i=1}^{n} y_i - a \sum_{i=1}^{n} x_i - nb.$$

Solving for b, we get:

$$b = \frac{\sum_{i=1}^{n} y_i}{n} - a \frac{\sum_{i=1}^{n} x_i}{n}$$

$$= \bar{y} - a\bar{x}, \qquad\qquad (16.11)$$

where we define

$$\bar{x} = \frac{x_1 + x_2 + \cdots + x_n}{n} \quad \text{and} \quad \bar{y} = \frac{y_1 + y_2 + \cdots + y_n}{n}.$$

We next find the minimizing a. By (16.10),

$$0 = -\sum_{i=1}^{n} \frac{\partial}{\partial a} (y_i - (ax_i + b))^2$$

$$= 2 \sum_{i=1}^{n} (y_i - (ax_i + b)) \cdot x_i$$

$$= \sum_{i=1}^{n} y_i x_i - b \sum_{i=1}^{n} x_i - a \sum_{i=1}^{n} x_i^2. \qquad \text{(divide both sides by 2)}$$

To solve for a, it helps to first substitute in our optimizing b from (16.11):

$$0 = \sum_{i=1}^{n} y_i x_i - (\bar{y} - a\bar{x}) \sum_{i=1}^{n} x_i - a \sum_{i=1}^{n} x_i^2$$

$$0 = \sum_{i=1}^{n} x_i (y_i - \bar{y}) + \sum_{i=1}^{n} x_i a\bar{x} - a \sum_{i=1}^{n} x_i^2$$

$$\sum_{i=1}^{n} x_i (y_i - \bar{y}) = a \left(\sum_{i=1}^{n} x_i^2 - \sum_{i=1}^{n} x_i \bar{x} \right).$$

Hence,

$$a = \frac{\sum_{i=1}^{n} x_i (y_i - \bar{y})}{\sum_{i=1}^{n} x_i (x_i - \bar{x})}$$

$$= \frac{\sum_{i=1}^{n} x_i (y_i - \bar{y}) - \sum_{i=1}^{n} \bar{x} (y_i - \bar{y})}{\sum_{i=1}^{n} x_i (x_i - \bar{x}) - \sum_{i=1}^{n} \bar{x} (x_i - \bar{x})} \quad \text{since} \quad \sum_{i=1}^{n} (y_i - \bar{y}) = 0 = \sum_{i=1}^{n} (x_i - \bar{x})$$

$$= \frac{\sum_{i=1}^{n} (x_i - \bar{x})(y_i - \bar{y})}{\sum_{i=1}^{n} (x_i - \bar{x})^2}. \tag{16.12}$$

Hence, from (16.11) and (16.12), and substituting in $\hat{a}$ for a in (16.11), we have that

$$\hat{b} ((x_1, y_1), \ldots, (x_n, y_n)) = \bar{y} - \hat{a}\bar{x}$$

$$\hat{a} ((x_1, y_1), \ldots, (x_n, y_n)) = \frac{\sum_{i=1}^{n} (x_i - \bar{x})(y_i - \bar{y})}{\sum_{i=1}^{n} (x_i - \bar{x})^2}.$$

As these estimators are defined for all values of $(x_1, y_1), \ldots, (x_n, y_n)$, it follows that

$$\hat{b} ((X_1, Y_1), \ldots, (X_n, Y_n)) = \bar{Y} - \hat{a}\bar{X} \tag{16.13}$$

$$\hat{a} ((X_1, Y_1), \ldots, (X_n, Y_n)) = \frac{\sum_{i=1}^{n} \left(X_i - \bar{X} \right) \left(Y_i - \bar{Y} \right)}{\sum_{i=1}^{n} \left(X_i - \bar{X} \right)^2}. \tag{16.14}$$

Using $\hat{a}$ and $\hat{b}$ from (16.13) and (16.14) guarantees our linear fit has minimal **SASE**.

Question: There's a natural interpretation for $\hat{b}$ in (16.13). What is it?

Answer: We can rearrange (16.13) to say

$$\bar{Y} = \hat{a}\bar{X} + \hat{b},$$

which makes perfect sense since we want $Y_i = aX_i + b$, and $\overline{Y}$ is the sample mean of the Y_i's and $\overline{X}$ is the sample mean of the X_i's.

Question: There's also a natural interpretation for $\hat{a}$ in (16.14) if we multiply the numerator and denominator by $\frac{1}{n-1}$. What is it?

Answer:

$$\hat{a}\left((X_1, Y_1), \ldots, (X_n, Y_n)\right) = \frac{\frac{1}{n-1} \sum_{i=1}^{n} \left(X_i - \overline{X}\right)\left(Y_i - \overline{Y}\right)}{\frac{1}{n-1} \sum_{i=1}^{n} \left(X_i - \overline{X}\right)^2} = \frac{\text{Cov}(X, Y)}{\text{Var}(X)}. \quad (16.15)$$

Specifically, the denominator of (16.15) is the (unbiased) sample variance of the X_i's, from Definition 15.8, and the numerator is the (unbiased) sample covariance between the X_i's and Y_i's.

Question: What can we say about the sign of $\hat{a}$ based on (16.15)?

Answer: When the covariance is positive, $\hat{a}$ will also be positive, meaning that the slope of the line is positive. This makes sense because it says that X and Y are positively correlated, meaning that when X goes up, Y goes up as well. Likewise, when the covariance is negative, the slope of the line is negative.

When doing regression, the goodness of fit of the line is denoted by a quantity called R^2, where higher R^2 is better.

Definition 16.11 (R^2 goodness of fit) *Consider the set of data sample points* $\{(X_1 = x_1, Y_1 = y_1), \ldots, (X_n = x_n, Y_n = y_n)\}$ *with estimated linear fit:*

$$y = \hat{a}x + \hat{b}. \quad (16.16)$$

Define

$$\hat{y}_i \equiv \hat{a}x_i + \hat{b}$$

to be the estimated dependent value for the ith point. Let

$$\overline{x} = \frac{x_1 + x_2 + \cdots + x_n}{n} \quad \text{and} \quad \overline{y} = \frac{y_1 + y_2 + \cdots + y_n}{n}.$$

Then we define the **goodness of fit** *of the line (16.16) by*

$$R^2 = 1 - \frac{\sum_{i=1}^{n} (y_i - \hat{y}_i)^2}{\sum_{i=1}^{n} (y_i - \overline{y})^2}, \quad \text{where } 0 \leq R^2 \leq 1.$$

The R^2 metric is also called the **coefficient of determination**.

Question: How can we interpret R^2?

Answer: The subtracted term

$$\frac{\sum_{i=1}^{n} (y_i - \hat{y}_i)^2}{\sum_{i=1}^{n} (y_i - \overline{y})^2} = \frac{\frac{1}{n} \sum_{i=1}^{n} (y_i - \hat{y}_i)^2}{\frac{1}{n} \sum_{i=1}^{n} (y_i - \overline{y})^2} = \frac{\text{sample average squared error}}{\text{sample variance}}$$

can be viewed as the sample average squared error in the estimators normalized by the sample variance of the data set. This term is thus sometimes referred to as "the fraction of unexplained variance." The hope is that this term is a small fraction, which means that R^2 is close to 1.

16.8 Exercises

16.1 Estimating the bias of a coin
A coin comes up heads with probability p and tails with probability $1 - p$. We do not know p. We flip the coin 100 times and observe X heads. Derive $\hat{p}_{\text{ML}}(X)$, the ML estimator for p.

16.2 Battery lifetimes
We have a bunch of batteries whose lifetimes are i.i.d. $\sim \text{Exp}(\lambda)$. Our goal is to determine λ. To do this, we sample the lifetimes of 10 batteries, whose lifetimes we represent by $X_1, X_2, \ldots, X_{10}$. Derive $\hat{\lambda}_{\text{ML}}(X_1, X_2, \ldots, X_{10})$, the ML estimator for λ.

16.3 How many balls are blue?
Suppose that you have a bin with four balls. Each ball is either yellow or blue (you don't know which). Your goal is to estimate the number of blue balls in the bin, which we'll refer to as θ.

To obtain your estimate, you sample three balls with replacement from the bin and note their colors. We let X_i denote the color of the ith ball, where we say that $X_i = 1$ if the ball is blue and $X_i = 0$ otherwise. Let $\hat{\theta}_{\text{ML}}(X_1, X_2, X_3)$ denote the ML estimator for θ.

Suppose we observed the specific sequence of colors: $1, 1, 0$. What is $\hat{\theta}_{\text{ML}}(X_1 = 1, X_2 = 1, X_3 = 0)$?

16.4 Job CPU requirements follow a Pareto distribution
After reading Chapter 10, you are well aware that job CPU requirements follow a Pareto(α) distribution. But for which value of α? To answer this question, we sample the CPU requirements of 10 jobs picked independently at random. Let $X_1, X_2, \ldots, X_{10}$ represent the CPU requirements of these jobs. Derive $\hat{\alpha}_{\text{ML}}(X_1, X_2, \ldots, X_{10})$, the ML estimator for α.

16.5 **Estimating the max of a distribution**
In Example 16.8, we saw that the time that students spend on their probability homework is distributed as $\sim$ Uniform$(0, b)$. To estimate the maximum of this distribution, b, we surveyed three students independently at random, whose times we represented by X_1, X_2, X_3. We then derived the ML estimator $\hat{b}_{\text{ML}}(X_1, X_2, X_3)$ for b, showing that

$$\hat{b}_{\text{ML}}(X_1, X_2, X_3) = \max\{X_1, X_2, X_3\}.$$

(a) Is $\hat{b}_{\text{ML}}(X_1, X_2, X_3)$ an unbiased estimator of b?
(b) To make the estimator more accurate, we decide to generate more data samples. Suppose we sample n students. What is the ML estimator $\hat{b}_{\text{ML}}(X_1, X_2, \ldots, X_n)$? Is it biased when n is large?
(c) Can you think of an estimator $\hat{b}(X_1, \ldots, X_n)$ that is *not* the ML estimator, but is an unbiased estimator for all n? [Hint: You're going to want to scale up $\hat{b}_{\text{ML}}(X_1, \ldots, X_n)$.]

16.6 **Estimating the winning probability**
Team A has probability p of beating team B. We do not know p, but we can see that in the last 10 games played between A and B, team A won seven games and team B won three games. Assume that every game has a unique winner and that games are independent. Based on this information, formulate and compute the ML estimator for p.

16.7 **Disk failure probability estimation**
Suppose that every disk has probability p of failing each year. Assume that disks fail independently of each other. We sample n disks. Let X_i denote the number of years until the ith disk fails. Our goal is to estimate p. Derive $\hat{p}_{\text{ML}}(X_1, X_2, \ldots, X_n)$, the ML estimator for p.

16.8 **Practice with linear regression**
You are given five points: $(0, 5), (1, 3), (2, 1.5), (3.5, 0), (5, -3)$. Determine the best linear fit to these points and compute the R^2 goodness of fit for your estimate.

16.9 Acknowledgment

This chapter was written in collaboration with Weina Wang, who was a major contributor to the chapter contents and the exercises.

17 Bayesian Statistical Inference

In Chapter 16, we defined an estimator of some unknown quantity, θ, based on experimentally sampled data, X. This estimator, denoted by $\hat{\theta}_{\mathrm{ML}}(X)$, is called a *maximum likelihood (ML) estimator*, because it returns that value of θ that produces the highest likelihood of witnessing the particular sampled data. Specifically,

$$\hat{\theta}_{\mathrm{ML}}(X = x) \equiv \underset{\theta}{\operatorname{argmax}} \, \mathbf{P}\{X = x \mid \theta\}. \tag{17.1}$$

The ML estimator makes a lot of sense in situations where we have no a priori knowledge of θ. However, what do we do in situations where we have some knowledge about θ – for example, we know that θ is likely to be high? $\hat{\theta}_{\mathrm{ML}}(X = x)$ as defined in (17.1) doesn't have any way of incorporating this a priori knowledge.

In this chapter, we therefore introduce a new kind of estimator, called a maximum a posteriori (MAP) estimator. Like the ML estimator, the MAP estimator is again an estimator of an unknown quantity, θ, based on experimentally sampled data, X. However, the MAP estimator starts with a distribution Θ on the possible values of θ, allowing us to specify that some values are more likely than others. The MAP estimator then incorporates the joint distribution of Θ and the sampled data X to estimate θ.

Because it assumes a prior distribution, Θ, the MAP estimator is a **Bayesian estimator**, as compared with the ML estimator which is a classical estimator. We will start with a motivating example that sheds some light on how the MAP estimator and the ML estimator are related.

17.1 A Motivating Example

Example 17.1 (Gold or silver coin?)

In this example, you are given a coin that you can't see. The coin is either gold or silver. If the coin is gold, then it has bias $p = 0.6$ (chance $p = 0.6$ of heads). If the coin is silver, then it has bias $p = 0.4$.

We wish to determine whether $p = 0.6$ or $p = 0.4$. To do this, we flip the coin nine times. Let X denote the number of heads observed.

Question: Define the ML estimator to determine whether $p = 0.6$ or $p = 0.4$.

Answer:

$$\hat{p}_{\text{ML}}(X = x) = \underset{p \in \{0.4, 0.6\}}{\text{argmax}} \ \mathbf{P}\{X = x \mid p\}. \tag{17.2}$$

Question: Consider these two expressions: $\mathbf{P}\{X = x \mid p = 0.4\}$ versus $\mathbf{P}\{X = x \mid p = 0.6\}$. Which is bigger?

Answer: The answer depends on x.

$$\mathbf{P}\{X = x \mid p = 0.4\} = \binom{9}{x}(0.4)^x(0.6)^{9-x}$$

$$\mathbf{P}\{X = x \mid p = 0.6\} = \binom{9}{x}(0.6)^x(0.4)^{9-x}.$$

So $\mathbf{P}\{X = x \mid p = 0.4\}$ is larger if $x < 5$, and $\mathbf{P}\{X = x \mid p = 0.6\}$ is larger if $x \geq 5$.

Thus, we have that

$$\hat{p}_{\text{ML}}(X = x) = \begin{cases} 0.4 & \text{if } x \in \{0, 1, 2, 3, 4\} \\ 0.6 & \text{if } x \in \{5, 6, 7, 8, 9\} \end{cases}. \tag{17.3}$$

Example 17.2 (Gold or silver coin with added information)

Now suppose we are in the same setting as Example 17.1, but we are given the additional information that gold coins are four times more common than silver ones. So, absent any samples, with probability 80% our coin is gold.

To capture this, define a random variable (r.v.) P, where P represents the bias of the coin:

$$P = \text{bias of coin} = \begin{cases} 0.4 & \text{w/prob 20\%} \\ 0.6 & \text{w/prob 80\%} \end{cases}.$$

Question: How can we incorporate this distributional information about the bias into our ML estimator?

Answer: Our ML estimator, as defined in (17.2), does not have a way of incorporating the distributional information represented by P.

Question: Intuitively, how do you imagine that knowing that the bias is modeled by P might change the result in (17.3)?

Answer: It seems like the output of $p = 0.6$ should be more likely, given the fact that most coins are gold. Thus, even when the sampled data is $X = x < 5$, it may still be true that the best estimate for p is $p = 0.6$.

As an idea for how to incorporate the distributional information embodied by P, consider the weighted ML estimator, given in (17.4). This new estimator starts with the ML estimator given in (17.2), but multiplies the likelihood function by the prior:

$$\hat{P}_{\text{weightedML}}(X = x) = \underset{p \in \{0.4, 0.6\}}{\text{argmax}} \left(\underbrace{\mathbf{P}\{X = x \mid p\}}_{\text{likelihood}} \cdot \underbrace{\mathbf{P}\{P = p\}}_{\text{prior}} \right). \quad (17.4)$$

This "weighted ML" estimator clearly puts more weight on the output $p = 0.6$ as compared to $p = 0.4$. We will soon see that this weighted ML estimator in (17.4) is equivalent to the MAP estimator, which we define next!

17.2 The MAP Estimator

We will first define the MAP estimator in the context of Example 17.2 and then define it more generally a little later.

Definition 17.3 (MAP estimator for Example 17.2) *Our goal is to estimate $p \in \{0.4, 0.6\}$. We are given a **prior distribution** on the possible values for p, denoted by r.v. P (we intentionally use the capitalized form of p). We also have experimental data, denoted by r.v. X.*

*We say that $\hat{P}_{MAP}(X)$ is the **MAP estimator** of p. We use a capital $\hat{P}$ to denote that the estimator takes into account both the prior distribution P and the data X to create an estimate of p:*

$$\hat{P}_{MAP}(X = x) = \underset{p \in \{0.4, 0.6\}}{\text{argmax}} \mathbf{P}\{P = p \mid X = x\}. \quad (17.5)$$

Note that $\hat{P}_{MAP}(X)$ is a function of a r.v. X and thus is a r.v., while $\hat{P}_{MAP}(X = x)$ is a constant.

Let us compare $\hat{P}_{MAP}(X = x)$ in (17.5) with $\hat{p}_{ML}(X = x)$ in (17.2). Both of these are estimates of p based on data sample $X = x$. Both involve finding the value of

p which maximizes some expression. However, (17.5) uses the prior distribution P and has swapped the order of the conditional as compared to (17.2).

Question: Argue that $\hat{P}_{\text{MAP}}(X = x)$ from (17.5) is equal to $\hat{p}_{\text{weightedML}}(X = x)$ from (17.4).

Answer: Starting with $\hat{P}_{\text{MAP}}(X = x)$, and applying Bayes' Rule, observe that we are looking for the p that maximizes:

$$\mathbf{P}\{P = p \mid X = x\} = \frac{\mathbf{P}\{P = p \ \& \ X = x\}}{\mathbf{P}\{X = x\}} = \frac{\mathbf{P}\{X = x \mid P = p\} \cdot \mathbf{P}\{P = p\}}{\mathbf{P}\{X = x\}}.$$

But the $\mathbf{P}\{X = x\}$ term doesn't affect this maximization, so we're really looking for the p that maximizes

$$\underbrace{\mathbf{P}\{X = x \mid P = p\}}_{\text{likelihood}} \cdot \underbrace{\mathbf{P}\{P = p\}}_{\text{prior}}. \tag{17.6}$$

But this in turn is exactly the expression that we're maximizing in (17.4).

Question: Is there any situation where $\hat{P}_{\text{MAP}} = \hat{p}_{\text{ML}}$?

Answer: Yes, this happens when the prior, P, provides no additional information, in that all possible values of p are equally likely. For our current example, this would mean that the gold and silver coins are equally likely. In the case of a continuous setting, P would follow a Uniform distribution.

We now proceed to evaluate

$$\hat{P}_{\text{MAP}}(X = x) = \underset{p \in \{0.4, 0.6\}}{\text{argmax}} \ \mathbf{P}\{P = p \mid X = x\}.$$

Given that there are only two possible values of p, we simply need to compare the following two expressions:

$$\mathbf{P}\{P = 0.4 \mid X = x\} = \frac{\binom{9}{x} \cdot 0.4^x \cdot 0.6^{9-x} \cdot 20\%}{\mathbf{P}\{X = x\}} \tag{17.7}$$

$$\mathbf{P}\{P = 0.6 \mid X = x\} = \frac{\binom{9}{x} \cdot 0.6^x \cdot 0.4^{9-x} \cdot 80\%}{\mathbf{P}\{X = x\}}. \tag{17.8}$$

Question: How do we determine which of (17.7) and (17.8) is higher?

Answer: It's easiest to look at their ratio and see when the ratio exceeds 1:

$$\frac{\mathbf{P}\{P = 0.6 \mid X = x\}}{\mathbf{P}\{P = 0.4 \mid X = x\}} = 4 \cdot \left(\frac{3}{2}\right)^{2x-9}.$$

But

$$4 \cdot \left(\frac{3}{2} \right)^{2x-9} > 1 \qquad \Longleftrightarrow \qquad x \geq 3.$$

Thus, $p = 0.6$ is the maximizing value when $x \geq 3$. So

$$\hat{P}_{\text{MAP}}(X = x) = \begin{cases} 0.4 & \text{if } x \in \{0, 1, 2\} \\ 0.6 & \text{if } x \in \{3, 4, 5, 6, 7, 8, 9\} \end{cases} . \tag{17.9}$$

Thus,

$$\hat{P}_{\text{MAP}}(X) = \begin{cases} 0.4 & \text{if } X < 3 \\ 0.6 & \text{if } X \geq 3 \end{cases} . \tag{17.10}$$

Intuitively, this makes sense, since we are starting out with a coin that is gold with probability 80%.

We end this section by defining the MAP estimator in general settings, beyond the context of Example 17.2.

Definition 17.4 *Our goal is to estimate some unknown* θ. *We are given a* **prior distribution** *on the possible values for* θ, *denoted by r.v.* Θ. *We also have experimental data, denoted by r.v.* X.
We say that $\hat{\Theta}_{MAP}(X)$ *is our* **MAP estimator** *of* θ. *We use a capital* $\hat{\Theta}$ *in our estimator to denote that the estimator takes into account both the prior distribution* Θ *and the data* X *to create an estimate of* θ.

In the case where Θ is a discrete r.v., *the MAP estimator is defined by:*

$$\hat{\Theta}_{MAP}(X = x) = \underset{\theta}{\text{argmax}}\, \mathbf{P}\{\Theta = \theta \mid X = x\}$$

$$= \begin{cases} \underset{\theta}{\text{argmax}}\, \mathbf{P}\{X = x \mid \Theta = \theta\} \cdot \mathbf{P}\{\Theta = \theta\} & \text{if } X \text{ is discrete} \\ \underset{\theta}{\text{argmax}}\, f_{X \mid \Theta = \theta}(x) \cdot \mathbf{P}\{\Theta = \theta\} & \text{if } X \text{ is continuous} \end{cases}$$

In the case where Θ is a continuous r.v., *the MAP estimator is defined by:*

$$\hat{\Theta}_{MAP}(X = x) = \underset{\theta}{\text{argmax}}\, f_{\Theta \mid X = x}(\theta)$$

$$= \begin{cases} \underset{\theta}{\text{argmax}}\, \mathbf{P}\{X = x \mid \Theta = \theta\} \cdot f_{\Theta}(\theta) & \text{if } X \text{ is discrete} \\ \underset{\theta}{\text{argmax}}\, f_{X \mid \Theta = \theta}(x) \cdot f_{\Theta}(\theta) & \text{if } X \text{ is continuous} \end{cases}$$

Note that $\hat{\Theta}_{MAP}(X)$ *is a function of a r.v.* X *and thus is a r.v., while* $\hat{\Theta}_{MAP}(X = x)$ *is a constant.*

> **Definition 17.5** *While the r.v. Θ represents the prior distribution, the conditional r.v., $[\Theta \mid X = x]$, represents the* **posterior distribution** *since it represents the updated version of the prior distribution, given the value of the data. Likewise,* $\mathbf{P}\{\Theta = \theta \mid X = x\}$ *is called the* **posterior probability** *(where we write $f_{\Theta \mid X = x}(\theta)$ for the continuous case). Thus $\hat{\Theta}_{MAP}(X = x)$ represents the value of θ that maximizes the posterior probability.*

Remark: While $\hat{\Theta}_{\text{MAP}}(X)$ in Definition 17.4 depends on both the prior distribution Θ and also on X, we note that $\hat{\Theta}_{\text{MAP}}(X)$ is a function of just X. Specifically, once we specify the value of X, say $X = x$, then $\hat{\Theta}_{\text{MAP}}(X)$ becomes a constant.

17.3 More Examples of MAP Estimators

Example 17.6 (Estimating voting probability)

Suppose we want to estimate the fraction of people who will vote in the next election. Let's call this quantity p. To estimate p, we sample 100 people independently at random. Suppose that 80 of the sampled people say that they plan to vote. This feels high, so we go back to look at prior elections and how many people voted in prior elections. We find that the fraction of people who voted in prior elections is well modeled by the r.v. P, with density function:

$$f_P(p) = (1 - p)^2, \qquad \text{where } 0 \leq p \leq 1,$$

shown in Figure 17.1. Given this prior, P, and the sample $X = 80$, how can we estimate the true fraction of people, p, who will actually vote?

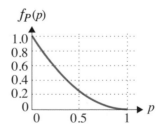

Figure 17.1 *Illustration of $f_P(p)$.*

In order to formulate this question in terms of Definition 17.4, we start with a few questions.

Question: If X denotes the number of people sampled, how is X distributed?

Answer: $X \sim \text{Binomial}(100, p)$.

Question: Which of the cases of Definition 17.4 should we be looking at?

Answer: $\Theta = P$ is continuous, and X is discrete. Thus,

$$\hat{P}_{\text{MAP}}(X = 80) = \underset{p}{\text{argmax}} f_{P|X=80}(p) = \underset{p}{\text{argmax}} \, \mathbf{P}\{X = 80 \mid P = p\} \cdot f_P(p).$$

Since $X \sim \text{Binomial}(100, p)$, we know that

$$\mathbf{P}\{X = 80 \mid P = p\} = \binom{100}{80} p^{80}(1 - p)^{20}.$$

Our posterior probability is thus:

$$\mathbf{P}\{X = 80 \mid P = p\} \cdot f_P(p) = \binom{100}{80} p^{80}(1 - p)^{20} \cdot (1 - p)^2$$

$$= \binom{100}{80} p^{80}(1 - p)^{22}.$$

To find the maximizing p, we differentiate the posterior with respect to p, ignoring the constant unrelated to p, and set the derivative equal to 0, yielding:

$$0 = p^{80} \cdot 22 \cdot (1 - p)^{21} \cdot (-1) + 80p^{79} \cdot (1 - p)^{22}.$$

This in turn is easily solved by dividing both sides by $(1 - p)^{21} \cdot p^{79}$, yielding:

$$p = \frac{80}{102}.$$

Thus,

$$\hat{P}_{\text{MAP}}(X = 80) = \frac{80}{102} \approx 78\%.$$

Question: This may still feel off to you. Shouldn't the prior matter more?

Answer: The answer lies in the number of people sampled. The fact that we sampled 100 people (picked uniformly at random) makes the prior distribution not so meaningful. Had we sampled a smaller number of people, then the prior distribution would matter much more.

Question: Repeat the voting example, where now we sample five people, uniformly at random and $X = 4$ report that they will vote. What is our estimate for p now?

Answer: You should get

$$\hat{P}_{\text{MAP}}(X = 4) = \frac{4}{7} \approx 57\%.$$

Observe that the prior distribution has much more of an effect now.

Another example of where estimation comes up has to do with signals that are (partially) corrupted by noise.

Example 17.7 (Deducing original signal in a noisy environment)

When sending a signal, θ, some random noise gets added to the signal, where the noise is represented by r.v. $N \sim \text{Normal}(0, \sigma_N)$. What is received is the sum of the original signal, θ, and the random noise, N. We represent the data received by r.v. X, where

$$X = \theta + N. \tag{17.11}$$

Suppose that we receive $X = x$. Based on that, we'd like to estimate the original signal, θ.

We will consider two situations: In the first, we have no prior information about the original signal. In the second, we have a prior distribution on the original signal.

Question: What is $\hat{\theta}_{\text{ML}}(X = x)$?

Since X is continuous, by Definition 16.6 we have that

$$\hat{\theta}_{\text{ML}}(X = x) = \underset{\theta}{\text{argmax}}\ f_{X|\theta}(x)$$

$$= \underset{\theta}{\text{argmax}}\ f_N(\theta - x), \qquad \text{by (17.11)}.$$

Question: Now, where does N have its highest density?

Answer: Since $N \sim \text{Normal}(0, \sigma_N)$, we know that it achieves its highest density at 0. Thus, $f_N(\theta - x)$ is highest when $\theta = x$. So

$$\hat{\theta}_{\text{ML}}(X = x) = x. \tag{17.12}$$

Since this holds for all x, we have that $\hat{\theta}_{\text{ML}}(X) = X$.

Question: Why does (17.12) make sense?

Answer: We are trying to estimate the original signal, θ. We know that the noise is symmetric, meaning that it is equally likely to add or subtract from the original signal. Thus, when we receive x, our best guess for the original signal is x.

Now consider that we have *additional information* in the form of a *prior distribution* on the original signal, represented by r.v. $\Theta \sim \text{Normal}(\mu, \sigma^2)$. Thus we can think of X as a sum of two independent random variables:

$$X = \Theta + N.$$

Again, we are trying to estimate the original signal, θ, given that we have received data $X = x$. To do this, we use a MAP estimator.

Question: What is $\hat{\Theta}_{\text{MAP}}(X = x)$?

Answer: By Definition 17.4,

$$\hat{\Theta}_{\text{MAP}}(X = x) = \underset{\theta}{\text{argmax }} f_{X|\Theta=\theta}(x) \cdot f_{\Theta}(\theta).$$

Now, since $X = \Theta + N$ and $\Theta \perp N$, we know that

$$[X \mid \Theta = \theta] \sim \text{Normal}(\theta, \sigma_N^2).$$

Hence,

$$f_{X|\Theta=\theta}(x) = \frac{1}{\sqrt{2\pi}\sigma_N} e^{-\frac{1}{2\sigma_N^2}(x-\theta)^2}. \tag{17.13}$$

So

$$\hat{\Theta}_{\text{MAP}}(X = x) = \underset{\theta}{\text{argmax }} f_{X|\Theta=\theta}(x) \cdot f_{\Theta}(\theta)$$

$$= \underset{\theta}{\text{argmax }} \left(\frac{1}{\sqrt{2\pi}\sigma_N} e^{-\frac{1}{2\sigma_N^2}(x-\theta)^2} \cdot \frac{1}{\sqrt{2\pi}\sigma} e^{-\frac{1}{2\sigma^2}(\theta-\mu)^2} \right)$$

$$= \underset{\theta}{\text{argmax }} \left(e^{-\frac{1}{2\sigma_N^2}(x-\theta)^2 - \frac{1}{2\sigma^2}(\theta-\mu)^2} \right) \qquad \text{(can ignore constants)}$$

$$= \underset{\theta}{\text{argmax }} \left(-\frac{1}{2\sigma_N^2}(x-\theta)^2 - \frac{1}{2\sigma^2}(\theta-\mu)^2 \right),$$

where the last line follows since it suffices to maximize the exponent. Let

$$g(\theta) = -\frac{1}{2\sigma_N^2}(x-\theta)^2 - \frac{1}{2\sigma^2}(\theta-\mu)^2.$$

To find the maximizing θ, we take the derivative and set it equal to 0, obtaining

$$0 = g'(\theta) = -\frac{1}{2\sigma_N^2} \cdot (-2)(x - \theta) - \frac{1}{2\sigma^2} \cdot 2(\theta - \mu),$$

which easily solves to

$$\theta = \frac{\frac{x}{\sigma_N^2} + \frac{\mu}{\sigma^2}}{\frac{1}{\sigma_N^2} + \frac{1}{\sigma^2}} = \frac{\sigma^2}{\sigma^2 + \sigma_N^2} \cdot x + \frac{\sigma_N^2}{\sigma^2 + \sigma_N^2} \cdot \mu.$$

Thus,

$$\hat{\Theta}_{\text{MAP}}(X = x) = \frac{\sigma^2}{\sigma^2 + \sigma_N^2} \cdot x + \frac{\sigma_N^2}{\sigma^2 + \sigma_N^2} \cdot \mu. \tag{17.14}$$

Question: What is the meaning behind the fact that the MAP estimate of θ in (17.14) looks like a weighted average?

Answer: Observe that (17.14) represents a weighted average of the received data, x, and the prior mean μ. So the MAP takes into account both the received data and also the prior distribution. Looking at the weights, we see that they depend on the variance of the original signal, σ^2, and also the variance of the noise, σ_N^2. If the variance of the noise is (relatively) low, then we weigh the received signal, x, more highly in our estimate. If the variance of the noise is (relatively) high, then we weigh the mean of the prior, μ, more highly in our estimate.

17.4 Minimum Mean Square Error Estimator

This chapter has been devoted to coming up with an estimator, in the case where we have a prior distribution, denoted by r.v. Θ, and also data, denoted by r.v. X. The idea has been to create a *posterior distribution*, denoted by

$$[\Theta \mid X = x].$$

Then, from Definition 17.4,

$$\hat{\Theta}_{\text{MAP}}(X = x) = \underset{\theta}{\text{argmax}} \, \mathbf{P} \{\Theta = \theta \mid X = x\}.$$

We can view $\hat{\Theta}_{\text{MAP}}$ as the **mode of the posterior** distribution. In the case of a discrete distribution, this represents the value, θ, that comes up most frequently in the posterior distribution. In the case of a continuous distribution, this represents the value with highest density.

One could alternatively define a different Bayesian estimator for θ that is the **mean of the posterior** distribution. We do this now.

Definition 17.8 *Our goal is to estimate some unknown θ. We are given a prior distribution Θ on the possible values for θ. We also have experimental data, denoted by r.v. X.*

We say that $\hat{\Theta}_{MMSE}(X)$ is the **minimum mean squared error (MMSE) estimator** *of θ, where*

$$\hat{\Theta}_{MMSE}(X) = \mathbf{E}\left[\Theta \mid X\right].$$

This is shorthand for saying that, for any x,

$$\hat{\Theta}_{MMSE}(X = x) = \mathbf{E}\left[\Theta \mid X = x\right].$$

Note that $\hat{\Theta}_{MMSE}(X)$ is a function of a r.v. X and thus is a r.v., while $\hat{\Theta}_{MMSE}(X = x)$ is a constant.

The estimator $\hat{\Theta}_{\text{MMSE}}(X = x)$ gets its name from the fact that this estimator in fact produces the minimum possible mean squared error of any estimator. We will prove this fact in Theorem 17.12. For now, let's consider a few examples of this new estimator to better understand how it compares with the MAP estimator.

Example 17.9 (Coin with unknown probability: revisited)

We revisit Example 7.14, where there is a coin with some unknown *bias*, where the "bias" of the coin is its probability of coming up heads. We are given that the coin's bias is drawn from distribution $P \sim \text{Uniform}(0, 1)$. We are also given that the coin has resulted in $X = 10$ heads out of the first 10 flips. Based on this, we would like to estimate the coin's bias.

Question: What is $\hat{P}_{\text{MMSE}}(X = 10)$?

Answer:

$$\hat{P}_{\text{MMSE}}(X = 10) = \mathbf{E}\left[P \mid X = 10\right].$$

To derive this, we need to first derive the conditional probability density function (p.d.f.) of P given $X = 10$:

$$f_{P|X=10}(p) = \frac{\mathbf{P}\left\{X = 10 \mid P = p\right\} \cdot f_P(p)}{\mathbf{P}\left\{X = 10\right\}}$$

$$= \begin{cases} \frac{t^{10} \cdot 1}{\mathbf{P}\{X=10\}} & \text{if } 0 \le p \le 1 \\ 0 & \text{otherwise} \end{cases}.$$

Here,

$$\mathbf{P}\{X = 10\} = \int_0^1 \mathbf{P}\{X = 10 \mid P = p\} \cdot f_P(p)dp$$

$$= \int_0^1 p^{10}dp$$

$$= \frac{1}{11}.$$

So,

$$f_{P|X=10}(p) = \frac{\mathbf{P}\{X = 10 \mid P = p\} \cdot f_P(p)}{\mathbf{P}\{X = 10\}}$$

$$= \begin{cases} 11p^{10} & \text{if } 0 \le p \le 1 \\ 0 & \text{otherwise} \end{cases} . \qquad (17.15)$$

Hence,

$$\hat{P}_{\text{MMSE}}(X = 10) = \mathbf{E}\,[P \mid X = 10] = \int_0^1 p11p^{10}dp = \frac{11}{12}.$$

Question: How does $\hat{P}_{\text{MMSE}}(X = 10)$ compare with $\hat{P}_{\text{MAP}}(X = 10)$?

Answer: The prior P is continuous and X is discrete, so using Definition 17.4 and (17.15), we have:

$$\hat{P}_{\text{MAP}}(X = 10) = \underset{p}{\text{argmax}}\ f_{P|X=10}(p) = \underset{p}{\text{argmax}}\ \left(11p^{10}\right) = 1.$$

Question: Which is the more believable estimator?

Answer: This is a matter of opinion, but it feels like the MMSE estimator does a better job of capturing the prior distribution than the MAP estimator.

Let's consider one more example comparing the MMSE estimator and the MAP estimator.

Example 17.10 (Supercomputing: estimating the true job size)

In supercomputing centers, users are asked to provide an upper bound on their job's size (running time). The upper bound provided by the user is typically several times larger than the job's actual size [49]. We can think of the upper bound provided as a scalar multiple of the original job size. The relationship between the original job and upper bound provided can be represented by:

$$X = S \cdot \Theta,$$

where Θ is a r.v. denoting the original job size, S is a scalar multiple where $S \geq 1$, and X is the reported upper bound. We will assume that $S \perp \Theta$. Given a value on the upper bound, $X = x$, how do we estimate the original job size, $\Theta = \theta$, from this? Specifically, we will be interested in deriving $\hat{\Theta}_{\text{MAP}}(X = x)$ and $\hat{\Theta}_{\text{MMSE}}(X = x)$.

To keep the computations from getting too messy, we assume: $\Theta \sim \text{Pareto}(\alpha = 3)$ and $S \sim \text{Pareto}(\alpha = 2)$. Hence,

$$f_\Theta(\theta) = 3\theta^{-4}, \qquad \text{if } \theta \geq 1$$
$$f_S(s) = 2s^{-3}, \qquad \text{if } s \geq 1.$$

Both estimators will require deriving $f_{\Theta|X=x}(\theta)$. To get there, we will have to start with the other direction, namely $f_{X|\Theta=\theta}(x)$.

Question: Given that $X = S \cdot \Theta$, what is $f_{X|\Theta=\theta}(x)$?

Hint: Is it $f_S\left(\frac{x}{\theta}\right)$?

Answer: The correct answer is

$$f_{X|\Theta=\theta}(x) = \frac{1}{\theta} \cdot f_S\left(\frac{x}{\theta}\right), \qquad x \geq \theta \geq 1.$$

To see why, recall that we need to make the arguments over probabilities, not densities:

$$\mathbf{P}\left\{X \leq x \mid \Theta = \theta\right\} = \mathbf{P}\left\{S \leq \frac{x}{\theta}\right\}$$

$$\int_{t=0}^{t=x} f_{X|\Theta=\theta}(t)dt = \int_{t=0}^{t=\frac{x}{\theta}} f_S(t)dt$$

$$\frac{d}{dx}\int_{t=0}^{t=x} f_{X|\Theta=\theta}(t)dt = \frac{d}{dx}\int_{t=0}^{t=\frac{x}{\theta}} f_S(t)dt$$

$$f_{X|\Theta=\theta}(x) = \frac{1}{\theta}f_S\left(\frac{x}{\theta}\right)dt \qquad \text{by FTC, see (1.6) and (1.7)}.$$

We use our conditional density to get the joint density as follows:

$$f_{X,\Theta}(x,\theta) = f_{X|\Theta=\theta}(x) \cdot f_\Theta(\theta) = \frac{1}{\theta} \cdot 2\left(\frac{x}{\theta}\right)^{-3} \cdot 3\theta^{-4} = \frac{6}{\theta^2 x^3}.$$

We can integrate the joint density to get $f_X(x)$, as follows:

$$f_X(x) = \int_{\theta=1}^{\theta=x} f_{X,\Theta}(x,\theta)d\theta$$

$$= \int_{\theta=1}^{\theta=x} \frac{6}{\theta^2 x^3}d\theta$$

$$= 6x^{-3} - 6x^{-4}, \qquad x \geq 1.$$

We are finally ready to obtain $f_{\Theta|X=x}(\theta)$:

$$f_{\Theta|X=x}(\theta) = \frac{f_{X,\Theta}(x,\theta)}{f_X(x)}$$

$$= \frac{\frac{6}{\theta^2 x^3}}{6x^{-3} - 6x^{-4}}$$

$$= \frac{x}{\theta^2 x - \theta^2}$$

$$= \frac{1}{\theta^2} \cdot \frac{x}{x-1}, \qquad x \geq \theta \geq 1.$$

Question: So what is $\hat{\Theta}_{\text{MAP}}(X = x)$?

Answer:

$$\hat{\Theta}_{\text{MAP}}(X = x) = \underset{\theta}{\text{argmax}}\ f_{\Theta|X=x}(\theta) = \underset{\theta}{\text{argmax}}\ \frac{1}{\theta^2} \cdot \frac{x}{x-1} = 1.$$

Question: What is $\hat{\Theta}_{\text{MMSE}}(X = x)$?

Answer:

$$\hat{\Theta}_{\text{MMSE}}(X = x) = \mathbf{E}\left[\Theta \mid X = x\right]$$

$$= \int_{\theta=1}^{\theta=x} \theta \cdot f_{\Theta|X=x}(\theta)d\theta$$

$$= \frac{x}{x-1} \int_{\theta=1}^{\theta=x} \frac{1}{\theta}d\theta$$

$$= \frac{x \ln x}{x-1}$$

$$= \ln x + \frac{\ln x}{x-1}.$$

Question: Which is the more believable estimator?

Answer: The MAP estimator is pretty useless, given that it simply returns an answer of $\theta = 1$. The problem is that the density of the prior is maximized at $\theta = 1$, and somehow this isn't improved when we look at the conditional density.

The MMSE estimator returns a more reasonable answer of $\theta \approx \ln x$. This makes more sense given that the upper bound on job size is x.

Question: You might wonder if the answers change if we make the problem a little more symmetric, where Θ and S have the same distribution. For example, what do you think might happen if $\Theta \sim \text{Pareto}(\alpha = 2)$ and $S \sim \text{Pareto}(\alpha = 2)$?

Answer: We find that, disappointingly, $\hat{\Theta}_{\text{MAP}}(X = x)$ remains at 1. However, now

$$\hat{\Theta}_{\text{MMSE}}(X = x) = \frac{x - 1}{\ln x}.$$

17.5 Measuring Accuracy in Bayesian Estimators

We have seen different estimators, producing different results. It is helpful to have some metrics for evaluating the *accuracy* of our estimators. One common metric for measuring the accuracy of estimators is the mean squared error (MSE).

Recall the MSE as given by Definition 15.4, when we were looking at non-Bayesian estimators. Here, θ was an unknown constant, X represented the sample data, and $\hat{\theta}(X)$ was our estimator for θ. Under this setting we defined:

$$\text{MSE}(\hat{\theta}(X)) = \mathbf{E}\left[(\hat{\theta}(X) - \theta)^2\right]. \tag{17.16}$$

For Bayesian estimators we need an *adaptation* of the definition in (17.16) because θ is no longer a constant, but rather is drawn from a prior distribution, Θ. For Bayesian estimators, we use Definition 17.11 for the MSE.

> **Definition 17.11** *Let* $\hat{\Theta}(X)$ *be an estimator where* Θ *represents the prior distribution and* X *the sample data. Then the* **mean squared error (MSE)** *of* $\hat{\Theta}(X)$ *is defined by*
>
> $$\text{MSE}(\hat{\Theta}(X)) = \mathbf{E}\left[(\hat{\Theta}(X) - \Theta)^2\right]. \tag{17.17}$$

Question: How should one interpret Definition 17.11? What is the expectation over?

Answer: Both terms within the expectation in (17.17) are random variables.

The first term is a r.v. which is a function of just X (once a value of X is specified, $\hat{\Theta}(X)$ becomes a constant). The second term is the r.v. Θ. The expectation in (17.17) is over the joint distribution of Θ and X (that is, it's a double sum).

At first, Definition 17.11 may seem a little strange. However, it's actually very similar to our definition in (17.16) except that now the value of θ is picked from the prior distribution. To see this, we condition on θ:

$$\mathbf{MSE}\left(\hat{\Theta}(X)\right) = \mathbf{E}\left[\left(\hat{\Theta}(X) - \Theta\right)^2\right]$$

$$= \int_\theta \mathbf{E}\left[\left(\hat{\Theta}(X) - \Theta\right)^2 \Big| \Theta = \theta\right] f_\Theta(\theta) d\theta$$

$$= \int_\theta \mathbf{E}\left[\left(\hat{\Theta}(X) - \theta\right)^2 \Big| \Theta = \theta\right] f_\Theta(\theta) d\theta.$$

Observe that the integrand looks very similar to (17.16). The point is, whatever our chosen value, θ, we want to say that our estimator, $\hat{\Theta}(X)$, is close to that value in expectation.

Now recall the estimator $\hat{\Theta}_{\mathrm{MMSE}}(X)$. Theorem 17.12 says that this estimator has the lowest MSE compared to all other estimators.

Theorem 17.12 $\hat{\Theta}_{MMSE}(X)$ *minimizes the MSE over all estimators* $\hat{\Theta}(X)$.

Proof: We start by defining:

$$\mathbf{MSE}\left(\hat{\Theta}(X = x)\right) = \mathbf{E}\left[\left(\hat{\Theta}(X) - \Theta\right)^2 \Big| X = x\right]. \qquad (17.18)$$

We will show that $\hat{\Theta}_{\mathrm{MMSE}}(X = x)$ minimizes $\mathbf{MSE}\left(\hat{\Theta}(X = x)\right)$ for all values of x. It then follows that $\hat{\Theta}_{\mathrm{MMSE}}(X)$ minimizes the MSE over all estimators $\hat{\Theta}(X)$.

$$\mathbf{MSE}\left(\hat{\Theta}(X = x)\right) = \mathbf{E}\left[\left(\hat{\Theta}(X) - \Theta\right)^2 \Big| X = x\right]$$

$$= \mathbf{E}\left[\hat{\Theta}(X)^2 - 2\hat{\Theta}(X)\Theta + \Theta^2 \Big| X = x\right]$$

$$= \hat{\Theta}(X = x)^2 - 2\hat{\Theta}(X = x)\mathbf{E}\left[\Theta \mid X = x\right]$$

$$+ \mathbf{E}\left[\Theta^2 \mid X = x\right]. \qquad (17.19)$$

We now want to find the minimizing $\hat{\Theta}(X = x)$ in (17.19). Recall that $\hat{\Theta}(X = x)$ is a constant function of x. We'll denote this by $c(x)$ and replace $\hat{\Theta}(X = x)$ with

$c(x)$ throughout, obtaining:

$$\mathbf{MSE}\left(\hat{\Theta}(X = x)\right) = c(x)^2 - 2c(x)\mathbf{E}\left[\Theta \mid X = x\right] + \mathbf{E}\left[\Theta^2 \mid X = x\right]$$
$$= (c(x) - \mathbf{E}\left[\Theta \mid X = x\right])^2 + \mathbf{E}\left[\Theta^2 \mid X = x\right]$$
$$- \mathbf{E}\left[\Theta \mid X = x\right]^2,$$

which is clearly minimized when the first term is 0, namely when

$$c(x) = \mathbf{E}\left[\Theta \mid X = x\right] = \hat{\Theta}_{\text{MMSE}}(X = x). \qquad \blacksquare$$

17.6 Exercises

17.1 Deducing original signal in a noisy environment
We have an original signal, represented by r.v. Θ, where $\Theta \sim \text{Normal}(0, 1)$. We also have noise, represented by r.v. N, where $N \sim \text{Normal}(0, 1)$. The received signal, represented by r.v. X, is then:

$$X = \Theta + N.$$

Derive the MMSE estimator, $\hat{\Theta}_{\text{MMSE}}(X = x)$. How does your answer compare to $\hat{\Theta}_{\text{MAP}}(X = x)$ under the same setting?

17.2 Mean squared error of the MMSE estimator
In Theorem 17.12, we saw that $\hat{\Theta}_{\text{MMSE}}(X)$ minimizes the MSE. But what exactly is this error? Prove that $\mathbf{MSE}\left(\hat{\Theta}_{\text{MMSE}}(X = x)\right)$ is the variance of the posterior distribution.

17.3 MMSE estimator for gold vs. silver coin problem
For the Bayesian coin problem from Example 17.2, derive the MMSE estimator, $\hat{P}_{\text{MMSE}}(X)$.

17.4 Hypothesis testing for COVID: MLE vs. MAP
To determine whether you have COVID, you take an antigen self-test. Rather than outputting "yes" or "no," the test outputs a number, L, from the set $\{0, 1, 2, 3\}$, where L indicates the level of antigen detected. The level L is not a perfect indicator. Table 17.1, called a "likelihood matrix," shows the probability distribution over the level output by the test, depending on whether you have COVID or not. For example, if you don't have COVID, then the test outputs $L = 0$ with probability 0.6 and $L = 1$ with probability 0.3, etc. By contrast, if you have COVID, the probability distribution is more biased toward higher levels.

	$L = 0$	$L = 1$	$L = 2$	$L = 3$
H_0: Don't have COVID	0.6	0.3	0.1	0.0
H_1: Have COVID	0.1	0.2	0.3	0.4

Table 17.1 *Likelihood matrix.*

Consider two hypotheses: H_0 that you don't have COVID and H_1 that you do.

(a) For each possible reading of L, determine which hypothesis is returned by the MLE, which returns the hypothesis with highest likelihood.

(b) For each possible reading of L, determine which hypothesis is returned by the MAP decision rule. Assume that $\mathbf{P}\{H_0\} = 0.8$ and $\mathbf{P}\{H_1\} = 0.2$.

17.5 Estimating the minimum: MLE vs. MAP
You observe 10 i.i.d. data samples, $X_1, X_2, \ldots, X_{10} \sim \text{Uniform}(a, 1)$. You know that $a \geq 0$ but not the exact value of a. Your goal is to estimate a.

(a) Determine $\hat{a}_{\text{ML}}(X_1, X_2, \ldots, X_{10})$, the ML estimator of a.

(b) Suppose that we have a prior on a, denoted by r.v. A, with p.d.f.:

$$f_A(a) = \begin{cases} \frac{20e^{-20a}}{1 - e^{-20}} & \text{if } 0 \leq a \leq 1 \\ 0 & \text{otherwise} \end{cases}.$$

Determine $\hat{A}_{\text{MAP}}(X_1, X_2, \ldots, X_{10})$, the MAP estimator of a.

17.6 Interaction graph
Annie, Ben, and Caroline are three CMU students. CMU has only two clubs: PnC club and Buggy club. Each student must join one and only one club. Suppose that you (as an outsider) know that Annie has joined the PnC club, but you cannot see which clubs Ben and Caroline join. However, you can see the interaction graph in Figure 17.2. The interaction graph tells us something about which students at CMU interact with other students. But

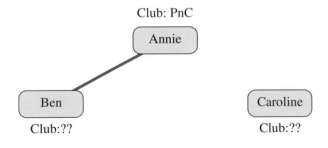

Figure 17.2 *Interaction graph for Exercise 17.6.*

the interaction graph is not perfect: An edge between two people exists with probability $\frac{1}{2}$ if the two people are in the same club and exists with probability $\frac{1}{6}$ if the two people are in different clubs.

(a) What is your ML estimate of the clubs Ben and Caroline each joins?

(b) Suppose that you know Ben and Caroline well enough to have the following prior: Ben joins PnC with probability $\frac{3}{8}$ and joins Buggy with probability $\frac{5}{8}$. Caroline joins PnC with probability $\frac{7}{8}$ and joins Buggy with probability $\frac{1}{8}$. They make their choices independently. What is your MAP estimate of the clubs Ben and Caroline each joins?

17.7 Error correcting codes

Suppose you want to transmit a message to your friend through a wireless channel. Your message, denoted as M, has three possible values with this distribution:

$$\mathbf{P}\{M = 0\} = \frac{1}{2}, \qquad \mathbf{P}\{M = 1\} = \frac{7}{16}, \qquad \mathbf{P}\{M = 2\} = \frac{1}{16}.$$

You have decided to use a 5-bit string, $U = U_1 U_2 U_3 U_4 U_5$ to encode message M as follows:

$$M = 0 \Longrightarrow U = 00000,$$
$$M = 1 \Longrightarrow U = 11110,$$
$$M = 2 \Longrightarrow U = 10101.$$

Here, the leftmost two bits, U_1, U_2, are used to differentiate among the values of M, and the remaining three bits, U_3, U_4, U_5 are redundant bits for error correcting – that is, the remaining bits reinforce the information in the first two bits. This coding scheme sets $U_3 = U_1$, $U_4 = U_2$, and $U_5 = U_1 + U_2 \mod 2$.

When you transmit the string U, each bit U_i gets flipped with probability $\epsilon = 0.2$, and $U_1, U_2, \ldots, U_5$ get flipped independently. Let $X = X_1 X_2 X_3 X_4 X_5$ denote the string that your friend receives. Your friend must estimate the value of M based on the received string. For two binary strings with the same length, the **Hamming distance** between the strings, denoted by $d_H(\cdot, \cdot)$, is defined to be the number of bits on which the two strings differ.

(a) Suppose your friend decodes X by comparing X with the three strings $\{00000, 11110, 10101\}$ and selecting the string that has the smallest Hamming distance to X. Then she declares that the value of M that corresponds to the selected string is the value transmitted. When there is a tie, she declares the smaller value for M. For example, if she receives $X = 10100$, then 10101 is the string from $\{00000, 11110, 10101\}$ that is the closest to X. So she declares that $M = 2$ is the value transmitted. If she receives $X = 11000$, then $d_H(X, 00000) = 2$, $d_H(X, 11110) = 2$, and $d_H(X, 10101) = 3$. So she breaks the tie and declares that $M = 0$.

    (i) What type of estimation is your friend doing?

    (ii) Suppose that the received string is $X = k \triangleq k_1 k_2 k_3 k_4 k_5$. How does your friend determine whether M equals 0 or 1 or 2? (Write down the probabilities involved).

(b) If your friend uses a MAP decoder to estimate M, what will she declare when she receives $X = 10100$?

17.8 MMSE estimator of temperature given noise

There is a heat source with temperature $T \sim \text{Normal}(100, 16)$. You want to know the value of the temperature, $T = t$, but you cannot directly access the source. You are, however, able to approximately measure the temperatures at two nearby locations: Let X_A denote your measurement of the temperature at location A, which is 1 mile away and known to have temperature $\frac{T}{2}$. Let X_B denote your measurement at location B, which is 2 miles away with temperature $\frac{T}{4}$. Unfortunately, X_A and X_B are both affected by noise, and hence what you actually read is:

$$X_A = \frac{T}{2} + W_A, \qquad W_A \sim \text{Normal}(0, 1),$$

$$X_B = \frac{T}{4} + W_B, \qquad W_B \sim \text{Normal}(0, 1),$$

where the noises W_A, W_B, and T are independent.

(a) What is the conditional p.d.f. of T given that you observe $X_A = x_A$ and $X_B = x_B$?

(b) What distribution does T follow given you observe $X_A = x_A$ and $X_B = x_B$?

(c) What is $\hat{T}_{\text{MMSE}}(X_A, X_B)$?

[Hint: If a r.v. Y has a p.d.f. of the form $f_Y(y) = C \cdot e^{-\frac{1}{2}(ay^2 + by + c)}$, where C, a, b, c are constants, independent of y, then $N \sim \text{Normal}\left(-\frac{b}{2a}, \frac{1}{a}\right)$.]

17.9 The MMSE is an unbiased estimator

Prove that the MMSE estimator is unbiased. That is, $\mathbf{E}\left[\hat{\Theta}_{\text{MMSE}}(X)\right] = \mathbf{E}[\Theta]$.

17.7 Acknowledgment

This chapter was written in collaboration with Weina Wang, who was a major contributor to the chapter contents and the exercises.

Part VI

Tail Bounds and Applications

In this part of the book we delve deeply into understanding the tail of a random variable, namely the probability that the random variable exceeds some value. While we briefly touched on this topic in Section 5.9, in Chapter 18 we derive much more sophisticated tail bounds, including Chernoff bounds and Hoeffding bounds.

Tail bounds are important in providing guarantees on the probability of some bad outcome. In Chapters 19 and 20, we study some common applications of tail bounds.

First, in Chapter 19, we look at how tail bounds allow us to create confidence intervals on a statistical estimate. We also study a popular problem in theoretical computer science, called the balls-and-bins problem, where balls are distributed independently at random among bins, and we prove bounds on the bin occupancy.

Next, in Chapter 20, we turn to the problem of designing and evaluating hashing algorithms. Here we show how our tail bounds and the balls-and-bins analyses from Chapter 19 give us bounds on the number of items in a hash bucket and the probability of a hash collision.

Tail bounds are extremely important in the analysis of many randomized algorithms. Randomized algorithms are covered in depth in Part VII of the book.

18   Tail Bounds

Until now, we have typically talked about the mean, variance, or higher moments of a random variable (r.v.). In this chapter, we will be concerned with the **tail probability** of a r.v. X, specifically,

$$\mathbf{P}\{X \geq x\} \qquad \text{or} \qquad \mathbf{P}\{X > x\}.$$

The tail behavior is very important for offering quality of service (QoS) guarantees. For example, we might have to pay a penalty if the response time exceeds 1 second, and thus we want to know the fraction of jobs whose response time exceeds 1 second. Equivalently, we might want to be able to formulate a service level objective (SLO), like "99% of jobs should experience response time less than 1 second." There are many other examples of tail behavior in computer science. For example, router buffers in a network need to be provisioned so that the probability of overflow is low. Likewise, when designing a hash table, we care not only about keeping the expected number of items in a bucket low, but also about ensuring that no bucket has a *huge* number of items. All these examples require deriving tail behavior.

While the variance of a r.v. tells us something about its deviation from its mean, the tail of the r.v. gives us a lot more information. Unfortunately, it is often not easy to reason about the tail behavior of even very simple random variables. Consider, for example, $X \sim \text{Binomial}(n, p)$:

$$\mathbf{P}\{X \geq k\} = \sum_{i=k}^{n} \binom{n}{i} p^i (1-p)^{n-i}. \tag{18.1}$$

We do not have a closed-form representation of the tail probability in (18.1). Specifically, we don't have a sense of what this tail probability looks like as a simple function of k, n, and p. The tail probability in (18.1) comes up in many applications. Suppose, for example, that you are distributing n jobs among n machines by assigning each job to a random machine. In expectation each machine should get one job. You would like to know the probability that a particular machine gets $\geq k$ jobs. This probability is represented by (18.1) in the case where $p = \frac{1}{n}$.

As another example, consider $X \sim \text{Poisson}(\lambda)$. Here, X is representative of the number of arrivals to a website during 1 hour, where arrivals come from many different sources at an average total rate of λ arrivals per hour (see Chapter 12). To understand the probability that there are $\geq k$ arrivals during the hour, we need:

$$\mathbf{P}\{X \geq k\} = \sum_{i=k}^{\infty} e^{-\lambda} \frac{\lambda^i}{i!}. \tag{18.2}$$

Again, we do not have a closed-form expression for the tail probability in (18.2).

The purpose of this chapter is to investigate *upper bounds* on these tail probabilities. These upper bounds are generally called **tail bounds**. Sometimes the goal is to upper bound a tail probability of the form $\mathbf{P}\{X \geq k\}$. Other times, our goal is to upper bound the tail of the distance of a r.v. from its mean, i.e., we're trying to upper bound:

$$\mathbf{P}\{|X - \mu| \geq k\}, \qquad \text{where } \mu \equiv \mathbf{E}[X].$$

In this latter case, our tail bound is more specifically referred to as a **concentration bound** or **concentration inequality**, because we're looking at the concentration of X around its mean.

We will start by reviewing the Markov bound and the Chebyshev bound before moving on to the much more powerful Chernoff bound.

Note: This chapter and the next few will require knowing asymptotic notation well. Before you continue, you should review Section 1.6. You will need to understand the definitions of $O(n)$, $o(n)$, $o(1)$, $\Omega(n)$, $\omega(n)$ and their significance for high n.

18.1 Markov's Inequality

> **Theorem 18.1 (Markov's inequality)** *Let X be a non-negative r.v., with finite mean* $\mu = \mathbf{E}[X]$. *Then,* $\forall a > 0$,
>
> $$\mathbf{P}\{X \geq a\} \leq \frac{\mu}{a}.$$

Proof: This was proved earlier as Theorem 5.16. ∎

Markov's bound is extremely weak.

Question: Suppose we flip a fair coin n times. Using Markov's inequality, what is an upper bound on the probability of getting at least $\frac{3}{4}n$ heads?

Answer: Let X denote the number of heads. Then $X \sim$ Binomial $\left(n, \frac{1}{2}\right)$.

$$\mathbf{P}\left\{X \geq \frac{3n}{4}\right\} \leq \frac{\mu}{\frac{3n}{4}} = \frac{\frac{n}{2}}{\frac{3n}{4}} = \frac{2}{3}. \tag{18.3}$$

This is clearly a terrible bound because it doesn't even involve n.

Question: Intuitively, as n gets higher, would you expect that the tail probability should get higher or lower?

Answer: Lower. As n gets higher, we would expect that we're unlikely to be so far from the mean.

The reason why Markov's inequality is so poor is that it only takes into account the mean of the r.v. Nevertheless, this is an important inequality because we will derive all our other inequalities from this one.

18.2 Chebyshev's Inequality

Chebyshev's inequality is a lot stronger than Markov's inequality because it takes into account the variability of the r.v. Chebyshev's inequality is derived by applying Markov's inequality to the deviation of a r.v. from its mean.

> **Theorem 18.2 (Chebyshev's inequality)** *Let X be a r.v. with finite mean $\mu = \mathbf{E}[X]$ and finite variance* $\mathbf{Var}(X)$. *Then,* $\forall a > 0$,
> $$\mathbf{P}\{|X - \mu| \geq a\} \leq \frac{\mathbf{Var}(X)}{a^2}.$$

Proof: This was proved earlier as Theorem 5.17. ∎

Using the notation σ_X to denote the standard deviation of X, where $\sigma_X^2 = \mathbf{Var}(X)$, and using $C_X^2 = \frac{\mathbf{Var}(X)}{\mathbf{E}[X]^2}$ to denote the squared coefficient of variation of X, we obtain a few additional interpretations of Chebyshev's inequality:

$$\mathbf{P}\{|X - \mu| \geq a\sigma_X\} \leq \frac{1}{a^2} \tag{18.4}$$

$$\mathbf{P}\{|X - \mu| \geq a\mathbf{E}[X]\} \leq \frac{C_X^2}{a^2}. \tag{18.5}$$

Now let's go back to the coin flipping example.

Question: Suppose we flip a fair coin n times. Using Chebyshev's inequality, what is an upper bound on the probability of getting at least $\frac{3}{4}n$ heads?

Answer: Again letting X denote the number of heads:

$$
\begin{aligned}
\mathbf{P}\left\{X \geq \frac{3n}{4}\right\} &= \mathbf{P}\left\{X - \frac{n}{2} \geq \frac{n}{4}\right\} \\
&= \frac{1}{2} \cdot \mathbf{P}\left\{\left|X - \frac{n}{2}\right| \geq \frac{n}{4}\right\} \\
&\leq \frac{1}{2} \cdot \frac{\mathbf{Var}(X)}{\left(\frac{n}{4}\right)^2} \\
&= \frac{1}{2} \cdot \frac{\frac{n}{4}}{\left(\frac{n}{4}\right)^2} \\
&= \frac{2}{n}.
\end{aligned}
\tag{18.6}
$$

Question: Where did the $\frac{1}{2}$ in the second line come from?

Answer: Since $X \sim \text{Binomial}\left(n, \frac{1}{2}\right)$, X is symmetric around $\frac{n}{2}$.

Assuming that $n > 3$, the $\frac{2}{n}$ bound in (18.6) is much tighter than the $\frac{2}{3}$ bound that we got from Markov's inequality. Furthermore, $\frac{2}{n}$ at least decreases with n.

18.3 Chernoff Bound

We derived the Chebyshev bound by squaring the r.v. $X - \mu$ and then applying Markov's inequality. To derive the Chernoff bound, we will first exponentiate the r.v. X and then apply Markov's inequality.

For any $t > 0$,

$$
\begin{aligned}
\mathbf{P}\{X \geq a\} &= \mathbf{P}\{tX \geq ta\} \\
&= \mathbf{P}\{e^{tX} \geq e^{ta}\} \\
&\leq \frac{\mathbf{E}\left[e^{tX}\right]}{e^{ta}}.
\end{aligned}
\tag{18.7}
$$

Question: Why were we allowed to apply Markov's inequality?

Answer: For any X and any t, we know that e^{tX} is a non-negative r.v.

Since (18.7) is true for all t, it follows that:

$$\mathbf{P}\{X \geq a\} \leq \min_{t>0} \frac{\mathbf{E}\left[e^{tX}\right]}{e^{ta}}.$$

Bounds on specific distributions are obtained by choosing the appropriate value of t. Even if a minimizing t cannot be found, it is still true that any t provides a tail bound.

Theorem 18.3 (Chernoff bound) *Let X be a r.v. and a be a constant. Then*

$$\mathbf{P}\{X \geq a\} \leq \min_{t>0}\left\{\frac{\mathbf{E}\left[e^{tX}\right]}{e^{ta}}\right\}. \qquad (18.8)$$

Question: Why should we expect that the Chernoff bound is stronger than the Chebyshev bound?

Hint: The Chebyshev bound got its strength by invoking the second moment of the r.v. What moments of the r.v. does the Chernoff bound invoke?

Answer: Notice the $\mathbf{E}\left[e^{tX}\right]$ in the Chernoff bound expression. This is a type of moment-generating function. It looks very similar to the Laplace transform, $\mathbf{E}\left[e^{-sX}\right]$. In fact, the nth derivative of $\mathbf{E}\left[e^{tX}\right]$, when evaluated at $t = 0$, yields the nth moment of X. Hence $\mathbf{E}\left[e^{tX}\right]$ encapsulates *all* moments of X.

Question: What do we do if we want to upper bound the other side of the tail, $\mathbf{P}\{X \leq a\}$?

Hint: Think about using $t < 0$.

Answer: For any $t < 0$,

$$\begin{aligned}
\mathbf{P}\{X \leq a\} &= \mathbf{P}\{tX \geq ta\} \\
&= \mathbf{P}\{e^{tX} \geq e^{ta}\} \\
&\leq \frac{\mathbf{E}\left[e^{tX}\right]}{e^{ta}} \qquad \text{(by Markov's inequality).}
\end{aligned}$$

Hence,

$$\mathbf{P}\{X \leq a\} \leq \min_{t<0} \frac{\mathbf{E}\left[e^{tX}\right]}{e^{ta}}. \qquad (18.9)$$

The Chernoff bound originated in this statistics paper [14], but it is widely used in theoretical computer science. We now consider several applications of the Chernoff bound to different distributions.

18.4 Chernoff Bound for Poisson Tail

We start by illustrating how the Chernoff bound can be used to bound the tail of X where $X \sim \text{Poisson}(\lambda)$, as in (18.2).

Let $X \sim \text{Poisson}(\lambda)$. For $t > 0$,

$$
\mathbf{E}\left[e^{tX}\right] = \sum_{i=0}^{\infty} e^{ti} \cdot \frac{e^{-\lambda} \cdot \lambda^i}{i!}
$$

$$
= e^{-\lambda} \cdot \sum_{i=0}^{\infty} \frac{(\lambda e^t)^i}{i!}
$$

$$
= e^{-\lambda} \cdot e^{\lambda e^t} \qquad \text{by (1.11)}
$$

$$
= e^{\lambda(e^t - 1)}.
$$

Let $a > \lambda$. Using the above, we have:

$$
\mathbf{P}\{X \geq a\} \leq \min_{t > 0} \left\{ \frac{\mathbf{E}\left[e^{tX}\right]}{e^{ta}} \right\}
$$

$$
= \min_{t > 0} \left\{ \frac{e^{\lambda(e^t - 1)}}{e^{ta}} \right\}
$$

$$
= \min_{t > 0} \left\{ e^{\lambda(e^t - 1) - ta} \right\}.
$$

It suffices to minimize the exponent of the above expression, $\lambda(e^t - 1) - ta$, which is minimized at

$$
t = \ln\left(\frac{a}{\lambda}\right),
$$

which is positive, since $a > \lambda$.

This yields

$$
\mathbf{P}\{X \geq a\} \leq e^{\lambda(e^t - 1) - ta}\Big|_{t = \ln\left(\frac{a}{\lambda}\right)}
$$

$$
= e^{\lambda\left(\frac{a}{\lambda} - 1\right) - a \ln\left(\frac{a}{\lambda}\right)}
$$

$$
= e^{a - \lambda} \cdot \left(\frac{\lambda}{a}\right)^a. \tag{18.10}
$$

Question: What is a bound on the probability that X is at least twice its mean?

Answer: From (18.10), we have $\mathbf{P}\{X \geq 2\lambda\} \leq \left(\frac{e}{4}\right)^{\lambda}$.

18.5 Chernoff Bound for Binomial

Chernoff bounds are most commonly applied to a sum of independent random variables, as in the case of a Binomial. In this section, we derive the Chernoff bound on the tail of X where $X \sim \text{Binomial}(n, p)$. There are many generalizations and variants of this result; see, for example, Exercises 18.15 and 18.20.

Theorem 18.4 (Pretty Chernoff bound for Binomial) *Let random variable* $X \sim \text{Binomial}(n, p)$, *where* $\mu = \mathbf{E}[X] = np$. *Then, for any* $\delta > 0$,

$$\mathbf{P}\{X - np \geq \delta\} \leq e^{-2\delta^2/n} \tag{18.11}$$
$$\mathbf{P}\{X - np \leq -\delta\} \leq e^{-2\delta^2/n}. \tag{18.12}$$

Observe that the bounds in Theorem 18.4 decrease with higher δ, as expected.

Question: One would likewise expect that the bounds in Theorem 18.4 decrease with higher n. Is this true?

Answer: This is a bit subtle:

- If δ is $\Theta(n)$, like the $\delta = \frac{n}{4}$ that we saw earlier, then the bound is of the form $e^{-\Theta(n)}$, which does in fact decrease with n, as we would expect. This is the strongest case of the bound. *This is the appropriate regime for using the pretty Chernoff bound.*
- If δ is $\Theta(\sqrt{n})$, then the bound appears to be constant in n. This makes sense because now we're looking at the probability of deviating from the mean by some number of standard deviations (again assuming p is a constant), which should become independent of n for high n and should just converge to a constant by the Central Limit Theorem (CLT).
- If δ is a constant, like 10, then the bound sadly grows with n. This is because the variance of $\text{Binomial}(n, p)$ is $np(1-p)$, which grows with higher n (assuming that p is a constant), so the probability of exceeding a constant δ increases as n gets bigger. This is the weakest case of the bound.

We will prove Theorem 18.4 in Section 18.7. But first we consider an example of its use.

Question: Suppose we flip a fair coin n times. Using the Chernoff bound, what is an upper bound on the probability of getting at least $\frac{3}{4}n$ heads?

Answer: Again letting X denote the number of heads:

$$\mathbf{P}\left\{X \geq \frac{3n}{4}\right\} = \mathbf{P}\left\{X - \frac{n}{2} \geq \frac{n}{4}\right\}$$

$$\leq e^{-2(n/4)^2/n}$$

$$= e^{-n/8}. \tag{18.13}$$

The bound in (18.13) goes to zero exponentially fast in n and is much tighter than the bound of $\frac{2}{n}$ that we obtained in (18.6) via Chebyshev's inequality.

18.6 Comparing the Different Bounds and Approximations

At this point, it is useful to step back and compare the bounds that we've seen (Markov, Chebyshev, Chernoff) with both the exact answer and the *approximation* given by CLT (Theorem 9.8). We focus on our usual question.

Question: What is the exact answer for the probability of getting at least $\frac{3}{4}n$ heads with a fair coin?

Answer:

$$\sum_{i=\frac{3n}{4}}^{n} \binom{n}{i} \cdot \left(\frac{1}{2}\right)^i \cdot \left(1 - \frac{1}{2}\right)^{n-i} = 2^{-n} \cdot \sum_{i=\frac{3n}{4}}^{n} \binom{n}{i}. \tag{18.14}$$

The exact answer has no closed form (which is why we've been looking for bounds), but we will evaluate it soon numerically so that we can see how it compares with the bounds that we've already computed.

CLT offers an *approximate* solution for the problem. Notice that all of our coin flips are independent, with probability $p = \frac{1}{2}$. If the number of these coin flips, n, is large, then the total number of heads, X, converges to a Normal distribution by the CLT.

Question: What is the mean and standard deviation of this Normal?

Answer: $\mathbf{E}[X] = \frac{n}{2}$. Since $X \sim \text{Binomial}(n, \frac{1}{2})$, we know $\mathbf{Var}(X) = \frac{n}{4}$, so $\sigma_X = \sqrt{\frac{n}{4}}$.

We now apply the CLT approximation by first formulating our question in terms of a standard Normal:

$$\mathbf{P}\left\{X \geq \frac{3n}{4}\right\} = \mathbf{P}\left\{X - \frac{n}{2} \geq \frac{n}{4}\right\}$$

$$= \mathbf{P}\left\{\frac{X - \frac{n}{2}}{\sqrt{\frac{n}{4}}} \geq \frac{\frac{n}{4}}{\sqrt{\frac{n}{4}}}\right\}$$

$$= \mathbf{P}\left\{\frac{X - \frac{n}{2}}{\sqrt{\frac{n}{4}}} \geq \sqrt{\frac{n}{4}}\right\}$$

$$= \mathbf{P}\left\{\text{Normal}(0, 1) \geq \sqrt{\frac{n}{4}}\right\}$$

$$= 1 - \Phi\left(\sqrt{\frac{n}{4}}\right).$$

Figure 18.1 compares the different approximations and bounds that we've seen, along with the exact result. As you can see, the Markov and Chebyshev bounds are both worthless for this example (we didn't even plot the Markov bound). The Chernoff bound is reasonable. The Normal approximation from the CLT is not a bound, but it's a really good approximation, particularly when n is high.

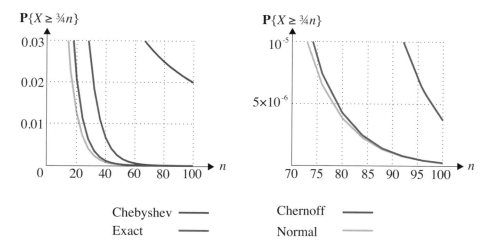

Figure 18.1 *Evaluation of* $\mathbf{P}\left\{X \geq \frac{3n}{4}\right\}$ *via Chebyshev, Chernoff, and Normal (CLT), where* $X \sim \text{Binomial}(n, 0.5)$. *Both graphs show the same comparison, but under different ranges. The first graph, with range* $1 \leq n \leq 100$, *shows that the Chebyshev bound is poor; the Chernoff bound is better; the Normal approximation from the CLT is very good. The second graph, with range* $n > 70$, *shows that, for higher n, Chebyshev is so bad that it doesn't even appear on the graph, and even the Chernoff bound doesn't look so great. Notice that the Normal approximation gets better and better with higher n.*

18.7 Proof of Chernoff Bound for Binomial: Theorem 18.4

The proof of Theorem 18.4 relies on Lemma 18.5. In the exercises, we will not in general have such a cute lemma to simplify our analysis, so the bounds that we will be able to prove will not always look as cute.

Lemma 18.5 *For any $t > 0$ and $0 < p < 1$ and $q = 1 - p$, we have that:*

$$pe^{tq} + qe^{-tp} \le e^{t^2/8}.$$

Proof: The proof only uses calculus and is deferred to Section 18.10.   ∎

Proof: [Theorem 18.4] We will prove (18.11). The proof of (18.12) is left as an exercise. It will help to view $X = \sum_{i=1}^{n} X_i$ where $X_i \sim \text{Bernoulli}(p)$.

For any $t > 0$,

$$
\begin{aligned}
\mathbf{P}\{X - np \ge \delta\} &= \mathbf{P}\{t(X - np) \ge t\delta\} \\
&= \mathbf{P}\left\{e^{t(X-np)} \ge e^{t\delta}\right\} \\
&\le e^{-t\delta} \cdot \mathbf{E}\left[e^{t(X-np)}\right] \\
&= e^{-t\delta} \cdot \mathbf{E}\left[e^{t((X_1-p)+(X_2-p)+\cdots+(X_n-p))}\right] \\
&= e^{-t\delta} \cdot \prod_{i=1}^{n} \mathbf{E}\left[e^{t(X_i-p)}\right] \quad \text{(because } X_i\text{'s are independent)} \\
&= e^{-t\delta} \cdot \prod_{i=1}^{n}\left(p \cdot e^{t(1-p)} + (1-p) \cdot e^{-tp}\right) \\
&\le e^{-t\delta} \cdot \prod_{i=1}^{n}\left(e^{t^2/8}\right) \quad \text{(by Lemma 18.5)} \\
&= e^{-t\delta + nt^2/8}. \qquad\qquad\qquad\qquad\qquad (18.15)
\end{aligned}
$$

We now want to find the $t > 0$ that minimizes this bound. It suffices to minimize the exponent in (18.15):

$$
\frac{d}{dt}\left(-t\delta + nt^2/8\right) = -\delta + \frac{2nt}{8}
$$

$$
\frac{d^2}{dt^2}\left(-t\delta + nt^2/8\right) = \frac{2n}{8} > 0.
$$

Hence the minimum is obtained by finding that $t > 0$ which satisfies:

$$-\delta + \frac{2nt}{8} = 0.$$

So

$$t = \frac{4\delta}{n},$$

which is positive, as desired. Substituting this value of t into (18.15), we have:

$$\mathbf{P}\{X - np \geq \delta\} \leq e^{-\frac{4\delta}{n} \cdot \delta + n\left(\frac{4\delta}{n}\right)^2/8}$$

$$= e^{-\frac{4\delta^2}{n} + \frac{2\delta^2}{n}}$$

$$= e^{-\frac{2\delta^2}{n}}.$$ ∎

18.8 A (Sometimes) Stronger Chernoff Bound for Binomial

The Chernoff bound that we derived in Theorem 18.4 was very pretty. However, it's not always as strong (tight) as possible. We now introduce another bound for the Binomial. In addition to sometimes being a lot stronger, this new bound holds for a **more general definition of a Binomial**, where the coins can have different probabilities. Specifically, imagine that we are again interested in the sum of n coin flips (call this X), but this time the ith coin has probability p_i of coming up heads.

> **Theorem 18.6 (Sometimes stronger Chernoff bound for Binomial)** *Define* $X = \sum_{i=1}^{n} X_i$ *where the* X_i's *are independent with* $X_i \sim$ *Bernoulli*(p_i) *and* $\mu = \mathbf{E}[X] = \sum_{i=1}^{n} p_i$. *Then,* $\forall \epsilon > 0$,
>
> $$\mathbf{P}\{X \geq (1 + \epsilon)\mu\} < \left(\frac{e^{\epsilon}}{(1 + \epsilon)^{(1+\epsilon)}}\right)^{\mu}. \qquad (18.16)$$
>
> *Furthermore, when* $0 < \epsilon < 1$,
>
> $$\mathbf{P}\{X \leq (1 - \epsilon)\mu\} \leq \left(\frac{e^{-\epsilon}}{(1 - \epsilon)^{(1-\epsilon)}}\right)^{\mu}. \qquad (18.17)$$

Proof: The proof is given in Exercises 18.20 and 18.21. ∎

To interpret the bound in Theorem 18.6, it helps to consider the inner expression:

$$f(\epsilon) = \frac{e^{\epsilon}}{(1 + \epsilon)^{(1+\epsilon)}}. \qquad (18.18)$$

Figure 18.2 shows a plot of this expression as a function of ϵ.

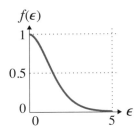

Figure 18.2 *Plot of expression (18.18). Higher ϵ leads to tighter bound.*

We make two observations: First, $\forall \epsilon > 0$, $f(\epsilon) < 1$. This implies that the bound in Theorem 18.6 is exponentially decreasing, as desired. Second, $f(\epsilon)$ decreases very quickly with higher ϵ. This too makes sense, since the Binomial should be concentrated around its mean. *The bound in Theorem 18.6 is particularly strong when ϵ is high.*

It is important to spend some time comparing the pretty bound for the Binomial in Theorem 18.4 with the (sometimes) stronger bound in Theorem 18.6. The following questions will help.

Question: Which is the better bound in the case where $p_i = p = \frac{1}{2}$, and where we are interested in the probability of at least $\frac{3n}{4}$ heads in n flips?

Answer: By Theorem 18.4, where $\delta = \frac{n}{4}$,

$$\mathbf{P}\left\{X \geq \frac{3n}{4}\right\} = \mathbf{P}\left\{X - \frac{n}{2} \geq \frac{n}{4}\right\} \leq e^{-\frac{n}{8}}.$$

By Theorem 18.6, where $\epsilon = \frac{1}{2}$,

$$\mathbf{P}\left\{X \geq \frac{3n}{4}\right\} = \mathbf{P}\left\{X \geq \left(1 + \frac{1}{2}\right) \cdot \frac{n}{2}\right\}$$

$$\leq \left(\frac{e^{.5}}{(1.5)^{1.5}}\right)^{\frac{n}{2}}$$

$$\approx (0.89)^{\frac{n}{2}}$$

$$\approx (1.54)^{-\frac{n}{8}}.$$

Thus, Theorem 18.4 produces a *tighter* bound than Theorem 18.6 in this case, although both bounds are reasonable. Observe that it should be unsurprising that Theorem 18.6 is not so great because ϵ is only 0.5 here, which is not a good value for Theorem 18.6 (see Figure 18.2).

Question: Which is the better bound, in the case where $p_i = p = \frac{1}{n}$, and where we are interested in the probability that $X \geq 21$?

Answer: By Theorem 18.4, with $\delta = 20$, we have:

$$\mathbf{P}\{X \geq 21\} = \mathbf{P}\{X - 1 \geq 20\} \leq e^{-2\cdot(20)^2/n} = e^{-\frac{800}{n}} \to 1 \text{ as } n \to \infty.$$

The issue here is that, although δ is high, it does not increase with n, and Theorem 18.4 is only really strong when δ is $\Theta(n)$.

By contrast, by Theorem 18.6, with $\epsilon = 20$, we have:

$$\mathbf{P}\{X \geq 21\} = \mathbf{P}\{X \geq (1 + 20) \cdot 1\} \leq \frac{e^{20}}{21^{21}} \approx 8.3 \cdot 10^{-20}.$$

So Theorem 18.6 yields a far stronger bound for large n (although it is weaker when n is small). Note that $\epsilon = 20$ here, which is in the ideal range for Theorem 18.6, as shown in Figure 18.2.

The above shows clearly that one has to be careful in choosing a good (tight) Chernoff bound for one's application.

18.9 Other Tail Bounds

There are many other tail bounds in the literature, which either generalize the Chernoff bound, or consider a more specialized case, or a little of both. One important bound is the Hoeffding bound:

Theorem 18.7 (Hoeffding's inequality) *Let* $X_1, X_2, \ldots, X_n$ *be independent random variables satisfying* $a_i \leq X_i \leq b_i$ *for all* i *where* $a_i \leq b_i$ *are real numbers. Let*

$$X = \sum_{i=1}^{n} X_i.$$

Then,

$$\mathbf{P}\{X - \mathbf{E}[X] \geq \delta\} \leq \exp\left(-\frac{2\delta^2}{\sum_{i=1}^{n}(b_i - a_i)^2}\right) \qquad (18.19)$$

$$\mathbf{P}\{X - \mathbf{E}[X] \leq -\delta\} \leq \exp\left(-\frac{2\delta^2}{\sum_{i=1}^{n}(b_i - a_i)^2}\right). \qquad (18.20)$$

Proof: The proof of Hoeffding's inequality is left to Exercise 18.24. It is similar to the Chernoff bound proofs, but relies on a convexity argument. ∎

Question: For Hoeffding's bound, do the X_i's need to be identically distributed?

Answer: Interestingly, the answer is no. The X_i's need to be independent, but they can each follow a different distribution, and in fact have their own lower and upper bounds. This makes the Hoeffding bound very general!

Notice that the format of the bounds in Theorem 18.7 is very similar to that in Theorem 18.4. The difference is that the n in the denominator of the exponent in Theorem 18.4 is now replaced by $\sum_{i=1}^{n}(b_i - a_i)^2$. Notice that the Hoeffding bound becomes smaller for higher δ, and becomes larger as $b_i - a_i$ increases.

18.10 Appendix: Proof of Lemma 18.5

This appendix contains the technical details needed to prove Lemma 18.5. We start with a basic identity from calculus:

> **Lemma 18.8** *If $g(0) = h(0)$ and $g'(k) \le h'(k)$ for all $k \ge 0$, then $g(t) \le h(t)$ for all $t \ge 0$.*

Proof:

$$h(t) - g(t) = (h(t) - g(t)) - (h(0) - g(0))$$
$$= \int_0^t (h'(k) - g'(k))dk$$
$$\ge 0, \qquad \text{because } h'(k) - g'(k) \ge 0. \qquad \blacksquare$$

> **Lemma 18.9** *For all $0 \le p \le 1$ and $t \ge 0$,*
> $$pe^{t(1-p)} + (1-p)e^{-tp} \le e^{\frac{t^2}{8}}. \qquad (18.21)$$

Proof: Multiplying both sides of (18.21) by e^{tp} yields

$$f(t) \equiv pe^t + 1 - p \le e^{tp + \frac{t^2}{8}}. \qquad (18.22)$$

Now taking the natural log of both sides of (18.22) yields

$$g(t) \equiv \ln(f(t)) = \ln\left(pe^t + (1-p)\right) \le \frac{t^2}{8} + tp \equiv h(t). \qquad (18.23)$$

It suffices to show that $g(t) \le h(t)$, $\forall t \ge 0$, as defined in (18.23).

Note that $f'(t) = f''(t) = pe^t$ and $0 \le f'(t) \le f(t)$, so $0 \le \frac{f'(t)}{f(t)} \le 1$.

Since $g(t) = \ln(f(t))$, we have that $g'(t) = \frac{f'(t)}{f(t)}$. Furthermore, using the fact that $f''(t) = f'(t)$, we have

$$g''(t) = \frac{f(t) f''(t) - f'^2(t)}{f^2(t)} = \left(1 - \frac{f'(t)}{f(t)}\right) \cdot \frac{f'(t)}{f(t)} \le \frac{1}{4}. \quad (18.24)$$

The last step involving the $\frac{1}{4}$ comes from the fact that, for all x, the quantity $(1 - x)(x)$ is maximized at $x = \frac{1}{2}$.

Since $g(0) = h(0)$, by Lemma 18.8 it suffices to show that $g'(t) \le h'(t)$ for all $t \ge 0$.

Since $g'(0) = h'(0)$, by Lemma 18.8 it suffices to show that $g''(t) \le h''(t)$ for all $t \ge 0$. But this latter statement is true because, by (18.24),

$$g''(t) \le \frac{1}{4} = h''(t). \qquad \blacksquare$$

18.11 Exercises

18.1 **Chebyshev bound**
A coin has probability $p = \frac{1}{3}$ of coming up heads on each flip. You flip the coin n times. Let X denote the number of heads you get. Use Chebyshev's inequality to upper bound the quantity: $\mathbf{P}\left\{X \ge \frac{1}{2}n\right\}$.

18.2 **Test scores: easy bounds**
Suppose I know only that the mean test score is 40%.
(a) What can I say about the fraction of the class with test score > 80%?
(b) Suppose I'm given further information that the standard deviation of test scores is 10%. What can I now say about the fraction of the class with test score > 80%?

18.3 **Reverse Markov inequality**
Let Y be a non-negative r.v. which is never greater than value b. Let $0 < a < b$. Prove:
$$\mathbf{P}\{Y \le a\} \le \frac{\mathbf{E}[b - Y]}{b - a}.$$

18.4 **The distribution of the average**
There are $n = 25$ students in my class. Their scores are independent

because they don't talk to each other, ever! Each student's score is well modeled by a r.v. (not necessarily Normal) with mean 40% and standard deviation of 10% (it's a hard class). Approximately what's the chance that the class average, A_n, exceeds 50%?
(a) What does Chebyshev's inequality tell us about $\mathbf{P}\{A_n > 50\%\}$?
(b) For large n, what does the CLT tell us about $\mathbf{P}\{A_n > 50\%\}$?

18.5 **Sunny Sundays**
Sundays are sunny with probability $\frac{7}{10}$, while all other days are, independently, only sunny with probability $\frac{7}{40}$. Upper bound the probability that in a sequence of n days (where n is a multiple of 7), at least half of the days are sunny. You'll want a bound that is exponentially decreasing in n.

18.6 **Kurtosis bound**
Let X be a r.v. and $a > 0$ be some constant. Define
$$\text{Kurt}(X) \equiv \mathbf{E}\left[(X - \mathbf{E}[X])^4\right].$$
The Chebyshev bound gives an upper bound on $\mathbf{P}\{|X - \mathbf{E}[X]| > a\}$ in terms of $\mathbf{Var}(X)$. Derive an upper bound on $\mathbf{P}\{|X - \mathbf{E}[X]| > a\}$ in terms of $\text{Kurt}(X)$.

18.7 **Coupon collecting**
There are n distinct coupon types that you would like to collect. Each day you are sent a random coupon from among the n types. Let X denote the number of days needed to collect all n distinct coupons, given that coupons are chosen randomly with replacement. The following identity is useful in answering some of the questions below:
$$\sum_{i=1}^{\infty} \frac{1}{i^2} = \frac{\pi^2}{6}.$$
(a) What is $\mathbf{E}[X]$? What does this approach for high n? Write your answer using $\Theta(\cdot)$.
(b) Derive $\mathbf{Var}(X)$. What does this approach for high n? Write your answer using $\Theta(\cdot)$.
(c) Derive an asymptotic upper bound on $\mathbf{P}\{X \geq 2n \ln n\}$ for large n using Markov's inequality.
(d) Derive an asymptotic upper bound on $\mathbf{P}\{X \geq 2n \ln n\}$ for large n using Chebyshev's inequality. Express your answer using $\Theta(\cdot)$.
Note: For $\mathbf{E}[X]$ in (c) and (d), use the asymptotic mean from part (a).

18.8 **Getting a job**
Jiacheng has independent probability 50% of being hired by each company at which he interviews. Suppose Jiacheng interviews at 20 companies. What is the probability that Jiacheng doesn't get a job?

(a) Use the Chernoff bound in Theorem 18.4 to upper bound the probability that Jiacheng doesn't get a job.

(b) Now use the Chernoff bound in Theorem 18.6 to upper bound the probability that Jiacheng doesn't get a job.

(c) Now compute the exact probability that Jiacheng doesn't get a job.

18.9 **Bounding wealth**

Keshav's Robinhood stock trading account loss limit is $1000 dollars. Thus on any given day Keshav's account value, V, can range from $-\$1000$ to ∞. Suppose that all we know about Keshav is that his average Robinhood account value is $3000 dollars. Can we say anything about the fraction of time that Keshav's account value is at least $9000? Find the tightest upper bound, t, such that

$$\mathbf{P}\{V \geq 9000\} \leq t.$$

(a) Find a bound t such that $\mathbf{P}\{V \geq 9000\} \leq t$.

(b) Prove that the t that you found in part (a) is tight. Specifically, show that there exists a distribution, V, such that $\mathbf{E}[V] = 3000$ and $V \geq -1000$ and $\mathbf{P}\{V \geq 9000\} = t$.

18.10 **The tightness of Markov's inequality**

Markov's inequality says that, for any non-negative r.v. X,

$$\mathbf{P}\{X \geq k\mathbf{E}[X]\} \leq \frac{1}{k}.$$

After reading this chapter, you likely got the impression that Markov's inequality is quite weak. Prove that Markov's Inequality is "tight" in the following sense: For any given $k \geq 1$, there exists a non-negative r.v. X such that $\mathbf{P}\{X \geq k\mathbf{E}[X]\} = \frac{1}{k}$.

18.11 **Tightness of Chebyshev's inequality**

Chebyshev's inequality tells us that for all random variables X,

$$\mathbf{P}\{|X - \mathbf{E}[X]| \geq a\} \leq \frac{\mathbf{Var}(X)}{a^2}.$$

Prove that Chebyshev's Inequality is "tight" in the following sense: Give a r.v. X (not equal to a constant) and a value $a > 0$ for which the above inequality is met at equality.

18.12 **Concentration bounds for pair-wise independent random variables**

Let $X_1, X_2, \ldots, X_n$ be pairwise-independent random variables, satisfying $\mathbf{Var}(X_i) \leq 10$ for all $i = 1, \ldots, n$. Let $X = \sum_{i=1}^{n} X_i$. Prove that for all $a > 0$,

$$\mathbf{P}\{|X - \mathbf{E}[X]| \geq a\} \leq \frac{10n}{a^2}.$$

18.13 Weak Law of Large Numbers
Let $X_1, X_2, X_3, \ldots$, be i.i.d. with finite mean $\mathbf{E}[X]$ and finite variance σ^2.
Let $S_n = \sum_{i=1}^{n} X_i$. Your goal is to prove the Weak Law of Large Numbers:

$$\forall \epsilon > 0, \quad \lim_{n \to \infty} \mathbf{P} \left\{ \left| \frac{S_n}{n} - \mathbf{E}[X] \right| > \epsilon \right\} = 0,$$

where $S_n = \sum_{i=1}^{n} X_i$. [Hint: Use Chebyshev's Inequality.]

18.14 Comparing bounds on tail of Exponential
Let $X \sim \text{Exp}(\lambda)$, where $\lambda > 0$. We will evaluate $\mathbf{P}\left\{X \geq \frac{a}{\lambda}\right\}$, the probability that X is at least a times its mean, where $a > 1$.
(a) What is $\mathbf{P}\left\{X \geq \frac{a}{\lambda}\right\}$ exactly?
(b) What does the Markov bound tell us about $\mathbf{P}\left\{X \geq \frac{a}{\lambda}\right\}$?
(c) What does the Chebyshev bound tell us about $\mathbf{P}\left\{X \geq \frac{a}{\lambda}\right\}$?
(d) What does the Chernoff bound tell us about $\mathbf{P}\left\{X \geq \frac{a}{\lambda}\right\}$?
[Hint: Pick t s.t. $0 < t < \lambda$.]
(e) How far off is the Chernoff bound from the correct answer?

18.15 Chernoff bound for Binomial with 1/−1 variables
Let $X_1, X_2, \ldots, X_n$ be i.i.d random variables, where

$$X_i = \begin{cases} 1 & \text{w/prob } 0.5 \\ -1 & \text{w/prob } 0.5 \end{cases}.$$

Let $X = \sum_{i=1}^{n} X_i$, where $\mu = \mathbf{E}[X] = 0$. Assume $a > 0$. Follow the steps below to prove from first principles that

$$\mathbf{P}\{X \geq a\} \leq e^{-\frac{a^2}{2n}}.$$

(a) Start by setting up the usual Chernoff-based inequality for $\mathbf{P}\{X \geq a\}$, based on exponentiating and then applying the Markov bound.
(b) Prove that $\mathbf{E}\left[e^{tX_i}\right] < e^{t^2/2}$, where $t > 0$. [Hint: Taylor series]
(c) Form a simple closed-form bound for $\mathbf{E}\left[e^{tX}\right]$ and use this to get a simple expression for $\mathbf{P}\{X \geq a\}$ in terms of t.
(d) Find the t that minimizes $\mathbf{P}\{X \geq a\}$ and use this to get the final result.
(e) What can you say about $\mathbf{P}\{|X| \geq a\}$?

18.16 Chernoff change of variable
Let $Y_1, Y_2, \ldots, Y_n$ be i.i.d. random variables, where

$$Y_i = \begin{cases} 1 & \text{w/prob } 0.5 \\ 5 & \text{w/prob } 0.5 \end{cases}.$$

Let $Y = \sum_{i=1}^{n} Y_i$, where $\mu = \mathbf{E}[Y] = 3n$. For $a > 0$, derive a bound on $\mathbf{P}\{Y - \mu \geq a\}$. To do this, you will exploit the result in Exercise 18.15 by defining a simple linear transformation between the Y_i's in this exercise and the $1/-1$ random variables in Exercise 18.15.

18.17 Chernoff bound for sum of Exponentials
Let $X = \sum_{i=1}^{n} X_i$, where the X_i's are i.i.d. and are Exponentially distributed with rate $\lambda > 0$. Use Chernoff bounds to derive an upper bound on the probability that X is at least twice its mean.

18.18 Tail on the sum of Uniforms
Let $X = X_1 + \cdots + X_n$ where the X_i's are i.i.d. with $X_i \sim \text{Uniform}(0, 1)$. What is an upper bound on $\mathbf{P}\left\{X \geq \frac{3n}{4}\right\}$? Please answer this question in two different ways:
  (a) Derive a Chernoff bound from scratch, following the usual process involving $\mathbf{E}\left[e^{tX}\right]$. [Hint: You will come across a term of the form $e^t - 1$. Please upper bound this by e^t to make your analysis nicer.]
  (b) Compute the answer given by the Hoeffding bound (Theorem 18.7).
  (c) Which bound do you expect to be better, (a) or (b)? Is that what happened?

18.19 Chernoff bound on Binomial
Complete the proof of Theorem 18.4 by proving (18.12).

18.20 Chernoff bound for Binomial with different probabilities
Prove (18.16) from Theorem 18.6, with extensions. Let $X = \sum_{i=1}^{n} X_i$, with independent $X_i \sim \text{Bernoulli}(p_i)$ and $\mu = \mathbf{E}[X] = \sum_{i=1}^{n} p_i$.
  (a) Prove that $\forall \epsilon > 0$,

$$\mathbf{P}\{X \geq (1 + \epsilon)\mu\} < \left(\frac{e^{\epsilon}}{(1 + \epsilon)^{(1+\epsilon)}}\right)^{\mu}.$$

Follow these steps, where $t > 0$:
  (i) Prove $\mathbf{E}\left[e^{tX}\right] < e^{(e^t - 1)\mu}$. [Hint: Use $1 + x < e^x$ from (1.12).]
  (ii) Apply the usual Chernoff bound technique to upper bound $\mathbf{P}\{X \geq (1 + \epsilon)\mu\}$. Write your answer as compactly as possible.
  (iii) Find a $t > 0$ that minimizes the answer in the previous step.
  (iv) Substitute in that t to yield the desired bound on $\mathbf{P}\{X \geq (1 + \epsilon)\mu\}$.
  (b) Follow the steps below to prove that, if $0 < \epsilon \leq 1$,

$$\mathbf{P}\{X \geq (1 + \epsilon)\mu\} < e^{-\frac{\epsilon^2 \mu}{3}}.$$

  (i) Using the result of part (a), write what you need to show as an inequality where the right-hand side is $(1 + \epsilon)\ln(1 + \epsilon)$.
  (ii) Derive the Taylor series expansion of $\ln(1 + \epsilon)$ where $0 < \epsilon \leq 1$. Then substitute this into your prior expression to prove the needed result.
  (c) From the result in part (b), deduce this immediate corollary:

$$\text{For } 0 < \gamma < \mu, \ \mathbf{P}\{X - \mu \geq \gamma\} \leq e^{-\frac{\gamma^2}{3\mu}}.$$

18.21 Chernoff bound for Binomial with different probabilities, continued
Prove (18.17) from Theorem 18.6, with extensions. Let $X = \sum_{i=1}^{n} X_i$, with
independent $X_i \sim \text{Bernoulli}(p_i)$ and $\mu = \mathbf{E}[X] = \sum_{i=1}^{n} p_i$.
(a) Show that for $0 < \epsilon < 1$,

$$\mathbf{P}\{X \le (1-\epsilon)\mu\} \le \left(\frac{e^{-\epsilon}}{(1-\epsilon)^{(1-\epsilon)}}\right)^{\mu}.$$

(b) Show that for $0 < \epsilon < 1$,

$$\mathbf{P}\{X \le (1-\epsilon)\mu\} < e^{-\frac{\epsilon^2 \mu}{2}}.$$

[Hint: start by proving that $\ln\left((1-\epsilon)^{(1-\epsilon)}\right) > -\epsilon + \epsilon^2/2$ by using a
Taylor series around 0.]

18.22 Approximating the tail of the Normal distribution
[Proposed by Arisha Kulshrestha] Recall that we have no closed-form
expression for the tail of the Normal distribution, which must be computed
by numerically evaluating the integral. Let $X \sim \text{Normal}(0, 1)$. Your goal
is to produce upper bounds on $\mathbf{P}\{X \ge a\}$, where $a > 0$.
(a) Use Markov's inequality to bound $\mathbf{P}\{X \ge a\}$. Note: This is not as
trivial as it might seem because X is *not* non-negative. It will help to
observe that:

$$\mathbf{P}\{X \ge a\} = \mathbf{P}\{X \ge a \mid X > 0\} \cdot \mathbf{P}\{X > 0\}.$$

Now define the non-negative r.v. $Y \equiv [X \mid X > 0]$ and note that
$\mathbf{P}\{X \ge a \mid X > 0\} = \mathbf{P}\{Y \ge a\}$.
(b) Use Chebyshev's inequality to bound $\mathbf{P}\{X \ge a\}$.
(c) Use Chernoff bounds following these steps:
   (i) Derive $\mathbf{E}\left[e^{tX}\right]$.
   (ii) Derive the Chernoff bound for $\mathbf{P}\{X \ge a\}$.

18.23 Negative Binomial tail
Suppose we are flipping a coin that lands on heads with probability $p > 0.5$. Let X be the number of heads that we see in n flips. Let Y be the
number of flips until we see the kth head. We say that $X \sim \text{Binomial}(n, p)$
and $Y \sim \text{NegBinomial}(k, p)$.
(a) Derive $\mathbf{E}[Y]$ and $\mathbf{Var}(Y)$.
(b) Prove that $\mathbf{P}\{Y > n\} = \mathbf{P}\{X < k\}$. (Just use words to explain why
each side implies the other.)
(c) Is $\mathbf{P}\{Y = n\} = \mathbf{P}\{X = k\}$? Explain.
(d) Use the above results and a Chernoff bound to derive an upper bound
on $\mathbf{P}\{Y > a\mathbf{E}[Y]\}$, where $Y \sim \text{NegBinomial}(k, p)$ and $a > 1$. You
should find that your upper bound decreases as k increases. (Please
don't worry about the fact that some quantities might not be integers.)

(e) In part (d) we used the Chernoff bound to derive an upper bound on Y's tail. Now instead use CLT. Apply CLT to approximate the probability that Y is at least twice its mean. You can leave your answers in terms of $\Phi(\cdot)$.

18.24 Hoeffding's inequality

[Proposed by Misha Ivkov] In this problem, you will prove Hoeffding's Inequality, Theorem 18.7, which states the following: Let $X_1, X_2, \ldots, X_n$ be independent random variables satisfying $a_i \leq X_i \leq b_i$ for all i where $a_i \leq b_i$ are real numbers. Let $X = \sum_{i=1}^{n} X_i$. Then,

$$\mathbf{P}\{X - \mathbb{E}[X] \geq \delta\} \leq \exp\left(-\frac{2\delta^2}{\sum_{i=1}^{n}(b_i - a_i)^2}\right),$$

$$\mathbf{P}\{X - \mathbb{E}[X] \leq -\delta\} \leq \exp\left(-\frac{2\delta^2}{\sum_{i=1}^{n}(b_i - a_i)^2}\right).$$

(a) Start with the usual Chernoff-based inequality for $\mathbf{P}\{X - \mathbb{E}[X] \geq \delta\}$, based on exponentiating and the Markov bound.
(b) Recall from Definition 5.21 that a real-valued function, $g(\cdot)$, defined on interval $S \subseteq \mathbb{R}$ is *convex* if $\forall \lambda \in [0, 1]$, and $\forall \alpha, \beta \in S$,

$$\lambda g(\alpha) + (1 - \lambda)g(\beta) \geq g(\lambda \alpha + (1 - \lambda)\beta). \qquad (18.25)$$

Draw a picture of (18.25) where $g(x) = e^x$ to illustrate that $g(x) = e^x$ is convex.
(c) Suppose that Y is a r.v. which satisfies $0 \leq Y \leq 1$ and has mean $\mathbf{E}[Y] = \mu$. Use the fact that e^x is convex to prove that

$$\mathbb{E}[e^{tY}] \leq \mu e^t + (1 - \mu). \qquad (18.26)$$

[Hint: You will start with (18.25), but replace λ with the r.v. Y, which is also in $[0, 1]$. You'll need to set $\alpha = t$, $\beta = 0$.]
(d) Use Lemma 18.5 to go from (18.26) to the expression below:

$$\mathbb{E}[e^{tY}] \leq e^{t\mu + t^2/8}. \qquad (18.27)$$

(e) Using part (d), derive a bound on $\mathbb{E}[e^{tX_i}]$ in terms of t, a_i, b_i, and μ_i, where μ_i is the mean of X_i. It will help to start by defining

$$Y = \frac{X_i - a_i}{b_i - a_i} \qquad \text{or, equivalently,} \qquad X_i = (b_i - a_i)Y + a_i.$$

(f) Form a simple closed-form bound for $\mathbb{E}[e^{tX}]$. Then use this bound to get a simple bound for $\mathbf{P}\{X - \mathbb{E}[X] \geq \delta\}$ in terms of t.
(g) Find the t that minimizes $\mathbf{P}\{X - \mathbb{E}[X] \geq \delta\}$ and use this to get the final result.
(h) Argue that the bound you showed for $\mathbf{P}\{X - \mathbb{E}[X] \geq \delta\}$ also works for $\mathbf{P}\{X - \mathbb{E}[X] \leq -\delta\}$.

19 Applications of Tail Bounds: Confidence Intervals and Balls and Bins

In Chapter 18 we saw several powerful tail bounds, including the Chebyshev bound and the Chernoff bound. These are particularly useful when bounding the tail of a sum of independent random variables. We also reviewed the application of the Central Limit Theorem (CLT) to approximating the tail of a sum of independent and identically distributed (i.i.d.) random variables.

These tail bounds and approximations have immediate application to the problem of interval estimation, also known as creating "confidence intervals" around an estimation. They also are very useful in solving an important class of problems in theoretical computer science, called "balls and bins" problems, where balls are thrown at random into bins. Balls-and-bins problems are in turn directly related to hashing algorithms and load-balancing algorithms. In this chapter, and the next, we will study these immediate applications of our existing tail bounds and approximations. In Chapters 21–23, we will move on to the topic of randomized algorithms, where we will see many more applications of our tail bounds.

19.1 Interval Estimation

In Chapter 15, we discussed estimating the mean, $\mathbf{E}[X]$, of a random variable (r.v.) X. We assume that we're given n i.i.d. samples of X, which we denote by $X_1, X_2, \ldots, X_n$. We then define our estimator of $\mathbf{E}[X]$ to be

$$\overline{X} \equiv \frac{X_1 + X_2 + \cdots + X_n}{n}.$$

We call $\overline{X}$ the **sample mean**. Importantly, $\overline{X}$ is a function of random samples and thus is itself a *random variable*, not a constant.

What we have not discussed, though, is: *How good is $\overline{X}$ at estimating $\mathbf{E}[X]$?*

Clearly, the estimator $\overline{X}$ gets closer and closer to $\mathbf{E}[X]$ as we increase the number of samples n. But it's hard to say how good $\overline{X}$ is because it's just a single value: a point estimator. What we really want is an interval around $\overline{X}$ where we can say that the true mean, $\mathbf{E}[X]$, lies within that interval with high confidence, say 95% probability. That is, we want an "interval estimator."

> **Definition 19.1** *Let θ be some parameter of r.v. X that we're trying to estimate, e.g., $\mathbf{E}[X]$. Let $X_1, X_2, \ldots, X_n$ be i.i.d. samples of X. Then we say that an* **interval estimator** *of θ with confidence level $1 - \alpha$ is a pair of estimators, $\hat{\theta}_{low}$ and $\hat{\theta}_{high}$, where*
>
> $$\mathbf{P}\left\{\hat{\theta}_{low} \leq \theta \leq \hat{\theta}_{high}\right\} \geq 1 - \alpha.$$
>
> *Importantly, the randomness here is due to $\hat{\theta}_{low}$ and $\hat{\theta}_{high}$, not θ. Here θ is a constant that we're trying to estimate, while $\hat{\theta}_{low}$ and $\hat{\theta}_{high}$ are both functions of the random data samples $X_1, \ldots, X_n$ and hence are random variables. Equivalently, we say that*
>
> $$\left[\hat{\theta}_{low}, \hat{\theta}_{high}\right]$$
>
> *is a $(1 - \alpha) \cdot 100\%$* **confidence interval** *for θ, with* **width** *$\hat{\theta}_{high} - \hat{\theta}_{low}$.*

For the purpose of our discussion we will be looking at creating 95% confidence intervals on $\mathbf{E}[X]$, which will take the form of

$$[\overline{X} - \delta, \overline{X} + \delta],$$

where 2δ represents the width of our confidence interval and $\overline{X}$ is the sample mean. It is generally desirable that the confidence interval has both a *high confidence level* (say 95%) and also a *low width*.

In Section 19.2 we'll see how to develop confidence intervals with guarantees. To do this, we will use Chernoff and Chebyshev bounds. Unfortunately, it is not always possible to develop these "exact" (guaranteed) confidence intervals. In Section 19.3 we show how to develop *approximate* confidence intervals. These rely on the CLT approximation.

19.2 Exact Confidence Intervals

In developing confidence intervals we start with the classical example of polling to determine the outcome of an election. Our goal here is to develop 95% confidence intervals, but this can easily be generalized to any confidence level.

19.2.1 Using Chernoff Bounds to Get Exact Confidence Intervals

Example 19.2 (Polling for election)

Imagine that we are trying to estimate the fraction of people who will vote for

Biden in the presidential election. Let p be the true fraction. Our goal is to figure out p.

To estimate p, we use the following algorithm:

1. Sample $n = 1000$ people independently at random. Let X_i be an indicator r.v., which is 1 if the ith person sampled says they'll vote for Biden.
2. Let $S_n = X_1 + X_2 + \cdots + X_n$.
3. Return the r.v.

$$\overline{X} = \frac{S_n}{n}$$

   as our estimate of p.

Question: Why is X_i a r.v.? How is it distributed?

Answer: Each individual either votes for Biden or doesn't, so there's no randomness in a particular individual. The *randomness* comes from the fact that we're picking *random* individuals. If we let X_i be our ith sample, then,

$$X_i = \begin{cases} 1 & \text{if person } i \text{ said yes} \\ 0 & \text{otherwise} \end{cases}.$$

Here $X_i \sim \text{Bernoulli}(p)$, because the probability that a randomly chosen person says "yes" is p.

Question: What do S_n and $\overline{X}$ represent? How are they distributed?

Answer: S_n represents the total number of people sampled who say they'll vote for Biden and $\overline{X}$ represents the fraction of people sampled who say they'll vote for Biden. Both are functions of random variables, so both are random variables.

$$S_n \sim \text{Binomial}(n, p) \qquad \overline{X} \sim \frac{1}{n} \cdot \text{Binomial}(n, p).$$

Our **goal** is to define a 95% confidence interval on p where:

$$\mathbf{P}\left\{ p \in [\overline{X} - \delta, \overline{X} + \delta] \right\} \geq 95\%.$$

Question: Given that n people are sampled, and we want a 95% confidence interval on p, how can we frame this as a Chernoff bound problem?

Hint: To use a Chernoff bound, we want to phrase the question as the probability that a Binomial deviates from its mean by some amount.

Answer: We need to find a δ such that

$$\mathbf{P}\left\{\left|\overline{X} - p\right| > \delta\right\} < 5\%, \tag{19.1}$$

or equivalently, such that

$$\mathbf{P}\left\{|S_n - np| > n\delta\right\} < 5\%. \tag{19.2}$$

We're thus considering the probability that S_n deviates from its mean, np, by $n\delta$. By using both parts of the Chernoff bound in Theorem 18.4, we have

$$\mathbf{P}\left\{|S_n - \mathbf{E}[S_n]| > n\delta\right\} \leq 2e^{-\frac{2(n\delta)^2}{n}}.$$

Hence, we need to find a δ such that

$$2e^{-2n\delta^2} < 0.05,$$

Equivalently,

$$\delta > \sqrt{\frac{-\ln 0.025}{2n}} = \sqrt{\frac{1.84}{n}}. \tag{19.3}$$

Question: How does the width of our confidence interval scale with the number of sampled people?

Answer: Observe that δ scales as $\frac{1}{\sqrt{n}}$. The bigger n is, the smaller δ can be.

Question: If we sample $n = 1000$ people, what is our confidence interval?

Answer: For $n = 1000$, we have $\delta \approx 0.043$. Hence $[\overline{X} - 0.043, \overline{X} + 0.043]$ forms a 95% confidence interval on the true p.

Question: Suppose that we need the width of our confidence interval to be no more than 1%, while still maintaining a 95% confidence level? How can we change n to achieve this?

Answer: We now have *two constraints*:

$$\delta > \sqrt{\frac{1.84}{n}} \qquad \text{and} \qquad \delta \leq 0.005.$$

So,

$$\sqrt{\frac{1.84}{n}} \leq 0.005,$$

or equivalently,

$$n \geq \frac{1.84}{(0.005)^2} = 73{,}600.$$

Of course, there are many more issues that come up in polling estimation. For example, it is not obvious how to get "independent," equally weighted samples.

19.2.2 Using Chebyshev Bounds to Get Exact Confidence Intervals

Question: Let's return to the problem of obtaining a 95% confidence interval on p given n sampled people, but this time we want to use Chebyshev's bound. Can we do it?

Answer: As in (19.2), we again need to find a δ such that

$$\mathbf{P}\{|S_n - np| > n\delta\} < 5\%.$$

By Chebyshev's Inequality (Theorem 18.2),

$$\mathbf{P}\{|S_n - np| > n\delta\} \leq \frac{\mathbf{Var}(S_n)}{(n\delta)^2} = \frac{np(1-p)}{n^2\delta^2}.$$

So we need to find a δ such that

$$\frac{p(1-p)}{n\delta^2} < 0.05. \tag{19.4}$$

But now we're stuck, because p is the parameter that we want to estimate, so how can we do this?

Question: What are some ideas for evaluating (19.4), given we don't know p?

Answer: One idea is to substitute $\overline{X}$ in for p, given that $\overline{X}$ is the estimator for p. However, this only gives us an approximate solution for δ, and we want a guaranteed bound. The idea we use instead is to bound $p(1-p)$.

Question: What is an upper bound on $p(1-p)$?

Answer: $\frac{1}{2} \cdot \frac{1}{2} = \frac{1}{4}$.

Thus, from (19.4), we are looking for δ such that

$$\frac{p(1-p)}{n\delta^2} < \frac{1}{4n\delta^2} < 0.05,$$

or equivalently,

$$\delta > \sqrt{\frac{5}{n}}.$$

Notice that this is slightly larger than the value we got in (19.3) via the Chernoff bound, which is to be expected since the Chebyshev bound is weaker than the Chernoff bound and we also upper-bounded the variance. However, like the result in (19.3), we still have the property that the width of the confidence interval shrinks as $\frac{1}{\sqrt{n}}$ as n grows.

19.2.3 Using Tail Bounds to Get Exact Confidence Intervals in General Settings

We now leave polling and return to the general setting of Section 19.1. We have a r.v. X whose mean, $\mathbf{E}[X]$, we are trying to estimate. We are given random i.i.d. samples of X, denoted by $X_1, X_2, \ldots, X_n$. This time we don't know that the X_i's are Bernoulli distributed. In fact, we assume that we know nothing about the distribution of the X_i's, but we do know $\mathbf{Var}(X_i) = \sigma^2$.

Question: How can we derive a 95% confidence interval on $\mathbf{E}[X]$?

Answer: Given that we don't know the distribution of the X_i's, it's hard to imagine how we can use a Chernoff bound. However, we can definitely use the Chebyshev bound. The process is almost identical to that in Section 19.2.2, except that we don't need to bound $\mathbf{Var}(S_n)$. Specifically, we again define

$$S_n = X_1 + X_2 + \cdots + X_n \qquad \text{and} \qquad \overline{X} = \frac{S_n}{n}.$$

Our confidence interval on $\mathbf{E}[X]$ again takes the form

$$\left[\overline{X} - \delta, \overline{X} + \delta \right],$$

where we're seeking δ such that

$$\mathbf{P}\left\{ \left| \overline{X} - \mathbf{E}[X] \right| > \delta \right\} < 5\%,$$

or equivalently, such that

$$\mathbf{P}\left\{ |S_n - n\mathbf{E}[X]| > n\delta \right\} < 5\%.$$

We now use the fact that we know that

$$\mathbf{Var}(S_n) = n\sigma^2$$

to invoke the Chebyshev bound. So we're seeking δ such that

$$\mathbf{P}\left\{|S_n - n\mathbf{E}\left[X\right]| > n\delta\right\} \le \frac{\mathbf{Var}(S_n)}{n^2\delta^2} = \frac{n\sigma^2}{n^2\delta^2} < 0.05.$$

Solving this, we have that

$$\delta > \frac{\sqrt{20}\sigma}{\sqrt{n}},$$

yielding the confidence interval

$$\left[\overline{X} - \frac{\sqrt{20}\sigma}{\sqrt{n}}, \ \overline{X} + \frac{\sqrt{20}\sigma}{\sqrt{n}}\right], \qquad (19.5)$$

where σ refers to σ_{X_i}.

As a final example, we consider how to generate confidence intervals around a signal in a noisy environment.

Example 19.3 (Interval estimation of signal with noise)

Suppose that we're trying to estimate a signal θ (this is a constant), but the signal is sent in a noisy environment where a noise, W, is added to it. The noise, W, has zero mean and variance σ_W^2. We obtain n samples, $X_1, \ldots, X_n$, where

$$X_i = \theta + W_i,$$

and where the W_i's are i.i.d. and $W_i \sim W$.

Again,

$$\overline{X} = \frac{X_1 + X_2 + \cdots + X_n}{n}$$

serves as a point estimator for θ.

Question: How can we produce a 95% confidence interval around θ?

Hint: Can we say that the X_i's are i.i.d.?

Answer: The X_i's are in fact i.i.d. Furthermore, $\mathbf{Var}(X_i) = \mathbf{Var}(W)$, which is known. Hence we can directly apply our result from (19.5) to get the following

95% confidence interval for θ:

$$\left[\overline{X} - \frac{\sqrt{20}\sigma_W}{\sqrt{n}} \, , \, \overline{X} + \frac{\sqrt{20}\sigma_W}{\sqrt{n}} \right]. \tag{19.6}$$

19.3 Approximate Confidence Intervals

In the previous section, we were able to use the Chernoff or Chebyshev bounds to derive guaranteed (exact) confidence intervals in many situations, subject to any desired confidence level. However there are also situations where this is not possible. Furthermore, there are situations where we might *choose* to derive an approximate confidence interval, despite being able to derive an exact confidence interval.

Question: Why would we ever want an approximate confidence interval when we can get an exact one?

Answer: Recall from Chapter 18 that, when the number of samples is high, CLT can offer a much better tail approximation than all existing tail bounds. Thus, even though CLT is just an approximation, we might prefer it to absolute bounds.

As an example of a situation where we might prefer an approximate confidence interval, let's return to the setup in Section 19.2.3. Here, we have a r.v. X whose mean, $\mathbf{E}[X]$, we are trying to estimate. We are given random i.i.d. samples of X, denoted by $X_1, X_2, \ldots, X_n$. All we know about the X_i's is their variance: $\mathbf{Var}(X_i) = \sigma^2$. Our point estimate for $\mathbf{E}[X]$ is

$$\overline{X} = \frac{X_1 + X_2 + \cdots + X_n}{n},$$

which is approximately Normally distributed. Our goal is to derive an interval of the form

$$[\overline{X} - \delta, \overline{X} + \delta],$$

where

$$\mathbf{P}\left\{ \left| \overline{X} - \mathbf{E}[X] \right| > \delta \right\} < 5\%.$$

Question: You may recall from Chapter 9 that with probability $\approx 95\%$ the Normal distribution is within 2 standard deviations of its mean.[1] Can we therefore

---

[1] While it is more precise to write 1.96 standard deviations, we're going with 2 for easy readability.

conclude that an approximate confidence interval for $\mathbf{E}[X]$ is

$$\left[\overline{X} - 2\sigma,\ \overline{X} + 2\sigma\right]?$$

Answer: No, this is wrong. We need to be using $\sigma_{\overline{X}}$ rather than σ, where

$$\sigma_{\overline{X}} = \frac{\sigma}{\sqrt{n}}.$$

The derivation of the approximate confidence interval proceeds as usual. Since $\overline{X}$ is a sum of i.i.d. random variables, we can write

$$Q = \frac{\overline{X} - \mathbf{E}[X]}{\sigma_{\overline{X}}} \sim \text{Normal}(0, 1), \qquad \text{when } n \to \infty.$$

Hence,

$$\mathbf{P}\{-2 \le Q \le 2\} \approx 95\%$$

$$\mathbf{P}\left\{-2 \le \frac{\overline{X} - \mathbf{E}[X]}{\frac{\sigma}{\sqrt{n}}} \le 2\right\} \approx 95\%$$

$$\mathbf{P}\left\{-2\frac{\sigma}{\sqrt{n}} \le \overline{X} - \mathbf{E}[X] \le 2\frac{\sigma}{\sqrt{n}}\right\} \approx 95\%$$

$$\mathbf{P}\left\{\overline{X} - 2\frac{\sigma}{\sqrt{n}} \le \mathbf{E}[X] \le \overline{X} + 2\frac{\sigma}{\sqrt{n}}\right\} \approx 95\%.$$

Thus, our confidence interval for $\mathbf{E}[X]$ is

$$\left[\overline{X} - 2\frac{\sigma}{\sqrt{n}},\ \overline{X} + 2\frac{\sigma}{\sqrt{n}}\right]. \tag{19.7}$$

Question: How does the confidence interval in (19.7) compare with what we derived earlier in (19.5)?

Answer: Clearly the confidence interval in (19.7) is way tighter, even though it's only an approximation.

Because CLT is so often used for confidence intervals, we summarize our results in Theorem 19.4.

Theorem 19.4 (CLT-based approximate confidence interval) *Let X be a r.v. whose mean, $\mathbf{E}[X]$, we are trying to estimate. We are given n random i.i.d. samples of X, denoted by $X_1, X_2, \ldots, X_n$. All we know about the X_i's is their variance:* $\mathbf{Var}(X_i) = \sigma^2$.
Let

$$\overline{X} = \frac{X_1 + X_2 + \cdots + X_n}{n}.$$

Let $\Phi(\cdot)$ be the cumulative distribution function (c.d.f.) of the standard Normal, and let

$$\Phi\left(z_{\frac{\alpha}{2}}\right) = 1 - \frac{\alpha}{2}, \qquad i.e., \quad z_{\frac{\alpha}{2}} \equiv \Phi^{-1}\left(1 - \frac{\alpha}{2}\right).$$

Then,

$$\left[\overline{X} - z_{\frac{\alpha}{2}} \cdot \frac{\sigma}{\sqrt{n}} \, , \, \overline{X} + z_{\frac{\alpha}{2}} \cdot \frac{\sigma}{\sqrt{n}}\right] \tag{19.8}$$

is a $(1 - \alpha) \cdot 100\%$ approximate confidence interval for $\mathbf{E}[X]$.

We now very briefly turn to the hardest case. Again X is a r.v. whose mean, $\mathbf{E}[X]$, we are trying to estimate. Again we are given n random i.i.d. samples of X, denoted by $X_1, X_2, \ldots, X_n$. However, this time we know *absolutely nothing* about the X_i's. We again wish to determine a $(1 - \alpha) \cdot 100\%$ confidence interval around $\mathbf{E}[X]$, but we do *not* know $\mathbf{Var}(X_i) = \sigma^2$, so we cannot directly use (19.8).

If we have an upper bound on $\mathbf{Var}(X_i)$, call it σ_{max}^2, then we can of course substitute σ_{max} in for σ in (19.8). However, if we don't even have a bound on σ, then our best bet is to use the sample standard deviation from (15.5):

$$S = \sqrt{S^2} = \sqrt{\frac{1}{n-1} \sum_{i=1}^{n} \left(X_i - \overline{X}\right)^2},$$

yielding the following $(1 - \alpha) \cdot 100\%$ confidence interval for $\mathbf{E}[X]$:

$$\left[\overline{X} - z_{\frac{\alpha}{2}} \cdot \frac{S}{\sqrt{n}} \, , \, \overline{X} + z_{\frac{\alpha}{2}} \cdot \frac{S}{\sqrt{n}}\right]. \tag{19.9}$$

Observe that (19.9) is now an approximation on two fronts. First, we're using CLT, which is an approximation, and second we're approximating $\mathbf{Var}(X_i)$ by the sample variance, S^2. Thus, in using (19.9) it is even more important that n is high.

19.4 Balls and Bins

We now turn to a very different application of tail bounds, illustrated in Figure 19.1, where balls are thrown uniformly at random into bins.

Figure 19.1 *Throwing balls into bins uniformly at random.*

Let's consider the simplest case where we have exactly n balls, each of which is thrown uniformly at random into one of n bins.

Question: On average, how many balls should each bin have?

Answer: Each bin should have one ball in expectation.

Question: What's the highest number of balls that a bin can have?

Answer: n.

This kind of problem comes up in many computer science applications. One example is load balancing of jobs among servers. Each job is routed to a random server, in the hope that all servers end up with an equal number of jobs. The reality, however, is that some servers will end up being sent a lot more jobs than others.

In Exercise 19.8 you will argue that, with high probability, some bin receives $\Omega\left(\frac{\ln n}{\ln \ln n}\right)$ balls. In fact, Exercise 19.7 points out that we expect to have several such "overly full" bins. This says that our attempt at random load balancing is not as "balanced" as we might think.

In Theorem 19.6, we will argue the other side, namely that with high probability no bin will have more than $O\left(\frac{\ln n}{\ln \ln n}\right)$ balls.

> **Definition 19.5** *The term* **"with high probability" (w.h.p.)** *generally refers to something on the order of* $1 - \frac{1}{n}$, *where n is the size of the problem. Sometimes the term is used a little more loosely to refer to something on the order of* $1 - \frac{1}{n^c}$, *where* $c > 0$ *is some constant. When making w.h.p. probabilistic guarantees, it is common to require that n is* **"sufficiently large."**

Question: How should we think about $\frac{\ln n}{\ln \ln n}$?

Answer: If we imagine that n is very large, then

$$1 \ll \frac{\ln n}{\ln \ln n} \ll \frac{\ln n}{10^9} \ll \ln n.$$

> **Theorem 19.6** *If n balls are thrown uniformly at random into n bins, then, with probability* $\geq 1 - \frac{1}{n}$, *every bin has* $\leq k$ *balls, where*
>
> $$k = \frac{3 \ln n}{\ln \ln n} - 1,$$
>
> *assuming sufficiently high n.*

Proof: Our approach will use Chernoff bounds. An alternative approach, not involving Chernoff bounds, is given in Exercise 19.6.

Consider only the jth bin. Let

$$B_j = \sum_{i=1}^{n} X_i = \text{\# balls in bin } j,$$

where

$$X_i = \begin{cases} 1 & \text{if ball } i \text{ goes in bin } j \\ 0 & \text{if ball } i \text{ doesn't go in bin } j \end{cases}.$$

Question: What is the distribution of B_j?

Answer: $B_j \sim \text{Binomial}(n, \frac{1}{n})$, where $\mathbf{E}\left[B_j\right] = 1$.

Question: We want to show that w.h.p. *every* bin has $\leq k$ balls. How can we do this? We'd like to reduce the problem to looking at an individual bin.

Hint: At first this seems complex, because the bins are clearly not independent. But independence is not necessary ...

Hint: We will invoke the *union bound* (Lemma 2.6), which says that for any events E and F,

$$\mathbf{P}\{E \text{ or } F\} \leq \mathbf{P}\{E\} + \mathbf{P}\{F\}.$$

Answer: We want to show that w.h.p. *every* bin has $\leq k$ balls. Equivalently, we want to show:

$$\mathbf{P}\{\text{There exists a bin with } > k \text{ balls}\} < \frac{1}{n}.$$

Equivalently, we want to show:

$$\mathbf{P}\{B_1 > k \text{ or } B_2 > k \text{ or } \cdots \text{ or } B_n > k\} < \frac{1}{n}.$$

But, invoking the union bound, it suffices to show

$$\mathbf{P}\{B_1 > k\} + \mathbf{P}\{B_2 > k\} + \cdots + \mathbf{P}\{B_n > k\} < \frac{1}{n}.$$

Thus it suffices to show that:

$$\mathbf{P}\{B_j > k\} < \frac{1}{n^2}$$

for every j.

We will now show that:

$$\mathbf{P}\{B_j \geq k + 1\} < \frac{1}{n^2}.$$

Question: Which Chernoff bound on the Binomial should we use: the pretty bound (Theorem 18.4) or the sometimes stronger bound (Theorem 18.6)?

Answer: We observe that k here (which represents δ in Theorem 18.4) grows as $\ln n$, but not as $\Theta(n)$. Hence it's not likely that Theorem 18.4 will give a great bound. If we look at the Chernoff bound given in Theorem 18.6, we see that the ϵ term there is high compared to $\mathbf{E}[B_j] = 1$. Thus, it is likely that Theorem 18.6 will produce a good bound.

Observing that $\epsilon = k$ and $\mu = 1$ in Theorem 18.6, we have:

$$\mathbf{P}\{B_j \geq 1 + k\} < \frac{e^k}{(1+k)^{(1+k)}}.$$

Hence, to prove that

$$\mathbf{P}\{B_j \geq 1 + k\} < \frac{1}{n^2},$$

it suffices to prove that:

$$\frac{e^k}{(1+k)^{(1+k)}} \leq \frac{1}{n^2}.$$

This latter inequality can be shown to hold by the following argument, which starts by taking logs of both sides:

$$\frac{e^k}{(1+k)^{(1+k)}} \leq \frac{1}{n^2}$$

$$\Updownarrow$$

$$k - (1+k)\ln(1+k) \leq -2\ln n$$

$$\Updownarrow$$

$$\frac{3\ln n}{\ln\ln n} - 1 - \frac{3\ln n}{\ln\ln n} \cdot \ln\left(\frac{3\ln n}{\ln\ln n}\right) \leq -2\ln n$$

$$\Updownarrow$$

$$\frac{3\ln n}{\ln\ln n} - 1 - \frac{3\ln n}{\ln\ln n} \cdot (\ln 3 + \ln\ln n - \ln\ln\ln n) \leq -2\ln n$$

$$\Updownarrow$$

$$\frac{3}{\ln\ln n} - \frac{1}{\ln n} - \frac{3}{\ln\ln n} \cdot (\ln 3 + \ln\ln n - \ln\ln\ln n) \leq -2$$

$$\Updownarrow$$

$$\frac{3}{\ln\ln n} - \frac{1}{\ln n} - \frac{3\ln 3}{\ln\ln n} - 3 + \frac{3\ln\ln\ln n}{\ln\ln n} \leq -2$$

$$\Updownarrow$$

$$o(1) + o(1) + o(1) - 3 + o(1) \leq -2. \qquad \blacksquare$$

Question: Our proof above requires that n is sufficiently large. Where is this needed?

Answer: In the last line of the proof, we state that a bunch of terms are $o(1)$. As explained in Section 1.6, such a statement requires that n is sufficiently large. Specifically, when we say that each term is $o(1)$, we mean that the term approaches 0 for sufficiently high n.

Question: You'll notice that we wrote each of the $o(1)$ terms with a positive sign. Does it matter if the $o(1)$ terms are positive or negative?

Answer: The sign of the $o(1)$ terms here doesn't matter. For high enough n, each $o(1)$ term is arbitrarily close to 0 (see Corollary 1.18). That is, we can think of each term as within 0.00001 of zero, so we don't care whether the terms are positive or negative.

19.5 Remarks on Balls and Bins

There are many more variants of the balls and bins problem, as this paradigm relates to many different computer science applications. For example, one might have m balls and n bins, where $m \neq n$. We will see an example of this when we discuss hashing in Chapter 20. One might have different "colors" of balls, say red balls and blue balls. The "balls" might represent jobs that arrive over time and are dispatched to random servers. One might also have reduced randomness in throwing the balls. For example, in the "power of two choices" version of the balls-and-bins problem, each ball chooses two random bins and then is thrown in the lesser-loaded of these two bins; see [60].

19.6 Exercises

19.1 **Confidence interval warm-up**
You have collected independent samples $X_1, X_2, \ldots, X_{400}$ from some unknown distribution represented by r.v. X. From these samples, you have derived the sample mean and sample variance:

$$\overline{X} = 10 \qquad S^2 = 144.$$

Construct an approximate 99% confidence interval for $\mathbf{E}[X]$.

19.2 **Confidence interval on mean when variance is known**
Suppose we have a r.v. $X \sim \text{Normal}(\mu, \sigma^2)$. Assume that we know σ^2, but we do not know μ. We would like to produce 95% confidence intervals for $\mu = \mathbf{E}[X]$. We have a *small* number n of i.i.d. random samples of X, denoted by $X_1, X_2, \ldots, X_n$. Unfortunately n is small. What is the tightest (least-width) 95% exact confidence interval that we can produce on $\mathbf{E}[X]$?

19.3 **Confidence intervals on vaccine efficacy**
[Proposed by Weina Wang] We are testing a new vaccine, and we want to determine its effectiveness. To do this, we hold a vaccine trial, where we administer the vaccine to all n of the participants. Two weeks later, we check to see the number of infected participants. We model infection as follows:
- With independent *known* probability z, each person will be exposed to the pathogen during the two-week post-vaccination period.
- If person i is exposed, then independently with *unknown* probability p, the vaccine worked and person i will not get sick.
- On the other hand, if the vaccine didn't work, then person i gets measurably sick upon exposure.

- We call z the exposure rate and p the efficacy rate.

Our goal is to estimate the efficacy rate, p. After the two-week period, we check to see whether each person got sick. Let Y_i be an indicator r.v. which is 1 if person i got sick. Let $\overline{Y} = \frac{1}{n}\sum_{i=1}^{n} Y_i$.

(a) Define the following estimator of p:

$$\hat{p}(Y_1,\ldots,Y_n) = 1 - \frac{\overline{Y}}{z}.$$

(i) Explain the logic behind this estimator.

(ii) Argue that $\hat{p}(Y_1,\ldots,Y_n)$ is an unbiased estimator of p, meaning that $\mathbf{E}\,[\hat{p}] = p$.

(b) Consider the following interval estimate for p, with $\epsilon = 0.01$:

$$[\hat{p}(Y_1,\ldots,Y_n) - \epsilon \,,\, \hat{p}(Y_1,\ldots,Y_n) + \epsilon].$$

(i) Using the Chernoff bound, find a study size n which ensures that the confidence level of the interval estimate exceeds 95%, regardless of the value of p.

(ii) Without using the Chernoff bound, find a study size n which ensures that the confidence level of the interval estimate exceeds 95%, regardless of the value of p.

19.4 Interval estimation

[Proposed by Weina Wang] I have a number, $\theta \in (0,1)$. You don't know θ, but you're allowed to make n guesses $X_1, X_2, \ldots, X_n$. You make your guesses independently and uniformly at random from $(0,1)$, so $X_i \sim \text{Uniform}(0,1)$. Your goal is to get within ϵ of θ where ϵ is some specific value in $(0,1)$. After you make your n guesses, I label those that are "below" θ in blue and those that are "above" in red, as shown in Figure 19.2. Let Y be the largest of the blue $X_1,\ldots,X_n$ (if there are no blue X_i, then $Y = 0$). Let $(Y, Y + \epsilon)$ (yellow interval) be an interval estimate of θ. You would like to be able to say that the interval $(Y, Y + \epsilon)$ contains θ with probability $\geq 1 - \delta$.

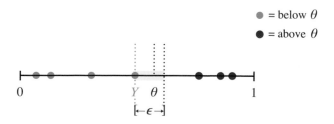

Figure 19.2 *The yellow interval is an interval estimate for Exercise 19.4.*

(a) Compute the c.d.f. of Y, denoted by $F_Y(y)$. Note the range of y.

(b) How large should n be to ensure that $\theta \in (Y, Y + \epsilon)$ with probability $\geq 1 - \delta$?

19.5 Expected size of fullest bin

In this chapter, we examined throwing n balls uniformly at random at n bins, and we looked at the fullest of the n bins. We proved that with high probability, the fullest bin has $\leq k$ balls, where $k = \frac{3 \ln n}{\ln \ln n} - 1$, assuming that n is sufficiently high. Explain why it follows that the expected size of the fullest bin is $O\left(\frac{\ln n}{\ln \ln n}\right)$.

19.6 High-probability upper bound on number of balls in max bin

Consider throwing n balls into n bins, uniformly at random. As usual assume that n is sufficiently large. Let $k = \frac{3 \ln n}{\ln \ln n}$. In this problem we will prove that the "max bin" (the one with the most balls) has $< k$ balls with high probability. Unlike the chapter, the proof will not use Chernoff bounds. Instead simpler bounds like the union bound will be useful. We will need several helping steps.

(a) First prove the following lemma, which you will need for later steps: If $1 < i < n$, then

$$\binom{n}{i} \leq \left(\frac{ne}{i}\right)^i . \tag{19.10}$$

[Hint: It helps to start by proving that $\binom{n}{i} < \frac{n^i}{i!}$.]

(b) Prove the following lemma, which you will need for later steps:

$$\text{If } k = \frac{3 \ln n}{\ln \ln n}, \text{ then } k^k \geq n^{2.99} .$$

[Hint: The argument here resembles that used at the end of this chapter.]

(c) Given that $k = \frac{3 \ln n}{\ln \ln n}$, prove that

$$\mathbf{P}\{\text{Bin } j \text{ has } \geq k \text{ balls}\} \leq \frac{1}{n^2} .$$

[Hint: Start by using a union bound over subsets to argue that

$$\mathbf{P}\{\text{Bin } j \text{ has } \geq k \text{ balls}\} \leq \binom{n}{k} \cdot \frac{1}{n^k} .$$

Then use part (a) and then part (b).]

(d) Prove that w.h.p. the maximum bin has $< k$ balls.

19.7 Lots of bins have lots of balls

Consider throwing n balls into n bins, uniformly at random. Let $k = \frac{c \ln n}{\ln \ln n}$, where $c = \frac{1}{3}$. Prove that the expected number of bins with at least k balls is $\Omega(n^{2/3})$, for n sufficiently large. We recommend the following steps:

(a) Prove that, for sufficiently high n,

$$\mathbf{P}\{\text{Bin } j \text{ has } \geq k \text{ balls}\} \geq \frac{1}{2ek^k}.$$

[Hint: It will suffice to lower bound the probability that bin j has exactly k balls. You will also use the fact that the function $\left(1 - \frac{1}{n}\right)^n$ is increasing with n, and thus exceeds half its limit for high n. It also helps to recall from (1.19) that $\binom{n}{k} > \left(\frac{n}{k}\right)^k$.]

(b) Prove the following lemma, which you will need in the next part:

$$\text{If } k = \frac{c \ln n}{\ln \ln n} \text{ then } k^k \leq n^c.$$

(c) Using parts (a) and (b), show that

$$\mathbf{E}[\text{Number of bins with } \geq k \text{ balls}] \geq \Omega(n^{1-c}).$$

Specifically, you will show that

$$\mathbf{E}[\text{Number of bins with } \geq k \text{ balls}] \geq \frac{1}{2e}n^{1-c} = \frac{1}{2e}n^{\frac{2}{3}}.$$

(d) Does part (c) imply that, in expectation, (at least) some constant proportion of the n bins has $\geq k$ balls? For instance, can we conclude that $1/4$ of the bins have $\geq k$ balls, or some other constant fraction?

19.8 High-probability lower bound on number of balls in max bin

Consider throwing n balls into n bins, uniformly at random. Let $k = \frac{c \ln n}{\ln \ln n}$, where $c = \frac{1}{3}$. Our goal is to show that with reasonably high probability, at least some bin has $\geq k$ balls.

Let X denote the number of bins with at least k balls. Observe that $X = \sum_{i=1}^{n} X_i$, where X_i is an indicator r.v. equal to 1 if bin i has $\geq k$ balls, and 0 otherwise. We want to prove that

$$\mathbf{P}\{X = 0\} \leq 4e^2 n^{-c} = \frac{4e^2}{n^{\frac{1}{3}}}.$$

(a) Use Chebyshev to upper bound $\mathbf{P}\{X = 0\}$ in terms of $\mathbf{Var}(X)$ and $\mathbf{E}[X]$.

(b) Prove that

$$\mathbf{Var}(X) \leq n.$$

In proving the above, you can assume the following fact (without proof):

$$\mathbf{Var}(X) = \sum_{i} \mathbf{Var}(X_i) + \sum_{i \neq j} \mathbf{Cov}(X_i, X_j)$$

where

$$\mathbf{Cov}(X_i, X_j) = \mathbf{E}\left[(X_i - \mathbf{E}[X_i])(X_j - \mathbf{E}[X_j])\right].$$

The term $\mathbf{Cov}(X_i, X_j)$ stands for "covariance of X_i and X_j," where positive covariance indicates that the random variables are positively correlated and negative covariance indicates that they are negatively correlated. [Hint: As part of your proof, you will need to prove that $\mathbf{Cov}(X_i, X_j) \le 0$.]

(c) Now use the result from Exercise 19.7(c) and your results from (a) and (b) to finish the proof.

19.9 Chernoff bound for real-valued random variables

[Proposed by Vanshika Chowdhary] Suppose that $X_1, X_2, \ldots, X_n$ are independent random variables with values in $[0, 1]$. Assume that $\mathbf{E}[X_i] = \mu_i$. Let

$$X = X_1 + \cdots + X_n.$$

You are given that $\mu = \mathbf{E}[X] \le 1$ and that $b = \frac{3 \ln n}{\ln \ln n}$. Show that

$$\mathbf{P}\{X \ge b\} \le \frac{1}{n^{2.99}}$$

for sufficiently high n. Please follow these steps:

(a) Start with the usual Chernoff bound approach to evaluating $\mathbf{P}\{X \ge b\}$. You will get an expression involving a product of $\mathbf{E}\left[e^{tX_i}\right]$ terms.

(b) Show that $\mathbf{E}\left[e^{tX_i}\right] \le e^{\mu_i(e^t - 1)}, \quad \forall t > 0$. Here are some helping steps:

   (i) Recall from Definition 5.21 that a real-valued function, $g(\cdot)$, defined on interval $S \subseteq \mathbb{R}$ is *convex* if $\forall \lambda \in [0, 1]$, and $\forall \alpha, \beta \in S$,

$$\lambda g(\alpha) + (1 - \lambda)g(\beta) \ge g(\lambda \alpha + (1 - \lambda)\beta).$$

   Now use the fact that e^x is a convex function and the fact that $X_i \in [0, 1]$ to show that: $e^{tX_i} \le X_i e^t + (1 - X_i)e^0$.

   (ii) Show that $\mathbf{E}\left[e^{tX_i}\right] \le e^{\mu_i(e^t - 1)}$.

(c) Substituting the result from (b) into (a), prove $\mathbf{P}\{X \ge b\} \le e^{b - b \ln b}$.

(d) Now plug in $b = \frac{3 \ln n}{\ln \ln n}$ to get the final result.

20 Hashing Algorithms

In the last two chapters we studied many tail bounds, including those from Markov, Chebyshev, Chernoff and Hoeffding. We also studied a tail approximation based on the Central Limit Theorem (CLT). In this chapter we will apply these bounds and approximations to an important problem in computer science: the design of hashing algorithms. In fact, hashing is closely related to the balls-and-bins problem that we recently studied in Chapter 19.

20.1 What is Hashing?

What exactly is hashing? Let's start with a simple example. Suppose you are the CMU student dean, in charge of maintaining a system that stores academic information on each student, such as the student's name, major, and GPA. You use social security numbers (SSNs) to identify students, so that not anybody can access the information. A student's SSN is called a **key**. When the student's SSN is entered, the system returns the student's academic information.

SSN	Academic Info
123456789	Mark Stein, Senior, GPA: 4.0
658372934	Tom Chen, Junior, GPA: 3.5
529842934	David Kosh, Freshman, GPA: 2.7
623498008	Divia Kana, Sophomore, GPA: 3.7
...	...

The main feature of the system is that search needs to be fast. Additionally, when new freshmen arrive, you need to insert their information into the system, and when seniors graduate, you need to delete their information from the system.

Suppose there are $m = 20,000$ students. How would you store this collection of student info? One solution is to use a linked list or unsorted array. Then insert is fast, but search and delete need to linearly scan the whole list, which takes $O(m)$ time. A better solution is to use a sorted data structure, such as a binary search tree that sorts student info by SSN. Then search, insert, and delete all take $O(\log m)$ time on average. None of these solutions is ideal.

Question: If space were not a consideration at all, is there a solution with $O(1)$ worst-case time for search, insert, and delete?

Answer: If space is not a consideration, one could use a huge array, A, where the SSN is the index in the array. For example, if Mark's SSN is 123456789, then his information will be stored in $A[123456789]$. The time for search, insert, and delete is $O(1)$. However, since there are 10^9 possible SSNs, the size of A needs to be 10^9. This is a waste of space for storing the info of only 20,000 students.

Question: Suppose that we're willing to give up on worst-case guarantees. Is there a solution with $O(1)$ *average time* for search, insert, and delete that uses just $O(m)$ space?

Hint: Here's an idea: Suppose we divide the students into $n = 10$ buckets according to the last digit of their SSN. Thus all students with SSN ending with 0 go into bucket 0, all students with SSN ending with 1 go into bucket 1, and so on. Then, if we want to search for Mark, we know that his SSN belongs to bucket 9, so we need only look within bucket 9. Assuming all bucket sizes are approximately equal, each bucket has about 2000 students, and our search time is 10 times faster than the single linked list. Can we take this idea further?

Answer: We can increase the number of buckets, n, to further improve the search time. For example, we can use the last *four* digits of the SSN. Then we will have 10,000 buckets, with ending digits 0000 to 9999. So, to search for Mark, we need only look within bucket 6789, which, assuming all bucket sizes are approximately equal, has only $\frac{20,000}{10,000} = 2$ students in expectation.

The solution is to use $n = O(m)$ buckets, which allows us to achieve $O(1)$ search time with $O(m)$ space!

This method is called **bucket hashing**. It makes searching, insertion, and deletion fast in expectation, because we need only search within a single small bucket.

Definition 20.1 A **bucket hash function** $h : U \rightarrow B$ *maps keys to buckets. For a key k, we call $h(k)$ the **hash** of k. The domain of h is U, the universe of all possible keys. The range of h is B, which is a subset of the non-negative integers, denoting the buckets. $K \subseteq U$ is the actual set of keys that we are hashing, where typically $|K| \ll |U|$. Let $|K| = m$ and $|B| = n$. We use r.v. B_i to denote the number of keys that hash to bucket i, also called the "size" of bucket i. The data structure which maps the m keys into n buckets using such a hash function is called a **hash table**.*

In the above example, U is all possible nine-digit SSNs ($|U| = 10^9$), K is the set of the SSNs of the 20,000 students, and B is the 10,000 buckets. As is typical, $m = |K| \ll |U|$, which allows us to get away with a small hash table.

When we adjusted the number of buckets above, we were trading off between space and search time. The ratio of keys to buckets is called the load factor, α.

Definition 20.2 *A hash table that stores m keys within n buckets is said to have a* **load factor** *of*

$$\alpha = \frac{Number\ keys}{Number\ buckets} = \frac{m}{n}.$$

It is typical to aim for a load factor that is a *small constant* above 1.

In general, we assume that hash functions have two desirable properties: (1) they are *efficient to compute*, and (2) they are *balanced* in that the keys are uniformly distributed between the buckets. If we're lucky and the keys are themselves uniformly distributed numbers, then a simple hash function like $h(k) = k \bmod n$ can work well. However, if the keys come from a more skewed distribution, it can be much harder to find a "balanced" hash function. Finding balanced and efficient hash functions is usually scenario-specific, so we won't dwell on this. For the purposes of analysis we will simply assume that our hash function is efficient and has a "balanced" property known as the *simple uniform hashing assumption*, defined next.

20.2 Simple Uniform Hashing Assumption

Definition 20.3 *A bucket hash function h satisfies the* **simple uniform hashing assumption (SUHA)** *if each key k has probability $\frac{1}{n}$ of mapping to any bucket $b \in B$, where $|B| = n$. Moreover, the hash values of different keys are independent, so for any subset of keys $k_1, k_2, \ldots, k_i \in K$, where $k_1 \neq k_2 \neq \cdots \neq k_i$ and $b_1, b_2, \ldots, b_i \in B$,*

$$\mathbf{P}\{h(k_1) = b_1\ \&\ h(k_2) = b_2\ \&\ \cdots\ \&\ h(k_i) = b_i\} = \frac{1}{n^i}.$$

SUHA is a lovely analytical convenience, but it may seem unattainable. Given that $h(k)$, the hash value of key k, is deterministic, how can we say that $h(k) = b$ with probability $\frac{1}{n}$? This is achieved by using a *universal family* of hash functions $h_1, h_2, \ldots, h_n$. The hash function to be used for a particular hash table is drawn, uniformly at random, from this universal family. Once a hash function, h_i, is picked, then that same hash function is used for all the keys of the table. In this way, the hash function is deterministic, but has appropriate random properties. We ignore questions on how to create universal families[1] and instead show how SUHA is used.

Question: Let B_i denote the number of keys which map to bucket i. Assuming SUHA, and assuming a load factor of α, what is $\mathbf{E}[B_i]$?

Answer: Assume that there are n buckets and m keys, and let $\alpha = \frac{m}{n}$. Let I_k be the indicator random variable that key k maps to bucket i. Then, by Linearity of Expectation,

$$\mathbf{E}[B_i] = \sum_{k=1}^{m} \mathbf{E}[I_k] = \sum_{k=1}^{m} \frac{1}{n} = \frac{m}{n} = \alpha.$$

So all buckets have the same size, α, in expectation.

Searching for a student involves hashing their SSN to some bucket i, and then searching through all the keys that mapped to that bucket. Traditionally, the keys that map to a single bucket are stored in a linked list at that bucket. This is called "bucket hashing with separate chaining," and will be the topic of Section 20.3. In Section 20.4, we will analyze a different way of storing keys that hash to the same bucket, called "bucket hashing with linear probing."

In both Sections 20.3 and 20.4, the goal is to use hashing to store information in a way that allows for fast search, insert, and delete, both on average and with high probability (w.h.p.). In Section 20.5 we will look at an entirely different use of hashing: how to verify the identity of a key without exposing the key (think here of the "key" as being a password that you want to ensure is correct without exposing it to an adversary). This will involve "cryptographic signature hash functions," where our goal will be to prove that, w.h.p., the hashing will not expose the identity of the key.

20.3 Bucket Hashing with Separate Chaining

In bucket hashing with separate chaining, the hash table is an array of buckets, where each bucket maintains a linked list of keys. Figure 20.1 shows our previous example, where the hash function maps an SSN to the last four digits of the SSN. To search for a key within a bucket, we traverse the linked list. To insert a key to a bucket, we first search within the linked list, and if the key does not exist, we append it to the linked list. To delete a key from a bucket, we first search for it

---

[1] See [16, p. 267] for a discussion of how number theory can be used to create a universal family of hash functions.

within the linked list, and delete it from the linked list if we find it. Thus the time complexity for all operations is dominated by the time complexity for search.

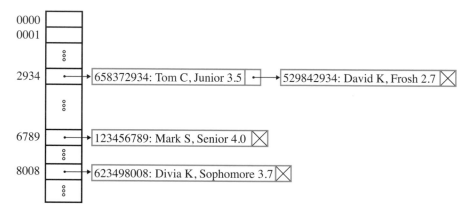

Figure 20.1 *Example of bucket hashing with separate chaining.*

We already saw that, under SUHA, and assuming a load factor of α, each bucket has α keys in expectation. Thus, the *expected* search time under bucket hashing with separate chaining is $O(\alpha)$. This is great because we typically imagine that α is a small constant. However, an individual bucket might have way more than α keys.

Question: What is the distribution on B_i, the number of keys in the ith bucket?

Hint: Remember that we're distributing m keys into n buckets, uniformly at random.

Answer:

$$B_i \sim \text{Binomial}\left(m, \frac{1}{n}\right).$$

Question: Assume that m and n are both high, while α is still a constant. What do we know about $\textbf{Var}(B_i)$?

Answer:

$$\textbf{Var}(B_i) = m \cdot \frac{1}{n} \cdot \left(1 - \frac{1}{n}\right) = \alpha \cdot \left(1 - \frac{1}{n}\right) \to \alpha.$$

In the setting when m and n are high, CLT tells us that the distribution of B_i approaches that of a Normal.

Question: So, when m and n are high, what, approximately, can we say is $\mathbf{P}\{B_i > \alpha + 2\sqrt{\alpha}\}$?

Answer: This is the probability that B_i exceeds its mean by more than 2 standard deviations. As the distribution of B_i approaches a Normal, this is approximately 2%.

So the number of keys in any individual bucket is likely to be small. The mean is α and the distribution approaches Normal(α, α) when m and n are high. But what about the *worst* bucket? How many keys does it have?

Question: In the case of $\alpha = 1$, what can we say with high probability (w.h.p.) about the *fullest* bin?

Answer: When $\alpha = 1$, we have $m = n$. In Section 19.4 we showed that if you throw n balls into n bins, uniformly at random, then w.h.p. the fullest bin will have $O\left(\frac{\ln n}{\ln \ln n}\right)$ balls. This is a w.h.p. bound on the cost of search when $\alpha = 1$.

We can imagine proving similar w.h.p. bounds on the cost of search for the case when $\alpha = 2$ or $\alpha = 3$. But what happens if α is high, say $\ln n$? One could imagine that the number of keys in the fullest bucket could be quite high now. Theorem 20.4 shows that this is not the case. Both the mean search cost and the w.h.p. search cost are $O(\alpha)$, for high α. Thus for the case where $\alpha = \ln n$, our w.h.p. bound on the cost of search is $O(\ln n)$, which is not that different than the case where $\alpha = 1$.

Theorem 20.4 *Under SUHA, for bucket hashing with separate chaining, assuming $m \geq 2n \ln n$ keys, and n buckets, then with probability $\geq 1 - \frac{1}{n}$ the largest bucket has size $< e\alpha$, where $\alpha = \frac{m}{n}$.*

Proof: Our proof follows along the same lines as that in Section 19.4. The idea will be to first prove that for any B_i,

$$\mathbf{P}\{B_i \geq e\alpha\} \leq \frac{1}{n^2}.$$

(We will show below how to do this).

Once we have that result, then by the union bound,

$$\mathbf{P}\{\text{Some bucket has} \geq e\alpha \text{ balls}\} \leq \sum_{i=1}^{n} \frac{1}{n^2} = \frac{1}{n}.$$

Thus, $\mathbf{P}\{\text{largest bucket has size} < e\alpha\} > 1 - \frac{1}{n}$ as desired.

All that remains is to prove that

$$\mathbf{P}\{B_i \geq e\alpha\} \leq \frac{1}{n^2}.$$

We start by observing that since $m \geq 2n \ln n$, we know that

$$\alpha = \frac{m}{n} \geq 2 \ln n.$$

Applying The Chernoff bound from Theorem 18.6, with

- $1 + \epsilon = e$ (so $\epsilon = e - 1 > 0$), and
- $\mu = \alpha \geq 2 \ln n$,

we have:

$$
\begin{aligned}
\mathbf{P}\{B_i \geq e\alpha\} &= \mathbf{P}\{B_i \geq (1+\epsilon)\mu\} \\
&< \left(\frac{e^\epsilon}{(1+\epsilon)^{1+\epsilon}}\right)^\mu \\
&= \left(\frac{e^{e-1}}{e^e}\right)^\alpha \\
&= (e^{-1})^\alpha \\
&\leq (e^{-1})^{2\ln n} \\
&= (e^{\ln n})^{-2} \\
&= \frac{1}{n^2}.
\end{aligned}
$$

■

20.4 Linear Probing and Open Addressing

In the previous section we studied bucket hashing with separate chaining, where each of the n buckets has a linked list ("chain") of keys that have mapped to that bucket. While chaining is easy to explain, it has some practical disadvantages. First, storing all those pointers is memory-intensive. More importantly, chaining is not cache friendly; the items in a given bucket list are typically scattered over the memory space. This section presents a more practical bucket hashing solution, called "bucket hashing with linear probing," that doesn't require pointers and is more cache friendly.

The high-level idea behind linear probing is that we store only *one* key in each cell of array B. If multiple keys have the same hash value, they are stored in the first available cell of array B. In this way, when searching for a key, one is always reading consecutive cells of an array, which are typically in the same cache line.

Here are the specifics: First, linear probing relies on using an array, B, with size $n > m$, where m is the number of objects stored. Typically when running linear probing, $n > 2m$, meaning that $\alpha < 0.5$, where α represents the load factor; this is in contrast with bucket hashing with separate chaining, where in general $\alpha > 1$. When we hash key k, if cell $h(k)$ of B is empty, then we place the record for key k into $B[h(k)]$. Later, if another key, k', has the same hash value as k, that is, $h(k') = h(k)$, then we cannot place k''s record into $B[h(k)]$. We instead search cell by cell, starting with cell $h(k) + 1$, then cell $h(k) + 2$, and so on, until we find the *first available empty cell*. We then insert k''s record into this first available cell. The process of probing consecutive cells to check if they're empty is called **linear probing**.

Question: What do you think happens if we get to the last cell of B and it is occupied?

Answer: The linear probing wraps around to the first cell. So when we talk about looking at cells $h(k)$, $h(k) + 1$, etc., we're really looking at cells $h(k)$ mod n, $h(k) + 1$ mod n, etc. We will leave off the "mod n" in our discussion to minimize notation.

Question: When searching for a key, k, how do we know k is not in the table?

Answer: We start by looking at cell $h(k)$, then $h(k) + 1$, and so on, until we come to an empty cell. The empty cell is our signal that k is not in the table.

Question: But what if the empty cell was created by a deletion?

Answer: When a key is deleted, we mark its cell with a special character, called a *tombstone*. The tombstone lets us know that the cell used to be full, so that we don't stop our search early. Thus, cells are never cleared in linear probing. When the number of tombstones gets too high, we simply recreate the table from scratch.

For the remainder of this section, we'll be interested in analyzing the *expected cost of search*. The cost of insert and delete can be bounded by the cost of search. Note that when we say "cost of search" we are referring to the cost of an unsuccessful search – that is, searching for a key that is not in the array. The cost of a successful search is upper-bounded by the cost of an unsuccessful search.

Unfortunately, bucket hashing with linear probing can often lead to *clustering* (long chains of full cells). Clustering is an artifact of using a linear probe sequence for inserting key k. When inserting key k, if cell $h(k)$ is already full, we next try for $h(k)+1$, and then $h(k)+2$. Thus, full cells are likely to be followed by more full cells.

Question: Any idea for how to get around this clustering problem, so that the full cells can be more uniformly spread out?

Answer: We can instead make the probe sequence for key k be a uniformly selected sequence of cells (a particular randomly-chosen *permutation* of cells in the table). Specifically, we denote the probe sequence for inserting key k by:

$$\langle h(k,1), h(k,2), h(k,3), \ldots, h(k,n) \rangle.$$

If key k finds a cell full, instead of trying the next consecutive cell in the array, it now tries the next cell in its probe sequence (its permutation).

In an ideal world, the probe sequence for each key is equally likely to be assigned any one of the $n!$ permutations of $\langle 1, 2, \ldots, n \rangle$. (Obviously the probe sequence corresponding to any particular key k is fixed.) This idea is called **open addressing with uniform probe sequences**. It leads to lower search times than linear probing. While open addressing does require skipping to different locations, at least all of these locations are within the same array, which keeps the pointer cost more reasonable.

> **Theorem 20.5** *Assume that m keys have been inserted into a table with n cells via open addressing with uniform probe sequences. The load factor is $\alpha = \frac{m}{n} < 1$. Then the expected cost of an (unsuccessful) search is at most $\frac{1}{1-\alpha}$.*

Proof: Let X denote the search cost. We will try to determine the tail of X and then sum that to get $\mathbf{E}[X]$.

$$\mathbf{P}\{X > 0\} = 1 \quad \text{(we always need to probe at least once)}$$
$$\mathbf{P}\{X > 1\} = \mathbf{P}\{\text{First cell we look at is occupied}\} = \alpha.$$

Let A_i denote the event that the ith cell that we look at is occupied. Then,

$$
\begin{aligned}
\mathbf{P}\{X > 2\} &= \mathbf{P}\{\text{First two cells we look at are occupied}\} \\
&= \mathbf{P}\{A_1 \cap A_2\} \\
&= \mathbf{P}\{A_1\} \cdot \mathbf{P}\{A_2 \mid A_1\} \\
&= \alpha \cdot \frac{m-1}{n-1} \quad (m-1 \text{ keys and } n-1 \text{ cells remain}) \\
&= \alpha \cdot \frac{\alpha n - 1}{n - 1} \\
&< \alpha \cdot \frac{\alpha n}{n} \\
&= \alpha^2.
\end{aligned}
$$

Using the chain rule from Theorem 2.10, we have:

$$\begin{aligned}
\mathbf{P}\{X > i\} &= \mathbf{P}\{\text{First } i \text{ cells we look at are occupied}\} \\
&= \mathbf{P}\{A_1 \cap A_2 \cap \cdots \cap A_i\} \\
&= \mathbf{P}\{A_1\} \cdot \mathbf{P}\{A_2 \mid A_1\} \cdots \mathbf{P}\{A_i \mid A_1 \cap A_2 \cap \cdots \cap A_{i-1}\} \\
&= \frac{m}{n} \cdot \frac{m-1}{n-1} \cdot \frac{m-2}{n-2} \cdots \frac{m-i+1}{n-i+1} \\
&\leq \alpha^i.
\end{aligned}$$

Finally, applying Theorem 4.9, we have:

$$\begin{aligned}
\mathbf{E}[X] &= \sum_{i=0}^{\infty} \mathbf{P}\{X > i\} \\
&\leq 1 + \sum_{i=1}^{n-1} \alpha^i \\
&\leq \sum_{i=0}^{\infty} \alpha^i \\
&= \frac{1}{1-\alpha}.
\end{aligned}$$

∎

Theorem 20.5 provides only an *upper bound* on expected search cost. Exercises 20.4 and 20.5 will provide *exact analysis*.

20.5 Cryptographic Signature Hashing

Up to now we have only talked about bucket hash functions, whose purpose is to support fast search speed. In this section we will talk about **cryptographic hash functions**. Their purpose has nothing to do with search speed, but rather they are used to encrypt (hide) information, for example, passwords.

Suppose you are again the CMU student dean, but this time you are managing services that only CMU students should be able to access. For example, a service might be course evaluations at CMU. To access the service, the CMU student enters her ID and password, and then the service becomes available. How do you design a system that allows you to check if a student's password is correct for her ID? We could store the IDs and corresponding passwords in a database. However, if the database is hacked, then all passwords will be compromised.

For example, let's say that Mark Stein's ID is *mstein* and his password is ILoveToHelp.

Question: Mark's ID is public. How can we identify Mark via his ID and password without ever storing his password?

Answer: The solution is to use a cryptographic hash function to hash passwords to signatures, and store *signatures* in the database instead.

Using a cryptographic hash function, we hash `ILoveToHelp` to a 32-bit signature $0x1b3a4f52$, and store the entry *mstein: $0x1b3a4f52$* into the database. Our database might look like Table 20.1.

ID	Signature of password
mstein	$0x1b3a4f52$
tchen	$0x51c2df33$
dkosh	$0xbb89e27a$
dkana	$0x2f85ad73$
...	...

Table 20.1 *Database storing signatures.*

Note: Table 20.1 is *not* a hash table. This is our database. Importantly, by looking at the database, you have no idea what passwords correspond to these IDs. Say Mark is trying to log into the course evaluations service with his ID *mstein* and password `ILoveToHelp`. To verify that Mark's password is correct, we apply a hash function to his entered password, obtaining:

$$h(\texttt{ILoveToHelp}) = 0x1b3a4f52.$$

Then we compare $0x1b3a4f52$ to the signature stored under *mstein* in the database. Since they're the same, we know that Mark (probably) entered the correct password. In this way, we can verify passwords without storing the actual passwords in the database.[2]

In general, when using cryptographic hash functions, we refer to the *passwords* whose identity we're trying to hide as the **keys**.

---

[2] In this section we will not be interested in the time to search our database, just in hiding the identity of passwords. However, if we were interested in search time, we could apply a bucket hash to the IDs in Table 20.1 to bring the search time down to $O(1)$. It is thus very reasonable to use bucket hashing and cryptographic signature hashing in conjunction.

> **Definition 20.6** A **cryptographic hash function** $h : U \rightarrow B$ *maps* **keys** *to* **signatures.** *For a key k, we call $h(k)$ the signature of k. The domain of h is U, the universe of all possible keys. The range of h is B, denoting all the possible signatures. $K \subseteq U$ is the actual set of keys that we are hashing. Let $|K| = m$ and $|B| = n$. Generally,*
>
> $$|U| \gg n \gg m,$$
>
> *because U represents a potentially infinite number of strings of any length, and we want $n \gg m$ to avoid collisions. Thus, $\alpha = \frac{m}{n} \ll 1$.*

Question: Which of n or m represents the number of entries in the database in Table 20.1?

Answer: The number of entries in the database is m, which is the number of actual keys (passwords) that we're hashing and also represents the number of actual IDs. However, the database is not our hash table. There is no "hash table," but rather just a hash function that maps the m passwords to a space of n possible signatures.

For cryptographic hash functions we typically want $n \gg m$, so that there are few "collisions." Thus, $\alpha \ll 1$.

> **Definition 20.7** A **hash collision** *occurs when two different keys have the same hash value. That is, $h(k_1) = h(k_2)$, where $k_1 \neq k_2$.*

Hash collisions are undesirable. It can be dangerous when multiple passwords map to the same signature because it increases the likelihood that an attacker can guess a password by trying multiple passwords with the same ID.

We'd ideally like there to be a one-to-one mapping between keys and signatures. Of course this is not possible, even with the best hash function, because $|U| \gg n$, and thus by the pigeon-hole principle, there exist keys with the same signature. The rest of this section is devoted to analyzing how large n needs to be to achieve a "low" probability of collision, given that m keys are being hashed.

Question: Suppose that an attacker tries m different passwords (keys). Each of the m keys is hashed, using a cryptographic hash function h, into a hash space of size $|B| = n$, where $n \gg m$. Assume SUHA so each key has probability $\frac{1}{n}$ of landing in any given bucket. What is the probability $p(m,n)$ that no collisions occur?

Hint: This should look a lot like the birthday problem from Exercise 2.10.

Answer: In the birthday problem, we had $m = 30$ people and $n = 365$ possible birthdays, and we looked for the probability of no duplicate birthdays, a.k.a., "no collisions." Repeating that analysis, let A be the event that no collisions occur, that is, no two keys have the same signature. We imagine that the keys are ordered, from 1 to m. Let A_i be the event that key i has a different signature from each of the first $i - 1$ keys. Now observe that

$$A = \bigcap_{i=1}^{m} A_i.$$

Thus,

$$\mathbf{P}\{A\} = \mathbf{P}\{A_1\} \cdot \prod_{i=2}^{m} \mathbf{P}\left\{A_i \,\middle|\, \bigcap_{j=1}^{i-1} A_j\right\}$$

$$= 1 \cdot \prod_{i=2}^{m}\left(1 - \frac{i-1}{n}\right)$$

$$= \prod_{i=1}^{m-1}\left(1 - \frac{i}{n}\right).$$

Now, by (1.14),

$$1 - \frac{x}{n} \le e^{-\frac{x}{n}}, \tag{20.1}$$

where this upper bound is close to exact for high n.

This yields the upper bound:

$$\mathbf{P}\{A\} \le \prod_{i=1}^{m-1} e^{-\frac{i}{n}} = \exp\left(-\frac{1}{n}\sum_{i=1}^{m-1} i\right) = \exp\left(-\frac{m(m-1)}{2n}\right).$$

This result is summarized in Theorem 20.8.

Theorem 20.8 (Probability no collisions) *If we use a simple uniform hashing function to hash m keys to a hash space of size n, then the probability that there are no collisions is denoted by $p(m, n)$, where*

$$p(m, n) = \prod_{i=1}^{m-1}\left(1 - \frac{i}{n}\right).$$

This is upper-bounded by:

$$p(m, n) \le e^{\frac{-m(m-1)}{2n}}.$$

Assuming that $n \gg m$, the upper bound is very close to exact.

Proof: The only part we have not proven yet is the tightness of the upper bound. Observe that (20.1) is close to an equality when $n \gg x$. In particular, if $n \gg m$, then the "upper bound" in Theorem 20.8 is a good approximation for each of the m terms in the product of $p(m, n)$. ∎

Corollary 20.9 *Assuming $n \gg m$, $\mathbf{P}\{no\ collisions\} \approx e^{-\frac{m^2}{2n}}$.*

Corollary 20.9 is interesting because it tells us that we need $m = \Theta(\sqrt{n})$ to ensure that the probability of no collisions is high. In fact, in Exercise 20.3, we'll derive formally that the expected number of keys that we can insert before we get a collision is $\approx 1 + \sqrt{\frac{\pi n}{2}}$.

We now use Corollary 20.9 to evaluate the effectiveness of the SHA-256 cryptographic hashing algorithm.[3] All you'll need to know for the evaluation is that the hash space, B, of SHA-256 is all 256-bit numbers.

Question: Suppose we are hashing 10 billion keys using SHA-256. Approximately what is the probability that there are no collisions?

Answer: Here, $m = 10^{10}$, so $m^2 = 10^{20}$, and $n = |B| = 2^{256} = 10^{77}$. Since $n \gg m$, we can use Corollary 20.9. Thus,

$$\mathbf{P}\{no\ collisions\} \approx e^{\frac{-m^2}{2n}} = e^{\frac{-10^{20}}{2\cdot10^{77}}} \approx e^{-10^{-57}}.$$

This is very close to 1, as desired.

Question: Approximately how many keys do we need to hash until the probability that there is a collision exceeds 1%?

Answer: Let

$$p = \mathbf{P}\{no\ collisions\} \approx e^{\frac{-m^2}{2n}}.$$

Then, $\ln p \approx \frac{-m^2}{2n}$, so $m \approx \sqrt{-2n \ln p}$.

Thus, setting $p = 99\%$, we see that, after hashing

$$m = \sqrt{-2 \cdot 2^{256} \ln 0.99} \approx 5 \cdot 10^{37}$$

keys, we will have a 1% probability of collision.

Question: Suppose a supercomputer can calculate 10^{10} hashes a second, and we have one billion such computers, and a year has about 10^7 seconds. How

---

[3] SHA stands for Secure Hash Algorithm.

many years will it take for us to hash enough keys to produce a 1% probability of collision in SHA-256?

Answer: It will take

$$\frac{5 \cdot 10^{37}}{10^{10} \cdot 10^9 \cdot 10^7} = 5 \cdot 10^{11} = 500 \text{ billion years!}$$

So it is virtually impossible to find a pair of keys that collides in SHA-256.

20.6 Remarks

This chapter was written in collaboration with Sheng Xu. The chapter presents only the briefest discussion of hashing, and instead emphasizes the probabilistic analysis. We have spent no time discussing data structures for implementing hashing. Our discussion of bucket hashing with open addressing and uniformly distributed probe sequences allows us to get away with some very simple analysis, which will be made exact in Exercise 20.5. By contrast, the analysis of search time under bucket hashing with linear probing is far harder, but is solved exactly in Knuth's book [46, section 6.4]. Finally, there are also many more advanced hashing schemes, including Bloom filters (see Exercise 20.6), cuckoo hashing [56], consistent hashing [44], and others which we didn't have room to cover, or whose analysis is beyond the scope of the book.

20.7 Exercises

20.1 **Expected hashes until buckets are full**

You are hashing keys, one at a time, into n buckets, where each key has probability $\frac{1}{n}$ of landing in each bucket. What is the expected number of keys hashed until every bucket has at least one key?

20.2 **Inspection paradox: the key's perspective**

You are hashing 100 keys into 100 buckets. One bucket ends up with 20 keys, another bucket ends up with 10 keys, and 70 buckets end up with 1 key each. The remaining 28 buckets end up with zero keys.

(a) From the perspective of the buckets, what is the average number of keys per bucket?

(b) When I search for a random key, on average, how many total keys do I find in the same bucket as my key (including my own key)?

The difference in your answers is the inspection paradox, see Section 5.11.

20.3 Expected hashes until collision

You are hashing keys, one at a time, into n buckets, where each key has probability $\frac{1}{n}$ of landing in each bucket. What is the expected number of keys hashed until you get a collision? Use this asymptotic result, proved by Ramanujan [28]:

$$\sum_{k=1}^{n} \frac{n!}{n^k(n-k)!} \sim \sqrt{\frac{\pi n}{2}},$$

to show that your answer grows as $\sqrt{n}$. Notice that you can think of this problem in terms of an n-sided die, where you ask how many times you have to roll the die, in expectation, until you get a number you've seen before. [Hint: You might want to get the mean by summing the tail. This problem will resemble the birthday paradox.]

20.4 Largest insert cost for open addressing with uniform probe sequences

Under open addressing with a uniform probe sequence, assume that we store m keys in a size n array with load factor $\alpha = 0.5$. We will prove that for the m keys that have been inserted, the expected largest insert cost among the m keys was $O(\log_2 m)$. Note that the insert cost of a key is equal to the number of cells probed by the key.

(a) For all $i = 1, 2, \ldots, m$, let

$$p_i = \mathbf{P}\{\text{the } i\text{th insertion requires} > k \text{ probes}\}.$$

Show that $p_i < 2^{-k}$.

(b) Let X denote the length of the longest probe sequence among all m keys. Show that the $\mathbf{P}\{X > 2\log_2 m\} < \frac{1}{m}$.

(c) Show that $\mathbf{E}[X] = O(\log_2 m)$. [Hint: Condition via (b).]

20.5 Open addressing with uniform probe sequences: exact analysis

In Theorem 20.5, we derived an upper bound on the expected cost of an (unsuccessful) search under open addressing with a uniform probe sequence. In this problem we will derive an exact expression for the expected cost, which is not far from the upper bound in Theorem 20.5. Use the same setup as in Theorem 20.5, again assuming that m keys have been hashed into an array of size n.

(a) First prove two useful lemmas (use counting arguments):
  (i) Lemma 1: $\binom{n'}{k}\binom{k}{1} = \binom{n'-1}{k-1}\binom{n'}{1}$.
  (ii) Lemma 2: $\sum_{r=1}^{n} \binom{n+1-r}{m-(r-1)} = \binom{n+1}{m}$.

(b) Prove that the probability that an (unsuccessful) search requires exactly r probes is $p_r = \frac{\binom{n-r}{m-r+1}}{\binom{n}{m}}$.

(c) Let U denote the cost of an (unsuccessful) search in this array of m keys. Prove $\mathbf{E}[U] = \frac{n+1}{n-m+1}$.

20.6 **Bloom filter hashing**

[Proposed by Priyatham Bollimpalli] Priyatham is creating new software to check music for copyright violations. For each candidate song, s, if s is the same as an already existing song, the software should output "copyright violation" with 100% certainty (all violations need to be reported). On the other hand, if s is an arbitrary new song, the software should output "new song" at least 99% of the time (it is okay to have a few false alarms).

(a) To maximize efficiency, Priyatham opts for a hash table implementation, with b buckets, where every song, i, is mapped to $h(i)$, which corresponds to one of the b buckets. (Assume that h obeys SUHA, mapping each key i to a uniformly random bucket.) To fill his hash table, Priyatham scrapes all one billion songs in the Internet and maps each to a bucket. Given a candidate song, s, Priyatham's software computes $h(s)$. If $h(s)$ is an empty bucket, the software outputs "new song," otherwise it outputs "copyright violation." Approximately how many buckets b are needed to achieve the desired correctness for an arbitrary song s? Hint: It will help to recall from (1.9) that, for large b,

$$\left(1 - \frac{1}{b}\right)^b \to e^{-1}.$$

(b) After determining that the above scheme uses too much space, Priyatham considers a new approach: He chooses 10 idealized, independent hash functions $h_1, \ldots, h_{10}$ that each map songs to the numbers 1 through 10 billion. He initializes an array A of 10 billion bits, initially set to 0. For each song s that he encounters, he computes $h_1(s), h_2(s), \ldots, h_{10}(s)$, and sets the corresponding indices of A to be 1 (that is, he sets $A[h_1(s)] := 1, A[h_2(s)] := 1$, etc.). Argue that after processing the one billion unique songs, we expect $\approx e^{-1} \approx 0.37$ fraction of the array elements to be 0. [Hint: Linearity of Expectation.]

(c) Now, given a song s, to check if s already exists, Priyatham computes the 10 hashes of s and checks if $A[h_1(s)] = A[h_2(s)] = \cdots = A[h_{10}(s)] = 1$. If so, he outputs "copyright violation," otherwise he outputs "new song." Prove that, if s is actually in your set of one billion songs, you will output "copyright violation" with probability 1. Likewise, if s is *not* in your set of one billion songs, you output "new song" with probability ≈ 0.99. [Hint: Use part (b).]

(d) In the above, we've assumed that the number of buckets (array A's size) is $b = 10$ billion and the number of independent hash functions is $k = 10$. Write a general equation that relates b to k, assuming that the Internet has one billion songs and that we desire no more than 1% false positives.

Note: This space-efficient probabilistic data structure is called a **Bloom filter**. It was conceived by Burton Howard Bloom in 1970 [9].

Part VII

Randomized Algorithms

This part of the book is devoted to randomized algorithms. A randomized algorithm is simply an algorithm that uses a source of random bits, allowing it to make random moves. Randomized algorithms are extremely popular in computer science because (1) they are highly efficient (have low runtimes) on every input, and (2) they are often quite simple.

As we'll see, while randomized algorithms are very simple to state, analyzing their correctness and runtime will utilize all the probability tools that we have learned so far, plus some new tools.

Chapter 21 covers randomized algorithms of the Las Vegas variety. These algorithms always produce the correct answer, but their runtime depends on the random bits.

Next, in Chapters 22 and 23 we cover randomized algorithms of the Monte Carlo variety. These algorithms are extremely fast, regardless of the random bits. However, they return the correct answer only some fraction of the time, where the fraction depends on the random bits.

We only provide the briefest introduction to randomized algorithms in the text. The exercises offer many more examples and illustrate further directions. There are also several textbooks that are devoted entirely to randomized algorithms; see for example [21, 41, 53, 54].

21 Las Vegas Randomized Algorithms

This chapter introduces randomized algorithms. We start with a discussion of the differences between randomized algorithms and deterministic algorithms. We then introduce the two primary types of randomized algorithms: Las Vegas algorithms and Monte Carlo algorithms. This chapter and its exercises will contain many examples of randomized algorithms, all of the Las Vegas variety. In Chapter 22 we will turn to examples of the Monte Carlo variety.

21.1 Randomized versus Deterministic Algorithms

In deriving the runtime of an algorithm, we typically assume that there is an *adversary* who provides the input, and we consider the runtime of the algorithm on this input.

A **deterministic algorithm** always follows the same sequence of steps, and the adversary knows what steps the algorithm takes. Thus, the adversary can feed the algorithm a "worst-case input" on which it will take an exceptionally long time. The **runtime** of the algorithm is specifically defined as the runtime on that worst-case input.

By contrast, a **randomized algorithm** is an algorithm that makes use of a random sequence of bits in deciding what to do next. The adversary still gets to choose which input to feed the algorithm. However, because the randomized algorithm makes **random moves**, it is very hard for an adversary to defeat – that is, there often is no longer a worst-case input.

This brings us to the **primary advantage** of randomized algorithms: they are likely to be very *efficient* (low runtime) on *every* input. The adversary is powerless when the algorithm is randomized since the particular steps that the algorithm will take depends on random numbers. This makes it hard for the adversary to foil a randomized algorithm with a bad input that takes a long time.

When we say that randomized algorithms are "likely" to be efficient on every input, we mean that the randomness is over the string of random bits; one could always have a very poor choice of random bits which results in inefficiency. Randomized algorithms are often much faster than deterministic ones because they don't have a worst-case input. That said, because the algorithm uses random bits, the execution time of the algorithm can vary even on the same fixed input; that is, the execution time on a given input is a random variable (r.v.).

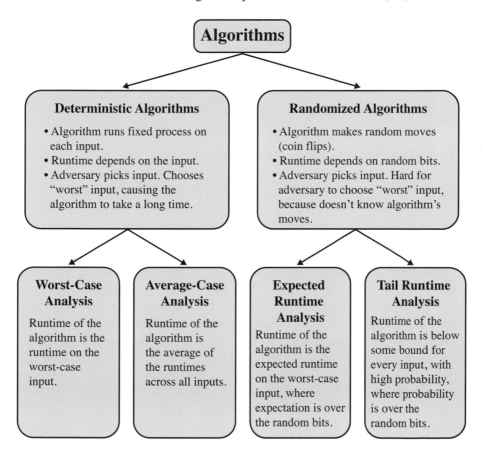

Figure 21.1 *Deterministic versus randomized algorithms.*

It is important not to confuse randomized algorithms with the **average-case analysis of deterministic algorithms**. In average-case analysis, the *input* is drawn from a distribution, and the goal is to show that the algorithm is efficient in expectation over all the inputs. That is, while there may be some bad inputs on which the deterministic algorithm takes a really long time, if those inputs occur with low probability, then we can say that the deterministic algorithm performs well in expectation, where expectation is taken over the space of *all* inputs. When we talk about average-case analysis we are no longer talking about an adversary providing the input, but rather we can think of having a random input.

In the exercises we will see examples of both randomized algorithms and average-case analysis, so that you can see the difference between the two.

A **secondary advantage** of randomized algorithms is that they are often much *simpler* than deterministic algorithms. In fact, many randomized algorithms sound impossibly stupid, but work well and are very easy to describe.

21.2 Las Vegas versus Monte Carlo

There are two types of randomized algorithms, which are actually quite different.

A **Las Vegas** algorithm will always produce the correct answer. However, its running time on a given input is variable, depending on the sequence of random bits. Although for some random bits its running time is high, its average running time is hopefully low (where the average is taken over the sequence of random bits).

A **Monte Carlo** algorithm typically runs in a fixed amount of time, which is very short and is typically independent of the random choices made. However, it only gives the correct answer some fraction of the time. For example, a Monte Carlo algorithm may only produce the correct answer half the time. This may seem really stupid. What's the point of having an algorithm that gives the wrong answer? However, it's not as bad as it seems: The error probability depends on the particular random bits. Hence, runs are independent of each other and one can improve the correctness by running the algorithm multiple times (with freshly drawn random bits).

An example of a Monte Carlo algorithm is the Stochastic Gradient Descent (SGD) algorithm, used extensively in machine learning for finding the minimum of a multi-dimensional function. SGD reduces computation time over traditional Gradient Descent by only doing the needed minimization computations at a few randomly selected points. While the result may not always be correct, it's extremely fast.

We now present some examples of Las Vegas algorithms, which always produce the correct answer. In the chapter we will concentrate on expected runtime; however, the exercises will also consider the tail of the runtime distribution.

Our first randomized algorithm is Randomized Quicksort. Before we describe it, it helps to review Deterministic Quicksort.

21.3 Review of Deterministic Quicksort

Quicksort is an efficient algorithm for sorting a list of n numbers: $a_1, a_2, \ldots, a_n$. Throughout our discussion we will assume for convenience that these numbers are distinct. The **size** of the problem is the number of elements in the list being sorted, namely n. The **runtime** of the algorithm is the number of comparisons needed to sort the list. Throughout, we will use

$C(n)$ = number of comparisons needed when the problem size is n.

In **Deterministic Quicksort**, the first element in the list (a_1) is designated as the *pivot*. All elements in the list are then compared with the pivot. Those elements less than the pivot are put into list $L1$, and those greater than the pivot are put into list $L2$, creating the list:

$$L1, \ a_1, \ L2.$$

Quicksort is then recursively applied to list $L1$ to obtain $L1s$ (sorted version of $L1$) and is recursively applied to list $L2$ to obtain $L2s$. The list returned is then

$$L1s, \ a_1, \ L2s.$$

Question: What is an example of a *bad* input list for Deterministic Quicksort?

Answer: In a sorted list, the pivot is always the smallest element in the list. Now all the elements end up in just *one* of the sublists, which is bad, because the size of the problem shrinks too slowly, resulting in high runtime.

Question: How many comparisons are needed in the case of a bad input list?

Answer: In the first step we compare the pivot with $n - 1$ elements. We then end up with a sublist of length $n - 1$, which requires $C(n - 1)$ comparisons to sort. Hence:

$$C(n) = (n - 1) + C(n - 1),$$

where $C(1) = 0$. Consequently $C(n) = O(n^2)$ on this bad input list.

Question: What is an example of a *good* input list for Deterministic Quicksort?

Answer: Ideally, we would like the pivot element to always be the median of the list. For example, consider the list:

$$\{5, 3, 2, 4, 7, 6, 8\},$$

which splits into:

$$\{3, 2, 4\}, 5, \{7, 6, 8\}$$

which further divides into:

$$\{2\}, 3, \{4\}, 5, \{6\}, 7, \{8\}.$$

Question: What is the number of comparisons needed by Deterministic Quicksort on a good input list?

Answer: Since the good input splits the list into two even lists at each step, we have approximately (ignoring rounding up or down):

$$
\begin{aligned}
C(n) &= n - 1 + 2C(n/2) \\
&= (n - 1) + 2\left(n/2 - 1 + 2C(n/4)\right) \\
&= (n - 1) + (n - 2) + 4C(n/4) \\
&= (n - 1) + (n - 2) + 4\left(n/4 - 1 + 2C(n/8)\right) \\
&= (n - 1) + (n - 2) + (n - 4) + 8C(n/8).
\end{aligned}
$$

Continuing in this fashion, we have that:

$$
\begin{aligned}
C(n) &= (n - 1) + (n - 2) + (n - 4) + (n - 8) + \cdots \\
&= n \lg n - \left(1 + 2 + 4 + \cdots + \frac{n}{2} + n\right) \\
&= n \lg n - 2n + 1 \\
&= O(n \lg n).
\end{aligned}
$$

21.4 Randomized Quicksort

We'd like the running time of Quicksort to be $O(n \lg n)$ on *every* input list. But how can we achieve this? The adversary can always choose to give us a bad input list that forces the running time to $O(n^2)$.

The solution is to use a randomized algorithm. Our **Randomized Quicksort** algorithm is identical to Deterministic Quicksort, except that the *pivot position* is chosen at random in each step. This makes it impossible for the adversary to give us a bad input list, which is the point of using randomness!

We will now prove that the expected running time of Randomized Quicksort is $O(n \lg n)$ on every input. Here, "expectation" is over all sequences of random pivot positions. In Exercise 21.13 you will invoke the Chernoff bound to show that *with high probability (w.h.p.)* the running time of Randomized Quicksort is $O(n \ln n)$ on every input.

Theorem 21.1 (Randomized Quicksort runtime) *Given any input list of n distinct elements, Randomized Quicksort will make $O(n \lg n)$ comparisons in expectation.*

Proof: Let $a_1, a_2, a_3, \ldots, a_n$ be an input. Let $s_1 < s_2 < s_3 < \ldots < s_n$ be the sorted version of this input. For $i < j$, let X_{ij} be an indicator random variable that takes on the value 1 if s_i and s_j are ever compared during the running of the algorithm and 0 otherwise. Note that s_i and s_j are compared at most once. Then, invoking Linearity of Expectation, we have:

$$C(n) = \sum_{i=1}^{n-1} \sum_{j=i+1}^{n} X_{ij}$$

$$\mathbf{E}[C(n)] = \sum_{i=1}^{n-1} \sum_{j=i+1}^{n} \mathbf{E}[X_{ij}].$$

Question: What is $\mathbf{E}[X_{ij}]$, namely the probability that s_i and s_j are compared?

Hint: Think about the following *sorted sublist*: $S = [s_i, s_{i+1}, s_{i+2}, \ldots, s_j]$ and condition on which element in S is the first to be chosen to be a pivot.

Answer: At any moment of time before one of the elements of S has been chosen as a pivot, all the elements of S must be in the same sublist. Now consider that moment when one of the elements of S is first chosen as a pivot. If the pivot element chosen is s_i, then s_i will get compared with all the elements in S, and hence s_i and s_j will get compared. The argument is the same if the pivot element chosen is s_j. On the other hand, if any element of S other than s_i or s_j is chosen as the pivot, then after the pivot operation, s_i and s_j will end up in different sublists and will never get compared. Hence,

$$\mathbf{P}\{s_i \text{ and } s_j \text{ get compared}\} = \frac{2}{j - i + 1}.$$

We thus have:

$$\mathbf{E}[C(n)] = \sum_{i=1}^{n-1} \sum_{j=i+1}^{n} \mathbf{E}[X_{ij}] = \sum_{i=1}^{n-1} \sum_{j=i+1}^{n} \frac{2}{j - i + 1}$$

$$= 2 \sum_{i=1}^{n-1} \sum_{k=2}^{n-i+1} \frac{1}{k} \qquad \text{where } k = j - i + 1$$

$$\leq 2 \sum_{i=1}^{n} \sum_{k=2}^{n} \frac{1}{k}.$$

Now, recalling the fact from (1.16) that

$$\sum_{i=1}^{n} \frac{1}{i} < 1 + \ln n,$$

we have:

$$\mathbf{E}\left[C(n)\right] \le 2 \sum_{i=1}^{n} \sum_{k=2}^{n} \frac{1}{k} < 2 \sum_{i=1}^{n} (1 + \ln n - 1) = 2n \ln n.$$

We have thus shown that $\mathbf{E}\left[C(n)\right] = O(n \ln n) = O(n \lg n)$ as desired. ∎

Summary: At this point, we have seen that Deterministic Quicksort, where the pivot is always chosen to be the first element of the list, has a worst-case input which forces $O(n^2)$ comparisons. By contrast, Randomized Quicksort, where the pivot is chosen randomly, has no worst-case input, and has an average runtime of $O(n \lg n)$, where this average is taken over the random choice of the pivot.

Question: Our analyses of both Deterministic Quicksort and Randomized Quicksort were *worst-case analyses* because the adversary was allowed to pick the worst possible input. What is meant by *average-case analysis of Quicksort*?

Answer: In average-case analysis, we are once again running Deterministic Quicksort, with our pivot always chosen to be the first element in the list, for example. However, rather than the input being chosen by an adversary, we assume that we have a *random input* – that is, a randomly ordered list. We derive the expected runtime, where the expectation is over the random ordering of the list.

Question: What is the runtime of Deterministic Quicksort under average-case analysis?

Answer: Because the input is randomly chosen, the adversary has no control over the first element in each sublist. So in each round, our pivot is effectively a random element in the list. Thus the computation of expected runtime is identical to what we saw for Randomized Quicksort, where we pick the pivot at random. Hence the expected runtime of the average-case analysis of Deterministic Quicksort is also $O(n \lg n)$.

21.5 Randomized Selection and Median-Finding

In the **k-Select** problem, we are given an unsorted list and asked to find the kth smallest element in the list. We'll assume that the list has n elements: $a_1, a_2, \ldots, a_n$. Again, for convenience, we assume that these numbers are distinct.

We will also ignore floors and ceilings in our discussion, so as to keep the notation from getting out of hand.

Question: What's an obvious way to solve k-Select in $O(n \lg n)$ time?

Answer: Sort the list, using Randomized Quicksort, and then return the kth element in the sorted list.

Our goal is to solve k-Select in $O(n)$ time.

Question: For certain values of k, it should be obvious how to achieve $O(n)$ time. What are these values?

Answer: If $k = 1$, then we can solve the problem just by walking through the list and keeping track of the smallest element so far. Similarly for $k = n$.

When $k = \frac{n}{2}$ (also known as the **Median-Select** problem), it is not at all obvious how to achieve $O(n)$ time.

We will present a very simple Las Vegas randomized algorithm for achieving $O(n)$ time on *every* input in expectation. The idea is to use random pivots as we did in the Randomized Quicksort algorithm. However, unlike the case of Quicksort, the pivot will allow us to throw away a part of the list.

Imagine that we start with a list of n elements, and our goal is to find the kth smallest element. We now pick a pivot at random. Suppose that our pivot happens to be the ith largest element in the list, s_i. In $O(n)$ time, we can subdivide the list into $L1$, those $i - 1$ elements smaller than our pivot, and $L2$, those $n - i$ elements bigger than our pivot. Our kth smallest element is either in $L1$ or $L2$, or it is equal to the pivot (if $k = i$).

Question: If $k < i$, then our problem reduces to ...

Answer: Finding the kth element in $L1$, a list of size $i - 1$.

Question: If $k > i$, then our problem reduces to ...

Answer: Finding the $(k - i)$th element in $L2$, a list of size $n - i$.

We refer to the above algorithm as **Randomized k-Select**.

Before we write up the formal analysis, let's do a quick thought-experiment.

Question: Suppose that the pivot element always exactly splits the list in half. How many comparisons, $C(n)$, will be needed by our algorithm?

Answer: We need $n - 1$ comparisons to split the list. After splitting the list, we'll have reduced the problem to selection in a list of length $n/2$. Ignoring floors and ceilings, we have:

$$
\begin{aligned}
C(n) &= (n-1) + C(n/2) \\
&= (n-1) + (n/2 - 1) + C(n/4) \\
&< n + n/2 + n/4 + n/8 + \cdots + 1 \\
&\leq 2n.
\end{aligned}
$$

So $C(n) = O(n)$ if the pivot is always picked *optimally*.

We will now show that, if we pick a *random pivot*, we can still achieve $O(n)$ comparisons. Here, expectation is over the choice of the random pivot. Our derivation is an *upper bound* because we will assume that we are always reduced to looking at the *longest sublist* of the two randomly created sublists. This time we won't ignore floors and ceilings, so that you can see how to argue this precisely.

> **Theorem 21.2 (Randomized k-Select runtime)** *For any list of n distinct elements, Randomized k-Select makes $\leq cn$ comparisons in expectation, where $c = 4$. This holds for any k.*

Proof: In general when writing a proof, one does not know exactly what the constant c will be. Thus, we will write our proof as if we are not given the value of c, and we will show how we can derive c as part of the proof, to get that $c = 4$.

Since the pivot is chosen randomly, it is equal to the ith largest element with probability $\frac{1}{n}$. Hence we have:

$$
\begin{aligned}
\mathbf{E}\left[C(n)\right] &\leq (n-1) + \sum_{i=1}^{n} \mathbf{P}\left\{\text{pivot is } s_i\right\} \cdot \mathbf{E}\left[C\left(\max\{i-1, n-i\}\right)\right] \\
&= (n-1) + \sum_{i=1}^{n} \frac{1}{n} \cdot \mathbf{E}\left[C\left(\max\{i-1, n-i\}\right)\right] \\
&\leq (n-1) + \frac{2}{n} \sum_{i=\lfloor \frac{n}{2} \rfloor}^{n-1} \mathbf{E}\left[C(i)\right].
\end{aligned}
$$

We will show that this results in $\mathbf{E}\left[C(n)\right] = O(n)$. We use induction. We claim that $\mathbf{E}\left[C(i)\right] \leq c \cdot i$ for some small integer $c \geq 1$ to be named later, and where $i < n$.

Since $\mathbf{E}\left[C(1)\right] = 0 \leq c \cdot 1$, the base case holds. Assuming that the inductive hypothesis holds for $i \leq n - 1$, we have:

$$\mathbf{E}\left[C(n)\right] \leq (n - 1) + \frac{2}{n} \sum_{i=\lfloor \frac{n}{2} \rfloor}^{n-1} c \cdot i$$

$$= (n - 1) + \frac{2c}{n} \cdot \frac{(n - 1) + \lfloor \frac{n}{2} \rfloor}{2} \cdot \left(n - 1 - \left\lfloor \frac{n}{2} \right\rfloor + 1\right)$$

$$\leq (n - 1) + \frac{2c}{n} \cdot \frac{(n - 1) + \frac{n}{2}}{2} \cdot \left(n - \frac{n - 1}{2}\right)$$

$$= (n - 1) + \frac{c}{n} \cdot \left(\frac{3n}{2} - 1\right) \cdot \frac{n + 1}{2}$$

$$= (n - 1) + \frac{c}{4n} \cdot (3n - 2) \cdot (n + 1)$$

$$= (n - 1) + \frac{3cn}{4} + \frac{c}{4} - \frac{2c}{4n}. \tag{21.1}$$

Our goal is to show that $\mathbf{E}\left[C(n)\right] \leq cn$. From (21.1), we can see that, if we set $c = 4$, then we have that:

$$\mathbf{E}\left[C(n)\right] \leq (n - 1) + \frac{3 \cdot 4 \cdot n}{4} + \frac{4}{4} - \frac{2 \cdot 4}{4n}$$

$$= (n - 1) + 3n + 1 - \frac{2}{n}$$

$$\leq 4n.$$

So

$$\mathbf{E}\left[C(n)\right] \leq 4n$$

is a solution to the original equation. We have thus proven the inductive case. ■

Question: Suppose we want to determine the median of a list of length n. How many comparisons are needed?

Answer: Still $O(n)$. If n is odd, we use Randomized k-Select with $k = (n+1)/2$. We refer to the median-finding algorithm as **Randomized Median-Select**.

21.6 Exercises

21.1 **Creating a fair coin**

You are given a biased coin that returns heads with probability 0.6 and tails otherwise. Let *Biased-Flip* be a routine that flips the biased coin once and returns the output. Design a Las Vegas algorithm, *Fair*, which

outputs heads with probability 0.5 and tails otherwise. Your algorithm, *Fair*, should only make calls to *Biased-Flip* and nothing else.
(a) State your *Fair* algorithm clearly.
(b) Prove that *Fair* outputs heads with probability 0.5 and Tails otherwise.
(c) Derive the expected number of calls to *Biased-Flip* required for *Fair* to produce an output.

21.2 Creating a three-way fair coin

Given a function *2WayFair* that returns 0 or 1 with equal probability, implement a Las Vegas function, *3WayFair*, that returns 0, 1, or 2 with equal probability. Aim to use a minimum number of calls to *2WayFair*.
(a) What is the expected number of calls to *2WayFair* made by *3WayFair*?
(b) Explain why *3WayFair* is a Las Vegas algorithm.
(Note: The solution is simple. Do not use any floating point arithmetic.)

21.3 Nuts-and-bolts problem

[Proposed by David Wajc] Imagine that you have n nuts, $N_1, N_2, \ldots, N_n$ with distinct sizes: $1, 2, 3, \ldots, n$. You also have n bolts, $B_1, B_2, \ldots, B_n$ with distinct sizes: $1, 2, 3, \ldots, n$, such that there is exactly one bolt that fits each nut. You can't see the nuts or the bolts, but you can perform a "trial" which consists of comparing one nut with one bolt. The result of a single trial is that either (a) they're a perfect fit, or (b) the bolt was too small, or (c) the bolt was too large. *You are not allowed to compare nuts with nuts or bolts with bolts.*
(a) Describe an efficient randomized algorithm for matching all n nuts to the n bolts in as few trials as you can. (Using $\Theta(n^2)$ trials is too many!)
(b) Derive the expected asymptotic running time of your algorithm.

21.4 Ropes problem

You have n ropes. Each rope has two ends. Consider the following randomized algorithm: At each step of your algorithm, you pick two random ends (these may be two ends from the same rope, or one end from one rope and one end from another rope), and tie these ends together. Keep going until there are no ends left. What is the expected number of cycles formed? Express your answer using $\Theta(\cdot)$.

21.5 Uniform sampling from a stream

[Proposed by David Wajc] Suppose you are walking down a long road, whose length you don't know in advance. Along the road are houses, which you would like to photograph with your very old camera. This old camera allows you to take as many pictures as you want, but only has enough memory to store *one* picture at a time. The street contains n houses, but you don't know n before you reach the end of the street.

Your goal is to end up with one photo in your camera, where that photo is equally likely to show any of the n houses.

One algorithm for achieving this goal is to walk all the way down the street, counting houses, so that we can determine n. Then we roll an n-sided die, where X denotes the roll outcome. Then we walk to the house numbered X and take its picture. However, you're a busy person and you don't want to walk down the street again. Can you achieve your goal by walking up the street only once? This problem is referred to as *uniform sampling from a stream with unknown length*.

(a) Propose a randomized algorithm for uniform sampling from a stream with unknown length. Your algorithm will involve replacing the item stored in memory with some probability as you walk (only once) down the street.

(b) Prove that, for all i, $\mathbf{P}\{i\text{th item is output}\} = \frac{1}{n}$.

21.6 **Pruning a path graph**

[Proposed by Vanshika Chowdhary] Figure 21.2 shows a path graph of n edges. At each round, you select a random edge of those remaining and cut it. Whenever an edge is cut, that edge and everything below that edge falls off. Let X be the number of edges that you cut until the entire path disappears (all edges are gone). What is $\mathbf{E}[X]$?

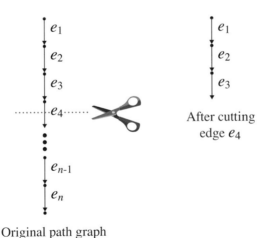

Figure 21.2 *For Exercise 21.6. Path graph with n edges, before and after pruning edge* e_4.

21.7 **Uniform sampling from a stream – generalized**

As in Exercise 21.5, you are walking down a long road with n houses, where you don't know n in advance. This time you have a *new camera* for photographing houses. This new camera has enough memory to store *s* photos at a time. You walk all the way down the street *just once* taking photos. By the end of your walk, you want to have stored a random subset of *s* homes. (Assume $n \geq s$.)

(a) Provide a randomized algorithm for achieving your goal.

(b) Let *S* denote the set of houses stored in your camera. Prove that, at the end of your walk, each of the *n* houses has an equal probability of being in *S*.

21.8 Finding the max – average-case analysis

Given an array *A* of length *n* containing distinct integers $a_1, a_2, \ldots, a_n$, the *FindMax* algorithm determines the maximum number in *A*. Assuming the inputs are given in a uniformly random order, what is the expected number of times that *currentMax* is updated? Provide upper and lower bounds for this expression.

Algorithm 21.3 (FindMax($a_1, a_2, \ldots, a_n$))

1. currentMax $= -\infty$

2. **for** $i = 1, \ldots, n$ **do**

        if $a_i >$ currentMax **then** currentMax $= a_i$.

3. **return** currentMax

21.9 Average-case analysis of Move-to-Front

Suppose you use a linked list to store *n* items: $a_1, a_2, \ldots, a_n$. Then the time to access the *i*th stored item in the list is *i*. If you know that certain items are accessed more frequently, you would like to store them at the *front* of the list, so that their access time is shorter. Unfortunately, you don't know the access probabilities of items, so you use the (deterministic) Move-To-Front (MTF) algorithm: Each time an item is accessed, you append it to the front of the list, so that its access time is 1 (for now). Assume that MTF has been running for a long time. Our goal is to understand the expected time to look up an item in the list, call it $\mathbf{E}[T]$, given that item a_i is accessed with probability p_i.

(a) Prove that

$$\mathbf{E}[T] = 1 + \sum_{i=1}^{n} p_i \sum_{j \neq i} \frac{p_j}{p_j + p_i}. \tag{21.2}$$

[Hint: Start by conditioning on the item, a_i, being accessed. The position of a_i can be expressed in terms of a sum of X_{ij} indicator random variables, where $\mathbf{E}[X_{ij}]$ is the probability that item a_j precedes a_i.]

(b) Verify your expression for $\mathbf{E}[T]$ in the case $p_i = \frac{1}{n}, \forall i$.

(c) Suppose that $p_i = C \cdot 2^{-i}$, $i = 1, 2, \ldots, n$, where *C* is the appropriate normalizing constant. Compute $\mathbf{E}[T]^{\text{MTF}}$ from (21.2), where $n = 5$ (you can write a small program). Now consider the case where we know the p_i's and we arrange the items according to the best arrangement (BA), namely in order of decreasing p_i. How does $\mathbf{E}\,[T]^{\text{BA}}$ compare with $\mathbf{E}\,[T]^{\text{MTF}}$?

21.10 How to find a mate – average-case analysis
[This is a repeat of Exercise 3.14, which is a nice example of average-case analysis.] Imagine that there are n people in the world. You want to find the best spouse. You date one person at a time. After dating the person, you need to decide if you want to marry them. If you decide to marry, then you're done. If you decide not to marry, then that person will never again agree to marry you (they're on the "burn list"), and you move on to the next person.

Suppose that after dating a person you can accurately rank them in comparison with all the other people whom you've dated so far. You do not, however, know their rank relative to people whom you haven't dated. So, for example, you might early on date the person who is the best of the n, but you don't know that.

Assume that the candidates are randomly ordered. Specifically, assume that each candidate has a unique score, uniformly distributed between 0 and 1. Our goal is to find the candidate with the highest score.

> **Algorithm 21.4 (Marriage algorithm)**
> 1. *Date $r \ll n$ people. Rank those r to determine the "best of r."*
> 2. *Now keep dating people until you find a person who is better than that "best of r" person.*
> 3. *As soon as you find such a person, marry them. If you never find such a person, you'll stay unwed.*

What r maximizes $\mathbf{P}\,\{$end up marrying the best of $n\}$? When using that r, what is the probability that you end up marrying the best person? (In your analysis, feel free to assume that n is large and $H_n \approx \ln(n)$.)

21.11 Finding the k largest elements
Given an array A of n distinct elements in random order, we will consider two algorithms which each output the k largest elements in sorted order.
(a) Randomized Algorithm 1 uses Randomized k-Select to find the kth largest element, x. We then walk through the array, keeping only those elements $\geq x$. Finally, we sort these k largest elements via Randomized Quicksort. Derive an asymptotic expression for the expected number of comparisons. Since Algorithm 1 is randomized, the expectation is over the random bits.
(b) Deterministic Algorithm 2 maintains a sorted list at all times, $S = [s_1 > s_2 > \cdots > s_k]$, of the top-$k$-so-far. We start by sorting the first k elements of A via Deterministic Quicksort and calling that S. We now take each element, x, of A, starting with the $(k+1)$th element,

$x = a_{k+1}$, and insert it into its place in S. To do this, we compare x with each element of S starting with s_k and then s_{k-1} (if needed), and then s_{k-2} (if needed) and so on until x finds its place in S. This is the first run. In the second run, we insert the $(k+2)$th element of A into its proper place in S. There will be $n - k$ runs, many of which will not change S at all. Prove that the expected number of comparisons made is $O(n + k^2 \log n)$. Since Algorithm 2 is deterministic, the expectation is over the randomly ordered input.

21.12 **Randomized dominating set**

A *dominating set*, D, in a connected undirected graph $G = (V, E)$, is a set of vertices such that, for each $v \in V$, either $v \in D$ or v is adjacent to some $v' \in D$ (in both cases we say that v is *covered* by D). Assume that $|V| = n$ and that G is *d-regular*, with $d \geq 2$, meaning that each vertex has exactly d neighbors. Our goal is to find the minimum sized D.

(a) Sheng proposes the following randomized algorithm to find a valid D: Each vertex picks a random number in the range $(0, 1)$. For each edge, (i, j), we pick the endpoint with the larger number to be in D. In this way, for every edge (i, j), we are guaranteed that at least one of i and j are in D. What is $\mathbf{E}\left[|D|\right]$ found by Sheng's algorithm?

(b) A better randomized algorithm is Algorithm 21.5. Derive $\mathbf{E}\left[|D|\right]$ for Algorithm 21.5. Here are some steps:
   (i) Express $\mathbf{E}\left[|D|\right]$ as a function of the p value in Algorithm 21.5.
   (ii) Find the p that minimizes $\mathbf{E}\left[|D|\right]$. Express $\mathbf{E}\left[|D|\right]$ for this p.
   (iii) Prove that $0 < \mathbf{E}\left[|D|\right] < n$. What happens to $\mathbf{E}\left[|D|\right]$ as d grows large?

> **Algorithm 21.5 (Dominating Set)**
> 1. *Given $G = (V, E)$, pick a random subset $D_0 \subseteq V$ where D_0 includes each $v \in V$ with probability p.*
> 2. *Let D_1 be all vertices in V that are not covered by D_0.*
> 3. *Return $D = D_0 \cup D_1$.*

21.13 **Bounding the tail of Randomized Quicksort**

Use Chernoff bounds to show that, w.h.p. $(1 - \frac{1}{n})$, Randomized Quicksort requires only $O(n \lg n)$ comparisons to sort a list of length n. Here are some steps to help you:

(a) Consider a particular run of Randomized Quicksort as shown in Figure 21.3. The tree shows the list L at each stage and then shows the sublists L_1 and L_2 under that, separated by the pivot, p. You can imagine drawing such a tree for any instance of Randomized Quicksort. Let T denote the total number of comparisons made by Randomized Quicksort. Explain why T is upper-bounded by the sum of the lengths of all root-to-leaf paths in the ternary tree. Note that pivots count as leaves as well, so every element is eventually a leaf. [Hint: For each leaf, think about the number of comparisons that it's involved in.]

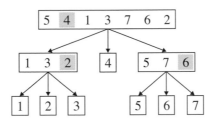

Figure 21.3 *Randomized Quicksort tree. The randomly selected pivot is in pink.*

(b) Now we'll argue that w.h.p. each root-to-leaf path is of length $O(\log n)$. Note: It's fine that some quantities are not integers.
   (i) Let's say that a node of the tree is "good" if the randomly chosen pivot separates the current list at the node into two sublists, each of size at most $\frac{3}{4}$ the size of the current list. Otherwise we say that the node is "bad." What is the probability that a node is "good"?
   (ii) Let g denote the maximum number of "good" nodes possible along a single root-to-leaf path. What is g as a function of n?
   (iii) Consider an arbitrary leaf i. We want to prove that the root-to-leaf path ending in i is not very long. Specifically, show that

$$\mathbf{P}\{\text{The root-to-leaf path ending in } i \text{ has length } \geq 6g\} \leq \frac{1}{n^2}.$$

   Here you're using the g from part (ii). Note that as soon as we see the first g "good" nodes, we'll be down to a single leaf.
(c) We have seen that with probability at least $1 - \frac{1}{n^2}$ a given root-to-leaf path is no longer than $6g$. What probabilistic statement about T follows from this?

21.14 **Randomized AND–OR tree evaluation**
   Min–max game trees are often represented by an AND–OR tree on binary inputs, where AND is equivalent to "Min" and OR is equivalent to "Max." In an AND–OR tree, there are alternating levels of ANDs and ORs. The leaves of the tree are all 0's and 1's. Recall that $\text{AND}(a, b) = 1$ only if $a = b = 1$, while $\text{OR}(a, b) = 1$ if either $a = 1$ or $b = 1$ or both. Each node in the tree has a value (computed bottom-up) based on its subtrees; the value of the entire tree is the value of the root node. T_k denotes a tree with k AND levels and k OR levels, having height $2k$ and $2^{2k} = 4^k$ leaves. Figure 21.4 shows T_2.
   (a) How many leaves must be evaluated in determining the value of T_k when a deterministic algorithm is used? What exactly will the adversary do to force you to evaluate that many leaves? The adversary

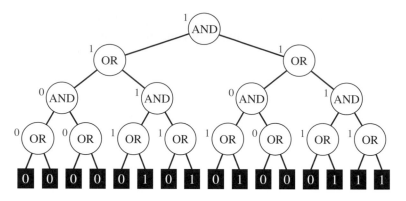

Figure 21.4 *This figure shows T_k, where $k = 2$. This means that there are $k = 2$ AND levels and $k = 2$ OR levels. The height of a T_k tree is $2k$. The values are computed bottom-up and are shown in red at each node. The final value of this tree is* 1.

knows the order in which your algorithm evaluates leaves and will give you the worst-case input.

(b) Consider the following *Randomized AND–OR algorithm*. This algorithm computes the value of each node in the tree, bottom-up. However, it *randomly* considers whether to first look at the left node or the right node, and then it doesn't bother looking at the remaining node unless necessary. Prove that the Randomized AND–OR algorithm requires $\leq 3^k$ leaf evaluations in expectation. Here, expectation is taken over the random bits used by the algorithm. As always, the adversary will try to give you the worst-case input; however, it will have a harder time because your moves are random.

   (i) Start with a tree of height 1, consisting of two leaves connected by an OR. How many leaves on average must be evaluated if the value of your tree is 1? How about if the value of your tree is 0?

   (ii) Now consider the tree T_k, where $k = 1$. This tree will have a single AND with two ORs underneath. How many leaves in expectation must be evaluated if the value of your tree is 1? What changes if the value of your tree is 0?

   (iii) Prove via induction that you can determine the value of T_k in $\leq 3^k$ leaf evaluations in expectation. Do this both when the value of the tree is 1 and when it is 0.

21.15 Multi-armed chocolate machine

[Proposed by Weina Wang] A chocolate machine has two arms, as shown in Figure 21.5. If you pull Arm 1, it gives you a chocolate with probability $p_1 = \frac{3}{4}$. If you pull Arm 2, it gives you a chocolate with probability $p_2 = \frac{1}{4}$. Unfortunately, you don't know the values of p_1 and p_2, or which one is bigger.

$p_1 = \tfrac{3}{4}$

$p_2 = \tfrac{1}{4}$

Figure 21.5 *Chocolate machine with two arms.*

Suppose pulling an arm once costs 1 dollar, and you have n dollars in total. Your goal is always to spend your n dollars to maximize the number of chocolates you receive in expectation.

(a) If you knew p_1 and p_2, how would you want to spend your n dollars? Let R^* denote the total number of chocolates you get. What is $\mathbf{E}[R^*]$?

(b) Since you do not know p_1 and p_2, you decide to pull each arm $\frac{n}{2}$ times (assume n is an even number). Let R_{rand} be the total number of chocolates you get. What is $\mathbf{E}[R_{\text{rand}}]$? Compare $\mathbf{E}[R_{\text{rand}}]$ with $\mathbf{E}[R^*]$.

(c) You figure that you can experiment with the arms a bit and decide how to use the rest of the money based on what you see. Suppose you pull each arm once to see which gives you chocolates.
   - If one arm gives a chocolate and the other one does not, you use the remaining $n - 2$ dollars on the arm that gives a chocolate.
   - Otherwise, you pick an arm uniformly at random and use the remaining $n - 2$ dollars on that arm.

Let R_{informed} be the total number of chocolates you get. What is $\mathbf{E}[R_{\text{informed}}]$? Compare $\mathbf{E}[R_{\text{informed}}]$ with $\mathbf{E}[R^*]$.

(d) You decide to experiment further. Suppose you pull each arm $m = 8 \ln n$ times. Let X and Y be the numbers of chocolates you get from Arm 1 and Arm 2, respectively. Then you do the following:
   - If $X \geq Y$, you use the remaining $n - 2m$ dollars on Arm 1.
   - Otherwise, you use the remaining $n - 2m$ dollars on Arm 2.

Let $R_{\text{well-informed}}$ denote the total number of chocolates you get. Derive a lower bound on $\mathbf{E}[R_{\text{well-informed}}]$. Show that $\mathbf{E}[R^*] - \mathbf{E}[R_{\text{well-informed}}] = O(\ln n)$.

For more general versions of this problem and more interesting algorithms, check out the multi-armed bandits literature (e.g. [47]).

21.16 Infinite highway problem

Imagine an infinitely long one-lane highway, starting at location 0 and

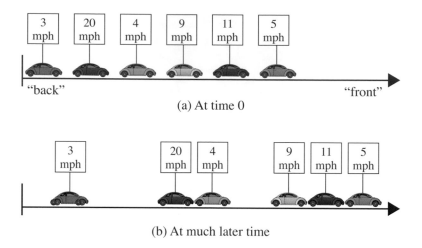

(a) At time 0

(b) At much later time

Figure 21.6 *One example of the infinite highway problem from Exercise 21.16.*

extending forever. There are n distinct cars, which start out evenly spaced. Each of the cars moves at some speed drawn independently from Uniform$(0, 100)$. The cars will drive forever on this one-lane highway, unable to pass each other, and faster cars will eventually get stuck behind slower cars that started in front of them. Over time, the cars will segregate into clusters. Figure 21.6 shows one particular example. Let X denote the number of clusters formed for a general instance of this problem.

(a) What is $\mathbf{E}[X]$?

(b) What is $\mathbf{Var}(X)$?

(c) Prove that X is less than $3\mathbf{E}[X]$ w.h.p. when n is high.

21.17 Independent set

[Proposed by Misha Ivkov] Let $G = (V, E)$ be a graph with $n = |V|$ vertices and $m = |E|$ edges. We say that $S \subset V$ is an independent set if no pair of vertices in S are connected by an edge. You will prove that G has an independent set S of size $\geq \frac{n^2}{4m}$. To do this, you will use the **probabilistic method**, which says: To prove that there is an independent set of size $\geq k$ in G, find a randomized algorithm which gives you an independent set of size S, where $\mathbf{E}[S] \geq k$. (Here S is a r.v. which depends on the random bits of the randomized algorithm.) Now you know there must be an independent set of size $\geq k$ in G.

Use the following Randomized Independent Set algorithm:

1. Pick each vertex of V to be in S with probability p.

2. If there exist two vertices in S that share an edge, randomly delete one.

Show that $\mathbf{E}[S] \geq \frac{n^2}{4m}$. Note: You will have to specify p.

22 Monte Carlo Randomized Algorithms

In the last chapter we studied randomized algorithms of the Las Vegas variety. This chapter is devoted to randomized algorithms of the Monte Carlo variety.

A **Monte Carlo** algorithm typically runs in a fixed amount of time, where the runtime is typically independent of the random choices made. However, it only produces the correct answer some fraction of the time (say half the time). The error probability depends on the particular random bits. Hence, runs are independent of each other, and one can improve the correctness by running the algorithm multiple times (with different sequences of random bits).

This definition is very abstract, so let's turn to some common examples.

22.1 Randomized Matrix-Multiplication Checking

One of the most common uses of randomized algorithms is to verify the correctness of a program, a.k.a. **program checking**. The typical scenario is that one has a program that one doesn't totally trust. One would like to check the correctness of the output very quickly – in way less time than it would take to run the computation from scratch.

As an example, consider the problem of multiplying two matrices.

Question: Using standard matrix multiplication, how many multiplications are needed to multiply two $n \times n$ matrices, $\mathbf{A}$ and $\mathbf{B}$?

Answer: $\Theta(n^3)$.

Question: How many multiplications are needed using the currently fastest method for multiplying matrices?

Answer: You've probably heard of Strassen's algorithm, which uses $O(n^{\log_2 7 + o(1)}) \approx O(n^{2.8})$ multiplications. Until recently, the fastest algorithm was due to Coppersmith and Winograd [15], using $O(n^{2.376})$ multiplications.

Recently, a CMU PhD student, Virginia Vassilevska, improved this to $O(n^{2.373})$ multiplications [79].

The Coppersmith and Winograd (C-W) algorithm is complex to implement, and the Vassilevska algorithm is even more so. Suppose that someone has an implementation of the Vassilevska algorithm. You might not trust their code.

You would ideally like to be able to check each output that the Vassilevska implementation gives you. That is, every time that you input two $n \times n$ matrices, **A** and **B**, into the Vassilevska implementation, and it outputs **C**, you'd like to check if in fact $\mathbf{A} \cdot \mathbf{B} = \mathbf{C}$.

Of course we could check that $\mathbf{A} \cdot \mathbf{B} = \mathbf{C}$ using standard matrix multiplication. But this would take $\Theta(n^3)$ time, which would defeat the whole point of using the $\Theta(n^{2.37})$ implementation.

We now illustrate a randomized algorithm due to Freivalds [29] that allows us to check whether $\mathbf{A} \cdot \mathbf{B} = \mathbf{C}$ using only $\Theta(n^2)$ multiplications. Hence, we can afford to run our checker every time that we run the Vassilevska implementation.

Algorithm 22.1 (Freivalds' matrix multiplication checking algorithm)
Inputs: **A**, **B**, **C** *all of dimension* $n \times n$, *with elements in* $\mathbb{R}$.

1. *Choose a random vector* $\vec{r} = (r_1, r_2, r_3, \ldots, r_n)$, *where* $r_i \in \{0, 1\}$.
2. *Compute* $\mathbf{B}\vec{r}$.
3. *Compute* $\mathbf{A}(\mathbf{B}\vec{r})$.
4. *Compute* $\mathbf{C}\vec{r}$.
5. *If* $\mathbf{A}(\mathbf{B}\vec{r}) \neq \mathbf{C}\vec{r}$, *then return:* $\mathbf{A} \cdot \mathbf{B} \neq \mathbf{C}$. *Otherwise, return* $\mathbf{A} \cdot \mathbf{B} = \mathbf{C}$.

Question: How many multiplications are needed by Freivalds' algorithm?

Answer: Each of steps 2, 3, and 4 only involve multiplication of a matrix by a vector, and hence use only $\Theta(n^2)$ multiplications.

Question: If Freivalds' algorithm returns $\mathbf{A} \cdot \mathbf{B} \neq \mathbf{C}$, is it correct?

Answer: Yes. Suppose, by contradiction, that $\mathbf{A} \cdot \mathbf{B} = \mathbf{C}$. Then, $\forall \vec{r}$, it must be the case that $\mathbf{A} \cdot \mathbf{B} \cdot \vec{r} = \mathbf{C} \cdot \vec{r}$.

Definition 22.2 *When* $\mathbf{A} \cdot \mathbf{B} \neq \mathbf{C}$, *and* $\vec{r}$ *is a vector such that*

$$\mathbf{A} \cdot \mathbf{B} \cdot \vec{r} \neq \mathbf{C} \cdot \vec{r},$$

then we say that $\vec{r}$ *is a* **witness** *to the fact that* $\mathbf{A} \cdot \mathbf{B} \neq \mathbf{C}$, *because it provides us with a proof that* $\mathbf{A} \cdot \mathbf{B} \neq \mathbf{C}$.

Thus the only time that Freivalds' algorithm might be wrong is if it returns $\mathbf{A} \cdot \mathbf{B} = \mathbf{C}$, even though $\mathbf{A} \cdot \mathbf{B} \neq \mathbf{C}$. This is referred to as **one-sided error**. Theorem 22.3 shows that the probability of this type of mistake is $\leq \frac{1}{2}$, given that $\vec{r}$ is chosen at random.

Theorem 22.3 (Freivalds error) *Let* $\mathbf{A}$, $\mathbf{B}$, *and* $\mathbf{C}$ *denote* $n \times n$ *matrices, where* $\mathbf{A} \cdot \mathbf{B} \neq \mathbf{C}$, *and let* $\vec{r}$ *be a vector chosen uniformly at random from* $\{0, 1\}^n$. *Then,*

$$P\{\mathbf{A} \cdot \mathbf{B} \cdot \vec{r} = \mathbf{C} \cdot \vec{r}\} \leq \frac{1}{2}.$$

Proof: [Theorem 22.3] Since $\mathbf{A} \cdot \mathbf{B} \neq \mathbf{C}$, we know that

$$\mathbf{D} \equiv \mathbf{AB} - \mathbf{C} \neq \mathbf{O},$$

where $\mathbf{O}$ is an $n \times n$ matrix of all zeros.

Now suppose that $\vec{r}$ is a vector such that

$$\mathbf{D}\vec{r} = \mathbf{AB}\vec{r} - \mathbf{C}\vec{r} = \vec{0},$$

as shown here:

$$
\begin{bmatrix}
d_{11} & d_{12} & d_{13} & \cdots & d_{1n} \\
d_{21} & d_{22} & d_{23} & \cdots & d_{2n} \\
d_{31} & d_{32} & d_{33} & \cdots & d_{3n} \\
\vdots & \vdots & \vdots & \vdots & \vdots \\
d_{n1} & d_{n2} & d_{n3} & \cdots & d_{nn}
\end{bmatrix}
\cdot
\begin{bmatrix}
r_1 \\ r_2 \\ r_3 \\ \vdots \\ r_n
\end{bmatrix}
=
\begin{bmatrix}
0 \\ 0 \\ 0 \\ \vdots \\ 0
\end{bmatrix}.
$$

Since $\mathbf{D} \neq \mathbf{O}$, we know that $\mathbf{D}$ must have at least one non-zero entry. For notational convenience, we will assume that this non-zero entry is d_{11} (you will see that this assumption is made without loss of generality).

Since $\mathbf{D}\vec{r} = \vec{0}$, we know that the product of the first row of $\mathbf{D}$ and $\vec{r}$ yields 0, that is,

$$\sum_{j=1}^{n} d_{1j} \cdot r_j = 0.$$

But this implies that

$$d_{11}r_1 + \sum_{j=2}^{n} d_{1j}r_j = 0$$

$$\Rightarrow r_1 = -\frac{\sum_{j=2}^{n} d_{1j}r_j}{d_{11}}. \tag{22.1}$$

Recall that $d_{11} \neq 0$ so the denominator of (22.1) is non-zero.

Question: Does (22.1) imply that r_1 is negative?

Answer: No, d_{1j} may be negative.

Now suppose that when choosing the random vector $\vec{r}$, we choose $r_2, \ldots, r_n$ *before* choosing r_1. Consider the moment just after we have chosen $r_2, \ldots, r_n$. At this moment the right-hand side of (22.1) is determined. Thus there is *exactly one choice* for r_1 (call this r_1^*) that will make (22.1) true.

Question: We now flip a 0/1 coin to determine r_1. What is $\mathbf{P}\left\{r_1 = r_1^*\right\}$?

Answer: There are two possible values for r_1 (namely 0 or 1). They can't both be equal to r_1^*. Thus, $\mathbf{P}\left\{r_1 = r_1^*\right\} \leq \frac{1}{2}$. Note this is not an equality because r_1^* can be any element of the Reals and thus is not necessarily $\in \{0, 1\}$. ∎

At this point we have proven that Freivalds' algorithm can check matrix multiplication in $\Theta(n^2)$ time with accuracy of at least $\frac{1}{2}$.

Question: How can we improve the accuracy?

Hint: Repeat Freivalds' algorithm with additional random vectors, $\vec{r} \in \{0, 1\}^n$.

Answer: Suppose we run Freivalds' algorithm using k randomly chosen $\vec{r}$ vectors. If for any vector $\vec{r}$ we see that $\mathbf{A}\,(\mathbf{B}\vec{r}) \neq \mathbf{C}\vec{r}$, then we output $\mathbf{A} \cdot \mathbf{B} \neq \mathbf{C}$; otherwise we output $\mathbf{A} \cdot \mathbf{B} = \mathbf{C}$. If in fact $\mathbf{A} \cdot \mathbf{B} = \mathbf{C}$, then all k runs will output "equal," and we will have the correct answer at the end. If $\mathbf{A} \cdot \mathbf{B} \neq \mathbf{C}$, then each run has independent probability $\geq \frac{1}{2}$ of discovering ("witnessing") this fact. Thus the probability that it is not discovered that $\mathbf{A} \cdot \mathbf{B} \neq \mathbf{C}$ is $\leq \frac{1}{2^k}$. The k runs require a total runtime of $\Theta(kn^2)$. If we make $k = 100$, yielding an extremely low probability of error, our overall runtime for using the Vassilevska implementation is still $\Theta(n^{2.37} + 100n^2) = \Theta(n^{2.37})$.

Question: Is it a problem if some of the random vectors $\vec{r}$ repeat? Does this change our confidence in the final answer?

Answer: This is not a problem. All that's needed is that the vectors are picked independently. Each time we pick a random $\vec{r}$, that choice will independently have probability $\geq \frac{1}{2}$ of being a witness.

Question: Suppose that the error in Freivalds' algorithm was not one-sided, but rather two-sided? Would we still be able to use this scheme?

Answer: The exact scheme we're using assumes one-sided error. However, we could use a related scheme in the case of two-sided error, where we take the "majority" output of several runs.

Question: Can we improve our confidence by choosing $\vec{r} \in \{0, 1, 2\}^n$?

Answer: Yes, this drops the probability of error to $\frac{1}{3}$ for each Freivalds check because, again, there is exactly one value of r_1^* that allows us to mess up, and our chance of now hitting that value is $\leq \frac{1}{3}$.

22.2 Randomized Polynomial Checking

We now apply a very similar idea to the question of multiplication of monomials over some real-valued variable x. Suppose we have a program that purports to multiply together monomials. For example, our program might take as input a string of three monomials:

$$(x - 3), \ (x - 5), \ (x + 7)$$

and output the third degree polynomial:

$$G(x) = x^3 - x^2 - 41x + 105.$$

Again, we'd like a way of *checking* the output of this multiplication program very quickly, in much less time than the runtime of the program. Here "runtime" refers to the number of multiplications.

Throughout, let's define $F(x)$ to be the (true) product of the monomials, that is,

$$F(x) \equiv (x - 3)(x - 5)(x + 7),$$

whereas $G(x)$ represents the output of our untrusted program. The goal of the checker is to determine whether $G(x)$ is equal to the product $(x-3)(x-5)(x+7)$ without computing $F(x)$.

Question: How many multiplications are needed to multiply d monomials?

Answer: $O(d^2)$. See Exercise 22.3.

We will now present a randomized checker that determines with high certainty whether our untrusted program is correct using only $\Theta(d)$ multiplications. As before, we start with a simple checker that makes mistakes, and then we improve the checker to lower its probability of mistakes.

Algorithm 22.4 (Simple Checker for multiplication of d monomials)

1. *Pick an integer, r, uniformly at random between 1 and 100d.*
2. *Evaluate $F(r)$. Evaluate $G(r)$.*
3. *If $F(r) = G(r)$, then output that the program is correct.
   Otherwise, output that it is incorrect.*

Question: What is the runtime of our Simple Checker?

Answer: $\Theta(d)$. Once you replace x by r, there are only d multiplications needed.

Question: Under what condition is the Simple Checker wrong?

Answer: If $F(x) = G(x)$, then the Simple Checker will always be correct. If $F(x) \neq G(x)$, then the Simple Checker might make an error if it only picks r values for which $F(r) = G(r)$. Again, this is a situation of **one-sided error**.

Question: So what is the probability that the Simple Checker is wrong?

Hint: If $F(x) \neq G(x)$, and each are polynomials of degree d, what is the maximum number of values of x on which they can nonetheless agree?

Answer: Assume that $F(x) \neq G(x)$. Let $H(x) = F(x) - G(x)$. $H(x)$ is at most a d-degree polynomial. As such, it has at most d roots (assuming $H(x) \neq 0$). Hence, there are at most d possible values of r, s.t. $H(r) = 0$. Equivalently, there are at most d possible values of r on which $F(x)$ and $G(x)$ agree. If we now limit the range of r from 1 to $100d$, then there are still at most d values of r for which $F(r) = G(r)$. Hence, the probability that we have found such an r is at most $\frac{d}{100d} = \frac{1}{100}$.

So our Simple Checker accurately tells us whether our program is correct with probability $\frac{99}{100}$ in only $\Theta(d)$ time.

Question: Suppose we'd like to know that our program is correct with probability $\frac{999,999}{1,000,000}$? How can we modify our Simple Checker to get this higher guarantee?

Answer: One idea is to pick our random r from a bigger range. For example, we can use a range from 1 to $10^6 d$. However, this may not be feasible for large d.

Answer: A better idea is to repeat our Simple Checker with different values of r. This will give higher accuracy, but require more time.

Algorithm 22.5 (Superior Checker)

1. *Repeat the Simple Checker k times, each time with some r drawn uniformly at random from the set of integers in $[1, 100d]$.*
2. *If $F(r) = G(r)$ for all k values of r, then output that the program is correct. Otherwise, output that the program is wrong.*

Question: What is the probability that the Superior Checker is wrong?

Answer: The Superior Checker only fails if $F(x) \neq G(x)$ and yet $F(r) = G(r)$ for all k values of r. But each time we draw a random r, that r has probability

$\geq \frac{99}{100}$ of resulting in inequality. So the probability that all k values of r result in equality is $\leq \frac{1}{100^k}$. With just $k = 3$, we already have our $\frac{999,999}{1,000,000}$ confidence.

Observe that the runtime of the Superior Checker is only $\Theta(kd)$.

22.3 Randomized Min-Cut

Throughout this section, we assume that we have an undirected graph $G = (V, E)$ with $|V| = n$ vertices and $|E| = m$ edges.

> **Definition 22.6** *A* **cut-set** *of a graph* $G = (V, E)$ *is a set of edges whose removal breaks the graph into two of more connected components.*

> **Definition 22.7** *A* **min-cut** *is a minimum cardinality cut set.*

The **Min-cut Problem** is the problem of finding a **min-cut**. Observe that there may be several minimum cardinality cut sets possible – we just want one of them. The Min-Cut problem has many applications, mostly dealing with reliability. For example, what is the minimum number of links that can fail before the network becomes disconnected?

We will now present a randomized algorithm for finding a min-cut that is both faster and simpler than any deterministic algorithm. Our algorithm is based on the idea of "contracting edges" until a cut-set results.

> **Definition 22.8** *The* **contraction of an edge** (v_1, v_2) *involves merging vertices* v_1 *and* v_2 *into a single vertex, v. Any edge* (v_1, v_2) *is removed. All edges that had an endpoint at either v_1 or v_2 (but not both) will now have an endpoint at the contracted vertex, v. Observe that the new graph may have parallel edges, but no self-loops.*

> **Algorithm 22.9 (Randomized Min-Cut algorithm)**
>
> 1. *Given a graph, G, repeat until only two vertices, u and v, remain:*
>   i. *Pick a random edge from all existing edges in the graph.*
>   ii. *Contract that edge.*
> 2. *Output the set of edges connecting u and v.*

Question: How many iterations are needed by the Randomized Min-Cut algorithm?

Answer: $n - 2$.

Figure 22.1 shows one example of Randomized Min-Cut that results in a min-cut and another that doesn't. In the example that works, the cut that is output should be interpreted as the two edges between vertex 5 and other vertices in the graph (looking at the original graph, we see that vertex 5 is only connected to vertices 3 and 4). In the example that doesn't work, the cut that is output should be interpreted as the three edges between vertex 2 and the other vertices in the graph (note that vertex 2 is only connected to vertices 1, 3, and 4 in the original graph).

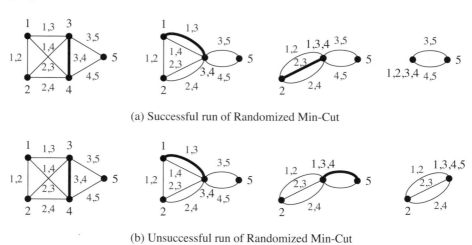

(a) Successful run of Randomized Min-Cut

(b) Unsuccessful run of Randomized Min-Cut

Figure 22.1 *Example of two runs of Randomized Min-Cut. The bold edge is the one about to be contracted.*

Question: Let $G = (V, E)$ refer to the original graph. Which, if any, of the following statements is true?

(a) Any cut-set of an intermediate graph is also a cut-set of G.
(b) Any cut-set of G is also a cut-set of every intermediate graph.

Answer: The first statement is true. Let C be a cut-set in an intermediate graph that separates vertices in S from those in $V - S$. All edges in C are edges from the original graph, $G = (V, E)$. Now suppose that there were additional edges between S and $V - S$ in the original graph, $G = (V, E)$. This couldn't happen because as soon as one of those was contracted away, then S and $V - S$ couldn't be separated. So C still forms a cut-set in G. The second statement is clearly false, as seen in Figure 22.1. The issue is that some edges of the cut-set of the original graph may have been contracted away.

So the output of Randomized Min-Cut is always a true cut-set of the original graph, but not necessarily a minimally sized cut-set.

We now state one more property of Randomized Min-Cut that will be useful in its analysis.

Lemma 22.10 *Let C be a cut-set of graph $G = (V, E)$. Let k be the cardinality of C. Suppose we run Randomized Min-Cut for the full $n - 2$ iterations. Then,*

C is output by Min-Cut $\Longleftrightarrow$ None of the k edges of C are contracted.

Proof:
($\Longrightarrow$) This direction is obvious in that C cannot be output if any of its edges are contracted.

($\Longleftarrow$) This direction is much less clear. For one thing, could it be that the cut that is output includes C *plus* some additional edge? For another thing, could it be that the cut that is output is *missing* some edge, $\vec{e}$, of C, because $\vec{e}$ got removed when a *parallel edge* to $\vec{e}$ got contracted?

We now address both issues. Suppose that C splits the graph into two components, called A and $\overline{A}$, as shown in Figure 22.2. Let E denote all edges in G. Let E_A, and $E_{\overline{A}}$ denote the set of edges in A, and $\overline{A}$, respectively. Hence $E = C \cup E_A \cup E_{\overline{A}}$.

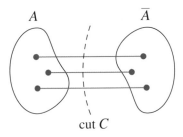

cut C

Figure 22.2 *By definition of C being a cut, we must have $E = E_C \cup E_A \cup E_{\overline{A}}$.*

Since cut C already splits graph G into A and $\overline{A}$, by definition there cannot be any "additional edges" beyond C that have one endpoint in A and one in $\overline{A}$. Thus it can't be the case that the final cut that is output includes C plus some additional edges. Likewise, since all edges outside of C must be in either A or $\overline{A}$, then contracting an edge outside of set C cannot result in some edge of C getting removed. ∎

Theorem 22.11 *The Randomized Min-Cut algorithm produces a min-cut with probability $\geq \frac{2}{n(n-1)}$.*

Proof: Let C be one of the min-cuts in the original graph, $G = (V, E)$. Let the cardinality of C be k. We will show that with probability $\geq \frac{2}{n(n-1)}$, C will be output by our algorithm.

By Lemma 22.10, the probability that C is output at the end of our algorithm is the probability that none of the k edges of C is contracted during the $n - 2$ iterations of the Randomized Min-Cut algorithm. To figure out this probability, it helps to first derive the number of edges in G.

Question: What is the minimum degree of vertices in G?

Answer: The minimum degree is k, because if some vertex had degree $< k$ then those edges would form a smaller cut-set.

Question: What is a lower bound on the number of edges in G?

Answer: G has at least $\frac{nk}{2}$ edges, from which edges are selected uniformly at random for contraction.

$$\mathbf{P}\{\text{no edge of } C \text{ is selected in the 1st round}\} \geq \frac{\frac{nk}{2} - k}{\frac{nk}{2}} = \frac{nk - 2k}{nk} = \frac{n-2}{n}.$$

Question: Why did we need a $\geq$ sign above?

Answer: Recall that $\frac{nk}{2}$ is a *lower bound* on the number of edges.

Suppose that after the first round, we did not eliminate an edge of C. We are left with a graph on $n - 1$ vertices. The graph still has a min-cut of C.

Question: Why does the graph still have a min-cut of C?

Answer: Any cut-set of the contracted graph is also a cut-set of the original graph. So if the graph has a min-cut smaller than $|C|$, then the original graph must have a cut-set smaller than $|C|$, which is a contradiction.

Since the contracted graph still has a cut-set of C, the graph must have $\geq \frac{k(n-1)}{2}$ edges. Given this lower bound on the number of edges, we have:

$$\mathbf{P}\{\text{no edge of } C \text{ is selected in the 2nd round} \mid \text{no edge selected in 1st round}\}$$
$$\geq \frac{\frac{(n-1)k}{2} - k}{\frac{(n-1)k}{2}} = \frac{(n-1)k - 2k}{(n-1)k} = \frac{n-3}{n-1}.$$

Generalizing, let E_i be the event that no edge of C is selected in the ith round. We want the probability that all of the first $n - 2$ events happen. By Theorem 2.10,

$$\mathbf{P}\{E_1 \cap E_2 \cap \cdots \cap E_{n-2}\} = \mathbf{P}\{E_1\} \cdot \mathbf{P}\{E_2 \mid E_1\} \cdots \mathbf{P}\{E_{n-2} \mid \cap_{i=1}^{n-1} E_i\}.$$

We have already shown that:

$$P\{E_1\} \geq \frac{n-2}{n} \quad \text{and} \quad P\{E_2 \mid E_1\} \geq \frac{n-3}{n-1}.$$

Via the same argument, we can see that:

$$P\{E_3 \mid E_1 \cap E_2\} \geq \frac{n-4}{n-2},$$

and so on. Hence we have:

$$
\begin{aligned}
&P\{\text{No edge of } C \text{ is ever contracted}\} \\
&= P\{E_1 \cap E_2 \cap \cdots \cap E_{n-2}\} \\
&= P\{E_1\} \cdot P\{E_2 \mid E_1\} \cdot P\{E_3 \mid E_1 \cap E_2\} \cdots P\{E_{n-2} \mid \cap_{i=1}^{n-3} E_i\} \\
&\geq \frac{n-2}{n} \cdot \frac{n-3}{n-1} \cdot \frac{n-4}{n-2} \cdot \frac{n-5}{n-3} \cdots \frac{3}{5} \cdot \frac{2}{4} \cdot \frac{1}{3} \\
&= \frac{\cancel{n-2}}{n} \cdot \frac{\cancel{n-3}}{n-1} \cdot \frac{\cancel{n-4}}{\cancel{n-2}} \cdot \frac{\cancel{n-5}}{\cancel{n-3}} \cdots \frac{\cancel{3}}{\cancel{5}} \cdot \frac{2}{\cancel{4}} \cdot \frac{1}{\cancel{3}} \\
&= \frac{2}{n(n-1)}. \qquad \blacksquare
\end{aligned}
$$

Observe that our algorithm has a high probability, $1 - \frac{2}{n(n-1)}$, of returning a cut-set that is *not* a min-cut.

Question: What can we do to reduce the probability that our algorithm is wrong?

Answer: We should run our algorithm many times and return the smallest cut-set produced by all those runs.

Claim 22.12 *If we run Randomized Min-Cut* $\Theta(n^2 \ln n)$ *times, and report the smallest cardinality cut-set returned, then with probability* $> 1 - \frac{1}{n^2}$ *our reported cut-set is a min-cut.*

Proof: The probability that our output is not a min-cut is upper-bounded by

$$
\begin{aligned}
\left(1 - \frac{2}{n(n-1)}\right)^{n^2 \ln n} &\leq \left(1 - \frac{2}{n(n-1)}\right)^{n(n-1) \ln n} \\
&= \left[\left(1 - \frac{2}{n(n-1)}\right)^{n(n-1)}\right]^{\ln n} \\
&< \left[e^{-2}\right]^{\ln n} \\
&= \frac{1}{n^2},
\end{aligned}
$$

where we've used the fact that $1 - x < e^{-x}$, for $0 < x < 1$, by (1.14). $\blacksquare$

Thus the total runtime of Randomized Min-Cut involves $\Theta(n^3 \ln n)$ contractions, which is still a very good runtime. Randomized Min-Cut also excels in its simplicity. There is of course some (tiny) possibility of error. However, here this error is not fatal in that the algorithm always gives a cut-set.

22.4 Related Readings

The Randomized Min-Cut algorithm is due to David Karger [42] and is famous for its simplicity. Since then many algorithms have been proposed with improved runtimes; see, for example, the Karger–Stein algorithm [43], which improves the runtime to $O(n^2 (\log n)^3)$ time.

22.5 Exercises

22.1 **From Las Vegas to Monte Carlo and back**
In this problem, you will show how to take a Las Vegas randomized algorithm and make it into a Monte Carlo algorithm, and vice-versa.
(a) Given a Las Vegas algorithm, A_{LV}, that solves a problem P in *expected* time t, describe a Monte Carlo algorithm for problem P that runs in time *at most* $50t$ and outputs the correct answer with probability at least 98%.
(b) Can you do the reverse? Suppose you have a Monte Carlo algorithm, A_{MC}, that runs in time *at most* t_{MC} and gives the correct answer with probability p. Suppose that there's a verification routine, V, that tells us with perfect accuracy whether A_{MC} is correct in time t_V. Can you use this to design a Las Vegas algorithm, A_{LV}? If so, what is the expected runtime of A_{LV}?

22.2 **Freivalds error**
In the proof of Theorem 22.3, we defined a matrix $\mathbf{D} \neq \mathbf{O}$, and stated without loss of generality that $d_{11} \neq 0$. Suppose that instead $d_{22} \neq 0$. Rewrite the proof of Theorem 22.3 to show that it holds here as well.

22.3 **Multiplication of monomials**
Let a "monomial in x" be an expression of the form $(x-c)$, where c is some constant. Prove that the number of multiplications needed to multiply d monomials in x is $O(d^2)$. Note that the problem is not saying that d^2 multiplications suffice. You might need $10d^2$ multiplications. You'll need to figure out the appropriate multiplier for d^2. [Hint: Use induction.]

22.4 **Randomized polynomial checking with knowledge**
Let $F(x) \equiv (x - c_1)(x - c_2)(x - c_3) \cdots (x - c_d)$ be the true product of d monomials. Let $G(x)$ be a degree d polynomial which is claimed to equal $F(x)$. Recall the Simple Randomized Checker from Algorithm 22.4. Now suppose you know a priori that the coefficients in $G(x)$ for $x^d, x^{d-1}, x^{d-2}, \ldots, x^{d/2+1}$ are all correct (say, someone else has checked those for you). Assume that d is even. Provide an upper bound on the probability of error of the Simple Randomized Checker.

22.5 **Randomized Max-3SAT**
You have a bunch of variables: $W, X, Y, Z, \ldots$ Each variable is allowed to be either 0 or 1. The term $\overline{X}$ denotes the negation of X. A *clause* is the OR of three *distinct* variables. For example: $(X \text{ or } Y \text{ or } \overline{Z})$. A clause is *satisfied* if it evaluates to 1. For example, under the assignment: $X = 1$, $Y = 0$, $Z = 0$, $(X \text{ or } Y \text{ or } \overline{Z})$ evaluates to 1, and hence is satisfied. A *3SAT expression* is the AND of a bunch of clauses: For example:

$$(X \text{ or } Y \text{ or } \overline{Z}) \text{ AND } (W \text{ or } \overline{X} \text{ or } \overline{Z}) \text{ AND } (Y \text{ or } \overline{X} \text{ or } Z).$$

The goal of Max-3SAT is to find an assignment of the variables that *maximizes* the number of satisfied clauses. For example, if we set $W = X = Y = Z = 1$ in the above 3SAT expression, then all three clauses will be satisfied. Max-3SAT is known to be NP-Hard.
(a) Propose a very simple Monte Carlo randomized algorithm for Max-3SAT. Let N denote the number of clauses satisfied by your algorithm. Show that $\mathbf{E}[N] = \frac{7}{8}m$, where m is the number of clauses.
(b) Prove that $\mathbf{P}\left\{N \leq \frac{3m}{4}\right\} \leq \frac{1}{2}$. [Hint: The Markov, Chebyshev, and Chernoff bounds won't work here. Look for a different inequality from Chapter 18 that goes in the right direction.]
(c) Let δ be an arbitrary small constant, $0 < \delta \ll 1$. How can we revise our algorithm to ensure that $\mathbf{P}\left\{N \leq \frac{3m}{4}\right\} \leq \delta$? [Hint: Your runtime will be a function of δ.]

22.6 **From Monte Carlo to Las Vegas**
[Proposed by David Wajc] Let $\mathcal{P}$ be a decision problem. Imagine that one has two Monte Carlo algorithms for deciding $\mathcal{P}$: Algorithm A is true-biased in that it always returns "true" when the answer is "true," but returns "true" with probability $p > 0$ when the answer is false (that is, it has false positives). Algorithm B is false-biased in that it always returns "false" when the answer is "false," but returns "false" with probability p when the answer is true (that is, it has false negatives). Suppose that the two Monte Carlo algorithms terminate in time n^c on inputs of size n (here c is a constant). Your goal is to create a Las Vegas algorithm, $\mathcal{L}$, whose expected runtime is polynomial. What is your Las Vegas algorithm, $\mathcal{L}$, and what is its expected runtime?

22.7 **Approximating π**

In this exercise, you will devise and analyze a Monte Carlo randomized algorithm to approximate π.

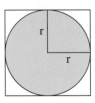

Figure 22.3 *For Exercise 22.7. A circle of radius r embedded within a square.*

(a) Suppose that you throw n darts uniformly at random within the square of Figure 22.3. Let X denote the number of darts which land within the circle. How is X distributed?

(b) Define a random variable Z (related to X) where Z is your "estimator of π." Prove that $\mathbf{E}[Z] = \pi$.

(c) We want to say that, with probability $1 - \epsilon$, Z is within δ of π. How high should n be to ensure this? Assume $0 < \delta \ll 1$ and $0 < \epsilon \ll 1$.

22.8 **Number of min-cuts**

For any graph G, with n vertices and m edges, let $S_1, S_2, \ldots, S_k$ denote the min-cuts of G. We want to prove an upper bound on the value of k.

(a) Let A_i denote the event that S_i is output by the Randomized Min-Cut algorithm. We proved a lower bound on $\mathbf{P}\{A_i\}$. What was that?

(b) Now consider the event: $[A_1 \cup A_2 \cup \cdots \cup A_k]$. By definition $\mathbf{P}\{A_1 \cup A_2 \cup \cdots \cup A_k\} \leq 1$. Use what you learned in part (a) to prove an upper bound on k.

22.9 **Randomized Max-Cut**

You are given a graph $G = (V, E)$ with n vertices and m edges. You want to divide the vertices into two disjoint sets, X and $\overline{X}$, where $X \cup \overline{X} = V$, so as to *maximize* the number of edges between X and $\overline{X}$. Rather than trying all ways of splitting V into two sets, you use this algorithm:

Algorithm 22.13 (Randomized Max-Cut algorithm)
Input: $G = (V, E)$.
Output: Disjoint sets, X and $\overline{X}$, where $X \cup \overline{X} = V$.

For each vertex $x \in V$, flip a fair coin:
  If heads, put x into set X.
  If tails, put x into set $\overline{X}$.

(a) What is the probability that a given edge $e = (x, y) \in E$ is in the cut-set? What is the expected size of the cut-set produced?

(b) Let

$$Y_e = \begin{cases} 1 & \text{if edge } e \text{ is in the cut-set} \\ 0 & \text{otherwise} \end{cases}.$$

Which of the following are true (may be more than one)?
   (i) The Y_e's are independent.
   (ii) The Y_e's pair-wise independent.
   (iii) The Y_e's are three-wise independent.
   (iv) None of the above.
   For anything you claimed to be true, provide a proof. For anything you claimed to be false, provide a counter-example.
(c) Use Chebyshev's inequality to show that with high probability, $\left(\geq 1 - O\left(\frac{1}{m}\right) \right)$, the size of the cut-set exceeds $m/4$.
(d) Why couldn't we use Chernoff bounds in part (c)?

22.10 Amplification of confidence (boosting)
We are given a Monte Carlo algorithm, $\mathcal{M}$, which always runs in some fixed time t. Given an input, $\mathcal{M}$ returns the correct answer for that input with probability $\frac{2}{3}$ (assume that there is a unique correct answer for each input). With probability $\frac{1}{3}$, $\mathcal{M}$ makes up a value and returns that. Note that the made-up value might be different each time. You do not know whether the output of $\mathcal{M}$ is correct or not.
(a) Given $\epsilon > 0$, explain how to create a new randomized algorithm, $\mathcal{N}$, which outputs the correct answer with probability at least $1 - \epsilon$.
(b) What is the explicit runtime of $\mathcal{N}$ (in terms of t)?

22.11 BogoSort
I have an array A of length n containing distinct integers $a_1, a_2, \ldots, a_n$ in a random order. I decide to sort these using a stupid randomized algorithm:

> **Algorithm 22.14 (BogoSort($a_1, a_2, \ldots, a_n$))**
>
> 1. *Check if $a_1, a_2, \ldots, a_n$ are sorted. If so, return the sorted array.*
> 2. *Randomly permute $a_1, a_2, \ldots, a_n$. Then return to step 1.*

Determine the expected number of comparisons needed for BogoSort:
(a) Let C be the number of comparisons needed for line 1 (the check step). What is $\mathbf{E}[C]$? For large n, can you approximate this within 1?
(b) What is the expected number of iterations needed in BogoSort?
(c) What is the expected total number of comparisons needed for BogoSort? (Note: Step 2 doesn't need comparisons.)

22.12 Monte Carlo control groups
In running an experiment, it is often useful to have two "equal" sets of people, where we run the experiment on one set, and the other set is used

as a control group. However, dividing people into two "equal" sets is non-trivial. Consider the example shown in the table below: We have m men who are rated on a 0/1 scale in terms of n features. We would like to divide the m men into two groups so that each group is approximately equal with respect to each feature.

	Looks	Brains	Personality
Mike	1	1	0
Alan	0	0	1
Richard	1	0	1
Bill	1	1	0

(a) Intuitively, which grouping is better in terms of creating balance between the groups across each feature:
   (i) Group 1: Alan with Richard   Group 2: Mike with Bill
   (ii) Group 1: Mike with Alan   Group 2: Richard with Bill
(b) Mathematically, we express the above table by an $m \times n$ matrix $\mathbf{A}$, where

$$\mathbf{A} = \begin{bmatrix} 1 & 1 & 0 \\ 0 & 0 & 1 \\ 1 & 0 & 1 \\ 1 & 1 & 0 \end{bmatrix}.$$

Consider an m-dimensional row vector $\vec{b} = (b_1, b_2, \ldots, b_m)$, where $b_i \in \{1, -1\}$. Let

$$\vec{b} \cdot \mathbf{A} = \vec{c}.$$

Here, the 1's in $\vec{b}$ indicate the men in group 1 and the -1's in $\vec{b}$ indicate the men in group 2. Observe that $\vec{c}$ is an n-dimensional row vector, where c_i indicates the total score for group 1 on feature i minus the total score for group 2 on feature i. Using the above notation, we rephrase our problem as: How can we find a $\vec{b}$ which minimizes $\max_j |c_j|$? Suppose we choose $\vec{b}$ randomly: we set $b_i = 1$ with probability $\frac{1}{2}$ and set $b_i = -1$ with probability $\frac{1}{2}$. Prove

$$\mathbf{P}\left\{ \max_j |c_j| \geq \sqrt{4m \ln n} \right\} \leq \frac{2}{n}.$$

[Hint 1: Start by deriving $\mathbf{P}\left\{ |c_j| \geq \sqrt{4m \ln n} \right\}$.]
[Hint 2: You will want to use the result in Exercise 18.15.]
[Hint 3: Don't worry about the fact that c_j might have fewer than m summands. Your bound for the case of m summands will still work.]

22.13 **Fixed-length path**

Given a graph G with n vertices, you want to decide whether there exists a path in G containing ℓ *distinct* vertices. The naive brute force algorithm has runtime $O(n^\ell)$. Consider instead this Monte Carlo algorithm:

1. Label each vertex independently and uniformly at random from $\{1, \ldots, \ell\}$.
2. Using breadth-first search (or something similar), check if there is a path $(v_1, \ldots, v_\ell)$ such that for all $1 \leq i \leq \ell$, v_i has label i. If yes, return true. Otherwise return false.

You may assume that this Monte Carlo algorithm runs in time $O(n^2)$.

(a) Show that this algorithm has a one-sided error of at most $1 - \frac{1}{\ell^\ell}$.

(b) How can we lower the error probability to $\frac{1}{n}$? What is the runtime of your new algorithm? [Hint: Recall from (1.12) that $1 + x \leq e^x$, $\forall x \geq 0$.]

22.14 **Generating a random permutation**

We are given an array A containing distinct integers $a_1, a_2, \ldots a_n$. We want to perfectly shuffle the array. That is, every one of the $n!$ permutations should be equally likely to be the result of our shuffle. Below are two potential algorithms. For each algorithm either prove that it results in a perfect shuffle, or provide a counter-example. [Hints: Induction is useful in proofs. Counter-examples shouldn't need more than three integers.]

Algorithm 22.15 (Shuffle attempt 1)

for $i = n, n - 1, \ldots, 2$ **do**
    $j = $ *random integer with* $1 \leq j \leq i$
    exchange $A[j]$ *and* $A[i]$
return A

Algorithm 22.16 (Shuffle attempt 2)

for $i = n, n - 1, \ldots, 2$ **do**
    $j = $ *random integer with* $1 \leq j \leq n$
    exchange $A[j]$ *and* $A[i]$
return A

22.15 **Approximate median**

In Chapter 21 we saw how to find the exact median of an unsorted list, $L = \{a_1, a_2, \ldots, a_n\}$ of n elements in expected $O(n)$ comparisons using the Median-Select algorithm. Now we present an algorithm to find an "ϵ-approximation of the median" in only expected $O\left(\frac{\log n}{\epsilon^2}\right)$ comparisons. Specifically, if $L' = \{s_1, s_2, \ldots, s_n\}$ denotes a sorted version of L, where $s_{(n+1)/2}$ is the exact median (assume n is odd), then our algorithm returns an element of L' in the sublist $S = \{s_{low}, \ldots, s_{high}\}$, where $low = (\frac{1}{2} - \epsilon)n$ and $high = (\frac{1}{2} + \epsilon)n$. See Figure 22.4. For simplicity, assume that low, $high$, and $(n+1)/2$ are all integers.

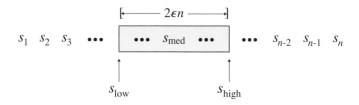

Figure 22.4 *For Exercise 22.15. The approximate median is anything in the box.*

Our approximate-median algorithm works as follows: We select a random element from L t times (the same element might get picked more than once). Let M denote the set of the chosen t elements. Now perform Median-Select on M and return its median, m, as our approximate-median (assume t is odd). You will need to find a t that is sufficiently high for our approximate-median, m, to be within the sublist $S = \{s_{low}, \ldots, s_{high}\}$ with high probability.

22.16 **Knockout tournament**

In a knockout tournament, the goal is to determine the "best" of n sports teams. Teams are paired against each other according to the tree structure shown in Figure 22.5. Each *round* starts with some number of "remaining teams." These remaining teams are paired up according to the tree structure. Each pair of teams (A,B) plays k games, where the team with the majority of the wins (say, A), moves up to the next round, and the other team (B) is dropped. Assume ties are impossible and k is odd. Assume also that $n = 2^m$ for some positive integer m. In Figure 22.5, we see that the number of teams starts at $n = 8$, but after one round we're down to four remaining teams, and after the second round, we're down to two teams, and so on.

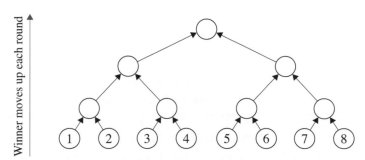

Figure 22.5 *Illustration of knockout tournament with $n = 8$ teams and $m = 3$ rounds.*

Assume that there is a "best" team, b, such that if b is paired against any team j, b will beat j with probability $\geq \frac{1}{2} + \epsilon$, where $0 < \epsilon \leq \frac{1}{2}$. Prove that when $k \geq \frac{4m}{\epsilon^2}$, team b wins the tournament with high probability $(1 - \frac{1}{n})$.
[Hint 1: It will be convenient to use the result from Exercise 18.21(b).]
[Hint 2: The following fact will simplify the algebra: Let N be an integer random variable and k be odd. Then $\mathbf{P}\{N \leq \frac{k-1}{2}\} = \mathbf{P}\{N \leq \frac{k}{2}\}$.]
[Hint 3: You will want to show that the probability that team b loses a single round is upper-bounded by e^{-2m}.]
There is a rich literature on applying Chernoff bounds to tournament design (e.g., [1, 2, 78]). This problem is based on [2].

22.17 Adding n-bit numbers – average-case analysis
Mor is implementing a bitwise adder to add two *random* n-bit binary numbers $a_1 a_2 \ldots a_n$ and $b_1 b_2 \ldots b_n$ for her operating system. She notices that the conventional adder needs to traverse all n bits of the two numbers from the lowest bit to the highest bit, propagating carry-ins when necessary (when we add a 1 to a 1, we need to carry-in a 1 to the next highest bit). To add faster, Mor constructs the following Near Adder whose work can be parallelized: instead of adding all n-bits sequentially, the Near Adder divides them into $\frac{n}{d}$ segments of size d-bits each. The Near Adder then uses the conventional adder to add consecutive overlapping $2d$-bit "blocks" in *parallel*, as shown in Figure 22.6, where the carry-in to each block is assumed to be 0. Thus the runtime of the Near Adder is $O(2d)$ rather than $O(n)$.
Observe that every (blue) $2d$-bit block (other than the rightmost one) has a shaded (pink) part for the least-significant d bits, and an unshaded part for the most-significant d bits. The Near Adder returns only the most significant d bits (the unshaded part) of each block as the sum of the two n-bit numbers. Notice that the $2d$-bit blocks purposely overlap. Only the most significant d bits of each $2d$-bit computation are returned, because they are likely to be uncorrupted. The pink parts are likely wrong because of the assumed 0 carry-in.
(a) Does the Near Adder always output the correct final sum? If not, when does it fail?
(b) Define a **propagate pair** to be a pair of bits (a_i, b_i) such that either $a_i = 1$ and $b_i = 0$, or $a_i = 0$ and $b_i = 1$. Prove Claim 22.17:

> **Claim 22.17** *The Near Adder is incorrect if and only if the true carry-in to a $2d$-bit block is 1 and all the lower d pairs of bits in that block are propagate pairs.*

(c) Say we want the Near Adder to output the correct sum with probability $1 - \epsilon$. How large should we pick d to be? Does picking a large d increase or decrease our accuracy? Here are some steps to follow:

     (i) First prove that the probability that the carry-in bit to a $2d$-bit block is 1 is strictly less than $\frac{1}{2}$.

    (ii) Now use step (i) to derive an upper bound on the probability that an arbitrary $2d$-bit block causes an error. Use Claim 22.17.

   (iii) Apply a union bound over all blocks to determine the probability of error of the Near Adder as a function of d and n.

   (iv) What value of d suffices to ensure that the Near Adder provides the correct answer with probability $> 1 - \epsilon$?

    (v) Does picking a larger d decrease or increase the error?

(d) (Optional!) Peter wants an Adder which is 100% accurate. Mor proposes that Peter can build upon her Near Adder to achieve 100% accuracy with low *expected* runtime. Propose an algorithm that could achieve this. You do not have to provide details or analysis, just a general idea.

This problem is based on a collaboration between Peter and Mor in [31].

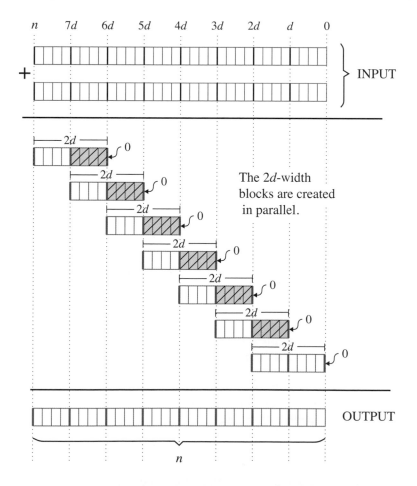

Figure 22.6 *Picture of Near Adder from [31].*

23 Primality Testing

One of the most important problems in the field of computer science is a math problem as well: *How can we determine if an integer n is prime?*

This chapter is devoted to primality testing. Primality testing has applications in many fields, including cryptography (see, for example, the RSA [61] algorithm), hash function design, pseudo-random number generation, and many others.

23.1 Naive Algorithms

Question: Think for a minute on how you might try to determine if n is prime or composite.

Answer: Back in grade school, you might have approached this question by considering every integer $k \in S = \{2, 3, 4, \ldots, n - 1\}$ and asking whether k divides n, written $k \mid n$.

> **Definition 23.1** *If we find some $k \in S = \{2, 3, 4, \ldots, n - 1\}$ such that $k \mid n$, then we say that k is a **witness** to the fact that n is composite. To be specific, we will say that k is a **divisor witness** to n being composite.*

You might improve upon this method by only considering divisors up to $\lfloor \sqrt{n} \rfloor$, that is, $S = \{2, 3, 4, \ldots, \lfloor \sqrt{n} \rfloor\}$. You can improve further by eliminating all multiples of 2 in S, other than 2, and then removing all multiples of 3 in S, other than 3, and so on. This process of removing all multiples of every prime in sequence is known as the Sieve of Eratosthenes.

Question: Suppose we've winnowed down the set S of potential divisors of n to just those primes which are smaller than n. It seems our test set should now be small. How big is our test set?

Answer: It turns out that the number of primes less than n is $\Theta\left(\frac{n}{\ln n}\right)$. This result is known as the Prime Number Theorem (see [24, 68]). Thus, even the winnowed down set S still has size which grows quickly with n.

Our goal in this chapter is to find a constant-time Monte Carlo style test to determine, with high probability, whether n is prime.

Importantly, this high probability of correctness should apply equally well to every n.

Question: For example, what's wrong with an algorithm that checks only if n is divisible by 2, 3, and 5, returning "probably prime" if none of those are divisors?

Answer: There is a significant fraction of composite numbers whose compositeness would never be detected by the above test. We want *every* n to have a high probability of correctly being evaluated, where the probability of error is exponentially decreasing in the number of random trials.

In Sections 23.2 and 23.3 we introduce the Fermat Primality Test. This test has the advantage of being very simple. Unfortunately, there is a *tiny* fraction of composite numbers, known as Carmichael numbers, for which the Fermat test will almost always return "prime." Thus the Fermat Primality Test is not a true test for primality.

In Section 23.4 we introduce a more complex test, called the Miller–Rabin test. The Miller–Rabin test works for all numbers, including Carmichael numbers. The Miller–Rabin test builds upon the Fermat test, so it's worth going through the sections in order. The Miller–Rabin test is the most practical and most widely used primality testing algorithm. It appears in software libraries for encryption schemes, such as RSA.

23.2 Fermat's Little Theorem

We normally think of a prime number as a whole number, greater than 1, whose only positive divisors are 1 and itself. The Fermat test is based on Fermat's Little Theorem, which provides an alternative characterization of prime numbers.

Theorem 23.2 (Fermat's Little Theorem) *The number n is prime if and only if*

$$a^{n-1} \equiv 1 \bmod n$$

for every integer $a \in S = \{1, 2, 3, \ldots, n-1\}$.

We will prove Theorem 23.2 later in this section. For now, observe that Theorem 23.2 says two things:

- If n is **prime**, then $a^{n-1} \equiv 1 \bmod n$, for every $a \in S$.
- If n is **composite**, then $a^{n-1} \not\equiv 1 \bmod n$, for at least one $a \in S$.

Definition 23.3 *Suppose n is composite. Consider*

$$T = \{a : a < n \text{ and } a^{n-1} \not\equiv 1 \bmod n\}.$$

The elements of T are called **Fermat witnesses** *to the fact that n is composite.*

Question: We have talked about two different types of witnesses to n being composite: divisor witnesses and Fermat witnesses. For a given composite n, are there more Fermat witnesses, or divisor witnesses?

Answer: It turns out that there are typically way more Fermat witnesses than divisor witnesses, which makes it much easier to find a Fermat witness. In fact, every divisor witness is also a Fermat witness.

For example, consider $n = 15$. The divisor witnesses of n's compositeness are 3 and 5. However, the set of Fermat witnesses is $\{2, 3, 5, 6, 7, 8, 9, 10, 12, 13\}$.

Theorem 23.4 *For every composite number n, every divisor witness of n is also a Fermat witness.*

Proof: Let $d > 1$ be a divisor of n. We'll show that d is a Fermat witness for n.

Suppose by contradiction that

$$d^{n-1} \equiv 1 \bmod n.$$

This means that there's some integer q such that

$$d^{n-1} = qn + 1. \tag{23.1}$$

But (23.1) can't be true because d divides the first term and the second term (since d divides n), but not the third term. Hence we have a contradiction. ∎

Before we can prove Fermat's Little Theorem (Theorem 23.2), we need one quick fun fact about prime numbers.

> **Lemma 23.5 (Fun fact about primes)** *If $p > 2$ is prime, then $\forall$ integers a, b,*
>
> $$(a + b)^p \equiv a^p + b^p \bmod p$$
> $$(a - b)^p \equiv a^p - b^p \bmod p.$$

Proof: If we write out the binomial expansion of $(a + b)^p$, it will be the case that every term in the expansion, other than the first or last term, is divisible by p. To see this, consider an arbitrary term in the expansion, say one with coefficient

$$\binom{p}{k} = \frac{p(p - 1)(p - 2) \cdots (p - k + 1)}{k(k - 1)(k - 2) \cdots 1}.$$

Observe that there is a factor p in the numerator, which is prime and thus not canceled by any terms in the denominator. Hence this term equals $0 \bmod p$. The case of $(a - b)^p$ is similar, but requires that p is odd. ∎

We are now ready to prove Fermat's Little Theorem (Theorem 23.2).

Proof: [Theorem 23.2] Suppose n is composite. We need to show that there's at least one integer $a < n$ such that $a^{n-1} \not\equiv 1 \bmod n$. This is easy: We know that n has some divisor, d. But then, by Theorem 23.4, we know that d is also a Fermat witness. Thus $d^{n-1} \not\equiv 1 \bmod n$.

Suppose now that n is prime. If $n = 2$, Fermat's Little Theorem holds trivially. So assume $n > 2$. Let's define set W to be the following set of integers:

$$W = \{x : x^n \equiv x \bmod n\}.$$

Question: Is the integer 1 contained in W?

Answer: Yes.

Question: Once we know that 1 is in W, what does the Fun Fact tell us about 2?

Answer: 2 is also in W.

In fact, the Fun Fact tells us that the set W is closed under addition and subtraction. To see this, observe that if $a, b \in W$, then $(a + b)^p \equiv a^p + b^p \equiv a + b \bmod p$, so $a + b \in W$ as well. The argument is similar for $a - b$.

So W contains all integers!

Now consider any integer $x \in S = \{1, 2, 3, \ldots n - 1\}$, where n is a prime. We will use the fact that any such $x \in S$ is also in W to show that x has the property that $x^{n-1} \equiv 1 \bmod n$.

First observe that since $x \in W$, we know that n divides $x^n - x$, so

$$n \mid x\left(x^{n-1} - 1\right). \tag{23.2}$$

But since $x < n$, we also know that x is not divisible by n. So, since n is prime, and it doesn't divide the first term in (23.2), it must divide the second term, $x^{n-1} - 1$. Thus,

$$x^{n-1} - 1 \equiv 0 \bmod n$$

and we're done.   ∎

Let's define one more type of witness for compositeness:

Definition 23.6 *Given a composite number n, let $a \in \{1, 2, \dots n - 1\}$ have the property that $\gcd(a, n) > 1$. Then we say that a is a **gcd witness** of n's compositeness.*

Theorem 23.4 can be made more general, as shown in Theorem 23.7.

Theorem 23.7 *For every composite number n, every divisor witness of n's compositeness is also a gcd witness, and every gcd witness is also a Fermat witness.*

Proof: See Exercise 23.1.   ∎

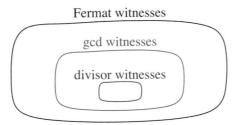

Figure 23.1 *Illustration of Theorem 23.7.*

Again, what's important is that while the number of divisor witnesses and gcd witnesses is very small, the number of Fermat witnesses is typically very high, making them easy to find. As another typical example, consider $n = 415,693$. There are only two divisor witnesses of n, namely 593 and 701. While there are more gcd witnesses, the proportion of gcd witnesses is still less than 1% (most numbers are relatively prime to n). By contrast, the proportion of Fermat witnesses is over 99%.

23.3 Fermat Primality Test

The Fermat Primality Test is motivated by the fact that there are typically so many Fermat witnesses. Given an integer n, the test considers a random number less than n and checks whether that number is a Fermat witness.

Algorithm 23.8 (Fermat Primality Test)
We are given an integer n which we wish to classify as prime or composite. Repeat the following for k rounds:

1. *Choose $a \in S = \{1, 2, 3, \ldots, n - 1\}$ uniformly at random.*
2. *If $a^{n-1} \not\equiv 1 \bmod n$, return COMPOSITE and stop.*

If we haven't stopped after k rounds, then return PROBABLY PRIME.

The Fermat Primality Test has **one-sided error**. If the test returns "composite" then n is provably composite (since a Fermat witness of compositeness was found). On the other hand, if the test returns "probably prime" then n might be prime, or we might simply have gotten unlucky and not found a Fermat witness.

So *mistakes* happen when n is composite but a Fermat witness is not found. What is the probability of a *mistake*?

We know, by Theorem 23.4, that every composite number, n, has at least two Fermat witness (the divisors of n are Fermat witnesses). To understand the probability of a mistake, we need to understand:

> *Given that n is composite, how many Fermat witnesses does n have?*

Question: Suppose that we could say that for every composite number n, at least half the $a \in S = \{1, 2, 3, \ldots, n - 1\}$ are Fermat witnesses. What would be the accuracy of the Fermat Primality Test?

Answer: In the case where n is composite, the Fermat Primality Test would return "composite" with probability at least $1 - 2^{-k}$. Note that there's never any error in the case where n is prime.

Unfortunately, while the proportion of Fermat witnesses is typically very high, it is not always true that at least half the $a \in S$ are Fermat witnesses. Here is what we do know: Consider the set $\mathcal{F}$ of Fermat witnesses of some composite number n, as shown in Figure 23.2. By Theorem 23.7, all gcd witnesses of n are automatically included in $\mathcal{F}$; we refer to these gcd witnesses as **trivial Fermat witnesses**. Unfortunately, there are typically very few gcd witnesses, and thus very few trivial Fermat witnesses. Suppose now that there is a **non-trivial Fermat**

witness for n, that is, some $a \in \{1, 2, \ldots, n-1\}$ where a is relatively prime to n and is a Fermat witness. Theorem 23.9 tells us that as soon as there is a single *non-trivial* Fermat witness, then we know that the total proportion of Fermat witness is at least half.

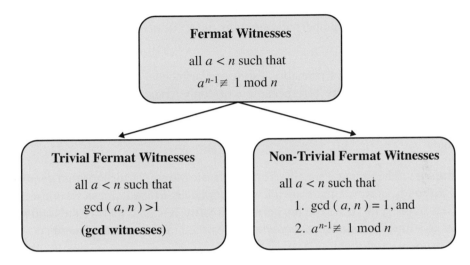

Figure 23.2 *Two types of Fermat witnesses for composite number n.*

Theorem 23.9 *For composite number n, suppose that there is at least one a in $S = \{1, 2, 3, \ldots, n-1\}$ such that a is a Fermat witness for n and $\gcd(a, n) = 1$. Then at least half the elements of S are Fermat witnesses for n.*

Proof: We defer the proof to Section 23.6.   ∎

So it seems that if there's even just *one* non-trivial Fermat witness for n, then it follows that there are plenty of Fermat witnesses for n. Unfortunately, there exists a very small set of composite numbers for which there are *zero* non-trivial Fermat witnesses. These numbers are called Carmichael numbers.

Definition 23.10 *A* **Carmichael number** *is a composite integer n such that,* $\forall a \in S = \{1, 2, 3, \ldots, n-1\}$:

$$\text{if } \gcd(a, n) = 1, \quad \text{then} \quad a^{n-1} \equiv 1 \bmod n.$$

Because this holds for all a, the Carmichael numbers have zero non-trivial Fermat witnesses.

The Carmichael numbers are named after Robert Carmichael [12, 13]. The first few numbers are:

$$561 \qquad 1105 \qquad 1729$$

Carmichael numbers are still a topic of current study by number theorists. The Carmichael numbers have several interesting properties (see [30]). They are odd, each having at least three distinct prime factors. They are square free (not divisible by the square of any prime), and for every Carmichael number n with prime factor p, it holds that $p - 1$ divides $n - 1$. In 1994 it was proved that, although Carmichael numbers are very rare, there are an infinite number of them [3].

From the perspective of primality testing, a Carmichael number, n, is likely to fail the Fermat Primality Test, because n has only trivial Fermat witnesses, and the number of trivial witnesses is small compared to n, so it is unlikely that we'll find a Fermat witness to n's compositeness, even when the test is run for many rounds.

Summary: The Fermat Primality Test is a classic Monte Carlo algorithm, requiring k rounds, however, there are a few integers n for which it doesn't work well. Given an integer n, if we run the Fermat Primality Test on n for k rounds and no Fermat witness is found, then *either n is one of the rare Carmichael numbers, or* n is prime with probability $\geq 1 - 2^{-k}$.

23.4 Miller–Rabin Primality Test

Unlike the Fermat Primality Test, the Miller–Rabin Primality Test works on every number n. Like the Fermat Primality Test, the Miller–Rabin test always returns "prime" if n is prime. For every composite n (including Carmichael numbers), it returns "composite" with probability $> \frac{3}{4}$ in each round. Thus with probability $> 1 - 4^{-k}$ a composite number will be witnessed in k rounds.

23.4.1 A New Witness of Compositeness

The Miller–Rabin test is based on using a new witness of compositeness. We've seen that finding a divisor witness proves n is composite. We've also seen that finding a Fermat witness proves that n is composite. A third way to prove that n is composite is to find a non-trivial square root of 1 mod n. The idea is based on the following theorem.

> **Theorem 23.11** *If p is prime, then all integer roots of*
> $$x^2 \equiv 1 \bmod p$$
> *satisfy $x \equiv 1 \bmod p$ or $x \equiv -1 \bmod p$.*

Proof:

$$x^2 \equiv 1 \bmod p \implies p \mid \left(x^2 - 1\right)$$
$$\implies p \mid (x - 1)(x + 1).$$

Hence, since p is prime, either $p \mid (x - 1)$ or $p \mid (x + 1)$ or both.[1] But this says that either $x - 1 \equiv 0 \bmod p$ or $x + 1 \equiv 0 \bmod p$, or both.

This says that the only possible roots are $x \equiv 1 \bmod p$ and $x \equiv -1 \bmod p$. To complete the proof, we note that both these potential roots in fact satisfy the equation $x^2 \equiv 1 \bmod p$. ∎

Corollary 23.12 *Given integers n and x, such that $x^2 \equiv 1 \bmod n$. If $x \not\equiv \pm 1 \bmod n$, then n must be composite.*

Suppose that

$$x^2 \equiv 1 \bmod n. \tag{23.3}$$

We say that $x \equiv \pm 1 \bmod n$ are *trivial* roots of (23.3). By contrast, if $x \not\equiv \pm 1 \bmod n$ satisfies (23.3), then we say that x is a *non-trivial* root of (23.3).

Definition 23.13 *Given a composite number n, we say that x is a **root witness of n's compositeness** if $x^2 \equiv 1 \bmod n$ and $x \not\equiv \pm 1 \bmod n$. A root witness is by definition a **non-trivial root**.*

23.4.2 Logic Behind the Miller–Rabin Test

The Miller–Rabin Primality Test is unintuitive when you hear it, so, rather than just stating it, we will develop it ourselves from scratch. The test attempts to determine that n is composite by looking for one of *two different types of witnesses*, either a Fermat witness *or* a root witness. It is thus much more powerful than the Fermat Primality Test.

We assume $n > 2$, and choose a randomly from $S = \{1, 2, \ldots, n - 1\}$. We also assume that n is odd, because if n is even we immediately output "composite."

---

[1] This follows from the Unique Prime Factorization Theorem (UPFT). UPFT states that every integer $n > 1$ can be written as a unique product of primes:

$$n = p_1^{c_1} \cdot p_2^{c_2} \cdots p_k^{c_k},$$

where the p_i's are distinct primes and the c_i's are non-negative integers. From UPFT, it follows that if $p \mid ab$, then either $p \mid a$ or $p \mid b$, since either a or b (or both) must contain p in its unique factorization.

Given that n is odd, we will consider $n - 1$, which must be even.

Since $n - 1$ is even, it contains at least one factor of 2. Let's peel off all the factors of 2 in $n - 1$. We are left with

$$n - 1 = 2^r \cdot d, \tag{23.4}$$

where $r > 0$ is the number of factors of 2 in $n - 1$, and d is by definition odd.

The Fermat test tells us that if

$$a^{n-1} \not\equiv 1 \bmod n, \tag{23.5}$$

then a is a Fermat witness of compositeness. By contrast if $a^{n-1} \equiv 1 \bmod n$, then we haven't learned anything, that is, n might still be prime.

We can rewrite (23.5) in terms of r and d, via (23.4), to say that if

$$a^{2^r \cdot d} \not\equiv 1 \bmod n,$$

then we have a Fermat witness of compositeness, so we return "composite" and we're done.

Now suppose instead that:

$$a^{2^r \cdot d} \equiv 1 \bmod n. \tag{23.6}$$

Question: We haven't found a Fermat witness, but is there a test that we can do to look for a root witness?

Hint: Think about (23.6) as a square equation. What is its root?

Answer: Let's rewrite (23.6) as follows:

$$\left(a^{2^{r-1} \cdot d}\right)^2 \equiv 1 \bmod n. \tag{23.7}$$

Now we can ask whether (23.7) has a non-trivial root.

If

$$a^{2^{r-1} \cdot d} \not\equiv \{1, -1\} \bmod n,$$

then we have found a root witness of compositeness, so we return "composite" and we're again done.

Now suppose instead that:

$$a^{2^{r-1} \cdot d} \equiv \{1, -1\} \bmod n.$$

Question: Do we get another chance to try to find a root witness?

Answer: If

$$a^{2^{r-1} \cdot d} \equiv -1 \bmod n, \tag{23.8}$$

there's nothing we can do. In this case we're done testing. Given that we haven't found any witness, we should return "probably prime," and we're done. However, if

$$a^{2^{r-1} \cdot d} \equiv 1 \bmod n, \tag{23.9}$$

and $r - 1 > 0$, then we do in fact get *another chance* to find a root witness of compositeness.

Question: Back in (23.8) we said that if $a^{2^{r-1} \cdot d} \equiv -1 \bmod n$, then we're done. How do we not know that some lower exponent (some future square root) won't give us another opportunity to find a non-trivial square root of 1?

Answer: To witness a non-trivial square root of 1, we need to again experience an equation of the form $x^2 \equiv 1 \bmod n$, where x is some lower power of a obtained by taking future square roots. However, this can't happen. Observe that once we see that some power of a is equivalent to 1 mod n, then all future squares will also be congruent to 1 mod n. So given that $a^{2^{r-1} \cdot d} \equiv -1 \bmod n$, it is impossible that some future square root will be congruent to 1 mod n.

23.4.3 Miller–Rabin Primality Test

Algorithm 23.14 shows a version of the Miller–Rabin algorithm based on our arguments in Section 23.4.2. For simplicity, this is shown for only a *single round*, that is, a single choice of $a \in \{1, 2, \ldots, n - 1\}$. In practice, Algorithm 23.14 would be repeated with k different randomly chosen a values. Only if no witness is found in all k iterations do we return a final "probably prime." Otherwise we return "composite."

Algorithm 23.14 (Miller–Rabin Primality Test: Single Round – Take 1)
Given: Integer $n > 2$, where n is odd:

1. *Express $n - 1 = 2^r \cdot d$ for some odd d.*
2. *Choose $a \in \{1, 2, \ldots, n - 1\}$ uniformly at random.*
3. *If $a^{2^r \cdot d} \bmod n \not\equiv 1$, return COMPOSITE-Fermat, and stop.*
4. *For $y = r - 1$ to $y = 0$:*
   - *If $a^{2^y \cdot d} \bmod n \not\equiv \{1, -1\}$, return COMPOSITE-Root, and stop.*
   - *If $a^{2^y \cdot d} \bmod n \equiv -1$, return PROBABLY PRIME, and stop.*
   - *(If we get here then we know that $a^{2^y \cdot d} \bmod n \equiv 1$, so we have another chance to find a non-trivial root, assuming $y > 0$.)*
5. *Return PROBABLY PRIME.*

While Algorithm 23.14 is entirely correct, it is more computationally expensive than needed, because it requires first computing $a^{2^r \cdot d}$. This is achieved by starting with a^d and then repeatedly squaring that quantity r times. It is possible to restate Algorithm 23.14 where we compute only those powers of a that are needed. Algorithm 23.15 shows the more efficient version.

Algorithm 23.15 (Miller–Rabin Primality Test: Single Round – Take 2)
Given: Integer n > 2, where n is odd:

1. *Express $n - 1 = 2^r \cdot d$ for some odd d.*
2. *Choose $a \in \{1, 2, \ldots, n - 1\}$ uniformly at random.*
3. *Let $y = 0$.*
   - *If $a^{2^y \cdot d}$ mod $n \equiv 1$, return PROBABLY PRIME, and stop.*
     (Notice all future squares will be 1, so there will be no root witnesses. When we reach $y = r$, the Fermat test will also output probably prime.)
   - *If $a^{2^y \cdot d}$ mod $n \equiv -1$, return PROBABLY PRIME, and stop.*
     (Notice that all future squares will be 1 so there will be no root witnesses. When we reach $y = r$, the Fermat test will also output probably prime.)
   - *(If we get here then we still have hope of returning COMPOSITE-Root, if $a^{2^1 \cdot d}$ mod $n \equiv 1$.)*
4. *For $y = 1$ to $y = r - 1$:*
   - *If $a^{2^y \cdot d}$ mod $n \equiv 1$, return COMPOSITE-Root, and stop.*
   - *If $a^{2^y \cdot d}$ mod $n \equiv -1$, return PROBABLY PRIME, and stop.*
     (Notice that all future squares will be 1, so there will be no root witnesses and the Fermat test will return 1 when $y = r$.)
   - *(If we get here then we have the potential for witnessing a root witness if the next round yields a 1.)*
5. *Return COMPOSITE.*

Observe that Algorithm 23.15 will often stop before having to compute all the powers of a.

Question: Why in Algorithm 23.15 did we only go up to $y = r - 1$. Don't we need to check $y = r$ as well? Also, why does the algorithm end by returning "composite"?

Answer: Suppose that we haven't stopped after $y = r - 1$. Then it must be the case that $a^{2^{r-1} \cdot d} \not\equiv \{1, -1\}$ mod n. Now, if $a^{2^r \cdot d} \equiv 1$ mod n we have a root witness, so we should return COMPOSITE-Root. If, on the other hand, $a^{2^r \cdot d} \not\equiv 1$ mod n, then we have a Fermat witness and should return COMPOSITE-Fermat. Either way, n is provably composite, so there is no need to check the result of the rth power.

What's shown in Algorithm 23.15 is a single round of the Miller–Rabin Primality

Test. In reality this test is run for k rounds (k instances of a), where the test stops if any round finds a witness of compositeness. If no witness of compositeness is found after k rounds, then the test outputs "probably prime."

As in the case of the Fermat Primality Test, if n is prime, then the Miller–Rabin Primality Test will always output "prime." It can be proven that if n is composite, the Miller–Rabin Primality Test will output composite on a randomly chosen a with probability $> \frac{3}{4}$, for every composite n. This result is due to Michael Rabin and is non-trivial to prove; see [57]. We have chosen to omit the proof because the focus of this book is not on number theory.

Question: If the Miller–Rabin Primality Test is run for k rounds on a composite n, what is the probability that a witness of compositeness is found?

Answer: $> 1 - \left(\frac{1}{4}\right)^k$.

Summary: Recall that the Fermat Primality Test failed on certain composite numbers, the Carmichael numbers, for which very few Fermat witnesses exist. By including a test for a root witnesses, in addition to Fermat witnesses, the Miller–Rabin test improves the probability of witnessing any composite n (including the case where n is Carmichael) all the way to $\frac{3}{4}$. This probability can then be improved with independent runs. Like the Fermat test, the Miller–Rabin test always outputs the correct result when n is prime. Thus there are no numbers on which the Miller–Rabin Primality Test fails to yield a correct result with high probability.

23.5 Readings

For the reader who is interested in reading more on primality testing, with complete proofs, we recommend [30]. In particular, [30, proposition 5.8] provides a proof for why the Miller–Rabin Primality Test is able to detect the compositeness of Carmichael numbers. The proof makes use of some of the unique properties of Carmichael numbers, mentioned earlier.

23.6 Appendix: Proof of Theorem 23.9

Restatement of Theorem 23.9: Let n be composite. Let $S = \{1, 2, \ldots, n-1\}$. Suppose that there exists at least one $a \in S$ such that a is a Fermat witness for n

and $\gcd(a, n) = 1$. Then at least half the elements of S are Fermat witnesses for n.

Proof: [Theorem 23.9] We partition the set S into four disjoint subsets: A, B, C, and D, where

$$A = \{a \in S \text{ such that } a^{n-1} \equiv 1 \bmod n \quad \text{and} \quad \gcd(a, n) = 1\}$$
$$B = \{b \in S \text{ such that } b^{n-1} \not\equiv 1 \bmod n \quad \text{and} \quad \gcd(b, n) = 1\}$$
$$C = \{c \in S \text{ such that } c^{n-1} \not\equiv 1 \bmod n \quad \text{and} \quad \gcd(c, n) > 1\}$$
$$D = \{d \in S \text{ such that } d^{n-1} \equiv 1 \bmod n \quad \text{and} \quad \gcd(d, n) > 1\}.$$

Question: We claim set D is empty. Why is this?

Answer: To see why, suppose integer $k = \gcd(d, n) > 1$. Now suppose also that

$$d^{n-1} \equiv 1 \bmod n.$$

Then, there is some integer q such that

$$d^{n-1} - 1 = q \cdot n.$$

But this is impossible because k divides the term d^{n-1} and also divides the qn term, but k does not divide -1.

Question: Which set is the trivial Fermat witnesses?

Answer: C.

Question: What does set B represent?

Answer: Set B is the non-trivial Fermat witnesses. We're trying to show there are lots of these.

Question: Do we know that sets A, B, and C are all non-empty?

Answer: Yes. Set A must at least contain the number 1. The theorem statement tells us that there is at least one element in B. Set C is non-empty because n is composite.

Restating the theorem statement in terms of these sets, we are trying to show that

$$\text{Given } \exists b \in B, \quad \text{then} \quad |B \cup C| \geq \frac{1}{2}|S|.$$

Let's assume, by contradiction, that $|B \cup C| < \frac{1}{2}|S|$. Then $|A| > \frac{1}{2}|S|$.

We will refer to the elements of A as $\{a_1, a_2, \ldots, a_k\}$, where $k > \frac{1}{2}|S|$.

Now let's take our $b \in B$ and multiply it by all the elements in A, creating the set Ab, which we define as follows:

$$Ab = \{a_1 b \bmod n, \quad a_2 b \bmod n, \quad \ldots, \quad a_k b \bmod n\}.$$

We will now show two properties of the set Ab:

1. $Ab \subset B$.

   To see this, note that every element $j \in Ab$ obeys the three properties needed to be in B. Specifically, if we assume without loss of generality that $j = a_i b \bmod n$, then we have that:
   i. $j^{n-1} \not\equiv 1 \bmod n$.
      (This follows because: $j^{n-1} \equiv (a_i b)^{n-1} \equiv a_i^{n-1} \cdot b^{n-1} \equiv 1 \cdot b^{n-1} \not\equiv 1 \bmod n$.)
   ii. $\gcd(j, n) = 1$
      (This follows because $\gcd(a_i, n) = 1$ and $\gcd(b, n) = 1$, so $\gcd(a_i b, n) = 1$.)
   iii. $j \in S$.
      (By definition j is an integer from 0 to $n - 1$. Furthermore, since $\gcd(j, n) = 1$, we known that $j \not\equiv 0 \bmod n$.)

2. The elements of Ab are distinct.

   To see this, suppose by contradiction that

   $$a_i b \bmod n = a_j b \bmod n, \quad \text{where} \quad a_i \neq a_j.$$

   Then $(a_i - a_j) b \equiv 0 \bmod n$. So $n | (a_i - a_j) b$. But $\gcd(n, b) = 1$, so it must be the case that

   $$n | (a_i - a_j). \tag{23.10}$$

   But $a_i < n$ and $a_j < n$ implies that $-n < a_i - a_j < n$, so (23.10) is false, yielding the contradiction.

Properties 1 and 2 together imply that there are at least k elements in B where $k > \frac{1}{2}|S|$. But this is a contradiction. ∎

23.7 Exercises

23.1 **Witnesses of compositeness**

Let n be a composite number. Prove that every divisor witness for n is also a gcd witness. Prove that every gcd witness is also a Fermat witness.

23.2 **Fermat test error**

Suppose that $n < 561$, and we are trying to determine whether n is prime or composite. Upper bound the probability of error in the k-round Fermat Primality Test.

23.3 Number theory reduction
Prove the following lemma that applies to many statements in this chapter:
Let a, b, c, n be positive integers.
If $ab \equiv ac \bmod n$ and $\gcd(a, n) = 1$,   then $b \equiv c \bmod n$.

23.4 Miller–Rabin
In the Miller–Rabin algorithm, we are given a number $n > 2$, where n is odd. We express $n - 1$ in the form:

$$n - 1 = 2^r \cdot d.$$

We then pick a random $a \in \{1, 2, 3, \ldots, n - 1\}$.
Suppose that we know that $a^{2^{r-1} \cdot d} \not\equiv 1 \bmod n$ and $a^{2^{r-1} \cdot d} \not\equiv -1 \bmod n$.
What does this tell us about n? Choose one answer and explain.
(a) n is prime.
(b) n is composite.
(c) n is composite type Fermat witness.
(d) n is composite type Root witness.
(e) There is insufficient information to deduce any of these.

23.5 Generating a random prime number
How can we generate a random prime of value smaller than n with probability larger than $1 - \epsilon$? Consider the following algorithm:

Algorithm 23.16 (Random prime)

1. *Choose an integer r from $\{1, 2, \ldots, n - 1\}$ uniformly at random.*
2. *Run the Miller–Rabin test on r for k runs.*
   - *If the test outputs "probably prime" for all k runs, output r as the generated prime and stop.*
   - *If the test outputs "composite" (of any type) in any of the k runs, go back to Step 1.*

In Algorithm 23.16 we say that we are starting a new *"round"* every time we call Step 1. Assume throughout that n is large.
(a) Find an approximate value for k such that the algorithm succeeds with probability larger than $1 - \epsilon$.
(b) Explain why Algorithm 23.16 is not a Las Vegas algorithm.
(c) Explain why Algorithm 23.16 is not a typical Monte Carlo algorithm.
(d) Analyze the expected number of rounds of Algorithm 23.16.

Part VIII

Discrete-Time Markov Chains

This final part of the book is devoted to the topic of Markov chains. Markov chains are an extremely powerful tool used to model problems in computer science, statistics, physics, biology, and business – you name it! They are used extensively in AI/machine learning, computer science theory, and in all areas of computer system modeling (analysis of networking protocols, memory management protocols, server performance, capacity provisioning, disk protocols, etc.). Markov chains are also very common in operations research, including supply chain, call center, and inventory management.

Our goal in discussing Markov chains is two-fold. On the one hand, as always, we are interested in applications and particularly applications to computing. On the other hand, Markov chains are a core area of probability theory and thus we have chosen to cover the theory of Markov chains in some depth here.

In Chapter 24, we introduce finite-state Markov chains, limiting distributions, and stationary distributions.

In Chapter 25, we delve into the theory of finite-state Markov chains, discussing whether the limiting distribution exists and whether the stationary distribution is unique. We also introduce time reversibility, time averages, and mean passage times. A more elementary class might choose to skip this chapter, but it is my experience that undergraduates are fully capable of understanding this material if they proceed slowly and focus on examples to help illustrate the concepts.

In Chapter 26, we turn to infinite-state Markov chains. These are great for modeling the number of packets queued at a router, or the number of jobs at a data center. Although we skip the hardest proofs here, there is still a lot of intuition to be gained just in understanding definitions like transient and positive-recurrent.

All these chapters are full of examples of the application of Markov chains for modeling and solving problems. However, it is the final chapter, Chapter 27 on queueing theory, which really ties it all together. Through queueing theory, we see a real-world application of all the abstract concepts introduced in the Markov chain chapters.

24 Discrete-Time Markov Chains: Finite-State

This chapter begins our study of Markov chains, specifically discrete-time Markov chains. In this chapter and the next, we limit our discussion to Markov chains with a finite number of states. Our focus in this chapter will be on understanding how to obtain the limiting distribution for a Markov chain.

Markov chains come up in almost every field. As we study Markov chains, be on the lookout for Markov chains in your own work and the world around you. They are everywhere!

24.1 Our First Discrete-Time Markov Chain

Love is complicated. Figure 24.1 depicts the day-by-day relationship status of CMU students.

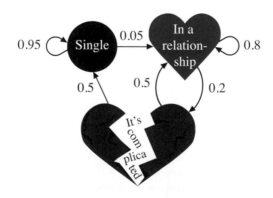

Figure 24.1 *The states of love, according to Facebook.*

There are three possible states for the relationship status. We assume that the relationship status can change only at the end of each day, according to the probabilities shown. For example, if we're "single" today, with probability 0.95 we will still be single tomorrow. When entering the "relationship" state, we stay there on average for five days (note the Geometric distribution), after which we move into the "it's complicated" state. From the "it's complicated" state, we're equally likely to return to the single state or the relationship state.

For such a Markov chain, we will ask questions like: *What fraction of time does one spend in the "relationship" state, as opposed to the "single" state?*

24.2 Formal Definition of a DTMC

Definition 24.1 *A discrete-time Markov chain (DTMC) is a stochastic process* $\{X_n, n = 0, 1, 2, \ldots\}$, *where* X_n *denotes the state at (discrete) time step* n *and such that* $\forall n \geq 0$, $\forall i, j$, *and* $\forall i_0, \ldots, i_{n-1} \in \mathbb{Z}$,

$$\mathbf{P}\left\{X_{n+1} = j \mid X_n = i, X_{n-1} = i_{n-1}, \ldots, X_0 = i_0\right\}$$
$$= \mathbf{P}\left\{X_{n+1} = j \mid X_n = i\right\} \quad \text{(Markovian property)}$$
$$= P_{ij} \quad \text{(stationary property)},$$

where P_{ij} *is independent of the time step and of past history.*

Let's try to understand this definition line-by-line.

Question: First, what is a "stochastic process"?

Answer: A **stochastic process** is simply a sequence of random variables. In the case of Markov chain, this is a sequence of the states at each time step.

Question: What is being stated in the equality in marked "Markovian property" in the definition?

Answer: In a nutshell, past states don't matter. Only the current state matters.

Definition 24.2 *The* **Markovian property** *states that the conditional distribution of any future state* X_{n+1}, *given past states* $X_0, X_1, \ldots, X_{n-1}$, *and the present state* X_n, *is independent of past states and depends only on the present state* X_n.

Question: What is being stated in the equality marked "stationary property" in the definition?

Answer: The **stationary property** indicates that the transition probability, P_{ij}, is independent of the time step, n.

> **Definition 24.3** *The* **transition probability matrix** *associated with any DTMC is a matrix,* **P**, *whose* (i, j)*th entry,* P_{ij}, *represents the probability of moving to state j on the next transition, given that the current state is i.*

Observe that, by definition, $\sum_j P_{ij} = 1$, $\forall i$, because, given that the DTMC is in state i, it must next transition to some state j.

Finite state versus infinite state: This chapter and the next will focus on DTMCs with a finite number of states, M. In Chapter 26, we will generalize to DTMCs with an infinite (but still countable) number of states.

DTMCs versus CTMCs: In a DTMC, the state can only change at synchronized (discrete) time steps. This book focuses on DTMCs. In a continuous-time Markov chain (CTMC) the state can change at any moment of time. CTMCs are outside the scope of this book, but we refer the interested reader to [35].

Ergodicity issues: In working with Markov chains, we will often be trying to understand the "limiting probability" of being in one state as opposed to another (limiting probabilities will be defined very soon). In this chapter, we will *not* dwell on the question of whether such limiting probabilities exist (called *ergodicity* issues). Instead we simply assume that there exists some limiting probability of being in each state of the chain. We defer all discussion of ergodicity to Chapter 25.

The three Ms: Solving Markov chains typically requires solving large systems of simultaneous equations. We therefore recommend taking the time to familiarize yourself with tools like Matlab [52], Mathematica [80], or Maple [50].

24.3 Examples of Finite-State DTMCs

We start with a few examples of simple Markov chains to illustrate the key concepts.

24.3.1 Repair Facility Problem

A machine is either working or is in the repair center. If it is working today, then there is a 95% chance that it will be working tomorrow. If it is in the repair center today, then there is a 40% chance that it will be working tomorrow. We are interested in questions like, "What fraction of time does my machine spend in the repair shop?"

Question: Describe the DTMC for the repair facility problem.

Answer: There are two states, "Working" and "Broken," where "Broken" denotes that the machine is in repair. The transition probability matrix is

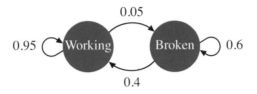

$$\mathbf{P} = \begin{array}{c} W \\ B \end{array} \begin{bmatrix} 0.95 & 0.05 \\ 0.40 & 0.60 \end{bmatrix}.$$

The Markov chain diagram is shown in Figure 24.2.

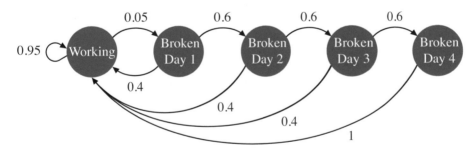

Figure 24.2 *Markov chain for the repair facility problem.*

Question: Now suppose that after the machine remains broken for four days, the machine is replaced with a new machine. How does the DTMC diagram change?

Answer: The revised DTMC is shown in Figure 24.3.

Figure 24.3 *Markov chain for the repair facility problem with a four-day limit.*

24.3.2 Umbrella Problem

An absent-minded professor has two umbrellas that she uses when commuting from home to office and back. If it rains and an umbrella is available in her location, she takes it. If it is not raining, she always forgets to take an umbrella. Suppose that it rains with probability p each time she commutes, independently of prior commutes. Our goal is to determine the fraction of commutes during which the professor gets wet.

Question: What is the state space?

Hint: Try to use as few states as possible!

Answer: We only need three states. The states track the number of umbrellas available at the current location, regardless of what this current location is. The DTMC is shown in Figure 24.4.

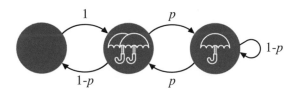

Figure 24.4 *DTMC for the umbrella problem.*

The transition probability matrix is $\mathbf{P} = \begin{array}{c} \\ 0 \\ 1 \\ 2 \end{array} \begin{array}{c} \\ \left[\begin{array}{ccc} 0 & 1 & 2 \\ 0 & 0 & 1 \\ 0 & 1-p & p \\ 1-p & p & 0 \end{array} \right]. \end{array}$

The probability of getting wet is the probability that it rains during a commute from a location with zero umbrellas.

24.3.3 Program Analysis Problem

A program has three types of instructions: CPU (C), memory (M), and user interaction (U). In analyzing the program, we note that a C instruction with probability 0.7 is followed by another C instruction, with probability 0.2 is followed by an M instruction and with probability 0.1 is followed by a U instruction. An M instruction with probability 0.1 is followed by another M instruction, with probability 0.8 is followed by a C instruction, and with probability 0.1 is followed by a U instruction. Finally, a U instruction with probability 0.9 is followed by a C instruction, and with probability 0.1 is followed by an M instruction.

In the exercises for this chapter and the next, we answer questions like, "What is the fraction of C instructions?" and "How many instructions are there on average between consecutive M instructions?" For now, we simply note that the program can be represented as a Markov chain with the transition probability matrix:

$$\mathbf{P} = \begin{array}{c} \\ C \\ M \\ U \end{array} \begin{array}{c} \begin{array}{ccc} C & M & U \end{array} \\ \left[\begin{array}{ccc} 0.7 & 0.2 & 0.1 \\ 0.8 & 0.1 & 0.1 \\ 0.9 & 0.1 & 0 \end{array} \right]. \end{array}$$

24.4 Powers of P: *n*-Step Transition Probabilities

> **Definition 24.4** *Let* $\mathbf{P}^n = \mathbf{P} \cdot \mathbf{P} \cdots \mathbf{P}$, *multiplied n times. Then* $(\mathbf{P}^n)_{ij}$ *denotes the* (i, j)*th entry of matrix* $\mathbf{P}^n$. *Occasionally, we will use the shorthand:*
>
> $$P_{ij}^n \equiv (\mathbf{P}^n)_{ij} \, .$$

Question: What does $(\mathbf{P}^n)_{ij}$ represent?

Answer: To answer this, we first consider two examples.

Example 24.5 (Back to the umbrellas)

Consider the umbrella problem from before, where the chance of rain on any given day is $p = 0.4$. We then have:

$$\mathbf{P} = \begin{bmatrix} 0 & 0 & 1 \\ 0 & .6 & .4 \\ .6 & .4 & 0 \end{bmatrix} \qquad \mathbf{P}^5 = \begin{bmatrix} .06 & .30 & .64 \\ .18 & .38 & .44 \\ .38 & .44 & .18 \end{bmatrix} \qquad \mathbf{P}^{30} = \begin{bmatrix} .230 & .385 & .385 \\ .230 & .385 & .385 \\ .230 & .385 & .385 \end{bmatrix} .$$

Observe that all the rows become the *same*! Note also that, for all the above powers, each row sums to 1.

Example 24.6 (Back to the repair facility)

Now, consider again the simple repair facility problem, with general transition probability matrix $\mathbf{P}$:

$$\mathbf{P} = \begin{bmatrix} 1 - a & a \\ b & 1 - b \end{bmatrix}, \qquad 0 < a < 1, \, 0 < b < 1.$$

You should be able to prove by induction that

$$\mathbf{P}^n = \begin{bmatrix} \frac{b+a(1-a-b)^n}{a+b} & \frac{a-a(1-a-b)^n}{a+b} \\ \frac{b-b(1-a-b)^n}{a+b} & \frac{a+b(1-a-b)^n}{a+b} \end{bmatrix}$$

$$\lim_{n \to \infty} \mathbf{P}^n = \begin{bmatrix} \frac{b}{a+b} & \frac{a}{a+b} \\ \frac{b}{a+b} & \frac{a}{a+b} \end{bmatrix} .$$

Question: Again, all rows are the same. Why? What is the meaning of the row?

Hint: Consider a DTMC in state i. Suppose we want to know the probability that it will be in state j two steps from now. To go from state i to state j in two steps, the DTMC must have passed through some state k after the first step. Below we condition on this intermediate state k.

For an M-state DTMC, as shown in Figure 24.5,

$$\left(\mathbf{P}^2\right)_{ij} = \sum_{k=0}^{M-1} P_{ik} \cdot P_{kj}$$

= Probability of being in state j in two steps, given we're in state i now.

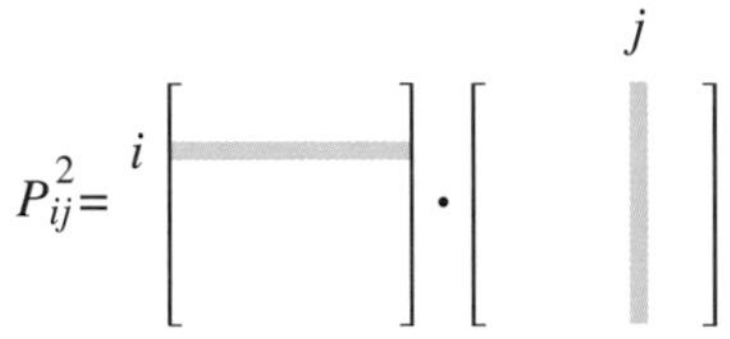

Figure 24.5 $\left(\mathbf{P}^2\right)_{ij}$.

Likewise, the n-wise product can be viewed by conditioning on the state k after $n - 1$ time steps:

$$\left(\mathbf{P}^n\right)_{ij} = \sum_{k=0}^{M-1} \left(\mathbf{P}^{n-1}\right)_{ik} P_{kj}$$

= Probability of being in state j in n steps, given we are in state i now.

24.5 Limiting Probabilities

We now move on to looking at the limit. Consider the (i, j)th entry of the power matrix $\mathbf{P}^n$ for large n:

$$\lim_{n \to \infty} \left(\mathbf{P}^n\right)_{ij} \equiv \left(\lim_{n \to \infty} \mathbf{P}^n\right)_{ij}.$$

This quantity represents the limiting probability of being in state j infinitely far into the future, given that we started in state i.

Question: So what is the limiting probability of having zero umbrellas?

Answer: According to $\mathbf{P}^{30}$, it is 0.23.

Question: The fact that the rows of $\lim_{n \to \infty} \mathbf{P}^n$ are all the same is interesting because it says what?

Answer: The fact that $(\mathbf{P}^n)_{ij}$ is the same for all values of i says that the starting state, i, does not matter.

Definition 24.7 *Let*

$$\pi_j = \lim_{n \to \infty} (\mathbf{P}^n)_{ij}.$$

π_j *represents the* **limiting probability** *that the chain is in state j, independent of the starting state i. For an M-state DTMC, with states $0, 1, \ldots, M-1$,*

$$\vec{\pi} = (\pi_0, \pi_1, \ldots, \pi_{M-1}), \quad where \sum_{i=0}^{M-1} \pi_i = 1,$$

represents the **limiting distribution** *of being in each state.*

Important note: As defined, π_j is a limit. Yet it is not at all obvious that the limit π_j exists! It is also not obvious that $\vec{\pi}$ represents a distribution (that is, $\sum_i \pi_i = 1$), although this latter part turns out to be easy to see (Exercise 24.2). For the rest of this chapter, we will assume that the limiting probabilities exist. In Chapter 25 we look at the existence question in detail.

Question: So what is the limiting probability that the professor gets wet?

Answer: The professor gets wet if both (1) the state is 0, that is, there are zero umbrellas in the current location (π_0); and (2) it is raining ($p = 0.4$). So the limiting probability that the professor gets wet is $\pi_0 \cdot p = (0.23)(0.4) = 0.092$.

Question: Can you see why the limiting probability of having one umbrella is equal to the limiting probability of having two umbrellas?

Answer: Let's go back to Figure 24.4. Suppose now that we're only trying to determine the fraction of time that we're in a location with one umbrella versus the fraction of time that we're in a location with two umbrellas. In that case, all that matters is the number of visits to state 1 versus the number of visits to state 2. But, over a long period of time, the number of visits to state 1 and the number to state 2 are equal. To see this, if one considers only those two options of 1 and 2, then the chain from Figure 24.4 collapses to that shown in Figure 24.6. But the chain in Figure 24.6 is symmetric, hence the equal limiting probabilities.

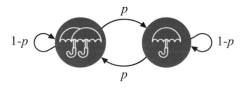

Figure 24.6 *Compressed umbrella problem.*

24.6 Stationary Equations

Question: Based only on what we have learned so far, how do we determine $\pi_j = \lim_{n \to \infty} (\mathbf{P}^n)_{ij}$?

Answer: We take the transition probability matrix $\mathbf{P}$ and raise it to the nth power for some large n and look at the jth column, any row.

Question: Multiplying $\mathbf{P}$ by itself many times sounds quite onerous. Also, it seems one might need to perform a very large number of multiplications if the Markov chain is large. Is there a more efficient way?

Answer: Yes, by solving stationary equations, given in Definition 24.8.

Definition 24.8 *A probability distribution* $\vec{\pi} = (\pi_0, \pi_1, \ldots, \pi_{M-1})$ *is said to be* **stationary** *for the Markov chain with transition matrix* $\mathbf{P}$ *if*

$$\vec{\pi} \cdot \mathbf{P} = \vec{\pi} \quad and \quad \sum_{i=0}^{M-1} \pi_i = 1.$$

Figure 24.7 provides an illustration of $\vec{\pi} \cdot \mathbf{P} = \vec{\pi}$.

$$\begin{bmatrix} \pi_0 & \pi_1 & \pi_2 \end{bmatrix} \begin{bmatrix} P_{00} & P_{01} & P_{02} \\ P_{10} & P_{11} & P_{12} \\ P_{20} & P_{21} & P_{22} \end{bmatrix} = \begin{bmatrix} \pi_0 & \pi_1 & \pi_2 \end{bmatrix}$$

Figure 24.7 *Visualization of* $\vec{\pi} \cdot \mathbf{P} = \vec{\pi}$ *for the case of* $M = 3$ *states.*

Doing the row-by-column multiplication in Figure 24.7 results in the following **stationary equations**:

$$\pi_0 \cdot P_{00} + \pi_1 \cdot P_{10} + \pi_2 \cdot P_{20} = \pi_0$$
$$\pi_0 \cdot P_{01} + \pi_1 \cdot P_{11} + \pi_2 \cdot P_{21} = \pi_1$$
$$\pi_0 \cdot P_{02} + \pi_1 \cdot P_{12} + \pi_2 \cdot P_{22} = \pi_2$$
$$\pi_0 + \pi_1 + \pi_2 = 1.$$

These stationary equations can be written more compactly as follows:

$$\sum_{i=0}^{M-1} \pi_i P_{ij} = \pi_j, \forall j \quad \text{and} \quad \sum_{i=0}^{M-1} \pi_i = 1. \tag{24.1}$$

Question: What does the left-hand side of the first equation in (24.1) represent?

Answer: The left-hand side represents the probability of being in state j one transition from now, given that the current probability distribution on the states is $\vec{\pi}$. So (24.1) says that if we start out distributed according to $\vec{\pi}$, then one step later our probability of being in each state will still follow distribution $\vec{\pi}$. Thus, from then on we will always have the same probability distribution on the states. Hence, we call the distribution "stationary," which connotes the fact that we stay there forever.

24.7 The Stationary Distribution Equals the Limiting Distribution

The following theorem relates the *limiting distribution* to the *stationary distribution* for a finite-state DTMC. Specifically, the theorem says that for a finite-state DTMC, the stationary distribution obtained by solving (24.1) is unique and represents the limiting probabilities of being in each state, assuming these limiting probabilities exist.

> **Theorem 24.9 (Stationary distribution = limiting distribution)** *In a finite-state DTMC with M states, let*
> $$\pi_j = \lim_{n \to \infty} (\mathbf{P}^n)_{ij}$$
> *be the limiting probability of being in state j (independent of the starting state i) and let*
> $$\vec{\pi} = (\pi_0, \pi_1, \ldots, \pi_{M-1}), \quad where \sum_{i=0}^{M-1} \pi_i = 1,$$
> *be the limiting distribution. Assuming that $\vec{\pi}$ exists, then $\vec{\pi}$ is also a stationary distribution and no other stationary distribution exists.*

Question: What's the intuition behind Theorem 24.9?

Answer: Intuitively, given that the limiting distribution, $\vec{\pi}$, exists, it makes sense that this limiting distribution should be stationary, because we're not leaving the limit once we get there. It's not as immediately obvious that this limiting distribution should be the only stationary distribution.

Question: What's the impact of Theorem 24.9?

Answer: Assuming that the limiting distribution exists, Theorem 24.9 tells us that to get the limiting distribution we don't need to raise the transition matrix to a high power, but rather we can just solve the stationary equations.

Proof: [Theorem 24.9] We prove two things about the limiting distribution $\vec{\pi}$:

1. We will prove that $\vec{\pi} = (\pi_0, \pi_1, \pi_2, \ldots, \pi_{M-1})$ is a stationary distribution. Hence, at least one stationary distribution exists.
2. We will prove that any stationary distribution must be equal to the limiting distribution.

Important: Throughout the proof, $\vec{\pi} = (\pi_0, \pi_1, \pi_2, \ldots, \pi_{M-1})$ is used to refer to the *limiting distribution*.

Part 1: Proof that $\vec{\pi} = (\pi_0, \pi_1, \pi_2, \ldots, \pi_{M-1})$ is a stationary distribution:

Intuitively, this should make a lot of sense. If we have some limiting distribution, then once you get there, you should stay there forever.

$$\pi_j = \lim_{n \to \infty} \left(\mathbf{P}^{n+1}\right)_{ij} = \lim_{n \to \infty} \sum_{k=0}^{M-1} (\mathbf{P}^n)_{ik} \cdot P_{kj}$$

$$= \sum_{k=0}^{M-1} \lim_{n \to \infty} (\mathbf{P}^n)_{ik} P_{kj}$$

$$= \sum_{k=0}^{M-1} \pi_k P_{kj}.$$

Hence $\vec{\pi}$ satisfies the stationary equations, so it's also a stationary distribution.

Part 2: Proof that any stationary distribution, $\vec{\pi}'$, must equal the limiting distribution, $\vec{\pi}$:

Let $\vec{\pi}'$ be any stationary probability distribution. As usual, $\vec{\pi}$ represents the limiting probability distribution. We will prove that $\vec{\pi}' = \vec{\pi}$, and specifically that $\pi'_j = \pi_j, \forall j$.

Suppose we start at time 0 with stationary distribution $\vec{\pi}' = (\pi'_0, \pi'_1, \ldots, \pi'_{M-1})$. After one step, we will still be in distribution $\vec{\pi}'$:

$$\vec{\pi}' \cdot \mathbf{P} = \vec{\pi}'$$

But this implies that after n steps, we will still be in distribution $\vec{\pi}'$:

$$\vec{\pi}' \cdot \mathbf{P}^n = \vec{\pi}'. \tag{24.2}$$

Looking at the jth entry of $\vec{\pi}'$ in (24.2), we have:

$$\sum_{k=0}^{M-1} \pi'_k (\mathbf{P}^n)_{kj} = \pi'_j.$$

Taking the limit as n goes to infinity of both sides, we have:

$$\lim_{n\to\infty} \sum_{k=0}^{M-1} \pi'_k (\mathbf{P}^n)_{kj} = \lim_{n\to\infty} \pi'_j = \pi'_j.$$

We are now ready to prove that $\pi'_j = \pi_j, \forall j$:

$$\pi'_j = \lim_{n\to\infty} \sum_{k=0}^{M-1} \pi'_k (\mathbf{P}^n)_{kj} = \sum_{k=0}^{M-1} \pi'_k \lim_{n\to\infty} (\mathbf{P}^n)_{kj}$$

$$= \sum_{k=0}^{M-1} \pi'_k \pi_j$$

$$= \pi_j \sum_{k=0}^{M-1} \pi'_k = \pi_j. \qquad \blacksquare$$

Note that we were allowed to pull the limit into the summation sign in both parts because we had finite sums (M is finite).

One more thing: In the literature you often see the phrase "consider a stationary Markov chain," or "consider the following Markov chain in steady state ..."

Definition 24.10 *A Markov chain for which the limiting probabilities exist is said to be* **stationary** *or in* **steady state** *if the initial state is chosen according to the stationary probabilities.*

Summary: Finding the limiting probabilities in a finite-state DTMC:

By Theorem 24.9, provided the limiting distribution $\vec{\pi} = (\pi_0, \pi_1, \pi_2, \ldots, \pi_{M-1})$ exists, we can obtain it by solving the stationary equations:

$$\vec{\pi} \cdot \mathbf{P} = \vec{\pi} \quad \text{and} \quad \sum_{i=0}^{M-1} \pi_i = 1,$$

where $\vec{\pi} = (\pi_0, \pi_1, \ldots, \pi_{M-1})$.

24.8 Examples of Solving Stationary Equations

Example 24.11 (Repair facility problem with cost)

Consider again the repair facility problem represented by the finite-state DTMC shown again in Figure 24.8.

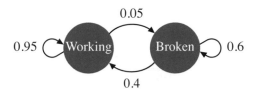

Figure 24.8 *Markov chain for the repair facility problem.*

We are interested in the following type of question.

Question: The help desk is trying to figure out how much to charge me for maintaining my machine. They figure that it costs them $300 every day that my machine is in repair. What will be my annual repair bill?

To answer this question, we first derive the limiting distribution $\vec{\pi} = (\pi_W, \pi_B)$ for this chain. We solve the stationary equations to get $\vec{\pi}$ as follows:

$$\vec{\pi} = \vec{\pi} \cdot \mathbf{P}, \text{ where } \mathbf{P} = \begin{pmatrix} 0.95 & 0.05 \\ 0.4 & 0.6 \end{pmatrix}$$

$$\pi_W + \pi_B = 1.$$

This translates to the following equations:

$$\pi_W = \pi_W \cdot 0.95 + \pi_B \cdot 0.4$$
$$\pi_B = \pi_W \cdot 0.05 + \pi_B \cdot 0.6$$
$$\pi_W + \pi_B = 1.$$

Question: What do you notice about the first two equations above?

Answer: They are identical! In general, if $\vec{\pi} = \vec{\pi} \cdot \mathbf{P}$ results in M equations, only $M - 1$ of these will be linearly independent (this is because the rows of $\mathbf{P}$ all sum to 1). Fortunately, the last equation above (the normalization condition) is there to help us out. Solving, we get $\pi_W = \frac{8}{9}$ and $\pi_B = \frac{1}{9}$.

By Theorem 24.9, the stationary distribution also represents the limiting probability distribution. Thus my machine is broken one out of every nine days on average. The expected daily cost is $\frac{1}{9} \cdot 300 = \$33.33$ (with an annual cost of more than $12,000).

Example 24.12 (Umbrella problem)

Consider again the umbrella problem depicted in Figure 24.9.

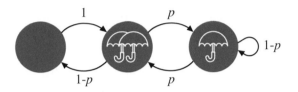

Figure 24.9 *DTMC for the umbrella problem.*

Rather than raising the transition matrix $\mathbf{P}$ to a high power, this time we use the stationary equations to obtain the limiting probabilities for general p:

$$\pi_0 = \pi_2 \cdot (1 - p)$$
$$\pi_1 = \pi_1 \cdot (1 - p) + \pi_2 \cdot p$$
$$\pi_2 = \pi_0 \cdot 1 + \pi_1 \cdot p$$
$$\pi_0 + \pi_1 + \pi_2 = 1.$$

Their solution is

$$\pi_0 = \frac{1 - p}{3 - p} \qquad \pi_1 = \frac{1}{3 - p} \qquad \pi_2 = \frac{1}{3 - p}.$$

Question: Suppose the professor lives in Pittsburgh, where the daily probability of rain is $p = 0.6$. What fraction of days does the professor get soaked?

Answer: The professor gets soaked if she has zero umbrellas and it is raining: $\pi_0 \cdot p = \frac{0.4}{2.4} \cdot 0.6 = 0.1$. Not too bad. No wonder I never learn!

24.9 Exercises

24.1 **Solving for limiting distribution**
    For the program analysis problem from Section 24.3.3, solve the stationary equations to determine the limiting distribution, (π_C, π_M, π_U).

24.2 **Powers of transition matrix**
Given any finite-state transition matrix, $\mathbf{P}$, prove that for any positive integer n, $\mathbf{P}^n$ maintains the property that each row sums to 1.

24.3 **Random walk on clique**
You are given a clique on $n > 1$ nodes (a clique is a graph where there is an edge between every pair of nodes). At every time step, you move to a uniformly random node *other* than the node you're in. You start at node v. Let T denote the time (number of hops) until you first return to v.
(a) What is $\mathbf{E}[T]$?
(b) What is $\mathbf{Var}(T)$?

24.4 **Card shuffling**
You have n distinct cards, arranged in an ordered list: $1, 2, 3, \ldots, n$. Every minute, you pick a card at random and move it to the front of the ordered list. We can model this process as a DTMC, where the state is the ordered list. Derive a stationary distribution for the DTMC. [Hint: Make a guess and then prove it.]

24.5 **Doubly stochastic matrix**
A doubly stochastic matrix is one in which the entries in each row sum up to 1, and the entries in each column sum up to 1. Suppose you have a finite-state Markov chain whose limiting probabilities exist and whose transition matrix is doubly stochastic. What can you prove about the stationary distribution of this Markov chain? [Hint: Start by writing some examples of doubly stochastic transition matrices.]

24.6 **Randomized chess**
In chess, a rook can move either horizontally within its row (left or right) or vertically within its column (up or down) any number of squares. Imagine a rook that starts at the lower left corner of an 8×8 chess board. At each move, a bored child decides to move the rook to a random legal location (assume that the "move" cannot involve staying still). Let T denote the time until the rook first lands in the upper right corner of the board. Compute $\mathbf{E}[T]$ and $\mathbf{Var}(T)$.

24.7 **Tennis match**
[Proposed by William Liu] Abinaya and Misha are playing tennis. They're currently tied at deuce, meaning that the next person to lead by two points wins the game. Suppose that Misha wins each point independently with probability $\frac{2}{3}$ (where Abinaya wins with probability $\frac{1}{3}$).
(a) What is the probability that Misha wins the game?
(b) What is the expected number of remaining points played until someone wins?

24.8 **Markovopoly**

[Proposed by Tai Yasuda] Suppose you are playing a board game where the board has 28 locations arranged as shown in Figure 24.10. You start at the "Go" square, and, at each turn, you roll a six-sided die and move forward in the clockwise direction whatever number you roll. However, the dark squares in the corners are jail states, and once you land there, you must sit out for the next three turns (for the next three turns, you stay in jail instead of rolling a die and moving). On the fourth turn, you can roll the die again and move. Your goal is to figure out the fraction of the turns that you are in jail. (You are "in jail" if you are in a jail square at the end of your turn.) Write stationary equations to determine this fraction.

Figure 24.10 *Markovopoly for Exercise 24.8.*

24.9 **Axis & Allies**

In the game Axis & Allies, the outcome of a two-sided naval battle is decided by repeated rolling of dice. Until all ships on at least one side are destroyed, each side rolls one six-sided die for *each* of its existing ships. The die rolls determine casualties inflicted on the opponent; these casualties are removed from play and cannot fire (roll) in subsequent rounds.

There are two types of ships: battleships and destroyers. For a battleship, a die roll of four or lower is scored as a "hit" on the opponent. For a destroyer, a die roll of three or lower is scored as a "hit" on the opponent. It takes two hits (not necessarily in the same round) to destroy a battleship and only one hit to destroy a destroyer. (Note: Battleships are twice as expensive as destroyers.)

For example: Suppose side A has two destroyers and one battleship. Suppose side B has one destroyer and three battleships. Side A rolls two dice for its destroyers (rolling, say, 3 and 6) and one die for its battleship (rolling, say, 5). This means that side A generates one hit against side B.

At the same time, side B rolls one die for its destroyer (rolling, say 5) and three dice for its battleships (rolling, say, 1, 4, and 6). This means that side B generates two hits against side A.

The defender gets to decide to which ship to allocate the hit; we assume that the defender chooses intelligently. In the above example, side A will choose to be left with one destroyer and one weakened battleship. Side B will choose to be left with one destroyer, one weakened battleship and two undamaged battleships.

If two destroyers (side A) engage a battleship (side B) in a battle, what is the probability that the destroyers win? What is the probability that the battleship wins? [Hint: Raise a matrix to a large power.] [Note: A tie is also possible.]

24.10 The SIR epidemic model

The SIR model is commonly used to predict the spread of epidemic diseases. We have a population of n people. The state of the system is (n_S, n_I, n_R), where

- n_S is the number of people who are *susceptible* (healthy/uninfected);
- n_I is the number of people who are *infected*;
- n_R is the number of people who are *recovered*. In the SIR model, "recovered" includes both those recovered and deceased. The point is that "recovered" people are no longer susceptible to the disease.

Clearly $n_S + n_I + n_R = n$.

Each individual of the population independently follows this transmission model:

- If the individual is susceptible, then:
  - with probability $p \cdot \frac{n_I}{n}$, the individual will be infected tomorrow;
  - with probability $1 - p \cdot \frac{n_I}{n}$, the individual will stay susceptible tomorrow.
- If the individual is infected, then:
  - with probability $\frac{1}{21}$, the individual will be recovered;
  - with probability $\frac{20}{21}$, the individual will stay infected.
- If the individual is recovered, then with probability 1 the individual stays recovered.

The goal of the SIR model is to predict what *fraction* of people are in the "susceptible" state when the epidemic ends (that is, $n_I = 0$). These are the people who never got sick and thus have the potential to get sick if the disease resurfaces. You will determine this fraction as a function of the parameter p. You will do this by first determining the appropriate probability transition matrix and then raising this matrix to a very high power. For both steps you'll want to use a computer program like Matlab. For the sake of this problem, please assume $n = 3$ (but feel free to try out higher values of n as well).

(a) How many states are there in this system?

(b) How many absorbing states are there in this system, and what are they? Absorbing states are states that you never leave once you enter them. [Hint: What is n_I for an absorbing state?]

(c) Derive the transition probability from state $(2, 1, 0)$ to $(1, 1, 1)$. Be careful to think about all the ways that this transition can happen. Plug in the values of n_I and n and use $p = 0.5$ so that your final answer is a constant.

(d) Use a computer program to generate the entire transition matrix $\mathbf{P}$. Assume that $p = 0.5$. Print out the row corresponding to state $(2, 1, 0)$. Now raise $\mathbf{P}$ to some very high power and watch what happens to row $(2, 1, 0)$. You'll want a high enough power that most of your entries are smaller than 0.01. What is the meaning of the row corresponding to state $(2, 1, 0)$?

(e) The parameter p can be thought of as a social distancing parameter, where lower p represents better social distancing practices. Consider values of p between 0 and 1. For each value of p, determine the expected fraction of the population who are left in the susceptible state when the outbreak is over (you will do this by conditioning on the probability of ending up in each absorbing state). Assume that you start in state $(2, 1, 0)$. Your final output will be a graph with p on the x-axis, but you can alternatively create a table with values of p spaced out by 0.05.

25 Ergodicity for Finite-State Discrete-Time Markov Chains

At this point in our discussion of discrete-time Markov chains (DTMCs) with M states, we have defined the notion of a *limiting probability of being in state j*:

$$\pi_j = \lim_{n \to \infty} (\mathbf{P}^n)_{ij},$$

where the limiting distribution is

$$\vec{\pi} = (\pi_0, \pi_1, \pi_2, \ldots, \pi_{M-1}), \quad \text{where} \quad \sum_{i=0}^{M-1} \pi_i = 1.$$

We have also defined the notion of a *stationary distribution, $\vec{\pi}$*, as a distribution that satisfies

$$\vec{\pi} \cdot \mathbf{P} = \vec{\pi} \quad \text{and} \quad \sum_{i=0}^{M-1} \pi_i = 1,$$

or, equivalently,

$$\pi_j = \sum_{i=0}^{M-1} \pi_i P_{ij} \quad \text{and} \quad \sum_{i=0}^{M-1} \pi_i = 1.$$

We also proved Theorem 24.9 for finite-state chains that says that, assuming the limiting distribution exists, the limiting distribution is a stationary distribution and no other stationary distribution exists. This theorem is important because it allows us to simply solve the stationary equations to get the limiting distribution.

In Chapter 24, we did *not* spend time on questions like the following:

1. Under what conditions does the limiting distribution exist?
2. How does π_j, the limiting probability of being in state j, compare with p_j, the long-run time-average fraction of time spent in state j?
3. What can we say about m_{jj}, the mean time between visits to state j, and how is this related to π_j?

This entire chapter is devoted to these and other theoretical questions, all related to the notion of *ergodicity*, to be defined soon. This chapter will only address ergodicity questions for finite-state chains. Infinite-state chains are deferred to Chapter 26.

25.1 Some Examples on Whether the Limiting Distribution Exists

We dive right into the question of existence of the limiting distribution, with a few examples.

Question: What is an example of a valid two-state transition matrix for which π_j does not exist?

Answer: Figure 25.1 shows an example of a chain with transition matrix

$$\mathbf{P} = \begin{bmatrix} 0 & 1 \\ 1 & 0 \end{bmatrix}.$$

Figure 25.1 *Limiting distribution does not exist.*

The problem is that the chain $\mathbf{P}$ is *periodic*; specifically, a given state is only visited every *other* time step (we will formally define the term "periodic" soon). Observe that $\pi_j = \lim_{n \to \infty} (\mathbf{P}^n)_{jj}$ does not exist, although $\lim_{n \to \infty} (\mathbf{P}^{2n})_{jj}$ does exist.

Question: Does this chain have a stationary distribution?

Answer: Yes, the stationary distribution *does* exist. To see this, let's set up the stationary equations $\vec{\pi} \cdot \mathbf{P} = \vec{\pi}$:

$$\pi_0 = \pi_1$$
$$\pi_1 = \pi_0$$
$$\pi_0 + \pi_1 = 1.$$

Solving these, we get $\vec{\pi} = (\frac{1}{2}, \frac{1}{2})$.

Question: If you walk along the Markov chain for a long time, what fraction of time, p_j, do you spend in state j?

Answer: $p_0 = p_1 = \frac{1}{2}$. These match the stationary probabilities. This is no coincidence. We will see that for any Markov chain, the p_j's satisfy the stationary equations and thus form a stationary distribution.

Question: Is there another two-state example for which the limiting distribution does not exist?

Answer: Consider the transition matrix $\mathbf{Q}$:

$$\mathbf{Q} = \begin{bmatrix} 1 & 0 \\ 0 & 1 \end{bmatrix}.$$

The corresponding chain is shown in Figure 25.2.

Figure 25.2 *Limiting distribution does not exist.*

The chain $\mathbf{Q}$ has the problem that the limiting state depends on where you start. Recall that the limiting probability of being in state j is supposed to be independent of the start state, i, that is, for transition matrix $\mathbf{Q}$ we want

$$\pi_j = \lim_{n \to \infty} (\mathbf{Q}^n)_{ij}$$

to be independent of i.

However, in our example, if you start in state 1, then you stay there forever, and if you start in state 0, then you stay there forever. Similarly, p_1, the long-run time-average fraction of time spent in state 1, isn't well defined, since it depends on the start state.

Question: What is the stationary distribution of chain $\mathbf{Q}$?

Answer: Chain $\mathbf{Q}$ has an infinite number of stationary distributions!

Examples like these illustrate why we need to differentiate between the stationary probability of being in state j, the limiting probability of being in state j, and the long-run fraction of time spent in state j.

Question: As a final example, does chain $\mathbf{R}$ have limiting probabilities?

$$\mathbf{R} = \begin{bmatrix} 0 & 0 & 1/2 & 1/2 \\ 1 & 0 & 0 & 0 \\ 0 & 1 & 0 & 0 \\ 0 & 1 & 0 & 0 \end{bmatrix}.$$

Answer: No, chain **R** is also periodic – it is just a little harder to see.

25.2 Aperiodicity

> **Definition 25.1** *The* **period** *of state j is the greatest common divisor (gcd) of the set of integers n, such that $(\mathbf{P}^n)_{jj} > 0$. A state is* **aperiodic** *if its period is 1. A chain is said to be aperiodic if all of its states are aperiodic.*

To understand the reasoning behind the definition of aperiodic, we recall the Chicken McNugget theorem. Once upon a time, a mathematician walked into McDonald's, hoping to buy food for all his n friends. He wanted to feed them each one chicken nugget (now you know why mathematicians are so skinny). Unfortunately the chicken nugget boxes only came in sizes of 4 nuggets/box or 9 nuggets/box. The mathematician (who was not just skinny but also thrifty) started to wonder if he could express n as a linear combination of 4 and 9, so that no nuggets would go to waste. As often happens, all this thinking led to a theorem, which is called the Chicken McNugget Theorem.

> **Theorem 25.2 (Chicken McNugget Theorem)** *There exists a positive integer n_0, such that, for all integers n, where $n \geq n_0$, we can express n as a non-negative linear combination of 4 and 9. Specifically, we can write:*
>
> $$n = a \cdot 4 + b \cdot 9,$$
>
> *where a and b are non-negative integer coefficients.*

The Euclidean Number Property extends the Chicken McNugget Theorem to other-sized nugget boxes.

> **Theorem 25.3 (Euclidean Number Property)** *Suppose we're given k positive integers, $i_1, i_2, \ldots, i_k$, where $\gcd(i_1, i_2, \ldots, i_k) = 1$. Then there exists a positive integer n_0, such that for all integers n, where $n \geq n_0$, we can express n as a non-negative linear combination of $i_1, i_2, \ldots, i_k$. Specifically, we can write:*
>
> $$n = a_1 \cdot i_1 + a_2 \cdot i_2 + \cdots + a_k \cdot i_k$$
>
> *where the a_i's are non-negative integer coefficients.*

Question: Returning to Markov chains, suppose there's a j to j path of length 4 and also one of length 3, as shown in Figure 25.3. Since $\gcd(3, 4) = 1$, state j by definition has period 1. But why *intuitively* does state j have period 1?

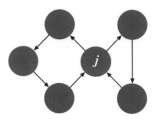

Figure 25.3 *There's a j-to-j path of length 3 and 4.*

Answer: By the Euclidean Number Property we know that for every integer n, greater than some n_0, we can express n as a linear combination of 3 and 4, with non-negative integer coefficients. Thus, there exists a j-to-j path of length n_0, as well as a j-to-j path of length $n_0 + 1$, as well as a j-to-j path of length $n_0 + 2$, and so on. Since there's a j-to-j path of length k for *every* sufficiently large k, we say that the period of j is 1.

Question: Why is it necessary that j be aperiodic for the limiting probability π_j to exist?

Answer: If j has period $d > 1$, then we can't say that there's a j-to-j path of length k for every sufficiently large k (in fact, it turns out we will only end up visiting j once every d steps). But this means that we can't talk about a limiting probability of being in state j independent of the time step n.

25.3 Irreducibility

We've seen that aperiodicity is necessary for the limiting probabilities to exist. Even when a DTMC is aperiodic, there's another problem that could come up: it is possible that the limiting probabilities could depend on the start state, whereas we want

$$\pi_j = \lim_{n \to \infty} (\mathbf{P}^n)_{ij}$$

to be the same for all start states i.

If we also want the limiting probabilities to be independent of the start state, we need one more condition, known as *irreducibility*, which says that from any state one can get to any other state.

Definition 25.4 *State j is **accessible** from state i if $(\mathbf{P}^n)_{ij} > 0$ for some $n > 0$. States i and j **communicate** if i is accessible from j and vice-versa.*

> **Definition 25.5** *A Markov chain is **irreducible** if all its states communicate with each other.*

Question: Why is irreducibility important for the limiting probabilities to exist?

Answer: The chain might consist of two disconnected components, as in Figure 25.4(a). Here the limiting probability of being in state j depends on the starting state, which is not allowed. Note, however, that irreducibility is not always *necessary* for the existence of the limiting probability. Consider for example Figure 25.4(b), which is also not irreducible, yet the limiting probabilities are all well defined.

(a) No limiting distribution   (b) Limiting distribution exists

Figure 25.4 *Both (a) and (b) show chains which are not irreducible. In (a) the limiting distribution does not exist, because it depends on the start state. In (b) the limiting distribution is $\vec{\pi} = (0, 1)$.*

Question: Do you think that aperiodicity and irreducibility are enough to guarantee the existence of the limiting distribution?

Answer: As we see in Theorem 25.6, for a *finite-state* DTMC, aperiodicity and irreducibility are all that are needed to ensure that the limiting probabilities exist, are positive, sum to 1, and are independent of the starting state. This is convenient, as it is often easy to argue that a DTMC is aperiodic and irreducible.

25.4 Aperiodicity plus Irreducibility Implies Limiting Distribution

> **Theorem 25.6 (Aperiodicity + irreducibility implies limiting distribution)**
> *Given an aperiodic, irreducible,* finite-state *DTMC with transition matrix* **P**, *as $n \to \infty$,* $\mathbf{P}^n \to \mathbf{L}$, *where* **L** *is a limiting matrix all of whose rows are the same vector,* $\vec{\pi}$. *The vector* $\vec{\pi}$ *has all positive components, summing to 1.*

Question: What does L_{ij} represent?

Answer: The (i, j)th element of $\mathbf{L}$ represents $\lim_{n \to \infty} (\mathbf{P}^n)_{ij}$, namely the limiting probability of being in state j given we started in state i.

Question: What does the ith row of $\mathbf{L}$ represent?

Answer: The ith row of $\mathbf{L}$ is the vector of limiting probabilities $(\pi_0, \pi_1, \ldots, \pi_{M-1})$, where $\pi_j = \lim_{n \to \infty} (\mathbf{P}^n)_{ij}$, and M is the number of states in the DTMC.

Question: Why is it important that the rows of $\mathbf{L}$ are the same?

Answer: The fact that row i and row k are the same says that

$$\lim_{n \to \infty} (\mathbf{P}^n)_{ij} = \lim_{n \to \infty} (\mathbf{P}^n)_{kj},$$

which says that the starting state does not affect the limiting probability of being in state j.

As a concrete example of Theorem 25.6, suppose that

$$\mathbf{P} = \begin{bmatrix} 1/2 & 1/3 & 1/6 \\ 1/3 & 1/3 & 1/3 \\ 1/8 & 3/4 & 1/8 \end{bmatrix}.$$

Then Theorem 25.6 is saying that $\mathbf{P}^n$ converges to a matrix $\mathbf{L}$ all of whose rows are the same. That is,

$$\mathbf{P}^n \longrightarrow \begin{bmatrix} 0.34 & 0.43 & 0.23 \\ 0.34 & 0.43 & 0.23 \\ 0.34 & 0.43 & 0.23 \end{bmatrix} = \mathbf{L}.$$

Proof: [Theorem 25.6] The remainder of this section is devoted to the proof of Theorem 25.6. This is a long proof and will require introducing a couple claims along the way. We are trying to show that $\mathbf{P}^n$ converges to a matrix where all rows are the same. Equivalently, we are trying to show that, for any j, the jth column of $\mathbf{P}^n$ converges to a vector whose components are all the same.

Let $\vec{e}$ represent the *column vector* of dimension matching $\mathbf{P}$, whose jth component is 1 and whose remaining components are all 0. That is,

$$\vec{e} = \begin{bmatrix} 0 \\ \vdots \\ 0 \\ 1 \\ 0 \\ \vdots \\ 0 \end{bmatrix}.$$

We are trying to show that

$$\mathbf{P}^n \cdot \vec{e}$$

converges to a vector all of whose components are the same. The idea is to view

$$\mathbf{P}^n \vec{e} = \mathbf{P}(\cdots(\mathbf{P}(\mathbf{P}(\mathbf{P}\vec{e}))))).$$

Consider the innermost product $\mathbf{P}\vec{e}$. Because $\mathbf{P}$ is a matrix of probabilities, where each row sums to 1, the effect of multiplying $\vec{e}$ by $\mathbf{P}$ is to replace each component of $\vec{e}$ by a value that is a *weighted average* of all the components. In particular, the effect is to bring all the components of $\vec{e}$ closer together. That is, the difference between the maximum component and the minimum component should decrease.

Here is an example of the effect of successive multiplications by $\mathbf{P}$:

$$\mathbf{P}\vec{e} = \begin{bmatrix} 1/2 & 1/3 & 1/6 \\ 1/3 & 1/3 & 1/3 \\ 1/8 & 3/4 & 1/8 \end{bmatrix} \cdot \begin{bmatrix} 0 \\ 1 \\ 0 \end{bmatrix} = \begin{bmatrix} 1/3 \\ 1/3 \\ 3/4 \end{bmatrix}.$$

$$\mathbf{P}(\mathbf{P}\vec{e}) = \begin{bmatrix} 1/2 & 1/3 & 1/6 \\ 1/3 & 1/3 & 1/3 \\ 1/8 & 3/4 & 1/8 \end{bmatrix} \cdot \begin{bmatrix} 1/3 \\ 1/3 \\ 3/4 \end{bmatrix} = \begin{bmatrix} 0.40 \\ 0.47 \\ 0.39 \end{bmatrix}.$$

Observe that after just two successive multiplications by $\mathbf{P}$, the components are already quite close!

We now claim that the difference between the maximum and minimum components of $\mathbf{P}^n \vec{e}$ shrinks as we increase n.

Claim 25.7 *Let M_n denote the maximum component of $\mathbf{P}^n \vec{e}$ and let m_n denote the minimum component of $\mathbf{P}^n \vec{e}$. Then*

$$M_n - m_n \leq (1 - 2s)(M_{n-1} - m_{n-1}), \tag{25.1}$$

where s is the smallest element in $\mathbf{P}$.

Proof: [Claim 25.7] To see intuitively why Claim 25.7 is true, consider the vector $\vec{y} = \mathbf{P}^{n-1}\vec{e}$. By our definition, the maximum component of $\vec{y}$ is M_{n-1} and the minimum is m_{n-1}. Now, if we multiply $\vec{y}$ by $\mathbf{P}$ (obtaining $\mathbf{P}\vec{y} = \mathbf{P}^n\vec{e}$), we are replacing each component of $\vec{y}$ by a weighted average of all the components of $\vec{y}$.

Question: More formally, what is an upper bound on the largest possible component, M_n, in $\mathbf{P} \cdot \vec{y} = \mathbf{P} \cdot \left(\mathbf{P}^{n-1}\vec{e}\right)$?

Answer: The largest possible M_n value is obtained when $\mathbf{P}$ is multiplied by $\vec{y}$ where all but one of the elements of $\vec{y}$ are M_{n-1}, with the remaining one being m_{n-1}, that is, $\vec{y}$ has only one small component.

To maximize M_n, we now want to make sure that the small m_{n-1} component of $\vec{y}$ is multiplied by the *smallest* possible value of $\mathbf{P}$, namely s. To do this, we consider the row, i, of $\mathbf{P}$ that contains s. Suppose s occurs in the jth column of $\mathbf{P}$. Then we make sure that m_{n-1} is likewise in the jth component of $\vec{y}$. This forces m_{n-1} to be multiplied by s. The remaining total weight in row i of $\mathbf{P}$ is $1 - s$, which gets multiplied by only M_{n-1} terms in $\vec{y}$. Thus an upper bound on M_n is given by:

$$M_n \leq s \cdot m_{n-1} + (1 - s) \cdot M_{n-1}. \tag{25.2}$$

Question: What is a lower bound on the smallest possible component, m_n in $\mathbf{P} \cdot \vec{y} = \mathbf{P} \cdot \left(\mathbf{P}^{n-1}\vec{e}\right)$?

Answer: Similarly, the smallest possible m_n value is obtained if all but one of the elements of $\vec{y}$ are m_{n-1}, with the remaining one being M_{n-1}. This time we want to make sure that the M_{n-1} component of $\vec{y}$ is weighted by the smallest possible value of $\mathbf{P}$, namely s. This allows the biggest possible remaining row weight of $1 - s$ to be applied to m_{n-1}. Thus a lower bound on m_n, the smallest component of $\mathbf{P} \cdot \vec{y}$, is:

$$m_n \geq (1 - s) \cdot m_{n-1} + s \cdot M_{n-1}. \tag{25.3}$$

Thus,

$$\begin{aligned}
M_n - m_n &\leq (25.2) - (25.3) \\
&= s \cdot m_{n-1} + (1 - s) \cdot M_{n-1} - (1 - s) \cdot m_{n-1} - s \cdot M_{n-1} \\
&= (1 - 2s)(M_{n-1} - m_{n-1}).
\end{aligned}$$ ∎

From Claim 25.7, it seems that the difference between the maximum and minimum elements of $\mathbf{P}^n\vec{e}$ continues to decrease as we continue to multiply by $\mathbf{P}$, until eventually all elements are the same, so we're done with the proof. This is true, except for a small hole ...

Question: Can you see the hole in the argument?

Answer: If $\mathbf{P}$ contains a zero element, then $s = 0$. In this case Claim 25.7 does not result in convergence, because $(1 - 2s) = 1$.

Question: How can this be fixed?

Hint: Even if $\mathbf{P}$ contains some zero elements, what do we know about $\mathbf{P}^n$ for high enough n, given that $\mathbf{P}$ is aperiodic and irreducible?

Answer: When $\mathbf{P}$ is aperiodic and irreducible, we will now show that even if $\mathbf{P}$ contains some zero elements, for all n beyond some point, $\mathbf{P}^n$ has all positive elements.

Claim 25.8 *Given $\mathbf{P}$ is aperiodic and irreducible, there exists some n_0, such that $\forall n \geq n_0$, $\mathbf{P}^n$ has all positive elements.*

Proof: [Claim 25.8] The proof is a consequence of the Euclidean Number Property (Theorem 25.3), as follows: Consider an arbitrary (j, j) entry of $\mathbf{P}$.

Question: If $P_{jj} > 0$, can we conclude that $(\mathbf{P}^n)_{jj} > 0$, $\forall n$?

Answer: Yes. The fact that there's a path of length 1 from j to j implies that there's a path of length n from j to j.

So suppose that $P_{jj} = 0$. By irreducibility, there exist paths from j to j. By aperiodicity, the gcd of these j-to-j paths is 1. Suppose, for example, the j-to-j paths have lengths x, y, and z, where $\gcd(x, y, z) = 1$. Hence, by the Euclidean Number Property, $\exists n_0(j, j)$, s.t., $\forall n \geq n_0(j, j)$, n can be expressed as a linear combination of x and y and z with non-negative integer coefficients; hence, $\forall n \geq n_0(j, j)$, there is a path of length n from j to j, and thus the (j, j)th entry of $\mathbf{P}^n$ is positive.

Now repeat this argument for all (i, i) pairs (there are only a finite number).

Next, consider two arbitrary states, i and j, where $i \neq j$. By irreducibility, there is some x s.t. there is a path from i to j of length x. However, since we also know that $\forall n \geq n_0(i, i)$ there is a path of length n from i to i, it follows that $\forall n \geq n_0(i, i) + x$ there's a path of length n from i to j. Define $n_0(i, j) = n_0(i, i) + x$.

Finally, define

$$n_0 = \max_{i,j}\{n_0(i, j)\}.$$

Now, for all $n \geq n_0$, $\mathbf{P}^n$ has all positive elements. ∎

To complete the proof of Theorem 25.6, we now define $\mathbf{P}' = \mathbf{P}^{n_0}$. Then,

$$\mathbf{P}^n = (\mathbf{P}^{n_0})^{n/n_0} = (\mathbf{P}')^{n/n_0} .$$

Now repeat the argument in Claim 25.7, except that rather than the decrease by a factor of $(1 - 2s) < 1$ occurring with each multiplication of $\mathbf{P}$, this decrease only happens every n_0 multiplications of $\mathbf{P}$. However, because $n/n_0 \to \infty$ as $n \to \infty$, we still have an infinite number of these decreases, meaning that

$$(\mathbf{P}')^{n/n_0} \to \mathbf{L}, \quad \text{as } n \to \infty.$$

Note that this argument still works even if n/n_0 is a fraction. In that case we define $n = m \cdot n_0 + r$, where $r < n_0$ and use m in place of n/n_0 in our argument. Here,

$$\mathbf{P}^n = \mathbf{P}^r \cdot (\mathbf{P}^{n_0})^m,$$

where the rightmost term converges to $\mathbf{L}$ as $m \to \infty$, and the $\mathbf{P}^r$ term doesn't affect this limit.

To finish off the proof of Theorem 25.6, we note that by Exercise 24.2, all powers of $\mathbf{P}$ have the property that the components of each row sum to 1. Furthermore, because $\mathbf{P}^{n_0}$ has all positive elements, and because multiplying by $\mathbf{P}$ only creates weighted averages of already positive values, then $\mathbf{P} \cdot \mathbf{P}^{n_0}$ still has all positive elements and so forth as we continue to multiply by $\mathbf{P}$. Hence the limiting matrix $\mathbf{L}$ will still have all positive elements and will have the property that the components of each row sum to 1. ∎

Summary: We have proven that for any aperiodic, irreducible, finite-state Markov chain, the limiting probabilities exist and are all positive.

> **Definition 25.9** *We say that a* finite-state *DTMC is* **ergodic** *if it has both desirable properties: aperiodicity and irreducibility. For the case of an infinite-state DTMC, ergodicity requires one more property (see Chapter 26).*

25.5 Mean Time Between Visits to a State

Consider the mean time between visits to state j, which we'll call m_{jj}. It seems that m_{jj} should be related to π_j, the limiting probability of being in state j. Theorem 25.12 shows that m_{jj} and π_j are in fact reciprocals.

> **Definition 25.10** *Let m_{ij} denote the expected number of time steps needed to first get to state j, given we are currently at state i. Likewise, let m_{jj} denote the expected number of steps between visits to state j.*

> **Theorem 25.11** *For an irreducible finite-state DTMC, m_{ij} is finite, for all i, j.*

Proof: See Exercise 25.19. ∎

Theorem 25.12 *For an irreducible, aperiodic finite-state Markov chain with transition matrix* **P**,

$$\pi_j = \frac{1}{m_{jj}} > 0,$$

where m_{jj} is the mean time between visits to state j and $\pi_j = \lim_{n \to \infty} (\mathbf{P}^n)_{ij}$.

Proof: We derive m_{ij} by conditioning on the first step, as follows:

$$m_{ij} = P_{ij} \cdot 1 + \sum_{k \neq j} P_{ik}(1 + m_{kj})$$

$$= 1 + \sum_{k \neq j} P_{ik} m_{kj}. \tag{25.4}$$

Likewise,

$$m_{jj} = P_{jj} \cdot 1 + \sum_{k \neq j} P_{jk}(1 + m_{kj})$$

$$= 1 + \sum_{k \neq j} P_{jk} m_{kj}. \tag{25.5}$$

We will now express (25.4) and (25.5) using matrix notation. All the matrices in this proof are of the same dimension as **P**. Let **M** be a matrix whose (i, j)th entry is m_{ij}. For purposes of the proof, it will be convenient to express **M** as a sum of two matrices,

$$\mathbf{M} = \mathbf{D} + \mathbf{N},$$

where **D** is a matrix whose entries are all zero, except for its diagonal entries: $d_{jj} = m_{jj}$, and **N** is a matrix whose diagonal entries are all zero, but where $N_{ij} = m_{ij}, \forall i \neq j$. Finally, let **E** be a matrix with *all* entries 1. Then we can express (25.4) and (25.5) as:

$$\mathbf{M} = \mathbf{E} + \mathbf{PN}. \tag{25.6}$$

Rewriting (25.6), we have

$$\mathbf{N} + \mathbf{D} = \mathbf{E} + \mathbf{PN}$$
$$(\mathbf{I} - \mathbf{P}) \cdot \mathbf{N} = \mathbf{E} - \mathbf{D}.$$

From Theorem 25.6, since we have aperiodicity and irreducibility, we know that the limiting distribution, $\vec{\pi}$, exists. Multiplying both sides by $\vec{\pi}$, we have:

$$\vec{\pi} \cdot (\mathbf{I} - \mathbf{P}) \cdot \mathbf{N} = \vec{\pi}(\mathbf{E} - \mathbf{D}). \tag{25.7}$$

Question: What do we know about the left-hand side of (25.7)?

Hint: Remember that $\vec{\pi}$ is also a stationary distribution, by Theorem 25.6.

Answer:

$$\vec{\pi}\mathbf{P} = \vec{\pi}$$
$$\Rightarrow \vec{\pi}(\mathbf{I} - \mathbf{P}) = \vec{0}$$
$$\Rightarrow \vec{\pi}(\mathbf{I} - \mathbf{P})\mathbf{N} = \vec{0}.$$

Thus, from (25.7) we have:

$$\vec{0} = \vec{\pi}(\mathbf{E} - \mathbf{D})$$
$$\vec{\pi}\mathbf{E} = \vec{\pi}\mathbf{D}$$
$$(1, 1, \ldots, 1) = (\pi_0 m_{00}, \pi_1 m_{11}, \ldots, \pi_{M-1} m_{M-1, M-1})$$
$$\pi_i m_{ii} = 1, \quad \forall i$$
$$\pi_i = \frac{1}{m_{ii}} > 0, \quad \forall i,$$

where the last line follows from the fact that m_{ii} is finite by Theorem 25.11. ∎

Corollary 25.13 *For an irreducible,* periodic *finite-state Markov chain,*

$$\pi_j^{stationary} = \frac{1}{m_{jj}} > 0,$$

where m_{jj} is the mean time between visits to state j and $\pi_j^{stationary}$ is the stationary probability of being in state j.

Proof: This is an easy consequence of the proof of Theorem 25.12 and is shown in Exercise 25.5. ∎

25.6 Long-Run Time Averages

For the purpose of this section, we imagine that we have an ergodic, finite-state DTMC, such as that shown in Figure 25.5.

A **random walk** is a walk through a Markov chain, where we move *indefinitely* between the states of the Markov chain according to the probabilities of the chain. For example, we might start at some state like *Blah*, and next move to *Tired* and then to *Wasted* and from there maybe back to *Blah*, and so on. Of course, you might take a different random walk through the chain, where you again start at state *Blah*, but this time next move to state *Achy* and from there back to state *Blah* and so on. Each random walk is often referred to as a **sample path** in that

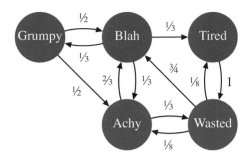

Figure 25.5 *The moods of students in the aftermath of Carnival festivities.*

it depends on the random coin flips. We say sample *path* rather than a sample *point*, because the walk is infinitely long.

Let $N_j(t)$ be the number of visits to state j by time t on our random walk. Our goal is to formally define p_j, the long-run proportion of time that a random walk spends in state j.

Question: How might we define p_j using $N_j(t)$?

> **Definition 25.14** *Given an irreducible DTMC, we define the* **long-run time-average fraction of time** *that a random walk on the DTMC spends in state j as:*
>
> $$p_j = \lim_{t \to \infty} \frac{N_j(t)}{t},$$
>
> *where $N_j(t)$ is the number of times that the random walk enters state j by time t (in the first t time steps).*

Question: Why does Definition 25.14 start by specifying that the DTMC is irreducible?

Answer: If the DTMC were not irreducible, then the time-average fraction of time spent in state j might depend on where we start, which would make it undefined.

In this section we ask: *How does p_j compare to π_j?*

Recall the definition of π_j, the **limiting probability** of being in state j:

$$\pi_j = \lim_{n \to \infty} (\mathbf{P}^n)_{ij}.$$

While p_j is an average over a *single* sample path, π_j is an average over *many* sample paths. To see this, let's consider the quantity

$$(\mathbf{P}^n)_{ij} \, .$$

This represents the probability of being in state j after n steps, given that we started in state i. If we consider $n = 1$, $(\mathbf{P}^1)_{ij} = P_{ij}$, namely the probability that in the first step we move to state j. On the other hand, $(\mathbf{P}^2)_{ij}$ is the weighted average over M two-step sample paths (the intermediate state could be any of the M states). Similarly, $(\mathbf{P}^3)_{ij}$ is the weighted average over M^2 three-step sample paths, and so on. We refer to

$$\pi_j = \lim_{n \to \infty} (\mathbf{P}^n)_{ij}$$

as an **ensemble average**, meaning that it is an average over *many* sample paths, in fact an infinite number.

Question: Does $p_j = \pi_j$?

Answer: It is not at all obvious that p_j, the *time-average* fraction of time spent in state j on a *single* sample path, should equal π_j, the *ensemble average* fraction of time spent in state j, averaged over *all* sample paths. The purpose of this section is to prove that, when π_j exists, then, on "almost all" sample paths, $p_j = \pi_j$. We will spend the rest of this section making this claim precise and proving it.

Before we get into it, we note one important way in which π_j and p_j differ.

Question: Recall that aperiodicity was required for π_j to exist. Is aperiodicity required for p_j to exist?

Answer: No. Irreducibility is all that is needed to ensure p_j is well defined.

To prove our claim that $p_j = \pi_j$, we will need to first understand the Strong Law of Large Numbers and then to learn a little renewal theory.

25.6.1 Strong Law of Large Numbers

The Strong Law of Large Numbers (SLLN) is an extremely important result in probability theory, but it is difficult to prove. We refer the interested reader to [22].

Theorem 25.15 (SLLN) *Let $X_1, X_2, \ldots$ be a sequence of independent, identically distributed (i.i.d.) random variables each with finite mean $\mathbf{E}[X]$. Let $S_n = \sum_{i=1}^n X_i$. Then, with probability 1,*

$$\lim_{n \to \infty} \frac{S_n}{n} = \mathbf{E}[X] \, .$$

While we omit the proof in this book, we will spend time discussing the meaning of the result. Let's consider, for example, that

$$X_i \sim \text{Bernoulli}\,(0.5)\,,$$

that is X_i represents the ith flip of a fair coin. Here, S_n represents the sum of the first n coinflips, and $\frac{S_n}{n}$ represents the average over the first n coinflips. SLLN says that, when n gets large, this average should converge to 0.5.

At first this sounds entirely obvious. After all, what else could the average be?

Looking a little closer, we note that SLLN says this happens **"with probability 1."** The term "with probability 1" is roughly saying that the statement is true on *almost every* sample path. A sample path here refers to a sequence of instances of $X_1, X_2, X_3, \ldots$ Each sample path is infinitely long, and there are infinitely many sample paths (there are two values possible for each X_i). More precisely, the statement "with probability 1" says that if we consider the number of "bad" sample paths on which the convergence doesn't happen and divide that by the total number of sample paths, then:

$$\frac{\text{Number bad sample paths up to length } n}{\text{Total number sample paths up to length } n} \to 0 \ \text{ as } n \to \infty.$$

Let's consider whether this makes sense.

Question: What's an example of a "bad" sample path?

Answer: $00000\ldots$ or $11111\ldots$

Question: Are there a finite or infinite number of bad sample paths?

Answer: Infinite.

Question: Is the number of bad sample paths countably infinite or uncountably infinite?

Answer: Uncountably infinite. Here's how to see this. Let's refer to the sequence 110 as a "red car" and to the sequence 101 as a "blue car" (Figure 25.6). Now any sequence made up of red and blue cars is clearly bad, because it has twice as many 1's as 0's. However, there are an uncountable number of possible sequences of red and blue cars (by Cantor's diagonalization argument [11]).

Figure 25.6 *Any sequence of red and blue cars is a bad sample path.*

Given that there are an uncountably infinite number of bad sample paths, it should be a little clearer why it's not so obvious that the fraction of bad sample paths goes to 0. This explains the power of SLLN.

25.6.2 A Bit of Renewal Theory

> **Definition 25.16** *A **renewal process** is any process for which the times between events are i.i.d. random variables, with a non-negative distribution X.*

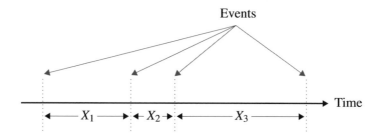

Figure 25.7 *A renewal process. $X_i \sim X$, for all i.*

An example of a renewal process is shown in Figure 25.7. Let $N(t)$ denote the number of renewal events by time t. Then, we have the following theorem:

> **Theorem 25.17 (Renewal Theorem)** *For a renewal process, if $\mathbf{E}[X] > 0$ is the mean time between renewals, where $\mathbf{E}[X]$ is finite, we have*
>
> $$\lim_{t \to \infty} \frac{N(t)}{t} = \frac{1}{\mathbf{E}[X]} \text{ with probability 1.} \tag{25.8}$$

Proof: The basic idea in this proof is to apply SLLN, which gives us the convergence on all sample paths with probability 1 (abbreviated, w.p.1). Let S_n be the time of the nth event. Then we have, $\forall t$,

$$S_{N(t)} \quad \leq \quad t \quad < \quad S_{N(t)+1}$$

$$\frac{S_{N(t)}}{N(t)} \quad \leq \quad \frac{t}{N(t)} \quad < \quad \frac{S_{N(t)+1}}{N(t)}.$$

Looking at the leftmost term, we have:

$$\frac{S_{N(t)}}{N(t)} = \frac{\sum_{i=1}^{N(t)} X_i}{N(t)} \longrightarrow \mathbf{E}[X] \text{ as } t \to \infty \quad \text{w.p.1 (SLLN)}.$$

Looking at the rightmost term, we have:

$$\frac{S_{N(t)+1}}{N(t)} = \frac{S_{N(t)+1}}{N(t)+1} \cdot \frac{N(t)+1}{N(t)} \longrightarrow \mathbf{E}[X] \cdot 1 \text{ as } t \to \infty \quad \text{w.p.1 (SLLN)}.$$

So, by the sandwich theorem, the center term likewise converges to $\mathbf{E}[X]$, namely:

$$\frac{t}{N(t)} \longrightarrow \mathbf{E}[X] \text{ w.p.1},$$

which implies that

$$\Rightarrow \frac{N(t)}{t} \longrightarrow \frac{1}{\mathbf{E}[X]} \text{ as } t \to \infty \text{ w.p.1}.$$

∎

25.6.3 Equality of the Time Average and Ensemble Average

We are finally ready to relate p_j, the time-average fraction of time that a DTMC spends in state j, to π_j, the limiting probability of being in state j.

> **Theorem 25.18** *For a finite-state irreducible DTMC, with probability 1,*
>
> $$p_j = \frac{1}{m_{jj}}.$$
>
> *For a finite-state, irreducible, and aperiodic DTMC, with probability 1,*
>
> $$p_j = \pi_j.$$

Proof: By Theorem 25.11, we know that m_{jj} is finite. Thus we can apply the Renewal Theorem (Theorem 25.17) to say that

$$p_j = \lim_{t\to\infty} \frac{N_j(t)}{t} = \frac{1}{m_{jj}} \quad \text{w.p.1},$$

where $N_j(t)$ is the number of visits to state j by time t.

Now, if we have both irreducibility and aperiodicity, we can invoke Theorem 25.12 which says that

$$\pi_j = \frac{1}{m_{jj}}.$$

Thus, $\pi_j = p_j$, w.p.1.

∎

25.7 Summary of Results for Ergodic Finite-State DTMCs

So far we've seen that for a finite-state DTMC which is both aperiodic and irreducible, the limiting distribution, $\vec{\pi}$ exists. This $\vec{\pi}$ is also the unique stationary distribution and furthermore represents the time-average probabilities of being in each state. In Theorem 25.19 we summarize all the results we've seen about ergodic finite-state DTMCs.

Theorem 25.19 (Summary theorem for ergodic, finite-state DTMCs) *In a finite-state DTMC, the word* ergodic *refers to two properties: aperiodic and irreducible. Given an ergodic finite-state chain, the following results hold:*

- *(Theorem 25.6) The limiting distribution exists and has all-positive components.*
- *(Theorem 25.12)* $\pi_j^{limiting} = \frac{1}{m_{jj}}$.
- *(Theorem 24.9) The stationary distribution is unique and is equal to the limiting distribution.*
- *(Theorem 25.18) Time-average* $p_j = \frac{1}{m_{jj}}$, *w.p.*1.
- *Putting it all together, we have that:*

$$0 < \frac{1}{m_{jj}} = \pi_j^{limiting} = \pi_j^{stationary} = p_j, \ w.p.1.$$

25.8 What If My DTMC Is Irreducible but Periodic?

So life is great when your DTMC is ergodic. But suppose instead you have a finite-state DTMC that is irreducible but periodic.

For any *periodic* chain, the limiting distribution does not exist (because the probability of being in a state depends on the time step).

However, it turns out that if the finite-state DTMC is irreducible, that alone suffices to ensure that the stationary distribution *exists* and is *unique* [35, section 9.8]. We saw an example of such an irreducible periodic chain in Figure 25.1. For such chains, the stationary distribution represents the long-run time-average proportion of time spent in each state, that is, the p_j's.

Very roughly the proof in [35, section 9.8] starts with the observation that when a chain is irreducible, all states have the *same* period d (see Exercise 25.17). Thus, it turns out that we can divide all the states into d residue classes, where some states are visited at times 0 mod d, some at times 1 mod d, ..., and some are visited at times $d - 1$ mod d. Thus, while $\lim_{n \to \infty} (\mathbf{P}^n)_{ij}$ does not exist, $\lim_{n \to \infty} (\mathbf{P}^{nd})_{ij}$ does exist, where d is the period of the chain. Thus we can think of the limiting distribution as existing if we only observe the chain every dth time step; and when the limiting distribution exists, we get a unique stationary distribution.

Since the case of irreducible, periodic finite-state DTMCs comes up quite a bit, we provide another summary theorem with everything you need to know about this case.

Theorem 25.20 (Summary for irreducible, periodic, finite-state DTMCs)
For a finite-state DTMC that is irreducible, but periodic:

- *The limiting distribution does not exist (it depends on the time step).*
- *The stationary distribution exists and is unique [35].*
- *(Theorem 25.11) For every state j, m_{jj} is finite.*
- *(Corollary 25.13) $\pi_j^{stationary} = \frac{1}{m_{jj}}$.*
- *(Theorem 25.18) Time-average $p_j = \frac{1}{m_{jj}}$, w.p.1.*
- *Putting it all together, we have that:*

$$0 < \frac{1}{m_{jj}} = \pi_j^{stationary} = p_j, \text{ w.p.1.}$$

25.9 When the DTMC Is Not Irreducible

In the case of a finite-state DTMC that is *not* irreducible, the limiting distribution may or may not exist.

For examples of chains which are not irreducible and the limiting distribution *does not* exist, see Figure 25.2 and Figure 25.4(a). Generally, a lack of existence happens if the DTMC consists of two completely disconnected components. In such situations, the limiting probability of being in state j is not independent of the starting state i. Note that while the limiting distribution doesn't exist, in Exercise 25.20 we prove that (at least one) stationary always exists for any finite-state chain.

An example of a chain which is not irreducible, yet the limiting distribution nevertheless *exists*, is given in Figure 25.4(b), where the limiting distribution is $\vec{\pi} = (0, 1)$, even though the chain is not irreducible and the period is undefined. In cases when the limiting distribution *does* exist, it is no longer the case that the limiting probability of every state j is positive, as we had in Theorem 25.12, since some states may not be reachable, or there may be an "absorbing" state (or states), from which one never leaves, as is the case in Figure 25.4(b).

Even if the entire chain is not irreducible, the chain can still be subdivided into irreducible components (sometimes individual states), where an irreducible component may function as its own ergodic chain.

In the next section, we will encounter some examples of chains that are not irreducible and illustrate the above points.

25.10 An Application: PageRank

We now consider an application of finite-state DTMCs and some of the ergodicity concepts that we've been studying.

Question: How many web search engines can you name?

Answer: Here are a few: W3Catalog (1993), WebCrawler (1994), Lycos (1994), AltaVista (1995), Excite (1995), Yahoo! (1995), Google (1998), Bing (2009).

The goal of a web search engine is not just to find a page that contains the item that you're searching for, but to find *the best* page that contains that item. For example, your name might appear on a lot of web pages: chess tournaments, swim competitions, theater productions, etc. Every search engine will show all these different pages. However what makes a search engine good is its ability to **rank** the pages, showing the most important pages first, so that someone searching for you will first see your Homepage or Linked In page, rather than that picture of you as a third grader.

Of course, how can a search engine know exactly which of the thousand pages is the most relevant one?

A common solution is to rank the pages in order of the number of links to that page (often called **backlinks** of the page), starting with the page that has the highest number of pointers into it. We refer to this strategy as *citation counting*.

Citation counting is a very commonly used measure of importance. For example, many tenure decisions are determined not by your number of publications, but by the number of citations to your publications.

Question: Suppose that we could determine the number of backlinks of each page (number of links pointing to the page). Why would that *not* necessarily be a good measure of the importance of the page?

Answer:

(1) Not all links are equal. If a page is pointed to from *cnn.com*, that link should be counted much more than if a page is pointed to from Joe Schmo's page.

(2) The citation counting scheme is easily tricked. Suppose I want my web page to have a high rank. I simply create a thousand pages that each point to my web page. Now my web page has a thousand pointers into it, so it should be ranked highly. (Hmmm ... not a bad way to handle the tenure citation issue too).

Okay, so citation counting is not the best of schemes. While it is insufficient to just count the number of pages pointing into a page p, we might do better by weighting each pointer by the number of pages pointing into it.

Question: Why is this system also easy to fool?

Answer: I can again create a thousand dummy web pages and have them all point to each other, in a clique, as well as pointing to my page. Now my web page has a high number of backlinks, all of which also have a high number of backlinks.

Google's PageRank Solution: Google's solution is to define PageRank recursively: *"A page has high rank if the sum of the ranks of its backlinks is high."* Observe that this covers both the case when a page has many backlinks and when a page has a few highly ranked backlinks.

Question: It is easy to say that "a page has high rank if the sum of the ranks of its backlinks is high," but how does that help us figure out the rank of a page?

Answer: The "aha" that the Google founders made was to realize that the recursive definition is actually saying

$$\pi_j = \sum_{i=1}^{n} \pi_i P_{ij},$$

where n is the number of pages.

That is, the only way for page j to have high limiting probability is if the pages i pointing into j have high limiting probability. Remind you of anything?

The rank of a page is thus just its stationary probability in a Markov chain!

Algorithm 25.21 (Google's PageRank algorithm)

1. *Create a DTMC transition diagram where there is one state for each web page and there is an arrow from state i to state j if and only if page i has a link to page j.*
2. *If page i has $k > 0$ outgoing links, then set the probability on each outgoing arrow from state i to be $1/k$.*
3. *Solve the DTMC to determine stationary probabilities. Pages are then ranked based on their stationary probabilities (higher probability first).*

This simple algorithm was the original basis behind the entire Google company. Today, Google has incorporated additional heuristics.

Example 25.22 (Well-behaved web graph)

Suppose the entire web consists of the three pages shown in Figure 25.8(a). Then the corresponding DTMC transition diagram is shown in Figure 25.8(b).

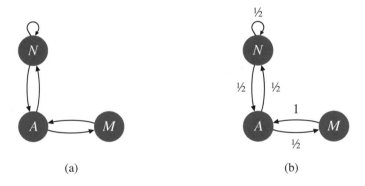

(a)   (b)

Figure 25.8 *(a) Links between web pages. (b) Corresponding DTMC transition diagram.*

We now solve the stationary equations:

$$\pi_A = \frac{1}{2}\pi_N + \pi_M$$

$$\pi_N = \frac{1}{2}\pi_A + \frac{1}{2}\pi_N$$

$$\pi_M = \frac{1}{2}\pi_A$$

$$1 = \pi_A + \pi_M + \pi_N.$$

This results in: $\pi_A = \pi_N = \frac{2}{5}$; $\pi_M = \frac{1}{5}$.

Intuition behind the PageRank algorithm: Imagine that each page initially has one unit of importance. At each round, each page shares whatever importance it has among its successors. Pages with a lot of incoming links will receive lots of importance (will be visited frequently in the DTMC).

25.10.1 Problems with Real Web Graphs

Unfortunately, PageRank does not work well on all web graphs. Consider the following two examples.

Example 25.23 (Dead end or spider trap)

Consider Figure 25.8(a), where this time there is either no outgoing link from page M (in this case M is called a "dead end") or there is a self-loop at state M (in this case M is called a "spider trap"). In either case, Figure 25.9 shows the corresponding DTMC transition diagram.

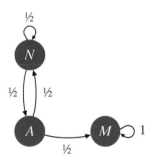

Figure 25.9 *DTMC for a web graph with a dead end or spider trap at M.*

The stationary equations are:

$$\pi_N = \frac{1}{2}\pi_A + \frac{1}{2}\pi_N$$

$$\pi_M = \frac{1}{2}\pi_A + \pi_M$$

$$\pi_A = \frac{1}{2}\pi_N$$

$$\pi_A + \pi_N + \pi_M = 1.$$

The solution to these equations is $\pi_M = 1$, $\pi_N = 0 = \pi_A$. These are also the limiting probabilities (note that the start state does not matter). Somehow this solution is very unsatisfying. Just because person M chooses to be anti-social and not link to anyone else, it should not follow that person M is the only important person on the web. Our solution does not match our intuitive view of surfing a web graph.

Example 25.24 (Two spider traps)

Now imagine that both M and N are anti-social and link only to themselves. The resulting DTMC transition diagram is shown in Figure 25.10.

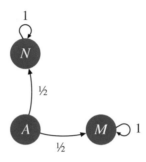

Figure 25.10 *DTMC for a web graph with two spider traps.*

The corresponding stationary equations are:

$$\pi_N = \frac{1}{2} \cdot \pi_A + \pi_N$$

$$\pi_M = \frac{1}{2} \cdot \pi_A + \pi_M$$

$$\pi_A = 0$$

$$\pi_A + \pi_N + \pi_M = 1.$$

Again our graph is not irreducible. Observe that there are now an infinite number of possible stationary solutions. This is because the limiting probabilities depend on the start state. Again the solution is very unsatisfying.

25.10.2 Google's Solution to Dead Ends and Spider Traps

Google's initial solution to dead ends and spider traps is to "tax" each page some fraction of its "importance" and then distribute that taxed importance equally among all pages in the web graph. This "tax" keeps the DTMC from getting trapped in a dead end or spider trap.

Figure 25.11 shows the effect of applying a 30% tax on the DTMC of Figure 25.9. First, every original transition is multiplied by 70%. Then, for each state s in an

M-state chain, we add a transition of weight $\frac{30\%}{M}$ from state s to every other state, including itself. Thus in the three-state chain in Figure 25.9, we add a transition of weight 10% from each state to every other state.

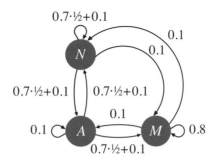

Figure 25.11 *Corresponding DTMC transition diagram.*

Observe that the spider trap is now no longer a problem, and we can easily solve for the limiting probabilities:

$$\pi_A = 0.19 \qquad \pi_M = 0.55 \qquad \pi_N = 0.26.$$

The problem now is that these limiting probabilities are highly dependent on the amount of tax!

25.10.3 Evaluation of the PageRank Algorithm and Practical Considerations

PageRank is intended to give an indication of the popularity of a page. This works well when the graph is irreducible, but it is problematic when there are spider traps or dead ends. The taxation solution for solving the spider trap problem seems ad hoc. If the tax is too small, then we still end up with too high a limiting probability at the spider trap state (as in $\pi_M = 0.55$ in Section 25.10.2). Thus we need to use a high tax. Yet a high tax seems totally unrealistic, because it leads to every state being of equal weight.

There's also the practical consideration: How does Google go about solving the DTMC for the stationary probabilities, given that it is a huge (finite) DTMC? Solving such a large number of simultaneous equations seems difficult.

Question: Is there another approach to obtain the limiting probabilities?

Answer: Yes, we can take powers of **P**, the transition probability matrix. This turns out to be faster when **P** is large and sparse and only an approximate solution is needed. This is the approach employed by Google.

25.11 From Stationary Equations to Time-Reversibility Equations

Thus far, to derive the limiting distribution of a DTMC, we solve the stationary equations. The purpose of this section is to consider a few *alternative systems of equations*. We will introduce "balance equations," which are only a small twist on stationary equations, and then introduce "time-reversibility equations," which are entirely different and sometimes greatly simplify the process.

All this is best illustrated via an example. Consider the DTMC in Figure 25.12 and its corresponding stationary equations.

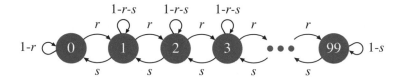

Figure 25.12 *A finite-state DTMC. Assume that* $0 < r, s < 1$.

Stationary equations for DTMC in Figure 25.12:

$$\pi_0 = \pi_0(1 - r) + \pi_1 s$$
$$\pi_1 = \pi_0 r + \pi_1(1 - r - s) + \pi_2 s$$
$$\pi_2 = \pi_1 r + \pi_2(1 - r - s) + \pi_3 s$$
$$\cdots$$
$$\pi_i = \pi_{i-1} r + \pi_i(1 - r - s) + \pi_{i+1} s$$
$$\cdots$$
$$\pi_{99} = \pi_{98} r + \pi_{99}(1 - s)$$
$$\sum_{j=0}^{99} \pi_j = 1.$$

These stationary equations are solvable (see Exercise 25.6), but are cumbersome.

Now consider an alternative to stationary equations, called **balance equations**.

> **Definition 25.25** *The* **balance equations** *for a Markov chain equate the total rate of leaving each state with the total rate of entering the state.*

Question: For a DTMC with transition probability matrix **P**, what is the rate of leaving state i?

This may be hard to think about, so let's start with an easier question:

Question: For a DTMC with transition probability matrix $\mathbf{P}$, what is the rate of transitions from state i to state j?

Answer:

$$\pi_i P_{ij} = \text{rate of transitions from state } i \text{ to state } j.$$

To see this, note that the "rate" of transitions from state i to state j is defined as the number of transitions per time step that have their start point in i and end point in j. To understand this quantity, observe that the DTMC is in state i for π_i fraction of all time steps. For P_{ij} fraction of those time steps, the DTMC will next move to state j. Hence, for $\pi_i P_{ij}$ fraction of all time steps, the DTMC is in state i *and* will move to state j in the next transition. Thus, if we look over t time steps (let t be large), then $\pi_i P_{ij} t$ total transitions will have their start point in i and their end point in j. Dividing by t, we see that the *rate* of transitions (number of transitions per time step) that go directly from i to j is $\pi_i P_{ij}$.

Question: So what is the total rate of transitions out of state i?

Answer: The expression $\sum_j \pi_i P_{ij}$ represents the total rate of transitions out of state i, including possibly returning right back to state i (if there are self-loops in the chain). If we want the total rate of transitions out of state i not including returning back to i, then we write: $\sum_{j \neq i} \pi_i P_{ij}$.

Definition 25.26 *The **balance equations** for a DTMC with transition matrix $\mathbf{P}$ is the set of equations*

$$\sum_{j \neq i} \pi_i P_{ij} = \sum_{j \neq i} \pi_j P_{ji} \quad and \quad \sum_i \pi_i = 1. \tag{25.9}$$

These hold for every state i. They equate (balance) the rate that we leave state i to go to a state other than i, with the rate that we enter state i from a state other than i.

Balance equations for DTMC in Figure 25.12:

$$\pi_0 r = \pi_1 s$$
$$\pi_1(r+s) = \pi_0 r + \pi_2 s$$
$$\pi_2(r+s) = \pi_1 r + \pi_3 s$$
$$\cdots$$
$$\pi_i(r+s) = \pi_{i-1} r + \pi_{i+1} s$$
$$\cdots$$
$$\pi_{99}(s) = \pi_{98} r$$
$$\sum_{j=0}^{99} \pi_j = 1.$$

It is easy to see that the balance equations for Figure 25.12 are equivalent to the stationary equations (we've basically just ignored the self-loops in the chain to create simpler equations). Intuitively, the balance equations make sense because every time we leave state i, we cannot again leave state i until we first return to state i.

> **Theorem 25.27** *Given a DTMC with transition matrix* **P**, *the balance equations for the DTMC are equivalent to the stationary equations. Thus, satisfying either set of equations is equally good.*

Proof: Recall the stationary equation for state i:

$$\pi_i = \sum_j \pi_j P_{ji}. \tag{25.10}$$

We also know that

$$\pi_i = \pi_i \sum_j P_{ij} = \sum_j \pi_i P_{ij}. \tag{25.11}$$

Combining (25.10) and (25.11), we have:

$$\pi_i = \sum_j \pi_i P_{ij} = \sum_j \pi_j P_{ji}. \tag{25.12}$$

We now subtract $\pi_i P_{ii}$ from both sides of (25.12):

$$\sum_j \pi_i P_{ij} - \pi_i P_{ii} = \sum_j \pi_j P_{ji} - \pi_i P_{ii}$$

$$\sum_{j \neq i} \pi_i P_{ij} = \sum_{j \neq i} \pi_j P_{ji}.$$

Hence we obtain the balance equations.   ∎

Balance equations can also be applied to a set of states as well as to a single state. For example, if a Markov chain is divided into two sets of states – call these S and S^c (here S^c denotes the complement of S) – then we can write equations equating the rate of transitions (the "flux") from S to S^c with the rate of transitions from S^c to S.

Question: Why does it make sense that the total flux from S to S^c should equal that from S^c to S?

Answer: The argument is identical to what we observed for a single state. Every time a transition takes us from S to S^c, we have left the states in S. We therefore cannot have another transition from S to S^c until we reenter the states in S, but this requires a transition from S^c to S.

We now return to the DTMC in Figure 25.12, and try to write even simpler equations. Such equations are referred to as **time-reversibility equations**.

Definition 25.28 *The* **time-reversibility equations** *for a DTMC with transition matrix* $\mathbf{P}$ *is the set of equations*

$$\pi_i P_{ij} = \pi_j P_{ji}, \quad \forall i, j \qquad \text{and} \qquad \sum_i \pi_i = 1. \qquad (25.13)$$

These equations apply to every pair of states, i, j. Specifically, there is one equation written for each pair of state, i, j. They equate the rate of transitions from i to j with the rate of transitions from j to i.

Time-reversibility equations for DTMC in Figure 25.12:

$$\pi_0 r = \pi_1 s$$
$$\pi_1 r = \pi_2 s$$
$$\pi_2 r = \pi_3 s$$
$$\cdots$$
$$\pi_i r = \pi_{i+1} s$$
$$\cdots$$
$$\pi_{98} r = \pi_{99} s$$
$$\sum_{j=0}^{99} \pi_j = 1.$$

The time-reversibility equations are *much* simpler than the stationary equations.

Question: Are the time-reversibility equations above equivalent to the stationary equations or balance equations that we've seen?

Answer: No!

While the time-reversibility equations look very different from the stationary and balance equations, it turns out that they *do* yield the correct stationary distribution for the chain in Figure 25.12. This seems impossible, but try it!

Question: Given an aperiodic, irreducible DTMC, are the time-reversibility equations always satisfied?

Answer: No.

Question: What's an example of a chain where the time-reversibility equations are not satisfied?

Answer: Imagine a chain which is irreducible, but where there is an edge from

i to j, but no edge from j to i. Then the rate of transitions from j to i is by definition 0, although the rate of transitions from i to j is non-zero.

In Theorem 25.29, we prove that *if* we can find π_i's that satisfy the time-reversibility equations, then those π_i's are the stationary probabilities. In that case, we say that the chain is called "time-reversible." If we can't find π_i's that satisfy the time-reversibility equations, this does not imply that there's no stationary distribution. It just means that we have to start from scratch with the (more complicated) stationary equations.

Theorem 25.29 (Time-reversibility implies stationarity) *For a DTMC with transition matrix* **P**, *suppose we can find* $x_0, x_1, x_2, \ldots$ *such that,* $\forall i, j$:

$$x_i P_{ij} = x_j P_{ji} \qquad and \qquad \sum_i x_i = 1. \qquad (25.14)$$

Then the vector $\vec{x} = (x_0, x_1, x_2, \ldots)$ *is a stationary distribution, and we say that the DTMC is* **time-reversible**.

Proof:

$$x_i P_{ij} = x_j P_{ji}, \qquad \forall i, j$$
$$\Rightarrow \sum_i x_i P_{ij} = \sum_i x_j P_{ji}$$
$$\Rightarrow \sum_i x_i P_{ij} = x_j \sum_i P_{ji}$$
$$\Rightarrow \sum_i x_i P_{ij} = x_j.$$

Hence, together with $\sum_i x_i = 1$, the x_j's satisfy the stationary equations. ∎

Remark 1: In some books, the definition of "time-reversible" requires additionally that the chain be ergodic, but we won't be making ergodicity a requirement.
Remark 2: Theorem 25.29 does not require that the number of states is finite.

Question: The time-reversibility equations are much simpler than the stationary or balance equations, but they aren't always solvable. For the chain in Figure 25.12, the time-reversibility equations had a solution. What was special about this chain?

Answer: The chain in Figure 25.12 has the property that the rate of transitions from state i to state j is always equal to the rate of transitions from state j to state i. To see this, notice first that if j is anything other than $i + 1$ or $i - 1$, then the rate of transitions from i to j is zero, and, likewise, the rate of transitions from j to i is zero. Now suppose $j = i + 1$. The *number* of transitions from i to

$i + 1$ during time t is the same (within 1) of the *number* of transitions from $i + 1$ to i. This is because every time we go from state i to $i + 1$, we can't repeat that transition until we first go from $i + 1$ to i. This translates to the *rates* being the same when we divide by time.

As we'll see in the exercises (see, for example, Exercises 25.9 and 25.18) there are plenty of Markov chains that are time-reversible, but it is not always easy to guess in advance which chains will have this beautiful property. When trying to determine the stationary solution, you *first try to solve the time-reversibility equations*. If those yield a solution, then you're done (your solution also satisfies the stationary equations). If the time-reversibility equations are not solvable, then you'll need to try solving the stationary or balance equations.

Question: A final reminder: Solving the stationary equations, or balance equations, or time-reversibility equations, yields a stationary distribution. What does that tell us about the limiting distribution?

Answer: The fact that we have a stationary distribution, $\vec{\pi}$, does not tell us anything about whether a limiting distribution exists. However, if we have a finite-state, irreducible, aperiodic DTMC, then, by Theorem 25.19, $\vec{\pi}$ is also the limiting distribution.

25.12 Exercises

25.1 **Two finite-state chains**
Figure 25.13 depicts two finite-state chains. For each chain, answer the questions below.

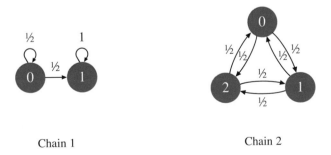

Chain 1   Chain 2

Figure 25.13 *Two finite-state chains for Exercise 25.1.*

(a) Is the DTMC irreducible?
(b) Is the DTMC aperiodic?

(c) Does the DTMC have a limiting distribution? If so, what is it? If not, why not?

(d) Does the DTMC have a stationary distribution? If so, what is it? If not, why not?

Explain each answer by citing the appropriate theorems.

25.2 **Passing around a ball**

[Proposed by Sam Yeom] In answering these questions, cite the theorems that you use in making your claims.

(a) Five people stand in a circle, passing a ball around. Suppose that each person either passes the ball right or left with 50% probability each. What is the stationary distribution? Is this also the limiting distribution?

(b) Five people stand in a circle, passing a ball around. Suppose that each person passes the ball to their right with probability 1. What is the stationary distribution? Is this also the limiting distribution?

(c) Now suppose that the five people are standing in a line. Each person passes the ball to their right or left with 50% probability each, except for the two people at the ends who always pass it to their one neighbor. What is the stationary distribution? Is this also the limiting distribution?

(d) Again the five people are standing in a line. Again each person passes the ball to their right or left with 50% probability each, except for the two people at the ends who always hold on to the ball instead of passing it. What is the stationary distribution? Is this also the limiting distribution?

25.3 **Multiple stationary distributions**

Ishani's finite-state DTMC has multiple stationary distributions. We do not know whether the chain is aperiodic or irreducible. What can we conclude?

(a) Ishani's DTMC has multiple limiting distributions.

(b) Ishani's DTMC has no limiting distribution.

(c) Ishani's DTMC has exactly one limiting distribution.

(d) We can't conclude any of these for sure.

Provide full justification for your answer by citing the appropriate theorems.

25.4 **Practice with the definitions**

Consider each of the two simple DTMCs shown in Figure 25.14. For each chain, please answer the following questions. Justify your answers by citing theorems.

(a) Is the chain aperiodic?

(b) Is the chain irreducible?

(c) Is the chain ergodic?

(d) Does the limiting distribution exist? If so, what is it? If not, why not?

(e) Does one or more stationary distributions exist? If so, what are the stationary distribution(s)?

(f) Is p_c, the time-average fraction of time spent in state c, well defined? If so, what is it?

(g) Consider m_{cc}, the mean time until we again visit state c, given we are in state c. Is m_{cc} well-defined? If so, what is it?

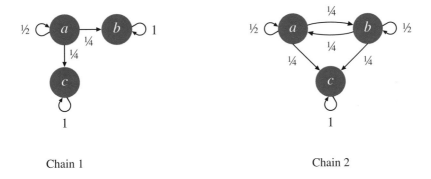

Chain 1   Chain 2

Figure 25.14 *Chains for Exercise 25.4.*

25.5 **Proof of Corollary 25.13**

Prove Corollary 25.13.

25.6 **A simple finite-state chain**

For the DTMC shown in Figure 25.15, explain how we know that the limiting distribution exists by citing theorems from the chapter. Then

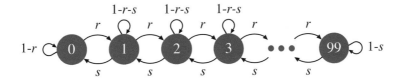

Figure 25.15 *Chain for Exercise 25.6.*

solve for the limiting distribution via these steps:

(a) From the stationary equations, express π_1 in terms of π_0. Then express π_2 in terms of π_0.

(b) You will notice a pattern that will help you make a guess for how to express π_i in terms of π_0 for any i.

(c) Determine π_0 by using $\sum_i \pi_i = 1$ and verify the correctness of your guess.

25.7 Some example DTMCs

For each chain shown in Figure 25.16, answer the following questions:
(a) Is the chain irreducible?
(b) Is the chain aperiodic?
(c) Does a stationary distribution exist?
(d) Does the limiting distribution exist?
Provide a one-line explanation for your answer, citing theorems.

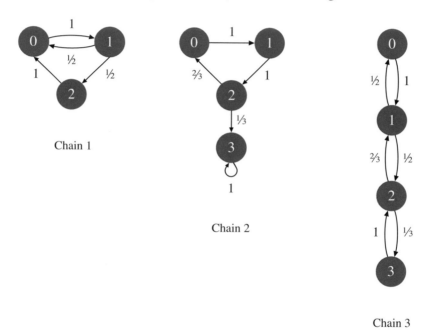

Figure 25.16 *Markov chains for Exercise 25.7.*

25.8 Caching

If you think about it, web browsing is basically a Markov chain – the page you will go to next depends on the page you are currently at. Suppose our web server has three pages, and we have the following transition probabilities:

$P_{1,1} = 0$ $\qquad$ $P_{1,2} = x$ $\qquad$ $P_{1,3} = 1 - x$
$P_{2,1} = y$ $\qquad$ $P_{2,2} = 0$ $\qquad$ $P_{2,3} = 1 - y$
$P_{3,1} = 0$ $\qquad$ $P_{3,2} = 1$ $\qquad$ $P_{3,3} = 0,$

where $P_{i,j}$ represents the probability that I will next request page j, given that I last requested page i. Assume that $0 < x < y < \frac{1}{2}$.

Recall that web browsers cache pages so that they can be quickly retrieved later. We will assume that the cache has enough memory to store two pages. Whenever a request comes in for a page that is not cached, the browser will store that page in the cache, replacing the page *least likely* to be referenced next based on the current request. For example, if my cache contained pages {2,3} and I requested page 1, the cache would now store {1,3} (because $x < 1 - x$).

(a) Find the proportion of time that the cache contains the following pages: (i) {1,2}   (ii) {2,3}   (iii) {1,3}. [Hint 1: You will need to think carefully about what information you need in your states to create the appropriate DTMC.] [Hint 2: When solving your DTMC, you will find that two of the states are only visited a finite number of times, with probability 1, so the long-run fraction of time spent there is 0. You can thus ignore these states and just solve for the stationary probabilities of the remaining states.]

(b) Find the proportion of requests that are for cached pages.

25.9 Practice with balance equations and time-reversibility equations
Consider the following Markov chains:

$$\mathbf{P}^{(1)} = \begin{pmatrix} 0 & 2/3 & 0 & 1/3 \\ 1/3 & 0 & 2/3 & 0 \\ 0 & 1/3 & 0 & 2/3 \\ 2/3 & 0 & 1/3 & 0 \end{pmatrix}$$

$$\mathbf{P}^{(2)} = \begin{pmatrix} 1/3 & 2/3 & 0 & 0 \\ 1/3 & 0 & 2/3 & 0 \\ 0 & 1/3 & 0 & 2/3 \\ 0 & 0 & 1/3 & 2/3 \end{pmatrix}.$$

(a) Draw the corresponding Markov chains for $\mathbf{P}^{(1)}$ and $\mathbf{P}^{(2)}$.

(b) Solve for the time-average fraction of time spent in each state for both $\mathbf{P}^{(1)}$ and $\mathbf{P}^{(2)}$. First try to use the time-reversibility equations, and if they do not work, then use the balance equations.

(c) Was $\mathbf{P}^{(1)}$ time-reversible? Was $\mathbf{P}^{(2)}$ time-reversible?

(d) For those chain(s) that were time-reversible, explain why it makes sense that for all states i, j in the chain, the rate of transitions from i to j should equal the rate of transitions from j to i.

25.10 Data centers, backhoes, and bugs
Our data center alternates between "working" and "down." There are two reasons why our data center can be down: (1) a backhoe accidentally dug up some cable, or (2) a software bug crashed the machines. Suppose that if the data center is working today, it will be down tomorrow due to backhoe reasons with probability $\frac{1}{6}$ or will be down tomorrow due to a software bug with probability $\frac{1}{4}$. A data center that is down today due to backhoe reasons will be up tomorrow with probability 1. A data center that is down today due to a software bug will be up tomorrow with probability $\frac{3}{4}$.

(a) Draw a DTMC for this problem.

(b) Is your DTMC ergodic? Why or why not?

(c) Is your DTMC time-reversible? Why or why not?

(d) What fraction of time is the data center working?

(e) What is the expected number of days between backhoe failures?

25.11 **CLT versus SLLN**

Consider a sequence of i.i.d. random variables $X_1, X_2, \ldots$ with finite mean $\mathbf{E}[X]$ and finite variance σ. Let $S_n = \sum_{i=1}^{n} X_i$. Now consider the quantity:

$$\frac{S_n - n\mathbf{E}[X]}{n}.$$

What does the Strong Law of Large Numbers (SLLN) say about this quantity as $n \to \infty$? What does the Central Limit Theorem (CLT) say about this quantity as $n \to \infty$? Are they in contradiction?

25.12 **Walks on undirected weighted graphs**

This problem comes up in many areas. Consider any undirected connected graph with weights: $w_{ij} = w_{ji}$ is the weight on edge (i, j) where $w_{ij} \geq 0$, $\forall i, j$. See for example Figure 25.17. A particle moves between nodes in a weighted graph as follows: A particle residing at node i will next move to node j with probability P_{ij}, where

$$P_{ij} = \frac{w_{ij}}{\sum_j w_{ij}}.$$

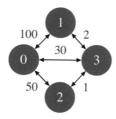

Figure 25.17 *A weighted graph with M = 4 nodes describing a particle's motion.*

Your goal is to determine the long-run proportion of time that the particle is in state i.

(a) Play around with the example in Figure 25.17. Which node do you think is visited most often?

(b) You'll now need to guess a solution for a *general weighted graph* and show that your solution satisfies the stationary equations. It will help a lot, both in making your guess and in verifying your guess, if you write out the time-reversibility equations rather than the stationary equations.

25.13 **Finite-state chain with equal weights**

Consider the finite-state chain in Figure 25.18.

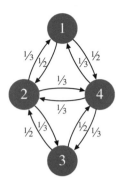

Figure 25.18 *Markov chain for Exercise 25.13.*

(a) Is the chain ergodic?
(b) Is the chain time-reversible?
(c) What is the limiting probability of being in each state?
(d) The finite-state chain in Figure 25.18 has two properties:
  (i) **Balanced weights**: This is the property that the probabilities on each of the arrows leaving a state are equal.
  (ii) **Bidirectional edges**: This is the property that if there's an edge from i to j, then there's also an edge from j to i.

  Look at the structure of the limiting probabilities that you obtained for Figure 25.18. To see the structure, it will help to write these over the same common denominator. Now imagine an *arbitrary* ergodic finite-state chain with n states that has both the "balanced weights" property and the "bidirectional edges" property. What can you say about π_j, the limiting probability of being in state j? Make a guess and verify it.

25.14 **Gas migration**

You have a box with n gas molecules, with a divider in the middle that the molecules can pass through. As shown in Figure 25.19, there is an A side and a B side to the box. Assume that n is even.

All the molecules start out on the A side. Every second, we pick a random gas molecule out of the n molecules and transfer it to the other side.

(a) Determine the proportion of time that the box has the same number of molecules on the A side and the B side. Start by drawing a Markov chain!

(b) Let N_B denote the number of molecules in the B side of the box.
  (i) What is $\mathbf{E}\left[N_B\right]$?
  (ii) What is $\mathbf{Var}(N_B)$?

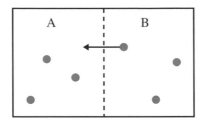

Figure 25.19 *Box of gas molecules for Exercise 25.14.*

[Hint: What do you know about N_B's distribution over a long time?]

25.15 **Randomized chess**
This problem concerns the behavior of various chess pieces as they move randomly around the board. Chess is played on an 8×8 board divided into 64 squares that alternate from white to black. The *king* can move one square in any direction (including the diagonal). The *bishop* can move any number of squares, but only in the diagonal directions. The *knight* moves in an L-shape. That is, the knight moves two squares to either side (left or right) and one square up or down. Or, the knight can move two squares up or down and one square to the side (left or right).
(a) You are given an empty chessboard with a lone king placed in one corner. At each time step, the king will make a uniformly random legal move. Is the corresponding Markov chain for this process irreducible? Is it aperiodic?
(b) What if a bishop is used instead?
(c) What if a knight is used instead?
(d) Now take advantage of Exercise 25.12 on undirected weighted graphs and time-reversibility to calculate the expected time for the king to return to the corner. Think about how hard this would be without time-reversibility. [Hint: The calculation should be very simple.]
(e) Do the same for the bishop.
(f) Do the same for the knight.

25.16 **Interpreting the stationary probabilities as fractions of time**
Assume that you have an irreducible, finite-state DTMC with M states (numbered $0, 1, \ldots, M - 1$) and transition matrix **P**.
Define

$$\phi_j = \lim_{n \to \infty} \frac{\sum_{i=1}^{n} p_j(i)}{n},$$

where $p_j(i)$ is the probability that the chain is in state j at time step i.
(a) What is the meaning of ϕ_j? Please follow these steps:
    (i) What does $\sum_{i=1}^{n} p_j(i)$ mean?

   (ii) What does $\frac{\sum_{i=1}^{n} p_j(i)}{n}$ mean?

   (iii) What does $\phi_j = \lim_{n \to \infty} \frac{\sum_{i=1}^{n} p_j(i)}{n}$ mean?

(b) Prove that the distribution $\vec{\phi} = (\phi_0, \phi_1, \ldots, \phi_{M-1})$ is a stationary distribution. Please follow these steps:

   (i) Express $p_j(i)$ in terms of a sum involving $p_k(i-1)$.

   (ii) Show that ϕ_j satisfies the stationary equations.

   (iii) Don't forget to prove the needed condition on $\sum_{j=0}^{M-1} \phi_j$.

25.17 In an irreducible DTMC, do all states have the same period?
Given an irreducible DTMC, either prove that all states have the same period, or find a counter-example.

25.18 How rare are time-reversible DTMCs?
Edward feels that time-reversible chains are very rare. Erica disagrees. Erica claims that it's easy to create time-reversible chains, via the idea of Exercise 25.12.

(a) Consider the DTMC in Figure 25.20 whose transitions are unlabeled. Use what you've learned in Exercise 25.12 to label each edge (i, j) of the DTMC with a transition probability p_{ij} such that $0 < p_{ij} < 1$ and such that the DTMC is time-reversible. Then write the *limiting distribution* of your chain.

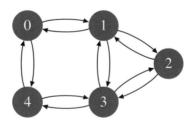

Figure 25.20 *Markov chain for Exercise 25.18.*

(b) How many possible answers are there to question (a)? That is, how many choices of transition probabilities are there that create a time-reversible DTMC? Pick the correct answer and give a one-line explanation:

   (i) exactly one

   (ii) a finite number

   (iii) countably infinite

   (iv) uncountably infinite

25.19 Irreducible finite-state chains have finite mean time to return
Prove Theorem 25.11: For a finite-state, irreducible DTMC, m_{ij} is finite, for every i, j.

25.20 **Every finite DTMC has at least one stationary distribution**
[Proposed by Misha Ivkov] In this problem we will prove that every *finite-state* DTMC has at least one stationary distribution. Note, we are not making any assumptions about the DTMC.
(a) First, prove that a finite DTMC must have at least one recurrent state.
   (i) Let i be a state in the Markov chain. Argue that there exists some state j such that $\sum_{n=0}^{\infty} (\mathbf{P}^n)_{ij} = \infty$.
   (ii) Now argue that $\sum_{n=0}^{\infty} (\mathbf{P}^n)_{jj} = \infty$.
(b) Let j be the recurrent state identified above, and let S be the set of states that are accessible from j. Show that S is an irreducible DTMC.
(c) As explained in Section 25.8, since S is irreducible, we know that it has a stationary distribution; let's call that $\vec{\pi}'$. We now define $\vec{\pi}$ as

$$\pi_i = \begin{cases} \pi_i' & \text{if } i \in S \\ 0 & \text{otherwise} \end{cases}.$$

Prove that $\vec{\pi}$ is a stationary distribution for the original DTMC.

26 Discrete-Time Markov Chains: Infinite-State

So far we have only talked about *finite*-state discrete-time Markov chains (DTMCs) with M states. Now we move on to infinite-state DTMCs. For a Markov chain with an infinite number of states, one can still imagine a transition probability matrix, $\mathbf{P}$, but the matrix has infinite dimension.

For an infinite-state DTMC, we denote the limiting probability distribution on the states by

$$\vec{\pi} = (\pi_0, \pi_1, \pi_2, \ldots) \quad \text{where} \quad \pi_j = \lim_{n \to \infty} (\mathbf{P}^n)_{ij} \quad \text{and} \quad \sum_{j=0}^{\infty} \pi_j = 1.$$

We say that distribution $\vec{\pi}$ is stationary if

$$\pi_j = \sum_{k=0}^{\infty} \pi_k P_{kj} \quad \text{and} \quad \sum_{j=0}^{\infty} \pi_j = 1.$$

Infinite-state Markov chains are common in modeling systems where the number of customers or number of jobs is unbounded, and thus the state space is unbounded. The typical example is a queue of jobs or packets, where the queue can grow arbitrarily long.

This chapter will introduce infinite-state DTMCs. We will see that many of the definitions, solution techniques, and theorems from finite-state DTMCs carry over to infinite-state DTMCs. However, there is one crucial difference, which comes up in the definition of ergodicity and the existence of a limiting distribution. This difference will be discussed starting in Section 26.4.

26.1 Stationary = Limiting

We have seen that for a finite-state DTMC, if the limiting distribution exists, then the limiting distribution and stationary distribution are equivalent (Theorem 24.9). The same result holds for infinite-state DTMCs.

> **Theorem 26.1 (Stationary distribution = limiting distribution)** *Given an infinite-state DTMC, let*
>
> $$\pi_j = \lim_{n \to \infty} (\mathbf{P}^n)_{ij}$$
>
> *be the limiting probability of being in state j and let*
>
> $$\vec{\pi} = (\pi_0, \pi_1, \pi_2, \ldots), \quad \text{where} \quad \sum_{i=0}^{\infty} \pi_i = 1,$$
>
> *be the limiting distribution. Assuming that the limiting distribution exists, then $\vec{\pi}$ is also a stationary distribution and* no other *stationary distribution exists.*

Proof: The proof follows along the lines of the proof of Theorem 24.9; however, it is a little more technical because we can't simply interchange the limit and the summation as we did in that proof, because we have an infinite sum over states. Fortunately, one can get around this difficulty by lower-bounding the infinite sum by a finite sum, which allows us to exchange the limit and the summation. After the exchange, we then consider the limit as the number of items in the finite sum approaches infinity. The details of this trickery are given in [35, section 8.9]. ∎

26.2 Solving Stationary Equations in Infinite-State DTMCs

So we can obtain the limiting distribution, $\vec{\pi}$, by solving the stationary equations. Yet there are an infinite number of stationary equations! How do we solve them?

Consider an example of a router that has infinite capacity for packets, called an **unbounded queue** (Figure 26.1). Packets arrive at the router and queue up there. We think of the router as a "server" since it serves packets. The server processes the packet at the head of the queue, and when it finishes processing that packet, it moves on to the next packet.

Figure 26.1 *Illustration of a server with unbounded buffer.*

Suppose at every time step, with probability $p = \frac{1}{4}$ one packet arrives, and independently, with probability $q = \frac{1}{3}$ one packet departs. Note that during a time step we might have both an arrival and a transmission, or neither. That is, a packet can "arrive" and "depart" within the same time step, leaving the system in the same state.

We will be interested in answering questions like: *What is the average number of packets in the system?*

To answer this question, we model the problem as a DTMC with an infinite number of states: 0, 1, 2, ..., representing the number of packets at the router. Let $r = p(1-q) = \frac{1}{6}$ and $s = q(1-p) = \frac{1}{4}$, where $r < s$. Figure 26.2 shows the Markov chain for our problem.

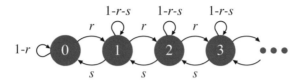

Figure 26.2 *DTMC for a server with unbounded queue.*

Here the transition probability matrix is infinite!

$$
\mathbf{P} = \begin{pmatrix}
1-r & r & 0 & 0 & \cdots \\
s & 1-r-s & r & 0 & \cdots \\
0 & s & 1-r-s & r & \cdots \\
0 & 0 & s & 1-r-s & \cdots \\
\vdots & \vdots & \vdots & \vdots & \vdots
\end{pmatrix}.
$$

The stationary equations look like this:

$$
\begin{aligned}
\pi_0 &= \pi_0(1-r) + \pi_1 s \\
\pi_1 &= \pi_0 r + \pi_1(1-r-s) + \pi_2 s \\
\pi_2 &= \pi_1 r + \pi_2(1-r-s) + \pi_3 s \\
\pi_3 &= \pi_2 r + \pi_3(1-r-s) + \pi_4 s \\
&\vdots
\end{aligned}
$$

$$
\pi_0 + \pi_1 + \pi_2 + \pi_3 + \cdots = 1.
$$

Question: How are we going to solve this infinite number of equations?

Answer: It might be easier to write the time-reversibility equations (Theorem 25.29):

$$
\begin{aligned}
\pi_0 \cdot r &= \pi_1 \cdot s \\
\pi_1 \cdot r &= \pi_2 \cdot s \\
\pi_2 \cdot r &= \pi_3 \cdot s \\
&\vdots
\end{aligned}
$$

which yield

$$\pi_1 = \left(\frac{r}{s}\right) \cdot \pi_0$$

$$\pi_2 = \left(\frac{r}{s}\right) \cdot \pi_1 = \left(\frac{r}{s}\right)^2 \cdot \pi_0$$

$$\pi_3 = \left(\frac{r}{s}\right) \cdot \pi_2 = \left(\frac{r}{s}\right)^3 \cdot \pi_0$$

$$\vdots$$

We can now make a general "guess":

$$\pi_i = \left(\frac{r}{s}\right)^i \pi_0.$$

Question: How do we verify that this guess is correct?

Answer: To verify your guess, you need to show that it satisfies the stationary equations:

$$\pi_i = \pi_{i-1}r + \pi_i(1 - r - s) + \pi_{i+1}s$$

$$\left(\frac{r}{s}\right)^i \pi_0 = \left(\frac{r}{s}\right)^{i-1} \pi_0 r + \left(\frac{r}{s}\right)^i \pi_0(1 - r - s) + \left(\frac{r}{s}\right)^{i+1} \pi_0 s. \quad \checkmark$$

Question: Okay, but we still do not know π_0. How can we determine π_0?

Answer: To determine π_0, we make use of the fact that $\sum_i \pi_i = 1$.

This says that

$$\pi_0 \cdot \left(1 + \frac{r}{s} + \left(\frac{r}{s}\right)^2 + \left(\frac{r}{s}\right)^3 + \cdots\right) = 1$$

$$\pi_0 \cdot \left(\frac{1}{1 - \frac{r}{s}}\right) = 1$$

$$\pi_0 = 1 - \frac{r}{s}.$$

So,

$$\pi_i = \left(\frac{r}{s}\right)^i \cdot \left(1 - \frac{r}{s}\right).$$

Question: What is the average number of packets in the system?

Answer: Let N denote the number of packets in the system. Then

$$\mathbf{E}[N] = \pi_0 \cdot 0 + \pi_1 \cdot 1 + \pi_2 \cdot 2 + \pi_3 \cdot 3 + \cdots$$

Question: Can we get a closed-form expression for $\mathbf{E}[N]$?

Answer: Yes! It will help to define

$$\rho = \frac{r}{s}$$

for shorthand. Then,

$$\pi_i = \rho^i(1 - \rho).$$

So,

$$
\begin{aligned}
\mathbf{E}[N] &= 1\rho(1 - \rho) + 2\rho^2(1 - \rho) + 3\rho^3(1 - \rho) + \cdots \\
&= (1 - \rho) \cdot \rho \cdot \left(1 + 2\rho + 3\rho^2 + 4\rho^3 + \cdots\right) \\
&= (1 - \rho) \cdot \rho \cdot \frac{1}{(1 - \rho)^2} \qquad \text{by (1.4)} \\
&= \frac{\rho}{1 - \rho}.
\end{aligned}
\tag{26.1}
$$

Wow! Equation (26.1) is a really simple formula. For our example, $\rho = \frac{\frac{1}{6}}{\frac{1}{4}} = \frac{2}{3}$ and $\mathbf{E}[N] = \frac{\frac{2}{3}}{1 - \frac{2}{3}} = 2$. So on average there are two packets in the system.

26.3 A Harder Example of Solving Stationary Equations in Infinite-State DTMCs

Of course not all infinite-state DTMCs are as easy to solve as the one in the previous section. Consider the DTMC shown in Figure 26.3.

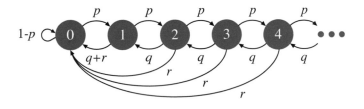

Figure 26.3 *DTMC for processor with failures.*

This kind of chain is often used to model a processor with failures. The chain tracks the number of jobs in the system. At any time step, either the number of jobs increases by 1 (with probability p), or decreases by 1 (with probability q), or a processor failure occurs (with probability r), where $p + q + r = 1$. In the case of a processor failure, all jobs in the system are lost.

To derive the limiting distribution for this chain, simply writing stationary equations will not lead us to the solution. In this case, the z-transform approach (generating functions) from Chapter 6 is very useful. Exercise 26.24 walks you through the steps.

26.4 Ergodicity Questions

We now turn to ergodicity questions.

Recall that in Chapter 25 we asked the following questions for *finite-state* DTMCs:

1. Under what conditions does the limiting distribution exist?
2. How does π_j, the limiting probability of being in state j, compare with p_j, the long-run time-average fraction of time spent in state j?
3. What can we say about m_{jj}, the mean time between visits to state j, and how is this related to π_j?

Recall that in the case of an *ergodic* (aperiodic and irreducible) finite-state DTMC with M states, everything behaves as we would like. Specifically, by Theorem 25.19,

$$0 < \frac{1}{m_{jj}} = \pi_j^{\text{limiting}} = \pi_j^{\text{stationary}} = p_j, \text{ w.p.1.}$$

When the finite-state chain is periodic but irreducible, then the limiting distribution doesn't exist but there's a unique stationary distribution. Specifically, by Theorem 25.20,

$$0 < \frac{1}{m_{jj}} = \pi_j^{\text{stationary}} = p_j, \text{ w.p.1.}$$

For the case of an infinite-state DTMC, we will see that the story is the same when the chain is ergodic. However, the definition of *ergodic* needs to be *strengthened*. The remainder of this chapter is devoted to understanding how to strengthen the definition of *ergodic*. We will figure this out together!

Infinite-state chains are infinitely more complex than finite-state chains. For example, for infinite-state chains, unlike their finite-state counterparts, we will see that when the DTMC is *not* ergodic, even the stationary distribution might not exist. Because of the added complexity inherent in infinite-state chains, we will have to omit some of the proofs in this text. We refer the interested reader to [35] for the omitted proofs.

Consider the three infinite-state DTMCs shown in Figure 26.4.

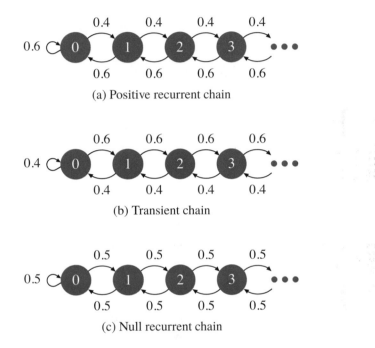

(a) Positive recurrent chain

(b) Transient chain

(c) Null recurrent chain

Figure 26.4 *Examples of three chains.*

Question: Which of these chains are aperiodic and irreducible?

Answer: All of them.

Question: For *finite-state* DTMCs that are aperiodic and irreducible, does a limiting distribution always exist?

Answer: Yes, by Theorem 25.6.

Question: Does a limiting distribution exist for all the chains in Figure 26.4?

Answer: We will see that a limiting distribution exists only for chain (a). For chain (a), we saw in Section 26.2 that there is a well-defined stationary probability of being in each state, and these stationary probabilities sum to 1. For the other two chains, we will show that the limiting probability of being in each state is

0, and the limiting probabilities do not sum to 1; hence there does not exist a limiting distribution. Chain (a) has a property called "positive recurrent." Chain (b) is what we call "transient," and chain (c) is "null recurrent." We explain all these terms in this chapter and how they relate to the existence of limiting distributions.

Question: Intuitively, what is the problem with chains (b) and (c) in Figure 26.4?

Figure 26.5 *Will the fish return to shore?*

Answer: To get some intuition, it helps to think about π_0, the limiting probability of being in state 0.

Chain (b) can be viewed as an ocean, where the shore is at state 0. Imagine you're a little fish swimming in the ocean. There is a drift away from shore. Think of this as a strong tide, pulling you deeper and deeper into the ocean. Given this drift, it is not obvious that you will keep returning to shore. In fact, we will show that after some point you never return to the shore. Thus, $\pi_0 = 0$. But this same argument holds for any state k that we call the "shore," so $\pi_k = 0$ for all k.

Chain (c) is the most confusing. It's not obvious whether the fish keeps returning to shore. We will show that the fish does in fact always return to shore. However, we will see that the time it takes for the fish to return is infinite. This ends up again resulting in $\pi_k = 0$ for all states k.

To formalize all of this, it helps to first understand the difference between a "recurrent" chain and a "transient" one.

26.5 Recurrent versus Transient: Will the Fish Return to Shore?

> **Definition 26.2** *We define $f_j =$ probability that a chain starting in state j ever returns to state j.*

> **Definition 26.3** *A state j is either recurrent or transient:*
>
> - *If $f_j = 1$, then j is a **recurrent** state.*
> - *If $f_j < 1$, then j is a **transient** state.*

Question: What is the distribution of the number of visits to a transient state j?

Answer: Every time we visit state j we have probability $1 - f_j$ of never visiting it again. Hence the number of visits is a Geometric random variable (r.v.) with mean $1/(1 - f_j)$.

> **Theorem 26.4** *With probability 1, the number of visits to a **recurrent** state is infinite. With probability 1, the number of visits to a **transient** state is finite.*

Proof: If a state j is recurrent, then starting in state j, with probability 1 (w.p.1) we will visit j again. Thus, repeating this argument, we see that w.p.1 state j will be visited an infinite number of times. In contrast, if state j is transient, then every time we visit state j, there is some probability $(1 - f_j)$ that we will never again visit j. With probability 1, that $1 - f_j$ probability event will eventually happen. That is, w.p.1, after some point we will never again revisit state j. ∎

> **Theorem 26.5** *Let $P_{ij}^n = (\mathbf{P}^n)_{ij}$ denote the probability that the chain will be in state j after n steps, given that the chain is in state i now.*
>
> - *If state i is recurrent, then $\sum_{n=0}^{\infty} (\mathbf{P}^n)_{ii} = \infty$.*
> - *If state i is transient, then $\sum_{n=0}^{\infty} (\mathbf{P}^n)_{ii} < \infty$.*

Proof: Observe that $\sum_{n=0}^{\infty} (\mathbf{P}^n)_{ii} = \mathbf{E}$ [Number visits to state i].

To see this, note that if N is the number of visits to state i, then we can write

$$N = I_1 + I_2 + I_3 + \cdots,$$

where I_n is an indicator r.v. which equals 1 if we're in state i at the nth time step.

Thus:

$$\mathbf{E}[N] = \mathbf{E}[I_1] + \mathbf{E}[I_2] + \mathbf{E}[I_3] + \cdots \qquad \text{(Linearity of Expectation)}$$

$$= \left(\mathbf{P}^1\right)_{ii} + \left(\mathbf{P}^2\right)_{ii} + \left(\mathbf{P}^3\right)_{ii} + \cdots$$

$$= \sum_{n=0}^{\infty} (\mathbf{P}^n)_{ii}.$$

Finally, by Theorem 26.4, for a recurrent state $\mathbf{E}[N] = \infty$, while for a transient one, $\mathbf{E}[N] < \infty$. ■

> **Theorem 26.6 (Recurrence class property)** *If state i is recurrent and i communicates with j, (written $i \longleftrightarrow j$), then j is recurrent.*

We start with the intuition for Theorem 26.6. Consider Figure 26.6. We know that we come back to i infinitely many times. By the definition of "communicates," every time we are in i, we have some probability of taking the road to j, and once we are in j, we have some probability of taking the road to i. So, for every visit to i, there's some non-zero probability that we'll also visit j. Therefore the number of visits to j is proportional to the number of visits to i. Because the number of visits to i is infinite, so is the number of visits to j.

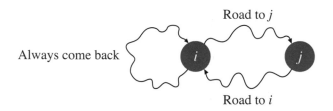

Figure 26.6 *Proof of Theorem 26.6.*

Now for the formal proof.

Proof: We know that i communicates with j. Thus, there exists an m such that $(\mathbf{P}^m)_{ji} > 0$ and there exists n such that $(\mathbf{P}^n)_{ij} > 0$. We also know that $\sum_{s=0}^{\infty} (\mathbf{P}^s)_{ii} = \infty$, because state i is recurrent.

What we want to show is that $\sum_{t=0}^{\infty} (\mathbf{P}^t)_{jj} = \infty$.

Now

$$\sum_{t=0}^{\infty} (\mathbf{P}^t)_{jj} \geq \sum_{s=0}^{\infty} (\mathbf{P}^{m+s+n})_{jj}, \qquad (26.2)$$

since the left-hand side of (26.2) considers all j-to-j paths, while the right-hand side considers only those of length at least $m + n$.

We can now further constrain our j-to-j paths by insisting that we must use the first m steps of our path to go from j to i and the last n steps to go from i to j. Specifically:

$$\sum_{t=0}^{\infty} \left(\mathbf{P}^t\right)_{jj} \geq \sum_{s=0}^{\infty} \left(\mathbf{P}^{m+s+n}\right)_{jj}$$

$$\geq \sum_{s=0}^{\infty} \left(\mathbf{P}^m\right)_{ji} \left(\mathbf{P}^s\right)_{ii} \left(\mathbf{P}^n\right)_{ij}$$

$$= \left(\mathbf{P}^m\right)_{ji} \left(\mathbf{P}^n\right)_{ij} \sum_{s=0}^{\infty} \left(\mathbf{P}^s\right)_{ii} \quad \text{(pulling out positive constants)}$$

$$= \infty \quad \text{(because state } i \text{ is recurrent).}$$

We have thus proven that state j is recurrent. ∎

Theorem 26.7 (Transience class property) *If state i is transient and i communicates with j, $(i \longleftrightarrow j)$, then j is transient.*

Proof: This follows directly from the previous Theorem 26.6. Suppose by contradiction that state j is recurrent. Then because j and i communicate, i is recurrent as well, which is a contradiction to the assumption. ∎

We have thus seen that *in an irreducible Markov chain, either all states are transient, or all are recurrent!*

Theorem 26.8 *For a transient Markov chain,*

$$\lim_{n \to \infty} \left(\mathbf{P}^n\right)_{ij} = 0, \quad \forall j.$$

Hence, the limiting distribution does not exist.

Proof: As we have seen, in a transient Markov chain there is some point after which we never visit state j again. So the probability of being in state j after n steps is zero as $n \to \infty$, that is,

$$\lim_{n \to \infty} \left(\mathbf{P}^n\right)_{ij} = 0,$$

and this holds for every state j.

Now

$$\sum_{j=0}^{\infty} \pi_j = 0$$

because the sum of a countable number of 0's is still 0. Thus the limiting distribution does not exist. ∎

> **Theorem 26.9** *For Markov chains where the limiting probabilities are all zero, no stationary distribution exists.*

Proof: The fact that no stationary distribution exists follows from an argument similar to that in the proof of Theorem 26.1. For details, see [35]. ∎

26.6 Infinite Random Walk Example

It's not so obvious how to argue whether a chain is transient or recurrent. The following example illustrates how this is done.

Consider the random walk shown in Figure 26.7, where at each step a gambler either gains a dollar (with probability p) or loses a dollar (with probability $q = 1 - p$). We'd like to determine whether the chain is transient or recurrent.

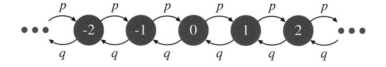

Figure 26.7 *Gambler's walk.*

Because all states communicate, it follows from Theorems 26.6 and 26.7 that either *all* states are transient or all are recurrent. Hence to determine whether the chain is recurrent or transient, it suffices to look at state 0.

To determine whether state 0 is transient or recurrent, we invoke Theorem 26.5. Let

$$V = \sum_{n=1}^{\infty} (\mathbf{P}^n)_{00}$$

denote the expected number of visits to state 0. If V is finite, then state 0 is transient. Otherwise it is recurrent.

Since one cannot get from 0 to 0 in an odd number of steps, it follows that

$$V = \sum_{n=1}^{\infty} (\mathbf{P}^n)_{00} = \sum_{n=1}^{\infty} \left(\mathbf{P}^{2n}\right)_{00} = \sum_{n=1}^{\infty} \binom{2n}{n} p^n q^n. \tag{26.3}$$

We now simplify this equation using Lavrov's lemma.

Lemma 26.10 *(Due to Misha Lavrov) For $n \geq 1$,*

$$\frac{4^n}{2n+1} < \binom{2n}{n} < 4^n. \tag{26.4}$$

Proof: By simple binomial expansion,

$$\sum_{k=0}^{2n} \binom{2n}{k} = (1+1)^{2n} = 2^{2n} = 4^n.$$

Since $\binom{2n}{n}$ is the largest term in the sum, it follows that it is bigger than the average term, $4^n/(2n+1)$. However, it is also smaller than the total sum, 4^n. ∎

Substituting (26.4) into (26.3), we get that

$$\sum_{n=1}^{\infty} \frac{4^n}{2n+1} p^n q^n < V < \sum_{n=1}^{\infty} 4^n p^n q^n. \tag{26.5}$$

If we substitute $p = q = \frac{1}{2}$ into the left-hand side of (26.5), we get that

$$V > \sum_{n=1}^{\infty} \frac{4^n}{2n+1} \cdot \frac{1}{4^n} = \sum_{n=1}^{\infty} \frac{1}{2n+1} = \infty. \tag{26.6}$$

If instead we assume $p \neq q$ and consider the right-hand side of (26.5), we get that

$$V < \sum_{n=1}^{\infty} (4pq)^n < \infty \quad \text{(since } 4pq < 1\text{)}. \tag{26.7}$$

Thus by (26.6) and (26.7) we see that $V = \sum_{n=1}^{\infty} (\mathbf{P}^n)_{00}$ is infinite if and only if $p = \frac{1}{2}$. So the chain is recurrent if and only if $p = \frac{1}{2}$.

We have thus proven Theorem 26.11.

Theorem 26.11 *The Gambler's walk shown in Figure 26.7 is recurrent only when $p = \frac{1}{2}$ and is transient otherwise.*

26.7 Back to the Three Chains and the Ergodicity Question

Let's return to the three infinite-state chains in Figure 26.4, repeated in Figure 26.8:

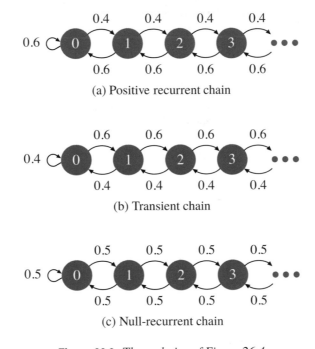

(a) Positive recurrent chain

(b) Transient chain

(c) Null-recurrent chain

Figure 26.8 *Three chains of Figure 26.4.*

26.7.1 Figure 26.8(a) is Recurrent

From what we've learned, chain (a) is recurrent, simply by virtue of the fact that we know that it has a stationary distribution (recall from Theorem 26.9 that, for a transient chain, no stationary distribution exists).

26.7.2 Figure 26.8(b) is Transient

Chain (b) is transient. Intuitively, imagine that j is very high. If you're in state j, the world looks very much like a 2D-infinite Gambler's walk where the drift goes to the right. However, this is not a formal proof of transience. Theorem 26.12 provides a proof by precisely relating chain (b) to the two-way Gambler's walk.

Theorem 26.12 *Chain (b) in Figure 26.8 is transient.*

Proof: [This cute proof is due to Misha Ivkov.] The proof relies on looking at two other chains which we have already analyzed, shown in Figure 26.9.

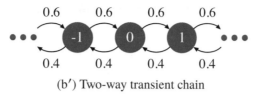

(b′) Two-way transient chain

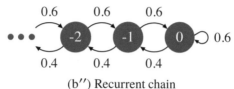

(b″) Recurrent chain

Figure 26.9 *Some helper chains for proving Theorem 26.12.*

We define a few quantities:

$$f_0 = \mathbf{P}\,\{\text{return to 0 in chain (b)}\}$$
$$f_0' = \mathbf{P}\,\{\text{return to 0 in chain (b′)}\}$$
$$f_0'' = \mathbf{P}\,\{\text{return to 0 in chain (b″)}\}$$
$$f_{ij} = \mathbf{P}\,\{\text{eventually visit } j, \text{ given currently in } i \text{ in chain (b)}\}$$
$$f_{ij}' = \mathbf{P}\,\{\text{eventually visit } j, \text{ given currently in } i \text{ in chain (b′)}\}$$
$$f_{ij}'' = \mathbf{P}\,\{\text{eventually visit } j, \text{ given currently in } i \text{ in chain (b″)}\}.$$

To show that chain (b) is transient, it suffices to show that $f_0 < 1$. By conditioning we have:

$$f_0 = (0.4) \cdot 1 + (0.6) \cdot f_{10}. \tag{26.8}$$

Now observe that

$$f_{10} = f_{10}'. \tag{26.9}$$

This is due to the fact that chain (b′) looks identical to chain (b) except for the states to the left of state 0; however, those states left of 0 don't matter in computing f_{10} or f_{10}'. Substituting (26.9) into (26.8) we have:

$$f_0 = (0.4) \cdot 1 + (0.6) \cdot f_{10}'. \tag{26.10}$$

Now observe that

$$f_{10}' < 1. \tag{26.11}$$

Equation (26.11) follows from this series of equations:

$$1 > f_0' \quad \text{because chain (b') is transient}$$
$$= (0.4) \cdot f_{-1,0}' + (0.6) \cdot f_{10}' \quad \text{by conditioning}$$
$$= (0.4) \cdot f_{-1,0}'' + (0.6) \cdot f_{10}' \quad \text{what's right of state 0 doesn't matter}$$
$$= (0.4) \cdot 1 + (0.6) \cdot f_{10}' \quad \text{because (b'') is recurrent}$$

Thus $0.6 > (0.6) \cdot f_{10}'$, and hence $f_{10}' < 1$.

Combining (26.11) and (26.10), we have:

$$f_0 = (0.4) \cdot 1 + (0.6) \cdot f_{10}' < (0.4) \cdot 1 + (0.6)1 = 1. \qquad \blacksquare$$

26.7.3 Figure 26.8(c) is Recurrent

Chain (c) is recurrent. This follows from the fact that f_0, the probability of returning to state 0, is at least as high in chain (c) as in the Gambler's walk of Figure 26.7 with $p = 0.5$, and we've shown that $f_0 = 1$ for the Gambler's walk with $p = 0.5$.

Question: Given that chain (c) is recurrent, does this mean that the limiting distribution exists for this third chain? If so, what is it?

Answer: Although this chain (c) is recurrent, and irreducible and aperiodic, it turns out that these are *not* enough to guarantee the existence of the limiting distribution. To see why, we turn to Theorem 26.13, known as the Ergodic Theorem of Markov Chains.

26.8 Why Recurrence Is Not Enough

Theorem 26.13 (Ergodic Theorem of Markov Chains) *Given a recurrent, aperiodic, irreducible DTMC, $\pi_j = \lim_{n \to \infty} (\mathbf{P}^n)_{ij}$ exists and*

$$\pi_j = \frac{1}{m_{jj}}, \ \forall j.$$

The Ergodic Theorem of Markov Chains is saying the same thing that we saw in Theorem 25.12, about π_j being the reciprocal of m_{jj}. However, those theorems were restricted to *finite*-state chains. The fact that we now allow for infinite-state chains makes the proof *much* more technical than for the case of a finite number of states, and we refer the reader to [35, section 9.10].

Question: The Ergodic Theorem (Theorem 26.13) *seems* to suggest that recurrent + aperiodic + irreducible suffices for the limiting distribution to exist. What's wrong with this?

Answer: There's an important distinction. While π_j exists, it is not necessarily positive. We're told that

$$\pi_j = \frac{1}{m_{jj}},$$

but m_{jj} can be infinite!

In the case of a finite irreducible chain, we were guaranteed that m_{jj} is finite, but that's not necessarily true for an infinite state chain. In particular for the chain in Figure 26.8(c), Theorem 26.14 shows that $m_{jj} = \infty$ for all states j. Hence the limiting probability of being in state j exists, but is zero. Consequently, the limiting distribution does not exist (since a countable number of 0's can't sum to 1). Furthermore, by Theorem 26.9 no stationary distribution exists for this chain either.

Theorem 26.14 *For chain (c) in Figure 26.8, $m_{jj} = \infty$, for all states j.*

Proof: We show that $m_{00} = \infty$. Suppose by contradiction that m_{00} is finite.

Observe that

$$m_{00} = 1 + \frac{1}{2} \cdot 0 + \frac{1}{2} \cdot m_{10}.$$

Thus, given that m_{00} is finite, it must also be the case that m_{10} is finite. Now observe that

$$m_{10} = 1 + \frac{1}{2} \cdot 0 + \frac{1}{2} \cdot m_{20}$$
$$= 1 + \frac{1}{2} \cdot (m_{21} + m_{10})$$
$$= 1 + \frac{1}{2} \cdot 2m_{10}$$
$$= 1 + m_{10}.$$

But the only way that

$$m_{10} = 1 + m_{10}$$

is if $m_{10} = \infty$, which is a contradiction. Hence,

$$m_{00} = \infty.$$

The argument is very similar to show that $m_{jj} = \infty$, where $j \geq 1$, and we leave it as Exercise 26.12. ∎

We have seen that while chains (a) and (c) in Figure 26.4 are both recurrent, they differ in the mean time to return to a state.

> **Definition 26.15** *Recurrent Markov chains fall into two types:* **positive recurrent** *and* **null recurrent**. *In a positive-recurrent MC, the mean time between recurrences (returning to the same state) is finite. In a null-recurrent MC, the mean time between recurrences is infinite.*

Both positive recurrence and null recurrence are class properties.

> **Theorem 26.16 (More class properties)** *If state i is positive recurrent and $i \longleftrightarrow j$, then j is positive recurrent. If state i is null recurrent and $i \longleftrightarrow j$, then j is null recurrent.*

Proof: See Exercise 26.23. ∎

26.9 Ergodicity for Infinite-State Chains

> **Definition 26.17** *An* **ergodic** *DTMC is one that has all three desirable properties: aperiodicity, irreducibility, and positive recurrence.*

> **Theorem 26.18** *For an ergodic DTMC, the limiting distribution exists.*

Proof: By Theorem 26.13, the limiting *probabilities* (the π_j's) exist. By positive recurrence, they are all positive. All that remains is to show that $\sum_j \pi_j = 1$. To see this, recall p_j, the time-average fraction of time that the chain spends in state j. We proved in Section 25.6 that, for finite-state irreducible, aperiodic chains,

$$p_j = \frac{1}{m_{jj}} \quad \text{w.p.1.}$$

This was proven via invoking the Strong Law of Large Numbers (SLLN).

Question: What was the one thing needed for SLLN to hold?

Answer: We needed the mean time between renewals, m_{jj}, to be finite.

For the case of infinite-state DTMCs, the same argument as in Section 25.6 goes through, provided that m_{jj} is finite, which it is for a positive recurrent chain.

Now, observe that

$$\sum_{j=0}^{\infty} p_j = 1,$$

since a random walk must be in *some* state at all time steps, so the fraction of time it spends in each state must total to 1. Hence, since

$$p_j = \frac{1}{m_{jj}} = \pi_j,$$

it also follows that

$$\sum_{j=0}^{\infty} \pi_j = 1. \qquad\blacksquare$$

Remark: For a finite-state DTMC, positive recurrence is a consequence of irreducibility. This fact was proven in Exercise 25.19. Hence, for finite-state chains, aperiodicity and irreducibility suffice for ergodicity.

To summarize, infinite-state DTMCs are much more complicated than finite-state DTMCs because positive recurrence is required for the limiting distribution (and stationary distribution) to exist and we don't always have positive recurrence. Fortunately, as explained in the Theorem 26.19 and the associated Remark, we never need to check for positive recurrence.

Theorem 26.19 (Summary theorem) *An irreducible, aperiodic DTMC belongs to* **one** *of the following two classes:*

Either:

(i) *All the states are transient, or all are null recurrent. In this case $\pi_j = \lim_{n \to \infty} (\mathbf{P}^n)_{ij} = 0$, $\forall j$, and there does not exist a limiting distribution or a stationary distribution.*

Or:

(ii) *All states are positive recurrent. Then the limiting distribution $\vec{\pi} = (\pi_0, \pi_1, \pi_2, \ldots)$ exists, and there is a positive probability of being in each state. Here,*

$$\pi_j = \lim_{n \to \infty} (\mathbf{P}^n)_{ij} > 0, \quad \forall i$$

is the limiting probability of being in state j. In this case $\vec{\pi}$ is a stationary distribution, and no other stationary distribution exists. Also, $\pi_j = \frac{1}{m_{jj}}$, where m_{jj} is the mean number of steps between visits to state j.

Proof: We know by Theorems 26.16 and 26.7 that transience, null recurrence, and positive recurrence are class properties, meaning that in an irreducible Markov chain all the states are of the same one type.

If all states are transient, then by Theorem 26.8, the limiting probabilities are all zero and no limiting distribution exists. Further, by Theorem 26.9, no stationary distribution exists.

If all states are null recurrent, then by Theorem 26.13, all the limiting probabilities are zero, so they can't add up to 1, hence no limiting distribution exists. Also, again by Theorem 26.9, no stationary distribution exists.

If all states are positive recurrent, then by Theorem 26.18, the limiting distribution exists. Finally, by Theorem 26.1, when the limiting distribution exists, it is equal to the unique stationary distribution.   ∎

> **Important Remark:** What is nice about Theorem 26.19 is that it tells us that we never have to actually determine whether our DTMC is positive recurrent. It suffices to simply check for irreducibility and aperiodicity and then solve the stationary equations. If these stationary equations yield a distribution, then that distribution is also the limiting probability distribution.

26.10 Exercises

26.1 **Irreducibility, aperiodicity, and positive recurrence**
For each of the following transition matrices: (i) Is the DTMC irreducible? (ii) Is it aperiodic? (iii) Is it positive recurrent? [Note: If the period is not defined, then the chain is *not* aperiodic.]

(a) $\begin{pmatrix} \frac{1}{4} & \frac{1}{4} & \frac{1}{2} \\ 0 & 0 & 1 \\ 1 & 0 & 0 \end{pmatrix}$ (b) $\begin{pmatrix} 0 & 1 & 0 \\ 0 & 0 & 1 \\ 1 & 0 & 0 \end{pmatrix}$ (c) $\begin{pmatrix} \frac{1}{3} & 0 & \frac{2}{3} \\ \frac{1}{4} & \frac{3}{4} & 0 \\ 0 & 0 & 1 \end{pmatrix}$ (d) $\begin{pmatrix} 0 & 1 & 0 \\ 0 & 1 & 0 \\ 1 & 0 & 0 \end{pmatrix}$

26.2 **Time to empty**
Consider a router where, at each time step, the number of packets increases by 1 with probability 0.4 and decreases by 1 with probability 0.6. How long does it take for the router to empty? The Markov chain depicting the number of packets is shown in Figure 26.10. Let $T_{1,0}$ denote the time to get from state 1 to state 0. (a) Compute $\mathbf{E}\left[T_{1,0}\right]$. (b) Compute $\mathbf{Var}(T_{1,0})$.

[Hint: The variance computation is a little tricky. Be careful not to lump together distinct random variables.]

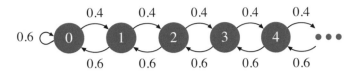

Figure 26.10 *Number of packets at router.*

26.3 Time to empty – extra strength

Consider the same setup as in Exercise 26.2. Let $T_{n,0}$ denote the time to get from state n to state 0. (a) Compute $\mathbf{E}\left[T_{n,0}\right]$. (b) Compute $\mathbf{Var}(T_{n,0})$.

26.4 Gambling game

Dafna starts out with zero dollars. Every day she gains a dollar with probability p, stays put with probability s, or loses all her money (goes broke) with probability b, where $p + s + b = 1$. Dafna plays the game forever. Use a DTMC to determine the stationary probability that Dafna has i dollars. What happens to your stationary probability when $s = 0$? What is Dafna's long-run expected money (for any general s)?

26.5 Reviewing the definitions

For the DTMC shown in Figure 26.11, circle all the statements that are *true*. Provide a one-line explanation for every item that you circled.

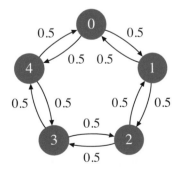

Figure 26.11 *Chain for Exercise 26.5.*

(a) The chain is null recurrent.
(b) The chain is positive recurrent.
(c) The chain is time-reversible.

(d) $\sum_{n=0}^{\infty} (\mathbf{P}^n)_{00}$ is finite.

(e) The chain is irreducible.

(f) The chain is aperiodic.

(g) There are an infinite number of stationary distributions.

(h) $m_{00} = 0.5$.

(i) $\lim_{t \to \infty} \frac{N_0(t)}{t} = 0$.

(j) The chain is ergodic.

(k) $m_{00} = \infty$.

(l) The limiting distribution exists.

(m) $f_0 < 1$.

(n) $(\mathbf{P}^5)_{00} = 2^{-5}$.

Glossary:

$\mathbf{P}$ is the transition probability matrix

f_j = probability that we ever return to state j given that we start in state j.

$N_j(t)$ = number of visits to state j by time t.

m_{jj} = mean number of time steps to return to j given we're in state j.

26.6 Equivalent definitions

Given an ergodic DTMC with transition matrix $\mathbf{P}$, make as few equivalence classes as you can out of the expressions below. For example, your answer might be:

$$a = b = d = i = j; \qquad c = g = h; \qquad e; \qquad f = j.$$

(a) $\lim_{n \to \infty} (\mathbf{P}^n)_{jj}$

(b) $\frac{1}{p_j}$

(c) $\frac{1}{m_{jj}}$

(d) π_j

(e) $\sum_{n=0}^{\infty} (\mathbf{P}^n)_{jj}$

(f) $1 + \sum_{k \neq j} P_{jk} \cdot m_{kj}$

(g) $\sum_k \pi_k P_{kj}$

(h) $\lim_{t \to \infty} \frac{N_j(t)}{t}$

(i) $\lim_{n \to \infty} (\mathbf{P}^n)_{kj}$

(j) f_j

Glossary:

$P_{ij} = (i, j)$th entry of transition matrix $\mathbf{P}$.

m_{jj} = mean number of time steps to return to j given we're in state j.

π_j = limiting probability of being in state j.

p_j = time-average fraction of time that chain spends in state j.

f_j = probability that a chain starting in state j ever returns to state j.

$N_j(t)$ = number of visits to state j by time t.

26.7 A positive recurrent chain
Recall the chain in Figure 26.12 that we've seen many times before.

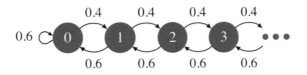

Figure 26.12 *Chain for Exercise 26.7.*

(a) Use Theorem 26.19 to explain how we know that the chain is positive recurrent.
(b) Derive m_{00} via conditioning on the next step. Then use a theorem to explain why your answer makes sense.

26.8 Stationary but not limiting
We've seen several examples of finite-state DTMCs for which the stationary distribution exists, but the limiting distribution does not. Provide an example of an *infinite-state*, irreducible DTMC for which there is a unique stationary distribution, but no limiting distribution exists. Solve for the stationary distribution.

26.9 Expected time until k failures
This is a repeat of Exercise 4.18, where we want to derive the expected number of minutes until there are k consecutive failures in a row, assuming that a failure occurs independently every minute with probability p. However, this time, solve the problem by finding the limiting probability of some Markov chain. Include a picture of your Markov chain. [Hint: You will have to think a bit to see how to convert from the limiting probabilities of the Markov chain to what you really want.]

26.10 Threshold queue
Figure 26.13 depicts a "threshold queue" with integer parameter t.

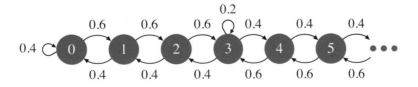

Figure 26.13 *For Exercise 26.10. Markov chain for threshold queue with $t = 3$.*

When the number of jobs is $< t$, then the number of jobs decreases by 1 with probability 0.4 and increases by 1 with probability 0.6 at each time step. However, when the number of jobs increases to $> t$, then the reverse is true and the number of jobs increases by 1 with probability 0.4 and decreases by 1 with probability 0.6 at each time step.

(a) Derive the stationary probability distribution as a function of t, for arbitrary threshold t.

(b) Given that you have a stationary distribution, explain why it follows that this distribution is the limiting distribution.

(c) Compute the mean number of jobs, $\mathbf{E}[N]$, as a function of t.

(d) What happens to $\mathbf{E}[N]$ when $t = 0$? Does this answer make sense?

26.11 **I am one with the chain**

[Proposed by Misha Ivkov] For the two chains in Figure 26.14, determine if each is positive recurrent, transient, or null recurrent. (Do not do anything complicated – just look and make a simple argument.)

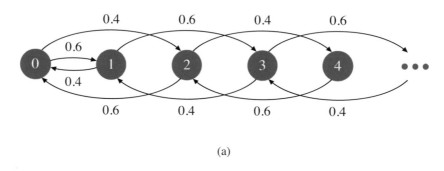

(a)

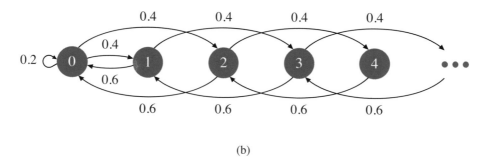

(b)

Figure 26.14 *Markov chains for Exercise 26.11.*

26.12 **Finish proof of Theorem 26.14**

Complete the proof of Theorem 26.14 in the chapter.

26.13 **Deriving the mean time between visits**

Consider the two DTMCs in Figure 26.15. For each chain, derive m_{00}, the mean number of time steps between visits to state 0. If you claim that

$m_{00} = \infty$, you need to prove it. If you claim that $m_{00} < \infty$, you need to specify what m_{00} is.

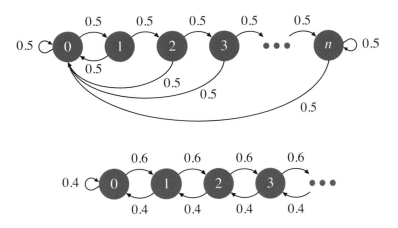

Figure 26.15 *Two chains for Exercise 26.13.*

26.14 **Walking in a winter wonderland**

[Proposed by Misha Ivkov] Figure 26.16 shows an infinite binary tree representing a DTMC, where $p + q + r = 1$. Label the layers where node 1 is layer 0, nodes 2 and 3 are layer 1, and nodes 2^k through $2^{k+1} - 1$ comprise layer k.

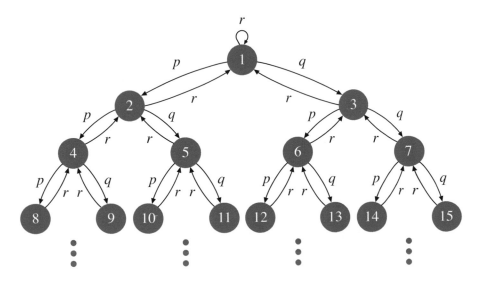

Figure 26.16 *Markov chain for Exercise 26.14.*

(a) Under what conditions does the limiting distribution exist (explain)? What is that limiting distribution? [Hint: It suffices to derive the following: (i) Express π_{2i} in terms of π_i; (ii) Express π_{2i+1} in terms of π_i; (iii) Derive π_1.]

(b) What is the long-run expected layer?

26.15 Pricing model

You are the market maker for GOGO. You have no clue whether GOGO stock will rise or fall, but you are obligated to buy or sell single shares from customers at all times. However, you do get to set the share price. To control the size of your position (number of shares of GOGO you own), when you are long (that is, own) GOGO, you set the price so that with probability $p < \frac{1}{2}$ your next trade is a buy, and with probability $q = 1 - p$ your next trade is a sell. In contrast, if you are short (that is, owe) GOGO, you set the price so that with probability p your next trade is a sell, and with probability q your next trade is a buy.

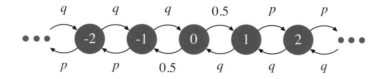

Figure 26.17 *Bidirectional chain for pricing.*

Your position is represented by the bidirectional chain in Figure 26.17. A negative state indicates how many shares you owe, and a positive state indicates how many shares you own.

(a) Given this pricing, what does your position tend to revert to?
(b) Derive the time-average fraction of time spent in each state.
(c) Why weren't you asked to find the limiting probabilities?
(d) What is the expected (absolute value) size of your position?

26.16 Brownian motion

Brownian motion models the walk of a drunkard, as depicted by Figure 26.18. Assume that the drunkard starts in state 0 and makes one move per day.

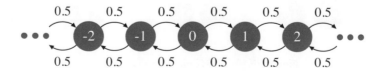

Figure 26.18 *Brownian motion.*

(a) Let $T_{0,n}$ denote the number of days it takes the drunkard to get from state 0 to state n. What is $\mathbf{E}\left[T_{0,n}\right]$? Prove it formally.

(b) Let $D_{0,n}$ denote the number of days until the drunkard first achieves distance n from its origin (that is, the drunkard first hits either state n or $-n$). Prove that $\mathbf{E}\left[D_{0,n}\right] = n^2$. Provide any proof that you like. The steps below are (optional) helping steps:

   (i) Define $D_{i,j}$ to be the number of days until the drunkard first gets to either state j or state $-j$, given that the drunkard starts in state i. Argue that $D_{0,n} = D_{0,1} + D_{1,2} + D_{2,3} + \cdots + D_{n-1,n}$.

  (ii) What is $\mathbf{E}\left[D_{0,1}\right]$? Derive $\mathbf{E}\left[D_{1,2}\right]$. Derive $\mathbf{E}\left[D_{2,3}\right]$. Do you see a pattern?

 (iii) Guess a formula for $\mathbf{E}\left[D_{i,i+1}\right]$ and verify that your guess is correct.

 (iv) Returning to step (i), derive $\mathbf{E}\left[D_{0,n}\right]$.

26.17 **Wandering around the Pittsburgh airport**
[Proposed by Adrian Abedon] At the Pittsburgh international airport, each of the terminals A, B, C, and D now have an infinite number of gates. A weary traveler in the airport wanders the gates at random, starting from the central hub (0). The traveler's movement is modeled by the Markov chain in Figure 26.19.

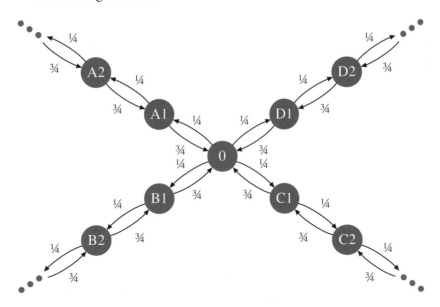

Figure 26.19 *DTMC for Exercise 26.17.*

(a) Find the stationary distribution $\pi_{Ai}, \pi_{Bi}, \pi_{Ci}, \pi_{Di}$, and π_0.

(b) Find $m_{0,A2}$, the expected time for the traveler to get to their gate $A2$.

26.18 **Gambler ruin problem**

Imagine a gambler who is equally likely to win a dollar or to lose a dollar every day (see Figure 26.20). The gambler starts out with i dollars. What is $P_{i,n}$, the probability that he makes it to n dollars before going bankrupt? [Hint: It helps to guess an expression for $P_{i,n}$ in terms of $P_{i+1,n}$.]

Figure 26.20 *State i indicates that there are i more tails than heads.*

26.19 **Mouse in infinite maze**

[Proposed by Misha Ivkov] A mouse is trapped in a maze with an infinite number of layers. At each time step, with probability $\frac{2}{3}$, the mouse decreases its layer by 1, and with probability $\frac{1}{3}$ it increases its layer by 1, as shown in Figure 26.21. The mouse can only escape from layer 0. Suppose that we drop the mouse into this maze at a random layer ≥ 1, where the mouse is dropped at layer i with probability $\frac{1}{2^i}$. Let T denote the number of steps until the mouse escapes (gets to layer 0).

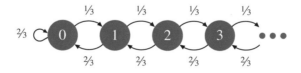

Figure 26.21 *Markov chain for Exercise 26.19, where the state represents the mouse's current layer.*

(a) Derive the z-transform, $\widehat{T}(z)$. It helps to define T in terms of T_i, where T_i is the time to escape when starting in layer i. Follow these steps:
  (i) Start by deriving the z-transform of T_1. [Hint: You will need to use the fact that $\widehat{X}(z) = 1$ when $z = 1$ for any discrete r.v. X.]
  (ii) Now derive the z-transform of T_i in terms of T_1.
  (iii) Finally derive the z-transform of T by conditioning on the starting state i.
(b) Differentiate your answer to (a) to get $\mathbf{E}\,[T]$.

26.20 **2D gambler's walk**

[Proposed by Weina Wang] A drunkard walks on the two-dimensional plane depicted in Figure 26.22. Formally prove or disprove that this is a recurrent chain. You will need to make use of the following equations:[1]

$$\sum_{k=0}^{n} \binom{n}{k}^2 = \binom{2n}{n} \geq \frac{4^{n-1}}{\sqrt{n}}.$$

[Hint: This will look a lot like Section 26.6. In expressing the V quantity, it helps to use a *single* summation over k, rather than a double summation.]

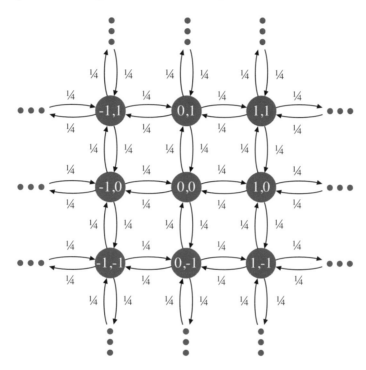

Figure 26.22 *Markov chain for Exercise 26.20.*

26.21 **Hellbound**

[Proposed by Alec Sun] Every lifetime Iggy is reincarnated into either heaven or hell. Since Iggy is a bad boy, reincarnations occur as follows:

– If Iggy is in heaven, then he will always be reincarnated into hell.
– If Iggy is in hell and has been in hell for $j \geq 1$ consecutive lifetimes since last being in heaven, then with probability $0 < p_j < 1$ he is reincarnated into heaven and with probability $1 - p_j$ he is reincarnated into hell.

Figure 26.23 depicts the infinite-state DTMC showing Iggy's state:

(a) Is the DTMC in Figure 26.23 irreducible, assuming that every value of p_j satisfies $0 < p_j < 1$?

---

[1] The equality is a special case of Vandermonde's identity. The inequality can be derived from Stirling's approximation. See Section 1.5 for a discussion of both.

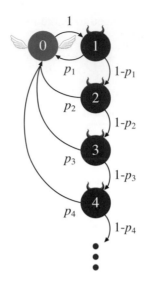

Figure 26.23 *DTMC for Exercise 26.21.*

(b) Let $c \in (0, 1)$ be a constant and suppose $p_j = c$ for all $j \geq 1$. Is our DTMC transient, positive recurrent, or null recurrent? Prove your answer.

(c) Suppose $p_j = \frac{1}{j+1}$ for all $j \geq 1$. Is this DTMC transient, positive recurrent, or null recurrent? Prove your answer. [Hint: It may be easier to consider $1 - f_0$.]

(d) Suppose $p_j = 2^{-j}$ for all $j \geq 1$. Is this DTMC transient, positive recurrent, or null recurrent? Prove your answer. [Hint: Compute f_0.]

26.22 Irreducible finite-state chains are positive recurrent ... again
This is a repeat of Exercise 25.19. Once again, you're being asked to prove that in a finite-state, irreducible DTMC, all states are positive recurrent. This time, follow these steps:
(a) First show that all states are recurrent.
(b) Now show that there exists at least one positive recurrent state.
(c) Now make use of Theorem 26.16 to finish the proof.

26.23 Proving that positive recurrence and null recurrence are class properties
Prove Theorem 26.16, which states that positive recurrence and null recurrence are class properties. [Warning: This is a difficult exercise.]

26.24 Processor with failures
The DTMC in Figure 26.24 is used to model a processor with failures. The chain tracks the number of jobs in the system. At any time step, either

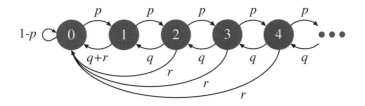

Figure 26.24 *DTMC for processor with failures.*

the number of jobs increases by 1 (with probability p), or decreases by 1 (with probability q), or a processor failure occurs (with probability r), where $p + q + r = 1$. In the case of a processor failure, all jobs in the system are lost. Derive the limiting probability, π_i, of there being i jobs in the system.

You will want to use the z-transform approach that you learned in Chapter 6. Here are some steps to help remind you how this works:

(a) Write the balance equation for state 0. Now express π_1 in terms of π_0.

(b) Write the balance equations for state $i \geq 1$.

(c) Let $\hat{\Pi}(z) = \sum_{i=0}^{\infty} \pi_i z^i$. Derive an expression for $\hat{\Pi}(z)$ in terms of π_0. You should get

$$\hat{\Pi}(z) = \frac{\pi_0 - z\pi_0 - z\frac{r}{q}}{z^2 \frac{p}{q} - z\frac{1}{q} + 1}.$$

(d) Rewrite $\hat{\Pi}(z)$ with its denominator factored into $\left(1 - \frac{z}{r_1}\right)\left(1 - \frac{z}{r_2}\right)$, where r_1 and r_2 are roots that you specify, where $r_1 < r_2$.

(e) Determine π_0. You will need three steps:
   (i) Explain why $\hat{\Pi}(z)$ is bounded for all $0 \leq z \leq 1$.
   (ii) Now show that $0 \leq r_1 < 1$.
   iii. We thus can conclude that $\hat{\Pi}(r_1) < \infty$. Thus, since r_1 is a root of the denominator of $\hat{\Pi}(z)$, it must also be a root of the numerator of $\hat{\Pi}(z)$. Use this to get π_0. [Note: Although you now have π_0, wait until the very end of the problem to substitute in this value.]

(f) Apply partial fraction decomposition to $\hat{\Pi}(z)$.

(g) $\hat{\Pi}(z)$ should now be very simple. Rewrite $\hat{\Pi}(z)$ as a geometric series.

(h) Match coefficients to get the π_i's.

(i) Verify that your solution for π_i satisfies the balance equations.

27 A Little Bit of Queueing Theory

We have alluded to the fact that probability is useful in the performance analysis and design of computer systems. Queueing theory is an area of applied probability which directly targets systems performance. Here the "system" might refer to a computer system, a call center, a healthcare system, a manufacturing system, a banking system, or one of many other examples. Markov chains (particularly continuous-time chains) are just one of many tools used in queueing theory. In this final part of the book, we provide a very brief introduction to queueing theory. For a much more in-depth coverage, see [35].

27.1 What Is Queueing Theory?

Queueing theory is the theory behind what happens when you have lots of jobs, scarce resources, and subsequently long queues and delays. It is literally the "theory of queues": what makes queues appear, how to predict the queue lengths, and how to improve system design by making the queues get shorter or go away.

Imagine a computer system, say a web server, where there is only one job. The job arrives, it uses certain resources (say some CPU, some I/O, some bandwidth), and then it departs. If we know the job's resource requirements, it is very easy to predict exactly when the job will depart. There is no delay because there are no queues. If every job indeed got to run in isolation on its own computer system, there would be no need for queueing theory. Unfortunately, that is rarely the case.

Queueing theory applies anywhere that queues come up (see Figure 27.1). We have all had the experience of waiting in line at the bank, wondering why there are not more tellers, or waiting in line at the supermarket, wondering why the express lane is for 8 items or less rather than 15 items or less, or whether it might be best to actually have *two* express lanes, one for 8 items or less and the other for 15 items or less. Queues are also at the heart of any computer system. Your CPU uses a time-sharing scheduler to serve a queue of jobs waiting for CPU time. A computer disk serves a queue of jobs waiting to read or write blocks. A router in a network serves a queue of packets waiting to be routed. The router queue is

Arriving customers ⟶

Server

Figure 27.1 *Illustration of a queue, in which customers wait to be served, and a server. The picture shows one customer being served at the server and five others waiting in the queue.*

a finite-capacity queue, in which packets are dropped when demand exceeds the buffer space. Memory banks serve queues of threads requesting memory blocks. Databases sometimes have lock queues, where transactions wait to acquire the lock on a record. Server farms consist of many servers, each with its own queue of jobs. Data centers often have a single central queue, where each job requests some number of resources to run. The list of examples goes on and on.

The goals of a queueing theorist are three-fold. The first is *predicting* the system performance. Typically this means predicting mean delay or delay variability or the probability that delay exceeds some service level agreement (SLA). However, it can also mean predicting the number of jobs that will be queueing or the mean number of servers being utilized (e.g., total power needs), or any other such metric. The second goal is *capacity provisioning*, namely determining how many resources are needed to achieve certain performance goals. One might want to provision to ensure that the system is stable, meaning that the queue lengths don't grow unboundedly. Or one might provision to ensure that certain SLAs are met. The third goal is finding a superior system *design* to improve performance. This often takes the form of a smarter scheduling policy or routing policy to reduce delays.

27.2 A Single-Server Queue

Figure 27.2 illustrates a single-server queue. The circle represents the server. One job can be served (worked on) at a time. New jobs arrive over time. If the server is free, the arriving job is served immediately; otherwise, the job has to queue. Unless stated otherwise, we assume that the jobs queue in First-Come-First-Served (FCFS) order.

Figure 27.2 *Single-server queue. The height of the rectangle indicates the size of the job.*

We formally define these quantities associated with the single-server queue:

Service order This is the order in which jobs (packets) will be served by the server. Unless otherwise stated, assume FCFS.

Average arrival rate This is the average rate, λ, at which jobs arrive to the server. For example, $\lambda = 3$ jobs/s, indicates that on average 3 jobs are arriving every second. Of course, some seconds might see more than 3 jobs, and others might see fewer than 3 jobs.

Interarrival time, mean interarrival time It is common to imagine that the times between arrivals are independent and identically distributed (i.i.d.), where there is a random variable (r.v.), I, which represents the time between successive job arrivals. In this case, $\mathbf{E}[I]$ would represent the mean interarrival time.

> **Question:** How can we think of $\mathbf{E}[I]$ in terms of what we've already seen?
>
> **Answer:** By definition, $\mathbf{E}[I] = \frac{1}{\lambda}$. Thus, in our example, the mean interarrival time would be $\frac{1}{\lambda} = \frac{1}{3}$ seconds. Note that we have not said anything about what the distribution of the interarrival time looks like. It might be Deterministic, meaning that exactly one job arrives every $\frac{1}{3}$ seconds, or it might be Exponential with rate 3, meaning that on average the time between arrivals is $\frac{1}{3}$, but it might be anywhere from 0 to infinity.

Service requirement, size It is common to assume that the sizes of jobs are i.i.d. and are denoted by the r.v. S. The size of a job is also called its service requirement. S is expressed in units of time and denotes the time it would take the job to run on this server if there were no other jobs around (no queueing). Importantly, the size is typically associated with the server.

Mean service time This is $\mathbf{E}[S]$, namely the average time required to serve a job on this server, where again "service" does not include queueing time. For example, we might have $\mathbf{E}[S] = 0.25$ seconds.

Average service rate This is the average rate, μ, at which jobs are served.

> **Question:** How can we think of μ in terms of what we've already seen?

Answer: By definition, $\mu = \frac{1}{E[S]} = 4$ jobs/s. Again, we have not said anything about the job size distribution. S might follow a Deterministic job size distribution, where every job has exactly size 0.25 seconds, or, for example, a Pareto distribution, with mean 0.25 seconds.

Observe that this way of speaking is different from the way we normally talk about servers in conversation. For example, nowhere have we mentioned the absolute speed of the server; rather, we have only defined the server's speed in terms of the set of jobs that it is working on.

Imagine that the server is a CPU with a FCFS queue of jobs. In **normal conversation**, we might say:

- The average arrival rate of jobs is 3 jobs per second.
- Jobs have different service requirements, but the average number of cycles required by a job is 2,000 cycles per job.
- The CPU speed is 8,000 cycles per second.
- That is, an average of 6,000 cycles of work arrive at the CPU each second, and the CPU can process 8,000 cycles of work per second.

In the **queueing-theoretic** way of talking, we would never mention the word "cycle." Instead, we would simply say:

- The average arrival rate of jobs is 3 jobs per second.
- The average rate at which the CPU can service jobs is 4 jobs per second.

This second way of speaking suppresses some of the detail and thus makes the problem a little easier to think about. You should feel comfortable going back and forth between the two.

27.3 Kendall Notation

In queueing theory there is a shorthand notation, called Kendall notation, which is used to represent simple commonly seen queueing systems consisting of just a single queue. Kendall notation is in no way expressive enough to represent all queueing systems (in particular, it is not useful for representing systems consisting of multiple queues, like networks), but it is still worth learning this shorthand.

As we saw in the previous section, what's most relevant is the distribution of the interarrival times of jobs and the distribution of the job sizes (service times). In Kendall notation there are typically three slots. The first indicates the distribution of the interarrival times; the second indicates the job size distribution; and the third indicates the number of servers. So, for example, writing:

$$D/\text{Pareto}(\alpha)/1$$

indicates that we're talking about a single-server queue where the interarrival times follow a Deterministic distribution and the job sizes follow a Pareto(α) distribution. Likewise, the notation

$$M/M/1$$

indicates that we're talking about a single-server queue where both the interarrival times and the job sizes are Exponentially distributed; the letter M is reserved for the Exponential distribution, and denotes the Markovian (memoryless) property of that distribution.

One thing that we have not discussed is independence. Kendall notation typically assumes (unless otherwise indicated) that the interarrival times are all independent random variables drawn from some distribution, and likewise that the job sizes are independent random variables drawn from some distribution, and that there is no correlation between interarrival times and the job sizes.

We also have not discussed the scheduling policy. Kendall notation typically assumes FCFS scheduling. If the service order is something other than FCFS, such as Shortest-Job-First, that information is sometimes included in a fourth slot. However we'll see that the fourth slot can be used for other things as well, such as indicating that the buffer capacity (number of jobs that can be in the system) is limited.

Question: Recall that back in Section 26.2, we talked about a queue where time was discretized. At each discrete time step, with probability p a packet (job) arrived, and with probability q a packet (job) departed, if there was a packet there. How can we represent such a system via Kendall notation?

Answer: Geometric(p)/Geometric(q)/1.

27.4 Common Performance Metrics

We consider these common **performance metrics** for queueing systems:

- **Response time, time in system, T:** We define a job's response time by

$$T = t_{\text{depart}} - t_{\text{arrive}},$$

where t_{depart} is the time when the job leaves the system, and t_{arrive} is the time when the job arrived to the system. We are interested in $\mathbf{E}[T]$, the mean response time; $\mathbf{Var}(T)$, the variance in response time; and the tail behavior of T, $\mathbf{P}\{T > t\}$.

- **Waiting time, delay, T_Q**: This is the time that the job spends in the queue, not being served. It is also called the "time in queue" or the "wasted time."
- **Number of jobs in the system, N**: The r.v. N includes those jobs in the queues, plus any jobs in service.
- **Number of jobs in queue, N_Q**: The r.v. N_Q denotes only the number of jobs waiting (in queues).

Question: For a single-server queue, with FCFS service order, as in Figure 27.2, what is the relationship between T and T_Q?

Answer: In a single-server queue with FCFS service order, waiting time can be defined as the time from when a job arrives to the system until it first receives service. Here $T = T_Q + S$.

27.4.1 Immediate Observations about the Single-Server Queue

There are some immediate observations that we can make about the single-server queue. First, observe that as λ, the mean arrival rate, increases, all the performance metrics mentioned earlier increase (get worse). Also, as μ, the mean service rate, increases, all the performance metrics mentioned earlier decrease (improve).

We require that $\lambda \leq \mu$ (we always assume $\lambda < \mu$).

Question: If $\lambda > \mu$ what happens?

Answer: If $\lambda > \mu$ then it seems like the queue length grows over time. We refer to this as **instability**. If the queue were represented by a Markov chain, this would be a transient chain.

Question: Can you provide the intuition for why the number of jobs in the system grows over time?

Answer: Consider a large time t. Let $N(t)$ be the number of jobs in the system at time t. Let $A(t)$ (respectively, $C(t)$) denote the number of arrivals (respectively, completions) by time t. Then we have:

$$N(t) = A(t) - C(t)$$
$$\mathbf{E}\left[N(t)\right] = \mathbf{E}\left[A(t)\right] - \mathbf{E}\left[C(t)\right]$$
$$\geq \lambda t - \mu t$$
$$= t(\lambda - \mu)$$
$$\to \infty \text{ as } t \to \infty \qquad \text{(when } \lambda > \mu \text{).}$$

(The inequality comes from the fact that the expected number of departures by time t is actually smaller than μt, because the server is not always busy.)

Throughout this book, we assume $\lambda < \mu$, which is needed for **stability**, which is defined as keeping queue sizes from growing unboundedly with time. When we later deal with networks of queues, we will also assume stability.

Question: Given the previous stability condition ($\lambda < \mu$), for a $D/D/1$ queue, what is T_Q? What is T?

Answer: $T_Q = 0$, and $T = S$.

Therefore queueing (waiting) results from *variability* in service time and/or inter-arrival time distributions. Here is an example of how variability leads to queues: Let's discretize time. Suppose at each time step, an arrival occurs with probability $p = 1/6$. Suppose at each time step, a departure occurs with probability $q = 1/3$. Then there is a non-zero probability that the queue will build up (temporarily) if several arrivals occur without a departure.

27.5 Another Metric: Throughput

We have already seen four performance metrics: $\mathbf{E}\left[N\right]$, $\mathbf{E}\left[T\right]$, $\mathbf{E}\left[N_Q\right]$, and $\mathbf{E}\left[T_Q\right]$. Now we introduce two new performance metrics: throughput and utilization. Throughput is arguably the performance metric most used in conversation. Everyone wants higher throughput! Is higher throughput related to lower response time? Let's see.

Question: In Figure 27.3, which system has higher throughput?

Answer: You might be tempted to think that the top queue has higher throughput, since its server is faster and thus jobs complete more quickly. While the top queue does have lower mean response time, both queues have the *same* throughput.

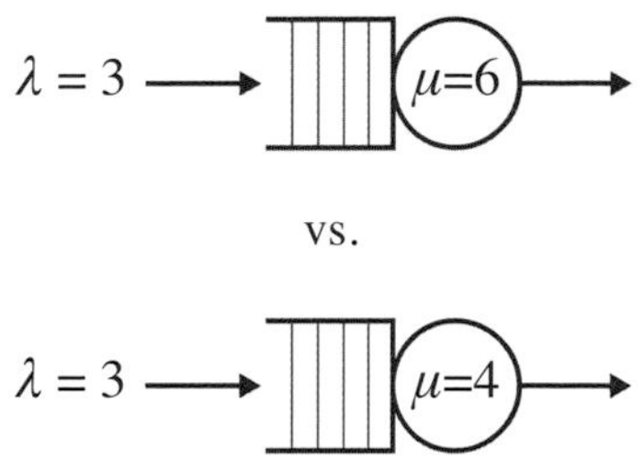

Figure 27.3 *Comparing throughput of two systems.*

Definition 27.1 Throughput, *denoted by X, is the long-run rate of job completions over time. We write:*

$$X = \lim_{t \to \infty} \frac{C(t)}{t},$$

where $C(t)$ denotes the number of completions by time t. Note that X is traditionally capitalized even though it's not a random variable.

Question: What is the throughput, X, of the queues in Figure 27.3?

Answer: Both systems have the same throughput of $X = \lambda = 3$ jobs/s. No matter how high we make μ, the completion rate is still bounded by the arrival rate: "Rate in = Rate out." Changing μ affects the *maximum possible X*, but not the *actual X*.

We now move on to understanding throughput for more complex systems.

27.5.1 Throughput for $M/G/k$

Figure 27.4 illustrates a k-server queueing system with a single shared queue. Whenever a server is free, it picks the job at the head of the queue to work on; if there is no job there, it sits idling until a job arrives. Because there is only one queue, we can describe this with Kendall notation. For example, this might be an $M/G/k$ queue with arrival rate λ jobs per second, where the M indicates that the interarrival times are distributed as $\text{Exp}(\lambda)$. The G here denotes that job sizes are i.i.d. following some general distribution, which we haven't specified. We use r.v. S to denote job size where the service rate at each server, μ, is defined to be $\mu = \frac{1}{E[S]}$. Here there are k servers, and a single FCFS queue, where the servers all pick their jobs from the same queue.

Question: What condition is needed to keep the system in Figure 27.4 stable?

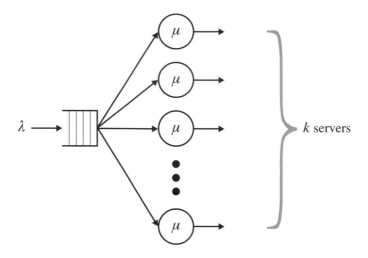

Figure 27.4 *A k-server queueing system.*

Answer: To keep the queue from growing unboundedly, we need to ensure that the total arrival rate of jobs into the system, λ, is less than the total rate at which jobs can leave the system, $k\mu$. So we want $\lambda < k\mu$.

Question: What is the throughput of the system in Figure 27.4?

Answer: Assuming a stable system, what comes in all goes out, so the completion rate is the arrival rate, namely $X = \lambda$.

In today's data centers, it is commonly the case that a *job occupies multiple servers simultaneously* rather than just occupying a single server. Exercise 27.7 examines how the above answers change in these multi-server job settings.

27.5.2 Throughput for Network of Queues with Probabilistic Routing

Figure 27.5 shows a network of queues. Here, server i receives external arrivals ("outside arrivals") with average rate r_i. However, server i also receives internal arrivals from some of the other servers. A job that leaves server i next goes to server j with probability P_{ij}. Server i processes jobs with average rate μ_i.

Note that we have not said anything about the distribution of the interarrival times or the service times, but that won't matter for questions of stability or throughput.

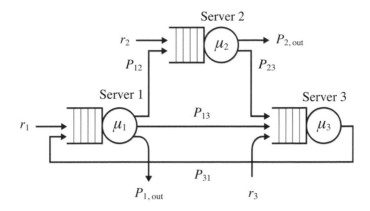

Figure 27.5 *Network of queues with probabilistic routing.*

Question: Assuming that the system is stable, what is the system throughput, X in Figure 27.5?

Answer: All jobs that arrive will also leave, so the rate of departures is the total rate of arrivals, namely: $X = \sum_i r_i$.

Question: What is the throughput at server i, X_i?

Answer: X_i is the rate of completions at server i. Let λ_i denote the *total* arrival rate into server i (including both external and internal arrivals). Then $X_i = \lambda_i$. But to get λ_i we need to solve these simultaneous equations:

$$\lambda_i = r_i + \sum_j \lambda_j P_{ji}. \tag{27.1}$$

Here, r_i denotes the rate of outside arrivals into server i, while $\lambda_j P_{ji}$ denotes the rate of internal arrivals into server i from server j. Note that λ_j here represents the total departure rate from server j (which is equal to the total arrival rate into server j).

Question: How are the r_i's constrained in these equations?

Answer: To maintain stability, we must have $\lambda_i < \mu_i$, $\forall i$, and this constrains the r_i's (see Exercise 27.8).

27.5.3 Throughput for Network of Queues with Deterministic Routing

In the queueing network in Figure 27.6, all jobs follow a predetermined route: CPU to disk 1 to disk 2 to disk 1 to disk 2 to disk 1 and then out.

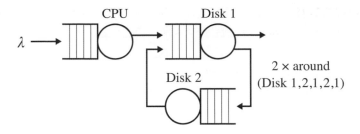

Figure 27.6 *Network of queues with non-probabilistic routing.*

Question: What is X in Figure 27.6?

Answer: $X = \lambda$.

Question: What are X_{Disk1} and X_{Disk2}?

Answer: $X_{\text{Disk1}} = 3\lambda$ and $X_{\text{Disk2}} = 2\lambda$.

27.5.4 Throughput for Finite Buffer

The queue in Figure 27.7 has finite capacity. The outside arrival rate is λ and the service rate is μ. Any arrival that finds no room is dropped.

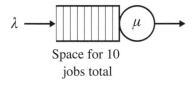

Space for 10
jobs total

Figure 27.7 *Single-server network with finite buffer capacity.*

Question: What is X?

Answer: Here, $X < \lambda$ because not all arrivals are admitted. The exact formula is $X = \lambda \cdot \mathbf{P}\{\text{job is admitted}\}$.

27.6 Utilization

When we talk about "utilization," we're almost always talking about the utilization of a single device (think single server), which we call "device utilization."

> **Definition 27.2** *The **device utilization**, denoted by ρ, is the long-run fraction of time the device is busy. This is also called the **device load**.*

Think about watching the device for a long period of time, t. Let $B(t)$ denote the total time during the observation period that the device is non-idle (busy). Then

$$\rho = \lim_{t \to \infty} \frac{B(t)}{t}.$$

Question: Looking at the two queues in Figure 27.3, what do you think ρ is for each server?

Answer: Intuitively it seems that $\rho = \frac{3}{6} = \frac{1}{2}$ for the top server, while $\rho = \frac{3}{4}$ for the bottom one. For example, for the bottom queue we imagine that there are 3 jobs coming in per second, and each occupies the server for $\frac{1}{4}$ second on average, so the server is occupied for $\frac{3}{4}$ fraction of each second. This is NOT a proof! In Section 27.11, we will *formally prove* that

$$\rho = \frac{\lambda}{\mu} \tag{27.2}$$

in the case of a single-server queue with arrival rate λ and service rate μ.

Although utilization almost always refers to a single device, if all the devices in a system are homogeneous and receive stochastically the same arrivals, then we often define the **system load** to be the same as a single server load.

For example, in the $M/G/k$ of Figure 27.4, we would say:

$$\text{system load} = \frac{\lambda}{k\mu}. \tag{27.3}$$

To see this, observe that, by symmetry, an individual server receives $\frac{1}{k}$ of the arrivals, on average, so its arrival rate is $\frac{\lambda}{k}$ and its service rate is μ, leading to a server utilization of $\frac{\lambda/k}{\mu} = \frac{\lambda}{k\mu}$. The case where a job occupies multiple servers is not much more complicated, see Exercise 27.7.

27.7 Introduction to Little's Law

Thus far, we have not discussed how one can determine the response time in a queueing system. One way in which this is done is to first represent the queueing system via a Markov chain. Then we solve for the stationary distribution of the Markov chain, which gives us $\mathbf{E}[N]$, the mean number of jobs in the system. We then use a beautiful theorem, called Little's Law, which allows us to convert from $\mathbf{E}[N]$ to $\mathbf{E}[T]$, the mean response time. The purpose of this section is to present and prove Little's Law.

As a side note: Not all queueing systems can be represented easily as Markov chains. The

$$\text{Geometric}(p)/\text{Geometric}(q)/1$$

queue forms a nice discrete-time Markov chain (DTMC), because the Geometric distribution is memoryless. Likewise, the $M/M/1$ queue (for the same reason of memorylessness) can be represented by a Markov chain, but this time a continuous-time Markov chain (CTMC) is required. However, what do we do when the interarrival times or service times are not memoryless? It turns out that one can usually approximate general distributions by mixtures of memoryless distributions, see [35, chpt. 21]. This ends up being very convenient for modeling queueing systems via Markov chains. On the other hand, there are also many techniques for getting to $\mathbf{E}[T]$ without going through a Markov chain.

Little's Law does more than relate $\mathbf{E}[N]$ to $\mathbf{E}[T]$. It provides a formal law for obtaining an average by dividing two averages, a trick that has many applications! One important application of Little's Law is that it allows us to prove the formula for device utilization ($\rho = \frac{\lambda}{\mu}$) that we saw in (27.2).

One of the reasons that Little's Law is so powerful is that it holds for *any ergodic queueing system*, no matter how complex, no matter how many queues, no matter what routing between the queues, no matter what service order within each queue, etc.

Question: What do we mean when we talk about an "ergodic system"?

Answer: Recall that for a Markov chain, we said that the Markov chain is ergodic if it is (1) irreducible, (2) aperiodic, and (3) positive recurrent. These ergodicity properties were sufficient to ensure that the time-averages were equal to their ensemble-average counterparts with probability 1. Even if we're not explicitly talking about a Markov chain, the same points apply. Generally, any "well-behaved" system is ergodic. By "well-behaved" we mean that the system is stable, in that queue lengths do not grow to infinity, and that the mean time between the system emptying is finite (as in positive recurrent).

27.8 Intuitions for Little's Law

Before we state Little's Law, it is worth trying to guess what it might say on your own. It should seem intuitive that $\mathbf{E}[T]$ and $\mathbf{E}[N]$ are proportional. For example, a fast-food restaurant gets people out fast (low $\mathbf{E}[T]$) and also does not require much waiting room (low $\mathbf{E}[N]$). By contrast, a slow-service restaurant gets people out slowly (high $\mathbf{E}[T]$) and therefore needs a lot more seating room (high $\mathbf{E}[N]$). Thus it seems that $\mathbf{E}[T]$ should be directly proportional to $\mathbf{E}[N]$.

Let's see if you can "guess" what it might be, by just looking at a single-server queue. Figure 27.8 shows an illustration of a single-server queue with outside arrival rate λ jobs/s, and mean job size $\mathbf{E}[S] = \frac{1}{\mu}$ seconds/job.

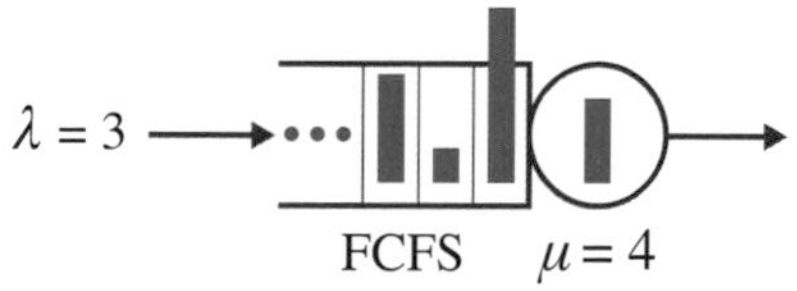

$$\lambda = 3 \longrightarrow \cdots$$

FCFS $\mu = 4$

Figure 27.8 *Single-server queue. The height of the rectangle indicates the size of the job.*

Question: Suppose we know the mean number of jobs in this system, $\mathbf{E}[N]$. Is there a way to convert that to the mean response time, $\mathbf{E}[T]$?

Here's a (WRONG) attempt: Let's think of $\mathbf{E}[T]$ as adding up the work in the system as seen by an arrival, where S_i denotes the size of the ith job, maybe something like:

$$\mathbf{E}[T] = \mathbf{E}[N] \cdot \mathbf{E}[S].$$

Intuitively the above attempt seems right because an arrival sees $\mathbf{E}[N]$ jobs, and each of these requires $\mathbf{E}[S]$ service time. However, it is WRONG for several reasons. First of all, N and S are not independent. Second, we're not taking into account the remaining service time on the job in service; remember that the job in service is typically partially complete. Third, this logic in no way generalizes to larger systems with many queues and servers.

The correct answer is:

$$\mathbf{E}[T] = \frac{\mathbf{E}[N]}{\lambda}. \tag{27.4}$$

Question: Can you explain *intuitively* why (27.4) makes sense for a single-server queue?

Answer: Think about a single FCFS queue, as shown in Figure 27.8. From a time-average perspective suppose that there are $\mathbf{E}[N]$ jobs in the system. Now observe that, on average,

$$\mathbf{E}[\text{Time between completions}] = \frac{1}{\lambda},$$

not $1/\mu$, because the average rate of completions is $X = \lambda$ (note that $1/\lambda$ is larger than $1/\mu$). Hence, intuitively, the expected time until the customer leaves is $\mathbf{E}[T] \approx \frac{1}{\lambda} \cdot \mathbf{E}[N]$. This is NOT a proof, only intuition. Theorem 27.3 will give us a proof, and that proof will hold for any network of queues.

27.9 Statement of Little's Law

Theorem 27.3 (Little's Law) *For any ergodic system (including arbitrarily complex networks of queues) we have that:*

$$\mathbf{E}[N] = \lambda \mathbf{E}[T], \tag{27.5}$$

where $\mathbf{E}[N]$ *is the expected number of jobs in the system,* λ *is the average arrival rate into the system, and* $\mathbf{E}[T]$ *is the mean time jobs spend in the system.*

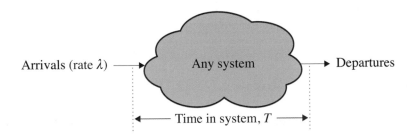

Figure 27.9 *Little's Law is extremely general.*

It is important to note that Little's Law makes no assumptions about the arrival process, the number of servers or queues, the service time distributions at the servers, the network topology, the service order, or anything! Also, since any *portion* of a queueing network is still a queueing network, Little's Law will apply to that portion as well.

Observe that, because we're considering ergodic systems, every job that arrives will complete in finite time (the mean time until the whole system empties is finite), so we know that

$$\lambda = X$$

in Figure 27.9. Here,

$$\lambda = \lim_{t \to \infty} \frac{A(t)}{t} \quad \text{and} \quad X = \lim_{t \to \infty} \frac{C(t)}{t},$$

where $A(t)$ is the number of arrivals by time t and $C(t)$ is the number of system completions (departures) by time t.

Restatement via Time Averages

Theorem 27.4 is a restatement of Little's Law in terms of time averages. This is the version that we'll actually be proving.

Theorem 27.4 (Little's Law restated) *Given any system, let $M(s)$ denote the number of jobs in the system at time s. Let T_i denote the response time of the ith arriving job.*

$$\overline{N}^{Time\ Avg} = \lim_{t \to \infty} \frac{\int_0^t M(s)ds}{t} \quad \text{and} \quad \overline{T}^{Time\ Avg} = \lim_{t \to \infty} \frac{\sum_{i=1}^{A(t)} T_i}{A(t)}.$$

For any system where the above limits exist and where $\lambda = X$, then,

$$\overline{N}^{Time\ Avg} = \lambda \cdot \overline{T}^{Time\ Avg}. \tag{27.6}$$

Observe that Little's Law as stated in Theorem 27.4 is an equality between *time averages* on a single sample path, while Little's Law from Theorem 27.3 is an equality between *ensemble averages*.

Question: Does Theorem 27.4 imply Theorem 27.3?

Answer: Yes! Theorem 27.3 assumes ergodicity, which subsumes the assumption that $\lambda = X$, which is needed in Theorem 27.4.[1] As we've seen in Chapters 25 and 26, if we have an *ergodic* system then the time average equals the ensemble average with probability 1. So proving that the time-average equality (27.6) holds suffices to guarantee that the ensemble averages are equal too. The reason we need the stronger assumption of ergodicity in Theorem 27.3 is just to make sure that the ensemble averages exist. Thus, assuming ergodicity, we can apply Little's Law in an ensemble average sense, which is what we do.

27.10 Proof of Little's Law

We are now ready to prove Little's Law.

Proof: [Theorem 27.4] Let T_i denote the time that the ith arrival to the system spends in the system, as shown in Figure 27.10. Thus the rectangle T_i marks the time from when the first job arrives until it completes (this includes time that the job is being served and time that it spends waiting in various queues).

---

[1] Ergodicity says that the mean time between empties is finite, so clearly every job completes in finite time, so the long-run rate of arrivals and completions converge.

Now, for any time t, consider the area, $\mathcal{A}$, contained within all the rectangles in Figure 27.10, up to time t (this includes most of the rectangle labeled T_5).

The key idea in proving Little's Law is that this area $\mathcal{A}$ is the same, whether we view it by summing *horizontally* or by summing *vertically*. We will first view $\mathcal{A}$ by summing horizontally, and then, equivalently, view it again by summing vertically.

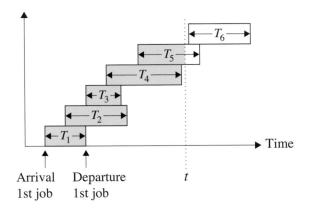

Figure 27.10 *Graph of arrivals.*

The horizontal view consists of summing up the T_i's as follows: We observe that

$$\sum_{i=1}^{C(t)} T_i \le \mathcal{A} \le \sum_{i=1}^{A(t)} T_i,$$

where $\sum_{i=1}^{C(t)} T_i$ denotes the sum of the time in system of those jobs that have completed by time t, and $\sum_{i=1}^{A(t)} T_i$ denotes the sum of the time in system of those jobs that have arrived by time t (a slight abuse of notation).

The vertical view of $\mathcal{A}$ adds up the number of jobs in the system at any moment in time, $M(s)$, where s ranges from 0 to t. Thus,

$$\mathcal{A} = \int_0^t M(s)ds.$$

Combining these two views, we have

$$\sum_{i=1}^{C(t)} T_i \le \int_0^t M(s)ds \le \sum_{i=1}^{A(t)} T_i.$$

Dividing by t throughout, we get:

$$\frac{\sum_{i=1}^{C(t)} T_i}{t} \le \frac{\int_0^t M(s)ds}{t} \le \frac{\sum_{i=1}^{A(t)} T_i}{t},$$

or, equivalently,

$$\frac{\sum_{i=1}^{C(t)} T_i}{C(t)} \cdot \frac{C(t)}{t} \leq \frac{\int_0^t M(s)\,ds}{t} \leq \frac{\sum_{i=1}^{A(t)} T_i}{A(t)} \cdot \frac{A(t)}{t}.$$

Taking limits as $t \to \infty$,

$$\lim_{t \to \infty} \frac{\sum_{i=1}^{C(t)} T_i}{C(t)} \cdot \lim_{t \to \infty} \frac{C(t)}{t} \leq \overline{N}^{\text{Time Avg}} \leq \lim_{t \to \infty} \frac{\sum_{i=1}^{A(t)} T_i}{A(t)} \cdot \lim_{t \to \infty} \frac{A(t)}{t}$$

$$\Rightarrow \overline{T}^{\text{Time Avg}} \cdot X \leq \overline{N}^{\text{Time Avg}} \leq \overline{T}^{\text{Time Avg}} \cdot \lambda.$$

Yet we are given that X and λ are equal. Therefore,

$$\overline{N}^{\text{Time Avg}} = \lambda \cdot \overline{T}^{\text{Time Avg}}.$$ ∎

Question: Are we assuming FCFS service order in this argument?

Answer: No, this argument does not depend on service order. Observe that the second arrival departs *after* the third arrival departs.

Question: Are we assuming anywhere that this is a single-server system?

Answer: No, this argument holds for any system. In fact, Little's Law can also be applied to any part of a system, so long as that part is well behaved (ergodic). We'll see this in Example 27.8.

A final remark on the proof: The proof assumes $\lim_{t \to \infty} \frac{\sum_{i=1}^{C(t)}}{C(t)} = \lim_{t \to \infty} \frac{\sum_{i=1}^{A(t)}}{A(t)}$. To see why, observe that the difference in the numerators is just the total work in the system at time t, which is finite, whereas the denominators grow with time. Thus the difference disappears in the limit as $t \to \infty$.

27.11 Important Corollaries of Little's Law

Corollary 27.5 (Little's Law for time in queue) *Given any system where* $\overline{N}_Q^{\text{Time Avg}}$, $\overline{T}_Q^{\text{Time Avg}}$, λ, *and X exist and where* $\lambda = X$, *then*

$$\overline{N}_Q^{\text{Time Avg}} = \lambda \cdot \overline{T}_Q^{\text{Time Avg}},$$

where N_Q represents the number of jobs in the queues in the system and T_Q represents the time jobs spend in queues.

Question: How would you prove Corollary 27.5?

Answer: Same proof as for Theorem 27.4, except that now instead of drawing T_i, we draw $T_Q^{(i)}$, namely the time the ith arrival to the system spends in queues (wasted time). Note that $T_Q^{(i)}$ may not be a solid rectangle. It may be made up of several rectangles because the ith job might be in a queue for a while, then in service, then waiting in some other queue, then in service again, etc.

> **Corollary 27.6 (Utilization Law)** *Consider a single device i with its own queue, possibly within a network of queues. Suppose that the average arrival rate into device i is λ_i jobs/s and the average service rate of device i is μ_i jobs/s, where $\lambda_i < \mu_i$. Let ρ_i denote the long-run fraction of time that device i is busy. Then,*
>
> $$\rho_i = \frac{\lambda_i}{\mu_i}.$$
>
> *We refer to ρ_i as the "device utilization" or "device load."*

Proof:

Question: Do you see where to apply Little's Law to queue i?

Hint: What should the "system" be for applying Little's Law?

Answer: Let the "system" consist of just the "service facility" (the server part *without* the associated queue), as shown in the shaded box of Figure 27.11. Now the number of jobs in the "system" is always just 0 or 1.

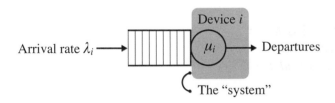

Figure 27.11 *Using Little's Law to prove the Utilization Law.*

Question: What is the expected number of jobs in the system as we have defined it?

Answer: The number of jobs in the system is 1 when the device is busy (this happens with probability ρ_i) and is 0 when the device is idle (this happens with probability $1 - \rho_i$). Hence the *expected* number of jobs in the system is ρ_i. So, applying Little's Law, we have:

ρ_i = Expected number jobs in service facility for device i

 = (Arrival rate into service facility) $\cdot$ (Mean time in service facility)

 = $\lambda_i \cdot \mathbf{E}$ [Service time at device i]

 = $\lambda_i \cdot \dfrac{1}{\mu_i}$.   ■

We often express the Utilization Law as:

$$\rho_i = \tfrac{\lambda_i}{\mu_i} = \lambda_i \mathbf{E}\,[S_i] = X_i \mathbf{E}\,[S_i]\,,$$

where ρ_i, λ_i, X_i, and $\mathbf{E}\,[S_i]$ are the load, average arrival rate, average throughput, and average service requirement at queue i, respectively.

Suppose we have some arbitrary network of queues. We'd like to again relate $\mathbf{E}\,[T]$ to $\mathbf{E}\,[N]$ for the system. However, we are only interested in "red" jobs, where "red" denotes some type of job. Specifically, we'd like to understand how $\mathbf{E}\,[N_{\text{red}}]$, the mean number of red jobs in the system relates to $\mathbf{E}\,[T_{\text{red}}]$, the mean response time of red jobs.

Question: Suppose we want to apply Little's Law to just a particular class of jobs, say the "red" jobs. Can we do this?

Answer: Yes.

Theorem 27.7 (Little's Law for red jobs) *For any ergodic system we have that:*

$$\mathbf{E}\,[N_{\text{red}}] = \lambda_{\text{red}}\mathbf{E}\,[T_{\text{red}}]\,,$$

where $\mathbf{E}\,[N_{\text{red}}]$ is the expected number of red jobs in the system, λ_{red} is the average arrival rate of red jobs into the system, and $\mathbf{E}\,[T_{\text{red}}]$ is the mean time that red jobs spend in the system.

Proof: The proof is exactly the same as for Little's Law, but only the T_i's corresponding to the red jobs are included in Figure 27.10.   ■

Example 27.8 (Repair center)

Repairs don't always work. In Jenny's repair center, shown in Figure 27.12, every arriving item undergoes a "repair attempt," but with probability 0.9 the item needs to go in for another round. We say that the total time for repair, T, is the time from when the item first arrives until it is fully repaired. Based on

Jenny's measurements, on average, $\lambda = 2$ items arrive to the repair center every hour, the average repair attempt takes $\mathbf{E}[S] = 2$ minutes, and $\mathbf{E}[T] = 10$ hours.

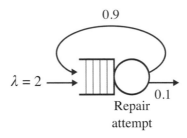

Figure 27.12 *Jenny's repair center.*

Question: What fraction of time is the repair center busy?

Answer: To answer this, we draw a gray box around just the server, as shown in Figure 27.13.

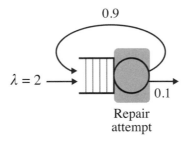

Figure 27.13 *The "system" here is the gray box.*

Applying Little's Law to this gray box system, we have:

$$\mathbf{E}[N_{\text{box}}] = \lambda_{\text{box}} \cdot \mathbf{E}[T_{\text{box}}].$$

Observe that $\mathbf{E}[N_{\text{box}}] = \rho$. Furthermore, $\mathbf{E}[T_{\text{box}}] = \mathbf{E}[S] = \frac{2}{60}$ hours. To get λ_{box}, we note that, on average, an item requires 10 repair attempts. Hence

$$\lambda_{\text{box}} = 10 \cdot \lambda = 20 \text{ items/hour.}$$

Little's Law thus yields:

$$\mathbf{E}[N_{\text{box}}] = \lambda_{\text{box}} \cdot \mathbf{E}[T_{\text{box}}]$$
$$\rho = 20 \cdot \frac{2}{60} = \frac{2}{3}.$$

Question: What is the expected number of items in the repair center, $\mathbf{E}[N]$?

Hint: This can be solved in two different ways, depending on how we define our system of interest in Figure 27.14.

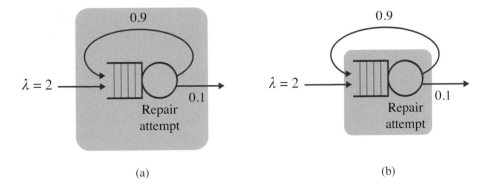

Figure 27.14 *Two different views of the "system," both with the same* $\mathbf{E}[N]$.

Answer: If we draw our gray box around the entire system, as shown in Figure 27.14(a), then $\lambda_{\text{box}} = \lambda = 2$. This yields:

$$\mathbf{E}[N_{\text{box}}] = \lambda_{\text{box}} \cdot \mathbf{E}[T_{\text{box}}]$$
$$\mathbf{E}[N] = \lambda \cdot \mathbf{E}[T]$$
$$= 2 \cdot 10 = 20 \text{ items.}$$

On the other hand, if we draw our gray box around a single attempt, as shown in Figure 27.14(b), then $\lambda_{\text{box}} = 10\lambda$. However, $\mathbf{E}[T_{\text{box}}]$ is only $\frac{\mathbf{E}[T]}{10}$ since there are 10 attempts on average. This yields:

$$\mathbf{E}[N_{\text{box}}] = \lambda_{\text{box}} \cdot \mathbf{E}[T_{\text{box}}]$$
$$\mathbf{E}[N] = (10\lambda) \cdot \mathbf{E}[T_{\text{attempt}}]$$
$$= (10 \cdot 2) \cdot \frac{\mathbf{E}[T]}{10}$$
$$= 20 \cdot \frac{10}{10} = 20 \text{ items.}$$

Unsurprisingly, the answer is the same, since Little's Law applies to any system or portion of a system.

27.12 Exercises

27.1 **Professors and students**
A professor practices the following strategy with respect to taking on new PhD students. On the even-numbered years, she takes on two new PhD students. On the odd-numbered years, she takes on one new PhD student.

All students graduate and the average time to graduate is six years. How many PhD students on average will the professor have in her group? Prove your answer.

27.2 **Professors and students, revisited**
A professor practices the following strategy with respect to taking on new PhD students. On the even-numbered years, she takes on two new PhD students. On the odd-numbered years, she takes on one new PhD student. Not all students graduate. Of the students whom the professor takes on, $\frac{1}{3}$ end up staying for one year on average and then leave the program; $\frac{1}{6}$ graduate after four years; $\frac{1}{6}$ graduate after five years; $\frac{1}{6}$ graduate after six years; and $\frac{1}{6}$ graduate after seven years. How many PhD students on average will the professor have in her group? Prove your answer.

27.3 **Mean response time at router with infinite capacity**
Recall in Section 26.2 we derived the mean number of packets in a router with infinite capacity, where at every time step, with probability $p = \frac{1}{4}$ one packet arrives, and, independently, with probability $q = \frac{1}{3}$ one packet departs. What is the mean response time, $\mathbf{E}\left[T\right]$, for this particular system?

27.4 **Mean response time at router with finite capacity**
As in Exercise 27.3, we return to the router in Section 26.2, but this time, the router only has room for a total of 3 packets. Specifically, if a packet arrives when the state of the DTMC is 3, then the packet is dropped and the state of the system doesn't change. What is the mean response time, $\mathbf{E}\left[T\right]$, of those packets that are *not* dropped. [Hint: To create an ergodic system, you'll want to think about the "system" as consisting only of the arrivals that enter.]

27.5 **The single-server queue**
Kunhe's system consists of a single-server queue. Based on Kunhe's measurements, the average arrival rate is $\lambda = 5$ jobs/s; the average job size is $\mathbf{E}\left[S\right] = 0.1$ s; and the average number of jobs is $\mathbf{E}\left[N\right] = 10.5$ jobs.
(a) What is the fraction of time that Kunhe's server is busy?
(b) What is the average time that jobs spend queueing in Kunhe's system, $\mathbf{E}\left[T_Q\right]$?

27.6 **The Arthur Ravenel bridge**
The Arthur Ravenel bridge in Charleston allows walkers and joggers to get to downtown Charleston. During my visit to Charleston, I observed that:
- On average, 20 walkers arrive per hour and take an average of 1 hour to cross the bridge.

- On average, 10 joggers arrive per hour and take an average of 20 minutes to cross the bridge.

Based on this data, estimate the average number of people (walkers plus joggers) on the bridge at any time.

27.7 **Data center utilization**

The Clouds-R-Us company runs a data center with 10,000 servers shown in Figure 27.15. Jobs arrive to the data center with average rate $\lambda = 2$ jobs/s. Each job requires some number of servers K, where $K \sim \text{Binomial}(1000, 0.05)$. The job holds onto these K servers for some time S seconds, where $S \sim \text{Exp}(0.02)$, and then releases all its servers at once. Assume that K and S are independent. Jobs are served in FCFS order. If a job gets to the head of the queue, but the number of servers that it needs exceeds the number of idle servers, then the job simply waits (blocking those jobs behind it in the queue) until that number of servers becomes available. You may assume that the system is ergodic. On average, how many jobs are running at a time?

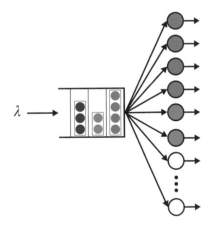

Figure 27.15 *Data center for Exercise 27.7.*

27.8 **Maximum outside arrival rate**

For the network-of-queues with probabilistic routing given in Figure 27.5, suppose that each server serves at an average rate of 10 jobs/s; that is, $\mu_i = 10$, $\forall i$. Suppose that $r_2 = r_3 = 1$. Suppose that $p_{12} = p_{2,out} = 0.8$, $p_{23} = p_{13} = 0.2$, $p_{1,out} = 0$, and $p_{31} = 1$. What is the maximum allowable value of r_1 to keep this system stable?

27.9 **Simplified power usage in data centers**

Given that power is expensive, it is common practice to leave servers on only when they are being used and to turn them off whenever they are not in use. Assume that the following power-aware algorithm is used: When a job arrives, it instantly turns on a fresh server (assume zero setup cost). When the job completes service, it instantly turns off that server. Assume that there is always a server available for every job (i.e., there is no queueing). Your goal is to derive the time-average rate at which power is used in our system. Assume that when a server is on, it consumes power at a rate of $\mathcal{P} = 240$ watts. Assume $\lambda = 10$ jobs arrive per second and that the service requirement of jobs is Uniformly distributed, ranging from 1 second to 9 seconds.

27.10 Going to the DMV

When getting your driver's license at the DMV, you have to pass through two stations: the photo-taking station and the license-creation station. Unfortunately, at the end of license-creation, with probability 25% they find something wrong with the photo, and the whole process has to start all over again. Figure 27.16 shows the process. As shown in the figure, the average arrival rate of people to the DMV is $r = 15$ people per hour, the average number of people in the photo station is 10, and the average number in the license station is 20. Assume that the system is stable in that the total arrival rate into each station is less than the service rate at the station. Derive the mean time from when you walk into the DMV until you walk out with your driver's license.

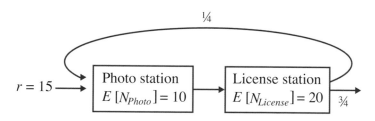

Figure 27.16 *The DMV process for Exercise 27.10.*

27.11 Network that looks like a flip flop

Tianxin's network, shown in Figure 27.17, looks like a flip flop. Jobs arrive to Tianxin's network at a rate of $r = 1$ jobs per second. The routing probabilities are shown. The service rate at station A is $\mu_A = 3$ jobs per second, and that at station B is $\mu_B = 4$ jobs per second. An individual job might pass through Station A, then B, then A, then B, etc., before it eventually leaves. Tianxin has observed that the expected number of jobs at station A is $\mathbf{E}[N_A] = 2$ and the expected number of jobs at station B is $\mathbf{E}[N_B] = 1$.

(a) Let T denote the response time of a job, i.e., the time from when it arrives until it departs. What is $\mathbf{E}[T]$?

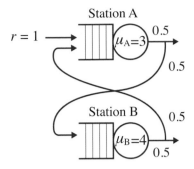

Figure 27.17 *Tianxin's network for Exercise 27.11.*

(b) Let λ_A denote the total arrival rate into station A. Let λ_B denote the total arrival rate into station B. What are λ_A and λ_B?

(c) What is the throughput of the system? What is the throughput of station A? Which is higher?

(d) Let T_A denote the time it takes for a job to make a *single* visit to station A (this includes queueing and then serving at station A). Likewise, let T_B denote the time it takes for a job to make a *single* visit to station B. What are $\mathbf{E}\,[T_A]$ and $\mathbf{E}\,[T_B]$?

(e) Let T_Q denote the total time that a job spends queueing while in the system. This includes the total time that the job is in queues from when it arrives until it leaves the system. What is $\mathbf{E}\left[T_Q\right]$?

27.12 Finally a haircut!

For over a year in lockdown, I haven't been able to get my hair cut, but finally I can return to the salon! At my salon there are two stations: the washing station and the cutting station, each with its own queue. The people who work at the washing station only wash hair. The people who work at the cutting station only cut hair. When a washing person frees up, they take the next person in the wash line, and similarly for the cutting line.

My salon is very quick. The average wash time is only $\mathbf{E}\,[S_{\text{wash}}] = \frac{1}{13}$ hours and the average cut time is only $\mathbf{E}\,[S_{\text{cut}}] = \frac{1}{7}$ hours. Unfortunately, they're so quick that they sometimes forget to rinse the shampoo, so, with probability $\frac{1}{4}$, I will need to rejoin the wash line after my wash is complete. There are two types of customers at my salon: the "wash-and-cut" customers, who get their hair washed and then cut, and the "cut-only" customers who only get their hair cut (no wash).

Figure 27.18 shows the salon. Assume that 54 customers enter the salon per hour. Assume that $\frac{2}{3}$ are wash-and-cut customers and $\frac{1}{3}$ are cut-only customers.

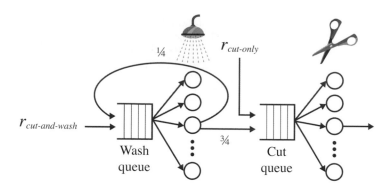

Figure 27.18 *Hair salon for Exercise 27.12.*

(a) What is the bare minimum number of staff (washers + cutters) that are needed to ensure that the hair salon is stable?

(b) On average, the number of customers at the wash station (either in the wash queue or having their hair washed) is 9. On average, the number of customers at the cutting station (either in the cut queue or having their hair cut) is 18.

  (i) What is the expected response time of a random customer (we're not told the type of customer)?

  (ii) What is the expected response time of a cut-only customer? [Hint: Think about the experience of a cut-only customer.]

27.13 Little's Law and the vaccine center

Our local COVID vaccine center is structured as a multi-server queue, where there are five nurses providing vaccines, and a queue of patients waiting to receive vaccines, as in Figure 27.19. When a patient is getting their vaccine, they sit in one of the five chairs. Due to social distancing rules, there is a limit of 25 on the total number of people allowed in the vaccine center (this includes the five nurses). There is an overflow queue of patients outside the vaccine center, waiting to get in. The total number of patients, N, grows and shrinks over time, but, on average there are $E[N] = 80$ patients in total (including both the vaccine center and the overflow queue). The long-run average rate of patients joining the queue is $\lambda = 40$ patients per hour.

(a) What is the expected total response time (from arrival to departure)?

(b) Suppose we model $N \sim \text{Geometric}\left(\frac{1}{80}\right)$. Let N_{center} denote the number of people inside the vaccine center (gray area). Let T_{center} denote the time spent inside the vaccine center. What is $E[T_{\text{center}}]$?

[Hint: Start by expressing N_{center} in terms of N. You will need a "min" term. Then derive $E[N_{\text{center}}]$ and apply Little's Law.]

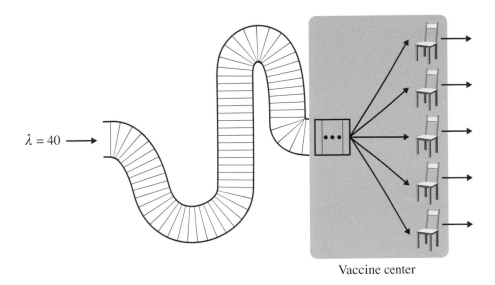

Figure 27.19 *Vaccine center.*

27.14 **Mean slowdown**

The slowdown metric is related to response time, but is somewhat more practical. A job's slowdown is defined as its response time divided by its size:

$$\text{Slowdown of job } j = \frac{\text{Response time of } j}{\text{Size of } j}. \tag{27.7}$$

The idea is that large jobs (like downloading a whole movie) can tolerate larger response times (while you go make popcorn), while small jobs (like downloading a web page) can tolerate only very small response times. The slowdown metric captures this tolerance better than response time.

(a) Jobs arrive at a server that services them in FCFS order (Figure 27.20).

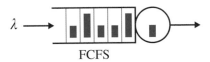

FCFS

Figure 27.20 *Figure for Exercise 27.14.*

The average arrival rate is $\lambda = \frac{1}{2}$ job/s. The job sizes (service times) are i.i.d. and are represented by r.v. S, where

$$S = \begin{cases} 1 & \text{w/prob } \frac{3}{4} \\ 2 & \text{otherwise} \end{cases}.$$

You have measured the mean response time, $\mathbf{E}[T] = \frac{29}{12}$. Based on this information, compute the mean slowdown, $\mathbf{E}[\text{Slowdown}]$.

(b) If the service order in part (a) had been Shortest-Job-First, would the same technique have worked for computing mean slowdown?

References

[1] Ilan Adler, Yang Cao, Richard Karp, Erol A. Pekoz, and Sheldon M. Ross. Random knockout tournaments. *Operations Research*, 65(6):1429–1731, 2017.

[2] Micah Adler, Peter Gemmell, Mor Harchol-Balter, Richard M. Karp, and Claire Kenyon. Selection in the presence of noise: The design of play-off systems. In *Proceedings of 5th ACM-SIAM Symposium on Discrete Algorithms*, pages 546–573, Arlington, VA, January 1994.

[3] W.R. Alford, A. Granville, and C. Pomerance. There are infinitely many Carmichael numbers. *Annals of Mathematics*, 140:703–722, 1994.

[4] Tom Anderson, David Culler, and David Patterson. A case for networks of workstations. *IEEE Micro*, 15(1):54–64, 1995.

[5] Nikhil Bansal and Mor Harchol-Balter. Analysis of SRPT scheduling: Investigating unfairness. In *Proceedings of ACM SIGMETRICS*, pages 279–290, Cambridge, MA, June 2001.

[6] Amnon Barak, Shai Guday, and Richard G. Wheeler. *The Mosix Distributed Operating System: Load Balancing for Unix*. Springer-Verlag, 1993.

[7] Paul Barford and Mark E. Crovella. Generating representative Web workloads for network and server performance evaluation. In *Proceedings of the ACM SIGMETRICS Conference on Measurement and Modeling of Computer Systems*, pages 151–160, Madison, WI, July 1998.

[8] David P. Blinn, Tristan Henderson, and David Kotz. Analysis of a wi-fi hotspot network. In *International Workshop on Wireless Traffic Measurements and Modeling*, pages 1–6, Seattle, WA, June 2005.

[9] Burton H. Bloom. Space/time trade-offs in hash coding with allowable errors. *Communications of the ACM*, 13(7):422–426, 1970.

[10] Paul Bratley, Bennett Fox, and Linus Schrage. *A Guide to Simulation*. Springer-Verlag, 2nd ed., 1983.

[11] Goerg Cantor. Über eine elementare frage der mannigfaltigkeitslehre. *Jahrensbericht der Deutschen Mathematiker-Vereinigung*, 1:75–78, 1891.

[12] R. D. Carmichael. Note on a new number theory function. *Bulletin of the American Mathematics Society*, 16:232–238, 1910.

[13] R. D. Carmichael. On composite p which satisfy the Fermat congruence $a^{p-1} \equiv 1 \bmod p$. *American Mathematics Monthly*, 19:22–27, 1912.

[14] Herman Chernoff. A measure of asymptotic efficiency for tests of a typothesis based on the sum of observations. *Annals of Mathematical Statistics*, 23:493–507, 1952.

[15] D. Coppersmith and S. Winograd. Matrix multiplication via arithmetic progressions. *Journal of Symbolic Computation*, 9:251–280, 1990.

[16] T. H. Cormen, C. E. Leiserson, R. L. Rivest, and C. Stein. *Introduction to Algorithms*. MIT Press, 3rd ed., 2009.

[17] Mark Crovella, Bob Frangioso, and Mor Harchol-Balter. Connection scheduling in web servers. In *USENIX Symposium on Internet Technologies and Systems*, pages 243–254, Boulder, CO, October 1999.

[18] Mark E. Crovella and Azer Bestavros. Self-similarity in World Wide Web traffic: Evidence and possible causes. In *Proceedings of the 1996 ACM SIGMETRICS International Conference on Measurement and Modeling of Computer Systems*, pages 160–169, May 1996.

[19] Mark E. Crovella, Murad S. Taqqu, and Azer Bestavros. Heavy-tailed probability distributions in the world wide web. In *A Practical Guide To Heavy Tails*, pages 1–23. Chapman & Hall, 1998.

[20] Allen B. Downey. The inspection paradox is everywhere. towardsdatascience.com/the-inspection-paradox-is-everywhere-2ef1c2e9d709, August 2019.

[21] D. Dubhashi and A. Panconesi. *Concentration of Measure for the Analysis of Randomized Algorithms*. Cambridge University Press, 2012.

[22] Richard Durrett. *Probability: Theory and Examples*. Cambridge University Press, 2019.

[23] E. O. Elliott. Estimates of error rates for codes on burst-noise channels. *Bell Systems Technical Journal*, 42:1977–1997, 1963.

[24] P. Erdös. On a new method in elementary number theory which leads to an elementary proof of the prime number theorem. *Proceedings of the National Academy of Science*, 35:374–384, 1949.

[25] Michalis Faloutsos, Petros Faloutsos, and Christos Faloutsos. On power-law relationships of the internet topology. In *Proceedings of SIGCOMM*, pages 251–262, Cambridge, MA, August 1999.

[26] Scott Feld. Why your friends have more friends than you do. *American Journal of Sociology*, 96(6):1464–1477, 1991.

[27] William Feller. *An Introduction to Probability Theory and Its Applications*, volume II. John Wiley and Sons, 2nd edition, 1971.

[28] P. Flajolet, P. J. Grabner, P. Kirschenhofer, and H. Prodinger. On Ramanujan's Q-function. *Journal of Computational and Applied Mathematics*, 58:103–116, 1995.

[29] R. Freivalds. Probabilistic machines can use less running time. In *Information Processing*, pages 839–842, 1977.

[30] Jean Gallier and Jocelyn Quaintance. Notes on primality testing and public key cryptography part 1: Randomized algorithms Miller–Rabin

and Solovay–Strassen tests. www.cis.upenn.edu/~jean/RSA-primality-testing.pdf.

[31] Pete Gemmell and Mor Harchol. Tight bounds on expected time to add correctly and add mostly correctly. *Information Processing Letters*, 49:77–83, 1994.

[32] E. N. Gilbert. Capacity of a burst-noise channel. *Bell Systems Technical Journal*, 39:1253–1265, 1960.

[33] Varun Gupta, Michelle Burroughs, and Mor Harchol-Balter. Analysis of scheduling policies under correlated job sizes. *Performance Evaluation*, 67(11):996–1013, 2010.

[34] Mor Harchol-Balter. Task assignment with unknown duration. *Journal of the ACM*, 49(2):260–288, 2002.

[35] Mor Harchol-Balter. *Performance Modeling and Design of Computer Systems: Queueing Theory in Action*. Cambridge University Press, 2013.

[36] Mor Harchol-Balter, Mark Crovella, and Cristina Murta. On choosing a task assignment policy for a distributed server system. *Journal of Parallel and Distributed Computing*, 59(2):204–228, 1999.

[37] Mor Harchol-Balter and Allen Downey. Exploiting process lifetime distributions for dynamic load balancing. In *Proceedings of ACM SIGMETRICS*, pages 13–24, Philadelphia, PA, May 1996.

[38] Mor Harchol-Balter and Allen Downey. Exploiting process lifetime distributions for dynamic load balancing. *ACM Transactions on Computer Systems*, 15(3):253–285, 1997.

[39] Mor Harchol-Balter, Bianca Schroeder, Nikhil Bansal, and Mukesh Agrawal. Size-based scheduling to improve web performance. *ACM Transactions on Computer Systems*, 21(2):207–233, 2003.

[40] Madeline Holcombe and Theresa Waldrop. More infectious delta variant makes up 83% of new US coronavirus cases as vaccine hesitancy persists. CNN, July 2021.

[41] Juraj Hromkovic. *Design and Analysis of Randomized Algorithms: Introduction to Design Paradigms*. Springer-Verlag, 2005.

[42] D. Karger. Global min-cuts in RNC and other ramifications of a simple mincut algorithm. In *4th Annual ACM-SIAM Symposium on Discrete Algorithms*, pages 21–30, January 1993.

[43] D. Karger and C. Stein. A new approach to the minimum cut problem. *Journal of the ACM*, 43(4):601–640, 1996.

[44] David Karger, Eric Lehman, Tom Leighton, Rina Panigrahy, Matthew Levine, and Daniel Lewin. Consistent hashing and random trees: Distributed caching protocols for relieving hot spots on the world wide web. In *Proceedings of the Twenty-Ninth Annual ACM Symposium on Theory of Computing*, pages 654–663, El Paso, TX, May 1997.

[45] S. Karlin and H. M. Taylor. *A First Course in Stochastic Processes*. Academic Press, 2nd ed., 1975.

[46] Donald Knuth. *The Art of Computer Programming, Volume 3*. Addison Wesley Longman Publishing Co., 1998.

[47] Tor Lattimore and Csaba Szepesvari. *Bandit Algorithms*. Cambridge University Press, 2020.

[48] Averill M. Law and W. David Kelton. *Simulation Modeling and Analysis*. McGraw-Hill, 2000.

[49] Cynthia Bailey Lee, Yael Schwartzman, Jennifer Hardy, and Allan Snavely. Are user runtime estimates inherently inaccurate? In *Proceedings of the 10th International conference on Job Scheduling Strategies for Parallel Processing*, pages 253–263, New York, NY, June 2004.

[50] Maplesoft. Mathematica. www.maplesoft.com/products/Maple/.

[51] Milefoot.com Mathematics. Joint continuous probability distributions. www.milefoot.com/math/stat/rv-jointcontinuous.htm.

[52] MathWorks. Matlab. www.mathworks.com/products/matlab.html.

[53] M. Mitzenmacher and E. Upfal. *Probability and Computing*. Cambridge University Press, 2005.

[54] R. Motwani and P. Raghavan. *Randomized Algorithms*. Cambridge University Press, 1995.

[55] Jayakrishnan Nair, Adam Wierman, and Bert Zwart. *The Fundamentals of Heavy Tails: Properties, Emergence, and Estimation*. Cambridge University Press, 2022.

[56] Rasmus Pagh and Flemming Friche Rodler. Cuckoo hashing. In *9th Annual European Symposium on Algorithms*, Aarhus, Denmark, August 2001.

[57] Michael O. Rabin. Probabilistic algorithm for testing primality. *Journal of Number Theory*, 12(1):128–138, 1980.

[58] I.A. Rai, E. W. Biersack, and G. Urvoy-Keller. Size-based scheduling to improve the performance of short TCP flows. *IEEE Network*, 19:12–17, 2005.

[59] I.A. Rai, G. Urvoy-Keller, and E. W. Biersack. LAS scheduling approach to avoid bandwidth hogging in heterogeneous TCP networks. *Lecture Notes in Computer Science*, 3079:179–190, 2004.

[60] Andréa Richa, Michael Mitzenmacher, and Ramesh Sitaraman. The power of two random choices: A survey of techniques and results. In P. Pardalos, S. Rajasekaran, and J. Rolim, editors, *Handbook of Randomized Computing*. Kluwer Press, 2001.

[61] R. L. Rivest, A. Shamir, and L. Adleman. A method for obtaining digital signatures and public-key cryptosystems. *Communications of the ACM*, 21(2):120–126, 1978.

[62] Sheldon M. Ross. *Stochastic Processes*. John Wiley and Sons, 1983.

[63] Sheldon M. Ross. *Simulation*. Academic Press, 2002.

[64] Sheldon M. Ross. *Introduction to Probability Models*. Elsevier, 2007.

[65] J Graham Ruby, Megan Smith, and Rochelle Buffenstein. Naked mole-rat mortality rates defy Gompertzian laws by not increasing with age. *eLife*, 7:e31157, 2018.

[66] L. E. Schrage. A proof of the optimality of the shortest remaining processing time discipline. *Operations Research*, 16:687–690, 1968.

[67] L. E. Schrage and L. W. Miller. The queue M/G/1 with the shortest remaining processing time discipline. *Operations Research*, 14:670–684, 1966.

[68] A. Selberg. An elementary proof of the prime number theorem. *Annals of Mathematics*, 50:305–313, 1949.

[69] Anees Shaikh, Jennifer Rexford, and Kang G. Shin. Load-sensitive routing of long-lived IP flows. In *Proceedings of ACM SIGCOMM*, pages 215–226, Cambridge, MA, September 1999.

[70] Edward H. Simpson. The interpretation of interaction in contingency tables. *Journal of the Royal Statistical Society, Series B*, 13:238–241, 1951.

[71] George B. Thomas and Ross L. Finney. *Calculus and Analytic Geometry*. Addison-Wesley, 9th ed., 1996.

[72] Muhammad Tirmazi, Adam Barker, and Nan Deng et al. Borg: The next generation. In *Proceedings of the Fifteenth European Conference on Computer Systems (EuroSys '20)*, pages 1–14, Heraklion, April 2020.

[73] Abhishek Verma, Luis Pedrosa, and Madhukar et al. Korupolu. Large-scale cluster management at Google with Borg. In *Proceedings of the Tenth European Conference on Computer Systems*, pages 1–17, Bordeaux, France, April 2015.

[74] Abraham Wald. On cumulative sums of random variables. *The Annals of Mathematical Statistics*, 15(3):283–296, 1944.

[75] Stefan Waner and Steven R. Costenoble. Normal distribution table for finite mathematics. www.zweigmedia.com/RealWorld/normaltable.html.

[76] Eric W. Weisstein. Stirling's Approximation. mathworld.wolfram.com/StirlingsApproximation.html.

[77] John Wilkes. Google cluster-usage traces v3, November 2019. http://github.com/google/cluster-data.

[78] Virginia Vassilevska Williams. Fixing a tournament. In *Proceedings of AAAI*, pages 2992–2999, Atlanta, GA, June 2010.

[79] Virginia Vassilevska Williams. Multiplying matrices faster than Copper-Winograd. In *Proceedings of 44th ACM Symposium on Theory of Computing*, pages 887–898, New York, NY, May 2012.

[80] Wolfram. Mathematica. www.wolfram.com/mathematica/.

[81] Zippia. The 10 largest shoe brands in the United States, August 2022. www.zippia.com/advice/largest-shoe-brands/.

[82] Daniel Zwillinger. *CRC Standard Mathematical Tables and Formulae*. Chapman & Hall, 31st ed., 2003.

Index